JEWISH HYMNOGRAPHY

THE LITTMAN LIBRARY OF
JEWISH CIVILIZATION

MANAGING EDITOR
Connie Webber

Dedicated to the memory of
Louis Thomas Sidney Littman
who founded the Littman Library
for the love of God
and in memory of his father
Joseph Aaron Littman
יהא זכרם ברוך

'Get wisdom, get understanding:
Forsake her not and she shall preserve thee'
PROV. 4: 5

Jewish Hymnography

A LITERARY HISTORY

LEON J. WEINBERGER

London · Portland, Oregon
The Littman Library of Jewish Civilization
1998

The Littman Library of Jewish Civilization

Published in the United Kingdom by
Vallentine Mitchell & Co. Ltd.
Newbury House, 900 Eastern Avenue,
London IG2 7HH

Published in the United States and Canada by
Vallentine Mitchell & Co. Ltd.
c/o ISBS, 5804 N.E. Hassalo Street,
Portland, Oregon 97213-3644

A catalogue record for this book is available from the British Library

Library of Congress Cataloging-in-Publication Data

Weinberger, Leon J.
Jewish hymnography : a literary history / Leon J. Weinberger.
p. cm.—(The Littman library of Jewish civilization)
Includes bibliographical references and index.
1. Piyutim—History and criticism. I. Title. II. Series.
BM678.W45 1997 296.4' 52' 09—DC21 97-10193 CIP r97

ISBN 1-874774-30-7

Copy-editing: Sarah Barrett
Indexes: Leon J. Weinberger
Publishing co-ordinator: Janet Moth
Design: Pete Russell, Faringdon, Oxon.
Typeset by Footnote Graphics, Warminster, Wilts.
Printed by: Biddles Ltd., Guildford & King's Lynn

For my grandchildren

NATHAN, REBEKAH AND LILLIAN
JACOB AND MICHAEL, AND GRIFFIN

Foreword

THE SYNAGOGAL HYMNS constitute the richest vein of Hebrew poetry, in terms of quantity and quality. Tens of thousands of them are extant, and while some are short and simple others are very long and complex. Some are content to follow well-worn furrows of convention verging in some cases on the banal, but others display breathtaking originality and inventive daring, and the best of them rank among the most brilliant creations of any language or culture.

The beginnings of Jewish hymnography are lost in time. The Temple had its psalms, and the recent discoveries in the Judaean desert have brought to light sectarian hymns of groups that replaced the worship of the Jerusalem Temple with their own associations. The Graeco-Roman Diaspora had its *proseuchai*, or prayer-houses, whose hymns are mainly lost, though snatches of them have been preserved by the Christian Church. Some early rabbinic compositions survive within the folios of the Talmud. But it was the cantor-poets of Byzantine Palestine who inaugurated the tradition of synagogal hymnography in the Hebrew language that, through successive upheavals and transformations, was destined to remain a standard feature of Jewish religious life for fifty generations and more.

The word *piyyuṭ*, like the word 'hymn', is of Greek origin, and it is no accident that the *piyyuṭ* first saw the light in a region where Greek and semitic cultures met and mingled. The same is true of classical Christian hymnography, whose formative figures Ephrem (in the fourth century) and Romanos (in the sixth) were both born and bred in Syria. The poetry of the Byzantine synagogue, like its architecture, its decorative art, and no doubt its music, is of mixed Greek and semitic parentage; it is an expression of that near-eastern Hellenism that is so well captured by Glen Bowersock in his book *Hellenism in Late Antiquity*. Hellenism in this sense is not in conflict with semitic tradition but enhances it and enables it to express itself with lucidity and beauty.

The precise relationship between Jewish and Christian hymnography has not yet been established. Downplayed by some scholars, it is variously considered by others as an outstanding example of the influence of Christian upon Jewish culture, or the reverse. H. W. Haussig, a leading scholar of Byzantium, considers that the synagogal hymn made an important contribution to Christian worship from the sixth century on, and that it also influenced the execution and style of Bible manuscripts, the cycle of biblical readings, and the notation indicating the biblical chant. 'Thus', he argues, 'all things considered, it is true to say that Jewish culture played a considerable part in the development of Byzantine church poetry and in the development of the Byzantine liturgical service' (*A History of Byzantine Civilization*, trans. J. M. Hussey, p. 48).

From Byzantine Palestine the *piyyuṭ* spread not only to Constantinople and to other parts of the Byzantine Empire, but into north-western Europe, and also eastwards to the heartland of oriental Judaism in Babylon, from where after the Arab conquests it advanced along the north shore of Africa to Spain. Wherever it went it took root in the hearts of the local Jewish communities, adapting itself to their varying aesthetic and religious needs. It occupied a major place in the public worship of the synagogue, but it also entered into the Jewish home, that veritable sanctuary and second of the twin pillars of the Jewish religion. Hymns were sung, as they still are, around the table at family gatherings for Sabbaths and festivals, and at weddings and other celebrations. Some acquired the status of popular songs, and many Jews who could recite no other post-biblical Hebrew poetry knew and cherished some of the *piyyuṭim*.

The *piyyuṭim* occupied a formative role in Jewish education. By means of these hymns, along with the prayers of the synagogue, Jewish worshippers were introduced to the elements of Jewish theology. Even the Thirteen Principles of Maimonides have been better known in their versified form, as the *Yigdal*, than in Maimonides' own formulation. However, as Jakob Petuchowski has rightly observed, the hymns, far from imposing a theological orthodoxy, tend to embody and maintain the individual creativity which is the hallmark of Jewish theology. 'Statements and arguments which, in prose, would immediately be branded as "heretical" have become, once they were couched in poetic form, ingredients of the liturgy, and continue to be rehearsed—often with more devotion than comprehension—by multitudes of the unsuspecting pious who would be utterly shocked to discover the true intent of their authors' (*Theology and Poetry*, p. 5).

The hallowed place of the *piyyuṭ* in Jewish life has not been achieved without opposition. Leading authorities in Babylon resisted its introduction for centuries. Maimonides found in the recitation of the *piyyuṭim* 'the major cause for the lack of devotion of the masses', and a similar consideration led the nineteenth-century Reformers to excise most of the *piyyuṭim* from the liturgy, in their efforts to bring the length of the synagogue service within the concentration-span of the average worshipper. It is a testimony to the enduring popularity of the *piyyuṭim* that they have survived against all opposition, and that even in Reform and Conservative congregations today they are sung with gusto.

Against this background it is surprising that there has hitherto been no general account of Jewish hymnography in English. All of us who have an interest in Hebrew literature or Jewish culture must be grateful to Professor Leon Weinberger for remedying this deficiency. He is well qualified to undertake this task, having himself edited hundreds of *piyyuṭim* from manuscripts in the course of a distinguished academic career. (His latest collection, *Rabbanite and Karaite Liturgical Poetry in South-Eastern Europe*, contains more than 480 items composed by 112 different authors.) His book takes us on a veritable odyssey around the greater and lesser islands of Jewish culture and through more than ten centuries. All the great names are here, and very many less famous ones as well, and we catch glimpses of the theological and political debates that have animated the Jewish communities in various times and places. His readers will be particularly grateful to Professor Weinberger for carefully distinguishing and explaining the different genres of the *piyyuṭ*, and for freely illustrating his account with extracts, many of them here translated into English for the first time.

For the uninitiated, this book will draw aside the curtain and open up a way into one of the most fascinating, edifying, and appealing areas of Hebrew literature. But even those who already possess some acquaintance with the world of the *piyyuṭ*, whether from the synagogue or the study, will benefit from this learned yet approachable history.

NICHOLAS DE LANGE

Preface and Acknowledgements

WHILE PREPARING this volume for publication I thought of the many teachers and colleagues who guided me in my studies of the synagogue liturgy during the past four decades. To the late lamented pioneers in the field, S. Bernstein, A. M. Habermann, Ḥ. Schirmann and S. Spiegel, I shall always be grateful for their generous support and encouragement.

I have benefited from the writings of my distinguished contemporaries, most notably Professors A. Mirsky and E. Fleischer. All students of the liturgy are indebted to them.

I am thankful for the help from librarians at the Bodleian, Oxford University; the British Library, London; Cambridge University Library; Munich's National Library; New York's Jewish Theological Seminary Library; the Bibliothèque Nationale in Paris; and the Vatican Library. Special thanks are extended to Dr Abraham David of the National and University Library, Jerusalem, for his unfailing assistance. For permission to publish specific extracts from their archives I am grateful to the following institutions: the Bibliothèque Nationale, Paris (Heb. MS 606, p. 103b); the Bodleian Library, Oxford (MS Opp. Add. 4°.80, fos. 108–10, 114^{v}–120^{v}, 131^{v}–141^{v}); the British Library, London (MS Add. 27086); the Jewish National and University Library, Jerusalem (MS 8° 421); the Library of the Jewish Theological Seminary of America (MS 4588, fos. 4a and 17b; MS 4580, fo. 1a).

I am grateful to my colleague Nicholas de Lange, who gave me the idea for this book, and to Connie Webber, who helped give it structure and coherence. I thank Sarah Barrett for her work as copy-editor and Janet Moth as publishing co-ordinator.

My wife, Marcy, has been consistently supportive of my work and I am most fortunate to have her at my side.

It is fitting that a study of the synagogue liturgy should begin with a benediction:

> *Praised are You, Lord our God, King of the universe, for granting us life, for sustaining us, and for helping us reach this day.*

Tuscaloosa, Alabama L.J.W.

Contents

3 Cantor-Rabbis in Italy, Franco-Germany and England

5 Cantor-Poets on Greece's Periphery: Macedonia, Bulgaria, Corfu, Kaffa (Crimea) and Crete

A Note on Transliteration

The transliterations from the Hebrew in this book are designed to give the general reading public a sense of its sound and structure while representing accurately the letters of the Hebrew alphabet so that Hebraists can better recognize words and understand the subtle meanings of the Hebrew texts. Following the scientific transliteration system of the *Encyclopedia Judaica* I have distinguished between *'alef* (= ') and *'ayin* (= ') and drawn other distinctions as follows: *bet* = *b*; *vet* = *v*; *waw* = *w*; *ḥet* = *ḥ*; *tet* = *ṭ*; *yod* = *y*; *kaf* = *k*; *khaf* = *kh*; *pe* = *p*; *fe* = *f*; *ṣaddiq* = *ṣ*; *qof* = *q*; *šin* = *š*; *sin* = *s*. I have not distinguished between *samekh* and *sin* because they are often interchangeable in Jewish hymnography of the period considered here.

The letter *e* is used to indicate the *segol*, as in *ḥomer* and *qedem*; the *ṣereh*, as in *nerot* and *yošev*; and the *šewa' na'*, as in *qerovah* and *telunah*. The letter *a* indicates the *pataḥ*, as in *baqqašah*; *qameṣ*, as in *magen*; and the *ḥaṭaf pataḥ*, as in *maḥazor*. The doubling of letters, as in *'ammim*, *ḥuqqim*, indicates a *dageš ḥazaq*. My references in the transliteration have been Ḥ. Yalon's *Quntres Torat Ha-Niqqud* (Jerusalem, 1937) and *Gesenius' Hebrew Grammar*, ed. A. Cowley (Oxford, 1966).

Some exceptions have been made to these general rules for personal names where established usages exist. For example, I have followed the generally accepted renditions of Yannai and Amittai and Ephraim rather than change them to Yannay, Amittay and Efrayim.

Abbreviations

b	*Babylonian Talmud*, ed. Romm (Vilna, 1881); English trans. ed. I. Epstein (London, 1948–52)
EJ	*Encyclopaedia Judaica* (10 vols., Berlin, 1928–34, incomplete; 16 vols., Jerusalem, 1972)
HUCA	*Hebrew Union College Annual*
j	*Jerusalem Talmud* (New York, 1959)
JQR	*Jewish Quarterly Review*
m	*Mišnah,* var. eds.; English trans. H. Danby (Oxford, 1933)
MGWJ	*Monatsschrift für Geschichte und Wissenschaft des Judentums*
REJ	*Revue des études juives*
t	*Tosefta*, ed. M. S. Zuckermandel (Pasewalk, 1881)

Tractates of the Talmud

AZ	*ʿAvodah Zarah*
BB	*Bavaʾ Batraʾ*
Ber	*Berakhot*
Beṣ	*Beṣah*
Bikk	*Bikkurim*
BM	*Bavaʾ Meṣiʿaʾ*
BQ	*Bavaʾ Qammaʾ*
ʿEruv	*ʿEruvin*
Giṭ	*Giṭṭin*
Ḥag	*Ḥagigah*
Hor	*Horayot*
Ḥul	*Ḥullin*
Ket	*Ketubot*
Makk	*Makkot*
Meg	*Megillah*
MQ	*Moʿed Qaṭan*
Pes	*Pesaḥim*
Qid	*Qiddušin*
RH	*Roš ha-Šanah*
Šab	*Šabbat*
San	*Sanhedrin*
Šeq	*Šeqalim*
Soṭ	*Soṭah*
Sukk	*Sukkah*
Taʿan	*Taʿanit*
Yev	*Yevamot*

Hispano-Hebrew Metres

Metric forms were derived from declensions of the Hebrew verb *pa'al*, yielding configurations like *nif'al* (– –), *nif'alim* (– – –), *pe'ulim* (v – –), *mefo'alim* (v – – –), *mitpa'alim* (– – v –), *po'alim* (– v –), *pa'alulim* (– v – –), and *mef'olelim* (v – v –). Below are the main metric patterns in Hebrew hymnography and their Arabic sources. The scansion reads from right to left.

Ha-'arokh (source: Arabic *ṭawīl*), the most frequently used configuration (reading from right to left; – indicates a long syllable and v a short syllable):

– – – v /– – v /– – – v /– – v //– – – v /– – v /– – – v /– – v (I)

Variant:

– – – /– – v /– – – /– – v //– – – /– – v /– – – /– – v (II)

Ha-šalem (source: Arabic *kāmil)*

– v– – /– v– – /– v– – //–v– – /– v– – /– v– – (I)

Variants:

– – – /– v– – /– v– – //– v– – /– v– – /– v– – /– v– – (II)

– – – /– v– – /– v– – //– – – /– v– – /– v– – (III)

Ha-merubbeh (source: Arabic *wāfir*):

– – v /– – – v /– – – v //– – v /– – – v/– – – v

Ha-marnin (source: Arabic *hazaj*):

– – – v /– – – v//– – – v/– – – v

Ha-mitpaššeṭ (source: Arabic *basīṭ*):

–v– /– v– –/– v–/–v– –//– v –/– v– – /– v – /– v– – (I)

Variants:

– – /– v– – /– v – /– v – – //– v –/– v – – /– v –/– v – – (II)

– – /– v – – /– – /– v – – //– – /– v – –/– –/– v – – (III)

Ha-qal (source: Arabic *khafīf*):

– v– – /– v – v /– – v –//– – v –/– v – v /– – v –

Ha-mahir (source: Arabic *sari*‘):

– v – /– v – – /– v – – //– v – /– v – – /– v – – (I)

Variant:

– – /– v – – /– v – – // – – /– v – – /– v – – (II)

Introduction

SINCE LEOPOLD ZUNZ'S literary history of pre-modern synagogue poetry (*piyyuṭ*) and Ismar Elbogen's history of the Jewish liturgy,[1] dramatic advances have been made in the study of Hebrew hymnography. These were due in large part to Solomon Schechter's discovery in 1896 of the Cairo Geniza (storeroom). Given the Jewish practice of not destroying texts in which the name of God was written, synagogues would preserve their business documents and letters, and their prayer-books when these were no longer fit for public use. The Jews in Old Cairo (Fustat) purchased their synagogue from the Copts in 882. In 1012 the building was destroyed by vandals and later rebuilt. The new edifice included an attic for the purpose of storing these texts. Schechter took with him some 100,000 fragments from the Cairo storeroom to Cambridge, where he was a Reader in Rabbinics. Geniza materials were also obtained at that time by the British Museum; the Bodleian, Oxford; St Petersburg Library; the Hungarian Academy of Budapest; Dropsie College Library, Philadelphia; and the Jewish Theological Seminary Library, New York, among others. In 1902 Schechter became president of the Jewish Theological Seminary and brought some of the Cairo Geniza texts with him. Israel Davidson, a member of Schechter's faculty, found among the fragments the writings of Yannai (6th c.), one of the earliest Ereṣ Yisra'el synagogue poets, and in 1919 he published a collection of his works (*Maḥazor Yannay*). Davidson's studies led him to produce his monumental bibliography in four volumes, *Thesaurus of Mediaeval Hebrew Poetry* (New York, 1923–33).

Exploiting the Cairo Geniza treasure trove, scholars in Berlin and later in Jerusalem published the works of hitherto unknown synagogue poets. Pioneering in this effort were H. Brody and his collaborators, M. Zulay, Ḥ. Schirmann and A. Habermann, at the Research Institute of Hebrew Poetry, and their students working at the new Research Institute of the Piyyuṭ in the

[1] *Literaturgeschichte der synagogalen Poesie*; Elbogen, *Der jüdische Gottesdienst in seiner geschichtlichen Entwicklung*.

Geniza. Following the publication of Davidson's *Thesaurus* the research moved in two separate, albeit at times intersecting, directions. The prime focus of Brody and his colleagues was the study of post-biblical Hebrew poetry in its regional setting. The results were Zulay's publications on the poets (*payṭanim*) of Ereṣ Yisra'el and Babylon; Schirmann's work on hymnography in Italy, Spain and Provence; and Habermann's studies of the Franco-German and English hymnists.

With the publication of Schirmann's *New Hebrew Poems from the Geniza* (Jerusalem, 1965) the research into the tens of thousands of liturgical fragments from the Geniza gained momentum, leading to the discovery of long-forgotten poets such as Simeon b. Megas (*Liturgical Poems of Simeon bar Megas*, ed. J. Yahalom, Jerusalem, 1984), a contemporary of Yannai, and the ninth-century 'Anonymous', author of some 580 choral refrains designed to enhance the hymns of Simeon b. Megas (*The Pizmonim of the Anonymous*, ed. E. Fleischer, Jerusalem, 1974). Moreover, the Research Institute of the Piyyuṭ in the Geniza aided scholars through its efforts in cataloguing the numerous fragments according to incipit and conclusion, form, rhyme, refrain, acrostic and genre. As a result, researchers have been able to reconstruct long-forgotten hymns (*piyyuṭim*) and provide improved versions of poems already published.

The Geniza find was enhanced by the discovery of *piyyuṭim* in lost or forgotten manuscripts and printed books in archival collections, including, happily, the great libraries in the former Soviet Union, now accessible to scholars. These developments made possible the recent textual studies with a regional focus, including the publications of A. Mirsky, Z. M. Rabinovitz, E. Fleischer, J. Yahalom, Naḥum Weissenstern, S. Eliṣur and W. J. van Bekkum on the poets of Ereṣ Yisra'el; J. Tobi, T. Beeri and Eliṣur on the Babylonians; Y. David and Fleischer on the Italians; D. Yarden, D. Pagis, I. Levin, Z. Malachi, M. Schmelzer, R. Scheindlin and R. Brann on the Hispanics; D. Goldschmidt and Y. Frankel on the Franco-Germans; S. Bernstein and L. J. Weinberger on the Balkan poets; E. Ḥazan and B. Bar-Tiqvah on the North Africans; and Y. Ratzaby and Tobi on the Yemenites.

The textual studies focused mostly on deciphering, reconstructing, and editing the texts and providing their literary sources and influences. The dramatic surge in publications prompted an interest in literary analysis of medieval Hebrew poetry and a study of its poetics. Dramatic findings in this area were made by M. Zulay in his philological study of the style and mannerisms of Eleazar Qillir (6th c.) in contrast to the hymnography of Sa'adyah Ga'on (882–942). A. Mirsky's investigation of the conceptual prototypes common to both rabbinic literature and synagogue poetry opened a fertile area of research. E. Fleischer's attempt to identify the forms and genres in Hebrew hymnography and their growth and development in regional settings yielded new insights into the dynamic character of the liturgy. Seminal contributions were made by E. Werner in his study of the Ereṣ Yisra'el *piyyuṭ* and its relation to Byzantine church hymnography, and by J. Yahalom on the rhetoric and syntax of the early *payṭanim* in the Byzantine environment.

All of these publications, with the exception of those of E. Werner, are written in modern Hebrew, and are accessible to a relatively limited readership. Hence the need for this volume, which will focus on the historical development of ideas and regional themes as expressed in the genres and forms employed by the synagogue poets. Given the recent advances in research, it is now possible to present a general introduction to Hebrew hymnography from its origins in the eastern Mediterranean to its emergence in southern and central Europe, the Iberian peninsula and the Balkans. Although we are not yet able to write a comprehensive literary analysis of medieval Hebrew poetry or a full exposition of its poetics, there is sufficient material for a literary history of the major centres of Jewish liturgical writing.

Synagogue hymnography, compared to its Christian and Muslim counterparts, is distinctive in both its focus and its volume. The Church liturgy centres on the mystery of the eucharist (= thanksgiving) as the offering of 'the holy bread of eternal life and the chalice of eternal salvation' (Canon of the Roman Mass, 4th–5th c.). It is a memorial to the Church's founder, who at the Last Supper took bread and wine and urged his disciples to do likewise ('Do this in remembrance of me,' 1 Cor. 11: 24). The eucharist, whether interpreted as the symbolic or real presence of Christ, involves the Christian in an action—the taking of bread and wine—with a salvific effect.

The focus in Islamic prayer (*ṣalat*) is the acknowledgement of God's unique and real presence ('I testify that there is no god but God' (*ashhadu an lā ilāha illā allāh*)) and His greatness ('God is most great' (*allāhu akbar*)). The verbal testimony is accompanied by a series of body movements which include bowing and descending to a prostrate position, with knees and toes on the floor and the forehead touching the floor with palms flat on the surface on either side of the head. The cycle of postures is designed to involve the body in the act of submission (*islām*) to God.

Although synagogue practice generally confines bodily activity to standing and a few bows during the Eighteen Benedictions and bowing when chanting the Adoration (*'aleynu le-šabbeaḥ*, 'It is incumbent upon us to praise'), its principal prayer, the *šema'* ('Hear, O Israel: The Lord is our God, the Lord alone,' Deut. 6: 4–9), is similar in purpose to the Muslim's 'testimony'. While reciting the *šema'*, the Jewish worshipper accepts the rule of God's kingship (*qabbalat 'ol malkhut šamayim*) and the obligation to live by His commandments (*qabbalat 'ol miṣwot*). Following the *šema'* are the 'Eighteen Benedictions', thirteen of which are petitions. This arrangement is modelled after the oriental court, where the subordinate first acknowledges the sovereignty of his lord and the obligation to serve him and then allows himself the liberty to petition for favours. The liberty of the Jew to address his

God derives from biblical models in which Israel's patriarchs and prophets had an ongoing dialogic relationship with deity. The dynamic divine–human dialogue is a distinctive feature in the synagogue, and the worshipper is urged by the rabbis (in *ʾAvot* 2. 13) to do his part creatively and with reverent imagination: 'Be careful when you recite the *šemaʿ* and the *tefillah* [Eighteen Benedictions, also known as *ʿamidah,* standing]. When you recite the *tefillah* do not make your prayer a prescribed routine but a plea for mercy and grace before God.'

The immense volume of Jewish liturgical writing is undoubtedly related to its dialogic focus. Davidson's *Thesaurus* lists some 35,000 poems by 2,836 poets. More than half were designed for liturgical use in over sixty different synagogue rituals in Europe, Asia and Africa.[2] These numbers are almost matched by the continually emerging discoveries of forgotten remnants from the Cairo Geniza. There is nothing comparable in Christianity or Islam to the vast Jewish liturgical corpus. The disparity in output is due both to the difference in focus and to the rabbinic encouragement to be creative in prayer. Lay leaders in the synagogue responded enthusiastically to the rabbinic advice, and urged their cantor-poets to compose additions to the obligatory *šemaʿ* and *ʿamidah,* as well as celebrations and observances of life-cycle events. A constant feature of the Jewish experience emerged with the hymnic ritualization of the great events of human life: birth, puberty, marriage and death; the feasts and fasts of the religious calendar; and the changes in the natural world—the appearance of the new moon and solar and lunar eclipses.

There is also a difference in the historical experience of the Jews exiled from their national home. Unlike Christians and Muslims, who in the Middle Ages were relatively secure in their separate sovereign states, Jews could only simulate their national independence by recalling in their prayers the courses (*mišmarot*) of the priestly families in the Temple, or the service (*ʿavodah,* pl. *ʿavodot*) of the High Priest on the Day of Atonement. Given a life in exile, the synagogue poet would often appeal to God for national restoration. Three of the petitions in the *tefillah* ('Have mercy, Lord, and return to Jerusalem'; 'Bring to flower the shoot of your servant David'; and 'May we witness your merciful return to Zion') express the hope for exile's end. Such hopes were echoed in thousands of *piyyuṭim* in every synagogue.

Our study of Jewish hymnography in the eastern Mediterranean and in western and central Europe will also reveal that its literary history was largely determined by contemporary culture. For example, liturgical writing

[2] Many *piyyuṭim* are no longer in active use. The old French ritual preserved in the *Maḥazor Witry* was neglected after the expulsion of the Jews from France in the 14th c. The Babylonian rite preserved by Hispanic Jews fell into desuetude after their expulsion in 1492. The Provençal prayer-book serving the once-thriving cities of Avignon, Carpentras and Montpellier has been all but forgotten with the demise of their Jewish population. The same holds true for the prayer-books of Algeria and Tunis in North Africa, for Asti, Fossano and Moncalvo in Italy's Piedmont, and for other dwindling Jewish communities.

in Babylonia (Iraq) and North Africa changed from earlier Ereṣ Yisra'el practices because of a newly introduced annual Torah-reading cycle in which the Pentateuch was divided into fifty-four sections (*parašiyyot*) supplanting the older triennial cycle. A distinctive feature of the early Ereṣ Yisra'el poets, Yannai, Simeon b. Megas and Qillir, was the liturgical embellishment of the *'amidah* in a multi-part composition known as the *qedušta'* (holy, based on Isa. 6: 3) for the Sabbath and festival morning service. The theme of the *qedušta'* was related to the week's Scripture lesson, whose verses were added to its poetic parts. When the Babylonians opted for an annual cycle, the older Ereṣ Yisra'el hymns had to be adapted and restructured. Another change in older forms was prompted by Qillir's introduction of popular choral refrains into the *qedušta'*. Since the *qedušta'* hymns of Yannai and Simeon b. Megas lacked these refrains, they were often neglected, or provided with choral accompaniments by later poets. A notable example is the liturgical compositions of an anonymous ninth-century Ereṣ Yisra'el poet whose choral refrains were attached to Simeon's *qedušta'ot* in order to make them more appealing.

Thematic changes in Jewish hymnography which emerged in the writings of Sa'adyah Ga'on included issues of contemporary philosophy and science. His reason for this practice was probably the same as the one he offered in the introduction to his philosophical work, The Book of Doctrines and Beliefs (*Sefer Ha-'Emunot We-Ha-De'ot*), where he expressed the hope that his work would provide guidance in a time of confusion and religious disputes. Philosophical themes continued to be included in the liturgy during the Andalusian Golden Age in the eleventh and twelfth centuries. Their range of conceits encompassed both Judah Ha-Levi's fervent Jewish nationalism, as seen in his laments for the fall of Jerusalem and its Temple (zionides), and Ibn Gabirol's universalism, in which he affirms that 'every creature' is God's servant and wishes to draw near to Him (*Keter Malkhut*, No. 8).

The environment of the Italians, the Franco-Germans and the Byzantine Romaniotes in the High Middle Ages differed from that of their Iberian colleagues. Whereas the latter participated in the intellectual life of a pervasive Judeo-Arabic courtly society, the central and east Europeans were largely isolated and generally indifferent to the achievements of their Christian neighbours. Unlike the Golden Age Andalusians, the Italians, Franco-Germans and Romaniotes were faced with an actively hostile environment, ranging from forced conversions under the Byzantine emperors Basil I (867–86), Leo VI (886–912) and Romanus I (920–44) to the annihilation of Jewish settlements in the Rhine valley during the First and Second Crusades. These experiences were reflected in their hymnographies with prominence given to themes like the Binding of Isaac (*'aqedah*). Jews facing martyrdom were reminded of Abraham's son, willing to give his life in response to the divine command. The *gezerot* (government decrees leading to anti-Jewish riots) were the new genres in the liturgy memorializing the victims, and appeals for exile's end and national restoration were repeated with increased urgency. Although the traumatic experiences of the central and east Europeans emboldened their rhetoric of grievance and resentment, they consistently protected the traditional theodicy by accepting the blame for their own suffering.

Contemporary culture also affected the language of hymnography. The linguistic stylings of Qillir, while often incomprehensible to moderns, were the common parlance of his day. The symbiosis between popular taste and liturgical practice is also reflected in Qillir's and his contemporaries' extensive use of rabbinic fables designed to hold the interest of their congregations. With the emergence of Judeo-Arabic courtly culture in Spain and North Africa, popular taste was largely determined by courtier-rabbis and patrons of the arts like Ḥisday Ibn Shaprut (*c.*915–*c.*970) and Samuel Ibn Nagrela (993–1056). The poets were part of the patron's entourage, dependent upon his generosity and reflecting his literary taste. A prominent feature of the Jewish courtly culture was the idealization of the Hebrew scriptures in much the same way as Arab courtiers celebrated the Qur'ān, Allah's 'flawless' Arabic speech (Qur'ān 39: 27). Jewish pride in the eloquence of biblical Hebrew was extended to synagogue hymnography, and focused on clarity of expression based on sound scriptural usages; Qillir's excesses were no longer fashionable. Abraham Ibn Ezra (1089-1164), the last of a celebrated quintet of Hispano-Hebrew poets that included Samuel Ibn Nagrela, Solomon Ibn Gabirol (*c.*1020–*c.*1057), Moses Ibn Ezra (*c.*1055–d. after 1135) and Judah Ha-Levi (b. before 1075, d. 1141), condemned Qillir (in a commentary on Eccles. 5: 1) for his liberties with the Hebrew language and his tendency to impose rabbinic fables and legends upon the religious service.

The *piyyuṭ* was for a time frowned upon by rabbinic authorities like Yehuday Ga'on, head of the Sura academy (*c.*757–61) and his pupil, Pirqoy ben Baboy as an unwarranted intrusion into the synagogue liturgy. In the following century the *piyyuṭ* gained respectability and was included in Sa'adyah Ga'on's *Siddur* (Order of Prayers). Later it served as a medium for prayer and teaching by the Rhineland's eminent rabbi-poets, Simeon b. Isaac b. Abun (*c.*950) and Rabbenu Geršom b. Judah (950–1028), master of the academy at Mainz. An indication of the changed status of the *piyyuṭ* and its author is seen in the treatment of the *'ofan,* a hymn embellishing an obligatory benediction of the *šema'* in the Sabbath and festival morning service. The *'ofan,* based on Isa. 6: 3, refers to celestial creatures singing God's praises as they carry His 'chariot throne'. The early Ereṣ Yisra'el poets, Yannai and Qillir, were careful not to elaborate on this hymn. Presumably they were sensitive to the rabbinic injunction (in *mḤag* 2. 1) which forbids public speculation on the matter of the chariot throne (*ma'aseh merkavah*). Later Rhine valley rabbi-poets, as well as the early Italian rabbinic judge Amittai b. Šefatiah (late 9th c.), were not as restrained in their poetic embellishments on the esoteric theme. As the leading rabbinic authorities in their communities, they could assert themselves in a manner that earlier poets were fearful of adopting.

Our study reveals the distinctive features of Jewish hymnography in its varied settings in the Mediterranean world and in central and northern Europe. Ereṣ Yisra'el was the birthplace of the *piyyuṭ* and the home of the anonymous poets (4th–6th c.) who generally followed biblical models—most notably the book of Psalms—in their liturgical writings. Some of their structural and stylistic innovations prompted the more imaginative creativity of their successors. Yose b. Yose (4th–5th c.), the first hymnist to be identified by name, expanded the musical devices of the hymn with strophic rhyming patterns, alliteration and assonance, and enhanced the hymn with legends from the rabbis. He employed figurative language in the form of metonymy—the emblematical use of words—and recontextualized biblical phrasing for assignment in the synagogue hymn. Yose is best known for his *'avodot*, additions to the Day of Atonement prayers giving an account of the High Priest's service on that day in the Temple.

Yose was followed by the recently rediscovered hymnography of Yannai, the stylistic master of the pattern poem, and an innovator in synthetic parallelism based on the biblical model in Ps. 42: 1. Yannai's efforts in enhancing the aesthetic quality of the worship service were in line with the rabbinic comment (in *Mekhilta de-R. Išmael*, No. 3) on Exod. 15: 2, '"This is my God, and I will glorify Him . . ." Is it possible for a man of flesh and blood to add glory to his creator? It simply means: I shall be beautiful before Him in observing the commandments.' The first Hebrew poet to sign his name in an acrostic, Yannai combined in his writings the aesthetic function with the didactic role of the poet. With regard to the latter, he took a stand on matters of Jewish law and urged his congregation to remain in their native land despite its occupation by foreigners. Yannai's role as teacher to his congregation is seen in some of his hymns for the New Year in which he reviews the laws relating to the sounding of the *šofar*. The practice of instructing the congregation in laws pertaining to forthcoming festivals and holy days was followed by the Ereṣ Yisra'el cantor-poet Phineḥas Ha-Kohen (7th c.) and by his European colleagues in later generations.

Eleazar Qillir (or Qallir), presumably a younger contemporary of Yannai, was the most prolific of the Ereṣ Yisra'el poets. His opaque style, with its neologisms, allusions and elliptic syntax, and his two-root-consonant rhyme were to influence later Italian, Romaniote and Franco-German poets. He and Yannai pioneered the *qedušta'*, hymns adorning the benedictions of the *'amidah*, and the *yoṣer* cycle of poems embellishing the blessings preceding and following the *šema'*. The multi-part *qedušta'* and *yoṣer* became the centrepieces of the synagogue liturgy in their time and in European congregations during the High Middle Ages. Ezra Fleischer appropriately referred to the age of Yannai and Qillir as the 'classical period' in Jewish hymnography.

Qillir was at his lyrical best in the elegies he composed for the Ninth of 'Av, the anniversary of the destruction of the first and second Temples. Drawing upon rabbinic sources, his lament takes the form of a dialogue between God and Israel in which the mourning parties find relief in mutual consolation. The dialogue as a rhetorical medium for dramatic effect was also employed by Andalusian and Romaniote poets. Distinctive in Qillir's writing is his epic narrative for the Ninth of 'Av in which he reassures the faithful of their reward 'at the end of days'. The narrative describes a future encounter between the mythical creatures Leviathan and Behemoth. In this contest designed for the entertainment of the righteous, both monsters are slain and their flesh is eaten at the festive meal. In the narrative Qillir gives coherence to the scattered references in rabbinic literature to the Leviathan–Behemoth contest. His sources may have come from folklore, a common practice of the *payṭan*, or from his rich imagination. It is likely that folklore was a factor in Qillir's Pentecost hymns, in which God is portrayed as matchmaker for the Torah. In his account, the Torah rejects the suitors Adam, Noah and the Patriarch, citing their deficiencies. Only Moses is worthy of her hand. This legend is not preserved in rabbinic sources, presumably because it casts aspersions on biblical worthies. Qillir appears to have been undeterred, presumably because the story was entertaining and would hold the attention of his congregation. The aesthetic function in Qillir's writing is prominent in his pioneering the *qiqlar* in the *qedušta'*. In this hymn comprising sets of rhymed triads with choral responses, the poet was able to enhance the musical component in worship and provide for a larger involvement of the laity in the service. Like Yannai, Qillir performed a didactic function and his *dibrin* (command) hymns for Pentecost are a notable example. In them he expanded on each of the commands in the Decalogue. Related to the teaching mission of Yannai and Qillir were their polemical broadsides against a repressive Byzantine empire. The practice was to be widely followed by later *payṭanim* living under Christian and Muslim rule.

A new era in Jewish hymnography begins with decline of the Ereṣ Yisra'el centres of learning beginning with the Arab conquest in 634 and the corresponding emergence of academies in Babylonia. With the adoption by the latter of the annual cycle of Scripture reading, the hymns that were designed for the triennial cycle had to be revised. Hybrid *piyyuṭim* appeared which combined both traditions, and new genres reflecting the changed environment. The Babylonians' preference for musical enhancement of the liturgy is evidenced by the sizeable number of choral refrains composed by the Anonymous for the *qedušta'ot* of Simeon b. Megas. Notable among the new genres was an introduction to the *yoṣer* named the *maṣdar* (opening). In this short (generally one-strophe) hymn, the poet would sign his name, and would then append his *maṣdar* to the larger, multi-part *yoṣer* which was composed by an earlier master. Poets who composed in this genre were either unwilling or not sufficiently gifted to write their own *yoṣerot* and were content with a mere introduction. In the hands of talented poets like Joseph Al-Baradani (*c*.929–99), who lived in a Baghdad suburb, the *maṣdar* was expanded, and subsequently developed into an independent choral unit. In this period of radical change in Scripture reading and in the *qedušta'* and *yoṣer*, many cantor-poets began to treat the hitherto connected hymns of these two genres as independent units.

Seeking to remedy the prevailing chaos in the synagogue liturgy, Sa'adyah Ga'on composed his *Siddur*. Guided by the principle of relevance with regard to the *piyyuṭ*, he permitted only those poetic embellishments which were in line with the theme of the obligatory benediction. He also stressed the need for sound biblical usage in writing for the synagogue, and was hailed as a model in this regard by the discriminating Abraham Ibn Ezra. The didactic element in Sa'adyah's poetry is evident in the philosophical themes which he introduces as a means of aiding his perplexed congregation. The aesthetic function of his hymnography appears in the flexible rhymed strophe which he pioneered, and which became standard practice in the poetry of the European *payṭanim*. The preferred choral enhancement of the service with congregational responses marked a change from earlier practices, when prayers were chanted mostly by the cantor-poet alone. The increased involvement of the laity led to the personalization of prayers in the form of 'supplications' composed by Sa'adyah and individual 'confessions' by Nissi al-Nahrawani (9th–10th c.). Sa'adyah's 'supplications' were recommended by the poet for private home use. Sa'adyah was to have a decisive influence on the Hebrew poets of Andalusia, even as Qillir was to become the mentor of the early Italians, Franco-Germans and Romaniotes.

Notable among Sa'adyah's successors were Samuel *Ha-Šeliši* (the third) b. Hošanah (d. after 1012) who held the third rank in the seating order at the Jerusalem academy, and Ha'yyay ben Šerira (939–1038), *ga'on* (eminence) of the academy at Pumbedita. Samuel, who later moved to Fostat, witnessed the anti-Jewish riots in that city and was among the community leaders who were arrested by the provincial governor. The third of Ševat, 4772 (31 December 1011) when the riots began, was declared a fast-day, and Samuel's personal account of his vexing experience and his recording of the events were included in the Fustat liturgy on the anniversary of the riots. Samuel's chronicle (*Megillat Miṣrayim*) was to be imitated by the Franco-Germans recounting the tragic fate of Rhineland Jewry during the First and Second Crusades. Ha'yyay Ga'on, who lived in the twilight of Babylonian Jewry's Golden Age, reveals an uncommon rhetorical boldness in his liturgical writing. In his penitential hymns (*seliḥot*), he argues that God has failed to carry out His obligations under the covenant while Israel has kept her part of the agreement under adverse conditions in exile.

The eleventh- and twelfth-century Hispanic synagogue poets Solomon

Ibn Gabirol, Judah Ha-Levi and Moses and Abraham Ibn Ezra were the literary heirs of Sa'adyah Ga'on. Their insistence on employing the language of Scripture for the worship service was modelled after the Ga'on's practice, as was their tendency to use the liturgy as a means of helping their congregations cope with current philosophical issues. The zeal of Gabirol and his contemporaries for biblical Hebrew reflected their nationalistic pride and that of their patrons. Although the Andalusians adopted much of the prevailing culture, their Arabism was tempered by the reality of being exiled from their national home. The degree to which Arabism was pervasive is seen in the Andalusians' attempt to adapt Arabic-style quantitative metrics for use in their writings for the synagogue. They also composed their *piyyuṭim* in the prevailing styles of Arabic prosody, the *qaṣīdah*, a monorhyme hymn in metrically balanced hemistichs, and *muwashshaḥ*, a hymn where the rhyme is variable in the strophes and constant in the refrain. They introduced into their synagogue poetry (and their secular writings) a disdain for personified Time (Arab. *zamān* and *dahr*) and the World (Arab. *dunyā*), a theme traceable to Arabic elegiac pre-Islamic poetry. Anticipating John Ruskin's 'pathetic fallacy', both Time and the World are seen as pernicious and untrustworthy. Ibn Gabirol exhorts his soul to 'belittle the World's goods' and not 'be tricked by wealth, honour and offspring' and Abraham Ibn Ezra prays to 'be saved / from Time's snares'.

Distinctive in the Hispanic *piyyuṭ* is the poet's signature in the acrostic. Unlike earlier modest practices in which the poet merely signed his name, the Hispanics prefaced their signature with 'I' (*'ani)*. The change is probably due to the difference in role and function between the east Mediterranean and Iberian cantor-poets. Whereas the former was supported by his congregation, the latter depended on the generosity of his courtier-patron, who also functioned as head of the synagogue community.

Given the intense competition among court poets vying for the favours of the patron, the temptation to 'borrow' from one's rival was ever present. Gabirol's complaint to a competitor, 'Admit that you stole and falsified my words,' was not uncommon—hence the preface to the signature, '"I" am the author.' To guard further against plagiarism, the poet would add to his name in the acrostic that of his father and his city of residence. The habit of proudly proclaiming authorship was also related to the Arabic literary mannerism of *fakhr* (self-glorification), a poetic practice dating from pre-Islamic times. Gabirol is said to have written about himself, 'I am the one who before he was born had the understanding of a man of eighty,' a common form of boasting that was also typical of his contemporaries. Added to the self-glorification was an Andalusian habit of adding to the signatures in the acrostic the word *qaṭan* (the humble), thus: 'I am Moses Ibn Ezra, the humble (*ha-qaṭan*).' This bit of verbal irony was not lost on the poet's congregation.

Although much indebted to Sa'adyah Ga'on, the Hispanics would also enhance the tonal quality of their hymns with intensive alliteration and assonance in the style of Yannai. They also imitated Qillir's dialogue hymns, which served as a rhetorical medium in communicating with their congregations. Enhancing the dialogue was figurative language and imagery focused on the relationship between God and Israel. Drawing upon Canticles and Arabic love poetry (*ghazal*), the Hebrew-Hispanics in their *piyyuṭim* imagined a distraught Israel recalling her youthful days when she followed her Lord into an unsown wilderness (based on Jer. 2: 2). Now she is an exiled wife scouring the highways and awaiting the return of her Beloved. Helping her endure the pangs of separation is the recollection of their idyllic past and the hope of reconciliation. The *payṭan*, in the manner of the chorus in the Greek drama, comments on her predicament. The *piyyuṭ* ends with the Beloved's reassurance that He has not forgotten his commitment and that they will soon renew their betrothal in their national home.

Although the Hispanics composed in most of the older genres, including the *'avodah*, *seliḥah*, *qeduša'* and *yoṣer*, they added some distinctive features. Notable was their treatment of the *mi kamokha* (Who is like You, Lord, among all that is worshipped?) in the *yoṣer* cycle embellishing the benedictions of the *šema'*. Unlike earlier modest renditions of the *mi kamokha*, those of Spanish poets were more expansive and they found the hymn a useful means of elaborating on themes in contemporary philosophy. This type of cosmic preface to the central idea in the *mi kamokha*, the 'majesty' and 'splendour' of God, became a hallmark of Gabirol and his contemporaries and was widely imitated in European liturgies.

A change in the fortunes of Iberian Jewry in the latter half of the twelfth century resulted from the invasions of the Muslim Almoravids and Almohades. With the Christian reconquest, the earlier courtly life and culture came to an end. The celebrated Andalusian poets became vagabonds and their grandee patrons were replaced by an emerging middle class. The new cantor-poets, sensitive to the more modest needs of their constituents, fashioned a conservative tone in liturgical writing. The earlier virtuosity in rhythm and metre gave way to a reflective focus on meaning in place of style. Notable among the synagogue poets of this period were two Gerona cantor-rabbis, Moses b. Naḥman (Naḥmanides, b. 1194) and Mešullam b. Šelomo Dapiera (*c.*1260). Departing from earlier Hispanic practices, they mostly avoided using Arabic metres and often favoured rabbinic over biblical literary construction. Unlike the courtly Andalusians, Naḥmanides and Dapiera were fond of loading their hymns with allusions to talmudic and midrashic sources. As in the earlier Babylonian experience, the changed environment was reflected in the adaptive art of the synagogue poet.

In our study of the ninth- and tenth-century *payṭanim* in Byzantine Italy we are grateful to Aḥima'aṣ b. Palṭiel (b. 1017) and his Scroll (*Megillaṭ 'Aḥima'aṣ*), chronicling the life and times of his family. Thanks to his memoir, we know much about the early Italian hymnists, including the versatile Amittai b. Šefatyah of Oria (in Apulia), and his prankster colleague, Silano of Venosa. Amittai's *piyyuṭim* are revealing with regard to the choral preferences of his congregation. In a *yoṣer* for the Sabbath, the Apulian poet adds a refrain after each strophe, in contrast to the earlier Ereṣ Yisra'el practice by Qillir and his followers of inserting the choral response after sets of three strophes. In this manner, Amittai's congregation, like the Babylonian laity, favoured a greater participation in the synagogue service. Similar efforts by Amittai are seen in two of his songs (*zemarim*) for the synagogue found in the Cairo Geniza. The refrains calling for a congregational response are not in Hebrew but, presumably, in an Apulian dialect with which the laity was familiar. Later Romaniote poets Šemaryah Ha-Ikriti and Yose b. Abraham would insert Greek idioms in their Simḥat Torah (Festival of Rejoicing with the Torah) refrains with a like purpose in mind. Amittai is also credited with pioneering the genial side of the liturgy in his mock-serious dialogue between the vine and the tree. Gaity in the synagogue liturgy was a feature of the Franco-German Purim *piyyuṭim*, which celebrated the rabbinic dictum that one is required to 'mellow' oneself with wine on that day until one is oblivious to the difference between Haman and Mordecai.

The mid-tenth century found a neo-classical revival in Italy. Solomon Ha-Bavli of Rome reintroduced the Qilliric two-root-consonant rhyme, a practice that had been neglected by less gifted poets because of its severe constraints. Ha-Bavli built his hymns in a consistent word metre, and, unlike Amittai, relied heavily on rabbinic sources. Varying from his Ereṣ Yisra'el mentor, however, Ha-Bavli constructed his *yoṣer* without choral refrains. His neo-classicism was imitated by the Italian hymnist, Elia b. Šemayah of Bari (11th c.) and his Romaniote contemporary, Samuel Ha-Kohen b. Memeli. His hymns enjoyed a wide popularity and were included in most of the central and eastern European liturgies. Like many synagogue poets before him, Ha-Bavli wrestled with the problem of theodicy. In one of his hymns he suggests that Israel's powerlessness in exile—compared to the might of Christians and Muslims—is only apparent. Her real strength, which surpasses that of her neighbours, is her trust in God. Elia b. Šemayah, in addressing this issue, blames Israel's leaders for her loss of national independence. The question of blame for Israel's degradation would perplex cantor-poets in every age.

Notable among the Italian *payṭanim* were members of the Kalonymide family from Lucca and the Anaws (delli Mansi) of Rome. Mešullam b. Kalonymus (10th–11th c.) revived a pre-classical practice of omitting allusions to rabbinic literature. His hymns, distinguished for their clarity, were a welcome change for a laity with limited learning. Yeḥiel b. Abraham from the Anaw family is noted for his penitential hymn on the eclipse of the sun. The Jews, like all medieval humanity, regarded natural phenomena as mysterious and awesomely uncontrollable. Yeḥiel, aware of his people's fears, tells them not to 'dread the signs of the skies' which are under divine guidance, even as he condemns the foolish nations who are 'terrorized when the sun and moon change'.

In the twelfth century, Italian poets began to reflect the influence of their Andalusian colleagues. Yeraḥmiel b. Solomon (12th c.) was probably the first Italian poet to compose hymns for the synagogue in Arabic-style quantitative metres. This happened about the time of Abraham Ibn Ezra's sojourn in Italy in the 1140s. By the following century the new metrics were standard practice, and were put to good use in an ethical treatise (*Maʿalot Ha-Middot*) for the synagogue by Yeḥiel b. Yekutiel (d. *c.*1280), a member of the Anaw family. Notable in Yeḥiel's essay is his personification of Time, in the Hispanic style. Yeḥiel laments that Time has 'buffeted' and 'deceived' him. His treatise is a personal confession in which he regrets his failure as a father to his children ('My sons are gone . . . They are strangers to me'). The cause of his failure was that he was not ruled by 'reason' and did not trust divine wisdom. The pathos here is not mere poetic self-indulgence, but an attempt to help the congregation learn from the poet's experience.

In the cantos of Moses b. Isaac da Rieti's (b. 1398) *Miqdaš meʿaṭ* (Small Sanctuary) for the Italian synagogue, Arabic quantitative metrics were replaced by a Hebrew syllabic metre modelled after the *terza rima* of Dante's *Divina Commedia* (Divine Comedy). Da Rieti's syllabic metrics were later imitated by the Corfiote poet Moses Ha-Kohen in his *terza rima* treatment of the biblical Esther. Ha-Kohen's hymn *Sefer Yašir Mošeh* was chanted in Corfiote congregations on the Sabbath before Purim.

The mid-tenth century was also witness to a flowering of hymnography in the synagogues of the Rhineland. The rabbi-poets Simeon b. Isaac and Geršom b. Judah were the first of several learned notables who contributed to the liturgy. Joining them in this effort were the leading tenth- to twelfth-century rabbinic authorities in Europe, including Joseph Ṭov Elem of Limoges, Menaḥem b. Makhir and Ephraim b. Isaac of Regensburg, Meir b. Isaac and Ephraim b. Judah of Worms and Ephraim b. Jacob of Bonn and Barukh b. Samuel of Mainz. Distinctive features in the Franco-German worship service are the *ʿaqedah*, a penitential hymn on the Binding of Isaac (Gen. 22), pioneered by Meir b. Isaac, and the *gezerot* (mourning anti-Jewish decrees) and martyrologies of Rhineland Jewry during the First and Second Crusades. Most of the rabbi-poets listed above witnessed the actions of the unruly mobs or were personally affected. Among the latter was Geršom b. Judah's son, who in 1012 was forcibly converted to Christianity and died shortly thereafter. Ephraim b. Judah saw his wife and two daughters murdered by the rioters in 1197. Notable among the *ʿaqedah* hymns is Ephraim of Bonn's, in which Abraham is portrayed as having actually 'slaughtered' Isaac 'as required'. Isaac's death on the altar was 'a complete sacrifice prepared' and served as a model for the Jewish victims offering their lives in sanctifying the divine name. In Barukh b. Isaac's elegy on the death of a young man from Würzburg who chose martyrdom rather than baptism, he writes, 'The Binding of Isaac was clear to see / In the streets and byways to all revealed.'

Despite their hardships, Rhineland rabbi-poets relished festive life-cycle occasions. For the Sabbath following the nuptials, they would compose mock-heroic 'permission requests' (*rešuyyot*) inviting the bridegroom to read from the Scripture lesson of the week. Their Purim poems were flushed with exuberance over the fall of Haman, igniting the hope that the present-day tyranny would likewise end. Happily, the rabbi-poets enlivened their liturgy with legends ranging from a lively adaptation of the Judith story for recital on Ḥanukkah to an engaging account for the close of the Sabbath (*havdalah*) of Elijah the prophet, who is soon to arrive and announce the coming of the Messiah.

The influence of the Hispanic poets, evident among the Italians, extended to the Rhine valley as well. Meir b. Isaac, author of more than fifty Hebrew and Aramaic hymns (the languages of the Bible) in several genres, made one modest and unimpressive attempt at composing in Arabic metres. Later efforts by Ephraim of Regensburg and the French master Jacob b. Meir Tam (Rabbenu Tam, 1100–71) were likewise disappointing. Abraham Ibn Ezra and his countryman, Judah Al-Ḥarizi (d. before 1235), sneered at their poor performance as poets, although Ibn Ezra acknowledged that Rabbenu Tam, with whom he corresponded, had endearing qualities as a scholar.

Two students of Rabbenu Tam, Jacob of Orléans and Yom Ṭov b. Isaac of Joigny, settled in England during the benign reign of the Angevin king Henry II (1154–89) and established academies in York. Both men perished in the massacre of their congregations in 1190 by a Crusader mob. Their colleague Joseph of Chartres composed a strongly worded elegy on the martyrs of York in which he blamed the 'Kitium [English] herd' for shedding 'the blood of the innocent', and noted that 'from the day your king [Richard I 'Cœur de Lion'] was crowned [in 1189], woe has come to your land.' Other elegies lamenting the fate of English Jewry followed, including a hymn by Meir of Norwich following the expulsion of England's Jews in 1290. His *piyyuṭ* chanted at the close of the Sabbath was in 'remembrance of the severity of the exile.' As in Italy and in the Rhineland, the pervasive Hispanic influence is also evident in the poetry of Meir of Norwich. This may be seen in his metrically balanced *qaṣīdah*-style hymns, and in the Hispanic-style cosmic preface to his *mi kamokha*.

Romaniote hymnography in south-eastern Europe reveals a three-stage development that is similar to the Italian experience. The early poets in Balkan Byzantium, Benjamin b. Samuel (11th c.) and his contemporaries, Isaac b. Judah, Benjamin b. Zeraḥ and Samuel Ha-Kohen Memeli, imitated Solomon Ha-Bavli's neo-classical revival practices. Like the Italian master, they generally built their hymns in a consistent word metre and with two-morpheme rhyme endings. They also favoured the Qilliric-style neologisms and allusions to rabbinic sources. Memeli, like Ha-Bavli, omitted the choral refrain from his *yoṣer*. By the twelfth century the Hispanic influence was evident in the *piyyuṭim* of the Romaniotes Moses b. Ḥiyyah and Joseph Qalai. Their hymns show a preference for biblical phrasing and reference and display an occasional use of *muwashshaḥāt* and *qaṣīdah*-style forms. They also experiment with Arabic quantitative metrics. The fascination with the writings of Gabirol and his contemporaries shows in the themes of Jewish Neoplatonism and Aristotelianism that the Romaniotes embedded in their hymns. Notable in this effort were Šabbetai Ḥaviv b. Avišay (13th c.) of Zagora (in Bulgaria); Solomon Šarvit Ha-Zahav of Ephesus (*c.*1374) and his contemporary Elijah b. Eliezer Philosof of Crete; and Šalom b. Joseph Enabi of Constantinople (*c.*1460). The interest in philosophy and science was also prompted by the Italian Renaissance, to which synagogue poets Šemaryah Ha-Ikriti (from Crete, 1275–1355) and Elijah Philosof made important contributions: Ha-Ikriti translated classical Greek literature for Robert of Anjou, and Philosof was the author of treatises on Aristotelian logic. A *tour de force* of this involvement in the revival of classical arts and sciences was the *terza rima* poem in syllabic metre, *Sefer Yašir Mošeh*, by Moses Ha-Kohen of Corfu (15th c.), modelled on Dante's *Divina Commedia*.

The role of the rabbi-poet in Balkan Byzantium was similar to that of his Franco-German counterpart. Benjamin b. Samuel was referred to as 'our angelic honoured sage' in the *Sefer Ha-Pardes*, attributed to the renowned R. Solomon b. Isaac (RaŠI, 1040–1105), master of the academy at Troyes. Hillel b. Eliaqim (12th c.) of Selymbria (near Constantinople), author of penitential hymns for the Romaniote liturgy, was cited as a rabbinic authority by the French scholar Isaac b. Abba Mari (1122–93) and the Italian sage Isaiah b. Mali (13th c.) of Trani. Following a suggestion by the rabbis (in *bPes* 6a) that he review the laws of Passover for a month before the festival, Benjamin b. Samuel chose one of his hymns as a means of instructing his congregation in Passover obligations and traditions. This was also the practice of the French hymnist, Joseph Ṭov Elem, whose instructions to his congregation reflected regional traditions, as did Benjamin's. A notable disagreement between Benjamin and Ṭov Elem resulted from the difference in furniture fashions in the two regions. Benjamin, in line with rabbinic opinion (in *bPes* 115b), tells his laity to lift the Seder table during the Passover in order to prompt children to ask the reason, and be told of God's wonders during Israel's exodus from Egypt. Ṭov Elem, however, advises his congregation to lift the Seder plate only, because (we are told by RaŠI's comment on *bPes*) it was too burdensome to lift the large tables used in French homes, as opposed to the lighter tables of the eastern Mediterranean.

The Romaniote rabbi-poets, like their Franco-German and Italian colleagues, were not reticent about speculating on the nature of the divine chariot throne in their *'ofan* hymns. In a revealing *'ofan*, Benjamin b. Samuel discloses that he has reached God's 'concealed' abode: 'there shall I sing of His wonders.' Benjamin was undoubtedly familiar with the literature of the 'chariot' (*merkavah*) mystics and their meditations on the seven celestial palaces (*heykhalot*) through which the theosophist hopes to pass and reach the divine 'throne'. His disclosure suggests that, having armed himself with the requisite esoteric knowledge, he has succeeded in making the 'ascent' unharmed, as did Rabbi Akiva (in *bḤag* 14b).

Balkan Jews were spared the horrible experience of their Rhineland brethren during the First and Second Crusades. Although there are no martyrologies of the type composed by the Franco-Germans, some revealing *'aqedah* hymns by Benjamin b. Zeraḥ suggest that the Romaniotes were fully aware of events in the Rhine valley. The trauma of the Crusades prompted a rise in messianic expectations and hopes of the imminence of Israel's redemption. The Romaniote rabbinic authority and synagogue poet, Tobias b. Eliezer of Kastoria (11th c.) was of the opinion (in his *Midraš Leqaḥ Ṭov*, on Exod. 3: 20, written in 1097) that 'all the [time] limitations have passed, and redemption is now dependent upon repentance alone.' His countryman Menaḥem b. Elia (12th c.) wrote that 'the time of redemption has been computed, / Only a few years remain . . . The time of exile has elapsed; / The rod of wickedness is broken.' The tendency to calculate the time of redemption and the end of the 'birth-throes' of the Messiah was a prominent theme in Jewish hymnography during the period of the Crusades. Benjamin b. Zeraḥ, like Benjamin b. Samuel, was learned in *merkavah* mysticism. Known as the master of the mystical divine and angelic names, Benjamin b. Zeraḥ reports the taunt of Israel's enemies, 'You have calculated the times of redemption and they are now past.' It is likely that Benjamin may have attempted to put his knowledge of esoteric names to theurgic use in hastening the Messiah's arrival. As G. Scholem has observed, 'The chief peculiarity [of *merkavah* mysticism is] its emphasis on God's might . . . [this] opens the door to the transformation of mysticism into theurgy; there the master of the secret "names" himself takes on the exercise of power.'[3] In contrast to Benjamin b. Zeraḥ's emphasis on God's might leading to theurgic use is the profound awareness of God's majesty for its own sake by the Balkan poet Abraham b. Isaac of Thebes (12th c.). In an unpretentious 'I–You' construction, the latter accepts his role as God's creature: 'You are revered in the councils [of angels] . . . I am a clod of earth, ashamed to tell Your praise.'

Related to the awareness of the deity's majesty was the Romaniote fear of divine punishment. This is seen in the several *piyyuṭim* on 'Judgment and Punishment in the Grave' by their eleventh- to fourteenth-century poets Samuel Memeli, Moses b. Ḥiyyah, Moses Ḥazan b. Abraham of Thebes,

[3] *Major Trends in Jewish Mysticism*, p. 56.

Mordecai b. Isaac, Šabbetai b. Joseph and Šemaryah b. Elqanah of Crete. Elaborating on earlier, more reticent rabbinic sources, the poets admonished their laity to repent. In this effort they spared no details in describing the horrors that await the sinner in the grave, prior to being 'thrust into the fires of hell'.

The emphatic consciousness of sin and judgment is also reflected in a Romaniote penitential hymn with the distinctive refrain, 'We have sinned (*ḥaṭa'nu*), our Rock; forgive us, our Maker.' The *ḥaṭa'nu* hymn from its earliest form in Sa'adyah Ga'on's *Siddur* to the Romaniote version, generally recounts the martyrdom of the ten Jewish Sages at the hands of the Romans during the reigns of Trajan and Hadrian. In the Romaniote treatment by Joseph b. Šelaḥya Meyuḥas (from the Greek *eugenes*, 13th c.) and Ḥananyah b. Šelaḥyah (14th c.), the plea for God's forgiveness is made on the merit of the sacrificial death of the Sages who were without sin or blemish. Their cruel death is given meaning as a vicarious atonement for Israel's sins: their martyrdom is to be as effective as the altar offerings in the Temple. Meyuḥas prays that God will 'consider the blood of the holy [Sages] that was spilled by the hands of the pagans / Like fatlings that were offered on God's altar,' and Ḥananyah pleads with the deity to 'receive the blood that was spilled . . . as You would my sacred Temple gift and my burnt offering'.

On the lighter side of Romaniote hymnography is Solomon Šarvit Ha-Zahav's mock-serious debate between Sabbath and Ḥanukkah when the two festivals occur on the same day. Each party makes its claim to priority in rank. Although the arguments are based on Jewish law, the intent of the hymn is to amuse and entertain the congregation on Ḥanukkah, the Feast of Lights. The aesthetic function of the Balkan rabbi-poets was similar in many ways to that of their Hispanic colleagues. A zionide by Menaḥem Tamar (15th c.) is constructed in the style of Judah Ha-Levi, and hymns in homonym rhyme distichs with identical closing units of different meanings by Abraham b. Menaḥem (14th c.) and his contemporary Šemaryah Ha-Kohen b. Aaron were patterned after Spanish and Provençal models. The latter's influence is also seen in the ingenious strophic hymns by Kastoria's Menaḥem b. Elia and Constantinople's Elia b. Benjamin Ha-Levi. Menaḥem's poem in fourteen strophes comprises five cola in monorhyme with five units in each hemi-colon. Repeating each unit fifty times, the poet spells his name and that of his father. Not to be outdone, Elia Ha-Levi builds his hymn with 1,000 units beginning with the letter *bet*, and divides the whole into twenty strophes connected by anadiplosis: repetition of the units closing and opening the strophes. Balkan poets, while not as influential as Qillir, Sa'adyah, Solomon Ha-Bavli or the Andalusians, were their willing students, even as they were open to the new forms and ideas emerging in the Italian renaissance. To their credit, Romaniote hymns were included not only in southeastern European liturgies, as expected, but in Italian, Franco-German and Spanish prayer-books as well.

The Karaites, a Jewish sect originating in the first half of the eighth century, are distinctive mainly because of their refusal to accept the authority of the talmudic-rabbinic tradition. Although the Karaites were at odds with their Rabbanite brethren in matters relating to Jewish law, they readily adopted the latters' models in hymnography. The Karaite liturgy, which in the early years of the sect consisted of recitation from the Psalms and other scriptural readings, soon developed into rich and varied genres for fasts and feasts. The new hymnography was preserved in the thirteenth-century Karaite prayer-book edited by the scholar-poet Aaron b. Joseph the Elder from Crimea and Constantinople. Like their Rabbanite counterparts, Karaite hymnists served a didactic function, instructing the laity in their religious obligations. This was the purpose of Constantinople's Elijah Bašyatchi's (*c*.1420–90) listing of the positive and negative commands—modelled on a hymn by Solomon Ibn Gabirol—for the Karaite Pentecost service. Karaite poets also used the liturgy as a means of instructing their congregations in current philosophical issues, particularly those relating to Jewish Neoplatonism and the nature of the soul. In their aesthetic function, Karaite hymnists resembled the Rabbanite Hispanics, favouring Arabic quantitative metres and verse forms. Caleb Afendopolo (d. 1525) of Kramariya (near Constantinople) was the master of this poetic art, as seen in his liturgical (and secular) writings, including his moving elegies on the expulsion of Jews from Lithuania and Kiev in 1495.

It is hoped that this brief introduction will make the reader want to learn more about the literary history of the *piyyuṭ* embellishing the obligatory fixed prayers in the synagogue service, and the cantor-poets who chanted the hymns. In the following chapters as we trace the development of the *piyyuṭ* from its beginnings in Ereṣ Yisra'el to its later development in Europe, we shall learn more about the changes prompted by differences in culture and historical experience. We shall also observe that the status of the *piyyuṭ* itself changed from its humble beginnings as a grudging concession by Babylonian rabbis to a valued tool for prayer and teaching by rabbi-poets in central and eastern Europe. A difference in the function of the *piyyuṭ* will also appear in its Hispanic period, when it changed from an art form reflecting the taste of courtier-rabbis to a less self-conscious medium of worship for the middle class. These changes in theme, language, tone and pattern of the liturgical hymn were influenced by its creative practitioners, Qillir, Sa'adyah, Solomon Ha-Bavli and Ibn Gabirol and his contemporaries, among others. The constant in the literary history of the *piyyuṭ* is its organic character reflecting the dynamic life and times of its users, the Jewish people.

I

The Beginnings of Hymnography in Ereṣ Yisra'el and Babylon

THE EARLY PERIOD IN EREṢ YISRA'EL

GENERAL BACKGROUND

THE LITURGICAL HYMN or *piyyuṭ* is by definition a poetic work that is chanted and designed by its composer (*payṭan*) for use in Jewish worship. It is necessary to distinguish between the term *piyyuṭ* (from the Greek *poietes*) as a general designation of Hebrew poetry, such as the rabbinic mnemonic on the letters of the Hebrew alphabet (in *bŠab* 104a), and its specific function as part of the synagogue service. We will also differentiate between the older obligatory prayers (*tefillah šel ḥovah*) such as the *šema*ʿ, the *ʿamidah*, the *qeduššah* (based on Isa. 6: 3), the blessings of the priests (*birkat ha-kohanim*), the blessings after meals (*birkat ha-mazon*), the blessings over the wine on the Sabbath (*qidduš*) and the blessings over the wine at the end of the Sabbath (*havdalah*), among others, and the later poetic additions to the Jewish liturgy. Our primary focus will be on the latter embellishments of the older fixed prayers. These embellishments include *piyyuṭim* for the benedictions of the *šema*ʿ and *ʿamidah*, and a wide variety of penitentials (*seliḥot*), elegies, epithalamia and life-cycle celebrations.

In Judeo-Arabic circles the musical component of the liturgical hymn was in eight modes (*octoechos*), as attested by Saʿadyah Ga'on and Abraham Ibn Ezra (in his commentary on Ps. 6: 1). It is likely that the Franco-German synagogues also employed this eightfold system of modality, as reported by the Jewish traveller Petaḥyah b. Jacob of Ratisbon.[1] The *piyyuṭ* is also known by the Arabicized term *ḥizānah* derived from the Hebrew *ḥazzan*, a synagogue official who, in talmudic times, among his other responsibilities

[1] See *Literaturblatt des Orients*, 4 (1844), col. 541, n. 44.

such as bringing out the Torah scrolls for the weekly reading and sounding the *šofar* heralding the Sabbath and festivals, would also chant the prayers when requested. With the increase in the number and variety of liturgical works he assumed the responsibility of selecting and chanting the appropriate hymns and on occasion composing new ones. He now became the *ḥazzan ha-keneset*, synagogue cantor, or *šeliaḥ ṣibbur*, the emissary of the congregation before God, and received a stipend for his services.[2]

With regard to the beginnings of the liturgical hymn there is the testimony of the eighth-century North African worthy Pirqoy b. Baboy, who writes in the name of his teacher's teacher, Yehuday, *ga'on* of Sura,

> The [authorities in Byzantium] forced apostasy upon the settlers in the land of Israel and decreed that they not recite the *šemaʿ* nor offer prayers. For the morning service, they permitted the recitation and the chanting of the *maʿamadot* [i. e. *qerovot*, embellishments of the *ʿamidah*]. This they did out of necessity [*be'ones*].

I. Davidson (in *Maḥazor Yannay*, pp. xix–xx) suggested that the emergence of piyyutic additions was designed to teach Jewish law following the Emperor Justinian's *Novella* No. 146 (529 AD) forbidding the Jews to study the *deuterosis* (Oral Torah). However, it is likely that *piyyuṭim* were composed before Justinian's edict. From the comments of a polemicist and convert to Islam, the twelfth-century Samau'al Ibn Yaḥya' of Fez in his *Ifḥām al-Yahud* (Silencing the Jews), we learn the following:

> The Parsees forbade the Jews to recite their [obligatory] prayers . . . and when the Jews realized that the Parsees would not relent in this, they composed [new] prayers in which they embedded verses from their obligatory prayers and called them *al-ḥizānah*. For these prayers they arranged a musical setting and at the times appointed for prayer they would gather to sing and to recite them. The difference between the *ḥizānah* and the obligatory prayers [Arab. *ṣalāt*] is that the *ṣalāt* is recited without melody; the cantor alone reads the [obligatory] prayers, unlike the *ḥizānah* in which the congregation joins in the reading and singing . . . It is surprising, therefore, that when the Muslims [who conquered the Parsees] permitted the protected minorities [Jews and Christians] to fulfil their religious obligations and recite their obligatory prayers that the *ḥizānah* for festivals and intermediary days as well as for joyous occasions had taken on the character of an obligation. The *ḥizānah* now became a common practice, taking the place of the *ṣalāt*, although they were not forced to it.[3]

The view that the emergence of the liturgical hymn was prompted by anti-Jewish decrees is supported by Judah b. Barzillay (11th–12th c.) of Barcelona:[4]

> [Regarding] these *piyyuṭim* which are recited throughout the world . . . it is said that they were ordained only for the time of forced apostasy because they were unable to

[2] Cf. Baron, *Social and Religious History*, vii. 82–3; Werner, *The Sacred Bridge*, pp. 384–7.

[3] See Ginzberg, *Ginzey Schechter*, ii. 551–2; the excerpt from the *Ifḥam* was edited and translated by M. Schreiner in *MGWJ* 42 (1898), 217 ff.

[4] Judah b. Barzilay, *Sefer Ha-ʿIttim*, p. 252.

read from the Torah given that the enemy forbade the study of the Torah. Therefore their sages arranged for insertions within the prayers so as to instruct the laymen about the laws of the festivals . . . in the form of praise, thanksgiving, verse and poetry.

While not discounting these historical considerations, it is equally important to view the liturgical hymn as a natural expression of the lay congregation seeking a larger and more creative share in the worship service. Creativity and spontaneity in prayer were also urged by the rabbis, noted above (in *'Avot* 2. 18): 'Do not make your prayer a prescribed routine [*qevaʿ*] but a plea for mercy and grace before God.'

THE PRINCIPAL POETS

The Early Cantor-Poets and the Anonymous *Payṭanim*

Sa'adyah Ga'on in the Arabic introduction to his *Sefer Ha-'Egron*[5] lists the earliest synagogue poets: Yose b. Yose, Yannai, Eleazar [Qillir], Joshua and Phinehas, all natives of Ereṣ Yisra'el, according to recent research. Preceding them were anonymous poets presumed to have lived between the third and sixth centuries. They are credited with some thirty fragments of hymns preserved in rabbinic literature. Some *piyyuṭim* in common use like *U-v-khen ten paḥdekha* (And therefore let your awe be manifest) for the Days of Awe and *Ribbon kol ha-ʿolamim* (Sovereign of all worlds) for the preliminary morning service are attributed to the third-century Ereṣ Yisra'el *'amora'*, R. Yoḥanan b. Nappaḥa, while others, like the New Year *malkhuyyot*, *zikhronot*, *šoferot* compositions (Sovereignty, Remembrance, Trumpet) and their introit *ʿAleynu le-šabbeaḥ* (It is incumbent upon us to praise) are said to have been composed by Abba Arikha, a third-century *'amora'* from Babylon. The texts of several elegies surviving in rabbinic sources are said to have been written by the *tanna'* R. Pinḥas b. Ya'ir (*mSot* 9. 15) and the *'amora'im* Bar Qippoq and Bar Abin, contemporaries of R. Aši (375–427) of Babylon. Included in this collection is the anonymous 'Song of the Kine' (in *bAZ* 24b), which the Israelites are said to have sung when the Ark was to set out and Moses said: 'Advance O Lord . . . ' (Num. 10: 35):

> Sing, O sing acacia tree [= the ark, made of acacia wood,
>   Exod. 25: 10]
> Ascend in all your gracefulness
> With golden weave they cover you,
> The sanctuary-palace hears your eulogy,
> With divers jewels are you adorned.

[5] Sa'adyah Ga'on, *Sefer Ha-'Egron*, p. 154.

The considerable list of hymns from the period of the anonymous poets is given in L. Zunz's epochal work, *Literaturgeschichte der synagogalen Poesie* (pp. 11–22). Some common features help to identify hymns from this period.

1. The anonymous poets rarely used rabbinic sources, or metonymy.[6] Their language, based on biblical models, is generally clear and unambiguous.
2. They embellished their hymns with an alphabetic acrostic (after Ps. 145). The acrostic may begin with the first letter and end with the last, or begin with the last and end with the first (a form known as *taśraq*).[7]
3. Other embellishments included anadiplosis (*širšur*), word repetition that serves to link two units of discourse such as consecutive stanzas or sentences,[8] refrains, and introductory scriptural verses.
4. Bilateral symmetry with balance of units in the bicolon.
5. Alliteration and repetitive rhyme units.

Following is an example of bilateral symmetry from a Days of Awe introit for the cantor. Note the balance of four units in each bicolon:

'Oḥilah la-'el 'aḥalleh fanaw
'Eš'alah mimmennu ma'aneh lašon
'Ašer bi-qhal-'am 'aširah 'uzzo
'Abiy'ah renanot be-'ad mif'alaw

Hoping in God, I implore Him,
I seek the gift of eloquence;
I would sing His praise abroad,
I would rejoice in His deeds.

A sample of alliteration is seen in the *šiv'ata'* (= seven, a hymn embellishing the seven benedictions of the Sabbath and festival *'amidah* that did not include the *qeduššah*, the Trisagion, in Isa. 6: 3) for the Passover Prayer for Dew:

[6] An exception is the hymn *'El 'adon 'al kol ha-ma'asim* (God is Lord over all His works). The phrase 'He summoned the sun and it shed its light; He looked and ordained the form of the moon' (*ra'ah we-hitqin ṣurat ha-levanah*) is presumably based on the rabbinic comment (*Gen. Rabbah* 6. 1) that God created two in order to lessen the chance that they would be treated as divinities. An alternative reading proposed by R. Jacob b. Asher (d. 1340), 'He saw and lessened the form of the moon' (*ra'ah we-hiqtin ṣurat ha-levanah*), is clearly indebted to the rabbinic note (in *bḤul* 60b) that initially both sun and moon shed light in equal measure. However, when the moon became envious of the sun, God ordered, 'Go and make yourself smaller.' Cf. Ber, *Seder*, p. 212. Metonymy is found in Scripture; cf. Deut. 32: 4; Ps. 80: 3. The use of metonymy by an anonymous poet is seen in the Purim hymn *Šošanat ya'aqov* (Lily of Jacob). The words refer to the Jewish people.

[7] e.g. the Sabbath hymn *Tiqqanta šabbat*.

[8] Anadiplosis occurs in the Sabbath hymn *Ha-kol yodukha, we-ha-kol yešabḥukha*, following the benediction which ends, *'oseh šalom u-vore' 'et ha-kol*.

'Iddarta 'emunim 'aṣiley 'eytanim
Be-'ahavah baḥarta be-ḥodeš nisan.

You have exalted the faithful [= Israel], scion of the mighty
[= Patriarchs]
With love You have chosen the month of Nisan.

The following selection from a *qedušta'* (a nine-part hymn embellishing the benedictions of the *'amidah* and ending with the Trisagion (= *qeduššah*)) for Pentecost, expanding on the Fifth Commandment (Exod. 20: 8), illustrates the practice of repetitive rhyme units:

'Oznekha haṭṭeh le-'imrey 'avikha
Beni, šemor miṣwat 'avikha
Giddelkha 'al kappayim 'avikha.

Heed the words of your father;
My son, observe the rules of your father
Who lifted you up on his hands, your father.[9]

Yose b. Yose

The last text cited is by Yose b. Yose, a transitional figure who lived in the fourth or fifth century and was the first of the hymnists named by Sa'adyah Ga'on as an early synagogue poet. While retaining some of the literary mannerisms of the anonymous poets, he experiments with rhyming forms other than repetitive units and borrows more frequently from rabbinic literature, given that the Jerusalem Talmud, edited *c.*350, was now available. Although known primarily for his *'avodot*, poetic treatments of the Day of Atonement Temple service, of which three versions have survived, he also composed hymns for the New Year *malkhuyyot, zikhronot* and *šoferot* cycles accompanying the *šofar* soundings; a *seliḥah* (penitential hymn) for the Day of Atonement evening service; two surviving fragments of larger, as yet unidentified works; and a *widduy* (confessional). Although some *'avodot* from the period before Yose have survived in the Cairo Geniza, Yose's three versions became the models for the genre and were widely imitated by hymnists in Babylon, Italy and Spain.

Innovations in phrasing and rhetoric emerge in Yose's poetry. While relying, for the most part, on the language of Scripture, he allows himself to recontextualize a familiar usage. Following is an example from his *'avodah*, *'Azkir gevurot 'elohah* (I will recall God's mighty acts):[10]

[9] Habermann, *Toledot Ha-Piyyuṭ*, i. 26–32; Mirsky, 'Gidrey ha-piyyuṭs'; Fleischer, *Širat Ha-Qodeš*, pp. 87–9. See *Sefer Ha-Pardes*, pp. 223 ff.

[10] Mirsky, *Piyyuṭey Yose*, p. 122: 2.

'Aḥaraw 'eyn ba-ḥeled
Lefanaw 'eyn ba-šaḥaq
'Eyn bilto qedem
We-'eyn zulato be-ʿeyqev

There is no one since Him on earth,
No one preceded Him in heaven;
There is no one except Him in the east,
And there is none beside Him in the west.

In his innovative use of *be-ʿeyqev* as meaning 'in the west', Yose endows the term with a new connotation. He does this by constructing an antithetic parallelism between *qedem* (east) and *ʿeyqev* (west), similar to the earlier contrast between *ḥeled* (earth) and *šaḥaq* (heaven). Yose's source for this usage is Ps. 119: 112: 'I incline my heart to perform your statutes, *forever, to the end*' (Heb. *le-ʿolam ʿeyqev*).

Metonymy, sparsely employed by the anonymous poets, is widespread in the poetry of Yose. Metonymy is already present in Scripture. Terms like Rock (Heb. *ṣur*, Deut. 32: 4, 18, and 37), Shepherd of Israel (*roʿeh yisra'el*, Ps. 80: 2) and Enthroned on the Cherubim (*yošev ha-keruvim*, Ps. 80: 2) are familiar designations for the deity. However, in the conceit of Yose, metonymy functions not only as metaphor but also as a historic descriptor or extended paraphrase. An example of metonymy as descriptor is in Yose's *'Azkir gevurot*. There he uses the direct metaphor 'lamps' (Heb. *nerot*, l. 25) in referring to sun and moon, but Isaac is designated as the 'lamb' (*ṭaleh*, l. 95) based on the Binding of Isaac story (Gen. 22: 8). Yose's use of metonymy as paraphrase is seen in his reference to the Serpent in the Garden of Eden as 'dirt crawler' (*zoḥel ʿafar*, l. 45) after Gen. 3: 14. Another example of paraphrase metonymy is his use of 'the third' (*šeliši*, l. 105) in designating the tribe of Levi, the third of Jacob's sons.

Even as metonymy served the poet in bringing relief from the monotony of repetiton, his use of rhetorical devices enlivened his art and embellished his narrative. For example, in Yose's *'Azkir gevurot* (l. 35) the poet adds to the creation story in Genesis by probing God's mind as He is about to create the world:

He [God] thought to himself: Who will enjoy this world? [lit. who will enter here?] . . .
If I create [man] by my word, he will pose as God
And if he disobeys, I will return him to the dust.

Again, in the Binding of Isaac story (Gen. 22) the poet puts these words into God's mouth as Abraham is about to sacrifice his son (l. 94):

Do not kill the lad; your action is as
Pleasing as if you had sacrificed.

Another device designed to enhance the interest of the congregation is the rhetorical question. In Yose's hymn for the New Year, *ʼAhalelah ʼelohay*[11] (I will praise God), the poet asks (l. 4):

Who is it that excels in rank and excels in power?
And whose is the kingdom?

And again in his *ʼEfḥad be-maʻasay*,[12] (I fear for my [evil] deeds, l. 3):

When I come to judgment, who will be my stay?
And who will remember to defend me in my cause?

In improving on the anonymous poets Yose introduces a variety of voices into his hymnography. As emissary of the congregation he seeks God's mercy for his people, but he also identifies with the worshipper who communicates with the deity through him. At times the poet identifies with God, as it were, and speaks in His name words of comfort to Israel or threatens punishment to the nations that afflict His people. A personal touch is given to God's voice in His address to Israel (in the *seliḥah*, *ʼEten tehillah*[13] (I will give praise)) attributed to Yose (l. 37):

He called in a loud voice: I am God Almighty:
  Return to Me and I will return to you.

The second part of the colon is based on Joel 2: 12 and Mal. 3: 7, but the first part is in the poet's imagination as he seeks to convey the urgency of God's plea to His people.

Unlike the anonymous poets who rarely employ rabbinic sources, Yose, who lived at a time when the texts of the rabbis became available, used them more often. Note his *ʼAzkir gevurot* (l. 10):

A thousand generations before [creation] God considered
Using the Torah as a model for His building plans.

Yose's conceit is based on *Gen. Rabbah* 1. 4, where the Torah is said to have preceded the creation of the world. In *Gen. Rabbah* 1. 1 God is perceived as gazing upon the Torah while He creates the world. In the same work (l. 19) Yose observes that the fires of Hell were created on the second day:

When He separated the waters [Gen. 1: 7] he ignited
The bonfires of Hell beyond measure.

It is likely that Yose's source was *Gen. Rabbah* 4. 6: 'Why is "that it was good" [Gen. 1: 4] not written in connection with the second day? R. Yoḥanan explained . . . "Because on it Gehenna was created."'

[11] Mirsky, *Piyyuṭey Yose*, pp. 87–95.
[12] Ibid. 95–103.
[13] Ibid. 236–41.

Yose's experiments with rhyme were sporadic and limited. Most of his surviving works are unrhymed, or limited to unit repetition closing the colon or the strophe, in line with the style of the anonymous poets. Such is his practice in *'Ahalelah 'elohay* ending with the unit *melukhah*; *'Efḥad be-ma'asay*, ending with *zikkaron*; and *'Eftaḥ peh be-renen*,[14] attributed to him where the closing unit is *melekh*. However, in the hymn preserved in the Cairo Geniza, *'Ekhre'ah we-'evrekhah*, attributed to Yose, the versatile poet experiments with strophes in rhyming tercets and quatrains.[15]

In addition to his occasional use of rhyme, Yose also employs a metrical stress rhythm, as in his *'avodah, 'Attah khonanta*:[16]

'Àttah khoǹanta / 'òlam be-rov ḥesed / u-v̀o yitnaȟeg / 'ad qeṣ̌ ha-yaǹin
'Ašer lò' yiǹmoṭ / me-'awòn yeṣuřim / we-lò' yim'àd / mi-koved p̌eša' wa-ḥaṭa'ìm.

You have established the world with steadfast love, by which it is guided eternally
It is not to be moved by the sins of man, it will not totter from the weight of crimes and transgressions.

The strophe contains four major stresses in each of the four hemicola, as indicated by a diagonal stroke. Precedent for a stress pattern in Hebrew poetry is found in the work of Ben-Sira (2nd c. BC), who employs four stresses in each hemicolon, as does Yose. Later poets, like Qillir and the Italian Solomon Ha-Bavli who came under his influence, follow a carefully regulated stress pattern.[17]

Yose's pioneering efforts were tempered by his regard for older rhetorical figures. Following the practice of the anonymous poets, he favours anadiplosis (*širšur*), in which repeated units are used to link the strophes.[18] Like his predecessors, Yose often adorns his strophes with refrains, and employs the use of headers from Scripture in order to establish a frame of reference for his hymn. There is also a distinct clarity in Yose's style of writing which is similar to that of the anonymous poets. Little is known about the poet's life, other than that he lived in Ereṣ Yisra'el. References to Yose as 'the orphan' (*ha-yatom*), because he bore the name of his father, or 'the high priest' because

14 Mirsky, *Piyyuṭey Yose*, pp. 242–4.

15 Ibid. 244–8.

16 Ibid. 172–99. Fleischer, *Širat Ha-Qodeš*, pp. 84–5.

17 The principle of isosyllabism, the use of an established equal number of syllables for each colon, is found in early Syriac poetry and in Byzantine church hymnography; it is commonly employed by the church hymnist Ephrem the Syrian (*c*.306–73). Cf. Fleischer, *Piyyuṭey Šelomo Ha-Bavli*, pp. 86–9; Werner, 'Hebrew and Oriental Christian Metrical Hymns'.

18 *Širšur* was also favoured by later generations of Mediterranean and central European hymnists. It is seen as late as the 16th c. in the work of the Salonikan poet Solomon Mevorakh. Cf. Weinberger, 'Širim ḥadašim', I, pp. 60–2.

he lived during Temple times and composed *'avodot* describing the Temple service, are mere speculation.[19]

THE PRINCIPAL GENRES

Seliḥah

Among the earliest additions to the fixed prayers were the *seliḥot*, penitential prayers chanted on fast-days. The theme of the *seliḥah* is related to the sixth benediction of the *amidah*: 'Praised are You, Lord who welcomes repentance' (*ha-marbeh lisloaḥ*). On fast-days other than the Ninth of 'Av, the *seliḥah* addition was inserted in this benediction.[20] *Seliḥot* were also chanted in what came to be known as the 'rite of forgiveness' (*Seder ha-seliḥot*). This practice was observed during the Ten Days of Repentance from the New Year to the Day of Atonement and took place during midnight services or just before daybreak. Another early form of the *seliḥah* was the *tokheḥah* (self-rebuke). Penitential prayers in these forms were added to the Day of Atonement service to lengthen it as the entire day would customarily be spent in the synagogue.

'Azharah

This is a poetic listing of the 613 positive and negative commands in the Torah. The number is based on a comment attributed to R. Simlai (*c.*200) in *bMakk* 23b. *'Azharah* (warning) hymns were chanted on Pentecost, the traditional anniversary of the giving of the Torah. One of the earliest hymns in this genre, *'Azharat re'šit le-'ammekha* (A warning You gave to Your people), relates to the giving of the Torah by the term *re'šit* in Prov. 8: 22: 'The Lord created me [Wisdom/Torah] in the beginning [*re'šit*] of His work.'

'Avodah

The New Year and Day of Atonement services were enhanced with additional prayers, a practice noted in a rabbinic source (in *jBer* 1. 6), 'What benedictions are made long? The benedictions of the New Year.' Among the enhancements were the three sets of prayers added to the *'amidah*. These affirmed God as king (*malkhuyyot*), remembered Him as judge (*zikhronot*) and rejoiced in Him as redeemer (*šoferot*). Additions on the Day of Atonement included an expanded confessional service, and the *'avodah*, an account—based in large part on *mYoma'* 3–5—of the sacrificial ritual by the High Priest during the Temple period. Later treatments of the *'avodah* by

[19] See Mirsky, *Piyyuṭey Yose*, pp. 10–11.

[20] See *Seder Rav 'Amram Ga'on*, p. 95.

Yose b. Yose were expanded to include an introduction describing the creation of the world and Israel's early history, leading to the election of the Aaronic priesthood and the Temple service. Further embellishments of the *'avodah* begun by Yose and continued by his successors included the supplements *Mah nehdar* (How glorious) and *'Ašrey 'ayin* (Fortunate to behold). The first began 'Truly, how glorious was the High Priest as he left the Holy Place,' and was based in part on Ben-Sira 50: 5: 'How glorious was he [the High Priest] surrounded by the people, as he came out of the house of the curtain,' and on *mYoma'* 7. 4, 'And he [the High Priest] made a feast for his friends because he came out safely from the Holy Place.' The second hymn, opening with 'Happy is the eye that has seen all this; does not the soul languish hearing it?' was designed to draw the contrast between the happier time of Temple days and the priestly service and the tragic present, with the Temple in ruins and Israel in exile.[21]

THE CLASSICAL PERIOD IN EREṢ YISRA'EL

GENERAL BACKGROUND

Ezra Fleischer in his *Širat Ha-Qodeš Ha-'Ivrit Bi-ymey Ha-Beynayim* (Hebrew Liturgical Poetry in the Middle Ages) has divided the literary history of Jewish hymnography in the eastern Mediterranean into the pre-classical period of the anonymous poets and Yose b. Yose (4th–6th c.), the classical period featuring the contributions of Yannai and Qillir (6th–8th c.), and the post-classical period (mid 8th–11th c.), when Babylon (Iraq) and North Africa replaced Ereṣ Yisra'el as the centre of liturgical creativity.

A New Role for Cantor-Poets

The new additions to the obligatory prayers, the *šema'* and *'amidah*, were undoubtedly prompted to a large degree by lay congregations seeking a wider variety and greater involvement in the worship service. Did not the rabbis urge (in *'Avot* 2. 18) creativeness in prayer? However, given the time-consuming labours required to provide for one's family it was not always possible to give the needed attention to prayer, as did, for example, the pious men of old 'who used to wait an hour before praying in order that they might concentrate their thoughts upon their Father in heaven' (*mBer* 5. 1). Hence obligatory prayers at fixed times, like the *šema'* and the *'amidah*, were instituted. These were recited by individuals both at home and in the synagogue, and in the latter were also repeated by the cantor. This cantorial repetition of

[21] See Fleischer, *Širat Ha-Qodeš*, pp. 93, 176–7.

fixed prayers did not satisfy worshippers who sought wider expressions of their need to communicate with the deity. At the urging of the members of the congregation, cantors of the pre-classical period therefore obliged by composing hymns which they inserted into the obligatory prayers.[22]

The emergence of liturgical additions as a response to the needs of the lay congregation is supported by the comment of the eleventh-century hymnist, Benjamin b. Samuel from Byzantium:[23] 'When learning decreased [in Israel] and became marginal, they composed hymns in lieu of exegesis.' The symbiosis between the liturgical hymn and popular tastes may be seen in the uncommon liturgical usages of the early cantor-poets, notably those of Eleazar Qillir. S. Spiegel correctly surmised that while Qillir's neologisms may be reprehensible to purists like Abraham Ibn Ezra (1092–1167) and incomprehensible to moderns, they reflect contemporary vernacular usage and were easily understood by his congregation. The learned Benjamin b. Samuel's statement that the *piyyuṭ* emerged as a grudging concession to the unlearned is characteristic of the disdain in scholarly quarters for this intrusion into the worship service. Pirqoy b. Baboy, the eighth-century rabbinic scholar from North Africa, reflected the views of contemporary learned circles when he wrote:

> Now that the Holy One blessed be He has destroyed the kingdom of Edom [Byzantium] and has nullified their decrees, and the invading Ishmaelites have allowed them to study the Torah and recite the *šemaʿ* and pray, it is forbidden to pray in ways other than those ordained by our sages, of blessed memory.[24]

The cantor-poet performed not only an aesthetic function in ornamenting the fixed prayers in the synagogue service but also a didactic role in interpreting Jewish legend and law. One of his responsibilities was to translate the reading from the Torah (*jMeg* 4. 1, 42d) into the vernacular. In this practice he often incurred the wrath of the rabbis, who faulted him for translating in a manner that they perceived to be contrary to Jewish law. The following is an example. In Lev. 5: 1 the law requires a sin offering from a person who refuses to testify while knowing that his refusal to be a witness could lead to a miscarriage of justice. In the rabbinic interpretation, the sin offering is required of one *who has been sworn in as a witness* and then fails to give testimony (RaŠI on Lev. 5: 1). In the view of Yannai—supported by the translation of the verse from Leviticus by Jonathan b. Uzziel—a person must make a sin offering if he has seen or heard a transgression and fails to report it, *even if he has not been sworn in as a witness.* Here is Yannai's statement from his *qerovah* on Lev. 5: 1:

[22] See Elbogen, *Ha-Tefillah*, pp. 210–15; Fleischer, *Širat Ha-Qodeš*, pp. 47 ff.

[23] See *Sefer Ha-Pardes*, pp. 223 ff.

[24] See Spiegel, 'Kalir, Eleasar', *EJ* (1932), ix. 819; Yahalom, *Sefat Ha-Šir*, pp. 17–18. The source of Pirqoy's statement is in Ginzberg, *Ginzey Schechter*, ii. 552.

When you hear one swearing falsely
Or cursing the name of the Lord,
You are to hasten to the court-house
And not hesitate or waver.

Another disagreement between rabbis and cantor-poets can be traced to Pirqoy b. Baboy's strictures against those among the latter who elaborate upon the mysteries of the divine 'chariot throne', in violation of rabbinic law (in *mḤag* 2. 1). Although the poets generally restrained themselves in their embellishment of the morning service *'ofan* hymn which describes the adoration of God by the angels (based on Isa. 6: 3), they were less reticent in their *qedušta'ot*, the multi-part insertions into the *'amidah*. An example of their independence in this regard is the *qedušta'* of Yannai on Gen. 28: 12 ff., describing Jacob's ladder and the angelic traffic thereon. His expansive comments on this esoteric subject were based on the *heykhalot* tracts in Jewish mysticism, and presumably had wide appeal to and general support in the lay congregation.[25]

The autonomy and self-confidence of the hymnists is also seen in the sources they employ. As expected, Yannai, a native of Ereṣ Yisra'el, relies mostly on the Jerusalem Talmud and rarely on the Babylonian. Unexpected, however, is his use of legends from the *Testament of the Twelve Patriarchs*, a pseudo-epigraphic work that has been preserved in a Greek text but must have circulated in a Hebrew edition during the lifetime of the poet. In Yannai's citation from the *Testament* (2. 2) Simeon regrets the grief that he caused his brother Joseph whom he cast into a pit: 'I knew . . . that this [punishment] had happened to me because of Joseph, so I repented and wept.' Yannai's use of the citation is in his *qerovah* on Exod. 1: 1 listing the character of the twelve tribes who enter Egypt:[26] 'Simeon, the weapon of violence [after Gen. 49: 5] in his hand, / Confesses his sin.'

For the most part, however, the cantor-poets reflected the beliefs and opinions of the rabbis in such matters as the unique nature and interdependence of humankind created in God's image, and the sanctity of Israel's land. Yannai, in particular, lingers over the theme that all humans endowed with a spirit (*nefeš*) given by God are equal in His sight. The following is a section from his *qedušta'* on Lev. 25: 14: 'When you make a sale to your neighbour or buy from your neighbour, you shall not cheat one another.'[27]

All creatures are equal before You
As on the day they were born . . .
The servant as the master
The mistress as the maid.

[25] Rabinovitz, *Maḥazor . . . Yannai*, i. 375. [26] Ibid. 262. [27] Ibid. 472.

Pursuing this metaphor, Yannai echoes the bold conclusion of the rabbis (in *Lev. Rabbah* 4. 8) that the spirit with which man is endowed and God, who is pure spirit, are equal. This is how the poet puts it in his *qeduŝta'* on Lev. 4: 1: 'You have likened the spirit of the Father [God] to the spirit of the son [man] . . . She is unique and You are unique; she is eternal and You are eternal; she is pure and You are pure; she is never asleep and You are never asleep.' Moreover, the spirit that God breathes into man gives him the same freedom to make choices:[28]

> Good and evil, mercy and cruelty, life and death He has given to man,
> He prospers when virtuous, he finds relief through compassion, he lives when endowing others . . .

When man fails to choose wisely, God is merciful; His wish is for his creatures to succeed through obedience to His commands, which are both moral and rational. It is imperative that man understand the reasons for the commands, rather than obey them perfunctorily. For example, the ram's horn that is sounded on the New Year is required to be bent in shape and not upright, in order to teach the value of humility and that God will lift up the lowly. Likewise, man must be clear about the reason for the Temple and the altar offerings. The 'sweet savour for the Lord' of the burnt animal is not to be understood literally: God does not require food or drink. The purpose of the Temple was to provide an earthly dwelling-place for God. Yannai alludes to this in his *qeduŝta'* on Num. 15: 1–3:[29]

> Here I will sit on My throne;
> Here I will sleep in My bed.

This bold metaphor echoes the rabbinic observation (in *Cant. Rabbah* 3. 11: 'Look . . . at King Solomon . . . on the day of his wedding') that God said to Moses: 'If you make [the likeness] of this heavenly [tabernacle] below, I shall leave my heavenly council above and descend and confine My divine presence within the midst of you below.' To which a rabbi adds, commenting on 'on the day of his wedding': 'this refers to [the consecration of] the Tent of Meeting.' In this metaphor the Temple, recontextualized by the rabbis and Yannai, becomes the home of God the bridegroom and Israel His bride and is the place where He 'sits' and 'sleeps'.

Since the divine spirit is the common endowment of humankind, it follows that all are interdependent. The rich are exhorted not only to be generous to the poor but also to know that their continued well-being depends on the degree of their generosity:

[28] Ibid. 478. [29] Ibid. ii. 56.

Merit and blame You inscribe on Your right hand;
All the days are made of change.[30]

Here too the cantor-poet draws upon rabbinic commentary (in *Lev. Rabbah* 34. 9),

R. Abin observed: The poor man stands at your door and the Holy One, blessed be He stands at his right . . . If you give him something, reflect who stands on his right that will give you reward, and if you do not give him anything, reflect that He who stands at his right will punish you.

Like the rabbis, the cantor-poet reserves a special place for Israel, people and land. This people apart existed before the creation of the world, which was made for its sake. Although 'mountains may be removed . . . and hills collapse, you, Israel, will not fall,' writes Yannai. Eternal also is the relationship between God, the bridegroom and Israel, His bride, who is set as a seal upon His heart (after Cant. 8: 6 and the rabbinic comments in *Cant. Rabbah*). To this choice people is given a select land praised sevenfold (Deut. 8: 8), like its inhabitants:[31]

A land of wheat and barley to the first [fruits of His harvest] [Jer. 2: 3];
A land of vines to the fruitful vine [Ps. 128: 3];
A land of fig trees to the ripened fig [Hos. 9: 10] . . .
She is sacred and they are sacred; let my holy ones come and settle in the holy land.

They who live in the land of Israel are encouraged to remain, although foreign powers rule over it. Those faithful settlers are the guardians of the treaty that God made with the Fathers, as recorded in Lev. 26: 42: 'I will remember my covenant with Jacob . . . and I will remember the land.' Their presence in the land guarantees that God will remember to keep his word and hasten Israel's national restoration. Reassuring the remaining settlers, the poet reminds them that descendants from the royal house of David have survived, even as have the priestly families who served in the Temple's twenty-four divisions. He urges them not be dismayed because the land is desolate and sparsely settled. Remember that Sarah, Abraham's wife, was barren and no one thought that she would bear a child in her advanced age. Zion too, like Sarah, will be blessed with children who will come from the ends of the earth to build their homes there. Commenting on the light which was to burn continually in the Tabernacle (Exod. 27: 2) he dreams of Israel reborn, a beacon to the world:

Our light will not be extinguished again and our lamps will never again be put out;

[30] Rabinovitz, *Maḥazor . . . Yannai*, i. 474. [31] Ibid. 117.

We shall be a light to the world and by our light the nations shall walk
And each will say to the other: Come let us be guided by the Lord's light.[32]

The didactic role of the cantor-poet is further seen in his instructional hymns for the holy days and festivals. Yannai, in his *qedušta'* for the New Year, reviews the laws governing the sounding of the *šofar*; and Phinehas Ha-Kohen (7th c., the last of the early poets mentioned by Sa'adyah Ga'on) in his *yoṣer* (an embellishment of the first benediction before the *šema'*), *'Or 'arba'ah 'asar*, for the first day of Passover, teaches his congregation the laws of leavened and unleavened bread. In their rulings on Jewish law and practice, the cantor-poets must choose between the differing opinions of the rabbis. For example, Yannai states that a *šofar* made from the horn of a bullock must not be used because the *šofar*, which is to remind God of the merit of Israel's patriarchs, should not be associated with haughtiness. In this ruling the poet sides with one rabbinic opinion (in *jRH* 1. 1 and *bRH* 26a) against another that permits the horn of a bullock. Yannai's reason is similar to that of the rabbis who prohibit the *šofar* of a bull because the accuser may not act as defender. In this case, the accuser is the golden calf which the Israelites brazenly worshipped in the wilderness (Exod. 32: 1 ff.).[33]

Although the superscription to the *yoṣer* of Phinehas Ha-Kohen reads, 'A *yoṣer* for the first day of Passover', it is likely that the hymn was included in the service of the Sabbaths preceding Passover, as suggested by the rabbis (in *bPes* 6a): 'Questions are asked and lectures are given on the laws of Passover for thirty days before Passover. R. Simeon b. Gamaliel said: two weeks.' Like Yannai, Phinehas in his decisions on Passover practices chooses between differing rabbinic opinions, as in his ruling in the matter of the disposal of leaven before Passover:

And the remainder [of the leaven] you shall burn as you were commanded,
Or if you wish you may scatter it to the wind,
Or you may throw it into the sea.

The source of this ruling is *mPes* 2. 1: 'R. Judah said: There is no removal of leaven save by burning. But the Sages maintain: He also crumbles and throws it to the wind or casts it into the sea.' The cantor-poet, following the view of the Sages, allows the several methods of leaven disposal. Similarly on the question of who may complete work on the fourteenth day of Nisan, the Sages maintain (*mPes* 4. 6) that only three craftsmen may complete tasks on the eve of Passover until midday if the work was begun before the fourteenth: tailors, hairdressers and washermen. R. Jose b. R. Judah includes shoemakers.

32 Ibid. 345.

33 Ibid. ii. 203.

On this question Phinehas adopts the ruling of the latter, contrary to the view of the Sages:

> Hairdressers, tailors and washermen employed,
> And shoemakers in their trade may complete their work,
> Whereby they honour the Festival.

Both pre-classical and classical cantor-poets functioned as spiritual leaders and polemicists, defending their religious beliefs and praying for the fall of the Christian and Muslim powers. Yose b. Yose calls upon the nations to acknowledge the sovereignty of the kingdom of God over their own temporal power in his New Year hymn *'Ahalelah 'elohay*,[34]

> Approach, nations; come, rulers; see the glorious power of [God's] kingdom;
> Magnify Him with me and let us exalt His name together, and take no pride in the crown of the [temporal] kingdom.

In the above hymn, Yose supports his argument by pointing to God's role as the Lord of history and His proven ability to reward and punish kings and nations. Seeing that the temporal powers persist in their arrogance, Yose calls down God's wrath upon Edom's (= the Christian) realm:

> May the liberators [of Zion] do battle and remove the [royal] mantle from Edom
> And place upon the Lord the majesty of power.[35]

Yannai is no less sanguinary in his condemnation of the Christian ruling power. 'Uproot from the earth the kingdom of Dumah [= Edom, after Isa. 21: 11],' he cries, adding: 'Would that the ruler of Dumah be humbled and brought low and lick dirt like a worm.' So confident is Yannai that his prayer will be answered that he boldly predicts the fall of Christian Byzantium, which he equates with the fourth beast in Dan. 7: 7: 'terrifying and dreadful and exceedingly strong.' In a play on the words Edom and *dam* (= blood), Yannai censures the ruling power:[36]

> He loves [to shed] blood [*dam*], therefore is he named Edom,
> He is Esau and he is Edom.
> Remember, Lord, against the Edomites, the destruction she wrought, even Edom's daughter;
> Let there be great slaughter in the land of Edom, a glowing fire in Edom's fields.

The poet's deep resentment of the abuses of power reflects the worsening economic conditions of Jewish farmers in Byzantine Palestine under Justinian

[34] Fleischer, *Ha-Yoṣerot*, p. 117; Mirsky, *Piyyuṭey Yose*, p. 87.
[35] Mirsky, *Piyyuṭey Yose*, p. 87.
[36] Rabinovitz, *Maḥazor . . . Yannai*, i. 47.

(527–65). The extensive building programmes of the emperor resulted in an increase in the tax burden, which the farmers often paid by selling their lands. This condition is reflected in Yannai's lament, 'Our inheritance is given to strangers; our lands are sold to our enemies.' Justinian's harsh treatment was particularly galling in light of the generous policy of an earlier predecessor, the emperor Valens (364–78) under whose reign Jews prospered as farmers, artisans, merchants and shopkeepers. The latter, it is reported, presented his Jewish subjects with 'gardens for their . . . worship', and Jewish traditions appealed widely to Christians.[37]

Adding insult to injury, Justinian began to meddle in the religious life of the Jews. No new synagogue could be built, and repair of old synagogues was discouraged. Jews were forbidden to observe Passover if it fell on a day before the Christian Easter. The emperor reasoned that the latter should have precedence in the calendar year. Moreover, Justinian decreed that Jews should not insist on reading the weekly Torah lesson in Hebrew, although it could be read in Greek. Additionally, the emperor forbade the rabbinic interpretation (*deuterosis*) of the Torah which usually followed its reading, and he encouraged Jews to convert to Christianity. Some assimilated Jews did not need much encouragement, and there are recorded instances of voluntary conversions to the Church. Jewish leaders fearful for the survival of their community counselled their people not to associate with their Gentile neighbours, as may be seen in the following warning by Yannai:[38]

> Do not enter the homes of Esau's sons
> Do not approach the premises of the shameless folk
> Let not your foot tread where hunters of Israel live . . .
> Do not come to the meetings of apostates.

The worsening economic conditions combined with the emperor's restrictive decrees led the Jews to join with the Samaritans in the revolt of 555. The Samaritans had been equally burdened by Justinian's policies, which prohibited them from inheriting property and ordered their wives and children to be raised as Christians. It appears that there was a lively debate in the Jewish community whether to take up arms against the imperial house. Those in favour argued that they could count on support from political factions of the hippodromes in Constantinople and Antioch. Moreover, they believed that the Samaritans had sufficient influence at court, particularly with the Empress Theodora, to enable them to prevail against Justinian.

Those Jewish leaders opposed to armed revolt pointed to the failures of Bar Kokhba's revolution in 133–5 and the uprising in 351 against Gallus, Constantine's nephew and eastern commander. It appears that Yannai shared

[37] Ibid. 47–8.
[38] Ibid. i. 49; Baron, *Social and Religious History*, ii. 189; Sharf, *Byzantine Jewry*, p. 28.

their views and counselled against involvement in ousting the ruling power, as indicated in the following from his commentary on Deut. 2: 4–5: 'be very careful not to engage in battle with them [the sons of Esau]':[39]

Do not make war against the scoffers to expel them . . .
Hasten not to do battle with the soldiers in crimson [*me'uddamin*, a play on 'Edom'].

In order not to provoke the authorities, Yannai counsels his congregation not to purchase or rent property on a site belonging to an ecclesiastical authority. It is likely that the poet's concern reflects Justinian's *Novella* No. 146, which declared null and void the possession of a synagogue on land occupied by the Church. Yannai is equally concerned that Jews were aping Greek manners and morals by taking an active part in the circus life of hippodrome chariot races, organized under the two parties known as the Blues, representing the affluent, and the Greens, the poor: 'Do not associate with evil men who profit from [chariot] races.'[40]

When Jews prospered under the emperor Valens they were naturally drawn to the Blues, and as a result earned the enmity of the Greens. The latter, it is reported, destroyed synagogues and desecrated Jewish cemeteries following the abortive revolt—led by the Blues—against the emperor Zeno in 484.[41]

Added to the threat from Greek culture was the pervasive presence of the Christian Church supported by the imperial house. The fourth and fifth centuries witnessed an increase of church-building in heavily populated Jewish settlements in the Galilee, with Christians hoping thereby to win Jewish converts. These proselytizing efforts by Church leaders are reflected in Yannai's anti-Christian polemics in his comments on Lev. 12: 1 ff.:[42]

[O God], no father gave birth to You
Nor have You borne a son!

In this the poet echoes the observation of the third-century Ereṣ Yisra'el *'amora'*, R. Abbahu (in *Exod. Rabbah* 29. 5): 'A human king may rule, but he has a father or brother or son; but God said: I am not like that; I am the first, for I have no father, and I am the last, for I have no brother, and beside Me there is no God, for I have no son.' Yannai's outrage at the practices of the Church are seen in the following blistering attack:[43]

Let them be put to shame, disgrace and confusion:
Those who call the villain noble,
Who choose the loathsome abomination

39 Rabinovitz, *Maḥazor . . . Yannai*, i. 50; ii. 127.
40 Ibid. ii. 127.
41 Sharf, *Byzantine Jewry*, p. 28.
42 Rabinovitz, *Maḥazor . . . Yannai*, i. 51, 388.
43 Ibid. ii. 221.

And rejoice in the idol with the naked body;
They are drawn to the dead rather than the living
And pollute themselves with offerings of the dead.

The first colon is from the *ʿamidah* in Yannai's prayer-book. Colon two is based on Isa. 32: 5, where the word for noble is *šoaʿ*. The similarity between *šoaʿ* and *Yešuaʿ* (= Jesus) was not lost on Yannai's congregation, who probably understood the reference as a condemnation of Christians who call upon Jesus, the 'villain'. The 'idol with the naked body' probably refers to Jesus on the cross, and the 'offerings of the dead' suggest the communion bread symbolizing his body.

Yose and Yannai are not alone in condemning the ruling powers in Byzantine Palestine. They are joined by Simeon Ha-Kohen b. Megas who prays, in a play on words, that Edom may suffer the same fate as Sodom. Continuing his word-play, Simeon notes, 'She [Edom] is called Dumah / [May God grant] that she be silenced [Heb. *demamah*] / Make her weaker than 'Admah [the city that God destroyed along with Sodom and Gemorah; Deut. 29: 22]; / Hasten the day for the judgment of Dumah.' In Simeon's comments on the plagues that were visited upon the Egyptians (Exod. 11: 1), he voices the hope, 'Let Edom be undone, as were [Egypt's] first-born; may their captains founder on snares and thorns.' In a *qedušta'* on the death of the first-born in Egypt (Exod. 12: 29), the latter poet predicts, 'Judgment's wrath has been dealt to Egypt; the bitter cup has been decreed for Byzantium.'[44]

Simeon also encourages his congregation to persevere in the hope of Israel's national restoration that is to come. Commenting on Gen. 27: 1: '[Isaac] called his elder son Esau', the poet plays with the words 'elder' (*gadol*) and 'least' (*qaṭon*):[45]

His father and mother called him elder,
But You said, 'I will make you [Esau] least' [Obad. 2] . . .
Hasten the great day,
Hurry, that the smallest [Israel] become a mighty nation . . .
The prince [Joseph] who began [his search] with the eldest
[Gen. 44: 12]
[Bring nigh] the time when the lesser Messiah will issue from
him . . .
Send the mighty prince [Michael, Dan. 12: 1]
That he may save both great and small.

The reference to the Messiah from the tribe of Joseph (or Ephraim) whose coming will precede that of the Messiah, son of David (from the tribe of Judah), and who will die in battle with Israel's enemies, is found in a tannaitic

44 See Yahalom, *Piyyuṭey . . . Megas*, pp. 133, 190, 195. 45 Ibid. 92–3.

source (in *bSukk* 52a) and in *Targum* Pseudo-Jonathan on Exod. 40: 11. It is speculated that Messiah ben Joseph symbolizes the reunion of the ten northern tribes with their southern brethren and reflects the failed Bar-Kokhba revolt. The poet Simeon, aware of this tradition, finds it convenient for use in this pattern poem contrasting the great and the lesser. However, the bulk of Simeon's messianic reflections focus on Messiah ben David, 'the Comforter' (*menaḥem*):[46]

Send us the man called Menaḥem;
Vengeance will sprout from him
Let him come in our day
And may authority rest on his shoulders. [Isa. 9: 5]

Like Yannai and Simeon Ha-Kohen, Eleazar Qillir prays for judgment upon Byzantium in his *zulat* for Tabernacles, *'Anna' terev 'aliṣotekha*: 'Bring upon Esau's sons, the insolent villains, loss of children and widowhood.' In his *šoferot* hymn *'Esso' de'i be-ṣedeq* for the New Year, he identifies the Christian ruling power with the fourth beast in Dan. 7: 23 that 'shall speak words against the Most High', and he pleads that 'it be consumed by flashes of fire in a raging flame.' In the *silluq, 'Elleh 'asitem we-'elleh ta'asu*, to his *qedušta'* for the eighth day of Tabernacles (Šemini 'Aṣeret), Qillir compares the royal house of Edom to a lizard (Prov. 30: 28) which grows fat with the aid of heretics (i.e. the Church, Heb. *semamit mešummenet be-šimmon minit*). And in the *malkhuyyot* hymn for the New Year, *'Ansikhah malki*, he complains, 'The powers that subjugate [Your people], worship idols of stone; they pollute a beautiful craft and rule with arrogance.'[47]

Qillir sharply attacked what he perceived to be the idolatrous practices of Christians in Byzantium. In the following from his *qedušta'*, *'Ereṣ maṭah we-ra'ašah*, for Pentecost, he decries the practice, in a commentary on Exod. 20: 4, 'You shall not make for yourself an idol':[48]

[Do not make] idols of the wretched
They are blind and deaf and without speech;
They are carried, borne on shoulders;
Helpless [themselves], they can do nothing for you.

In his condemnation of Christian icon worship Qillir was not alone. The debate between the iconoclasts and those defending the icons nearly brought about the collapse of the Byzantine empire. As early as the fourth century, St Epiphanius condemned the use of images as an idolatrous practice prohibited by the Pentateuch. However, in the fifth century images of Jesus, Mary and the saints proliferated in the empire and were used in private worship and in

46 Yahalom, *Piyyuṭey . . . Megas*, p. 211.
47 See *Maḥazor Le-Sukkot*, pp. 93, 387; *Maḥazor Le-Yamim*, i. 264, 234.
48 *Maḥazor . . . Šavu'ot*, p. 113.

public street processions, hence Qillir's observation, 'They are carried, borne on shoulders.'

After Yose, Yannai, Simeon and Qillir, classical poets in Ereṣ Yisra'el like Yoḥanan Ha-Kohen b. Yehošua (7th c.) and his contemporary Phinehas Ha-Kohen voice their discontent with the newly arrived Muslim powers, in addition to berating Christian Byzantium. In a revealing strophe from Yoḥanan's *qedušta'*, *'Izzun šema' medubbar*, for Šabbat Šim'u (*devar 'adonay beyt ya'aqov*, Jer. 2: 4), Yoḥanan prays for the fall of Edom (= Byzantium) at the hands of the invading Arabs,[49]

Subdue Mount Seir and Edom;
Make haste to confirm Your decree;
Uproot the godless nation with Your mighty sceptre;
Strike them with the Arab [*pere'*, Gen. 16: 12] force
Until they become disabled.

However, in the *silluq* to his hymn for Ḥanukkah, Yoḥanan condemns the Arab powers with the same passion with which he castigated the Christians,[50]

Seir [= Byzantium] and his son-in-law [Islam, Gen. 28: 9] banish from the world;
Repay them according to their work
And according to the evil of their deeds.

It is likely that Yoḥanan's mixed feelings about the Muslims reflect the conditions in Palestine during the years of the Persian invasion in the first two decades of the seventh century. When the Persians were expelled from Syria and Palestine by Heraclius in 628–9, the Byzantine emperor promised Benjamin, head of the Jewish community in Tiberias, the site of an academy of learning (*yešivah*), to respect Jewish rights. (It should be mentioned that in his hymn, *'Izzun šema' medubbar*, Yoḥanan mentions 'the *yešivah*' (ll. 186, 230–2), a probable reference to the academy in Tiberias where he may have lived.) However, upon his entry into Jerusalem Heraclius was told of Jewish atrocities against Christians during the Persian occupation and as a result he was persuaded to break his promise. Shortly thereafter, the emperor expelled the Jews from Jerusalem and allowed, according to some sources, an indiscriminate slaughter against them.[51]

When the Arabs invaded Palestine in 630 the Jewish communities were hopeful that their rights would be respected. The poet Yoḥanan initially perceived the Arab invader as the 'sceptre' of God's wrath against Byzantium. Jewish nationalist feelings were revived with the Arab invasion and Jewish guerrilla forces joined battle against the Byzantine occupation. In a letter to

[49] Weissenstern, *Piyyuṭey R. Yoḥanan*, pp. 66, 78.
[50] Ibid. 318. [51] Cf. Sharf, *Byzantine Jewry*, p. 51.

Heraclius Jewish militants demanded, 'God gave our father Abraham this land for an inheritance and after him, to his offspring . . . we are the sons of Abraham; you have possessed our land long enough; depart from it peacefully . . . otherwise we shall seize it from you by force.'[52]

At first the hopes of the Jewish settlers were justified. Jews, as the 'people of the Book', were a protected minority (*dhimmis*) under Muslim law. They were permitted to live peaceably if they paid the *jizyā*, a poll-tax levied on all non-Muslims as the price of the free exercise of their religion, and the *kharaj*, a land-tax, in lieu of military service, calculated according to the productivity of the property.[53] However, Muslims were not kindly disposed to Jews (or Christians) who would not submit to their authority. Muḥammad had set a precedent when he punished Jewish tribes in Arabia, the Qurayẓa, the Qaynuqa' and the Naḍīr whom he suspected of disloyalty. The Arab invaders of Palestine were no less sanguine and presumably prompted Yoḥanan Ha-Kohen's outcry, 'banish [them] from the world'. In a decisive battle in 634 near Gaza it was reported that Arab armies killed 4,000 Jewish, Samaritan and Christian peasants. According to the chronicle of John of Nikiu, the Jews of Egypt, on hearing of the approach of the Arabs, fled 'in the fear of the Muslim, the cruelties [of their commander] 'Amar and the seizure of their possessions.'[54]

Phinehas Ha-Kohen b. Jacob from Kafra (= Tiberias), the last-mentioned in Sa'adyah's list of early poets, was presumably the last of the Ereṣ Yisra'el classical cantor-poets.[55] Like Yoḥanan Ha-Kohen, Phinehas condemns both the Christian and Muslim powers. In his Ḥanukkah *qerovah*, *'Eli be-nes hinsisi*, he recounts how God has judged the rulers of Babylon and Persia and will now 'command in a loud voice heard by all that Islam and Byzantium [Heb. *qedar we-'edom*] be annihilated.'[56]

Phinehas does not always mention both the Christian and Muslim powers in his diatribes and it is likely that, like Yoḥanan Ha-Kohen, he lived in the first half of the seventh century during the Arab invasion of Palestine. In his *mišmarot* for the twenty-four priestly divisions (*'Anna' 'ezon mennu*), he refers only to Christians and does not mention Muslims:[57]

> Destroy the power of Edom;
> Bring them down into darkness.

The latter work may have been written before the Arab invasion of Palestine in 630.

[52] Sharf, *Byzantine Jewry*, p. 52. [53] Ibid. 51. [54] Ibid. 52.

[55] Other classical Ereṣ Yisra'el cantor-poets not mentioned above are Hadutah, Yehošua Ha-Kohen (the Joshua mentioned fourth in Sa'adyah Ga'on's list), Joseph b. Nisan of Shaveh-Kiryataim (in Trans-Jordan), Elazar bar Phinehas and Mošeh. Cf. Zulay, 'Le-toledot', pp. 158–69.

[56] Zulay, 'Eine Ḥanukkah-qerovah', p. 169. [57] Zulay, 'Le-toledot', p. 139.

THE PRINCIPAL POETS

Yannai

Yannai, the second poet in Sa'adyah's list, identifies himself by signing his name in his hymns in acrostic form. His work, largely unknown before the Cairo Geniza find, represents a watershed in Hebrew hymnology. The use of rhymed strophes is now commonplace and rabbinic sources are frequently employed.

Of special interest are the pattern poems, in which each colon repeats a continuous range of syntactic, semantic and synthetic devices. The following is from Yannai's *qerovah* (a generic term for adornments of the *'amidah*) on Num. 23: 10:[58]

'Im ṭihartah, mi yeṭamme'?
'Im yiḥadtah, mi yafriš?
'Im kibbadtah, mi yeqallel?
'Im liwwitah, mi yaṭ'eh?

If You purify, who would pollute?
If You unite, who would divide?
If You honour, who would revile?
If You escort, who would stray?

The rhetorical pattern in the Hebrew of two fixed and two free units is a variation of parallel construction, already known from biblical literature where parallelism is synonymous (Ps. 15: 1), antithetic (Prov. 10: 1), repetitive (Pss. 29: 1–2 and 92: 9) or synthetic (Ps. 42: 1). In Yannai's pattern there is antithesis as regards syntax and semantics between word two, in the perfect with an affirmative meaning, and word four, in the imperfect with a negative sense. There is also synthetic parallelism after the model in Ps. 42: 1: 'As a hart longs for flowing streams, so longs my soul for You, O God.' In this construction the focus is not on equivalents or opposites but on the correspondence of the parts in the colon.

It is also likely, as A. Mirsky suggests, that the synthetic construction in some of R. Ishmael's thirteen principles of logic by which the Torah may be expounded served as a model for Yannai and Qillir. Consider R. Ishmael's third rule: 'A comprehensive principle [*binyan 'av*] is derived from one text, or from two related texts' (*Sifra*, ch. 1). The phrasing of this principle is in a synthetic construction as, for example, in the following rabbinic ruling (in *mMen* 12. 5), 'Just as we find [*mah maṣinu*] in the case of wine, which is offered as an obligation, that it may also be offered as a freewill offering, even so [*'af*] oil can be offered as an obligation and may be offered as a freewill

[58] Rabinovitz, *Maḥazor . . . Yannai*, ii. 97.

offering.' A similar construction is seen in another ruling (in *mḤul* 4. 4), 'Just as we find [*mah maṣinu*] that if [a beast] were *ṭerefah* that the slaughtering thereof renders it clean [so that it does not cause uncleanness], so [*'af*] the slaughtering of the beast [that is clean] shall render clean the member [that had protruded and it should not convey uncleanness].'[59]

Variations in the phrasing of synthetic parallelism abound in rabbinic literature. In addition to the *mah . . . 'af* construction, there is the *mah . . . kakh*, as seen in *Cant. Rabbah* 1. 2, 'Just as [*mah*] water stretches from one end of the world to another, as it says [in Ps. 136: 6], so [*kakh*] the Torah goes from one end of the world to another [as it says in Job 11: 9].' At times, the constructions are broadened to include a wider synthesis using the terms 'above . . . below', as in the following, attributed to R. Berekhia (in *Pes. de R. Kahane*, 1. 3): 'Just as [we find] above [*le-ma'alah*] seraphs stand [in attendance on Him (Isa. 6: 2)], so do the planks of acacia wood [in the Tabernacle, Exod. 26: 15] stand upright, below [*le-maṭṭah*]; just as above [*le-ma'alah*] the stars [shine], so the clasps [that couple the tent of the Tabernacle, Exod. 26: 11] shine below [*le-maṭṭah*].'

In an abbreviated phrasing of the synthetic parallel the terms *mah . . . 'af* (just as . . . even so) were assumed leaving only *le-ma'alah . . . le-maṭṭah* (above . . . below). This abbreviated construction was more often employed in rabbinic literature and was adapted in this form by Yannai in his *qerovah* for Ḥanukkah:[60]

> [Light from the clas]ps attached below [*be-maṭṭah*]
> Is esteem[ed as] the fixed stars above [*ma'alah*] . . .
> The seven-branched candelabra below [*maṭṭah*, Exod. 25: 37]
> Is esteemed as the seven constellations above [*ma'alah*] . . .
> Your Presence [*šekhinah*] in the Tabernacle below [*maṭṭah*]
> Is esteemed as Your Presence dwelling above [*ma'alah*].

Qillir

A variation in configuring the *mah . . . kakh* ('just as . . . so') parallel served the hymnist Eleazar Qillir, the third poet mentioned in Sa'adyah's list. The rabbinic construction of the parallel (in *Lev. Rabbah* 30. 12, expounding on Lev. 28: 40) reads:

> 'The fruit of the *hadar* tree' symbolizes Israel; just as [*mah*] the *etrog* has taste as well as fragrance, so [*kakh*] Israel have among them men who possess learning and good deeds. 'Branches of palm-trees,' too, applies to Israel; as [*mah*] the palm-tree has taste but not fragrance, so [*kakh*] Israel have among them such as possess learning but not good deeds.

[59] See Mirsky, 'Mahṣavatan', pp. 11–18.
[60] Rabinovitz, *Maḥazor . . . Yannai*, ii. 242.

Utilizing the essentials of this construction, Qillir increases its resonance (in his *silluq* (closing) to a *qerovah* for Tabernacles)[61] by substituting for *mah . . . kakh* the broader *u-khmo . . . ken* :

U-khmo be-ʿeṣ hadar reyaḥ we-taʿam
Ken be-ʿam zo baʿaley miṣwot we-dat noʿam;
U-khmo be-ʿeṣ tamar taʿam we-loʾ reyaḥ
Ken be-ʿam zo baʿaley miṣwot be-loʾ dat reyaḥ

Even as in the *hadar* fruit there is fragrance and taste,
So are there pious and learned among this people;
Even as in the palm tree there is taste without fragrance,
So are there pious and unlearned among this people.

Both units in this bicola construction are identical in meaning to the rabbinic model, but not in phrasing. In addition to fortifying the word pattern, Qillir asserts his independence by using the scriptural construction *u-khmo . . . ken* instead of the rabbinic *mah . . . kakh.*

Another example of synthetic parallelism deriving from the principles (*middot*) by which the Torah was expounded and whose phrasing in rabbinic sources served the classical-era synagogue poet is 'measure for measure'. The rabbinic formulation of this principle can take the form of 'he who . . . from him' (*mi . . . mimmennu*) as in the following from *Sifre* No. 18: 'He who [*mi*] began to sin, from him [*mimmennu*] begins the punishment.' A rabbinic variation on the construction of this principle is 'she [the woman suspected of adultery] . . . therefore' (*hiʾ . . . lefikhakh*), as in *tSot* 3. 3, 'She revealed her flesh to him, therefore the priest reveals her shame in public.' The latter formulation of 'measure for measure' is also employed by Yannai in modified form:

She [*hiʾ*] [cal]led out to the stranger and he embraced her belly,
Therefore [*lakhen*] her belly will swell and rot,
She [*hiʾ*] set her eyes upon an[other],
Therefore [*lakhen*] she will belong neither to her husband nor to another.

The construction in the *Tosefta'* and in Yannai is identical in meaning, except that Yannai, like Qillir after him, prefers the biblical term *lakhen* ('therefore') to the rabbinic *lefikhakh.*

In the classical period the rhymed strophe was an accepted practice. The strophic structures of Yannai and Qillir are regularly defined by rhyming patterns. The strophe, a unit of bicola or tricola construction demonstrating a stylistic and structural coherence, is already present in biblical literature,

[61] Mirsky, 'Maḥṣavatan', p. 29.

where it is defined by refrains (as in Ps. 42: 5–6, 11–12) or by alphabetical acrostics (Ps. 119). In the period of the anonymous poets, the alphabetical acrostic continued to designate the strophe, as in the Sabbath hymn *'El 'adon 'al kol ha-ma'asim*,[62] and in most of Yose's compositions. At times, however, Yose would add to the acrostic a rhyming pattern, as in the following from the hymn *'Ekhre'ah we-'evrekhah*, defining the strophe for the letter *lamed*:

Libbi 'afanneh / le-raḥameni yifneh / la-'arokh šewwa' be-ma'aneh / ṭerem 'eqra' we-ya'aneh
Milluli horot / mi-pi ve-mahamurot / mevasser ṭov be-tokh ḥavurot / 'azkir gevurot.

I will direct my heart that He may turn to me in mercy; I cry in my prayers; before I call He will answer;
My words will witness [that] my mouth in the heat of passion [seeks] the bearer of good tidings to the congregation when I will declare His might.

Yose's strophe comprises a quatrain of versets in the first colon, a triad of versets in the second, and the closing refrain from the first two units of his *'avodah*, *'Azkir gevurot 'eloha*.[63] With Yannai the strophe is defined by rhyming quatrains with three units in each quarter, as in his *qerovah* on Gen. 29: 31:

'Omṣakh 'ayom ba-šeḥaqim / boṭeh be-khol ṣwddy šewwaqim
Galuy-lakh 'ahavat ḥašuqim / daruš-lakh gam-sin'at 'ašuqim.[64]

Your fearsome might is displayed in the heavens; it is expressed on the street corners;
To You is revealed the love of the desiring [Israel]; the hated oppressed appeal to You.

Yannai's strophe of rhyming quatrains became the model for synagogue poets throughout the Mediterranean world and in central and eastern Europe. Its influence was felt in the hymns from Italy, the Rhine valley and Byzantium until the thirteenth century, when the newer Hispano-Hebrew *qaṣidah*-type poems and *muwashshaḥāt* attracted the hymnists. It is now generally agreed that the first use of a consistent rhymed strophe in world poetry is found in the *qedušta'ot* of the classical period. Qillir, following Yannai, embellished the rhyming strophe with a characteristic flourish by extending it to nine versets with three units in each third. Following is an excerpt from *'Essa' de'iy le-meraḥoq*, the fourth segment of his *qerovah* for the Day of Atonement, *Šošan 'emeq 'uyyemah*:[65]

62 See Ber, *Seder*, pp. 211–12.
63 See Mirsky, *Piyyuṭey Yose*, pp. 246, 122.
64 Rabinovitz, *Maḥazor . . . Yannai*, i. 22, 171.
65 See Schirmann, 'Hebrew Liturgical Poetry'; *Maḥazor Le-Yamim*, ii. 341.

ʾOrekhey šewaʿ la-rov / ḥin ʿerkam yaʿarov / peney ʾelohey mi-qarov
ʿAtirati ʾaz tiqrov / ʿaverati bal teʾerov / ʾelay le-val qerov
Zomem ʾim yizrov / ʿadat ʾel la-ḥarov / ʾeššaʿen be-masdiq we-qarov.

They present their pleas in abundance hoping that their prayers will find favour in God's presence.
I offer my petition hoping that my sins will not entrap me and stand in my way;
When the plotters make headway in seeking to destroy God's people, I shall rely upon Him nearby, vindicating me.

To further mark the borders of the strophe, Qillir added a short refrain of three versets and thereby pioneered a widely imitated genre known as the *qiqlar* (from the Greek *kuklos*, cycle). The *qiqlar* is a large and self-contained work with sets of rhymed triads interrupted by choral responses made up of three versets and ending with the unit *qadoš*. It was designed as a choral response by a professional choir employed by congregations in Ereṣ Yisra'el at the time of Qillir.[66]

Another characteristic of Yannai's hymnography is the wide deployment of verses from Scripture or from rabbinic literature that were inserted into the body of the hymn. Although earlier poets did embellish their work with biblical verses, it was inadvertently and on a modest scale. With Yannai such insertions are commonplace and integral to the poet's conceit, as in the following from his *qerovah* on Gen. 33: 18, relating the return of Jacob to his home in Shechem:[67]

When he [Jacob] left, the sun had set on his account,
For His [God's] belove[d is like] the parting sun;
[Upon his re]turn the sun arose
Since God is like a shield and sun to those who trust Him.

In the last colon the poet inserts a mix of two verses from Ps. 18: 31 ('He is a shield for all who take refuge in Him') and Ps. 84: 12 ('For the Lord God is a sun and shield'). Similarly in Yannai's *qerovah* on Lev. 14: 34 ('When you come into the land of Canaan, which I give you for a possession, and I put a leprous disease in a house in the land of your possession'), the poet prays that God's beloved (Israel) be healed and purified and that the 'pollution in the home where we live [Zion] be removed.' He closes with the lament, 'There is no blessing since the day that the Temple has been destroyed; there has been no day without a curse.' The latter is from the statement by Rabban Simeon b. Gamaliel (in *mSot* 9. 12).

[66] See Fleischer, *Širat Ha-Qodeš*, pp. 132, 148.
[67] Rabinovitz, *Maḥazor . . . Yannai*, i. 207.

Rhetorical flourishes abound in Yannai's poetry, ranging from play on words to alliteration and assonance, all of which are designed to enhance the aesthetics of his composition and hold the attention of his congregation. At times the hymnist will challenge the acumen of his congregation with word games and riddles. Following is an example from Yannai's *qerovah* on Exod. 32: 15 ('Then Moses turned and went down from the mountain, carrying the two tablets of the [covenant] witness in his hands, tablets that were written on both sides'):

> Good are the two / written from two / as witnesses two / from the One and not two;
> He assigned their writing five, five / to the bridegroom armed with five / in order that five should not rule them.[68]

Yannai hints at the solution to the riddle of the twos and fives by including the above verse from Exodus in the chain of biblical sentences following his first set of rhymed quatrains in the *qerovah*. This explains the first four hemistichs: good are the two covenant tablets written from two sides as two witnesses from the One [God who is] not two. Decoding the remaining triad, however, requires a familiarity with biblical and rabbinic sources.

In the latter triad Yannai is taking a position in a dispute between R. Ḥanina b. Gamaliel and the Sages (in *Mekhilta de-Rabbi Išma'el*, No. 8), and decides with the former that five commands were written on each side of the tablet and not ten on each side, as the Sages held. The 'bridegroom' of the Torah is Israel (Hos. 2: 21) who is prepared for battle (*ḥamušim*) with five kinds of weapon. According to the *Midraš Ha-Gadol* on Exod. 13: 18: '*Ḥamušim* means armed . . . teaching us that they were arrayed with five kinds of weapon: bow, club, shield, spear and sword.' Closing the triad, Yannai informs us that Israel is heavily armed in order to defend itself against the five angels of destruction who sought to do harm to Moses when he ascended the heavens to receive the Torah. The rabbinic source of this legend is in *Deut. Rabbah* 9. 12: 'When God said to Moses in heaven: "Arise, go down hastily from here," five angels of destruction overheard this and they sought to harm him.'

The classical age, a model for succeeding generations of cantor-poets, was dominated by Yannai and Qillir. Their wide-ranging innovations opened new opportunities for enhancing the aesthetic component of worship. The use of rhyme to define the strophe became commonplace, and generally followed an established pattern of *rime riche* calling for a uniform sound in the last syllable beginning with the consonant before the last vowel, and a uniform sound of two consonants belonging to the root of each rhyming word. Following is an example from Qillir's elegy for the Ninth of 'Av, *Šavat suru menni*:[69]

[68] Rabinovitz, *Maḥazor . . . Yannai*, p. 358.

[69] *Seder Ha-Qinot*, pp. 35–6.

'Al har [Ṣiyyon] ṣadu še'oney meDANAY
Ṣafu 'al ro'ši zeyDONAY
Ṣametu be-nov la-'amod zeDONAY
Ṣod noṣrat le'orer meDANAY
Ṣa'aq 'ammi bi-ymey ben-DINAY
Ṣaddiq hu' 'aDONAY.

On mount [Zion] the hosts of my enemies lay in wait;
The wicked closed over my head;
The insolent reduced me to a halt at Nov [Isa. 10: 32];
You kept my sin to arouse my enemies;
My people cried in the days of [Elazar] Ben Dinay
[*mSot* 9. 9; *Cant. Rabbah* 2. 7]:
Righteous is the Lord.

Qillir's rhyme patterns were to be widely imitated by hymnists in Italy, Byzantium and central Europe until superseded, in part, by the newer forms emerging from Spain under the influence of Arabic prosody. Other innovations during the classical period called for the introduction of choral responses in the *qiqlar* strophe of the *qedušta'ot* by Qillir. The choral response as part of the sacred service was standard in biblical times (2 Chr. 5: 12–14; 7: 6) and in the Temple ritual of the rabbinic period (*mTam* 7. 3–4). Even after the destruction of the Temple and the ban on vocal music (*bGit* 7a), a precentor with two assistants was selected to chant the prayers. The tenth-century chronicler Nathan Ha-Bavli describes the installation of the Babylonian exilarch at a Sabbath service conducted by a precentor accompanied by a trained chorus of young men.[70] Following the destruction of the Temple and prior to the tenth century, the only evidence of choral accompaniment is to be found in Qillir's compositions for the Sabbaths and festivals, when poetic insertions were designed for congregational response. This response, which presumably began as a sporadic utterance growing out of emotional involvement in the sacred service, was eventually formalized, emerging ultimately in the form of a professionally trained choir.

Of special interest in this regard is the poetry of Simeon Ha-Kohen b. Megas, probably a contemporary of Yannai. Like the latter, Simeon hails from Ereṣ Yisra'el and composes *qedušta'ot* for the triennial cycle of Torah readings, in line with the synagogue practice of his time. The bulk of Simeon's literary corpus, like that of Yannai's, was discovered in the Cairo Geniza. As his name *megas* (great) suggests, Simeon was born in a Greek-speaking environment, and his diatribes against the Christian ruling power point to a period before 634, the year that Ereṣ Yisra'el was conquered by the Arabs. Simeon's hymns, like those of Yannai, were chanted by the precentor

[70] See Werner, *The Sacred Bridge*, pp. 135–6.

alone, without choral accompaniment or congregational participation. This is indicated by the lack of a choral refrain (*qiqlar*) in the latter's hymns, such as we find in the compositions of Qillir. With Qillir's hymnody, the choral refrain gained wide appeal and became a common practice in the synagogue service. The fondness for the hymns of Yannai and Simeon continued long after their demise. Although they composed their works without choral refrains, later cantor-poets would attach choral stanzas to the hymns of Yannai and Simeon and have the best of two traditions. Such a practice has been preserved in the work of an anonymous ninth-century poet ('the Anonymous') who composed choral refrains (*pizmonim*) to the *qedušta'ot* of Simeon Ha-Kohen. Following is an excerpt from the sixth part of Simeon's *qedušta'* on the Torah reading from Lev. 18: 1–3: 'You shall not do as they do in the land of Egypt.' The poet is the speaker:[71]

Happy is the man who considers the pleasures of Torah [study];
His soft-spoken words are heeded;
He will be uplifted in the hope of the redeemed;
Happy is the man who does not walk in the path of sinners.
[Ps. 1: 1]

To this the Anonymous adds a choral refrain in which God is the speaker:[72]

Happy is the man:
He who pays heed to My words
Will witness the building of My Temple;
He will hear in My House
The shouts and happy songs;
He will see the coming of My anointed
As I have thought and spoken;
Happy is the man who listens to Me. [Prov. 8: 34]

As noted above, the language of the cantor-poets in the classical period, often incomprehensible to the modern ear, reflected common contemporary usage. The neologisms and allusions of Yannai, Qillir and their colleagues were easily understood by their congregants, who were well versed in rabbinic and folk sources. In their desire to communicate with the laity, the hymnists occasionally inserted foreign terms into their compositions for the synagogue. Such was the practice of Yannai and Simeon Ha-Kohen, who

[71] Yahalom, *Piyyuṭey . . . Megas*, pp. 133, 221.

[72] Fleischer, *Pizmoney Ha-'Anonymus*, p. 207. The 580 poems of this author were found in a Cairo Geniza MS, parts of which are preserved in the Cambridge University Library (Taylor-Schechter, Add. No. 3663). Menahem Zulay determined that they were the work of an unknown poet whom he named the 'Anonymous'.

lived in Ereṣ Yisra'el under the rule of Greek-speaking Byzantium. A case in point is Yannai's *qedušta'* for the New Year:[73]

> [The Judge sit]s on the throne of justice like a king;
> P[assin]g all before Him for judgment, from pauper to king.
> All who come into the world . . .
> Pass before him like troops.

Yannai uses the Greek *noumeron* for 'troops'. Later, the twelfth-century Greek hymnist Moses Ḥazan b. Abraham, in his penitential confession 'Man, consider the judgment decrees' (*'Enoš binah mišpat ha-ḥereṣ*), will do likewise. A similar tendency to resort to Greek usage is seen in the *qedušta'* of Simeon Ha-Kohen on Exod. 11: 1: 'I will bring but one more plague upon Pharaoh and upon Egypt':

> A sapphire-like [staff] in the hands of the master of names [Moses]
> Making miracles for the sinless folk [Israel].

The term 'sapphire-like' is from the Greek *sapfeirinon*. Later generations of synagogue poets from Byzantium, like Šemaryah b. Elia Ha-Ikriti and Abraham b. Jacob, also did not hesitate to employ Greek terms that were in common use by their congregants.[74]

However, the most telling innovations in language were the host of new usages that invaded the synagogue liturgy in the classical period. Purists like Abraham Ibn Ezra (in his commentary on Eccles. 5: 1) were outraged by the ungrammatical excesses. However, in fairness to the cantor-poets, it is likely that they merely reflected the vernacular habits of their congregations.[75]

THE PRINCIPAL GENRES

Qerovah

Qerovah is the generic name for the hymns embedded in the *'amidah*. Presumably the term is derived from the designation *qarova'* given the

[73] Rabinovitz, *Maḥazor . . . Yannai*, ii. 201.

[74] See Weinberger, *Širat Ha-Qodeš*, English section, pp. 10–12; Yahalom, *Piyyuṭey . . . Megas*, p. 184.

[75] Following are some examples of the new usages: (1) *Lamed he'* and *pe' nun* verbs are conjugated as if they were *'ayin yod*. Thus *nigaš* becomes *gaš*; *gilah* is *gal*; *nasa'* is *sa'*. (2) The letters *beyt*, *kaf*, *lamed*, *mem* (*bakhlam*) are joined to the noun. Instead of *ka-'ašer halekhu* (they went) there is *ke-halekhu*. (3) Verbs are treated as nouns by dropping the *nun* in the suffix. This yields *ḥinekhi* in place of *ḥinekhani* and *limmedi* instead of *limmedani*. (4) Preserving the *nun* in the *lamed nun* verb when it is identical with the suffix. Thus *natanenu* instead of *natenu* and *niš'anenu* in place of *niš'anu*. (5) Coining nouns from verbs and verbs from nouns. (6) Omitting the feminine endings of nouns and treating them as masculine. (7) Aramaic usages. Zulay, *Ha-'Askolah*, pp. 17–18.

cantor-poet (in Aramaic; in Hebrew *qarov*), the one who approached (*de-qarev*) the lectern to lead the congregation in prayer.[76]

The prolific Eleazar Qillir pioneered a *qerovah* for Purim with hymnic embellishments in rhyming sestets for each of the eighteen benedictions of the *ʿamidah.* Preceding the benediction, 'who destroys the enemy and humbles the arrogant' (*šover ʾoyevim u-makhniyʿa zedim*), the sequence of sestets is interrupted by an insertion in quatrains spanning two alphabetic acrostics and the poet's name twice repeated. Each of the eighteen words in Esther 2: 17, 'The king loved Esther more than all the other women,' etc., is used to open the eighteen tercets. Also for Šabbat Zakhor preceding Purim, Qillir composed a *qerovah*, *ʾAzkir selah zikhron maʿasim.* Its fourth section, beginning with *ʾAṣ qoṣeṣ*, has come to symbolize the poet's uncommon phonetically intensive style and mannerism:[77]

> *ʾAṣ qoṣeṣ / ben qoṣeṣ / qeṣuṣay le-qaṣṣeṣ*
> *Be-dibbur mefoṣeṣ / reṣuṣay le-raṣṣeṣ*
> *Leṣ be-voʾ le-loṣeṣ / pullaṣ we-nitloṣeṣ*
> *Ke-ʿaṣ meḥaṣaṣim le-ḥaṣṣeṣ / ke-neṣ ʿal ṣippor le-naṣṣeṣ.*

Employing a discontinuous rhyme, Qillir embellishes the strophe with sound parallels of both closing syllables and root letters, adding a lyrical quality to the hymn. Working through the elliptic syntax, metonymies and neologisms of this strophe was not too difficult for the cantor-poet's congregation, although for the modern reader decoding Qillir can be a formidable challenge. Following is a translation of the strophe:

> The wicked, son of the wicked, hastened to eliminate the humbled,
> And harm the dejected with vile slander;
> The scoffer while doing his mischief was stunned and scorned
> When he resolved to hunt the sages, like an eagle his prey.

Haman, descendant of Amaleq (wicked son of the wicked) seeks to murder the Jews (humbled, dejected) and is frustrated by Mordecai, one of the sages in the Sanhedrin (*bMeg* 16b).

Qedušta'

Innovations in genre are a distinctive feature of the classical period, when in addition to the earlier *seliḥah*, *ʾazharah* and *ʿavodah* new embellishments of the fixed prayers emerged. These included the *qeduštaʾ* adorning the benedictions of the *ʿamidah*, and the *yoṣer* cycle enhancing the blessings preceding and following the *šemaʿ*. Although these genres had their modest beginnings

[76] See *Midraš Tehillim*, on Ps. 19, and the term, *ḥazzanaʾ de-qarev*, the cantor who approaches (the lectern).

[77] Ber, *Seder*, pp. 674–84, 666–7.

in the pre-classical period, it was only through the efforts of Yannai and Qillir that the *qeduṣta'* and *yoṣer* became the centrepieces of the sacred service. The *qeduṣta'* belongs to the family of *qerovot*, poetic units embedded in the benedictions of the daily *'amidah*. The hymnic insertions of the *qedušta'*, however, were designed for the *'amidah* benedictions during the morning service (*šaḥarit*) on Sabbaths and festivals when the *qeduššah* (the Trisagion based on Isa. 6: 3 and Ezek. 3: 12) was recited. The *šiv'ata'*, a sister to the *qedušta'*, comprised verset embellishments of the seven benedictions of the *'amidah* during the addition (*musaf*) to the morning service when, in the old Ereṣ Yisra'el ritual, the *qeduššah* was not recited. The *qedušta'* was generally longer than the *šiv'ata'* and was, in large part, standardized in the classical period to include three broad poetic units encompassing the *'amidah* benedictions, 'shield [*magen*] of Abraham', 'who revives [*meḥayyeh*] the dead', and the *mešullaš* (threefold), leading up to the *qeduššah*. Within this threefold framework most of the *qedušta'ot* of the period contain eight separate hymns, with the exception of Yannai's, which have nine. The first two hymns, in rhymed quatrains, are identified by a full alphabetic acrostic and include the *magen* and *meḥayyeh* benedictions. The third hymn, the *mešullaš*, comprising four quatrains, reveals the poet's name in the acrostic and closes with the first verse from the reading from the Prophets for the Sabbath or festival. The *mešullaš* which closes the first poetic unit is intended as an introduction to the third benediction of the *'amidah*.

The second unit begins with a composition opening with *'El na'* (May it please God) and closes with *qadoš* (holy). This fourth hymn is a relatively short work in monorhymed prose, but without strophes and devoid of alphabetic acrostic. The fifth hymn in this unit was not standardized and its treatment varied. In Yannai's corpus the work comprises ten strophes—hence its name *'asiriyyah* (ten)—in diarhyme mostly, with alphabetic acrostic reaching the letter *yod*. Qillir built this hymn in rhymed quatrains, allowing the poet to sign his name and that of his father in the acrostic. This Qilliric practice is confined to hymn No. 5 in those of his *qedušta'ot* where he neglects to identify his father in the *mešullaš*.

The hymns in the third poetic unit of the *qedušta'* were also not standardized, and this led to a varied mix of forms and conceits. The sixth hymn opening this unit is usually a large and self-subsistent work. Yannai's sixth hymn is built in rhymed quatrains with a full alphabetical acrostic. In this practice he is followed by other early composers of *qedušta'ot*, like Haduta and Simeon b. Megas. However, Qillir characteristically charts a different course in his treatment of the sixth hymn in his pioneering of the *qiqlar*. The seventh hymn in the third unit also varies from poet to poet. Yannai's treatment of the seventh hymn, known as *rahiṭ* (furnishing), features virtuosic alliteration, anadiplosis and unstrophed patterns without rhyme and alphabetic acrostic. Occasionally Yannai, the eclectic, builds his *rahiṭ* in diarhymed strophes.

Qillir, too, experiments in composing his *rahiṭ*. He may choose a pattern poem with full alphabetic acrostic, or rhymed quatrains (or sestets) ending with a verse from Scripture. Most classical-era poets end the *qedušta'* with an eighth hymn, the *silluq* (closing), an elaborate construction mostly in rhymed prose resembling the fourth hymn. The *silluq* always ends with the verse from Isa. 6: 3: 'And one called to another and said: "Holy, holy, holy is the Lord of hosts." ' Yannai, unlike his successors, writes a relatively short *silluq*—also in rhymed prose—and adds to it a ninth hymn, the *qeduššah*. The latter, in rhymed prose as well, is a poetic embellishment of Isa. 6: 3 and Ezek. 3: 12: 'Blessed be the glory of the Lord.'

Some of the non-standardized hymns in the *qedušta'* were treated to extraordinary embellishment and innovation for the Day of Atonement service when the cantor-poet was challenged to engage the attention of the worshipper during the long fast-day. Among the hymns that lent themselves to elaboration was the sixth hymn, the *qiqlar*, which in Qillir's treatment for the Day of Atonement took on the character of a mini-*'avodah* and focused on the Temple service of the High Priest for that day. At times Qillir would attach to the Days of Awe *qiqlar* a poetic appendage built in sets of couplets with refrains repeated at the end of each strophe. This type of hymn with multiple refrains, known as *estribillo* or *estrioto*, was widely used in Provençal, Galician-Portuguese and Arab folk poetry and was popular in the Spanish court.[78]

Another innovation associated with the Days of Awe *qiqlar* was an insertion in the *qedušta'* of the New Year's morning service. The theme of the hymnic insertion which came after the *qiqlar* was God's sovereignty and man's creatureliness. The hymn, in rhymed tercets, featured *estribillo*-like, alternately repeated refrains. The first three versets, beginning with 'The King on high' (*Melekh 'elyon*) extol the might of deity and close with 'And He will rule forever'; the second tercet, opening with 'The wretched king' (*Melekh 'evyon*), points to the limited power of the human monarch and closes with 'How long will he rule?' In later editions of the Franco-German prayer-book the versets denigrating the ruling powers were eliminated for fear of reprisals.[79] Other variations in the *qedušta'* were seen in the additional service for the New Year, when the hymn was enlarged to include the three themes of the *šofar* service, *malkhuyyot*, *zikhronot* and *šoferot*. Treatment of the *šofar* themes, termed *teqi'ata'* (blasts), varied. Yose b. Yose and Qillir favoured strophic structures with monorhyme refrain, while the late-classical poet Phinehas Ha-Kohen preferred non-strophic forms.

The *qedušta'ot* for the three Pilgrimage Festivals are noted for their poetic embellishments of the Song at the Sea (Exod. 15: 1 ff.) on Passover, the Decalogue on Pentecost and the Death of Moses on the last day of Taber-

[78] See Fleischer, *Širat Ha-Qodeš*, p. 166; D. C. Clarke, *Encyclopedia of Poetry and Poetics*, ed. A. Preminger (Princeton, 1965), p. 257.

[79] See *Maḥazor Le-Yamim*, i. 105–9.

nacles. The exulting tone of Israel's victory song at the Sea of Reeds, the lesson read on the seventh day of Passover, readily lent itself to improvisation by early hymnists like Yannai and Simeon b. Megas[80] and later by Franco-German poets, Simeon b. Isaac 'the Great' of Mainz (b. *c.*950) and his contemporary Moses b. Kalonymous of Lucca, who, in the *rahiṭ* part of the *qedušta'*, composed poetic commentaries on each verse of the Reeds Song, beginning with 'Thus the Lord saved Israel that day from the Egyptians' (Exod. 14: 13).[81]

The stately strophes of the Decalogue, the required Torah reading for Pentecost, elicited a response from cantor-poets, who embellished the verses from Exod. 19: 25–20: 15 in the *rahiṭ* part of the *qedušta'*. Here, as for the Song at the Sea reading for Passover, the hymnist expanded on the scriptural verses and on each of the Ten Commandments. The poetic insertions, ornamented with alphabetic acrostic, name signature and anadiplosis and known as *seder dibrin* (order of commands), were composed by Qillir and his successors in central and southern Europe. Following is a selection from Qillir's commentary on the fifth command, 'Honour your father and your mother' (Exod. 20: 12), composed in twenty-four rhyming versets with a couplet refrain connected to the versets by anadiplosis and closing with the sixth command, 'You shall not murder' (Exod. 20: 13):[82]

> Obey your parents with faithful devotion; they bought you with prayer.
> They brought you into the patriarch's covenant; with breast milk you were amply nourished.
> They carried you on their shoulders and taught you; they laboured without stint in your behalf.
> If harm befell you they suffered; they led you to the fear of God.
> They made you know the laws and customs; they endowed you with home and treasure.
> They support you and help you find a mate; do their will and be not insolent . . .
> Minister to them like a servant to his master; accept their petitions and lengthen your days with years.
> Years you will lengthen and gain a clear conscience if the image [of God] you do not destroy.

On Pentecost, the anniversary of the giving of the Torah, the hymnists were attracted to the legend of God as matchmaker seeking a suitable mate for the Torah, who after rejecting Adam, Noah and the Patriarchs as unworthy of her, settled upon Moses as a fitting suitor. The core of this folklore,

[80] Rabinovitz, *Maḥazor . . . Yannai*, i. 308–9; Yahalom, *Piyyuṭey . . . Megas*, pp. 195–200.
[81] See *Sefer Qerovot*, pp. 77–91, 198–213.
[82] *Maḥazor . . . Savu'ot*, p. 115.

preserved only in the *piyyuṭ* and not in rabbinic sources, was expanded and set to verse by Qillir and his successors in Europe and North Africa and inserted into the *qedušta'*, in the *rahiṭ* section, following the *qiqlar*. The enhanced legend is headed by the verse from Prov. 8: 22, 'The Lord created me at the beginning of His work.' In its earliest treatment by Qillir the verses from Prov. 8: 22–9 are each embellished in rhymed strophes similar to the treatment of the Song at the Sea and the Decalogue. Later hymnists used only the scriptural opening in Prov. 8: 22. The legend itself comprised nine motifs:

1. The Torah entertains God for 2,000 years before the creation of the world.
2. God decides to create the world with wisdom for the sake of the Torah.
3. God consults the Torah before beginning the work of creation.
4. He determines that the world is needed in order to give honour to the Torah.
5. The Torah wants to be given only to the ministering angels and not to humankind.
6. God informs the Torah that her commands are intended only for humankind which is given the power to repent its sins.
7. God offers the Torah a choice of suitors who would bring her down to earth.
8. The Torah gives her reasons why Adam, Noah and the Patriarchs are not acceptable.
9. When Moses is presented to her she readily agrees.[83]

This legend, like much of folklore, often varied with the retelling, as may be seen in the different reasons given by the poets for the Torah's refusal to accept Abraham as her suitor. Following are two versions of the Torah's objections to Abraham, by Qillir and by Yoḥanan Ha-Kohen b. Yehošua:

[QILLIR]
Without trust and with ignorance,
He [Abraham] said [to God] without thinking:
How shall I know [that I am to possess the land]? [Gen. 15: 8]

[YOḤANAN]
He did not have pity upon his only son
And lifted his hand to shed blood like a savage . . .
He should have appealed to You and begged for mercy.[84]

The last day of Tabernacles, with its scriptural reading from Deut. 33: 1 ff. and the account of Moses' death, led the poets to meditate on man's mortality. One of the earliest compositions on the death of Moses, *'Ašer biglal 'avot*,

[83] Weinberger, 'Širim ḥadašim', ii. 2–7.
[84] Ibid. 5.

an unrhymed hymn from the period of the anonymous poets, ends with 'Moses died, who then shall not die?'[85] Later hymnists set to verse the tragedy of Moses who, after having led Israel out of Egypt and through the wilderness, is condemned to die and prevented from seeing the promised land. According to legends preserved in both rabbinic and hymnic sources, Moses pleads with God to let him live and complete his mission. Following is a moving rendition of Moses' plea for life from a *qedušta'-rahiṭ* in the form of a dialogue between God and Moses. The work is attributed to Phinehas Ha-Kohen:

[MOSES:]
I will not die! Why must I die?
Is it because of the plagues that I brought in Noph [Egypt],
Or because of the many I caused to drown in the sea?
I did according to Your will and if there were righteous among them, I am innocent!
Remember when their rabble received me asking, 'Who is God?'
Do not entrap me because of them.

The Mighty One [God] answered him the selfsame day:
'They were wicked indeed and pressured to exhaustion, a target for archers.
That is not why!'

[MOSES:]
If that is not why, then why must I die?

[GOD:]
Moses, ascend and die; it is decreed that you shall die.[86]

Whether or not Moses was mortal is debated in rabbinic sources (in *bSot* 13b and parallels in *Sifre* No. 357):

Others declare that Moses never died; it is written here [in Deut. 34: 5], 'So Moses died there,' and elsewhere [in Exod. 34: 28] it is written, 'And he was there with the Lord.' As in the latter passage it means standing and ministering, so also in the former it means standing and ministering.

Another rabbinic opinion (in *bSukk* 5a) disagrees:

Neither did the *šekhinah* ever descend to earth, nor did Moses and Elijah ever ascend to Heaven, as it is written [in Ps. 115: 16], 'The heavens are the heavens of the Lord, but the earth has He given to the sons of men.'

The emphatic tone of the latter statement suggests that it was intended as a polemic against the assumption of Moses. Among the hymnists there is likewise a difference of opinion on the question of Moses' mortality. Views

[85] *Maḥazor Le-Sukkot*, pp. 471–2.

[86] *Maḥazor Kol Ha-Šanah*, ii. 193b.

that argue for the assumption of Moses are preserved in several Mediterranean hymns. Characteristic of these is the poem *Ṣa'aqah yokheved be-qol*, preserved in North African congregations, in which the poet reports,

> The angels have raised him [Moses] to the highest heavens
> To the innermost place, the holy of holies.

Much bolder is the statement in another North African hymn, *Ṣa'aqah yokheved mi-ke'ev*:

> The *šekhinah* descended and Moses was raised.[87]

Balancing these views, however, is the early anonymous hymn *'Ašer biglal 'avot*, stressing the mortality of Moses, and the equally emphatic early Byzantine poet Samuel Ha-Kohen b. Memeli in his *zulat*, *'Uyyam ne'eman we-nikh'av*, even as he concedes that, unlike other mortals, Moses expired with a kiss from God:

> The pure one in the blessed circle
> The Lord kissed delicately
> And there died Moses, servant of the Lord.[88]

Yoṣer

The five poetic embellishments adorning the benedictions of the *šema'* in the weekday morning service take their names from the liturgical phrasing of the benedictions themselves. The first is called the *yoṣer* after the blessing before the recitation of the *šema'*, *yoṣer ha-me'orot*; the second is called the *'ahavah* after the second blessing before the *šema'*, *ha-boḥer be-'ammo yisra'el be-'ahavah*; the third, the *mi kamokha*, is named after the scriptural verse (from Exod. 15: 11) embedded in the blessing after the *šema'*; the fourth is named *'adonay yimlokh* or *'adonay malkenu* after the second verse in the latter blessing (from Exod. 15: 18); and the last, the *ge'ullah*, is taken from the blessing after the *šema'*, *ga'al yisra'el* or *ṣur yisra'el we-go'alo*.

On Sabbaths and festivals the *'ofan*, *me'orah* and *zulat* hymns are added to the *yoṣer* complex. The *'ofan*, named after the liturgical unit *we-ha-'ofannim we-ḥayyot ha-qodeš*, connects the verse from Isa. 6: 3 to the verse in Ezek. 3: 12 in the blessing before the *šema'*. The *me'orah* adorns the benediction *yoṣer ha-me'orot*, and the *zulat* embellishes the liturgical unit after the *šema'* beginning with the word *'emet* and ending with *'eyn 'elohim zulatekha*. The first hymn in the complex, called the *guf ha-yoṣer* (body of the *yoṣer*), was formalized by classical poets and generally included four sets of three tercets closing with a

[87] Weinberger, 'Midraš 'al peṭirat Mošeh', pp. 291–2.
[88] Weinberger, *Širat Ha-Qodeš*, p. 8.

scriptural verse. The sets were encompassed by a like number of choral refrains, *qiqlar* style, in tercets ending with the word *qadoš*. All tercets, in the sets and the refrains, were linked through anadiplosis, the repetition of a word or phrase ending one tercet and opening another. The four sets comprised a complete alphabetic acrostic and the choral stanzas held the name signature of the poets. In later variations, Byzantine and Spanish hymnists asserted their independence by spelling out their names beginning with the opening tercets. Transitional figures like the tenth-century Hispano-Hebrew poet Joseph Ibn Abitur and the twelfth-century Byzantine hymnist Joseph b. Jacob Qalai, combining classical mannerisms with the newer European forms, give both alphabetic acrostic and name signature in the sets and stanzas of the *yoṣer*.[89]

The *'ofan* following the *guf ha-yoṣer* in the classical period is generally a short quatrain comprising an abridged alphabetic acrostic. Later embellishments of this genre included three strophic sets of rhymed tercets with choral refrains of three versets, but without the *qadoš* ending. The thematic content of the *'ofan* focuses on the chorus of angelic hosts echoing God's praise as they bear His chariot throne. It is likely that the hymnists did not wish to elaborate on the theme of the chariot throne (*ma'aseh merkavah*), a subject forbidden in *mḤag* 2. 1, and therefore made do with a shortened *'ofan*. Moreover, the cantor-poets were undoubtedly sensitive to the strictures of the Babylonian rabbi Pirqoy ben Baboy condemning hymnists who comment on the chariot throne.[90]

Although they added embellishments in structuring the *'ofan*, the hymnists were careful to observe the standard form of the *me'orah* and *'ahavah*. From the time of Qillir these hymns, without exception, were composed in rhymed quatrains and were followed by a scriptural verse and the concluding benediction: in the *me'orah*, *yoṣer ha-me'orot* and in the *'ahavah*, *ha-boḥer be-'ammo yisra'el be-'ahavah*. It is likely, as E. Fleischer suggests, that the two hymns were intentionally shortened in order that the poet should not be tempted to stray from the theme of the blessing conclusion. This was in line with rabbinic teaching (in *bPes* 104a): 'He who recites *havdalah* must say [something] in the nature of the conclusion near to its conclusion.' It was also in keeping with the warning of Natronay Ga'on that 'people should say words tantamount to the blessing's introduction and conclusion.'[91]

Given the standardized limitations of the *me'orah* and *'ahavah*, the hymnists, like poets of a seventeen-syllable haiku, were challenged to enclose large conceits in small shapes. Following is a *me'orah* by a post-classical poet, Samuel *Ha-Šeliši*, on the reading from Gen. 47: 28 in which the poet meditates on the resurrection of the dead:

89 Weinberger, *Re'šit Ha-Payṭanut*, English section, p. 5.
90 Fleischer, *Ha-Yoṣerot*, pp. 264–5.
91 *'Oṣar Ha-Ge'onim*, i. *Ber* No. 178; Fleischer, *Ha-Yoṣerot*, pp. 268–9.

Concealed in the grave, hidden in the clefts of rocks, closed in the pit;
Their bones are dry, their skin shrivelled, their flesh withered;
Venerable [One], resurrect, summon the imprisoned, awaken them
Sprinkle them with radiant dew, revive them to sing and praise.[92]

Within the short space of four versets, the poet echoes a universal hope. Taking a cue from the demise of Jacob in the Torah reading, he commiserates with the fleshless dead imprisoned in their graves, even as he knows that they are not forsaken. God, the light's creator (*yoṣer ha-me'orot*) will revive them with His radiant dew.

The *guf ha-yoṣer*, *'ofan*, *me'orah* and *'ahavah* constitute the first unit of the Sabbath and festival *yoṣer*. The second unit begins with the *zulat* hymn and adorns the prayer after the *šema'* ending with *'eyn 'elohim zulatekha*. The *zulat* is generally a large work, matching the *guf ha-yoṣer* in size. Most poets constructed this hymn in rhymed quatrains with an ending (and at times an opening) verset from Scripture. The theme of the *zulat* may deal with the weekly reading from the Pentateuch and the Prophets, or it may focus exclusively on the lesson from the Pentateuch and avoid the Prophets, as was the practice of Qillir.[93] Since the *zulat* grew to inordinate length, it became a burden both for the cantor-poet who offered a solo rendition of the work and for the members of the congregation who remained silent throughout. To relieve the monotony of the *zulat* offering, Phinehas b. Jacob Ha-Kohen of Kafra is said to have introduced choral refrains into the *zulat*, giving the hymn a sonic balance and enhancing thereby its aesthetic value. Following Phinehas in this practice was Sa'adyah Ga'on (882–942) who regularly inserted choral responses in the *zulat*.[94]

Closing the *yoṣer* complex is the *mi kamokha* (Who is like You?) connecting the two scriptural verses (in Exod. 15: 11 and 15: 18) embedded in the *ge'ullah* blessing after the recitation of the *šema'*. In the classical period, the *mi kamokha* was perceived as an appendage to the *zulat* and generally comprised a one-stanza work in quatrains. When the poet chose to sign his first name in the acrostic to the *mi kamokha* he would add the versets needed to accommodate the signature.[95]

Ma'ariv

The liturgical units embedded in the evening services, the *ma'arivim*, can be traced to the pre-classical period. Most of the *ma'arivim* were shorter than the *qedušta'ot* and *yoṣerot*, partly because of the urgings of synagogue officials (*parnasim*) who wished to return home at a reasonable hour for the evening

[92] Fleischer, *Ha-Yoṣerot*, pp. 275–6.
[93] Ibid. 281–6. [94] Ibid. 294–6. [95] Ibid. 311–21.

meal. This may also explain why *ma'arivim* for weekdays and Sabbaths have not been preserved and only hymns designed for the evening service at festivals have survived. The evening service allowed for six stations where liturgical units could be placed. These included the two benedictions before the recitation of the *šema'*, the *ma'ariv 'aravim* and the *'ohev 'ammo yisra'el*; the two verses from Exod. 15: 11 (*mi kamokha*) and 15: 18 (*'adonay yimlokh*); and the two benedictions after the *šema'*, the *ga'al yisra'el* and the *ha-pores sukkat šalom 'aleynu we-'al kol 'ammo yisra'el we-'al yerušalayim.*

From the available sample of classical *ma'arivim* it appears that their authors did not invest the same effort and talent in their construction as was expended on larger works for the morning service. A notable exception is the following evening service hymn by an unknown poet, named Joseph in the acrostic. His hymn paraphrases Isa. 54: 1, the lesson from the Prophets read on one of the seven Sabbaths of Consolation between the Ninth of 'Av and the New Year:[96]

Sing O barren one! You who said, 'Who has borne me these?'
Your sons will multiply like the sand and their petitions I will fulfil;
Those hidden treasures of the sand I will reveal to them.'
Thus spoke the One who brings the evening, His name exalted
among them:

BLESSED ARE YOU WHO BRINGS ON THE EVENINGS
[*HA-MA'ARIV 'ARAVIM*]

'She who did not bear will conceive, her seedling is male;
From her land I will expel stranger and foreigner;
I will rage against her despoilers.'
His blessed and beloved will sing: He who avenges blood is
mindful of them.

BLESSED ARE YOU WHO LOVES HIS PEOPLE
[*'OHEV 'AMMO YISRA'EL*]

Sing, shout and rejoice, O pure without blemish;
In your midst all your multitudes will be gathered;
For they are blessed of the Lord;
And they will be welcomed, 'Blessed are you who come in God's
name';
Pleasant is their response, 'It is good to bless the Lord';
My Prince [Messiah] will come to them borne on the clouds;
They will rejoice and be happy in God's house,
And all your children shall be taught by the Lord,
They who give witness, 'Who is like You [*mi kamokha*], O God,
among the mighty?'

[96] Fleischer, *Širat Ha-Qodeš*, pp. 245–6.

Seliḥah

The penitential hymn (*seliḥah*) which originated in the pre-classical period was given new forms by classical poets. Among their innovations were the *pizmon* (from the Greek *prosomoion*) and the *ḥaṭa'nu*. The *pizmon* did not vary much from the regular *seliḥah*, save for its opening versets, which were repeated as refrains after each strophe. The *ḥaṭa'nu* got its name from the confessional formula, 'We have sinned, O our Rock; forgive us, our Creator', recited on the Day of Atonement. In the classical *ḥaṭa'nu* this formula was the refrain following the strophes which, in this genre, were often connected by anadiplosis.

Of special interest is the *ḥaṭa'nu* recited on the Day of Atonement, the Ninth of 'Av, and the Fast of Gedaliah recounting the tragic deaths of Judea's ten leading sages during the reigns of the Roman emperors Trajan and Hadrian. Based in part on the rabbinic account of the Ten Martyrs in *Lam. Rabbah* 2. 2 (ed. S. Buber 50b), the poet Yehudah (a contemporary of Yannai and Qillir), in his *ḥaṭa'nu*, *'Elleh 'ezkerah we-nafši 'alay 'ešpekhah*, blames the deaths of the sages on the sins of Israel: 'We have sinned, O our Rock.' Because the ten are without blemish their deaths are able to atone for Israel's sins, as did the sacrifices of unblemished animals in the Temple service. The nature of Israel's crime that warrants such drastic punishment is indicated in Deut. 24: 7: 'If someone is caught kidnapping another Israelite, enslaving or selling the Israelite, then that kidnapper shall die.' The kidnappers were the children of Jacob (= Israel) who sold their brother Joseph into slavery, and since the culprits, long since dead, have not been punished, it remains for the sinless ten to atone vicariously for their crime. The ten are informed that this is the divine decree:

> Accept Heaven's judgment upon you
> From their [Jacob's sons] days to the present no one is your equal;
> Were they alive, I would have judged them instead of you;
> And now you must bear the sins of your fathers.

Judgment comes upon Israel because of the sin committed by the sons of Jacob (= Israel), and atonement is granted through the sacrificial death of the unblemished ten.[97]

In their treatment of the atoning death of the sages, the hymnists, like the rabbis, draw on a theme from Isa. 53: 9–10 where the Lord's servant who has

[97] See Zulay, *Zur Liturgie*, p. 7; *Maḥazor Le-Yamim*, ii. 568–73. In a later treatment of this legend by the Franco-German poet Meir b. Yeḥiel in his elegy *'Arzey ha-levanon*, the remains (Heb. *noteret*) of the murdered sages are fed to the lions who devour them 'in a ritually clean place like a sin offering and a guilt offering.' The poet's referent is the text in Lev. 6: 9–10 regarding the meal offering: 'What remains [*we-ha-noteret*] of it [the offering] shall be eaten . . . in the sacred precinct . . . it is most holy, like the sin offering and the guilt offering.' Cf. *Seder Ha-Qinot*, pp. 82–5.

'done no injustice' and has 'spoken no falsehood' has been made 'an offering for guilt.' It is also likely that the hymnists were aware of the Hebrew text of 4 Maccabees where the pious Eleazar, a leader of the Judeans, prays before his martyr's death at the hands of the tyrant Antiochus, '[God], be merciful to Your people and let our punishment suffice for them. Make my blood their purification, and take my life in exchange for theirs.' Undoubtedly, the hymnists were familiar with the legends surrounding the Binding of Isaac (*'aqedah*) who, according to R. Eliezer b. Pedat (in *Sefer Ha-Yašar*, ed. Rosenthal, p. 81) 'did not die [in the *'aqedah*], [but] Scripture accounts it to him as though he had died and his ashes lay on top of the altar.' Therefore, say the rabbis (in *Tanḥuma Wa-Yera'*, 23), 'Whenever the children of Isaac sin and as a result come into distress, let there be recalled to their credit the *'aqedah* of Isaac and let it be regarded by You as though his ashes were heaped up on top of the altar, and forgive them and redeem them from their distress.'[98]

Qinah

The elegies (*qinot*) composed during the classical period, in particular those of Qillir for the Ninth of 'Av, are noted for their fervent nationalism and intense longing for Israel's restoration in her native land. It is certain that Qillir composed at least five and perhaps as many as forty elegies marking the anniversary of the destruction of the first and second Temples. The Qillir elegies cover a wide range of themes. He laments the abolition of the Temple cult and the twenty-four priestly divisions who administered it. He mourns that the *šekhinah* has been reluctantly removed from Jerusalem and lovingly describes its withdrawal in stages. He cries for the loss of Betar, Bar Kokhba's last stronghold in the war against Rome, and elegizes the death of Judea's King Josiah. His most moving laments are presented as dialogues between the vanquished nations, Judea and Samaria, mourning their fate, and between Jeremiah and the exiled widow Israel, dressed in rags. He relies heavily upon rabbinic legends even as he characteristically embellishes the sources from his own imagination, or from contemporary folklore. Following is part of Qillir's treatment of the Jeremiah–Israel dialogue from his elegy, 'Behold, at the time when [Israel] fair as Tirṣah [Cant. 6: 4], was in fullness of abundance [*'Az bi-mlo't sefeq yafah ke-tirṣah'*]:[99]

[98] The connection between Isaac and the ten was not lost on the hymnists; in one account by the Byzantine poet Ḥananyah b. Šelaḥyah in his *ḥaṭa'nu*, *Ḥeṭ'i ke-nifqad*, one of the ten, R. Ishmael, is referred to as *kofer 'eškol* after Cant. 1: 14, 'My beloved is unto me as a cluster of henna [*'eškol ha-kofer*]'. A similar designation is given to Isaac because, as *Cant. Rabbah* 1. 14 puts it, he 'was bound on the altar like a cluster [of grapes tied to a pole] [and] because he atones [*mekhapper*] for the iniquities of Israel.' See Weinberger, *Seder Ha-Seliḥot . . . Ha-Romaniotim*, pp. 111–12.

[99] *Seder Ha-Qinot*, pp. 101–2.

[JEREMIAH:]
In the name of God and man I bid you [Israel]:
Declare, are you a demon or a human?
Your elegant form resembles a human,
Yet you strike fear and terror as only angels can.

[ISRAEL:]
I am neither demon nor formless clay;
At [the time of] peace and tranquillity I was well known,
Whether to the three [Patriarchs] or the seventy-one [Sanhedrin],
Or the twelve [tribes] or the sixty myriad [who left Egypt], or the one [Abraham] . . .
How could I rejoice, or raise my voice?
My babes are delivered into hostile hands,
My prophets are beaten; they are dragged [into exile];
My kings have been exiled, my princes and priests are in chains.

At the close of the elegy, God intervenes and bids Jeremiah to appeal to the Patriarchs to intercede on Israel's behalf:

Arise Jeremiah! Why do you keep silent?
Go, call the Patriarchs, Aaron and Moses;,
Let the shepherds come and raise a lament,
For the desert wolves have torn the lamb.

In the latter conceit the poet draws upon the rabbinic legend (in *Lam. Rabbah*, Proem No. 24):

The Holy One, blessed be He, said to Jeremiah: 'I am now like a man who had an only son, for whom he prepared a marriage-canopy, but he died under it. Do you not feel anguish for Me and My children? Go, summon Abraham, Isaac and Jacob, and Moses from their graves, for they know how to weep.'

In Qillir's elegy 'Then Jeremiah went to the graves of the Patriarchs' (*'Az be-halokh yirmiyahu 'el qivrey 'avot*); he elaborates on the legend and portrays the panic-stricken prophet frantically calling upon Israel's founding fathers, 'Why are you lying there? Your children are exiled; they are pierced with daggers!' Then, turning to God, he asks, 'Where is the merit of the ancestors in the wasteland?' Now aroused, the fathers respond with cries and prayers to God, pleading, 'Where is Your assurance, "I will remember in their favour the covenant with their ancestors? [Lev. 26: 45]"' Responding, God reassures the fathers: 'I cannot help you; it is My decree.' Not wishing to leave them unsatisfied, He explains the reason for the decree. Israel is judged for her failure to live up to the covenant: 'They have exchanged My glory for vanity.'

Abraham, whom God tested and did not find wanting, is not satisfied and pursues the argument: 'Was I tried in vain on ten occasions on their behalf . . . Where is Your assurance, "Abraham do not fear! [Gen. 15: 1]"?' The fine point in this exchange between God and Abraham is not found in rabbinic sources and is probably Qillir's own embellishment. In the rabbinic version of the legend (in *Lam. Rabbah,* Proem No. 24) Abraham merely questions God's decree and is informed, 'Your children sinned,' etc. In Qillir's treatment the argument is then pressed by Isaac, who asks, as in *Lam. Rabbah*, if his willingness to be bound by his father and to sacrifice his life was in vain. He closes (like his father) with the reminder, 'And where is Your assurance, "My covenant I will establish with Isaac [Gen. 17: 21]"?'[100] Isaac's plea is followed by the entreaties of Moses and of Leah, Rachel, Bilhah and Zilpah, the wives of Jacob. The appeals of Bilhah and Zilpah are not preserved in rabbinic sources and are known only from Qillir's work. The elegy closes with God urging Israel to repent and assuring her that He too is exiled to Babylon for their sake. He ends with the promise: 'Behold, I will return your banished children!'

Hoša'not

Another occasion when hymnists were inspired to improvise was the seventh day of Tabernacles, Hoša'na' Rabbah. On this day, after seven processions around the altar chanting 'Save us we beseech You, O Lord' (Ps. 118: 25), willow-sprigs, representing the sins of the past, would be dashed against the synagogue floor. This was also a critical time for Israel's farmers, who believed that on Tabernacles God decreed the amount of rain that was to fall that year. In the old Ereṣ Yisra'el ritual the Prayer for Rain was recited immediately after the seventh procession on Hoša'na' Rabbah. Poetic embellishments for this day dating from the pre-classical period were generally expansions on Ps. 118: 25: 'Save us,' etc. (*hoši'ah na'*). The term was later abbreviated to *hoša'na'* (see *mSukk* 4. 5 and *bSukk* 30b). The earliest hymns for this day probably took the form of litanies chanted during the processions, with the worshippers responding to the cantor in the refrain 'Save us' (*Hoša'na'*). Variations on the litany form emerge in the classical period with the work of Qillir, whose *hoša'not* hymns feature alphabetic acrostic and rhyme, and are distinguished by their focus on the concerns of the farmer:

> Save man and beast . . .
> Save the planting of trees in the desolate earth
> Save the wine crop and and the grain
> Save the grape and the fruit trees on earth renowned . . .
> Save the flowers, strengthen them
> Save the plants that they may flourish.

[100] *Seder Ha-Qinot*, pp. 98–100.

Qillir is also sympathetic to the needs of the cattle-farmer on this critical day:

Save the animal that she not abort . . .
Save the herds from becoming lean
Save the sheep from destruction.[101]

The liturgies of Hoša'na' Rabbah, with their concern for the welfare of plant and animal life, bring into focus man's stewardship of God's worldly gifts. In the prayer for the autumn and winter rains that sustain life, Israelite man is dependent upon the seasonal changes ordained by God. He is likewise aware of the monthly changes in the lunar cycle and the appearance of the moon heralding the beginning of the month. The new moon determined the religious calendar, since the holy days of the year were to be observed on a given day of the lunar month.

Qidduš Yeraḥim

This term refers to the sanctification of the lunar cycle. In Temple times, when the new moon was sighted each month, celebrations and festive meals were held, complete with the sounding of the ram's horn and special benedictions over wine of the new month. The formal celebration—known as the Feast of the New Month or the Feast of the Sanctification of the Month—was generally held on the evening ending the Sabbath during the week of the sighting. The episode is described in *Exod. Rabbah* 16. 24: 'What blessing is to be recited by one who beholds the new moon? . . . Some of the rabbis hold: "Blessed be He who renews the months", some: "Blessed be He who consecrates the months", and others: "Who hallows Israel"; since unless Israel sanctify it, it is not sanctified at all.'[102]

Israel's role, then, is decisive in endowing the lunar cycle with sanctity, and accounts for the enthusiasm of the monthly celebration in Ereṣ Yisra'el, even after the pre-calculated calendar replaced lunar sightings as the method for determining the new month. The cantor-poets were also caught up in the excitement and were moved to embellish the benedictions recited at the festive meal. The hymnic insertions, appropriately titled 'Sanctification of the New Month', have been preserved in the Cairo Geniza in several versions, most notably in the work of Phinehas Ha-Kohen, who composed separate dedications for each of the months in the year. Following is his hymn to the month of 'Av :[103]

May the month of 'Av elicit joy
On its ninth, as its fifteenth [*mTa'an* 4. 1];
Father [*'av*] on high, favour your children;

[101] Fleischer, *Širat Ha-Qodeš*, pp. 70, 254–5.
[102] *bSan* 41b–42a.
[103] Marmorstein and Habermann, *Qiduš Yeraḥim*, pp. 38–9.

Merciful beloved, have pity like a father . . .
Thirty-nine vessels in Temple use
Return to honourable service;
Submit the plan to revive my holy ministers;
Renew my salvation as did the one coming in the fifth.

AS IT IS WRITTEN [Ezra 7: 8]: HE [Ezra] CAME TO JERUSALEM IN THE FIFTH MONTH; AND IT IS SAID [Jer. 31: 13]: THEN SHALL THE YOUNG WOMEN REJOICE IN THE DANCE; AND IT IS SAID [Ps. 104: 19]: YOU HAVE MADE THE MOON TO MARK THE SEASONS; THE SUN KNOWS ITS TIME FOR SETTING

BLESSED ARE YOU WHO SANCTIFIES ISRAEL AND THE NEW MONTHS.

Mišmarot

A leading source of inspiration for the hymnists of the classical period were the twenty-four divisions (*mišmarot*) of priestly and levitical service in the Temple. Each division enjoyed this privilege for two weeks during the year. The memory of the service divisions, including the particular weeks of service, was preserved by priestly families in Galilee long after the Temple was destroyed, even as it inspired poets like Qillir, Hadutah and Phinehas Ha-Kohen from Kafra in the Galilee. Whereas Qillir composed his *mišmar* hymn, *'Eykhah yaševah ḥavaṣṣelet ha-šaron we-damam ron* (Alas, the Rose of Sharon dwells [in exile], her song is silenced), as an elegy in quatrains for the Ninth of 'Av, Hadutah, a contemporary of Yannai and Qillir, and Phinehas wrote festive Sabbath *qerovot* for each of the twenty-four priestly families. Designated *qerovot* were chanted on the Sabbaths that corresponded to the two weeks of service for each family. This practice, which kept alive the memory of the Temple ritual, continued well into the eleventh century, when the cantors would announce at the Sabbath prayers the name of the priestly family division that served in the Temple for that week.[104]

Hadutah's *mišmarot qerovah* is an unexceptional work in rhymed strophes, while that of the later Phinehas is a more attractive pattern poem with rhyming sestets connected by anadiplosis with refrains in quatrains. In the latter work, each strophe begins with *'anna'* (please) and closes with the benediction, 'Blessed are You who makes peace.' The sestets enclose the complete alphabetic acrostic, while the refrains spell out the poet's name. Preceding the versets of the refrain is the name of the priestly family division. Following is the first strophe from Phinehas' *qerovah*, honouring the watch of the priestly family Yehoyariv (*jTa'an* 4. 8, p. 68d).

Please listen to our prayer and song,
May our cries rise before You in memory;

104 *Seder Ha-Qinot*, pp. 47–52; Zulay, 'Le-toledot', pp. 111–20.

Gather to your home the Rose of Sharon [Israel];
Restore the Temple and the Tent [of meeting] and the Ark;
Gather in truth Aaron's sons, even those who sleep in Hebron [the Patriarchs];
Strengthen in its time Yehoyariv, the [priestly] division from Meron [in the Galilee].

The division from Meron glorify at the end of days and always; shorten the days [of our exile] and hasten the end;
The first [priestly] watch remember to rouse with your salvation in abundant authority and peace without limit.

BLESSED ARE YOU WHO MAKES PEACE.

The superscription to Phinehas' *qerovah* refers to his hymn as belonging to the *'oseh ha-šalom* (who makes peace) genre because of its closing benediction. The genre, which was much in vogue in later Hispano-Hebrew hymnography, was presumably pioneered by Phinehas.[105]

Birkat Ha-Mazon

The *birkat ha-mazon* (grace after meals) is mentioned in rabbinic sources (in *bBer* 48b), 'Our Rabbis taught: Where is the saying of grace intimated in the Torah? In the verse [Deut. 8: 10], "And you shall eat and be satisfied and bless."' In addition to embellishing the benedictions for the morning and evening services, the hymnists would also enhance the blessings in the grace. Poetic insertions were commonly placed before the three benedictions of the grace after meals, the *Ha-zan 'et ha-kol*, *'Al ha-'areṣ we-'al ha-mazon* and *Boneh be-raḥamaw yerušalayim*, and each of the insertions was supported by a verse from Scripture. The theme of the hymns varied with the occasion: epithalamia for the wedding feast, elegiacs for the mourners' meal and prayers for the welfare of the newborn infant at the feast of circumcision. Other occasions for the poetic celebration of the grace benedictions were the Sabbaths and the three Pilgrimage Festivals, the New Moon, the New Year, Ḥanukkah and Purim. Since the hymns for grace were not standardized, the poets were at liberty to employ a variety of strophic forms including rhymed couplets, tercets and quatrains.

Following is an anonymous pattern-poem epithalamium for use in the grace following a wedding feast, with couplets alternating in praise of groom and bride:

Groom! I liken you to the canopied
Splendour of the seven chambers [*šiv'ah heykhalot*] in perfection.

105 Zulay, 'Le-toledot', pp. 137–46.

Bride! He [God] made her stand out in choice garments,
Stately as a palm tree, her breasts are like its clusters.
Groom! He entered you in Eden's garden to make you wise
And gave you bridegroom's blessings and dominion over all.
Bride! He brought them together and he loved her above all
[She is] Eve, the mother of all the living.

AS IS WRITTEN [Gen 3: 20]: THE MAN NAMED HIS WIFE EVE, AND [Ps. 145: 16]: YOU OPEN YOUR HAND, SATISFYING THE DESIRE OF EVERY LIVING THING.[106]

Noteworthy is the poet's use of *šiv'ah heykhalot* (l. 2), a term from Jewish mysticism preserved in the *heykhalot* tracts and referring to the seven celestial chambers, the last of which houses God's chariot throne.[107] Undoubtedly the poet's audience was familiar with the reference, even as it was familiar with the rabbinic comment in *Gen. Rabbah* 8. 13, where God is said to have officiated at the wedding of Adam and Eve when He blessed the bridegroom and adorned the bride. At the wedding feast of the remarried widow the hymnist gives voice to the triumph of the recently bereaved who now makes a new life for herself:[108]

Unhappy widow, build now a home complete;
Mature and eminent, God has raised your fallen home,
Even as He will appoint the builders' hands and Israel will be bereft no longer;
Remember the love of the faithful; favour us and may Your gifts sate us as manna.

The widow's triumph is a paradigm for Israel's congregation in exile—designated by the feminine form *keneset yisra'el*—who is bereft of her children. With divine help she too will rebuild her land and her Temple.

LANGUAGE AND STYLE

Folk Legends

The tension between the views of the rabbis and the needs of the laymen was partially allayed some decades following Pirqoy's strictures by Natronay, *ga'on* of Sura (853–6). The latter, successor to Yehuday—a vocal critic of additions to the fixed prayers—was more sympathetic to the new developments in the liturgy. He wrote that it is permissible 'to add material in any

106 Habermann, 'Berakhot', pp. 85–6.

107 Scholem, *Major Trends*, p. 54. Many *heykhalot* hymns were preserved in the Greater Heykhalot (*Heykhalot Rabbati*). Some hymns were designed to help the mystic make the 'ascent' to the celestial chambers. See Carmi, *Hebrew Verse*, pp. 195–200.

108 Habermann, 'Berakhot', pp. 89–90.

given blessing whose subject matter is relevant to that blessing [*me'eyn 'otah berakhah*].' He also allowed *piyyuṭim to* be recited 'on any particular holiday, and if the subject matter of the *piyyuṭ* is pertinent to the holiday.' Amram, following Natronay as *ga'on* of the Sura academy, was equally tolerant of added liturgical hymns, although his successor, Naḥšon, is said to have insisted that 'in the academy and wherever our rabbis live, they alter nothing of the prayers which our sages have instituted . . . [and they chant] no *piyyuṭ* and admit no *ḥazzan* who knows *piyyuṭim* to the synagogue. A congregation where *piyyuṭim* are recited is not a congregation of scholars.'[109]

Naḥšon's revealing comment that *piyyuṭim* are not for scholars is supported by Benjamin b. Samuel's observation that *piyyuṭim* came to be written 'when learning decreased'. With the emergence of an élite corps of Hebrew poets in Andalusia in the eleventh and twelfth centuries, criticism of the early *payṭanim* gained new impetus. Abraham Ibn Ezra, a member of high standing in the Andalusian circle and an advocate of clarity in phrasing and purity in language, was outraged by the linguistic excesses of the widely imitated Eleazar Qillir and his use of neologisms, periphrases and elliptic syntax. In his commentary on Eccles. 5: 1 Ibn Ezra wrote:

> The Holy Tongue [Hebrew] in the hands of R. Eliezer [Eleazar Qillir], may his soul rest in Eden, has become like an open unwalled city. He has made masculine into feminine and vice versa . . . I shall not be able to recount one-thousandth of the errors committed by the hymnists [*payṭanim*].

Moreover, charged Ibn Ezra, Qillir loads the worship service with unbecoming 'riddles and fables'. Earlier, Pirqoy b. Baboy in the name of Yehuday had chided the hymnists for adding lore and legend (*'aggadot*) to the benedictions of the *'amidah* and for discoursing in the *piyyuṭim* on the configuration of the divine chariot throne, a subject forbidden by the rabbis (in *mḤag* 2. 1) to be aired in public.[110]

However, the cantor-poets were undeterred. Some of the folk legends which they adapted for synagogue use are preserved only in the liturgy and are not to be found in the more discriminating rabbinic sources. One such legend relates how after the death of Moses, his mother, Jochebed, went to look for her son. She asks Mount Sinai and the Sea of Reeds, but they do not know. Continuing her frantic search, she hears the voice of angels informing her that Moses has been taken to the heavens and rests securely with God.[111]

109 See *'Oṣar Ha-Ge'onim*, i. *Ber.* Nos. 178–9; Hoffman, *Canonization*, pp. 66–71.

110 See Ginzberg, *Ginzey Schechter*, ii. 546.

111 Ibn Ezra in his commentary on Gen. 46: 23 refers to the Jochebed folk-tale and asks sarcastically, 'Is it not bad enough [that the rabbis (in *bBB* 120a–123b) state that Jochebed was born when Israel entered Egypt] but now come the hymnists [*payṭanim*] with their hymn, "[Moses:] Jochebed my mother, be comforted after me." This would make Jochebed 250 years old [since Israel stayed in Egypt 210 years and spent 40 in the wilderness; Moses was 80 when they left Egypt, making Jochebed 130 when she gave birth to Moses]!' See Weinberger, 'Midraš 'al peṭirat Mošeh', pp. 285–93.

Other legends adapted by the cantor-poets in their efforts to reach out to the lay public include the story of God as matchmaker for the Torah and the epic battle between the monsters Leviathan and Behemoth for the entertainment of the righteous in the Garden of Eden. These, like the Jochebed story, are preserved only in the synagogue liturgy.[112]

A review of the stories is required to show their popular appeal and to point out the problems they posed for the rabbis. In the tale of God as matchmaker outlined above on p. 54, the Lord tries to find a suitable mate for the Torah. The legend is presented in the form of a dialogue between God and the Torah and is preserved in several Pentecost *qedušta'ot*, the nine-part hymn which ends with the Trisagion and is designed to embellish the benedictions of the *'amidah*. Versions of these two hymns were composed by Qillir (Q1 and Q2), by the seventh-century poet Yoḥanan ha-Kohen b. Yehoshua (Byzantium); and by the tenth- to eleventh-century hymnists Simeon b. Isaac the Pious b. Abun the Great (Mainz), Solomon Suleiman Al-Sinjari (Babylon), Nehemiah b. Solomon b. Heman Ha-Nasi (Babylon), Solomon b. Judah Ga'on (Jerusalem), Benjamin b. Samuel (Constantinople) and Joseph b. Samuel Ṭov Elem (Bonfils) (Limoges).

The story is set in the year 2000 before the creation of the world, which is then inhabited only by God and the Torah. She (Torah, a feminine noun) is lodged near Him in her chamber and 'plays on His lap' (Q1: *mišta'ša'at 'al birko*). Now God decides to create the world for the Torah's sake and 'consults with her as if seeking permission' (Yoḥanan: *nimlaḥ bah, melekh 'olam, kemo nuṭṭal rešut livrot 'olam*), adding 'If it meets with your approval, then I will create the world (Yoḥanan: *'Im yiṭav na' be-'eynayikh, 'evra' 'olam*). The Torah is not eager to share God with the world, and argues that the world's inhabitants will fail to live by her commands. At last the Torah agrees to the world's creation, but only on the condition that she be given to angels and not to humans. God reminds the Torah that her commands are designed to guide only humans.

Very well, says the Torah, but who will be worthy to take me down to earth? When God suggests Adam, the Torah objects, 'If he could not keep one command, how will he observe the many [Simeon]!' God then presents Noah to the Torah; he too is rejected, because of his drinking habits. Abraham is next offered as a suitor to the Torah, and is also found wanting because he sought proof that he would inherit the land of Canaan (Gen. 15: 8). Moreover, Abraham was too eager to shed the blood of his son: 'He should have appealed to You and begged for mercy [Yoḥanan and Q2, Benjamin and Joseph].' When Isaac is presented to the Torah and praised for his willingness to be offered up as a sacrifice, she faults him for his preference of Esau over Jacob. Jacob, too, is refused because he deceived his father Isaac in order to

[112] See Weinberger, 'God as Matchmaker'; Schirmann, *The Battle Between Behemot and Leviathan*.

obtain his blessings. God then brings forward Moses and at last the Torah is satisfied. 'Him I desire [Yoḥanan],' she says, and consents to be his bride.

This legend, like much folklore, was preserved in oral form and was undoubtedly familiar to the hymnists' audience. The likely reason that it was not included in rabbinic literature is that it denigrates the lives of worthy men like Adam, Noah and the Patriarchs. The policy of the biblical writers who present the hero complete with his flaws is not shared by the rabbis, whose views on the notables of the past is best expressed (in *bŠab* 55b-56ab) by the Ereṣ Yisra'el *'amora'*, R. Samuel b. Naḥmani (3rd–4th c.): 'Whoever maintains that Reuben sinned . . . that the sons of Eli sinned . . . that Samuel's sons sinned . . . that Solomon sinned . . . that Josiah sinned is merely making an error.' By ingenious methods of exegesis the rabbis sought to explain away the transgressions of prominent biblical figures even when these are explicitly recorded in the scriptural text. The hymnists, it appears, were not constrained by such rabbinic considerations and, like the biblical editors, they relished a good story to share with an appreciative congregation.

With regard to the epic encounter between the mythical animals Leviathan and Behemoth (to which the rabbis refer indirectly), a full account is given only in the hymns, most notably in the *silluq* (closing), *Wa-yikkon 'olam* (He established the world), to a *qerovah* by Qillir. Here the setting is the Garden of Eden at the End of Days. It is time to reward the righteous with the promised banquet (1 Enoch 60: 7–10 and Apocalypse of Esdras 4: 49–52). They will feast on the flesh of the largest land and sea animals, Behemoth and Leviathan, but not before they are entertained by a contest in which the two monsters battle to the death, reminiscent of the Roman circus.

The earliest associations of Leviathan with sport occur in Ps. 104: 26: 'Leviathan that You formed to sport with.' The rabbis (in *bAZ* 3b) learn from this verse that God 'sits and sports with Leviathan.' Later rabbinic embellishments had God organizing a circus-like spectacle in which Leviathan would entertain the righteous (*Targum* on Ps. 104: 26). In further elaboration on this legend, the monster Behemoth was designated to be Leviathan's opponent in the spectacle. The righteous who refused to attend the Roman circus would now be rewarded with what one rabbi (in *Lev. Rabbah* 13. 3) termed a 'wild-beast contest of the gentiles.'

The rabbis content themselves with telling only the bare essentials of the battle ('Behemoth will, with its horns, pull Leviathan down and rend it, and Leviathan will, with its fins, pull Behemoth down and pierce it through'), even as they are careful to note that Behemoth was killed by a ritually valid slaughter (' "God said: A teaching will go out from Me" [Isa. 51: 4], meaning that an exceptional temporary ruling [permitting Behemoth to be slaughtered by piercing] will go forth from Me,' *Lev. Rabbah* 13. 3). However, it remained for Qillir and other hymnists to provide the details that gave the story its epic character. The others who added their embellishments include

Yose ben Yose, and the ninth- to eleventh-century poets Amittai b. Šefatiah, Solomon Ha-Bavli and Mešullam b. Kalonymous from Italy; Sa'adyah Ga'on and Solomon Suleiman Al-Sinjari from Babylon; Elijah (the Elder?, 11th c.) and Joseph Ṭov Elem from France; Simon b. Isaac the Pious and Meir b. Isaac from Germany, and Solomon Ibn Gabirol of Spain.

It is Qillir, however, who is the main architect of the epic narrative, now enlarged to include a detailed description of the primeval monsters, based in part on Job 40: 15–24 and 41: 1–34. In the biblical portrait, the awe-inspiring Behemoth lives atop a thousand mountains where he feeds, and he drinks from the four rivers emanating from Eden. He easily lifts his massive tail as thick as a cedar and his limbs are like bars of iron. Yet, in Qillir's treatment, he is a merciful giant who shelters other animals and protects them against predators. The poet's portrait of Leviathan, too, is an augmentation of what is known about him from Scripture and rabbinic legends. Equal in size and power to Behemoth, the monster fish is just as gentle. Although his tail is like a mammoth ring surrounding the 'Great Sea' (which in rabbinic legend encloses the earth) and he demolishes with his 'spike' all his enemies, whom he then devours, he also entertains the great fishes and merits the praise of angels.

Hence the great battle of the two mammoths is not to be compared with the contest between the Babylonian Marduk and Tiamat, or the biblical creator God with Leviathan and Rahab of the sea. While the latter is an epic struggle between the forces of order against the power of watery chaos, the former is a mock-epic combat between two archetypes of land and sea long since subdued by the Creator and now offered as entertainment for the righteous. The hymnists' description of the Leviathan–Behemoth struggle, though lacking the dramatic suspense of the Babylonian or biblical creation epic, was able to hold the attention of the congregation and thereby fulfil its purpose.

In staging the contest for the righteous, both combatants have to be brought to the Garden of Eden. This is not too difficult for the land-based Behemoth who already drinks from Eden's waters, but Leviathan refuses to be drawn out of the sea by a fishhook (Job 40: 25). Even the angels fail in the effort and are in dread of him (41: 17). God now takes command and orders the sea creature to present himself at the designated place in Eden. In the ensuing battle the two monsters wrestle in close combat with no opening between them. They lash out at each other with horns and fins and seem to be evenly matched until the sea mammoth breathes forth fire from his nostrils (Job 41: 11–13) and sets ablaze Behemoth's pubic hair. In pain, the land mammoth retreats, hiding among the fragrant ferns of Eden. These too are, inadvertently set on fire, giving rise to a perfumed cloud of incense which fills the Garden and rises to the heavens. At that moment a Bat Qol (voice from heaven) is heard paraphrasing Cant. 4: 16: 'Awake O north wind; come O south wind! Blow upon my garden that its perfume may spread.'

Now recovered from his wounds, Behemoth re-enters the fray and the two resume fighting, taking turns goring and stabbing. God intervenes, declaring a draw, as it were, and makes peace between them. He then slays them in a ritually valid slaughter and offers them as banquet fare to the righteous in Eden. The narration ends with praise to God who will reveal the End of Days and bless his anointed one (from the house of David) and his people Israel for ever. In recounting the epic contest between Behemoth and Leviathan, both rabbis and hymnists rely on traditions about the two giants preserved in Scripture and in folk sources. However, only the hymnists, notably Qillir, give the story its epic dimension and dramatic structure by adding the necessary details. Qillir has God summoning Leviathan to do battle in Eden after the angels fail. He adds suspense to the contest when the sea monster disables his rival with fire from his nostrils. He depicts Behemoth's brave return to the battle after his retreat. He paints flaming forests of Eden reflecting the destruction wrought by the combatants, even as they soothe the righteous with perfumed fragrance. These embellishments giving the story its epic character proceed from the need of the hymnist, who, unlike the rabbi, must inspire as well as entertain his congregation on the Sabbaths and festivals when no labour is permitted and there is little else to occupy the unlettered layman.

POST-CLASSICAL DEVELOPMENTS IN THE BABYLONIAN DIASPORA

GENERAL BACKGROUND

During the period of Arab domination of Ereṣ Yisra'el from 634 to 1099 Jewish hymnography declined in the land of its birth and flourished in Babylonia and North Africa. The reasons for the decline are not clear. The Arab conquerors did not change the administrative system, and preserved northern Ereṣ Yisra'el (the old Byzantine Palaestina Secunda) as the military province of Jordan with Tiberias as its capital, and southern Ereṣ Yisra'el (the Byzantine Palaestina Prima), comprising Judea and Samaria, as the military province of Palestine with Lydda as its capital. However, the exorbitant land-taxes (*kharaj*) that Muslims imposed on the farms of non-believers led many Jews to settle in cities where economic conditions were more promising and where they could safely practise their crafts such as dyeing and tanning. Tiberias remained the hub of Jewish religious life, much as it had been during the last century of Byzantine rule, and the Masoretes, who invented the Tiberian system of vocalizing Scripture, flourished in the city. Their system was to replace the older Palestinian and Babylonian vocalizations, and was adopted by Jewish communities throughout the world.

The academies of Jewish learning during the Arab period, first in Tiberias and later in Jerusalem and Ramle, could boast outstanding leaders like Aaron b. Meir (a contemporary and rival of Sa'adyah Ga'on), Solomon b. Judah (1025–51) and Daniel b. Azariah (1051–62). However, for reasons still unclear, economic conditions worsened in the cities. A letter (preserved in the Cairo Geniza) from Solomon b. Judah remarks that he was persuaded to become the prayer-leader (*ḥazzan*) of the Jerusalem synagogue and for two years was not paid for his services. One of Solomon's main functions was to raise funds from supporters in Egypt for the impoverished Jewish communities in the Holy Land. Adding to the prevailing penury was the decision of the Muslim Fāṭimid government which ruled in Palestine and Syria to withhold financial support for the Jerusalem academy. It is likely that this decision was taken during the reign of the sixth caliph of the Fatimid dynasty, Al-Ḥākim (996–1021), who in *c.*1012 is said to have burned synagogues and forced Jews to convert to Islam.[113] In the worsening economic and political conditions, the Jewish population began to decrease in Ereṣ Yisra'el by the end of the eleventh century and as a result lost some of its prestige and influence.

While Jewish life was declining in Ereṣ Yisra'el under the Fāṭimid caliphs, it flourished in Babylonia (Iraq) under Arab rule. The early Arab caliphs, beginning with Omar (634–44), were kindly disposed towards their Jewish subjects. The mid-seventh to the mid-eleventh centuries witnessed the golden age of the *ge'onim*, the heads of the prospering academies of Jewish learning in Sura and Pumbedita. This period coincided with an unparalleled efflorescence of Arabic culture during the Ummayad and Abbasid dynasties. The strength and influence of the Arab state during this period contributed to the growing importance of its Jewish leaders in relation to their counterparts in the eastern Mediterranean. As a result, the independence of the Babylonian *ge'onim* began to assert itself in matters of Jewish law and practice. One of their decisions was to adopt an annual Torah reading cycle, in contrast to the triennial cycle prevailing in Ereṣ Yisra'el.

This decision led to dramatic changes in those parts of the synagogue liturgy which were related to the weekly Scripture lesson, primarily the *qedušta'* and *yoṣer*. The *qedušta'ot* of Yannai, designed for the triennial cycle, had to be refashioned in hybrid formations combining the practice of both communities. In some cases the hymnist, mindful of the tolerance limits of his congregation, would drastically curtail the *qedušta'* to four short strophes, interspersed with lengthier *pizmonim* (choral refrains). This practice of emasculating the *qedušta'* led to further abuses of the genre, with the hymnist constructing his hybrid from the works of several classical poets and using *pizmonim* by different authors. The new construction also led to a pattern of composition in strophes and refrains in other genres.

[113] See Mann, *The Jews in Egypt and in Palestine*, ii. 69–70, 318.

THE PRINCIPAL POETS

Sa'adyah Ga'on

Innovations

Sa'adyah b. Joseph was *ga'on* (eminence) of the academy at Sura, father of medieval Jewish philosophy, translator of the Bible into Arabic, editor of the first methodically organized prayer-book, compiler of the first comprehensive Hebrew dictionary, including a rhyming dictionary for use by poets, and an innovative and influential poet. His liturgical writings represent a watershed in Jewish hymnography. M. Zulay has shown that Sa'adyah anticipated most of the innovations that were to characterize the later Hispano-Hebrew Golden Age poets.[114] Prominent among Sa'adyah's achievements were his pioneering changes in rhyming patterns that were to be imitated by cantor-poets in Spain, central Europe and Byzantium. The prevailing rhyme pattern in the classical period, be it the Qillirian type of rhyming two root-letters or its modification of one rhyming root-letter, allowed for only an end rhyme in the strophe, *aaaa*, *bbbb*, *cccc*, etc. However, in the work of Sa'adyah a pattern of multiple rhymes in one strophe can be seen, as in the following, *abab*, from his *'avodah* for the Day of Atonement:[115]

Ba-'adonay yiṣdequ we-yoduhu;
Penimah ḥokhmah lifnay;
'Emunato yede'u wi-yaḥaduhu;
'Omerey yeš 'adonay.

Be vindicated in the Lord and praise Him;
Wisdom leads you inside before Me;
Know His faithfulness and declare His unity;
Confirm the presence of God.

The strophes that follow in this *'avodah* are constructed in *bcbc*, *bdbd*, and *bebe*, constituting a sixteen-cola unit for the letter *'alef*. The poet continues the pattern for the remaining letters of the alphabet. Of equal interest is Sa'adyah's use of anadiplosis (*širšur*) not as a means of linking strophes, as was the practice in the classical period, but as the opening and closing units (*ba-'adonay . . . 'adonay*) in each strophe, as in the sample above.

Sa'adyah's innovations in a flexible rhymed strophe were to influence later hymnists from Babylon, such as the tenth-century Nehemiah b. Solomon b. Heman Ha-Nasi in his Prayer for Rain in seven parts (*šiva'ta'*) with full alphabetic acrostic.[116] However, unlike Sa'adyah's variable rhyme construction in the alphabet units, Nehemiah is content with an *abab* pattern for each letter

[114] Zulay, *Ha-'Askolah*, pp. 13–14, 99–107.
[115] Sa'adyah Ga'on, *Siddur*, p. 280.
[116] Zulay, 'Piyyuṭey Rabbi Neḥemiah', pp. 205–17.

throughout his twenty-cola structure. Sa'adyah also introduced what was to become the standard rhymed strophe for later hymnists in Italy, Spain and Byzantium, *aaab*, *cccb*, *dddb*, etc. Classical poets also occasionally used this form, but always with a repeated unit in the last colon and not a variable rhymeme, as was Sa'adyah's practice.

Philosophy in the Liturgy

Among the most far-reaching innovations of the Ga'on was the introduction into the liturgy of themes in medieval religious philosophy. This practice was to be followed by Hispano-Hebrew poets (and by hymnists from Byzantium), most notably by Solomon Ibn Gabirol (1021/2–*c*.1055) in his celebrated meditation *Keter Malkhut* (The Kingly Crown). In Sa'adyah's ten-part *qerovah*, 'Bless the Lord O my soul', for the Day of Atonement, in which he comments on the first four verses of Ps. 104, the Ga'on expatiates on the soul and its Creator; on the contrast between God and man; on the celestial fire; on supernal light and wisdom; on the nature of the heavens; and on the upper waters, the clouds, the spirits and classes of angels. Following is a sample from the second part of his *qerovah* commenting on Ps. 104: 1, 'O Lord my God, You are very great.' In drawing the contrast between God and man, Sa'adyah employs the rhetoric of the pattern poem, 'You are greater . . . they are less,' reminiscent of Yannai:[117]

> You are greater than all the astronomers;
> They measure the lower [world] upon which You built the higher;
> First You established the heavens underneath which You spread
> out the earth's lair.
> O Lord my God, You are very great.

Sa'adyah's *Siddur*

In the course of his tumultuous life Sa'adyah found himself embroiled in controversies with Aaron b. Meir, head of the Jerusalem academy, and Kohen Ṣedeq b. Joseph leader of the Pumbedita academy, as well as heretics like Ḥīwi al-Balkhī, and the Karaites. Sa'adyah's fearless independence of mind led him to the arguable assertion that 'there are no prayers other than these [eighteen benedictions of the *'amidah*].' In the dispute among the Babylonian rabbis whether it is permissible to embellish the fixed prayers, Sa'adyah allowed the addition of *qeduŝta'ot* and *qerovot* which he composed and included in his prayer-book. However, some of the changes that he proposed in the benedictions of the *šema'* generated new controversies. For example, he objected to the phrasing of the benediction, 'O cause a new light to shine upon Zion'. He argued that 'the light for which we give thanks to God every

[117] Zulay, *Ha-'Askolah*, p. 114.

day is the light of the sun itself, and nothing else.' The Ga'on also found fault with the benediction before the *'amidah*, 'Blessed are You O God, who has redeemed Israel,' preferring, 'Blessed are You, O God, king of Israel and his redeemer,' with its hopeful messianic overtone. Aware of the confusion in liturgical practices Sa'adyah noted that 'our people's traditions concerning prayers and benedictions . . . [have] been so neglected that they are completely forgotten.' In an apparent reference to the hybrid *qedušta'ot* and *yoṣerot* of the period, Sa'adyah wrote: 'others [of our prayers] were either so amplified or so truncated that they were completely altered and lost their original meaning and purpose.'[118]

It was this perceived chaos in the liturgy that prompted Sa'adyah to compose his prayer-book, which he titled *Kitāb Jāmī' aṣ-Ṣalawāt wat al-Tasābīḥ* (Collection of All Prayers and Praises). He compromised in the matter of poetic embellishments and allowed those that were consistent with the theme of the benediction. Noteworthy is his practice of rarely signing his name in the acrostic to his poetry. Perhaps he did not wish to be identified with the composers of *piyyuṭim*, given the opposition to their inclusion in the liturgy. The signature in most of Sa'adyah's liturgical work is that of a certain Solomon, who was probably the precentor in the Ga'on's congregation. Sa'adyah's prayer-book collection, a methodically arranged compilation in Arabic, was initially well received in Arabic-speaking countries. However, with the decline of the eastern Mediterranean centre Sa'adyah's prayer-book was forgotten. A critical edition by I. Davidson, S. Asaf and B. I. Joel bears the title *Siddur Rav Sa'adyah Ga'on* (Jerusalem, 1941).

Sa'adyah's Language

As noted above, Sa'adyah's supplications earned the unconditional praise of the perceptive Abraham Ibn Ezra, who celebrated their elegant biblical usages. However, some of his other hymns, like the Admonition, 'Whereas You, our Rock, chose this wretched man' (*'Im lefi boḥrekha ṣurenu ba-'adam ha-zeh ha-dal*) and the *yoṣer, 'Agarteley ḥemdi* (My desired vessels), on Lev. 9: 1[119] brim over with archaisms, neologisms and allusions largely incomprehensible to lay people and forbidding even to scholars. Was the Ga'on thereby showing a bias in favour of the learned, or was he trying to demonstrate that it takes scholarship to master the *piyyuṭ*, contrary to the views of critics who argued that '*piyyuṭim* are not for scholars'? An equal number of the Ga'on's hymns—in addition to the Supplications admired by Ibn Ezra—are easily comprehended. Following is an example from his *yoṣer*, *Naḥamu 'arusah mi-ma'amad sinay*, complete with choral refrains, on the reading from Isa. 40: 1 ff.:[120]

[118] Sa'adyah Ga'on, *Siddur*, pp. 10–11, 13, 17 n. 20.
[119] Zulay, *Ha-'Askolah*, pp. 149–61.
[120] Ibid. 197–200.

Be comforted, O hosts mobilized of old,
Soon you will see the wonders of the appointed time;
Your eyes who saw for themselves [what the Lord did to the Baal
of Peor; Deut. 4: 3] . . .
Be comforted, you who trusted your prophets;
A good glory will alight upon you,
See I have imparted to you [statutes and ordinances; Deut. 4: 5].

Sa'adyah's Legacy

Even as Eleazar Qillir had the most telling influence on the tenth- and eleventh-century Italian and Franco-German synagogue poets so Sa'adyah prefigured the conceits, rhetorics and poetics of Hispano-Hebrew hymnists like Joseph Ibn Abitur, Solomon Ibn Gabirol and Judah Ha-Levi. The Ga'on was both a traditionalist and innovator. Like the classical poets, he wrote *'avodot* for the Day of Atonement, *yoṣerot* and *šiv'atot* for Sabbaths and festivals, *dibrin* (commentaries on the Ten Commandments) and *'azharot* (catalogues of the 613 commandments) for Pentecost, and prayers for rain for the last day of Tabernacles. Although no formal *qedušta'ot* from Sa'adyah have been preserved, he did compose supplements to existing hymns in this genre. Sa'adyah's innovations as a hymnist lay in his new and imaginative usages of the prosody, imagery and rhetoric of Scripture as the medium of liturgical discourse. The Ga'on revived the use of the scriptural *waw* consecutive in the perfect and imperfect verbs, reintroduced the biblical forms for pronominal suffixes for nouns, *fimo*, *qodšehu*, *'eymatah* and others, and resorted to the infinitive absolute to emphasize the idea of the verb in the abstract. In addition, as noted above, he introduced alternating rhyme, pioneered new genres for both public and private use and combined Hebrew poetry with philosophy.[121]

Sa'adyah's Successors: Nehemiah b. Solomon, Samuel b. Hošanah and Ha'yyay Ga'on b. Šerirah

Although Sa'adyah was the best known and most influential of the post-classical poets, other hymnists whose liturgical writings have been discovered in the Cairo Geniza are impressive in their own right. Among these is the tenth-century Babylonian Nehemiah b. Solomon, a disciple of Sa'adyah and author of epic-length *šiv'atot* praying for rain (*tefillat gešem*), *'avodot* for the Day of Atonement and *qedušta'ot* for Pentecost. Like Sa'adyah, Nehemiah preserves features of the classical period in his stress on word metre (a constant number of units in each colon) even as he experiments with variable

[121] Ibid. 19–40.

rhyme forms. In his work with the newer rhyme patterns, Nehemiah was to influence Hispano-Hebrew poets who sought to imitate a celebrated sequence in Nehemiah's *tefillat gešem*, *'Im yimmal'u he-'avim*, for Tabernacles. In this sequence, *'Eloha ba-kol memšalto,* Nehemiah constructs a rhyming *tour de force* comprising a tenfold alphabetic acrostic of 220 bicola with monorhyme *ayim* ending and variable median rhymemes after each alphabet letter. Following are two sample cola from letters *'alef* and *bet*:[122]

'Eloha ba-kol memšalto / ne'ddar mi-qolot mayim
'Eḥad we-'efes bilto / ḥofen we-ḥošer mayim . . .
Be-ma'amarkha ha-kol bara'tah / we-nit'alletah 'al šamayim
Bi-yminkha ma'lah talitah / petukhim me-'eš u-mi-mayim.

God, ruler of all, mighty in the water's roar;
One and none beside Him, He lets the waters drip from His palm . . .
By Your word You made all and are exalted above the heavens;
With Your right arm You suspended the heights, a mixture of fire and water.

Following the Ga'on's example, Nehemiah infused his hymns with conceits from religious philosophy. However, unlike his mentor, who cleaves to established rabbinic views in his hymnography, Nehemiah in his *'avodah*, *'An'im gevurot 'el*,[123] echoes contemporary thinking in medieval metaphysics and botany. This may be seen in his use of terms like *meṣi'at 'olam* (= essence of the world), *yiḥud ha-'iyqar* (= unity of God) and *sekhel be-niqqayon* (= pure intellect), and his mention of the 1,290 types of flora. R. Nehemiah's occasional reference to the philosophy and science of his day became a common practice of the later Hispanics, Solomon Ibn Gabirol and Abraham Ibn Ezra, whose liturgical writing brimmed over with conceits from Neoplatonism.

Another prominent poet of the post-classical period was Samuel *Ha-Šeliši* (the third) b. Hošanah (d. after 1012), prolific author of some 400 hymns in every genre. Born in Ereṣ Yisra'el, where he attained the third rank in the seating order at the Jerusalem academy, he later settled in Fostat (Old Cairo). Like his predecessors Sa'adyah Ga'on and Nehemiah b. Solomon, Samuel often follows earlier models. He copies the forms of the classical *yoṣer,* although he takes liberties with the *'ofan,* which he builds in uncommon lengths of six sets in rhymed tercets with refrains, or in nine quatrains followed by choral stanzas in couplets.[124] Samuel's *me'orah,* 'Concealed in the

[122] Zulay, 'Piyyuṭey Rabbi Neḥemiah', p. 205.

[123] Ibid. 219–22.

[124] Cf. Wallenstein, *Some Unpublished Piyyuṭim from the Cairo Geniza*, pp. 78–81; Fleischer, *Ha-Yoṣerot*, pp. 264–5. As noted above, cantor-poets were generally sensitive to the charges of Pirqoy b. Baboy that they tend to elaborate on the forbidden (in *mḤag* 2. 1) mysteries of the divine 'chariot throne' in the *'ofan*.

grave', reveals his talent in condensing a universal theme within the confines of a sparse quatrain. Samuel also experiments with the newer *maṣdarim*, *rahaṭim*, and hymns with strophes and refrains after the fashion of contemporary hymnography. His work with the new alternating rhyme forms pioneered by Sa'adyah anticipate Solomon Ibn Gabirol in his treatment of the *mi kamokha*.

While living in Fostat, Samuel witnessed and wrote about the anti-Jewish riots in that city. The riots began on the third ofŠevat, 4772 (31 December 1011) and lasted for three days, after which they were ended by order of the caliph Al-Ḥākim.[125] In remembrance of the riots Samuel composed *qerovot*, *seliḥot* and a chronicle (*Megillat Miṣrayim*) describing his ordeal and the events leading up to it. From Samuel's sources it appears that Muslim rioters attacked a Jewish procession honouring the late Šemaryah b. Elḥanan, a prominent scholar and close friend of Samuel. The rioters then denounced the Jews to the provincial governor, who ordered twenty-three of them to be arrested, including Samuel. After appealing to the caliph for mercy, and then finding that there were not sufficient legal grounds for holding the prisoners, they were released. Jewish leaders then proclaimed an annual fast to be observed on the third ofŠevat.

It is likely that Samuel's *qerovot* and *seliḥot* marking the riots were initially composed for his private use, as were many of Sa'adyah's liturgical works. However, the superscription to his *qerovah*, *'Aromimkha 'adonay ki dillitanu*,[126] directs that it be recited in the synagogue on the fast of the third of Ševat. It is also likely that Samuel's other recordings of those events became a part of the fast-day service in Fostat congregations on the anniversary of the riots. In this, both the poet and the congregation anticipate the later practices of the Franco-Germans when they remembered, in *qinot*, *seliḥot* and chronicles, the anti-Jewish agitations during the First Crusade. Samuel's poetic record of the riots is graphic and intensely personal. Presumably, he was already advanced in age when forced to spend time in prison, and he complains about 'the chains on his legs and the [iron] collar around his neck.'[127] Although weakened by the experience, he begins a fast together with the other prisoners and describes his ordeal. His two *qerovot* opening with versets from Ps. 102: 5–13 and 30 respectively, elaborate on the harsh treatment that he endured in prison, and close on a note of thanksgiving:[128]

> 'You have turned my mourning into dancing' [Ps. 30: 11] . . .
> My strength and my fortress, You have inclined the king's heart to be gracious and merciful.

His *seliḥah*, *'Illu finu male' širah ka-yam*, probably written after the *qerovot*, focuses less on the poet's travail and more on God's redeeming power.[129]

[125] See Mann, *The Jews in Egypt and in Palestine*, i. 31.
[126] Zulay, 'Piyyuṭim', p. 168. [127] Ibid. 163. [128] Ibid. 172. [129] Ibid. 173–5.

The last of the prominent post-classical poets, Ha'yyay[130] ben Šerira (939–1038), was *ga'on* at the academy at Pumbedita. He composed mostly *rahaṭim* and an occasional *'adonay malkenu* hymn in strophes and refrains. He is also the author of two sets of uncommon *seliḥot* for the Ninth of 'Av . In the first set of six, Ha'yyay dispenses with rhyme in a manner reminiscent of the pre-classical poets. Yet, unlike them, he signs his name in an acrostic spanning the full alphabet. The sets are unusual in theme as well as form. The poet does not focus on Israel's sins or beg for forgiveness, as is common in the *seliḥah*. Instead he presents a list of complaints and charges addressed to God:[131]

> Whom have You abandoned eternally that You should cast us off
> forever?
> With whom have You always been indignant that You should be
> angry with us forever? . . .
> Have You not allowed an escape from every snare and have I not
> seen a limit to each travail?
> Why then is the time of my exile extended and widened,
> encompassing me from length to length?

The bitter rhetorical questions increase in boldness as the poet pursues his argument:

> He who remembers in mercy the alienated, why does He refuse to
> pity His intimates?
> He who is gracious and kind to strangers, why is He not
> compassionate with His own? . . .
> Seeing His children slaughtered before His eyes, how can He
> remain indifferent and restrained?

Even more remarkable is Ha'yyay's argument that Israel has not failed in her obligations under the covenant and is being punished unjustly:

> Come [O God] and see that we have been steadfast in observance,
> Even as our troubles have increased.

To be sure, most of these conceits have their parallels in Pss. 44 and 74. Even Ha'yyay's outcry, 'Woe, who is the hard-hearted Father who has been like an enemy to his children?' is based on Lam. 2: 5, 'The Lord has become like an enemy; He has destroyed Israel.' However, it is the poet's effort in choosing and editing for his own rhetorical purposes the several scriptural verses that sets these *seliḥot* apart.

130 This is the correct pronunciation of his name; see Habermann, *Toledot Ha-Piyyuṭ*, i. 112.
131 Brody, 'Piyyuṭim . . . Ha'yyay Ga'on', pp. 12–25.

THE PRINCIPAL GENRES

Revised *Qedušta'* and *Yoṣer*

Changes in the *qedušta'* are much in evidence in the post-classical period, due in large part to the introduction of trained choirs responding in choral refrains. Since the *qedušta'ot* of Yannai and Simeon b. Megas did not allow for choral responses, and given that post-classical congregations were attracted by the choir's aesthetic appeal, the hymnists had to compose their own *qedušta'ot* with refrains for choral accompaniment, or add to the works of Yannai and Simeon choral stanzas of their own. The latter choice was made by the anonymous ninth-century hymnist in Ereṣ Yisra'el (which by this time had adopted the annual Torah reading cycle), who designed choral additions to the *qedušta'ot* of Simeon b. Megas.[132]

However, not all the additions by the Anonymous are short choral refrains, after the model of Qillir's tercet *qiqlar* for the choir. The lengthier works of the Anonymous, while still attached to Simeon's *qedušta'ot*, served as intermezzi.[133] With the addition of choral refrains to the already large *qedušta'ot* of Yannai and Simeon, the tolerance threshold of the congregation was in jeopardy. To shorten the service, hymnists decided to limit the *qedušta'* and include only a few of its nine parts while preserving the choral refrains, which now became independent liturgical units.[134]

Post-classical poets showed a preference for composing *yoṣerot* over other genres, in part because the *yoṣer* was relatively neglected by earlier hymnists, who focused largely on refining the *qedušta'*. Since the *yoṣer* had not become standardized, the later poets were encouraged to compose in this genre. As a result, we are left with a sizeable corpus of *yoṣerot* for each of the fifty-four Scripture lessons in the annual cycle of Torah readings in Babylonian congregations.[135] The new reading practice resulted in changes in structuring the *yoṣer*. Much energy was expended by the post-classical poets in reconstructing the *yoṣer* series, with significant innovations in the liturgical unit following the *šema'* and ending with *'eyn 'elohim zulatekha*. In Qillir's treatment, the *zulat*, the second-longest hymn in the series after the *guf ha-yoṣer*, customarily built in quatrains and focused on the weekly reading from the prophets, was generally recited without accompaniment by choir. However, in the late classical

[132] See Fleischer, *Pizmoney Ha-'Anonymus*, pp. 11–60.

[133] This practice was similar to the *troparion* which allowed for a respite between the strophes of the *kontakion* in the liturgy of the Byzantine Church. See Werner, *The Sacred Bridge*, pp. 178 ff.; Fleischer, *Pizmoney Ha-'Anonymus*, p. 23 n. 39.

[134] This practice followed a similar pattern in the Byzantine Church, where the expanded *troparia* grew into the autonomous strophic and metric *stichera*. See Werner, *The Sacred Bridge*, p. 178.

[135] The annual cycle of Torah readings is implied in the discussion of the Babylonian rabbis (in *bMeg* 29b). The division into 54 pericopes was based on the need to read on each Sabbath three times what the Ereṣ Yisra'el congregations read. See Elbogen, *Jewish Liturgy*, pp. 132–4.

period beginning with Phinehas Ha-Kohen, choral refrains were introduced in the *zulat*. Another change occurred in the post-classical period when the Babylonian poet Solomon Suleiman Al-Singari built his *zulatot* in seven (or eight) short stanzas with a complete alphabetic acrostic and a closing scriptural verse. As a result of the change in Scripture reading practices, the hymn no longer dealt with the lesson from the Prophets as in classical times. Since changes were in order, Solomon Suleiman allowed himself to rebuild the other hymns in the *yoṣer* cycle, namely the *mi kamokha* and *'adonay yimlokh* (The Lord shall reign), or *'adonay malkenu* (The Lord is our King) in the *ge'ullah* blessing. His *mi kamokha* is built in three rhyming quatrains with an alphabetic acrostic reaching the letter *mem*. The *'adonay malkenu* then follows in a like number of quatrains completing the alphabetic acrostic and thereby linking the two hymns.

To appreciate fully this innovative change it should be remembered that behind each liturgical unit is an organic value concept. In the *ge'ullah* blessing, the value concept is God's love in redeeming Israel from Egyptian bondage, which the congregation acknowledges with gratitude: 'You have been the help of our fathers from of old; a shield and a saviour to their children in every generation.' In the closing lines of the blessing Israel, relying upon God's love, pleads for His aid: 'Rock of Israel, arise to help Israel; deliver Judah and Israel, as You have promised.' Fully aware of the organic unity in the *ge'ullah* blessing, Solomon Suleiman connects the *mi kamokha*, acknowledging God's love for Israel in ages past, with the *'adonay malkenu*, voicing the hope for Israel's national restoration. The manner in which the linkage is made dovetails with the structure of the twenty-four-letter acrostic, which divides evenly into three sets of quatrains. Conveniently for the poet, the second set comprising the *'adonay malkenu* begins with the letter *mem*, enabling the poet to open the plea for redemption with it:

Matay tirṣeh mi-yadenu 'olah u-minḥah?

When will You be pleased to receive from our hands burnt
offerings and meal offerings [in the rebuilt Temple]?[136]

The use of a trained choir to enhance the aesthetics of the synagogue service gained wide popularity in the post-classical period, as may be seen in the *me'orot*, *'ahavot*, *mi kamokha* and *'adonay malkenu* hymns of the period supplied with choral refrains. In the classical period these hymns were chanted by the precentor alone.

[136] See Kadushin, *Worship and Ethics*, pp. 94–5; Fleischer, *Ha-Yoṣerot*, pp. 310–17.

NEW GENRES

ʿOseh Ha-Šalom, Rahaṭ, Ševaḥ, Maṣdar and *Weʿal Zoʾt*

Among the new hymns that emerged in the post-classical Babylonian synagogue were those of the *ʿoseh ha-šalom* (who makes peace) genre adorning the closing benediction of the *ʿamidah*. In the classical period Phinehas Ha-Kohen's compositions on this theme were part of his triennial reading cycle *šivʿataʾ*, the seven-part embellishments of the benedictions of the *ʿamidah* for Sabbaths and festivals in Ereṣ Yisra'el when the *qeduššah* was not recited. In the post-classical age the *ʿoseh ha-šalom* hymn (referred to in some Cairo Geniza fragments as 'the Priestly Blessing' (*birkat kohanim*)) was severed from its connection to the *šivʿataʾ* and was recited as a separate liturgical unit. It is likely that the Babylonian hymnist, who was not bound by the restrictive conventions of the classical *šivʿataʾ*, was now free to close the *ʿamidah* with a poetic flourish—which the *ʿoseh ha-šalom* hymn afforded—and thereby impress his congregation. As in their hybrid *qeduštaʾot* the Babylonian cantor-poets built their *ʿoseh ha-šalom* hymns in the form of strophes and refrains. Following is an example from a post-classical poet named Phinehas:[137]

ʾArukkah me-ʾereṣ,
Be-ridtah me-ʿereṣ;
Goy ʾeḥad ba-ʾareṣ,
Neḥaluha be-šalom.

[The Torah,] its measure is longer than the earth,
Upon its descent from the skies;
[Israel,] a special nation on earth
Inherited her in peace.

The closing colon, ending with the unit *šalom* (peace), served as the choral response.

Another new genre from this period is the *rahaṭ*, which, like the *rahiṭ*, the lengthy seventh part of Qillir's *qeduštaʾot*, was recited hastily and without choral elaboration. Presumably the *rahaṭ* originated as an embellishment of the benedictions of the *ʿamidah*, but because of its inordinate length came to be seen as an independent liturgical unit. In the *rahaṭim* from the post-classical period, however, there is little evidence to connect the hymn thematically to the *ʿamidah*. In its later development, the *rahaṭ* came to be an all-purpose hymn serving both feasts and fasts. In addition to the *rahaṭ* the post-classical poets pioneered the *ševaḥ*, a prayer of praise. The latter hymn

[137] Fleischer, *Širat Ha-Qodeš*, pp. 297–9.

served as the introductory verses (*pesuqey de-zimra'*) of the Sabbath and festival services, and was adopted by the later Hispano-Hebrew poets for their liturgical use.

A new genre in the post-classical era was the *maṣdar* (opening), a one-strophe introduction to the *yoṣer*, giving the name of the hymnist and ending with a reference to the weekly Torah portion, in line with the prevailing practice. The *maṣdar* generally opens with praise of God and closes with the word *qadoš*. The purpose of this short hymn was to introduce the author of the *yoṣer* and to prepare the congregation for the poetic embellishments of the benedictions of the *šema'* that were to follow. The *maṣdar* was extensively used by poets who were unwilling or not talented enough to compose the several hymns of the *yoṣer* and contented themselves with prefacing the larger work with their short, signed introductions. In time the *maṣdar* too was separated from its connection to the *yoṣer*, and developed into an autonomous liturgical unit with choral refrains and poetic mannerisms designed to flatter its author.[138]

The early elegant and modest *maṣdarim* were written by Joseph Al-Baradani (*c*.925–99), a native of Baradan, a suburb of Baghdad, where he and his father Ḥayyim served as cantors in the local synagogue. Following is a *maṣdar*-epithalamium for the Sabbath following a wedding, when the bridegroom is called to the reading of the Torah:[139]

> May God take pleasure in His deeds,
> For He is exalted by His righteousness;
> Sun and moon He made, even all His works;
> To His servants He revealed the mystery of His creation . . .
> Bride and groom rejoicing are grateful to Him;
> He is the glory of His pious ones.

Already in Al-Baradani's occasional treatment of the *maṣdar* there are signs pointing to its subsequent development as an independent choral genre. This is seen in his *maṣdar* for the Sabbath which opens with a response for the choir from Ps. 33: 9:[140]

> Adore and glorify the Creator of all by His word:
> For He spoke and it came to be;
> He made the heavens and suspended the earth on His arms,
> For He spoke and it came to be . . .

Other innovations of the period include an introduction to the *mi kamokha* section of the *yoṣer*, beginning with 'Therefore' (*we-'al zo't*) and ending with 'Rejoicing, they sang: Who is like You . . . ? (*mi kamokha?*).[141] The

[138] Fleischer, *Širat Ha-Qodeš*, p. 307.
[139] Beeri, *Maṣdarim*, ii. 87.
[140] Ibid. 65.
[141] Fleischer, *Širat Ha-Qodeš*, p. 315.

new *we-'al zo't* genre, pioneered by the tenth-century Babylonian hymnist Judah b. Benjamin, established the thematic connection between the freeing of the Israelite slaves from Egyptian bondage in the past and the future redemption of Israel from exile. Following is Judah's *we-'al zo't* hymn for the Torah reading from Exod. 13: 17:[142]

> Therefore I will praise the Lord; who is like You among the gods
> Who divided the sea into twelve highways?
> When You return to rescue me from Ishmael's rule,
> The old and the young will adore You.

In addition to the revisions in the *qedušta'* and *yoṣer* and the emergence of new genres, the poets felt free to enlarge upon the standard signature acrostic in their hymns. They now added to their names the words *ḥazaq* (be strong), *ḥazaq we-'emaṣ* (be strong and bold), *yizkeh* (may he be worthy), *yizkeh le-ḥayyey 'olam* (may he be worthy of eternal life), *le-ḥayyey 'olam ha-ba'* ([may he be worthy] of life in the world to come).

Personal Prayers: Confession, Supplication and Admonition

The increased concentration on the aesthetic component in the post-classical Babylonian synagogue seen in the choral responses of trained choirs reflects a new emphasis on the needs of the individual in the worship service. From earliest times prayers were recited by the cantor-poet with only occasional responses by the congregation. The break with the earlier Scripture reading practice in Ereṣ Yisra'el led to changes in the focus of the service, which now became increasingly orientated towards individual needs for expression in prayer. This may be seen in the Confessions (*widduyim*) composed by the Babylonian Nissi Al-Nahrawani (9th–10th c.) and in the Supplications (*baqqašot*) of Sa'adyah Ga'on. Following is a portion of Nissi's 'Confession', a new genre in rhymed prose addressing itself to the concerns and anxieties of mortal man:[143]

> With what shall I come [before You] and what healing do I seek? I have been like a stubborn and rebellious son . . . That which You forbade, I have permitted . . . that which You hate I have loved . . . I did not intend to make You angry. I presume to come to You seeking forgiveness; my face is like that of a [shameless] dog, like a brazen whore. Humiliated, I approach You . . .

A similar tone pervades the Supplications of Sa'adyah Ga'on, which he recommends be recited by the individual at night in the privacy of his

[142] Elitzur, *Piyyuṭey Rabbi Yehudah*, pp. 32, 146.
[143] Habermann, *Toledot Ha-Piyyuṭ*, i. 102.

home.[144] The Ga'on's work in this genre is noted not only for its personal character but for its literary elegance, as attested by Abraham Ibn Ezra's comments (on Eccles. 5: 1): 'The Ga'on, R. Sa'adyah, guarded himself against the four [abuses of the language in Qillir's poetry], in his two "Supplications" which have no equal. They are based on the language of Scripture and on [sound] usage, and they are free of riddles, fables and legends.' Like Nissi's 'Confessions', Sa'adyah's Supplications in rhymed prose acknowledge man's dependence on his Creator and trust in His wisdom:

> Were I to heap praises like the ocean's waters and sing [them] with a mouth opened as wide as the vault of heaven; were I to keep watch like the cedars in Lebanon and stand fortified like Tabor and Hermon; were I to spread my hands [in prayer] like the wings of eagles and ever lift my eyes to the stars in heaven; were I to raise my voice like a hind longing for flowing streams and bend my knees while sleep flees from me during my allotted days, I would not do justice to a fraction of the benefits, mercies and blessings with which You have favoured me to this day . . .[145]

The Admonition (self-rebuke = *tokheḥah*), a genre originating in the preclassical period, was revived by Sa'adyah. Unlike earlier, modest treatments, the Ga'on raised the Admonition to epic proportions in rhymed prose spanning the complete alphabetic acrostic, fourfold. In his 'Whereas You, our Rock, chose this wretched man' (*'Im lefi boḥrekha ṣurenu ba-'adam ha-zeh ha-dal*) in this genre, the Ga'on considers the human condition with telling comments on the several ages of man. His observations begin with the very young 'who coo like a dove' seeking to satisfy their desires, but turn cruel after winning their prize, to the old who 'move from journey to journey to the land of gloom and chaos'. After a stark account of man's failures bordering on despair, the poet finds relief in the love of God reaching out to His creatures. It is likely that this Admonition in rhymed prose was also intended for private use, and not for congregational worship, where the hymns were mostly in rhymed strophes. In addition to pioneering meditations for private use, Sa'adyah proposed the bold thesis that prayer constitutes the eighteen benedictions of the *'amidah* and 'that there are no prayers other than those.' Therefore, the Ga'on advised, an individual may repeat the eighteen benedictions 'as many times as he wishes.' And if one desires to supplement the *'amidah* with additional prayers there are the several voluntary *baqqašot* which Sa'adyah composed in rhymed prose for private use and which are conveniently available in the Ga'on's *Siddur*.[146]

[144] Sa'adyah Ga'on, *Siddur*, p. 47.
[145] Ibid. 69.
[146] Ibid. 45, 403–9; Zulay, *Ha-'Askolah*, pp. 45–67; Fleischer, *Širat Ha-Qodeš*, pp. 317–18.

2

Hymnographic Developments in Spain

GENERAL BACKGROUND

Andalusia's Golden Age: New Directions in Hymnography

THE EMERGENCE of Hispanic[1] Jewry in the tenth and eleventh centuries as an influential cultural force was due, in large part, to the political power and stability of the Ummayad caliph 'Abd al-Raḥmān III (912–61). Cordoba, his capital, became a thriving commercial centre and a flourishing seat of Jewish life and learning. From the Cairo Geniza documents it is learned that the Mediterranean area during this period was an active free-trade community in which Jewish merchants from Spain prospered in trading silk, sugar, olives, pottery and corkwood. However, the largest percentage of Hispanic Jews were engaged in farming, manufacture and handicraft. In addition to Cordoba, Jews lived in Granada, Lucena, and Seville in Andalusia, where some were owners of huge estates which included entire villages.[2]

One of the early leaders of the Jewish community in Spain was the court physician Ḥisdai Ibn Shaprut (*c.*915–*c.*970), who also served as chief of customs and foreign trade. As a result of his influence at court, Ḥisdai became the acknowledged representative of Spanish Jewry. From this position he was able to appoint the learned Moses b. Ḥanokh, chief rabbi and head of the academy at Cordoba. With this action the Jews of Spain began to assert their independence and, to a great extent, ceased to rely on the Babylonian academies for rulings in matters of Jewish law.

By his support of Jewish scholars and poets like Dunaš b. Labrat and Menaḥem b. Saruq and his interest in the Cordoba academy, Ḥisdai was to set the standards for the Jewish courtier. Several decades later, Samuel Ibn Nagrela (993–1056), vizier to the Zirid rulers of Granada, would exemplify to

[1] The terms 'Hispanic', 'Spanish' and 'Iberian' are here used interchangeably.
[2] Goitein, *A Mediterranean Society*, i. 79.

perfection the multidimensional character of the court Jew. Among Nagrela's credits were his pedigree: he claimed that he was a direct descendant of 'the nobles of Jerusalem' who settled in the Spanish city of Merida.[3] Moreover, he was thoroughly familiar with classical Hebrew, Aramaic and Arabic literature, rabbinic studies and Greek learning encompassing physics, logic, mathematics, astronomy, ethics, metaphysics and rhetoric, all of which had been translated into Arabic. Added to this was his influence at court, where his responsibilities included commanding the Zirid armies of Kings Ḥabbus and Badis against their Andalusian rivals.

The lavish life-style of the Jewish courtier (modelled after his Arabic counterpart) included patronage of the arts and sciences. The courtier's home became the fashionable meeting-place for the leading scientists, philosophers and poets of the day. These were expected to entertain the patron and his guests at the regular drinking parties held in a perfumed garden. The company of friends, relatives and sycophants in the mansion of the Maecenas provided the setting for the court poet. The celebrated Hispanic Hebrew poets who flourished in Andalusia from the tenth to the middle of the twelfth century were, with the exception of Nagrela, impoverished and dependent upon the generosity of the patron. The poet could choose to live at court, serving the master by declaiming his virtues and abusing his enemies, or he could opt for the life of a vagabond, searching for an appreciative Maecenas.

Service at court required the poet to help celebrate the highlights of the patron's life. Weddings, his own and those of his family; the coming of age of his sons; the patron's appointment to office at the royal court; his return from a successful diplomatic mission; his recovery from illness—all were lauded in verse offerings. Likewise, the death of the patron or members of his family were duly lamented in *ad hoc* elegies. Added to these was the responsibility of the court poet to compose liturgical hymns for the synagogue which the patron attended and, in large part, supported. In contrast to the post-classical east Mediterranean cantor-poets who were employed by the laity in the congregation, Andalusian poets were dependent upon the generosity of the patron. Pleasing the hand that fed him became the poet's main concern in both his secular and his liturgical writings.

The Classical Revival in Christian Spain

Hebrew hymnography in the second half of the twelfth century reflected the changes in Jewish life following the decline of Judeo-Arabic courtly culture. The lavish life-style of the Andalusian court Jew completely disappeared after successive invasions by Muslim Almoravid and Almohad armies and the Christian reconquest. Among the Jewish exiles were Moses Ibn Ezra, Judah

[3] Ibn Daud, *Sefer Ha-Qabbalah*, pp. 79, 137.

Ha-Levi and Abraham Ibn Ezra. The latter two fled Spain never to return, while the former sought refuge in the Christian north and lived as a vagabond poet full of regret at the passing of the Andalusian Golden Age.

Like Moses Ibn Ezra, other Jews found refuge in the Spanish north where they prospered as farmers, craftsmen and merchants. An emerging Jewish middle class replaced the courtier grandees as the arbiters of taste in liturgical writing. From the literary remains of synagogue poets during this period it appears that the earlier much-admired virtuosity in rhythm and metre gave way to a more reflective emphasis. Pioneering the new trend were the eminent Bible commentator, legal authority, kabbalist and occasional poet Rabbi Moses b. Naḥman (Naḥmanides) of Gerona and his colleague, the esteemed kabbalist and poet Rabbi Mešullam b. Šelomo Dapiera.

Born in Catalonia, both men avoided, for the most part, the classical Arabic metres cherished by the Andalusians, and, unlike the latter, they wrote poetry that was integrated and unified. Whereas the Andalusian *qaṣidah* was only loosely connected, if at all, in its several and diverse parts,[4] Dapiera, in binding a set of themes in his hymns, pioneers an anadiplosis wherein a word or phrase from the first hemistich in the *qaṣidah* is used to open the following second hemistich. A variation of this anadiplosis is seen in the later *piyyuṭim* of Solomon Mevorakh of Salonika. In another departure from Judeo-Arabic courtly tastes, Dapiera prefers rabbinic and vernacular usage to biblical constructions and loads his poetry with talmudic and midrashic references.[5] Dapiera's poetic legacy includes several encomia dedicated to his circle of friends in Catalonia and Provence, a polemic against Maimonides, elegies and gnomic verses. Among the verses is a meditation, *Li rinanah ṣippor* (A dove sang for me), on the theme of repentance, in which the poet asks the dove bearing a message from his friend to hand it to him. Reading the note, he is cheered to learn that his friend admires his poetic skills. Suddenly he is overcome with guilt as he remembers a dream in which he is charmed by a young maiden. Would I be esteemed by friends if they knew my failing? he wonders. In a conceit reminiscent of the meditations of Sa'adyah Ga'on and Solomon Ibn Gabirol, Dapiera admonishes his body:[6]

> Why do you revert to childish days? Youth
> Has died and a different spirit lives within you;
> You have changed into another, mature in wisdom,
> Why would you disdain your soul's advice?

With Naḥmanides the rejection of Judeo-Arabic mannerisms in liturgical writing continues, and his few surviving hymns suggest a revival of earlier classical and late eastern models. Following is a part of his *mustajāb*, *Me-r'oš*

[4] Pagis, *Hidduš U-Masoret*, pp. 150–2.
[5] Brody, 'Širey Mešullam', pp. 9–10; 65, ll. 1–2, 5–6; 108, ll. 10–11.
[6] Ibid. 109; Fleischer, 'The "Gerona School"'.

mi-qqadmey ʿolamin, recited on the Day of Atonement in congregations in Barcelona, Algiers and Tunis. The poem is built in strophes of quatrains with rhyming tercets and closing scriptural verse ending with the word *melekh*:[7]

At first before earth's beginning
I (the soul) was there sealed in His treasure house;
From nothing He made me and after some time,
  I asked leave of the King [*melekh*].

My life began at the foundation of the world;
My image was drawn in a form prepared,
And examined by the hands of the Craftsman
  And brought to the treasure house of the King.

LANGUAGE AND STYLE

Arabic Metrics in Synagogue Hymnography

The Andalusian courtier-poets are the direct heirs of the post-classical late eastern hymnists. The writings of Saʿadyah Ga'on were the instruction manuals for the illustrious circle of Andalusians whose compositions heralded a Golden Age in Hebrew prosody. Saʿadyah's student in Baghdad, Dunaš ben Labrat, championed Arabic-style quantitative metrics for use in Hebrew poetry. In Spain the new metrics found ready followers in court poets whose patrons were widely attracted to Arabic culture in its many forms. Saʿadyah's emphasis on the language of Scripture as the preferred medium for liturgical writing was to become standard practice for Hispanic Hebrew poets. The love of Arabism (*al-ʿarabiyya*) notwithstanding, the latter, like the Andalusian grandees who supported them, could point with pride to the singular eloquence of biblical Hebrew in the service of synagogue hymnography.

The use of Arabic metrics had a slow start in Spain. The early poets, like Joseph Ibn Abitur (d. after 1012) and Isaac Ibn Mar Saul (10th–11th c.), were reticent in their use of the new metres for synagogue use and rarely employed them. Samuel Ibn Nagrela did consistently employ the new metrics in his hymnography, and it is likely that his example led to their wider use. In his three volumes of secular poetry, he pioneered a wide variety of metric forms. In the sizeable hymnographic corpus of the later Spaniards, Solomon Ibn Gabirol (b. 1021/2, d. between 1053 and 1058), Isaac Ibn Giy'at (1038–89), Moses Ibn Ezra (1055–1140), Judah Ha-Levi (1075-*c.*1141) and Abraham Ibn Ezra (1092–1167), Arabic metrics became a commonplace in embellishing the benedictions of the *šemaʿ* and *ʿamidah*, as well as in other liturgical additions.

Quantitative metrics are based on a consistent pattern of long and short

[7] Schirmann, *Ha-Širah Ha-ʿIvrit*, ii. 322–5.

syllables (not stressed and unstressed syllables, as in Yose b. Yose's *'Attah konanta 'olam*). Since Andalusian poets did not distinguish between Hebrew long and short syllables because the role of short syllables in Hebrew is minimal (compared to Arabic), the number of short syllables available for their use was relatively small. Despite this limitation Hebrew poetry adopted Arabic metric prototypes, using the *šewa' mobile* and its *ḥaṭaf* variables as short syllables (Heb. *yated*, v) and the other morphemes as long syllables (Heb. *tenu'ah*, –). This allowed the Hispanic Hebrews to adopt twelve of the sixteen basic metres codified by al-Khalīl Ibn Aḥmad (8th c.) and dozens of derivations. Following the Arabs, who used the standard Arabic verb *fa'al* in codifying their metric system, the Andalusians employed the Hebrew verb *pa'al*. Given the Arabic model, poets like Ibn Nagrela introduced a variety of metric forms deriving from declensions of the Hebrew verb and yielding configurations like *nif'al* (– –), *nif'alim* (– – –), *pe'ulim* (v– –), *mefo'alim* (v– – –), *mitpa'alim* (– –v–), *po'alim* (–v–), *pa'alulim* (–v– –) and *mefolelim* (v–v–). Combinations of these configurations constituted the main metric patterns in Hebrew Golden Age poetry. The most frequently employed Hebrew metres in distichs, and their Arabic sources are to be found on pp. xxii–xxiii.

Characteristic of metric poetry was the rhythmic balance of long and short syllables in a symmetrical configuration between the opening (*delet*) and the closing (*soger*) of the distich. Following is an unidentified tercet prayer by Ibn Nagrela. Its metre is *ha-šalem* II. The short syllables are underlined:[8]

Malkah reša'ah, mi-melokh hit'ahari, / sarah senu'ah —'al mesan'ayikh seri!
'Ofrat senir, 'orkhah tenumatekh 'aley / 'eres deway, hitna'ari, hit'orari,
Hitrappe'i, ki yeš le-makatekh sori, / hitnasse'i, ki yeš le-ṣidqatekh peri.

Evil queen [Edom], abdicate your throne! Sarah, despised, rule your foes!
Fawn of Senir [Israel], for too long have you slept on your sickbed; arise, awaken.
Be healed, there is balm for your hurt; be lifted up, there is a reward for your virtue.

Arabic *Qaṣīdah* and *Muwashshaḥ*

The pervasive fascination with Arabism by Hebrew Golden Age poets was now extended to the two types of Arabic prosody, the *qaṣīdah* and the *muwashshaḥ*. The former, originating in pre-Islamic Arabia, comprised

[8] Ibn Nagrela, *Ben Tehillim*, p. 318, No. 207.

metrically similar hemistichs in monorhyme versets with undulating rhythm. The latter, conceived by tenth-century Arabs in Andalusia, featured tercet strophes in variable rhyme and distichs in monorhyme versets. The *muwashshaḥ* held an added attraction in that its distichs could easily be converted to choral responses. Unlike post-classical eastern Mediterranean congregations, Spanish synagogues rarely used a professional choir. In its place was a practice which called for designated congregational responses in strophes and refrains. In this the Hispanics resembled their pre-classical Ereṣ Yisra'el counterparts, with solo precentor unaccompanied by choir and limited congregational responses. During the early years of their settlement, in the ninth and tenth centuries, Spanish congregations made use of post-classical hymns with choral responses embellishing the benedictions of the *šema'* and *'amidah*. However, without the enhancement of a trained choir, for which these hymns were designed, the worshipper found the service uninspiring. With the introduction in the late tenth century of the rhythmically rich *qaṣīdah* and the symmetrical *muwashshaḥ*, the aesthetics of the liturgy were enhanced and the congregation was allowed a wider involvement in the service. Both prosodic forms gained wide use by Hebrew hymnists in Spain, with the *muwashshaḥ*, in particular, becoming the medium of choice for congregational responses in the worship service.[9] Following is Solomon Ibn Gabirol's classic hymn, *Šaḥar 'avaqqeškha*, a *rešut* (permission) for the *nišmat* prayer (All living souls shall bless Your name) recited on the Day of Atonement. It is in *qaṣīdah*-type form comprising evenly balanced and metrically symmetrical hemistichs:

Šaḥar 'avaqqeškha, ṣuri u-misgabbi / 'e'erokh lefanekha šaḥri we-gam 'arbi;
Lifney gedullatakh 'e'emod we-'ebahel / ki 'eynkha tir'eh kol maḥševot libbi;
Ma-zeh 'ašer yukhal ha-lev we-ha-lašon / la'asot, u-mah koaḥ ruḥi be-tokh qirbi?
Hineh lekha tiṭav zimrat 'enoš; 'al ken / 'odakh be-'od tihyeh nišmat 'eloha bi.[10]

At the crack of dawn I seek You, my refuge and my rock, / offering You my prayer morn and eve;
I stand trembling before Your greatness; / Your eyes see my inner thoughts;
Can my heart and tongue do / aught and what strength can I claim?
Yet You will be pleased with this mortal's song; therefore / I'll ever praise You while my soul is in me.

[9] Fleischer, *Širat Ha-Qodeš*, p. 340. The *muwashshaḥ* in Arabic and Hebrew secular poetry would close with a *kharjah*, a distich in vernacular Arabic, or in Mozarabic, a blend of Romance and Arabic. The *kharjah* was excluded by the hymnists, who objected to the intrusion of a foreign language into the synagogue liturgy.

[10] Ibn Gabirol, *Širey Ha-Qodeš*, p. 79.

In composing the *muwashshaḥ* for synagogue use, the Hispanics were generally careful to observe its accepted standards. A good example of this strophic verse form is seen in Isaac Ibn Giy'at's *ge'ullah* (embellishing the benediction before the *šema'*, *ga'al yisra'el* (Redeemer of Israel)), *'Esbelah nedudi, 'agilah be-galuti.*[11] The hymn begins with the required *abab* opening called the *madrikh* (guide). This is followed by a set of tercets in hemistichs *cdcdcd,* followed by another set of *abab* hemistichs closing out the strophe. The process is repeated with no limit on the number of strophes, provided that the hemistichs of the 'guide' are in uniform rhyme. The rhyme of the tercet hemistichs may vary. The metre in the 'guide' and the tercet could be identical, as in Judah Ha-Levi's hymn for the Sabbath of Ḥanukkah, *Yešakha yazkiru,*[12] or it could vary, as in the above hymn of Ibn Giy'at.

Coping with the formidable metric and rhyming demands of the *muwashshaḥ* could become awkward. To overcome this problem the hymnists would often dispense with the metrics of long and short syllables and opt for a quantitative metre of long syllables only. Thus, while preserving the basic pattern of 'guides' and tercets, the hemistichs were balanced in a symmetry of morphemes, excluding the *šewa' mobile* and its *ḥataf* derivatives. Following is the last 'guide' to Judah Ha-Levi's *seliḥah* (penitential), *Yonati, laylah reḥovot sovavah,*[13] in the form of a *muwashshaḥ*:

Tiqwati / me-'itkha lo' nikhzevah
Nimšekhet / u-vritkha lo' kazvah.

My hope / in You will not be disappointed
It continues / and Your covenant will not fail.

Another alteration in the widely popular 'guide' (or 'belt')-poem served both the poet and the congregation. Since Spanish synagogues conducted services without benefit of a choir, the hymns were chanted by the precentor with congregational responses. These responses often echoed the couplet 'guide' in the *muwashshaḥ*. However, since the 'guide', whether in distichs or hemistichs, was often long and varied from strophe to strophe, it was not easy to learn. In order to simplify congregational responses, the 'guide' was shortened to one colon. To further ease the laity's involvement some poets decided not to vary the 'guide', which the congregation sang after each strophe in what was now a pseudo-*muwashshaḥ*.

In the ultimate simplification of the pseudo-*muwashshaḥ*, the one-colon refrain was a verse from Scripture, as in the following excerpt from the *mi kamokha, Mi kamokha 'amuqqot goleh*, by Judah Ha-Levi:[14]

[11] Ibn Giy'at, *Širey*, pp. 182–3.
[12] Ha-Levi, *Širey Ha-Qodeš*, pp. 341–3.
[13] Ibid. 766–7.
[14] Ibid. 723–33; Fleischer, *Širat Ha-Qodeš*, p. 353.

Who is like You revealer of the hidden,
Awesome in splendour, doing wonders? [Exod. 15: 11]

The Creator, who made all from nothing
Is revealed to the heart but not the eye;
Therefore, do not ask, how and wherefore—?
He completes heaven and earth,
Awesome in splendour, doing wonders.

Baroque variations on the pseudo-*muwashshaḥ* with scriptural ending were soon to follow in such forms as tercet strophes divided into metrically balanced quatrains. Closing out each strophe is a verse from Scripture. Following is a sample from the *'ofan*, *Mal'akhim mamlikhim*,[15] by Moses Ibn Ezra:

Šemo la'ad / be-rav ra'ad / be-'eymah hen / ya'ariṣun;
Še'on serafim / be-rom 'afim / ka-beraqim / yeroṣeṣun;
Šo'alim zeh / rešut mi-zeh / le-haqdiš 'el / be-mora'ot,
'Omerim: qadoš, qadoš, qadoš 'adonay ṣeva'ot.

His name eternally / with much trembling / and fear they / revere;
The rustle of seraphs / flying on high, / like lightning they hasten,
One requests / permission of the other / to sanctify the Lord; / in awe
They speak: 'Holy, holy, holy is the Lord of hosts!' [Isa. 6: 3]

Adventures in Rhyming

Not all of the liturgical hymns of the Andalusians were composed in Arabic metres. Many were patterned after earlier post-classical synagogue models of quatrain strophes opening in rhyming tercets and closing with scriptural refrains. A popular variation of this model had the strophe in quatrains with an *aabb* rhyme and closing verse from Scripture. In the *silluq* (closing), *Yir'ey 'adonay haleluhu*, to his *qerovah* for the New Year, the talented Judah Ha-Levi, seeking to enhance the rhythmic quality of the hymn, expands its strophe design with an elaborate rhyming structure. Its scansion is *aa* / *aabb* / scriptural verse / *ccdd* / *ee* / scriptural verse / *ff* / *gghh* / scriptural verse / etc. Bolder rhyming configurations were to follow, as in Ha-Levi's *ge'ullah* for the Sabbath before Pentecost, *Yonah nesa'tah 'al kanfey nešarim*, a metreless pseudo-*muwashshaḥ* with strophes of six hemistichs in irregular rhyme, followed by two rhyming 'guides', of which the last colon is a repeated verse from Ruth 4: 4. The first set of 'guides' is in variable rhyme while the rhyme of the second set is constant throughout the hymn. Its scansion is: *a* / *a* / *a* / *aa* / *aa* / *aa* / *bb* / *bb* / *cc* / verse / *dd* / *dd* / *dd* / *dd* / *dd* / *dd* / *ee* / *ee* / *cc* / verse from Scripture, etc.[16] When writing prayers for

[15] Schirmann, *Ha-Širah Ha-'Ivrit*, i. 410; Fleischer, *Širat Ha-Qodeš*, p. 354.
[16] Ha-Levi, *Širey Ha-Qodeš*, pp. 57–60, 412–16; Fleischer, *Širat Ha-Qodeš*, pp. 354–8.

private use, the Hispanics would completely dispense with rhymed strophes and, following the model of Sa'adyah Ga'on, they would compose in rhymed prose. Some, like the late eleventh-century Saragossan Levi Ibn al-Tabbān, gave themselves licence to rhyme with segmented morphemes, as in his *'ahavah*, *Livši bat nedivim*, where the word *bigdey* (apparel) is made to rhyme with the morpheme *de* in *dema'* (tears):

Livši bat nedivim bigdey / tif'artekh we-'edyekh . . .
Hoḥili we-ḥiš 'emḥeh de/ma' me-'al le-ḥayekh.

O daughter of princes, put on your splendid apparel and jewels . . .
Be hopeful, soon I will wipe the tears from your cheek.[17]

Scriptural Adornments

The Jewish Hispanic's attraction to Arabism did not lessen his fondness for the Hebrew Scriptures. Like his predecessors in classical and late eastern periods, the Andalusian poet, when writing for the synagogue, would embellish the hymn with scriptural verse-openings. This is seen in Ibn Gabirol's *'Omrah golah we-surah*,[18] headed by the verse from Ps. 90: 1, 'Lord, You have been our dwelling-place in all generations,' with repeated refrains from Isa. 26: 12, 'Lord, You will ordain peace for us.' At other times, the poet inserted the scriptural verse into the strophe itself and allowed the verse to rhyme with the other hemistichs in the strophe. The strophe then closed with a continuation of the verse which now served as a refrain. Following is a sample from the second strophe of Judah Ha-Levi's *qerovah*, *Ya'alu le-'elef we-li-revavah*, for the New Year:[19]

Ha-yom pequddot niqra'ot / we-tevel la-din niṣṣevet
U-vo heḥel ha-ṣur le-har'ot / gevurat yamin maḥaṣevet
U-vo konen kes nora'ot / ha-magbihi la-ševet
Ha-mašpili lir'ot / ba-šamayim u-va-'areṣ.

This day the officers are called / to summon the world to judgment;
On it the Rock intends to show / the might of His punishing arm;
On it the awesome seat is prepared / for the One seated on high
Who looks far down on the heavens and the earth.

The second hemistich in colon 3 and all of colon 4 are taken from Ps. 113: 5–6. An added benefit in having the biblical verse as a refrain was that it was easily recognized and readily chanted by the congregation. In the following example from Ha-Levi's *seliḥah*, *Be-šem 'adonay 'adamot u-meromot niqra'u*, for the midnight services during the month of 'Elul,[20] the hymn also opens with chanted refrains, *Be-šem 'adonay* (In God's name) and ends in chanted

[17] Ibn al-Tabbān, *Širey*, p. 80.
[18] Ibn Gabirol, *Širey Ha-Qodeš*, pp. 175–8.
[19] Ha-Levi, *Širey Ha-Qodeš*, pp. 55–7.
[20] Ibid. 582–8.

scriptural verses with monorhyme ending *ʿolam*. In the fourth strophe the poet proclaims:

> In God's name, the hidden creatures were raised from the great deep,
> Even blood and flesh and herds of cattle;
> The likeness changes, a generation comes and a generation goes
> But the world forever [*le-ʿolam*] [remains standing].

The last phrase in colon 3 and all of colon 4 are from Eccles. 1: 4. However, the poet abruptly breaks off the verse with the word *le-ʿolam*—which he needs for his rhyme scheme—and invites the congregation to participate in the service by supplying the missing word *ʿomedet* (remains standing).

Biblical literature was also employed for thematic purposes. This was accomplished by taking a verse out of context in order to serve the poet's conceit. Solomon Ibn Gabirol made a practice of recontextualizing Scripture in his celebrated *Keter Malkhut* (The Kingly Crown) recited on the Day of Atonement. In the section on God's unity (No. 2) he writes:[21]

> You are One, raised and exalted beyond subduing and falling
> Can the One alone ever fall?

The last colon is from Eccles. 4: 10, 'Woe to the one who is alone and falls and does not have another to help.' In its original context the subject is man who is fortunate if he has a friend to help him in need. However, in Gabirol's hymn the subject is the unique nature of God. Again in the same work Gabirol writes (in No. 4):

> You live and he who masters Your secrets gains eternal delight,
> He shall eat and live forever!

The last colon from Gen. 3: 22 is in the context of God's concern that man, having partaken of the tree of knowledge, will now eat from the tree of life and live forever. In the hymn, the verse serves to focus on God's eternal life and its mystery, to which man can be privy and in which he can rejoice. Another noteworthy example of recontextualization in the seventh hymn in Gabirol's *Keter Malkhut* is his discourse on God's relationship to light:

> You are the everlasting light and the intellect's eye longs for You beholding it;
> You shall see only part of it, and shall not see it all.

In the latter colon the poet employs the statement of an impatient Balak (in Num. 23: 13), who exhorts Balaam to curse Israel from a more favourable vantage-point. In the hymn the verse represents the response of the 'intellect's

[21] Ibn Gabirol, *Širey Ha-Qodeš*, p. 39.

eye', informing the seeker after the 'everlasting light' that he can view it only in part. This response is reminiscent of Exod. 33: 23 where God informs Moses: 'You shall see my back; but my face shall not be seen.' Gabirol, it appears, pioneered the bold art of recontextualizing verses from Scripture to serve the thematic needs of the hymn; the practice does not appear in the works of the late eastern post-classical poets. In his practice of interpreting a biblical text in a manner other than its plain meaning (*pešat*) Gabirol was undoubtedly familiar with the rabbinic teaching (in *bSan* 34a), 'One biblical verse may convey several meanings.' The rabbis based this opinion on the verse in Jer. 23: 29, 'And like a hammer that breaks the rock into pieces,' i.e. just as the rock is splintered into many pieces, so may the biblical text yield many meanings.

Acrostics and Signatures

Like earlier poets, the Hispanics were fond of acrostic and name signatures. Some poets not given to modesty signed their names several times in the hymn and prefaced the signature with *'ani*, 'I', as in 'I, Menaḥem b. Saruq'. Saruq, who lived in the tenth century, was probably the first Hispanic Hebrew poet to employ this device, which was widely imitated by his contemporaries, Dunaš b. Labrat, Joseph Ibn Abitur and their successors. The more modest post-classical poets did not place an 'I' before signing a liturgical hymn. The reason for the change was probably due to a difference in the role and function of the Iberian hymnist. Whereas the late eastern cantor-poets were supported by their congregations, their counterparts in Spain had to rely upon the generosity of courtier patrons like Ḥisdai Ibn Shaprut or Samuel Ibn Nagrela. The patron would support as many poets as his means and disposition would allow. The poet dependent upon a benefactor would, understandably, use his prosodic skills to compete for the master's favour. The rich and varied secular poetry honouring the Maecenas by the likes of Dunaš and Ibn Gabirol and their contemporaries testifies to a competitive life in the courtly culture of tenth- to eleventh-century Andalusia. The patron was not only influential at the royal court but governed Jewish affairs as well. Ibn Nagrela bore the title *nagid*—a term comparable to the Arabic *Ra'is al-yahud*—used to designate the leader of the Jewish community. Since the rivalry among poets vying for the patron's largesse often carried over from the court environment to the synagogue where the patron's presence was prominent, it is likely that the poet was tempted to boast in the signature to his hymn: I am the author.

Evidence of the rivalry among Hispanic poets often led to 'borrowing' from the writings of others. Reflecting this common practice is Solomon Ibn Gabirol's blunt accusation that his work has been plagiarized:[22]

[22] Ibn Gabirol, *Širey Ha-Ḥol*, p. 263.

Admit that you stole and falsified my words, and violently
overturned the standards [of good taste],
Hoping to exalt yourself with my poems and find relief from
distress.
Can humans ascend the heavens and conceal their luminaries from
the earth?
The matter is clear to me. Rivers will not be made dry by taking
from them a ladleful.

The manners of Judeo-Arabic courtly culture would also help explain Gabirol's lavish boast in which he compares his poems to 'luminaries' in the heavens and to flowing rivers. Although his writings have been expropriated by a rival, Gabirol is certain that his poetic gifts can never be diminished. Gabirol, like his older contemporary Samuel Ibn Nagrela, had no illusions about his abilities. Nagrela would compare his writing talents to those of King David. 'I am the David of my age,' he boasted in his meditation, *Šeʿeh minni ʿamiti we-ḥaveri*, while Gabirol would claim, 'I am the one who before he was born had the understanding of a man of 80.'[23] The swagger of Nagrela, Gabirol and their contemporaries is in imitation of mannerisms in Arab literary culture, where poems of self-praise (Arab. *fakhr*) were commonplace. Like his Arab contemporaries Gabirol combines self-praise with lampoon (Arab. *hijāʾ*). After lampooning his rival who hoped to 'exalt [himself] with my poems' he boasts, 'Can humans ascend the heavens and conceal their luminaries [Gabirol's poems] from the earth?'[24]

In the acrostic signature to their hymns for the synagogue, Gabirol and his contemporaries would often add the word *qaṭan*, 'the small' or 'the humble'. The full acrostic would read: 'I am Solomon Ibn Gabirol (or Moses Ibn Ezra), the humble.' The anomaly of the poet's boast that he is humble was not lost on his congregation, who may have perceived the addition as poetic play. It would appear that the practice of adding *qaṭan* to the signature was initiated by the Andalusians; it is not found in the writings of the late eastern or classical poets.

The additions of 'I' and 'the humble' to the acrostic was the Hispanic poet's way of injecting himself into the hymn. Not content with merely giving their names, Gabirol and his fellow Andalusians would add the names of their fathers, including their pedigree as priests or levites. Some would give their Arabic as well as Hebrew names and include their native city in the acrostic. In Ibn Gabirol's epic hymn for the Day of Atonement, *Mi kamokha šokhen ʿad loʾ reʾšit*, the acrostic reads, 'Solomon, *ʾalef–taw* [full alphabetic

[23] Ibn Nagrela, *Ben Tehillim*, p. 33; Ibn Gabirol, *Širey Ha-Ḥol*, p. 108.

[24] See Schoeler, 'Bashshār b. Burd', pp. 278–9. The 10th-c. Abbasid poet al-Mutanabbī, who composed some 12 poems of self-praise combined with contempt for humankind and the world, would write, 'If I have pride it is that of a prodigal man / Who does not see anyone above him. / I am the brother of glory, and the master of poetry; / I am the poison of my enemy and the torment of my rivals.' See Ullah, *Islamic Literature*, p. 59.

acrostic], I Solomon, the humble son of Judah Ibn Gabirol Málagi [from Málaga], be strong and fortify your hearts all who hope in the Lord of the Day of Atonement.'[25] Abraham Ibn Ezra in his *mi kamokha*, *'Otot 'el bema'asaw niṣṣavot*, gives the name both of the city where his father lived and of the city adjoining it: 'Abraham the son of Rabbi Meir Ezra from the city of Lucena in the vicinity of Estella, be strong, amen.' Possibly the most elaborate acrostic also comes from the pen of the latter poet in his epithalamium, *Mi kamokha 'el be-fil'o 'ašurennu*, where he writes his name and the name of the bridegroom and his family: 'Abraham, Abraham the son of Rabbi Meir ibn Ezra at the wedding of Judah the son of the honourable Rabbi Nissim the Nagid, son of the honourable Rabbi Maṣliaḥ.'[26]

Musical Devices

Reviving a practice of Yannai in the classical period, the Andalusians enhanced the tonal quality of their poetry with phonetically intensive alliteration and assonance. In a *silluq* to his *qerovah*, *Šulammit yasfah šaw'ah*,[27] Gabirol constructs a *tour de force* of resonating tones that span the length of the Hebrew alphabet. The twenty-two-strophe work assigns five units to each strophe with monorhyme ending. In the strophes, every unit in the first colon and the first two units in the following cola begin with letter *'alef*; units 3–5 in the cola open with the remaining letters of the alphabet:

'A'amir, 'a'addir, 'afuddat 'aguddat 'oratekha
'Ava'er, 'avarer, beriqat behiqat behiratekha
'Agdil, 'agbir, gulat gedullat gevuratekha
'Edgol, 'edroš, daharat divrat diratekha.

I will exalt, empower, the garment of Your light assembled;
I will explain and clarify the flash and glitter of Your light translucent;
I will enlarge, strengthen the crown of Your mighty power;
I will elevate and interpret the races of Your heavenly spheres.

Not to be outdone, Judah Ha-Levi weighed in with his *nišmat* hymn[28] in which twelve units in each of its five strophes contain one of the five letters of the author's name *YHWDH*:

Nišmat yedidim yeqarim yevo'un yeyaḥadun . . .
Nišmat ha-'am ha-doreš halikhot ha'-el ha-me'assef . . .
Nišmat weladim wetiqim wa'adu wa-yyit'attedu wa-yevaqšu . . .

[25] Ibn Gabirol, *Širey Ha-Qodeš*, pp. 98–116.
[26] A. Ibn Ezra, *Širey Ha-Qodeš*, ii. 329–40, 358–73.
[27] Ibn Gabirol, *Širey Ha-Qodeš*, pp. 243–4.
[28] Ha-Levi, *Širey Ha-Qodeš*, p. 720.

The souls of the beloved precious come to proclaim Your unity . . .
The souls of the people seeking God's path have gathered . . .
The souls of the earnest children have come together to stand [before You] . . .

Hispanic poets also experimented with rhyme forms in sound parallelism of consonantal roots and their endings. In the following *mešullas* to Ibn Gabirol's *qerovah*, *Šulammit yosfa śaw'ah*,[29] the poet's thirteen-strophe hymn in quatrains is in consistent monorhyme throughout its fifty-two units, reminiscent of the mannerisms of the Babylonian hymnist R. Nehemiah b. Solomon:

Šezufey feleṭay / 'afufey 'eyṭay / šoqeday we-'oṭeay / 'al saf rahiṭay
Beḥuray ḥaniṭay / yeladay me'uṭay / ba-'adat qešuṭay / kelalay u-fraṭay . . .

The wretched remnant surrounded by vultures, yet hastens to the house of prayer;
The flowering lads, their seeds are few, are gathered with the faithful, young and old . . .

In his *'ahavah* in the form of a pseudo-*muwashshaḥ*, Abraham Ibn Ezra combines alliteration with extended monorhyme and adds paronomasia (Arab. *tajnīs*), a punning play on words similar in sound but disparate in meaning. Below is the opening strophe:[30]

'Ani, 'ani / be-tokh 'ani
U-maḥani / kemo 'oni
Be-yam 'oni / we-hinnani
Be-ḥanneni / lema'ani / ke-'ovot.

I am he / who is in mourning;
My camp / is like a boat
In a sea of misery; / behold me
In my prayers / for me, / I am [weak] as a ghost.

The paronomasia is not continued in the remaining five strophes, which comprise eight hemistichs with separate monorhyme for each strophe, and a closing unit with a consistent rhymeme *'ot* in all the strophes.

Stylistic Rhetorics

Hispanic hymnists, like their predecessors in the east, sought to enhance the aesthetics of the worship service by embellishing the obligatory prayers. In

[29] Ibn Gabirol, *Širey Ha-Qodeš*, pp. 210–13.

[30] A. Ibn Ezra, *Širey Ha-Qodeš*, ii. 394.

addition, the synagogue hymn as a studied ornament of speech was designed to communicate traditional values. Among these was the call to repent during the Days of Awe, to rejoice on Sabbaths and festivals, to entertain the bride and groom and to console the mourners. In seeking to persuade their congregations the poets would enlist stylistic rhetorics. Among the rhetorical devices employed by classical poets was the dialogue hymn.[31] Eleazar Qillir set to verse the legend of God negotiating with the Torah over a suitable mate, and Phinehas Ha-Kohen in his *qedušta'-rahiṭ* details the exchange between God and Moses when the latter appeals for continued life. Phinehas again turns to the dialogue as a rhetorical tactic in his account of the Joseph story in the *zulat, 'Aḥ be-na'aleykhem mekhartem* (You sold a brother for a pair of shoes) based on Gen. 44: 14–17. In the exchange, Joseph condemns his brothers for selling him into slavery and Judah chastizes Joseph for making life difficult for his brothers when they went to purchase grain in Egypt. In the hymn, constructed in strophes of quatrains with closing refrain couplets, the identity of the parties to the dialogue, Joseph and Judah, is given in the refrains, which were presumably chanted antiphonally by segments of the congregational chorus.[32]

The Andalusian poets further advanced the rhetorical art of the dialogue in their *yoṣerot*. This hymn they built in rhyming strophes of tercets interrupted by choral refrains in tercets. The identity of the parties is given in short alternating introductions to the strophes, and their exchanges are presented in alternating strophes. Below is an example from a dialogue hymn by Ohev b. Meir Ha-Nasi, a contemporary of Moses Ibn Ezra, embellishing the Decalogue. The parties are God addressing Moses and the latter conveying God's words to Israel's elders:[33]

And God spoke to Moses:

'To you I shall reveal God's hidden wonders;
Prepare yourself to meet your Lord and begin
On the third month from the time of Israel's exodus . . . '

And Moses came and called out to the elders of the nation: . . .

'Faithfully and in unison with the many
Receive [it (the Torah)], both young and old,
Even all the words which the Lord has spoken.'

[31] The dialogue hymn appears in the early Syrian (Monophysite) Church under the name *sogitha* (or *sugitha*) from the Aramaic *sugya*, and in the 5th-c. *kontakion* of the Byzantine Church. The *kontakion*, which, like the *qerovot* of Yannai, feature introductions to the biblical lesson of the week, transitional strophes, acrostics and rhymes, also highlight dialogues between Mary and the Angel Gabriel and Mary and Joseph. See Schirmann, 'Hebrew Liturgical Poetry', pp. 158–9.

[32] Fleischer, *Ha-Yoṣerot*, pp. 139–41.

[33] Schirmann, 'Ha-mešorarim', pp. 278–81.

The hymn assigns ten strophes of rhyming tercets to the words of God and an equal number to those of Moses. The strophes alternate in sets of four, three and three and are prefaced by introductions of the speakers.

In Isaac Ibn Giy'at's treatment of a dialogue hymn for the New Year, the parties address each other directly, but are not identified by name, as in the following encounter between God and Israel:[34]

[GOD:]
Return to Me and I shall return to you: [Mal. 3: 7] . . .
My hands are stretched out
To receive My repentant children
  Return, return unto Me.

[ISRAEL:]
Here we come to You, for You are the Lord our God [Jer. 3: 22] . . .
If we have sinned much
We desire Your pardon;
  Return us, O our Father.

In another *yoṣer* for the Torah reading from Num. 22: 2 (*Balaq*) of which only a fragment has survived in the Cairo Geniza,[35] the dialogue is a direct exchange between the parties who are identified by name ('Balaq said to Balaam' and 'Balaam said to Balaq') in alternating order after each set of three strophes and refrain. This latter form of the dialogue embedded in the *yoṣer* was to be imitated by twelfth-century hymnists in Byzantium, like Moses b. Ḥiyyah and Joseph Qalai.

In a further variation of the dialogue, the parties are not identified by name, nor are their words introduced by an opening formula. However, their identities and the substance of their remarks are known from the context of the hymn. The following example is from Solomon Ibn Gabirol's *rešut* for Passover, *Ša'ali yefeh-fiyyah*, in which God is portrayed as Israel's bridegroom:[36]

[GOD:]
Ask, comely maid what you desire of Me
Your entreaties have reached My ears.

[ISRAEL:]
A lion met me and after him a leopard;
I fled from them and deserted my garden;
Soon thereafter a savage beast appeared
At midnight and occupied my land . . .

[34] Ibn Giy'at, *Širey*, pp. 470–3.

[35] Fleischer, *Ha-Yoṣerot*, p. 500 n. 25.

[36] Ibn Gabirol, *Širey Ha-Qodeš*, p. 332.

Israel, God's bride, laments that she has been exiled to Babylonian (= lion, Dan. 7: 3–6) and Christian (= leopard) lands. Having escaped, she is met by the Muslim (= savage beast, Heb. *pere'*, Gen. 16: 11–12) powers, who conquer her land and settle there.

Figurative language and imagery are often used by the hymnist as a rhetorical tactic of style in presenting the views of God and Israel and the themes of exile and redemption. Gabirol's dialogue between God and Israel as husband and wife in distress is enhanced by imagery originating in rabbinic explications of the Song of Songs. Scriptural, rabbinic and hymnic sources celebrate the early years of the happy couple when Israel followed her Lord in the unsown wilderness (Jer. 2: 2). When the wife proved to be unfaithful, her husband divorced her and she was made an object of scorn. Here is Abraham Ibn Ezra's treatment of the theme in his *muwashshaḥ*-elegy, *'Aḥ wa-'eved hadimmuni*, for the Ninth of 'Av. The selection is from the first strophe following the 'guide':[37]

Women, listen to the heavy burden I bear:
Am I made of iron; is my flesh like copper?
My lover beheld me, a captive, and bought me for a wife;
Into his home he brought me and dressed me in a new garment;
I betrayed my husband for another, on account of which I am divorced;
I am friendless; my family has risen up against me.

Behind the imagery is God, Israel's lover who helped her escape from Egyptian captivity and took her for a wife. When she betrays him, he leaves her to be abused by her family, i.e. Esau (= Christians) and Ishmael (= Muslims). Building on this image, the poet shows Israel repentant and regreting the loss of her kind and protecting husband. She is hopeful that he will return and waits for him at the crossroads on the highway. Again, Abraham Ibn Ezra in his *muwashshaḥ*, *'Em derekh ma-'amadi*:[38]

My stand is at the crossroads;
I strain to hear a voice;
Perhaps the messenger will come
With the good news bringing relief.

The messenger does not arrive and the dramatic tension builds. Israel, though she is abandoned, does not give up hope. She intensifies her search and scours the highways in the cities where she is exiled, seeking to retrace the steps her beloved may have taken. This segment of the drama is in Ibn Ezra's *me'orah*, *'Essa' 'eynay le-khol derekh*:[39]

[37] A. Ibn Ezra, *Širey Ha-Qodeš*, ii. 284–7.
[38] Ibid. i. 235–7. [39] Ibid. 106–7.

Mine eyes search out all the highways;
Where, from my presence, O where did my beloved flee? . . .
Would that I had died by his hand, a bride,
Before the foe subdued me day and night.

She wastes away and cannot sleep. She keeps her lonely vigil in the dark and searches the heavens for the morning light. She is desperate, but remains guarded in her impatience. Again, Ibn Ezra in his *muwashshaḥ*, *'Az ba-'alot mequṭṭeret mor*:[40]

Searching the highways, she asked, 'When will He return?
At night she stands watch with Orion and Pleiades enquiring
About him; if he tarries she will not complain and wait for him.

Helping her endure the pangs of separation and sleepless nights is the bright reminiscence of her past idyllic life in the company of her beloved. Following is the opening of Ibn Ezra's *muwashshaḥ*:

When the myrrh-scented maiden came up from the wilderness,
Like a graceful doe with good sense she nestled against her
beloved;
In younger days, the stag gently took her hand and she hastened
To his side like thirsty men to a river's stream; he aroused her—
Her heart raged overcome by desire as she spoke:
'Would my beloved tell me his pleasure and I will do his
bidding' . . .
She was preferred above all the maidens with surpassing affection;
He protected the delicate girl until he departed . . .

Ibn Ezra's imagery in this love drama is strikingly similar to its Arabic counterpart. The parting of lovers, the long night of watchful waiting, the nostalgic recollection of a happy past are conventional motifs in the opening (*nasīb*) of Arabic love poetry (*ghazal*), and these may have had some influence on the Hispanic poet, who undoubtedly was familiar with the genre. Ibn Ezra's primary source was presumably Canticles, where the beloved, a shepherd, departs from home and his betrothed searches for him among the flocks of his companions (Cant. 1: 7). At night in her bed she calls to him, and, upon receiving no reply, she rises and goes about the city in the streets and squares seeking to find him (Cant. 3: 1–2). Also in Canticles, the lover recalls her happy past in the company of her beloved (2: 3–4) and hopes for their reconciliation: 'O that his left hand were under my head, and his right hand embraced me' (2: 6).[41]

[40] A. Ibn Ezra, *Širey Ha-Qodeš*, i. 259–60.

[41] Ibid.

Philosophical Themes

Following the lead of Sa'adyah Ga'on, Hispanic poets introduced themes from contemporary philosophy and science into their writings for the synagogue. The extent of this practice and the reliance upon non-Jewish sources was far greater than seen in earlier eastern sources. Given that the Greek classics were now available in Arabic translations, poets like Gabirol, Ha-Levi and Abraham Ibn Ezra took part in the discussions of the philosophical issues of the day. This is seen in their monographs (Gabirol's *Meqor Ḥayyim*, Ha-Levi's *Kuzari* and Ibn Ezra's *Yesod Mora'*) and in their liturgical writings for a laity able to follow the fine points of their arguments. A prominent example of a synagogue hymn influenced by non-Jewish souces is Ibn Gabirol's *Keter Malkhut* which is based, in large part, on Ptolemaic cosmology and Neoplatonist psychology. Contemporary with Gabirol's writings were the Epistles of the Brethren of Purity (*Rasā'il Ikhwān aṣ-Ṣafā'*), a work edited in the late tenth or early eleventh century, probably by Ismaili Muslims in Basra. Some of the themes in the Epistles are echoed in Gabirol's *Keter Malkhut*. Among these is God's universalism, prominent in the Epistles where truth is believed to be 'one without its being the private work of anyone,' and the assertion that 'God has sent His spirit to all men, to Christians as well as to Muslims, to blacks as to whites.' This latter view, for example, is expressed in Gabirol's eighth hymn in his *Keter Malkhut*.[42]

Other points of contact between the Epistles and Gabirol include the stress both place on the divine will (Heb. *raṣon*) and on the influence of the sun in affecting political change, in agreement with God's design (*Keter Malkhut*, No. 15):

> He [the sun] uproots kingdoms and in their place raises and exalts others;
> He has the power to abase and lift up with force,
> All by the will of the Creator who made him with wisdom.

In *Keter Malkhut*, No. 17, Gabirol observes that when the moon stands directly before the sun she radiates his reflected light which 'illumines her whole face', and her splendour wanes to the degree that she declines from him. When the moon has been lessened to the extreme she comes into conjunction with the sun which 'cleaves to her' (*u-ve-hiddavqo 'immah*) and she is hidden in a secret place, after which she is renewed and returned to her old self. And the sun 'issues forth as a bridegroom from his chamber' (Ps. 19: 6). This perplexing analysis of the lunar circuit becomes clear in light of the Epistles where it is held that the Intellect, with the permission of God,

[42] A. L. Tibawi, 'Jāma'ah Ikhwān aṣ-Ṣafa', *Journal of the American University of Beirut* (1930–1), p. 60; Loewe, 'Ibn Gabirol's Treatment of Sources', p. 183.

animates the sun and moon who bring life to all creation through their union. This is achieved by virtue of their role as representatives of the male and female principles.[43]

To his description of the nine-level Ptolemaic universe, Gabirol adds a tenth, the Sphere of Intelligence, which, although made by God, has been separated from Him in the creative process and now seeks to return to its divine source (*Keter Malkhut*, No. 24):

> And it exists by Your power,
> And from You and to You it yearns,
> And unto You is its desire.

The latter colon, *we-'elekha tešuqato*, taken from God's conversation with Cain (Gen. 4: 7), is here recontextualized to designate the desire of a hypostatized creation to be reunited with its Maker. Here too, Gabirol reflects the Muslim Neoplatonist configuration which viewed God as 'the first beloved of the universe', and that the part of creation that is not God proceeds from Him and desires to be reunited with its sublime source. This attraction is the result of the universe's passionate desire (Arab. *'išq*) for its Creator, the only beloved (*ma'šuq*), and is the animating force which brings life into being and controls it. The Hebrew term *šwq* used in Gen. 4: 7 is a homonym of the Arabic *šawq* (= yearning) and is related to it in meaning as well. It is likely that the similarity of terms and themes was not lost on Gabirol or his congregation.[44]

God as the source of the universe and its beloved is a major theme in the Neoplatonism of Abraham Ibn Ezra, for whom 'God is the One and there is no being except by cleaving to Him [*we-'eyn heyot la-howeh raq 'im yidbaq bo*].'[45] The theme is repeated in his liturgical writings, in the *rešut*, *'Eykh teḥešeh nafši*,[46]

> How can my soul restrain itself from her desire
> To live on by cleaving ['*adey tidbaq*] to the Lord who made her?

The source for this conceit is Deut. 11: 22, 'If you will diligently observe this entire commandment . . . loving the Lord your God and holding fast to him [*u-le-dovqah bo*],' where it recommends the need to be faithful to God—and not to other gods—and to keep His commands. In Ibn Ezra's treatment, the verse is recontextualized to serve his view that God is the one totality of the universe and that being exists through God alone.[47]

[43] Loewe, 'Ibn Gabirol's Treatment of Sources', p. 184.
[44] Ibid. 184–5.
[45] A. Ibn Ezra, *Yesod Mora' We-Sod Torah*, in Levin, *Yalqut Avraham Ibn Ezra*, p. 337.
[46] A. Ibn Ezra, *Širey Ha-Qodeš*, i. 25
[47] See A. Ibn Ezra's commentaries on Gen. 1: 26: 'God is the One, He made all and He is all,' and on Exod. 23: 21: 'He is all and from Him comes all.'

Scriptural Usage and Plain Meaning

The Spanish hymnist's choice of language was directly related to the conditions of his employment. Unlike his eastern counterpart, who was hired by his congregation and was expected to compose new works for Sabbaths, festivals and holy days, the Spanish hymnist, in the service of discriminating patrons fiercely devoted to the Hebrew Bible, chose only those works which conformed to their critical standards. Despite their devotion to Arabic culture, the Hispanic Hebrews insisted on the excellence of the language of Scripture, which they championed in the service of the liturgy (and secular arts). Their zeal for biblical Hebrew was in line with the practice of the much-admired Sa'adyah Ga'on, and may have been motivated by a nationalistic pride in the superior quality of Israel's native tongue. Since patrons like Samuel Ibn Nagrela and Isaac Albalia were themselves expert Hebrew scholars the poets, dependent upon their generosity, had to be scrupulous in the use of Hebrew grammar based on biblical models.[48] Moses Ibn Ezra, in his Arabic book on poetics, *Kitāb al-muḥāḍara wa-l'-mudhākara*, warns his colleagues:[49]

> If you come upon a Hebrew root that is conjugated [in the Bible] only in the *nif'al* or *hitpa'el*, or if it appears in the *pa'ul* and not the *po'al*, you are obligated to conjugate it according to what is found [in the Bible] in the *nif'al* or *hitpa'el*, or in the metre of *pa'ul*, without *po'al*.

He also cautions that nouns and verbs should agree in gender and in number and that in all instances biblical usages should serve as a guide. Abraham Ibn Ezra is more outspoken in his criticism of earlier poets who, in his opinion, wrought havoc with the Hebrew language. As an example, the younger Ibn Ezra, in his commentary on Eccles. 5: 1, cites the work of the classical poet Eleazar Qillir, whom he faults on several counts. Qillir's hymns, he charges, are 'mostly riddles and allegories' and are overly dependent upon rabbinic usages in the Talmud which, as is known, borrows from other languages. Why then, Ibn Ezra asks, should we not follow the model of the established liturgical prayers, all of which are composed in unadulterated Hebrew, instead of 'praying in the language of the Medes and Persians, the Christians and Muslims?' Moreover, he complains, even when Qillir employs the language of Scripture, he commits gross grammatical errors. Lastly, Qillir is blamed for loading down his hymns with metaphors and legends. In support of his criticism, Ibn Ezra cites the rabbinic teaching (in *bŠab* 63a): 'A verse cannot depart from its plain meaning.' From this he concludes: 'Therefore it is seemly that prayers should be composed in language that does not depart

[48] Ibn Daud, *Sefer Ha-Qabbalah*, pp. 80–1; Zulay, *Ha-'Askolah*, pp. 19–20; Brann, *The Compunctious Poet*, pp. 23–4.

[49] The text below is from the Hebrew translation of *Kitāb al-muḥāḍara wa-l'-mudhākara*, *Širat Yisra'el*, ed. B. Halper (Leipzig, 1923–4), pp. 148 ff.

from its plain meaning and not in secret utterances and fables, or in rabbinic opinions that are not followed and can be given varying interpretations.'

Hispanic poets were also cautioned about clarity in phrasing their ornamented speech. The poem was required to have a defined goal and present a rational argument. In constructing a convincing argument, the poet should employ the figures that would achieve the desired dramatic effect. These may include the rhetorical question and the extended dialogue, among others. Of primary importance is that the poem's plain meaning should be understood without reference to sources outside the Scriptures. This would not disqualify the use of metaphors like 'dove' (*yonah*) for Israel, or 'Rock' (*ṣur*) for God, since they are commonly used in a biblical context.

Of questionable taste, however, would be metaphors and figures that can be understood only with reference to sources in rabbinic literature or Jewish mysticism.[50] These canons of good taste were, in large part, modelled after contemporary standards in Arabic prosody which were incorporated into the prevailing Judeo-Arabic culture. To a large extent the Iberians were faithful to the standards set by Moses and Abraham Ibn Ezra and their contemporaries. However, there were notable exceptions. A close reading of the hymns for the synagogue by Solomon Ibn Gabirol, Judah Ha-Levi and Abraham Ibn Ezra reveal an undeniable dependence on sources in rabbinic literature and in Jewish mysticism. Following is a strophe from Abraham Ibn Ezra's *'ofan* in the form of a pseudo-*muwashshaḥ*, *Maḥanot 'elyonim*. The citation can be understood only with reference to rabbinic and Ptolemaic astronomy:[51]

The hosts on high, with one voice recite the *qeduššah*
He created his ministers on seven levels;
Eve and morn they run their appointed rounds,
North and south encompassing the planets;
Some designate the days, others the months and the years.

The reference for the last strophe is the statement in *Pirkey de Rabbi Eliezer* (ed. Friedlander, p. 32), 'All the stars minister to the seven planets, and their names are: Sun, Venus, Mercury, the Moon, Saturn Jupiter and Mars . . . their service is . . . by night . . . by day . . . for the hours of the night . . . for the hours of the day.' In the same hymn Ibn Ezra refers to God as the 'example among His hosts' (*'ot bi-ṣva'o*). The same metaphor is used in a hymn for Passover by Isaac Ibn Giy'at: 'The Lord of Hosts is called an example' (*Yah bi-ṣva'ot niqra' 'ot*), and in the *'ofan* by Judah Ha-Levi, *Yaqdišun ha-yom šaloš*: 'He is sanctified among his hosts . . . He is set as an example upon all works' (*hu' ha-niqdaš ba-ṣeva'ot . . . sam 'al kol ha-mif'al 'ot*).[52] This metaphor can be made clear only in light of the legend (in *bḤag* 15a–16a)

[50] Fleischer, *Širat Ha-Qodeš*, pp. 413–18.
[51] A. Ibn Ezra, *Širey Ha-Qodeš*, i. 158.
[52] Yarden, *Sefuney Širah*, p. 11; Ha-Levi, *Širey Ha-Qodeš*, p. 741.

regarding the four who entered the 'Garden' (*pardes*). Of these only Rabbi Aqiva emerged unharmed because, according to Rabbi Yoḥanan, he was armed with the verse (from Deut. 33: 2): 'And He came from the myriad holy,' meaning that He is distinguished among His myriads. Therefore Aqiva was not misled to confuse God with his 'myriads'. Reš Laqiš said that Aqiva was spared because he remembered the verse (in Isa. 48: 2): 'The Lord of Hosts is his name,' meaning that 'He is the example [*'ot*, in the text from *'Eyn Ya'aqov*, in use by the Hispanics] among his hosts.[53]

Also based on non-scriptural models is Ibn Ezra's *tokheḥah* (self-rebuke), *Ben 'adamah yizkor be-moladto*,[54] recited in Spanish congregations at the concluding service (*ne'ilah*) on the Day of Atonement. In this hymn the poet sketches the several ages of man, from the infant of 5 to the hoary head of 80 and beyond. The source of the poet's conceit is found in the *Ethics of the Fathers*, 5. 24 and *Eccles. Rabbah* 1.3. Moreover, as indicated above, the Iberian poets did not hesitate to include in their hymns references to the dialogues of Plato and the physics of Aristotle.

Although Abraham Ibn Ezra did not himself adhere to the standards which he set for the hymnist, it is likely that he had a model poet in mind in his diatribe against the excesses of Qillir. And there is reason to suspect that his model was Samuel Ibn Nagrela. Samuel the Nagid, pre-eminent 'courtier-rabbi', was in the words of Gerson Cohen a 'typological figure', setting the standards for the rabbinate and the Jewish community,[55] and pioneering Arabic-style quantitative metres and prosodic forms.

Ibn Ezra was as effusive in his praise of Nagrela as were his contemporaries. In his *Sefer Moznayim*, a treatise on Hebrew grammar written in Rome in 1140, Ibn Ezra lauds Nagrela's work on this subject as 'second to none in excellence'. In this study, Ibn Ezra is presumably siding with Nagrela in the latter's dispute with the grammarian Jonah Ibn Janaḥ. In his *Sefer Ṣaḥot*, another grammatical work written in Mantua in 1145, Ibn Ezra writes, 'my view [with regard to the *'ayin waw* stem] approximates his [the Nagid's].' Some eighteen other references to the works of Nagrela are found in Ibn Ezra's Bible commentaries and the 'twenty-two books' written by the Nagid are cited in the latter's *Sefer Yesod Mora'* (1.2).[56]

Ibn Nagrela is best known for the secular poetry in his *Ben Tehillim*, *Ben Mišley* and *Ben Qohelet*. In these collections he frequently employs rabbinic language even as he innovates in the manner of Qillir and his contemporaries and coins terms not wholly sanctioned by scriptural usage. Moreover, he assumes that his audience is thoroughly familiar with rabbinic literature since many of his secular works can be understood only with reference to rabbinic

[53] Mirsky, 'Ha-ziqah', pp. 249–50.

[54] A. Ibn Ezra, *Širey Ha-Qodeš*, ii. 542.

[55] Ibn Daud, *Sefer Ha-Qabbalah*, p. 272.

[56] A. Ibn Ezra, *Sefer Mo'znayim*, ed. W. Heidenheim (Offenbach, 1791), p. 2a; idem, *Sefer Ṣaḥot*, in Levin, *Yalqut . . . Ibn Ezra*, p. 391; idem, *Sefer Yesod Mora'*, ibid. 316.

collections and gaonic writings and not in their plain meaning. Some examples follow.

In Nagrela's celebrated *širah* (poem) 'God of might' (*'Eloha 'oz*) marking his victory at Alpuente over his enemy Ibn 'Abbās of Almeria on 4 August 1038, he voices his fears at the start of the battle and utters a prayer:[57]

Father Jacob, pray for me, and [Moses] son of Amram stand by me in my distress;
You who are buried in the Makhpelah, how can you lie still on a day like this? Rise up from your cave
And take hold of God's throne and cry out to the merciful Lord and speak to him [about my] grief;
And if He asks: My beloved, what troubles you?
Answer him: Arise, awaken and rouse yourself!
And if You will not deign to have mercy upon Joseph [the Nagid's son], your young one, is there a chance of victory?

A reader unfamiliar with rabbinic literature will understandably wonder at the sudden transition from 'Answer him', etc. to 'have mercy upon Joseph, your young one.' Only with the aid of the proem in *Lam. Rabbah* 24 can the poet's conceit be fully appreciated. There we read that when God sought to destroy the Temple, Jeremiah went to the Cave of Makhpelah and said to the Patriarchs: 'Arise, for the time has come when your presence is required before the Holy One, blessed be He.' He then stood on the banks of the Jordan and called: 'Son of Amram, arise, the time has come when your presence is required before the Holy One, blessed be He.' When the Patriarchs appeared in heaven, God enquired of his Ministering Angels: 'Why should my beloved be in my house?' Then Abraham spoke before the Lord, 'Sovereign of the Universe, when I was 100 years old You gave me a son and when he reached the years of discretion . . . You ordered me, "Offer him as a sacrifice before Me." I steeled my heart against him and I had no compassion on him; but I myself bound him. Will You not remember this on my behalf and have mercy on my children?'

Another example of Nagrela's reliance on rabbinic sources is seen in his *tehillah* (praise) 'Will You always act on my behalf?' (*Ha-li ta'as be-khol šanah pe'ulim?*). In the hymn he celebrates his victory over the armies of Ismā'īl Ibn 'Abbād of Seville on 5 October 1039. In recounting the event, the Nagid, commanding the troops of Granada, is struck by the size and strength of the enemy. He thinks that they are vastly superior to the forces of Ibn 'Abbās whom he defeated the previous year. In the thick of battle, he sees the Angel of Death hovering over the men in combat. At that moment, he writes:[58]

[57] Ibn Nagrela, *Ben Tehillim*, p. 10. [58] Ibid. 20.

I raised my voice pronouncing the Name of God, honoured and
awesome, as do the seventy Standard-Bearers;
I had prepared it for use in times of distress in petitioning the
Dweller in the Heavens.

It would appear that Nagrela was privy to the Ineffable Name of God pronounced by the High Priest on the Day of Atonement in Temple times (*bYoma'* 39b). From a *tefillah* (prayer) by Sa'adyah Ga'on, 'He remembers the loving-kindness of the Fathers' (*Zokher ḥasdey 'avot*), we learn (ll. 179 ff.): 'Our Fathers knew how to pronounce the Ineffable Name; the Firm Foundations of the Earth invoked it whenever they were in danger.'[59] Understanding the reference to the seventy Standard-Bearers requires familiarity with *Pirqey de Rabbi Eliezer*, 24:

The Holy One Blessed be He called to the seventy angels who surround the throne of his glory, and He said to them: Come let us descend and let us confuse the seventy nations . . . The Holy One, blessed be He descended with the seventy angels who surround the throne of his glory, and they confused their speech into seventy nations and seventy languages.

Another case of rabbinic usage is seen in the Nagid's thanksgiving hymn, 'I am obliged to God for his goodness' (*Ṭovot le'el 'alay*).[60] After returning victorious from the wars Nagrela fell ill, and though not fully recovered he wrote this *širah* (poem). In it he draws a graphic portrait of the horrors of war and complains about the illness from which he has found little relief during the past three months. Yet 'there is a blessing in that', he writes (l. 41), 'since the suffering settles my account with God, although to some it is mere calamity.' Here too, the Nagid's consolation can only be understood in light of the rabbinic teaching (in *bBer* 5a): 'Sufferings wash away all the sins of a man.' A more subtle rabbinic reference is suggested in the war poem 'Men of Wisdom' (*Metey sekhel*)[61] marking his victory on 8 September 1047 over the forces of Malaga and Seville. In it he wrote that 'God condemned them to death towards evening [*danam be-diney nefašot*] and did not permit them to be ransomed with money [*lo' be-diney mamenot*].' The English translation, while accurate, does not fully convey the poet's conceit. The terms *diney nefašot* and *diney mamenot* originate in *mSan* 4.1: 'Civil suits [*diney mamenot*] are tried by day and concluded at night. But capital charges [*diney nefašot*] must be tried by day and concluded by day.'

These examples and others suggest that Nagrela's secular poems are often not understood in their plain meaning and require a familiarity with non-scriptural texts. This is not true of his liturgical writings. The Nagid's corpus of hymns for the synagogue is slim compared to his numerous wisdom poems, dirges, wine- and love-poems, war poems, encomia and derogatory

59 Zulay, *Ha-'Askolah*, p. 224.
60 Ibn Nagrela, *Ben Tehillim*, p. 54.
61 Ibid. 76.

poems and epigrams, among other genres which he pioneered. Only a dozen of his liturgical hymns have been preserved. These include several short *rešuyyot* and some longer *seliḥot*.

The Nagid's *seliḥot* contain all the conventional themes in what L. Zunz calls the 'Normal-*Seliḥah*'. The hymns in this genre are preserved in Nagrela's *Ben Tehillim*, and some may have been composed for his personal use. Others, like his *seliḥot* for the Day of Atonement, 'His is the sea and the dry land' (*'Ašer lo yam we-ḥaravah*), 'He who spreads out the heavens' (*'Ašer naṭah šeḥaqim*), and 'Confess the sins you committed in secret' (*Hodu be-ḥeṭ' seter*), are provided with a choral refrain and were undoubtedly designed for congregational use.[62]

There is general agreement that Ibn Nagrela was the first Hebrew poet to employ the *muwashshaḥ* adapted from Arabic models. It is noteworthy that none of the Nagid's surviving hymns for the synagogue was composed in this form, unlike the those of Solomon Ibn Gabirol, Isaac Ibn Giy'at, Abraham Ibn Ezra and their contemporaries, who frequently utilized the *muwashshaḥ* for their liturgical works. It would appear that the Nagid did not wish to use an alien form for purposes of prayer. The language of the Nagid in his *piyyuṭim* is for the most part based on sources in Scripture or upon early established prayers, as in the following from 'He who spreads out the heavens' (ll. 29, 32):

> You set kings on the throne [*we-'at mamlikh melakhim*] and give grace to the worthy . . .
> You are charitable [*we-'at gomel ḥasadim*] to hundreds and thousands . . .

The reference in the first line is to a *qerovah* for the Days of Awe, 'He who holds in his hand the measure of judgment' (*Ha-'oḥez be-yad middat mišpaṭ*) with its praise of deity, 'He sets kings on their throne, for dominion is his' (*ha-mamlikh melakhim we-lo ha-melakhah*). The reference in the second is to the benediction in the *'amidah*, 'He bestows loving-kindness' (*gomel ḥasadim ṭovim*).[63]

All of the Nagid's liturgical works can be understood in their plain meaning even when he uses rabbinic terms. In *'Ašer lo yam* (l. 7), 'Woe is to me, how can I explain what my sins have wrought [*garmu*]?', *garmu* is found in *bSan* 65b. In *'Ašer naṭah šeḥaqim* (l. 1), 'He spreads out the skies upon His earth like a dome' [*ke-qubbah*], the term is from *Baraita de-Šemuel ha-Qaṭan* 1. These samples suggest that Nagrela, unlike his younger contemporaries, was more discriminating in his liturgical writings, and may have been the model synagogue poet against whose standards Abraham Ibn Ezra judges the hymns of Qillir and his contemporaries.[64]

[62] Ibn Nagrela, *Ben Tehillim*, pp. 317–28.

[63] *Maḥazor Le-Yamim*, i. 9, 225.

[64] Weinberger, 'Liturgical Poetry of Samuel Ibn Nagrela'.

The Hispanics' mentor on the excellence of biblical usage and the need for precision in style and rhetoric was Sa'adyah Ga'on. In his strictures against the alleged shortcomings of Qillir, the younger Ibn Ezra, in the commentary on Eccles. 5: 1, invokes the *baqqašot* of Sa'adyah as the ideal in liturgical writing: 'The *ga'on* Rav Sa'adyah is innocent of these four [charges against Qillir] in his two *baqqašot* which have no equal in all literature; they are based on the language of Scripture and on sound grammatical usage, and are unencumbered by riddles, fables and legends.' It is likely that Sa'adyah also influenced the Andalusian poets in their emphasis on the universal validity of the rational search for God. This tendency is evident in Ibn Gabirol's eighth hymn in his *Keter Malkhut*:[65]

> You are God and every creature is Your servant and worshipper;
> Your glory is not lessened by those who worship others
> Since their intent is to come to You [*le-haggiy'a 'adekha*]
> Like blind men they seek to reach the King and stray . . .
> Your servants, though, are like the wise men steering a straight course.

In these lines Gabirol echoes medieval enlightenment thinking, which acknowledged the seeds of truth in every religious pursuit, even as it was confident in the guidance of reason ('the wise men'). Gabirol's conceit is anticipated by Sa'adyah Ga'on in his *baqqašah*, *'Attah hu' 'adonay levaddekha*:[66]

> You alone are master over all . . .
> Your might and majesty are never diminished . . .
> All come from You . . . and all tend towards You [*ha-kol 'adekha*]
> With their heart's wisdom they will look for You
> Seeking with their intellect, they will find You.

THE PRINCIPAL GENRES

'Avodah

Following the models of Yose b. Yose and Sa'adyah Ga'on, Hispanic poets composed *'avodot* for the Day of Atonement, often with lengthy introductions. Joseph Ibn Abitur adorned his *'avodot* with anadiplosis of two words connecting the strophes in quatrains after the manner of Sa'adyah, but, unlike the Ga'on, Abitur closed his strophes with a verse from Scripture. Abitur's *'avodot*, like those of Yose and Sa'adyah, comprised a historical prologue followed by a description of the Day of Atonement Temple service and of the role of the High Priest. Ibn Gabirol and Ibn Giy'at in their *'avodot*

[65] Ibn Gabirol, *Širey Ha-Qodeš*, p. 42.
[66] Sa'adyah Ga'on, *Siddur*, pp. 48–9; Scheindlin, *The Gazelle*, p. 12.

generally followed Abitur's structure, although they relied less on rabbinic sources and more on themes in contemporary philosophy and astronomy. Moses Ibn Ezra's *'avodah* dispensed with the traditional two-part division and simplified the anadiplosis by confining it to only one strophe-connecting word. Abraham Ibn Ezra returned to the classical form of the *'avodah*, eliminating anadiplosis from the strophes. His *'avodah* is distinctive in that it ends with a scriptural verse in which the name of God is mentioned.

In line with earlier practice, the Andalusians included the *'avodah* supplements *Mah nehdar* (How glorious) and *'Ašrey 'ayin* (Fortunate to behold). These were designed to show the contrast between the happier time of Temple days and the priestly service and the tragic present, with the Temple in ruins and Israel in exile. Spanish poets made much of this contrast, and some, like Ibn Gabirol, added a third hymn, beginning, 'And so it came to naught, the delight of every eye' (*U-v-khen hayah le-'ayin, maḥmad kol 'ayin*). The play on the words *'ayin* (naught) . . . *'ayin* (eye) was followed with an inventory of Israel's losses:[67]

A palace no longer; no longer a city;
Sanhedrin no longer; no longer a dwelling [for God's presence] . . .

'Azharah

For the festival of Pentecost, the anniversary of the Torah-giving at Mount Sinai, the Hispanics composed *'azharot*, a listing of the 613 commands. Their model was Sa'adyah Ga'on's treatment of this genre, which called for rhyming quatrains connected by anadiplosis. An exception to this practice was Ibn Gabirol's marvellous metric *'azharah*, *Šemor libbi ma'aneh*, comprising 164 strophes in monorhyme. The practice of writing *'azharot* for Passover and detailing the laws pertaining to the festival was pioneered, among the Hispanics, by Judah Ha-Levi and imitated by later hymnists in Italy, France and Byzantium. These hymnists also composed *'azharot* for the Days of Awe, Šabbat Šuvah and Tabernacles, focusing on the particular laws and traditions of each occasion. A precedent for this practice appears in the writings of Phinehas Ha-Kohen, who reviewed the laws of Passover in a *yoṣer* for that festival, and it is likely that Ha-Levi followed his model.

Qedušta'

The Andalusian laity, like many in eastern synagogues, found the classical *qedušta'* lengthy and unappealing. Faced with the need to redesign the genre, Hispanic poets eliminated the massive second section of the *qedušta'* while preserving the first, the *magen*, *meḥayyeh* and *mešullaš*, and the third,

[67] Fleischer, *Širat Ha-Qodeš*, pp. 381–3; Ibn Gabirol, *Širey Ha-Qodeš*, p. 281.

the *silluq*, which they expanded to compensate for the loss of the middle part. The embellishments of the first three benedictions of the *'amidah* were modelled after those of the classical poets, with sets of rhyming quatrains interrupted by verses related to the Scripture lesson. Faithful to the style of their classical forebears, the Hispanics refrained from injecting Arabic metrics into the traditional rhyming quatrains adorning the *magen* benediction. However, asserting their independence, they added a metric hymn with choral refrain, titled *pizmon*, after the first set of Scripture verses. Judah Ha-Levi's *pizmon* to his nine-part *qedušta'*, *'Et milḥamot 'adonay*, is one example of this innovation. His *pizmon* was chanted on Šabbat Zakhor and related to the Torah lesson from Exod. 17: 14, 18. The work is in the form of a pseudo-*muwashshaḥ* with an opening 'guide' of tercets in hemistichs ending with a verse from Ezek. 17: 24. Following the 'guide' are four strophes in quatrain hemistichs which close with the said verse from Ezekiel. The following is a translation of the 'guide':[68]

> When the enemy [Haman] advised trickery, his counsel was flawed;
> The Rock summoned his servants, 'You in exile, wait for me
> And know that I am the Lord who pierces darkness with light;
> I have laid low the tall tree and lifted the lowly one.

Of particular interest is the set of hymns designed for the Day of Atonement in the Hispanic synagogue. Known as *ma'amad*, the set comprises *qedušta'ot*, *yoṣerot*, *seliḥot* and other genres for the evening and morning services. The practice of composing a complete liturgical set, i.e. a *ma'amad*, instead of individual hymns for the fast-day, was initiated by Joseph Ibn Abitur and continued by Ibn Gabirol, Ibn Giy'at and Moses and Abraham Ibn Ezra. Due to its excessive length, the hymnist's *ma'amad* was rarely preserved intact by later precentors who, for reasons of their own, altered the structure of the liturgical set. Thanks to the discovery in the Cairo Geniza of large fragments from a *ma'amad* by Ibn Abitur, we are able to reconstruct a model of its original form.

The structure of the *qedušta'* in the Day of Atonement *ma'amad* varied from Ibn Abitur's monorhyme to Ibn Gabirol's strophics with closing scriptural verse repeated. Following Gabirol's model were Ibn Giy'at and Moses Ibn Ezra. The latter expanded on the *qedušta'* with the addition of a *qiqlar*, a refrain-type stanza following a set of strophes after the manner of the classical poets beginning with Qillir. In a further expansion on the *qedušta'*, the Hispanics employed the *estriota* (or *estribillo*) modelled after the Arabic *zéjel*, with its introductory strophe presenting the theme of the poem, followed by a monorhyme tercet and a repetition strophe rhyming with the intro-

[68] Ha-Levi, *Širey Ha-Qodeš*, p. 279.

duction.[69] The treatment of the *estriota* by Abitur began with an opening scriptural verse giving the theme to be developed in the hymn. This was followed by a monorhyme tercet with repeated refrain. Instead of rhyming with the opening verse the refrain ended with the word *qadoš*. Later, Gabirol added a rhyming couplet after the opening verse and followed it with a monorhyme tercet refrain to which he appended a strophe and another, different, refrain. Throughout the hymn the refrains alternate after each strophe.

A favourite *estriota* theme for Spanish poets was the story of Jonah, the second Scripture lesson for the Day of Atonement. Gabirol's *estriota* treatment of the reading from Jonah generally followed the biblical text, albeit with some embellishments. When the mighty storm comes upon the sea threatening to break up the ship, the sailors are in a state of intoxication:

When the drunken sailors [*halumim*, as Isa. 28: 1] ask, 'Tell us now
What is your country? Where do you come from?' [Jon. 1: 8]

The refrains allow the poet to comment, after the manner of the Greek chorus, on God's summons to Jonah and the latter's refusal to carry out his mission. In the first refrain, the poet speaks in God's name and affirms His omnipotence and omniscience. In the second refrain, coming after Jonah decides to flee to Tarshish, the poet, speaking for himself, warns that it is futile to run from God's presence:[70]

Almighty, You abide in the east and west;
Sadly, I cry, I am in your hands;
Where can I flee from Your presence, Holy One?

Another innovation in the Hispanic liturgy initiated by Ibn Gabirol was the *rešut*, a metric hymn inserted before the *qedušta'*, seeking permission to recite the Day of Atonement prayers. The following *rešut*, *Ša'ar petaḥ dodi* by Gabirol, was chanted, presumably, at the concluding (*ne'ilah*) service:[71]

Open the gate, my beloved, arise and open the gate;
My soul is struck with terror; I am horribly afraid;
My mother's haughty maid mocks me;
From the day that the Lord heard the cry of the lad
At midnight, the wild beast pursued me
After I had been trampled by the boar of the forest;
The end sealed up adds to my discontent;
No one can explain it to me and I am ignorant.

[69] Fleischer, *Širat Ha-Qodeš*, pp. 377–81; P. Le Gentil, 'À propos de la "strophe zéjelesque"', *Revue des langues romanes*, 70 (1949), pp. 119–34.

[70] Malachi, 'Sefer Yonah'; Ibn Gabirol, *Širey Ha-Qodeš*, pp. 216–18.

[71] Ibid. 469.

The 'gate' is a metaphor for the 'Gates of Mercy' which Israel hopes will remain open, allowing her to be granted forgiveness for her sins. Also, the reference may be to the 'Gate of Redemption' and relief from the 'haughty maid' (Hagar = Muslims, Gen. 21: 10), the pursuing Ishmaelites (= wild beast, Gen. 16: 11–12) and the barbaric Christians (= boar of the forest, Ps. 80: 14). Israel is confident that the 'gate' will eventually open, leading to her national restoration, even as she is frustrated in her effort to ascertain when that time will come. The 'end sealed up' is a reference to Dan. 12: 4, 'But you, Daniel, keep the words secret and the book sealed until the time of the end.'

A distinctive Hispanic hymn is the *mustajāb* (response, refrain), an Arabic term designating a pseudo-*muwashshaḥ* comprising a scriptural verse as 'guide' and refrain. The strophes are built in rhyming tercets with closing scriptural verses. The scriptural 'guide' is repeated at the end of each strophe and ends with the same unit as the verses following the tercets. The 'guide' verse is the thematic base of the *mustajāb* hymn constructed without metre in the following rhyming pattern: *a* [guide verse] / *bbb* / *a* [verse] / *a* [guide verse, etc. Abraham Ibn Ezra added anadiplosis (*širšur*) in his treatment of the *mustajāb*. Below is a section of Gabirol's composition in this genre. The 'guide' verse is from Ps. 144: 3:[72]

> Lord what is man . . .
> Wretched and afflicted in their obstinacy;
> Pitiful, they persevere in treason;
> Even when you see them you will ask, 'Where are they?'
> They are like waters dissipated from the sea
> Men are mere breath. [Ps. 62: 10]

The original purpose of the *mustajāb* was to embellish the verses from the Scripture lesson in the *qedušta'* for the Day of Atonement. However, owing to its popularity with both hymnists and congregation it was recited as a separate *seliḥah* apart from the *qedušta'*.

Yoṣer

Hispanic poets generally preserved the several components of the *yoṣer* complex, including the *guf ha-yoṣer*, *'ofan*, *me'orah*, *'ahavah* and *mi kamokha*. The latter hymn, however, was expanded beyond its conventional classical length. Often the Spanish *mi kamokha* comprised thirty or more strophes, unlike the earlier pithy, one-strophe forms of this genre. The reason for this liberty was that the *mi kamokha* (Who is like unto You O Lord?) lent itself more easily to elaboration than the other parts of the *yoṣer*, and thereby

[72] A. Ibn Ezra, *Širey Ha-Qodeš*, ii. 138–44; Ibn Gabirol, *Širey Ha-Qodeš*, p. 218.

enabled the poet to expatiate on popular themes in metaphysics and cosmogony. Following is Ibn Gabirol's *mi kamokha*, *Šalit yoṣer kol po'al*:[73]

By word He created the four elements
He established the heavens connecting their heights.

The reference to the four natural elements, air, fire, earth and water, from Aristotle's *Physics* (ed. R. Hope, 1. 6. 189b4), was co-opted to serve Jewish (and Muslim) cosmogony. Moreover, in elaborating on 'Who is like unto You?', Gabirol also enlisted figures from Jewish mysticism. The following citation from his *mi kamokha*, *Šokhen be-govhey meromim*, is based on *Sefer Yeṣirah*:[74]

The Rider of the Clouds [God, Ps. 68: 5] created thirty-two paths
With a ration of pure words, informing humankind.

The thirty-two secret paths of wisdom by which God created the world, as postulated in *Sefer Yeṣirah* 2. 2, are the ten *sefirot* added to the twenty-two letters of the Hebrew alphabet. Gabirol was undoubtedly aware of the speculation in *merkavah* (divine chariot throne) mysticism in which the four *sefirot* represent the four elements, described above, and the other six refer to the six dimensions of space.[75] *Sefer Yeṣirah* is a source used by Judah Ha-Levi as well, in his *mi kamokha* hymns. Below is the first strophe from his *Mi kamokha 'amuqqot goleh*:[76]

The Creator made all from nothing;
It is revealed to the heart
Do not ask how and wherefore;
'The heavens and earth I fill.' [Jer. 23: 24]

The source for the opening assertion of *creatio ex nihilo* is *Sefer Yeṣirah* 2. 5, and the source of l. 3 discouraging speculation on the subject of cosmogony (*ma'aseh bere'šit*) can be traced to *mḤag* 2. 1: 'Whoever puts his mind to these four matters it were better for him if he had not come into the world— What is above? What is below? What before? What after?'

A prominent subject in the *mi kamokha* is the nature of the soul. Ha-Levi, like Gabirol, embedded contemporary speculation on the qualities of the soul into hymns of this genre. The following is from the same *mi kamokha*:

Consider the hidden path of the soul;
Study it and be refreshed;
It will make you wise and you will be free,
Being that you are incarcerated in the prison that is the world.

[73] Ibn Gabirol, *Širey Ha-Qodeš*, p. 328.
[74] Ibid. 350.
[75] See Scholem, *Major Trends*, pp. 73–4
[76] Ha-Levi, *Širey Ha-Qodeš*, p. 723.

The latter conceit was in Ha-Levi's day a familiar Neoplatonic notion traceable to Plato's *Phaedo* (Plato, *Dialogues*, ed W. H. D. Rouse, p. 487): '"The lovers of learning understand," said he [Socrates], "that philosophy found their soul simply imprisoned in the body."'

Prayers for Dew and Rain

Other genres from earlier periods which attracted the attention of the Hispanic Hebrews were the Prayer for Dew on Passover and the Prayer for Rain on Tabernacles. Here too the Spaniards followed the earlier practices of Eleazar Qillir, even as they endowed the genre with a distinctive character. For example, Abraham Ibn Ezra's Prayer for Rain, unlike similar hymns by Qillir, is built in pseudo-*muwashshaḥ* metric strophes followed by scriptural verses. However, like Qillir (in his *'Elim be-yom meḥussan*), Ibn Ezra constructs his *tefillat ṭal*, *'Eloha ṭuvo lo' nikhḥad*, in twelve strophes corresponding to the signs of the zodiac and the months of the year. Below is the opening strophe:[77]

The Lord will not conceal His love; the glory of His saints will abide in His counsel
There is nothing to fear in the constellation Ram: the wolf and the lamb shall graze together;
Lord, in *Nisan* raise for your own a miracle, and when all anguish flees
The remnant in the midst of the many shall be as the dew from the Lord,

AS IT IS WRITTEN [Mic. 5: 6], 'THE REMNANT OF JACOB SURROUNDED BY MANY PEOPLES SHALL BE LIKE DEW FROM THE LORD LIKE SHOWERS ON THE GRASS WHICH DO NOT DEPEND UPON PEOPLE OR WAIT FOR ANY MORTAL.'

Rešut

The *rešut* (permission) hymn would be the poet's way of presenting himself to the congregation, or of introducing the prayer that he is about to chant. One of the distinguishing features of the Hispanic *rešut* is a tendency to dwell on themes in philosophy and mysticism. A telling example is Joseph Ibn Abitur's *rešut* to the prayer recited in the daily introductory service, 'Blessed be He who spoke and the world came into being' (*Barukh še-'amar we-hayah ha-'olam*). The Spanish *rešut* to this prayer generally comprised rhyming quatrains in alphabetic acrostic with each letter preceded by *barukh*:

[77] *Maḥazor Le-Šaloš Regalim*, pp. 77–9; A. Ibn Ezra, *Širey Ha-Qodeš*, ii. 210–15.

Blessed is He who founded heaven and earth with ten commands
and preserved them . . .
Blessed is He who created form [*ṣurah*] like the forms of creatures
with face, forehead and brow.

The reference for the first strophe is *'Avot* 5. 1, 'With ten utterances the world was created.' In the second strophe, however, Abitur used the term 'form' (*ṣurah*) not in its familiar biblical context, as in Ezek. 43: 11 ('the plan of the Temple'), but in the Aristotelian sense as *eidos* opposed to matter (Heb. *ḥomer*, Greek *ule*). The contrast between matter and form in Aristotle relates to the process of becoming, i.e. the transition from potentiality to actuality. Matter is the principle of actuality; form, that of potentiality. Aristotle used those two terms to explain the relationship of genus to species, designating the former as matter and the latter as form. (Aristotle, *Metaphysics*, H, 2, p. 1043, a, 19; H, 6, p. 1045, a, 33 ff.). Gabirol (in his *Fons Vitae*, ed. C. Baeumker, i, 10, 12–13, pp. 13–15) used Aristotle's model to explain that if substances of differing kinds show common characteristics, the similarity is due to a common substratum. In line with this thinking, Abitur names the stratum 'face, forehead and brow' with 'form' as their common substratum.[78]

Ibn Abitur's *rešut* to the *Barukh še-'amar* daily prayer was not widely imitated by the Andalusians, given that on weekdays men were anxious to get to work and were content to recite the required unembellished prayers. However, Abitur's pioneering *rešut* to the *nišmat kol ḥay* prayer ('The soul of every living being') recited on Sabbaths and festivals did gain considerable popularity. The latter hymn, generally built in tercets or tercet hemistichs, prefaced each strophe with the unit *nišmat*. The opening colon in each strophe ended in varying monorhyme units giving the name of the author. Other forms of this hymn were less ornate, comprising strophes in quatrains with an opening unit, *nišmat*. The *nišmat* hymns for Sabbaths and festivals were generally limited to some five strophes, but were considerably enlarged for the Day of Atonement service, when worshippers spent the entire day in the synagogue.

The *rešut* to the *nišmat* also served to highlight contemporary thinking on the nature of the soul. Jewish Neoplatonists like Ibn Gabirol and Abraham Ibn Ezra reaffirmed the view held in talmudic times that the soul, a spiritual being different from the body, originates in a suprasensual world. However, in their wider speculations on the subject, the Neoplatonists projected an odyssey of the soul forced to leave its heavenly home and descend earthwards into a human body to help make it virtuous. In its descent the soul acquired the impurities of the sub-celestial world and became alienated from its divine source. Its alienation was increased once it entered the body and surrendered

[78] Guttmann, *Philosophies of Judaism*, pp. 91–2.

to its passions. To guard against being mired in the material world, the soul is exhorted to remember its divine source and carry out its mission. In seeking to attain its goal, the soul is advised to pursue virtue through knowledge and the rule of reason, thereby enabling it to return to its primeval home after the death of the body. These speculations on the nature of the soul are preserved in hymns of various genres by Ibn Gabirol and Ibn Ezra. Below is a sample from the latter's *Nišmat šadday hevinatni*:[79]

Before creation His hand prepared me;
To acknowledge Him, He brought me hither!

In Ibn Ezra's commentary on Exod. 3: 15, he writes that the souls of humans originate in the supramundane world and that they have the same spiritual nature and intelligence as the angels. Like the latter, the souls receive their commission—to aid humankind in acknowledging God's sovereignty, a view ably expressed by Gabirol in his *Keter Malkhut*, No. 25:[80]

Who can fathom Your thoughts in the making of radiant souls
from Intelligence's sphere . . .
They are the angels by Your will; messengers of Your Presence . . .
They give witness that You have created us,
That You are our Lord who made us and not we ourselves,
That all of us are the work of Your hands,
And that You are our Master and we Your servants.

The soul that is unmoved by the temptations of the sensual world is ever mindful of her alienation. In his *Nišmat ʾeloha be-ʾappaw*, Abraham Ibn Ezra gives voice to the soul's yearning to be reunited with her divine source:[81]

The soul, the breath of life, desires the intimacy [*qirvat*]
Of the Name, high and exalted . . .

The drama of the soul's odyssey comes to an end with the death of the body and with the successful completion of her mission on earth. Thus, in Ibn Ezra's *Nišmat ʾel mi-meqor ḥayyim hiʾ nilqaḥah* (God's soul taken from the source of life),[82]

When her residence collapses she finds rest;
Light dawns for the righteous and joy for the upright in heart.

A prominent theme in the *rešut* to the *nišmat* is the disdain for personified Time (Heb. *zeman*; Arabic *zamān*, *dahr*) and the World (Heb. *tevel*, Arabic *dunyā*), a conceit traceable to Arab sources. Both are portrayed as pernicious

[79] A. Ibn Ezra, *Širey Ha-Qodeš*, i. 143.
[80] Ibn Gabirol, *Širey Ha-Qodeš*, pp. 52–4.
[81] A. Ibn Ezra, *Širey Ha-Qodeš*, ii. 229.
[82] Ibid. 398.

forces conspiring against the soul.[83] In the view of the Hispanic Hebrews, *tevel* (the world), a feminine noun, is conceived as the second wife, tempting man with worldly pleasures and keeping him from the spiritual joys of the world to come. Man will learn that the second wife (the world) is untrustworthy; she appears to be bountiful only to disappoint him. The revealing metaphor is found in the writings of Samuel Ibn Nagrela:[84]

My friend, do you hope to gain the world to come
While your feet hasten to the delights of the world at hand?
You are like a man with two wives;
When you please the one, you anger the other.

Time is no better than the World; it passes all too quickly and hastens man to old age and the grave. Time is personified as an enemy, trapping man into a false sense of confidence only to better ensnare him. Man's only recourse in his struggle with Time and the World is to arm himself with stoic indifference, as recommended by Ibn Gabirol:[85]

If you desire eternal life and fear the fires of hell,
Then belittle the World's goods and don't be tricked by wealth,
  honour and offspring . . .
Come to know your soul; she alone will survive you.

These views are echoed in Abraham Ibn Ezra's *rešut* to the *nišmat*, *'El 'el šuvi yeḥidah*:

O my soul, return to God and be saved
From Time's snare. How long must you crave foolishness?
Having considered the mystery of your birth, why do you rebel?
Your behaviour should disappoint you and make you ashamed.
Enough of chasing after Time's mistakes.
Do not weaken in your war against temptation;
Take hold of Wisdom and turn to the Intellect;
Pray night and morning and know Who [confronts you].
Put on Reason's valued garment; wrap it around you,
Never fail to keep the promise to your Master.
Fortify yourself with His love—and you will find peace
Forever in His holy heights, there rejoicing.[86]

Although many Hispanic poets perceived Time as blind fate with demonic authority over man, Samuel Ibn Nagrela and Judah Ha-Levi, among others,

[83] See Nicholson, *Studies in Islamic Poetry*, pp. 47, 211, 230; Levin, '"Zeman" we-"tevel"', pp. 68–79.
[84] Ibn Nagrela, *Ben Qohelet*, No. 354.
[85] Ibn Gabirol, *Širey Ha-Ḥol*, No. 176, p. 333.
[86] A. Ibn Ezra, *Širey Ha-Qodeš*, i. 49.

sought to accommodate Time's character to the religious belief in God's sovereignty and justice. The following is from Nagrela:[87]

All is in God's hands, and if He wishes,
He will command tempestuous Time;
And He grants what the other withheld,
And leaves in peace what the other disturbed.

Ha-Levi distinguishes between two types of service:

Time's servants are the servants of servants,
God's servant alone is free;
Therefore while every one goes out to seek his fortune,
My soul says, 'The Lord is my possession.'[88]

Whereas Time's servants are addicted to its transient pleasures, God's servant is free to choose an eternal reward. Moreover, whereas Time is in possession of the lives of his servants, the liberated soul can claim, 'The Lord is my possession.'

Like the *rešut* to the *nišmat*, the *rešuyyot* to the *qaddiš* and *barekhu* generally incorporate the themes of the latter two prayers. However, there are notable exceptions in the *rešuyyot* of Solomon Ibn Gabirol and Judah Ha-Levi. In the former's *Šokhev ʿaley miṭṭot zahav*, there is no indication whether the work is intended as a *rešut* to the *qaddiš* or *barekhu*. Instead, the metric hymn in four monorhyme hemistichs is cast as a lover's plea to be reunited with her beloved, based on themes from Canticles and Arab love poetry (*ghazal*). The speaker is Israel:[89]

You [God] lying upon Your golden bed [the Ark] in my Temple,
When will You prepare the couch for [the Messiah, son of] my ruddy one [1 Sam. 16: 12]?
Why sleep, sweet gazelle [God] when the morning star is risen like an ensign above Senir and Ḥermon?
Turn away from the savages [the nations] and come near the graceful doe [Israel];
I am meant for You as You are meant for me;
Come to my palace and find my treasure holding new wine, pomegranates, myrrh and cinnamon.

Judah Ha-Levi's metric *rešut* for Passover in five monorhyme hemistichs, *Yedidi, ha-šakhaḥta ḥanotakh be-veyn šaday*, is, like Gabirol's, without a clue as to whether it is related to the *qaddiš* or *barekhu*. And, like Gabirol's, Ha-

87 Ibn Nagrela, *Ben Qohelet*, No. 89.
88 Lam. 3: 24; Ha-Levi, *Diwan*, ii. 300. See Elitzur, '"We-ha-yamim"', pp. 42–3.
89 Ibn Gabirol, *Širey Ha-Qodeš*, p. 457.

Levi's hymn echoes Israel's yearning for national restoration couched in images drawn from scriptural and Arabic prosody. Here too, Israel is the speaker addressing God, her lover:[90]

> My beloved, have You forgotten the time You lingered between my breasts?
> Why have You sold me in perpetuity to my taskmasters?
> Did I not once chase after You in an unsown land?
> Are not Seir, Paran, Sinai and Sin's wilderness my witness?
> I was Your beloved and You had your way with me,
> Why do You pay Your respects to others in my place?
> Banished to Christian lands and thrust upon the Muslims,
> Tested in Greece's crucible and suffering under the Mede's yoke;
> Is there a redeemer beside You or a prisoner of hope other than I?
> Give me Your strength for I have given my love to You!

The manner in which the *rešuyyot* of the Hispanic hymnists became personalized is unprecedented in synagogue hymnography. The hymns emerge from a common framework of relationships, man to his soul and the beloved (Israel) to her lover (God). At times the poet identifies with one or the other of the parties, or he may distance himself and allow them to speak for themselves. In either case, his intimate familiarity with the parties allows for an easy transfer to the congregation, which responds to the shared intimacy.

Muḥarrak

The *nišmat* prayer, highly esteemed in Spain, became the beneficiary of multiple embellishments. In addition to the preceding *rešut*, its poets composed another hymn, the *muḥarrak* (Arabic 'mover') to be recited as an introduction (*petiḥah*) before the *rešut*. The *muḥarrak* was generally constructed in the form of a *muwashshaḥ*, and its theme was an exhortation to the soul to be mindful of its responsibility. After completing its mission, it is urged to return to its celestial home. In Isaac Ibn Giy'at's treatment, the poet appeals to reason in urging his soul not to fall prey to the connivance of material forces seeking to lead it astray. Following is his *Negdekha 'asim megammati*:[91]

> Violent men turning to idols
> Telling lies and losing their way;
> They argue, 'Your shepherds lead you astray!'
>   Yet I remain steadfast;
>   The memory of You [God] is my strength and song.

[90] Ha-Levi, *Širey Ha-Qodeš*, p. 327.

[91] Ibn Giy'at, *Širey*, p. 452.

Moses Ibn Ezra in his *muḥarrak*, *Ruaḥ sesoni we-ḥen man'ammaw*, identifies with his soul, now estranged from its source, and summons images from both Canticles and the Arabic *ghazal*. He calls upon the idyllic garden, reminiscent of Eden and the trysting place of lovers, to emit its fragrance in the hope that God, the soul's beloved, will make an appearance:[92]

> Hasten the myrrh and the hill of frankincense;
> Awake north wind; come south wind;
> Perhaps my beloved will come down to the garden
> To eat my fruit and gather my lilies
>   And renew the time of younger days.

Seliḥah

Following a practice established by the Babylonian *ge'onim*, Spanish congregations observed evenings of prayer called *ma'amadot* (stations) during the month of 'Elul and the Ten Days of Repentance. The prayers, known as *seliḥot* (penitentials), were recited from after midnight until dawn throughout the month and during the Repentance days. The Iberian congregations referred to the *ma'amadot* as *'ašmurot* (vigils), while the *seliḥot* were called *taḥanunim* (petitions). Due to popular demand, the poets obliged by composing a large selection of *taḥanunim* seeking forgiveness both for themselves and the congregation. Considerable latitude was permitted with regard to the structure of the petition. Most were in the form of a pseudo-*muwashshaḥ*; others were cast in non-metric or metric strophes counting long and short syllables, or long only. As a rule, the Spanish *seliḥah* was supplied with a refrain (*pizmon*) designed as a congregational response.[93]

The thematic content of the *seliḥah* was widened by the Hispanics. The several themes in the 'normal-*seliḥah*' are summarized by L. Zunz in his study of synagogue poetry.[94]

1. Repentance and regret. In the conceptual framework of the *seliḥah*, the petitioner confesses his sins while the gates of heaven are opened, and in this 'propitious time' (*'et raṣon*) prayer is the only recourse, since Temple sacrifices are no longer available.
2. The insignificance of man, whose days are as a fleeting shadow full of vanity. God, however, is eternal, almighty, merciful and omniscient.
3. Israel trusts in the covenant made with God. This trust is extended to the Torah and to God's thirteen attributes as well as to the Merit of the Fathers and the Binding of Isaac. Despite its long exile, Israel remains faithful to the model of trust exemplified by the Patriarchs and reaffirms

92 Schirmann, *Ha-Širah Ha-'Ivrit*, i. 411.

93 Fleischer, *Širat Ha-Qodeš*, p. 404.

94 Zunz, *Die synagogale Poesie des Mittelalters*, pp. 83 ff.

its belief in God's unity. Moreover, Israel is confident that its faithfulness will be rewarded, and it relies upon prayer, fasting and repentance to rebut the charges of the satanic adversary. It is hopeful that its repentance will be accepted and its sins remembered no more.

4. The plight of Israel's scattered remnant enduring the travails of the Exile. The powerlessness of God's congregation is seen in marked contrast to the overbearing might of its enemies. From the depths of despair Israel gives voice to intense nationalist longings for redemption and prays for the restoration of the Temple, the gathering in of its exiles and renewal of its days as in olden times.

Tokheḥah

Another related genre in the *seliḥot* class was the *tokheḥah* (self-rebuke), popularized by the Iberians. The hymn could serve the individual members of the congregation, or the poet himself. Whereas in the petition the poet would combine the request for forgiveness with the plea for national restoration, the admonition was exclusively personal in its focus on the human predicament. Following are strophes from Ibn Gabirol's admonition, *Šokheney batey ḥomer*, opening with a couplet refrain followed by quatrains with variable rhyme. The unusual (for an admonition) rhyming pattern is *aa // bbcc / aa / ddee / aa //*, etc. This popular hymn was chanted on the Day of Atonement in Spain as well as in Algeria, Tunis, Italy and Byzantium:[95]

Ye who dwell in homes of clay, why be arrogant?
Humans have no advantage over animals! [Eccles. 3: 19]

It is for us to know that we are worms;
Our defences are without substance; why then are we proud? . . .

Poor and wretched man, your fate is likened to a gourd
That shot up during the night and perished before dawn.

The poet draws a dismal portrait of the human condition but, withal, repentance and the grace of God are always available:

Let the evil man forsake his ways and repent before his Lord
Perhaps the Rock will respond and desist from his anger . . .

Show your mercy to those who knock at your door;
You are our Lord and our eyes look to You.

Teḥinnah

The centrepiece of the night vigil service was the reading of the Thirteen Divine Attributes from Exod. 34: 6–7, 'The Lord, the Lord is a gracious and

[95] Ibn Gabirol, *Širey Ha-Qodeš*, p. 213.

merciful God . . .', followed by the public confession of sins and a silent supplication recited while lying prostrate. (In its modern form, the worshipper merely sits and rests his brow on his arm while reciting the supplication.) The supplication began with the plea, 'O Lord, God of Israel, turn from your fierce wrath and renounce the plan to punish Your people' (Exod. 32: 12). Against this setting the Hispanics introduced their own supplication (*teḥinnah*) to be recited silently before the opening verse (from Exod. 32: 12) of the obligatory plea. They then co-opted the verse as a refrain to be repeated after the strophes. The Spanish *teḥinnah* began with 'O Lord'—as for the opening verse—and generally comprised strophes in tercets with rhyming couplets and terminal verset as a repeated unit. The theme of the supplication was a confession of sins, a plea for forgiveness and a hope for national restoration.

In the following *teḥinnah* from David b. Elazar Ibn Baqodah, a contemporary of Moses Ibn Ezra, the above themes are skilfully combined, with the prime focus on national restoration. The hymn was written at a time when Christians and Muslims fought for control of Jerusalem:[96]

> O Lord, my despair grows and I am jealous when I think about Jerusalem;
> They are assembled to lay waste our Temple; our feet were standing in your gates, Jerusalem . . .
> I speak from great anguish; may my tongue cling to my palate if I forget you, Jerusalem . . .
> May the voice soon be heard by a nation exiled and dispersed, 'Rejoice O Jerusalem.'

Gemar

The vigil nights also inspired poets to compose the *gemar* (conclusion). The *gemar* was initially designed as a coda to obligatory prayers. Isaac Ibn Giy'at's *'Anšey levav, šim'u li* is titled '*gemar* for *šema' yisra'el*'. In its later form it is likely the hymn was chanted as a refrain for the several vigil night *seliḥot* at the close of the service, hence the name 'conclusion'. When serving the *seliḥah*, the *gemar* usually opened with the verse from Dan. 9: 7 and was without metre and in monorhyme. The theme of the *gemar* focused on the contrast between man, the lowly sinner, seeking forgiveness of God seated on His judgment throne. In a vigil-nights setting the hymn first appears in the writings of the Saragossan poet Levi Ibn al-Tabbān (a contemporary of Moses Ibn Ezra). Following is his *gemar*, *Lekha 'adonay ha-ṣedaqah, 'eloha gozer u-meqim*, beginning with *laudes* and ending with a petition:[97]

[96] Schirmann, 'Ha-mešorarim', p. 292.
[97] Ibn Giy'at, *Širey*, pp. 181–2; Ibn al-Tabbān, *Širey*, p. 145.

'Righteousness is on your side, O Lord' [Dan. 9: 7], God who
  decrees and fulfils;
He bears the world by His might; His majesty is in the skies . . .
His sits on the judgment throne and His ordinances are just;
Be merciful and judge not your poor oppressed . . .
Be near to your supplicants, O God on cherubs seated.

Muqqadimah

The rich variety of hymns prompted by the night vigils of 'Elul and the Days of Repentance was extended to the *šofar* service during morning prayers for these periods. The series of *šofar* blasts was introduced by a recitation of appropriate scriptural verses (*mišpatiyyot*). In order to better prepare the worshipper for the *šofar* service, the hymnists prefaced the *mišpatiyyot* with an opening chant, titled *muqqadimah* (preface). The introduction began with a *mišpatiyyot* verse, presumably as a refrain. The strophes were in quatrains of rhyming tercets and terminal verset with repeated closing unit. The hymn was designed to introduce the three sets of *šofar* blasts, the *malkhuyyot*, *zikhronot* and *šoferot*. Following is a portion of Judah Ha-Levi's introductory hymn to *malkhuyyot*:[98]

'The Lord is our Master; He will redeem us' [Isa. 33: 22] . . .

May the prayers of the faithful please You;
They come to praise Your name
Even as they dread Your wrathful anger;
  Forgive our sins . . .

These many years we are ruled by our masters
And each day they afflict us;
Raging waters have swept us away;
Why have You utterly forgotten us?

Hištaḥawayah and *Meyuššav*

The supplications chanted during the vigil-nights service were an extension of the supplications recited after the *'amidah* during the daily morning service. Both during daily prayers and on vigil nights the worshipper prostrated himself. The practice was based on the rabbinic comment (in *mTam* 7. 3), 'The Levites chanted the psalm. When they came to a pause a *teqi'ah* [*šofar* blast] was blown, and the public prostrated themselves. At every pause there was a *teqi'ah* and at every *teqi'ah* a prostration.' Prostration (*hištaḥawayah*) hymns were composed for the vigil nights by the Hispanics, as were hymns to be chanted while sitting upright (*meyuššav*). Judah Ha-Levi is the author of a

[98] Ha-Levi, *Širey Ha-Qodeš*, pp. 9–10.

meyuššav, *Heykhal ʾadonay u-miqdaš hadomo*, for the vigil nights. Following is part of the five-strophe pseudo-*muwashshaḥ*:[99]

The exiles in the west, in Ethiopia and Egypt,
Turn their faces towards Jerusalem
To their Father who lives in the heavens
Hoping to serve Him and praise His name.

Baqqašah

In addition to the hymns designed especially for the vigil nights, the Spaniards co-opted the *rahiṭ* section of their *qedušta'ot*, which they converted into a *seliḥah*. The practice of co-opting hymns for uses other than originally intended was not uncommon. For example, the elegant metric *baqqašah* (appeal), *ʾEloha, ʾal tedineni ke-maʿli*, by the Lucenan hymnist Isaac Ibn Mar Saul, a contemporary of Ibn Abitur, was presumably written as a private meditation. However, because of its uncommon attraction it was adopted for congregational use on the Days of Awe by synagogues in Spain, Algiers, Tunis, Italy, Byzantium and Cochin. Ibn Mar Saul's supplication is built in rhyming hemistichs with a *ha-merubbeh* metre: – –v/– – –v/– – –v. The opening hemistich is repeated at the end, giving closure to the hymn. The Hispanics pioneered the metric *baqqašah*, usually in *ha-merubbeh* metre. Ibn Mar Saul's hymn in this genre became a model for succeeding generations of Hebrew poets. The following are selections from his *baqqašah*:[100]

Lord, do not judge me according to my deserts;
Do not measure into my lap [Isa. 65: 7] payment for my deeds;
In Your mercy show me Your grace and I shall live;
Please, Lord, do not pay me as I deserve;
My arrogant spirit is demeaned before You; in my anguish
I rend my heart, not my garment;
In agony I stand, depressed
On account of my wickedness and foolishness;
I am drunk with grief, not with wine; I stumbled
In my steps straying from Your path;
What can I say and where turn for help
On Judgment Day? To whom shall I flee? Who will defend me?

The *baqqašah* in rhymed prose, pioneered by Sa'adyah Ga'on, was continued by Ibn Gabirol in his magisterial *Keter Malkhut*; by Judah Ha-Levi in his fourteen-part hymn in this genre, *ʾAvarekh et-ʾadonay ʾašer yeʿaṣani*; and the virtuosic, *baqqašat ha-memim*, of the thirteenth-century Provençal poet

[99] Ibid. 591–2.

[100] Schirmann, *Ha-Širah Ha-ʿIvrit*, i. 50; iv. 489, 703.

Yedayah Ha-Penini. The latter work comprises 1,000 words beginning with the letter *mem*.

Widduy

The confession of sins (*widduy*) during the vigil nights and the Days of Awe followed a formula from earlier times in which all the letters of the Hebrew alphabet were enlisted: *ʾašamnu*, *bagadnu*, *gazalnu* (we have trespassed, we have dealt treacherously, we have robbed), etc. In this construction, the worshipper was made aware of the pervasive nature of his sinful behaviour. Later embellishments on this practice included the anonymous hymn *ʾAšamnu mi-kol ʿam; bošnu mi-kol dor*, preserving the alphabetic formula. Hispanic poets would often attach the confession to the *baqqašah*, as did later poets in the Balkans. This was the practice of Baḥya Ibn Paqudah (late 11th c.) and Judah Ha-Levi, whose *widduyyim* were composed in rhymed couplets. Unlike Baḥya, whose confession is stated in the plural, 'We have sinned', etc. as in earlier forms, Ha-Levi lists his sins in the singular, 'I have sinned', etc. In this Ha-Levi follows the practice of Solomon Ibn Gabirol, who added a confession in rhymed prose to his *baqqašah*, *Keter Malkhut*, No. 33 noting his sins in the singular.[101]

Ha-Levi's confession is of particular interest since it leaves the impression that he is as much sinned against as sinning:

> I have trespassed, even as they have laid waste the pasture of my home . . .
> I have been treacherous, even as traitors betrayed me . . .
> I have been presumptuous, even as wicked men had me in constant fear;
> I have framed lies even as liars have perverted my way;
> I have spoken falsely even as those who falsify Your words have scoffed at me.

Rehuṭah

In addition to the vigil-nights *seliḥot*, another hymn in this genre known as *rehuṭah* (fluency) gained entrance into the Hispanic ritual. Among its forms is Judah Ha-Levi's twelve-part *rehuṭah*, *Wa-yered ʾiš ʾelohim*, designed to embellish the Ten Commandments and their preceding verses (Exod. 19: 20–20: 15) and Abraham Ibn Ezra's more modest work in this genre, *ʾEštaḥaweh ʾappayim ʾarṣah*. Following the style of pre-classical poets, Ibn Ezra's *rehuṭah* is unrhymed and without strophes or refrains. The hymn was chanted without the usual pauses, i.e. with fluency, as its name suggests. The

[101] Ibn Paqudah, *Sefer*, pp. 611–12; Ha-Levi, *Širey Ha-Qodeš*, p. 163; Ibn Gabirol, *Širey Ha-Qodeš*, pp. 58–9.

only concession to contemporary practice is the poet signing his name in the acrostic. Ibn Ezra's *rehuṭah* was to become the model in both theme and structure for later poets like Isaac of Mont Ventoux (*Ha-Seniri*) in Provence (13th c.). Following is a sample from Ibn Ezra's *rehuṭah*:[102]

> My bowed face touches the ground; there is nothing lower.
> I lie prostrate before the Most High, exalted above all heights;
> With what shall I approach Him but my spirit, His creation, His own? . . .
> He is more distant than the highest heaven and nearer than my flesh and bone! . . .
> Are not the hosts of heaven and earth made like me!
> Why would I ask their help seeing that nature's aid is false?
> There is no relief for the slave save from the one who bought him.

Qinah

The elegy (*qinah*) also belongs to the *seliḥah* class, although its theme is distinctive. In their elegies the Hispanics, like their forebears in the east, lamented the times of trouble: the destruction of the Temple; the assassination of Gedaliah (2 Kgs. 25: 25); the murder of the prophet Zechariah b. Yehoyadah (*bGiṭ* 57b), and the fall of Betar (*bGiṭ* 57a) among others. Other elegies were more focused, like Joseph Ibn Abitur's *Bekhu 'aḥay we-gam sifedu*, composed in 1012, lamenting the decrees of the caliph Al-Ḥākim against Jewish communities in Ereṣ Yisra'el.[103] As with the *seliḥah*, the forms of the *qinah* varied. Ibn Abitur built his in strophes of rhyming couplets with *ha-marnin* (– – –v/– – –v) metre, while Isaac Ibn Giy'at's elegy for the Ninth of 'Av is a pseudo-*muwashshaḥ* with metre limited to long syllables. The zionides of Judah Ha-Levi, combining an ode to Zion with a lament for its fall, won special distinction and many imitators. These hymns, distinguished by their metric rhythm and elegantly balanced hemistichs, were included in the Ninth of 'Av liturgies of congregations in central Europe, the Mediterranean world and south Asia. Following is a sample from the best-known of Ha-Levi's laments for Zion, *Ṣiyyon halo' tišʾali li-šlom 'asirayikh*:[104]

> You [Zion] are the abode of kings, the seat of the Lord, though
> Slaves now occupy the throne of your princes!
> Would that I could wander in places where
> God revealed himself to your prophets and messengers;
> Who will make me wings that I could travel far?
> I would lay my broken heart among your shattered cliffs.

102 A. Ibn Ezra, *Širey Ha-Qodeš*, ii. 148; Schirmann, *Ha-Širah Ha-ʿIvrit*, ii. 283–4.
103 Ibid. i. 64.
104 Ha-Levi, *Širey Ha-Qodeš*, pp. 913–18.

Elegy-*Petiḥah*

Special occasions in the life of Spanish Jewry, like the death of a patron, a season of drought, or the introduction of restrictive government decrees, often elicited poetic responses in the form of an elegy-*petiḥah* (introduction). This introduction was generally built as a pseudo-*muwashshaḥ* without metre, unlike the more abundant non-liturgical elegies composed in metric hemistichs with monorhyme. Following is part of the lament *petiḥah* by Judah Ha-Levi in rhyming tercets with closing refrain, *'Emunot yehgeh ḥikki*. Of interest is the poet's use of the *ubi sunt?* (Where are they now?) theme, a popular motif in Arabic, Hebrew and Latin poetry in the Middle Ages:[105]

Ask, 'Where are the princes and where the mighty men?
Where are those memorialized in "The Chronicle of the Lord's Wars?"' (Num. 21: 14)

Those they loved are no more, even as those they envied are gone;
Their hatreds have vanished from underneath the skies of the Lord.

They were arrogant in their lifetime, unconcerned with the grave;
Yet even there is the presence of the Lord.

In the final strophe, the poet refers to the popular belief that the dead are judged in the grave (*din we-ḥibbut ha-qever*). This theme was extensively treated in the vigil-nights hymns of the Hebrew poets from Byzantium.

A fast-day was often decreed in time of drought during which prayers for rain were recited. These petitions were preceded by a *petiḥah*, as in the thirteen-strophe hymn by Judah Ha-Levi, *'Asimah megammati le-qonen 'al 'agmey mayim*. The work is constructed in quatrains with each colon—including the fourth, a scriptural verse—ending with the word *mayim* (water), as in this excerpt:[106]

I am in pain and have not been answered; mine eyes are pools of water;
My heart is torn for lack of flowing streams;
I have fasted for [relief from] the thirst that begs for water;
My eyes flow with tears.

Enhancing the musical quality of the poem is its phonetic-intensive assonance, alliteration and play on words. This may be seen in the Hebrew text of the above strophe:

[105] Ha-Levi, *Širey Ha-Qodeš*, p. 1075. [106] Ibid. 678.

'Unneyti we-lo' na'aneyti we-'eynay 'eynot mayim
Pullag levavi 'al ḥesron palgey mayim
Ṣom ṣamti 'al ṣimma'on 'ašer 'eyn mayim
'Eyni, 'eyni yoredah mayim.

Petiḥot with a narrower focus include Judah Ha-Levi's lament inspired by restrictive government decrees. It is likely that they were recited as part of a fast-day observance during which prayers were offered petitioning divine aid. Reflective of the hardships endured by Hispanic Jews is Ha-Levi's *petiḥah*, *'Aqonen 'al mar tela'otay*, written in the turbulent years of the early reconquest of Spain by Christian forces:[107]

Among the armies of Seir and Qedar [Christians and Muslims]
My soldiers are forlorn; absent
Are the men of Israel going to battle.
They fight their wars;
We are their casualties;
This is the way it has been in Israel.

On every side, a trap and snare
And there is no one to seek
The welfare of Israel.

Hymns for the Life-Cycle: Circumcisions and Epithalamia

Rites of passage generally combined the ritual act with liturgical sanction. To the obligatory benedictions solemnizing the required practice, Hispanic poets would add their own enhancements. The circumcision embellishment was often constructed in the form of a pseudo-*muwashshaḥ* and was largely uniform in theme, celebrating the new addition into the covenant of Abraham. Completing the hymn was a prayer that the infant grow into manhood learned in the Torah, sanctified by marriage and practised in good deeds. At times the poet would also pay tribute to the father and pray for his welfare, as in the following selection from the circumcision hymn *'Elohim [ye]motekha we-šanekha*, by Judah Ibn Giy'at, son of Isaac Ibn Giy'at. In the hymn the father of the infant is referred to 'the nobleman Isaac' (Heb. *ha-gevir Yiṣḥaq*), who was probably the poet's patron:[108]

Rejoice in your devoted son and with your family;
May he persevere in the practice of your hallowed traditions;
May he become an adorning crown for your head,
And a jewel for your necklace.

[107] Ibid. 693. [108] Schirmann, *Širim Ḥadašim*, p. 232.

Ascend the mighty heights, O noble Isaac,
And sup and rest on the lofty heavens;
And when Time's rascals make you fair game [when you die],
Your righteousness will escort you.

The epithalamia of Hispanic poets were generally short hymns constructed with metric hemistichs in monorhyme. The hymn would not only pay tribute to the young couple but extend greetings and praise to their families. The following epithalamium, *Šemeš ke-ḥatan ya'aṭeh sut 'or*, by Solomon Ibn Gabirol, is notable in that it focuses on the bridegroom exclusively, with stock images drawn from Ps. 19: 5–6:[109]

The bridegroom like the sun radiates light coverlets emanating
from His undiminished glory;
He has learned to encompass the western end as he bends low to
Your mighty throne . . .
Each day he bows down to You; cover him then with majesty's
garment.

Sabbath Hymns: *Zemer* and *Havdalah*

Since the Sabbath was a festive day which required the eating of three meals (*bŠab* 118a), it was customary to celebrate with songs (*zemirot*) interspersed among the several courses. An early Hispanic *zemer*, *Deror yiqra' le-ven u-l-vat*, bearing the acrostic 'Dunaš', is attributed to Dunaš b. Labrat (mid-10th c.). Judah Ha-Levi wrote several *zemirot* for the Sabbath. In his playful metric *zemer*, *'Al 'ahavatekha 'ešteh geviy'iy*, in the form of a pseudo-*muwashshaḥ*, he is impatient with the slow pace of weekdays and eagerly awaits the delights of the Sabbath:[110]

To you, beloved I drink my cup; peace upon you,
greetings to the Sabbath.
For six work days I slave for you;
Labouring thereon I am sated with restlessness;
For me the days are but few
Because of my love for you, O day of delight . . .

I hear good tidings from the fifth day:
Tomorrow your spirits will be refreshed;
To my work in the morning, freedom at eventide;
I am called to dine with my Lord and Shepherd . . .

[109] Ibn Gabirol, *Širey Ha-Qodeš*, p. 466.

[110] Ha-Levi, *Širey Ha-Qodeš*, pp. 643–4.

How sweet the time at sunset
Seeing Sabbath's face fresh and new;
Bring fruit and pour the wine
This is my day of rest, this, my beloved and friend.

The obligatory benedictions designed to distinguish between the sanctity of the Sabbath and the ordinary character of the weekdays are listed among those instituted by the men of the Great Assembly (*'Avot* 1. 1 and *bBer* 33a). The four *havdalah* (separation) benedictions—over wine, spices, light and the separation of the sacred from the secular—benefited from Hispanic adornments. A major theme in the *havdalah* hymns was the call to Elijah the Prophet to bring news of Israel's redemption. The earliest Spanish hymns on this theme appear at the time of Ibn Gabirol. Below is part of the Ibn Gabirol's metric *havdalah*, *Šelaḥ minzar*, in the form of a pseudo-*muwashshaḥ*:[111]

Send the prince [Elijah] to the exiled nation scattered here and abroad . . .
May he comfort the flock with news of the end time and desired day . . .
Hasten to prepare the divorcee's [Israel's] inheritance and may she rule over them [that possess it].

[111] Ibn Gabirol, *Širey Ha-Qodeš*, p. 512.

3

Cantor-Rabbis in Italy, Franco-Germany and England

GENERAL BACKGROUND

JEWISH SETTLEMENTS in Italy appeared as early as the Roman pagan era (2nd c. BC to AD 313). When Christianity became the *religio licita* of the Roman Empire the legal status of the Jews changed. They were not allowed to serve in the army, nor were they permitted to hold positions of honour in the civil service. Laws were passed forbidding the building of new synagogues or the repair of old ones. With the fall of the western Roman Empire in 476 and the troubles that followed, Jews emigrated to the relatively stable south of Italy, ruled by the Roman emperors in Byzantium. Although the Byzantine emperors Justinian and Heraclius enacted legislation designed to limit the practice of Judaism, the status of the Jews changed for the better in the ninth century under a more tolerant government. Now settled in the coastal cities Taranto, Trani, Oria, Venosa and Bari, Jewish merchants were active in the flourishing maritime trade with Greece, northern Africa and the eastern Mediterranean.

An insight into Jewish life in Byzantine Italy is provided by the family chronicle of Aḥima'aṣ ben Paltiel (b. 1017). Written in rhymed prose, the Aḥima'aṣ Scroll (*Megillat 'Ahima'aṣ*) recounts the achievements of the author's ancestors from the ninth to the eleventh centuries, beginning with Amittai (*c.*800) of Oria, in Apulia. According to the family legend, Amittai's family was brought to southern Italy by Titus after the fall of Jerusalem. Aḥima'aṣ boasts that his forebears were 'diviners of mysteries' and 'makers of verse' and describes Amittai as 'a poet and scholar'. The Italians were linked to the Franco-Germans by the Kalonymides of Lucca, Moses, Kalonymus and Mešullam (10th–11th c.) who moved to Mainz in the tenth century.

Jewish settlements in Germany date from the time of the Roman Emperor Constantine, who in 321 and 331 issued decrees affecting the Jews of Cologne. In the ninth century, under Carolingian rule, Jews are listed among the merchants near the Imperial Court at Aachen. By the end of the eleventh century Jewish settlements were situated throughout the valleys leading to the North Sea, and on the Danube. Jews were often invited by government authorities to improve the commercial life of the region. The Bishop of Speyer in 1084 offered such inducements as protection against 'the insolence of the populace' and the privilege of owning land. Settling in cities like Speyer, Regensburg, Cologne, Worms and Mainz, Jews would voluntarily segregate themselves in neighbourhoods in which they built the synagogue and established a cemetery.

When the Kalonymide family moved to Mainz in the tenth century, the city gained pre-eminence in Jewish scholarship. Mešullam, son of Moses b. Kalonymus, was the leading European rabbinic authority in his day and was consulted by Jewish communities in distant parts of Europe and North Africa. Several of his responsa (answers to enquiries on matters of Jewish law) were found in the Cairo Geniza. Moses and his son Mešullam were early contributors to what was to become the Franco-German (Aškenaz) prayer-book, and their hymns occupy a prominent place in the ritual. Adding to the lustre of Mainz was the eminent cantor-rabbi Simeon b. Isaac b. Abun (*c.*950) and Rabbenu Geršom b. Judah (950–1028), master of the academy at Mainz, which in his day became a magnet for Jewish students throughout Europe.[1] The Italian–Franco-German connection was transplanted in England by Jacob of Orleans and Yom Ṭov b. Isaac of Joigny, students of the French master Rabbenu Jacob Tam.

Although there is reason to suppose that Jews came to England with the Norman conquest in 1066, it is not until the mid-twelfth century that we hear of established Jewish communities in London, Lincoln, Winchester, York, Oxford, Bristol, Gloucester and Norwich. Under the rule of Henry I (1100–35) Jews were tolerated and, presumably, were granted a charter of liberties. With the death of Henry, Jews in Norwich (in 1144) and in Gloucester (in 1168) were charged with murdering Christians in order to obtain blood for the Passover. More such accusations followed in 1181, 1183 and 1192.

During the reign of Henry II, prosperous Jewish financiers like Aaron of Lincoln (*c.*1125–86) became an asset to the Crown. The benefit to the state from taxes raised from Jews almost equalled the amount gained from the general population. The accession to the throne of Richard I, 'Cœur de Lion', in 1189, brought a change for the worse in the lives of England's Jews. The religious excitement of the Crusades, in which Richard was a leading figure, led to outrages against Jewish settlements in Stamford and Norwich among others. When a mob threatened to massacre the York congregation in March 1190 the Jews, led by R. Yom Ṭov b. Isaac of Joigny, chose voluntary death rather than baptism.

The reign of Henry III initiated new restrictions against the Jews. By order of the Council of Oxford (in 1222), the ruling of the Fourth Lateran Council

[1] See Blumenkranz, 'Germany', pp. 163–4.

(1215) requiring Jews to wear a distinctive badge was enforced. Blood libel accusations continued, among which was the case of young St Hugh of Lincoln, said to have been murdered in 1255 for ritual purposes. Eighteen Jews were executed for this alleged offence. Heavy taxes impoverished Jews, rendering them of little value to the state. In light of this development, Edward I issued an edict on July 1290 which called for the expulsion of the Jews from England.

Jewish learning flourished in twelfth-century England. Two students of the French scholar R. Jacob Tam, R. Jacob of Orleans and R. Yom Ṭov b. Isaac of Joigny, settled in England and established academies of learning in York, though each met a martyr's death during the anti-Jewish riots brought on by Crusader zeal. Abraham Ibn Ezra visited London in 1158 and was warmly received. In the four weeks in June and July that he spent there, he completed his philosophical–ethical treatise, *Yesod Mora'*. The work was commisioned by his English patron, Joseph b. Jacob of Maudeville.

The Role of the Italian Synagogue Poet

Unlike the Hispanic courtier-poet beholden to his patron, Italian hymnists served the congregation in much the same way as their classical and late eastern predecessors. Between accounts of Aḥima'aṣ's illustrious kindred, Amittai and his son, Šefatyah, there are amusing anecdotes about congregational life in ninth-century Apulia. Amittai's colleague Silano of Venosa, a gifted synagogue poet in his own right, is portrayed as a prankster with the presence of mind to bring comic relief during a crisis in the congregation.

It happened that a visiting dignitary from Ereṣ Yisra'el came to Venosa and was to preach at the Sabbath service. When word of his visit spread, men and women from the nearby villages came to Venosa and, for reasons unknown, began brawling in the streets. Seeing that the Sabbath was approaching and the tension had not subsided, Silano, who had access to a copy of the visitor's sermon, made some changes in the text without the author's knowledge. The Scripture reading for the Sabbath dealt among other things with the wife who has gone astray (Num. 5: 12 ff.), and presumably the preacher related the reading to the rabbinic commentary in *Num. Rabbah* 12. 16: '"And they came, both men and women" [Exod. 35: 22]: they came on top of one another, men and women together in a promiscuous throng.' The preacher, caught up in the enthusiasm of his message, found himself reading Silano's emendation:

> When men came in wagons,
> The women emerged from their houses of ill repute
> And beat upon them with pitchforks.

This sudden shift from a biblical setting to recent contemporary events elicited a roar of laughter from both Silano and his congregation and helped defuse a tense situation. The preacher, however, was not amused, and upon his return to Ereṣ Yisra'el he reported the incident to his superiors. As a result Silano was scorned for many years by the Holy Land elders, who relented at last in response to the intercession of Aḥima'aṣ (the grandfather of the author of the famous *Megillah*). Several *seliḥot* by Silano, one of the earliest synagogue poets in Europe, have been preserved and are included in the Franco-German liturgy.[2]

Silano had access to the Sabbath sermon to be given by a visiting dignitary because it is likely that he was a synagogue employee. It is presumed that Silano's colleagues, Zevadiah, Šefatiah and his son Amittai, and David b. Huna, were also cantor-poets in the eastern tradition. In this role they were required to compose the expected embellishments of the obligatory prayers and, when the occasion required, to improvise. The Aḥima'aṣ Scroll relates one such incident, when Amittai, son of Šefatiah, was urged to extemporize an elegy on the death of a wayfarer at the Oria inn. The poet, who also served as a judge in the region's religious court, had left the city to tend to his vineyard when he was summoned by the elders of Oria to eulogize the deceased. Without much time to prepare, Amittai hastened back to the city to pay homage to the dead man. He began his elegy with a simile between the plight of a wayfarer in a strange city and the agony of Israel exiled to a foreign land:[3]

Alas, O wayfarer, alas, O exile;
Those not familiar with you will be unruly;
Whoever knows you and has had dealings with you will lament and bewail [your fate].

Among the mourners stood 'Moses the schoolteacher', a detractor of Amittai, who began to parody the elegy with a play on words:

Whoever knows you and has had dealings with you
Suffers from your judgments.

The reference to some of the harsh rulings of Amittai, the judge, was not lost upon the assembly, who undoubtedly relished the parody. The role of the cantor-poet as judge in a rabbinic court is continued in tenth-century Rhineland Jewry led by rabbis Simeon b. Isaac and Geršom b. Judah of Mainz.

2 *Megillat 'Aḥima'aṣ*, pp. 18–19; Habermann, *Toledot Ha-Piyyuṭ*, ii. 14.
3 Amittai, *Širey*, p. 119; Habermann, *Toledot Ha-Piyyuṭ*, ii. 18.

The Role of the Franco-German and English Synagogue Poets

Unlike the courtier-poets of Andalusia and the cantor-poets in Italy, the Franco-German rabbi-poets were the recognized religious authorities in their communities. Simeon b. Isaac, the earliest Rhine Valley poet born in Germany, was known by the title 'Our rabbi Simeon' (*Rabbana' Šim'on*). In this role he addressed a wide range of concerns to the Jewish public. In a revealing *qerovah* for Pentecost, *Šekhen ra'akha*, Simeon cautions his prospering congregation against greed and materialism:[4]

> [Man] fashioned from clay how does he profit?
> He lusts with a passion for what is not his!
> The rich have possessions that are not theirs [to keep];
> A purchase that is not yours, why make it?
> Would that he were wise and understanding in knowledge and reason,
> He would rejoice and take courage from his lot in life.

The prominence of R. Simeon b. Isaac as spiritual leader of the Mainz community is attested by the earliest chronicle (*Memorbuch*) from this region. In one entry he is cited as 'our master, Rabbi Simeon the Great'. From the entry we learn that R. Simeon successfully intervened with state authorities for the purpose of easing anti-Jewish decrees. His efforts, together with the intercession of Pope John XVIII through his legate the Bishop of Piperno, helped put an end to the persecutions of Jews and led to their return, in 1013, to Mainz, where they were protected in their persons and property by the state.[5] In his role as communal leader, R. Simeon was alert to any variants in Jewish religious practice that could lead to the kind of schism produced by the arguments of Karaites against their Rabbanite opponents in eastern Europe. In his *seliḥah*, *'Elohim, qamu 'alay zedim*, he denounces in harsh tones a group of dissenters—possibly Karaites or their sympathizers—within the Jewish community:[6]

> Lord, wicked men have risen against us
> Whose righteous deeds are like a filthy cloth;
> Traitors, they profane the covenant of the fathers;
> They anger us with their arrogance and scorn;
> Haughty is their speech; their faces bold;
> Their words are boastful; they slander and insult . . .
> They intend to profane the holy Sabbath;

[4] Habermann, *Piyyuṭey Rabbi Šim'on*, pp. 102–3.
[5] Blumenkranz, 'Germany', p. 174.
[6] Ankori, *Karaites in Byzantium*, pp. 252 ff.; Habermann, *Piyyuṭey Rabbi Šim'on*, p. 162.

Their meeting place, a den of robbers;
They disobey the Torah, forsake their duty.

The rabbi-poet Geršom b. Judah (960–*c*.1028) of Mainz, known as Rabbenu Geršom, the 'Light of the Exile'—a title applied to him by R. Solomon b. Isaac (RaŠI)—was a younger contemporary of R. Simeon b. Isaac. Rabbenu Geršom became the most influential teacher at the academy of Mainz, attracting students like R. Isaac b. Judah and R. Isaac b. Eliezer Ha-Levi. The latter were to become the mentors of RaŠI, the leading commentator on the Bible and the Babylonian Talmud and the author of several liturgical hymns. Although best known for the enactments (*taqqanot*) ascribed to him as appellate judge, and for his commentary on the Talmud, R. Geršom also wrote for the synagogue service.

Joseph b. Samuel Ṭov Elem (Bonfils) was a contemporary of R. Simeon and Rabbenu Geršom. Born in Provence, Ṭov Elem lived in Narbonne, Limoges and Anjou. A respected rabbinic authority whose opinions were cited by RaŠI and the Tosafists (authors of additional comments on the Talmud), he is the author of hymns in classical and late eastern genres. The other Franco-German cantor-poets and their students who settled in England also functioned as rabbinic authorities and communal leaders in addition to their duties as cantor-poets.[7]

THE PRINCIPAL ITALIAN POETS

Amittai

Amittai b. Šefatiah, the most prolific of the Apulians, is the author of a *qedušta'*, several *yoṣerot*, including the innovative *'Asiḥah be-divrey nifle'otekha*, *seliḥot*, *zemirot* and epithalamia. Some fifty of his hymns have been preserved in Mediterranean and Franco-German congregations. In addition to his standard liturgical work, Amittai experimented with a mock-serious dialogue in his *Wikuaḥ ha-gefen we-ha-'eṣim*. The poem, included in the synagogue ritual, features two protagonists, the vine and the tree. Both debate their relative merits in alternating strophes with closing scriptural verse:[8]

[THE VINE:]
My wine brings joy to men, a libation mixed with fire,
Giving breath to the weary wayfarer, moving the whispering lips;
See it strengthening the weak; Solomon made note of it:
'Give strong drink to one who is perishing and wine to those in bitter distress.' [Prov. 31: 6]

[7] Habermann, *Toledot Ha-Piyyut*, ii. 121–238.
[8] Ibn Nagrela, *Ben Tehillim*, p. 318, No. 207.

[THE TREE:]
That which you highly praise gives licence to the dejected,
Leads good men to shameless acts; it makes the virtuous quarrelsome,
Like Scorpio stinging the Pleiades; on the likes of it the parable speaks:
'Wine is a mocker; strong drink a brawler.' [Prov. 20: 1]

Amittai's use of rabbinic sources is limited. The following, from his *zemer* (song), *Ševaḥ rum šofer*, is an exception.[9]

Were all the moisture-laden heavens made of parchment
Written upon repeatedly, they would not suffice to encompass
The praises of the One who adorns the heavens and makes the eve and morn.

Were all the earth's spaces waters, even pits and clefts,
And though o'erladen with ink, they could not write
The praises [etc.]

Completing the conceit, the poet asserts that if all men were scribes and all the trees were pens, they would not be equal to the task of praising the One, etc. The source of the metaphor is a statement by Raba b. Meḥasia (in *bŠab* 11a): 'If all the seas were ink, reeds pens, the heavens parchment, and all men writers, they could not suffice to write down the intricacies of government.' The conceit also appears in the *Nišmat kol ḥay*, a prayer from the period of the anonymous poets, and in the writings of the late eastern poet Sa'adyah Ga'on, the Hispanics Menaḥem Ibn Saruq and Moses Ibn Ezra, and Franco-Germans Simeon b. Isaac and Meir b. Isaac.[10]

Amittai's moving refrain-hymn (*pizmon*), *'Ezkerah 'elohim we-'ehemayah*, gained wide popularity and was included in Italian and Franco-German liturgies. Chanted during the afternoon service on the Day of Atonement, its eloquence combines yearnings for Israel's national restoration with full confidence in God:[11]

When I remember, O Lord, I am filled with longing:
Every city built on its own site I see,
While the city of God is consigned to the realm of the dead;
Yet, withal, we are dedicated to God, our eyes are lifted up . . .

In addition to the ninth-century Apulians, Italian poets included Solomon Ha-Bavli of Rome (mid-10th c.); the Kalonymides of Lucca, Moses, Kalonymus, and Mešullam (10th–11th c.); Elia b. Šemayah of Bari (11th c.); members of

[9] Ibn Nagrela, *Ben Tehillim*, p. 118.
[10] Habermann, *'Iyyunim*, p. 55.
[11] *Maḥazor Le-Yamim*, ii. 663–4.

Rome's Anaw family, Yeḥiel b. Abraham (d. before 1070); Yeraḥmiel b. Solomon (12th c.); Zedekiah b. Benjamin and Yeḥiel b. Yekutiel (13th c.); thirteenth-century poets from Trani (in Apulia), Isaiah b. Mali and Isaiah b. Elijah; members of the deRossi family (*Ha-'Adummim*) in Rome, Solomon b. Moses (d. after 1284) and his son Emanuel; and Moses b. Isaac da Rieti (b. 1398), who composed decasyllabic Hebrew poetry in syllabic metre.[12]

Solomon Ha-Bavli

The mid-tenth-century poet Solomon Ha-Bavli, probably of Rome, heralds a neo-classical revival in synagogue hymnography. The term *bavli*, from the biblical 'Bavel', was commonly used by rabbinic sources (and in the New Testament) as a reference to Rome, and it is likely that Solomon lived there. Apart from the Qilliric two-root-consonant rhyme, and sporadic neologisms, allusions and Aramaisms, Ha-Bavli's rhetorics are not unlike those of the Apulians. Below is his argument with God in the *seliḥah*, *'Eyn ke-middat basar middotekha*:[13]

> Since Your character is unlike that of mortal man,
> Where is Your zeal and your eternal counsel?
> The daughter [Israel] whom You chose for Your gracious home,
> Lords have ruled her and she cannot join You.

In the penitential, *'Elleh be-šališemo*, based on Ps. 20: 8 ('Some take pride in chariots, and some in horses, but our pride is in the name of the Lord'), Ha-Bavli deals with the vexing problem of how to justify the subservient existence of Jews exiled to Christian and Muslim lands. Was not Israel God's favoured daughter? Why is she powerless while the rejected sons, Ishmael and Esau (Muslims and Christians) lead vast armies that rule the known world? Ha-Bavli insists that Israel's trust in God is a power greater that the military force of her enemies:[14]

> These trust their commanders; others, in their cavalry;
> Our faith is in Your Name and power to intervene;
> Dweller in the heights, bring near our redemption!
>
> These trust their legions; others take pride in their skills;
> Our faith increases in the One mighty to save;
> He aids the weak over the strong!

Ha-Bavli, the author of an *'avodah*, *'Adderet tilbošet*, and of several *yoṣerot* and *seliḥot*, gained wide acceptance in the Mediterranean world and his works

[12] For a more complete list of Hebrew poets in Italy, see Schirmann, *Mivḥar Ha-Širah*, pp. 9–24.
[13] Fleischer, *Piyyuṭey . . . Ha-Bavli*, p. 271.
[14] Ibid. 320–1.

were included in the Italian, Franco-German and Balkan prayer-books. His neo-classical leanings inspired several imitators, and his *yoṣer*, *'Or yešaʿ me'uššarim*, was a model for Italians and Franco-Germans like Mešullam b. Kalonymus and Simeon b. Isaac and the Byzantine poet Benjamin b. Samuel.[15]

Elia b. Šemayah

Solomon Ha-Bavli's influence is evident in the hymnography of Elia b. Šemayah of Bari (in Apulia), the author of some thirty-eight penitential hymns. Bari in the eleventh century was a thriving seaport city from which Christian pilgrims in 1064–5 began their journey in record numbers to the Holy Land. The story of the four rabbis from Bari (recorded in Ibn Daud's *Sefer Ha-Qabbalah*, pp. 43–9, 63–7) who, after being taken prisoner at sea in 972, were redeemed by Jewish communities in Alexandria, Tunisia, Kairouan and Cordoba, suggests that Apulia was a flourishing seat of Jewish learning. This view was supported by the statement of Rabbenu Tam (12th c.): 'From Bari goes forth the Torah and the word of God from Otranto.'

Bar Šemayah's hymns are in some respects more imitative of Qillir than are Ha-Bavli's. Note the dense alliterative chain in his *seliḥah*, recited during the Ten Days of Repentance. Following is the opening strophe:[16]

'Iwwitikha, qiwwitikha me-'ereṣ merḥaqqim;
Be-qirbi šiḥartikha, qera'tikha mi-maʿamaqqim . . .
Deraštikha biqqaštikha ba-reḥovot u-va-šewaqim . . .

You are my desire and my hope in distant lands;
With all my being I wait for You; I call You from the depths . . .
I seek You and ask for You on the streets and highways.

Images from pastoral life, drawn largely from biblical sources, figure prominently in the rhetoric of the Bari poet. In Bar Šemayah's *seliḥah*, *Taʿinu ke-ṣo'n 'ovedot*, Israel, the lamb, is left unguarded by her shepherds and is set upon by the wild boar (*ḥazir yaʿar*), a metaphor for Christians:[17]

We have wandered to the ends of the earth like sheep forsaken;
We prowl the streets, mountains and valleys;
Since shepherds have failed to defend us,
The wild boar boisterously sealed our fate.

Like Ha-Bavli, Bar-Šemayah addresses the problem of Jewish weakness and subservience to Christian power. Seeking an answer to Israel's loss of

[15] Fleischer, *Piyyuṭey . . . Ha-Bavli*, pp. 7–8, 378–9.
[16] Elia b. Šemayah, *Piyyuṭey*, p. 36.
[17] Habermann, *Toledot Ha-Piyyut*, ii. 23.

sovereignty and subsequent exile, he blames her leaders ('shepherds have failed to defend us').

The Kalonymides

In addition to Apulia and Rome, the city of Lucca in Lombardy was a centre of Jewish learning and liturgic creativity in the tenth and eleventh centuries. The earliest hymnist in this region, Moses ben Kalonymous (9th c.) is the author of *'Eymat nor'otekha*, a *qerovah* chanted in the Franco-German ritual on the last day of Passover. Built on earlier classical models, the hymn exudes a determined confidence, seen in the poet's account of Pharoah's fall and his suggestion that Israel's current enemy will meet a similar fate. Following is the *qiqlar* section of the hymn:[18]

What good will sin do to the sinner?
Can the might of the arrogant prevail?
Will He not repay each one for his deeds?
Can mere flesh rebel
Against the Maker of all by His word?

The second member of the illustrious Kalonymide family, Kalonymous b. Moses, known as Kalonymous the Elder, lived in the mid-tenth century. Although he is cited by his contemporary, Rabbenu Geršom b. Judah of Mainz, as a 'great scholar and a composer of hymns for all the festivals', only some fourteen of his *rahiṭim* for the Day of Atonement have been preserved in the Franco-German ritual and in prayer-books from Prague and Salonica. All of his *rahiṭim*, based on the verse from Jer. 10: 7, 'Who would not fear You, O King of the nations?', are in the form of a litany with consistent rhyming couplets. In the familiar *rahiṭ* pattern, each hymn is introduced by the above verse; the couplets are preceded by one of the units in the verse and that unit becomes the prime focus of the poem. Following is a portion of his *rahiṭ*, *Ha-goyim 'efes wa-tohu*, in which he draws a contrast between Israel and the nations:[19]

The nations are accounted before You as nothing and emptiness;
Your true and tried [Israel] are apart, not counted among them . . .
The nations consider holy the child born from lechery;
Your exalted [Israel] abhor the passion of the lewd woman.

The second couplet is an anti-Christian polemic based on a legend traceable to the pagan Celsus that Mary had been divorced by her husband, who suspected her of adultery, and that Jesus was born as a result of her affair with a Roman soldier (see Origen, *Contra Celsum*, i. 28, 32). The poet is equally blunt in a following couplet:

[18] *Maḥazor Le-Regalim*, p. 521.

[19] *Maḥazor Le-Yamim*, ii. 186–7.

The nations deify a corrupt symbolic image;
Your people give testimony to Your sovereignty, O God of gods.

The 'symbolic image' is presumably a reference to the crucifix. The characterization of Jesus as 'corrupt' can be traced to Rabbi Abbahu (*c*.300) of Caesarea, who is reported to have said (in *jTa'an* 2. 1): 'If a man says to you, I am god, he lies; [if he says], I am the son of man, he shall regret it; [if he says], I shall rise to heaven, he says it, but he shall not fulfil it.' Kalonymous b. Moses' *rahiṭ* on the 'nations' was generally omitted by editors of the prayer-book for fear of offending the Christian ruling power.

The son of Kalonymous the Elder, Mešullam (10th–11th c.), was probably born in Lucca, later moved to Rome and died in Mainz. He is the author of two *'avodot* in classical style, *'Ammiṣ koaḥ* and *'Asoḥeaḥ nifle'otekha*. Both are preserved in the Franco-German prayer-book.[20] As emissary of the congregation he reveals his inner fears in the eloquent *rešut*, in rhyming quatrains, *'Eymekha nasa'ti ḥin be-'orkhi*, for the morning service of the Day of Atonement. As in his *'avodot*, there are hardly any allusions to rabbinic sources; the clarity and directness of the hymn is its most appealing quality. Below is the opening strophe:[21]

I prepare my prayer burdened by the fear of You;
Your people have sent me; I bend my knee;
You took me from the womb; You light up my darkness;
Teach me clear speech, lead me in Your truth.

Another hymnist from the Kalonymide family was Šabbetai b. Moses, who held the title *ro'š qallah*, a high-ranking office in the academy at Rome. Presumably he was the father of R. Kalonymous b. Šabbetai *'iš romi* ('of Rome'), cited as a rabbinic authority by the Franco-Germans and highly esteemed by RaŠI.[22]

Rome's Anaw Family

Another of Italy's prominent families were the Anaws (or Anaus). Known in Italian as the Piatelli or delli Mansi, they could trace their descent to the nobles of Jerusalem brought to Rome by Titus. Nathan b. Yeḥiel (born *c*.1037) was the author of the lexicographical study *Sefer Ha-'Arukh*, and his son, the synagogue poet Yeḥiel b. Abraham (d. before 1070), wrote some twenty-three hymns, including a *qerovah* for the Fast of Esther, *yoṣerot* for Passover and Pentecost, and *seliḥot* and *qinot*. For reasons unknown, most of his works have survived in manuscript form only, and a few have been preserved in Italian prayer-books. Of particular interest is his penitential on the

[20] *Maḥazor Le-Yamim*, ii. 435 ff., 447 ff.
[21] Ibid. 112.
[22] See Zimmels, 'Scholars and Scholarship', p. 182.

eclipse of the sun, *ʾAttah galita sodekha*. The poet does not elaborate on the eclipse as an uncommon occurrence in the natural order; he is more concerned with describing the reaction of Rome's Christian population to the startling event. The poet's phenomenological approach to a rare natural event is unprecedented in Jewish hymnography.

The hymn opens with an affirmation that God controls the lights in the heavens and that Jews should not fear an eclipse of the sun. Moreover, the poet warns his congregation not to follow the idolatrous practices of the Christians who, in dread of changes in the natural order, turn to their statues of Jesus and Mary for help:[23]

Abhor the idols of the gentiles; do not envy them;
Reject the habits of the nations; be joined in the fear of Me . . .
Madmen and fools day and night act as if smitten
And terrorized when the sun and moon change;
Fear and tremble and be in awe of My Name
And do not dread the signs of the skies . . .
Your words have helped him who stumbles to remember the
  covenant;
Would that he put his faith in You and be blessed hereafter
Rather than hope in a man like him, splayed,
A statue he carved from the forest wood.

The 'man like him, splayed' is a reference to Jesus on the cross. In a revealing strophe the poet notes the panic of the frightened Christians seeking divine aid in the wake of the eclipse. He describes a religious procession in the streets of Rome in which statues, presumably of Jesus and Mary, were borne on the shoulders of the devout:

The idolaters kneel and bow down even as they stumble;
Destroy the platforms of the idols and bring dread to their palaces;
They have gathered to place the statue on their shoulders;
They carry it, since it cannot walk.

Other hymnists in the Anaw family of Rome included Benjamin b. Abraham, the physician (13th c.), and his son Zedekiah (d. after 1280), also a physician, and their contemporaries Abraham b. Joab, Moses b. Abraham and Yeḥiel b. Yequtiel who wrote in Spanish quantitative metres. Following is Zedekia b. Benjamin's entreaty (*teḥinnah*) titled 'On the time of troubles'. In it he prays for God's help from the accusations of the Franciscan monks:[24]

They mock me; with contempt they remove
  My mantle of many colours that I wore.

[23] Schirmann, *Le-Toledot Ha-Širah*, ii. 39–43.

[24] Schirmann, *Mivḥar Ha-Širah*, p. 100.

They are like worshippers of idols, these priests of paganism;
They act abominably, making false charges with lying deceit;
Like the contentious priest [Hos. 4: 4] they demand tithes and gifts;
They exalt themselves over me and devise strategies against me.

The phrase 'they remove / My mantle of many colours [Gen. 37: 3] that I wore' charges that the Franciscans are now claiming to be the 'true Israel' (*verus Israel*).

Anan b. Marino

From Siponto, another Jewish centre of learning in the tenth and eleventh centuries, came the synagogue poet Anan b. Marino, from whom only one hymn for the close of the Sabbath has been preserved. Many of Siponto's scholars were students of Ha'yyay Ga'on at the Pumpeditha academy in Babylon. Anan's *piyyuṭ* is in the form of a personal appeal to Elijah, urging him to hasten the redemption of Israel. According to rabbinic tradition, Elijah was expected to announce the coming of the Messiah at the close of the Sabbath, but not on the eve of the Sabbath or festival, so as not to disturb Jewish families in their preparations for the holy days (*bPes* 13a and *b'Eruv* 43b). The hymn opens with a rhyming quatrain followed by strophes of tercets. The last two cola of the quatrain are repeated after each strophe:[25]

O prophet Elijah, how long will you tarry?
The eyes of the dear lad [Israel] hang upon you and await your coming . . .
There is a time to be silent and a time to speak; how long will you hold your tongue . . .
Be brave, prepare and arm yourself, go to the son of Jesse.
Tell him that the flogged can only whisper their complaints to God;
Perhaps he will hasten his advent and save me from my seducers . . .
The wise and their followers who are privy to hidden truth
Know this from tradition:
The end will not come by the word of man!

The 'hidden truth' is that the Messiah will come only at the urging of Elijah the Prophet.

Yeraḥmiel b. Solomon and Yeḥiel b. Yekutiel

The visit of Abraham Ibn Ezra to Italy from 1140 to 1147 or 1148 was instructive for the cantor-poets in the region, who now dispensed with the Qilliric rhyme of two root-consonants and favoured the prosody of two metrically

[25] Habermann, *Toledot Ha-Piyyuṭ*, ii. 24–6.

balanced hemistichs after Hispanic models. Early in the twelfth century, Yeraḥmiel b. Solomon was the first Italian hymnist to compose in quantitative metre. In the following century the practice became commonplace, and skilled poets like Yeḥiel b. Yekutiel (d. *c.*1280), a member of Italy's venerable Anaw family, succeeded in arranging an ethical treatise of 175 cola in a consistent *ha-merubbeh* metre: – –v/– – –v/– – –v. The treatise, *Ma'alot Ha-Middot*, is modelled after an earlier work by Ha'yyay Ga'on titled *Musar Haskel*, and is similar in theme to the *Qa'arat Kesef* of the thirteenth-century Provençal poet Yehosef Ha-'Ezovi. Yekutiel's opus was probably chanted in the synagogue during the month of 'Elul and the Ten Days of Repentance. It is written in the first person singular, with the author confessing his frailties and lamenting his fate. His diatribe against the vagaries of personified Time is reminiscent of similar conceits in Judeo-Arabic poetry. Armed with his trust in God and relying on 'wisdom' and 'reason', he can overcome Time's treachery and help himself and others:[26]

Behold a man buffeted by Time, filled with anguish, overcome with shame and scorn . . .
Men who saw me were amazed and stupefied . . .
They counselled courage [saying]: . . .
Although Time has deceived you like a cheat,
Let your wisdom's spear strike it down . . .
Array your reason to stand against it
And take refuge under cover of the Dweller on High . . .
I now resolve to follow in the way of the wise and learned;
I shall instruct myself first . . . then teach the many others.

Following his resolve, the poet harks back to an earlier time and regrets his failure as a father to his children. This personal tragedy is his reason for writing this poetic treatise, which, he hopes, will provide ethical guidance and instruction to parents:

My sons are gone, no more;
They are strangers to me; they denounce me!
They have left me and I am alone . . .
They refused my counsel and went their way . . .
I mourned for them . . . and was ashamed . . .
Reasonable thoughts then turned me around;
They said, 'Have mercy on the foolish;
Remove the stumbling-block before them.'
This is the reason for this treatise in which I gathered
Sayings true and honest from Scripture and the sages . . .
To teach children respect and guard them from Time's sorrow.

[26] Ibid. 33–9.

Moses b. Isaac da Rieti

Born in 1398 in Rieti, R. Moses lived for a time in Rome, where he was the local rabbi and served as private physician to Pope Pius II. He died in Rome after 1460. His *Miqdaš me'aṭ* (Little Sanctuary) composed when he was 24, is a syllabic-metre Hebrew adaptation in *terza rima* of Dante's *Divina Commedia*. Whether Moses da Rieti was the first Jewish hymnist in Italy to employ syllabic metre is questionable in light of the discovery of syllabic-metre Hebrew poetry in the Cairo Geniza. Da Rieti's *Miqdaš me'aṭ* was to influence the Corfiote poet Moses Ha-Kohen, author of a *terza rima* hymn on the festival of Purim. Selected cantos from *Miqdaš me'aṭ* were chanted in the Italian synagogue service. Following is a selection from Part II, Canto I:[27]

> The holy chamber [*heykhal qodeš*] was located in the middle,
> The heads of the creatures and the concealed light
> Adorned its walls, extending to the edges.
>
> I saw it (the light) curling in the heights;
> There was no limit to the troops verging towards it,
> Ascending and descending the ladder's steps . . .
>
> Then I beheld the image of the chamber
> And its court inhabited by a growing throng;
> Master and student sat at their places.
>
> They discoursed on the Torah armed with talmudic
> Weapons in their hands, nor were they without
> The legends [*'aggadah*] that gladden the heart.

LANGUAGE AND STYLE IN ITALY

Rhyme and Metre

The rhyme of the Apulians was a modified Qilliric pattern with the rhymeme in the final syllable only. Terminal rhyme, replacing Qillir's two-root-letter rhyme, was already in vogue during the late classical era. One of its practitioners in the latter period was Phinehas Ha-Kohen, who probably found it too difficult to emulate Qillir's demanding practice. Solomon Ha-Bavli reintroduced the 'pure' two-root-letter Qilliric rhyme, and apparently influenced Elia b. Šema'yah to follow his example. Later Italian poets discontinued this practice.

The early Italian hymns featured a word metre in which each colon comprised a fixed number of units. This practice, which Ha-Bavli continued, was

[27] Schirmann, *Mivḥar Ha-Širah*, pp. 195–7.

a change from earlier eastern prosody of stress metre, wherein each colon presented an equal number of heavily stressed units. The latter included semantically significant words and excluded conjunctions, pronouns and adverbs joined by hyphens. In the Italian 'pure' stress all words were counted, regardless of their significance.[28]

The Italians also experimented with variations in syllabic metre. Following is an example of this by an anonymous Italian hymnist lamenting the anti-Jewish decrees of the Byzantine emperor Basileus (867–86). The hymn, in rhyming couplets, comprises lines of eight syllables:[29]

'Anas 'oti melekh 'edom
Bi-šma' yisra'el paṣ li dom . . .

Kenesiyyot nataṣ raša'
Lo' hitpallel ba-hem noša'.

Edom's king has violated me
After my 'Hear O Israel' he struck me dumb . . .

The wicked man destroyed the synagogues;
None survives to pray in them.

Another sample of syllabic metre from Apulia is seen in a *zemer*, *Hiddaleh dallat 'ummi*, by Amittai b. Šefatyah, preserved in the Cairo Geniza. It, too, is constructed in rhyming couplets and eight-syllable metre.[30] The syllabic metre of the Apulians anticipated the later Hispanic metrics. However, it is unlikely that there was a direct influence, given that the Spaniards, unlike the Italians, made a distinction between the *šewa' mobile* and the *ḥataf*, with the latter serving as a short syllable and the other morphemes as long syllables. These distinctions were based on models from long and short syllables in Arabic poetry, even as the several metric configurations utilized by Ibn Nagrela and his contemporaries were based on the work of al-Khalīl Ibn Aḥmad who codified the rules of Arabic poetry. However, the discovery in the Cairo Geniza of poetry in syllabic metre composed in ninth-century Italy necessitates a revision of earlier opinions that this practice was first introduced in Hebrew poetry by the fifteenth-century Italian hymnist Moses da Rieti.[31]

The language of the Apulians is based primarily on Scripture and is relatively free of neologisms and allusions. Occasionally, Amittai would refer to rabbinic sources. Ha-Bavli, too, modelled his hymns mostly on biblical sources, which he complemented periodically with Aramaic usages. His neologisms and allusions to rabbinic sources are evident, but are not pervasive.

[28] Fleischer, *Piyyuṭey . . . Ha-Bavli*, pp. 71–94.
[29] *Megillat 'Aḥima'aṣ*, p. 106; Fleischer, 'Hebrew Liturgical Poetry', p. 419.
[30] Amittai, *Širey*, p. 129.
[31] Pagis, *Ḥidduš U-Masoret*, pp. 294–9; Fleischer, 'Hebrew Liturgical Poetry', p. 420.

THE PRINCIPAL ITALIAN GENRES

ʿAvodah

One of the earliest Italian *ʿavodot* is *ʾAdderet tilbošet*, by Solomon Ha-Bavli. Characteristic of Ha-Bavli's neo-classicism, his *ʿavodah* is devoid of rhyme and its strophes are defined by the letters of the alphabet. In this practice he follows the model of Yose b. Yose's *ʿavodot*, *ʾAzkir gevurot ʾeloha*, and *ʾAttah konanta ʿolam be-rov ḥesed*. Like Yose's hymns in this genre, Ha-Bavli's divide the work into two parts, beginning with a narrative introduction relating Israel's sacred history until the time of Moses and Aaron and closing with an account of the Aaronic High Priest serving in the Temple on the Day of Atonement.[32] Later treatments of the *ʿavodah* by Mešullam b. Kalonymus include *ʾAmiṣ koaḥ* and *ʾAsoḥeaḥ nifleʾotekha*, both preserved in the Franco-German prayer-book. The former is, like Yose's and Ha-Bavli's, without rhyme, and the strophes are delineated by the letters of the alphabet. Mešullam's *ʾAsoḥeaḥ nifleʾotekha* is built in rhyming quatrains which define the strophes. His model for this practice may have been the classical poet Eleazar Qillir, who composed *ʿavodot* in rhyme. Mešullam also divides his *ʿavodot* in the style of his predecessors.[33]

Qeduštaʾ

As far as is known, only one *qeduštaʾ* from the early Italian period has been preserved. Amittai b. Šefatiah's epithalamium *qeduštaʾ*, *ʾAttah huʾ we-loʾ yittammu šenotekha*, is constructed in the classical manner, albeit with some minor variations. Instead of the standard set of quatrains in the *mešullaš* section, Amittai chooses tercets. He dispenses with the *qiqlar* and strays from tradition by signing his name after the alphabetic acrostic in the *rahiṭ*, 'Amittai *ḥazaqʾ*. He also deviates from the classical form of the genre by signing his name in three places (in the *mešullaš*, the *rahiṭ*, and in poem No. 5). His citations from Scripture are not related to the weekly lesson because the hymn has a specific purpose (celebrating a wedding) that is unrelated to the Sabbath Torah reading.[34]

Yoṣer

The early Italian hymnists were less inclined to follow classical models in their *yoṣer* than in their *qeduštaʾ* compositions. Part of the reason is that, unlike the *qeduštaʾ*, the several components of the *yoṣer* had not been standardized in

[32] Fleischer, *Piyyuṭey . . . Ha-Bavli*, pp. 38–43.
[33] *Maḥazor Le-Yamim*, ii. 435 ff., 447 ff.
[34] Amittai, *Širey*, pp. 9–31.

Amittai's time. It is also likely that the Italians, like some *ge'onim* in Iraq, were reluctant to add embellishments to the traditional benedictions of the *šema'*. The Italian hymnists who chose to compose *yoṣerot* had several options given the available variations in this genre.

Contrary to the choices of the Hispanics, who preferred the lyrical sections in the *yoṣer*, such as the *me'orah* ('Praised are You, Lord, creator of lights'), the *'ahavah* ('Praised are You, Lord, who loves His people Israel'), and the *mi kamokha* ('Who is like You, Lord?'), the Italian hymnists favoured the longer *guf ha-yoṣer* and *zulat* because they allowed greater opportunities for impressing the congregations who employed them. The *guf ha-yoṣer*, *zulat* and *'ofan* are the only three components in the early Apulian *yoṣer* complex. The *'ofan* (based on Isa. 6: 3 and Ezek. 3: 12) presumably appealed to the Italians because it afforded an opportunity to speculate on the divine 'chariot throne'.

The customary construction of the *guf ha-yoṣer*, beginning with Qillir, was in sets of three tercets interrupted by a choral response ending with the unit *qadoš*. The *yoṣer* for Šabbat Ḥatanim by Zevadiah, *'Afa'er šem melekh be-mošav maqhalotaw*, follows this earlier model. Amittai, in his *guf ha-yoṣer* for the Sabbath, *'Asiḥah be-divrey nifle'otekha*, deviates from this pattern by adding a *qadoš* refrain after each strophe. Presumably, his purpose in this effort was to allow for wider congregational participation in the synagogue service. Unlike the late eastern synagogues, the Apulians did not make use of a professional choir and were content to allow only the precentor to chant the prayers. In lieu of a choir, the Italians enlisted the aid of the congregation by adding response refrains to the standard poetic embellishments of the benedictions of the *šema'* and *'amidah*. Following is a sample from the five-strophe *'ofan*, *'Er'ellim u-mal'akhim*, by Amittai with a internal, rondeau-type refrain chanted by the congregation at the end of each strophe.[35]

Angels and messengers
Sanctify and bless
The King of kings.

They prepare and make ready
Their wings, a shelter;
Each day they enthrone
The King of kings.

The extraordinary efforts of the Apulians to involve the congregation in hymnic responses is seen in two *zemarim* (songs) by Amittai preserved in the Cairo Geniza. The non-Hebrew refrains repeated by the congregation in the *zemarim* are *Diqlo diqlo laḥ* and *Hiddaleh let dallah*. It is likely that the

[35] David, *Širey Zevadiah*, pp. 53–60; Amittai, *Širey*, pp. 25–31, 106; Fleischer, *Ha-Yoṣerot*, pp. 643–4.

language of the refrains is a contemporary Apulian vernacular with which the congregation was thoroughly familiar.[36]

Solomon Ha-Bavli has left us three *yoṣerot*. His *ʾOmeṣ dar ḥazaqim*, for the Sabbath, is built in a manner similar to the style of Amittai's *ʾAsiḥah be-divrey nifleʾotekha*, with choral refrains attached to each strophe. In his *ʾEl nissaʾ*, Ha-Bavli changes course and adds a mere two *qadoš* couplet refrains to the twenty-four-strophe hymn. There is a terse quality to this hymn, built in sets of cola comprising only two units. Ha-Bavli's third hymn in this genre is the magisterial *ʾOr yešaʿ meʾuššarim*, for Passover. This much-imitated poem is built in rhyming quatrains, with closing scriptural verses spanning the complete book of Canticles. The influence of Qillir is much in evidence. Like his mentor, Ha-Bavli adds a transitional set of strophes, the *silluq*, which connects the *guf ha-yoṣer* to the *ʾofan*. He also revives the Qilliric practice of the two root-consonant rhyme. However, unlike Qillir (and Amittai) the independent-minded Ha-Bavli builds his *ʾOr yešaʿ* in quatrains (not tercets) and omits the *qadoš* refrains. Presumably the choral component in this hymn was in the congregation responding with the scriptural citation from Canticles at the end of each strophe.[37]

ʾOfan

Echoes from Jewish mysticism are heard in Amittai's *ʾAttah ʾelohey ha-ruḥot* and David b. Huna's *ʾofan* for Passover, *Gan naʿul ʾussefu ʾerʾellim*. Decoding the latter hymn requires a knowledge of the *heykhalot* literature to which the poet's congregation was undoubtedly privy. In the eight-strophe hymn in quatrains, God is Israel's sought-after beloved. The poet's language and imagery are drawn largely from Canticles:[38]

> The *ʾerʾellim* [angels] were assembled in the sealed garden;
> There they play with Your shoots [Cant. 4: 12],
> Nard and crocus spread out in the valleys;
> Garden springs pulsating in their flow.
>
> Awaken, north wind, blow upon my garden;
> I entered the bower and drank my wine;
> My sleep flows on and my God protects me;
> I have put away my flute, the voice of my song . . .
>
> He who lives in the heights, His speech is most sweet;
> Where has He gone; I seek after Him in the streets;
> He has come down to raise me from the depths;
> I will praise Him in the thunderous choir.

[36] Amittai, *Širey*, pp. 128–9; Fleischer, 'Hebrew Liturgical Poetry', p. 424.
[37] Fleischer, *Piyyuṭey . . . Ha-Bavli*, pp. 191–223.
[38] Schirmann, *Mivḥar Ha-Širah*, pp. 17–18; Habermann, *Toledot Ha-Piyyuṭ*, ii. 19–20.

Zulat

Innovations in other components of the *yoṣer* are credited to Amittai in his five surviving *zulatot.* In eastern congregations the theme of the *zulat* centred on the weekly reading from the Prophets. Amittai appears to be unaware of this practice, or he is unwilling to follow it. The themes of his *zulatot* are diverse. One of the more colourful in this genre is his *'Az bi-hyot kallah*, for Šabbat Ḥatanim, when the bridegroom is called to the reading of the Torah. The epithalamium-style *zulat* is cast in the form of a dialogue and celebrates God's deliverance of the maiden Israel held captive by Putiel, Egypt's guardian angel. Based mostly on Ezek. 16, the hymn opens with God sending His messenger Moses to Putiel seeking the release of Israel, who has now come of age to be betrothed. When, after a heated exchange with Moses, the angel refuses, God intervenes, punishing Egypt and rescuing Israel, whom He takes for His bride:[39]

When the bride dwelt in the strange land
And matured, reaching the age of nubility,
He appointed an agent to set her free,
Since her girlhood days were over.
The messenger came to speak to Egypt's angel:
'Make not light of this matter!
Her bridegroom made you guardian to give her the best;
How can you permit yourself to enslave her, embitter her life?'

Putiel replied, 'Deceiving her now
Will only spoil her; you cannot help her;
Go your way and leave her be;
Delude her not, let her go back to work.'

THE PRINCIPAL FRANCO-GERMAN POETS

Simeon b. Isaac

The first hymnist known to have been born in Germany was Simeon b. Isaac of Mainz, author of *yoṣerot*, *qerovot* and *seliḥot.* Like Solomon Ha-Bavli and the classical poets, he favoured a carefully crafted word metre and at times loaded his hymns with neologisms, ellipses and allusions in Qilliric fashion. Like his predecessors, he embellished his hymns with anadiplosis—word repetition linking two strophes—and on occasion, as in his *seliḥah*, *'Ewili ha-mat'eh margiz*,[40] he employed internal rhyme. He is eclectic in his rhyming

[39] Amittai, *Širey*, p. 86

[40] Habermann, *Piyyuṭey Rabbi Šim'on*, p. 148.

tastes: his *seliḥah*, *'Akh bekha 'el*,[41] is in a modified free verse similar to pre-classical hymnody.

R. Simeon's *qedušta'ot* generally follow classical patterns, with occasional additions of *rešuyyot* and scriptural verses. The verses are set at the beginning, middle or end of his hymns. In the *guf ha-yoṣer*, *silluq*, *'ofan*, *zulat* and *ge'ullah* of his *'Ahuvekha 'ahevukha*, for Passover, he skilfully embeds into his strophes whole chapters from Canticles. This practice he probably learned from Solomon Ha-Bavli's *yoṣer*, *'Or yešaʿ me'uššarim*. The latter hymn was the likely model for R. Simeon's *yoṣer*. The Rhineland poet often expands on the verse with comments from rabbinic literature, as in the following from the *silluq*:[42]

> 'Your two breasts' [Cant. 4: 5]
> Are adorned with royalty and priesthood.

The referent is *Cant. Rabbah* 4: 5, ' "Your two breasts": these are Moses (royalty) and Aaron (priesthood).' A revealing aspect of the Rhineland poet is given in his *rešut*, *'Atiti le-ḥannenkha*, to a *qerovah* for the New Year. Here the rabbi-poet confesses the fear that he may be unworthy to lead his congregation in prayer:[43]

> I come beseeching with a heart torn and agitated;
> I seek Your mercy like a beggar at the door;
> Take pity on us; judge us not harshly
> Lord, open my lips . . .

Although Carolingian Jewish merchants generally prospered, restrictive decrees against them were not uncommon. They were accused of collusion with Muslims in the destruction of the Church of the Holy Sepulchre in Jerusalem by the Caliph al-Ḥākim, and of co-operating with Judaizing movements within the Church. In 1012 Emperor Henry II expelled the Jews from Mainz, which ultimately led to anti-Jewish excesses and forced baptisms. It is likely that Simeon's *yoṣer*, *'El 'el ḥay 'arannen*, was written against this background:[44]

> Exile overcomes me, poverty and emptiness,
> When I see baseness exalted among men;
> Oppressed by lying enemies seeking to excise Your name from
>   my lips;
> They forbid me entrance to Your mansion.
>   Do not keep silent!

The 'mansion' is a reference to the reward of the faithful in the world to come. The refrain 'Do not keep silent' was repeated by the congregation after

41 Habermann, *Piyyuṭey Rabbi Šimʿon*, p. 158. 42 Ibid. 27–33. 43 Ibid. 107.
44 Blumenkranz, 'Germany', pp. 172–4; Habermann, *Piyyuṭey Rabbi Šimʿon*, pp. 14, 40–1.

each strophe. It is likely that the later choral responses in the Franco-German synagogue were based on Simeon b. Isaac's model. Combined with this lament is the hope for national restoration in his *yoṣer*, *Melekh 'amon ma'amorkha*, for the New Year:[45]

> May the *šofar* in France and Spain proclaim the holy time
> When the Eternal will renew the scattered in all directions,
> And they will bow down to the Lord at the holy mountain [Zion].

On happier occasions the poet participated in his congregation's wedding celebrations. He is probably the first of the central European hymnists to compose epithalamia in the form of *rešuyyot* (permissions) preceding the marriage ceremony. His serious tone in this genre is in contrast to the Hispanic epithalamia, with their broad references to Canticles and the joys of love. Simeon focuses instead on God's mighty act as matchmaker, in his *Merešut šokhen ʿad*:[46]

> He prepares for each man a suitable mate according to his merit . . .
> It was as difficult to mate them as was dividing the sea for Israel.

The latter is based on *Lev. Rabbah* 8. 1.

Rabbenu Geršom b. Judah

A younger contemporary of Simeon b. Isaac, Rabbenu Geršom was personally affected by the anti-Jewish agitation in 1012, when his son was forcibly converted to Christianity and died shortly thereafter. Echoes of this tragedy are heard in his *seliḥah*, *'Attah mi-qedem 'eloheynu*, for Ḥanukkah:[47]

> In his folly, the Greek and his evil minions
> Sought to make Your people forget Your sweet Name;
> He planned to banish the children at play [Israel];
> He fell and was crushed and died afflicted with illness . . .

He is more direct in his reference to contemporary events in the hymn, *'Eleykha niqra'*:[48]

> They have decreed that we no longer call upon the Lord's name,
> Our redeemer, called the God of hosts;
> My Beloved, all radiant and ruddy, distinguished among ten
> thousands;
> [They would have us] despise His word and expunge Him.

45 Fleischer, *Širat Ha-Qodeš*, p. 458; Habermann, *Piyyuṭey Rabbi Šimʿon*, pp. 47–9.
46 Habermann, *Piyyuṭey Rabbi Šimʿon*, p. 184.
47 Habermann, *Toledot Ha-Piyyuṭ*, ii. 181–2.
48 Habermann, *Sefer*, p. 16.

R. Geršom seeks solace in memories of the Jerusalem Temple; and in a moving elegy, *'Avadnu me-'ereṣ ṭovah*, he mourns its destruction and the loss of the national home, even as he takes comfort in the Torah and its study:[49]

The holy city and its precincts are a prey and reproach;
All its precious wares are sunk and sequestered,
And only this Torah has remained.

R. Geršom was also the author of some ten *seliḥot*, all patterned after earlier classical and eastern models.[50]

Joseph Ṭov Elem

Joseph b. Samuel Ṭov Elem (Bonfils) was a contemporary of Simeon b. Isaac and Rabbenu Geršom. Born in Provence, Ṭov Elem lived in Narbonne, Limoges and Anjou. A respected rabbinic authority whose opinions were cited by RaŠI and the Tosafists, he is the author of hymns in classical and late eastern genres. Of special interest is his first-time use of the pseudo-*muwashshaḥ* for the French synagogue. Presumably, he was influenced by the Hispanics in this rhyming practice, since there is no evidence that it was employed by the early Italians. This rhyming pattern was later to be used by Meir b. Isaac of Worms who also experimented with quantitative metres. Following is part of Ṭov Elem's *seliḥah* for the Fast of Gedaliah, *'Ayaḥed ṣuri*. The hymn's opening verse, 'Hear O Israel' (Deut. 6: 4), is repeated in a refrain:[51]

The entangled thorns [i.e. the nations] who worship the idol [lit. Molokh]
May their mouths be stopped and they be cast like refuse in the streets;
He is glorified among His holy ones who circle [the heavens];
See, a king will reign in righteousness.

Ṭov Elem revived the long-neglected practice of composing *ma'arivim*, the six-strophe festival evening hymn, mentioned above. There is no evidence that the early hymnists in Italy wrote *ma'arivim*: it is presumed that precentors there were discouraged from this practice by a laity eager to join their families for the festive evening meal. Ṭov Elem also experimented with the newer constructions of the *guf ha-yoṣer*, pioneered by Amittai and Solomon Ha-Bavli. Instead of the traditional set of three tercet strophes followed by a tercet refrain ending with the word *qadoš*, the French poet and his colleagues enlarged both strophes and refrains in ratios of seven to four or five to two. In Ṭov Elem's *guf ha-yoṣer*, *'Arannen ḥasdekha la-boqer*, for the second Sabbath

[49] Habermann, *Toledot Ha-Piyyuṭ*, ii. 181.
[50] Ibid. 180.
[51] *Seder Ha-Seliḥot . . . Liṭa'*, pp. 162–3.

after Passover, the ratio of strophes to refrains is seven to four. In the hymn the poet deftly combines the themes of both holy days and closes with a celebration of married life and Sabbath rest:[52]

With His hands He made him [Adam] that he may prosper,
Gave him dominion over all in east and west;
He said, 'Man cannot be at peace alone!'
From his rib He removed a fruitful vine . . .
A day of rest He gave to the scattered folk [Israel] . . .
The Lord is robed and girded with strength

Menaḥem b. Makhir

A nephew of Rabbenu Geršom, R. Menaḥem b. Makhir of Regensburg, rabbinic authority and hymnist, witnessed the anti-Jewish excesses on the eve of the First Crusade in 1096 and the years following, and composed an elegy, *'Evel 'a'orer*, lamenting the havoc wrought among Rhineland Jewry. The elegy is both a supplication for divine aid and a historical record, complete with dates of the tragic events. The literary figures in the hymn are taken largely from Lamentations and adapted for contemporary use. The elegy is built in rhymed couplets with repeated alternating refrains modelled after classical forms:[53]

They humiliated my saints, profaned my sanctuary, degraded my holy places, alas!
In the year 4856 [1096], the eleventh year of the cycle 256, woe is me! . . .

The worshippers of Molokh waged war against God's forces and ruled the region, alas!
The unruly and unkempt [tyrannized] the pure Torah, woe is me! . . .

Clothed in vengeance, arise, stand and resist;
In the heights above, devise judgment for the fallen,
And restore the *šekhinah* to its place.

The term 'worshippers of Molokh' is a commonplace reference to Christians by Franco-German and Byzantine hymnists.[54]

In contrast to the sombre tone and angry lament in his elegy, R. Menaḥem celebrates, in his *baqqašah*, *Mah 'ahavti me'on beytekha*, the festive water-drawing ceremony in the Jerusalem Temple on the first day of Tabernacles. The hymn was part of the Franco-German ritual, where it was chanted on

[52] Ber, *Seder*, p. 729. [53] Habermann, *Sefer*, p. 63.
[54] Zunz, *Die synagogale Poesie*, p. 467.

that feast-day. The hymns' superscription in the 1331 Nuremberg Prayer-Book reads, 'A "Flute" [*ḥalil*] for the Water-Drawing Celebration.' Its theme is based on rabbinic accounts (in *mSukk* 5. 1–2) of the celebration in Temple times, enhanced by an orchestra of flutes. The *baqqašah* is built in six strophes of rhyming sestets with the name of the poet in the acrostic. The following is the second strophe:[55]

> Flute-playing [was offered] at the water-drawing, a precious practice from earliest times,
> On five days or six during the feast celebrated by the purchased congregation [Israel];
> At the conclusion of the first festival day they descended to the constructed court of women,
> Where they made a great enactment as decreed by custom;
> The city rejoiced and was pleased as a peaceful river stretched wide;
> Upon [the city] ascended the families, the tribes of God.

The hymn closes with a plea to renew the days of old, when pilgrims travelled thrice-yearly to Jerusalem and appeared before the Lord. Like Ṭov Elem, Menaḥem b. Makhir experimented with pseudo-*muwashshaḥ* rhyming schemes, and his *'ofan*, *Mal'akhey ṣeva'ot be-ʿelṣon*, is constructed in quatrains with internal rhyme and a scriptural verse serving as the closing 'belt'.[56]

Meir b. Isaac

The innovative R. Meir b. Isaac, *šeliaḥ ṣibbur* (precentor) of Worms, was a contemporary of Menahem b. Makhir. R. Meir died in 1096, shortly before the Crusader action against Rhineland Jews, in which his wife and his son, Isaac, were murdered. He wrote *qerovot*, *šivʿatot* (for Šabbat Zakhor and Šabbat Parah), *maʿarivim* and *seliḥot* in both Hebrew and Aramaic. To the *maʿarivim* he added a seventh strophe called *bikur* or *tosefet*.[57] R. Meir was the first central European poet to compose in Judeo-Arabic quantitative metre. He is best remembered for his *ʿaqedot* (Binding of Isaac (Gen. 22) hymns), which he pioneered in European synagogue hymnography, and his poems in Aramaic, like the *'Aqdamut millin*, for the first day of Pentecost. His *ʿaqedah* hymns struck a chord in the hearts of European Jews during the fearful days of 1096 and thereafter. Isaac's resolve to be sacrificed on Mount Moriah was seen a victory for the Jewish faithful who died sanctifying God's name during the Crusader outrages in the Rhineland. Following is the closing strophe of R. Meir's *ʿaqedah*, *'El har ha-mor givʿat horayah*, for the Day of Atonement in which God assures Abraham of His promise:[58]

55 Habermann, *Toledot Ha-Piyyuṭ*, ii. 182–4.
56 Fleischer, *Širat Ha-Qodeš*, p. 438.
57 Ibid. 466.
58 *Maḥazor Le-Yamim*, ii. 558–9.

I swear by My might,
That by this, your deed
I will hear the cry of your sons in pain . . .

'Aqdamut millin, initially written to introduce the Aramaic translation of the Torah lesson, continued to be chanted in Franco-German synagogues long after the practice of translating into Aramaic was discontinued. Its fifty-two couplets in monorhyme constitute a complete alphabetic acrostic, the author's name and a closing prayer, 'May he [the author] persevere in the Torah and in good deeds, amen; be strong and of good courage.'

Ephraim b. Isaac

The respected halakhic authority and hymnist of exceptional talent, Ephraim b. Isaac of Regensburg, lived through the anti-Jewish decrees of 1137 and the atrocities of the Second Crusade in 1146–7. He studied in France under Rabbenu Jacob Tam and before settling in Regensburg—where he served on its appellate court (*beyt din*)—he lived in Speyer and Worms. Author of some thirty-two liturgical hymns, including *yoṣerot* and *seliḥot*, R. Ephraim is predominantly sombre in his themes and reflects the anger, fears and hopes of his congregation. In a moving *yoṣer* for the Sabbath of Passover, *'Eloha bekha 'eḥaveq*, R. Ephraim trumpets Israel's resolve to remain faithful to its God, despite the attempts by Christians at conversion:[59]

He bows to one hung on a rack,
And counsels me to deny You,
And bend the knee to a block of wood;

I will not run to feed after him;
I know that he and his will be put to shame;
Harm awaits him who stands surety [for a stranger]!

'Hung on a rack' and a 'block of wood' are references to Jesus on the cross. The last line is based on Prov. 11: 15 and is interpreted by the poet as a warning against trusting 'strange' gods. In a revealing line from his *'ahavah* for Pentecost, *'Otekha kol ha-yom qiwwinu*, he struggles to remain hopeful of Israel's ultimate redemption:[60]

I am compelled to be exchanged [for another];
Moreover, forlorn is my trust
In the End of Days [redemption];
How long O Lord?

[59] Habermann, 'Piyyuṭey R. Ephraim . . . mi-Regensburg', p. 130.

[60] Ibid. 137.

Despite his doubts, in his *seliḥah*, *'Elohim 'adonay ḥeyli*, he affirms the conventional theodicy by blaming himself for his fate.[61]

> My affliction is in proportion to my sins;
> Sackcloth and ashes are my blanket,
> Therefore I am deeply moved.

R. Ephraim's mastery of the poetic craft is seen in his ten hymns composed in quantitative metre, after the manner of the Hispanics. In his *baqqašah*, *'Ašer 'eyn lo temurah*,[62] he experiments with an uncommon metre, – –v/ – – –v/– –v/– – –v, a variation of the familiar *ha-'arokh*: – – –v/– –v/– – –v/ – –v (both are to be read from right to left). In this usage R. Ephraim may have been influenced by Samuel Ibn Nagrela, who employs a similar metre in his liturgical hymn *'Ašer naṭah šeḥaqim*.[63] True to Hispanic practice, R. Ephraim's *baqqašah* is constructed in two metrically identical halves, after the *qaṣīdah* model. His example in composing hymns with quantitative metrics was followed by his contemporaries R. Barukh b. Samuel of Mainz and R. Jacob b. Meir Tam.

R. Ephraim's treatment of the *zulat* varies from eastern models in its change of focus. Like other hymns in this genre for the Sabbath by Rhineland poets, R. Ephraim's deals with Israel's travail in exile. Following is the refrain in his *zulat*, *'Eli, 'eli lammah*, for the fifth Sabbath after Passover:[64]

> My God, my God
> Why are my sighs hidden from You?
> Behold, I am a dove afflicted.

The influence of Golden Age Hispanic poets is clearly evident in the poetry of R. Ephraim. Following the model of the Regensburg hymnist Solomon Ibn Gabirol, he plays on words—here 'length' (*le-'orekh*) and 'your light' (*le-'orekh*)—to recontextualize verses from Scripture for emphasis. Following is an example from his *zulat*, *'Elohim lo' 'eda' zulatekha*:[65]

> How long will I be oppressed?
> They have put stumbling-blocks in my path
> The nations who walk its length [*le-'orekh*].

The last line is from Isa. 60: 3, 'Nations shall come to your light' (*le-'oreḵh*). Likewise in the *zulat*, *'Eli, 'eli lammah*, he prays:

> Cast away the exile that it may not be found;
> Bring light to the eyes of the formidable [Israel],
> For they are overcast [*ki 'afilot hemmah*].

[61] Habermann, 'Piyyuṭey R. Ephraim . . . mi-Regensburg', p. 147.
[62] Ibid. 159.
[63] Ibn Nagrela, *Ben Tehillim*, p. 322.
[64] Habermann, 'Piyyuṭey R. Ephraim . . . mi-Regensburg', p. 135.
[65] Ibid. 132.

The latter is based on Exod. 9: 32, 'But the wheat and the emmer were not hurt [from the hail], for they ripen late [*ki 'afilot hemmah*].'

Ephraim b. Jacob

Born in 1133, Ephraim b. Jacob of Bonn, eminent halakhist and author of *novellae* on the Talmud, kept a record in his *Memorbuch* of the atrocities committed during the Second Crusade in 1147. He is the author of some thirty Hebrew and Aramaic synagogue hymns in several genres. In addition to his moving *ʿaqedah*, *'Et 'avotay 'ani mazkir*, he wrote an *'ahavah*, *'Ayummati 'ahavtikh*, in the form of a dialogue in alternating strophes between God and Israel.[66]

[GOD:]
My beloved, My mercies have contained My anger, now reversed;
The time to be gracious to you has come;
Why do you say, 'My hope is lost!'? . . .
If I forget you I forsake My right arm;
Is God's hand unable to save the dearest?
Is He not permitted to treat the son of the loved one [Jacob] as
the first born? [cf. Deut. 21: 16]

[ISRAEL:]
My fair Beloved, I know that You can gladden me;
In my hand is the marriage document [*ketubah*],
A reliable witness of the purchase inscribed,
But my hopes continue to be frustrated;
Every day I am always in distress;
I have been killed for Your sake, slaughtered and made desolate,
But my love is as strong as death.

The form of the hymn is styled after the dialogue *'ahavah*, *Segullati melukhah 'azartikh*, attributed to Mešullam b. Moše (11th c.) of the Kalonymides. The dialogue as rhetorical device, observed earlier in the work of Amittai, was often employed by the Franco-Germans.

In the *'ofan* to his *yoṣer*, *'El 'eḥad yaḥid*, R. Ephraim of Bonn permits himself to speculate on the divine chariot throne. This is in line with the practice of the Franco-German rabbi-poets, who were less reticent in this respect than their classical and late eastern predecessors. In the *'ofan*, R. Ephraim paraphrases the legend of the angel Sandalfon, who approaches the chariot throne bearing a crown from the collective prayers of Israel. He elicits a promise from the crown that it will ascend and rest upon God's head.[67]

[66] Habermann, 'Piyyuṭey R. Ephraim . . . mi-Bonn', pp. 234–6.

[67] Ibid. 241–2.

Sandalfon consults with Wisdom on fashioning knots for the crown,
Exacting a promise that it will ascend on the head of the Fearful and Awesome;
Fair is the crown made from the prayers of the pure,
Carried from the womb, praising the Lord, a people yet unborn. [Ps. 102: 19]

The poet's source is a rabbinic comment (in *bḤag* 14b) on Ezek. 1: 15, '"Now as I beheld the living creatures [*ḥayyot*], I saw a wheel on the earth beside the living creatures," [it means] a certain angel who stands on the earth and his head reaches unto the living creatures . . . his name is Sandalfon . . . he stands behind the chariot [throne] and weaves crowns for his Maker. But is it so? Is it not written [in Ezek. 3: 12]: "Blessed be the glory of the Lord from His place"? accordingly, no one knows His place! He [Sandalfon] pronounces the (Divine) Name over the crown, and it goes and rests on His head.'

Barukh b. Samuel

The mid-twelfth-century cantor-rabbi Barukh b. Samuel of Mainz is the author of hymns in the *yoṣer* series, *zemirot*, *rešuyyot* and *seliḥot*. A prominent halakhist and author of responsa in Jewish law, R. Barukh studied under R. Ephraim b. Isaac of Regensburg and served as circuit judge (*dayyan*) for Mainz and surrounding villages. Many of his hymns reflect the hardships of Rhineland Jewry during his lifetime. With the certainty that God is faithful, R. Barukh reminded the Lord of His obligation to His son Israel, in the *zulat*, *'Aḥarey nimkar*:[68]

Is it not the duty of a father to redeem his son;
Why have You forgotten him? Should You not take him back?
Yours is the obligation to redeem him again;
You are bound to protect him and put him on his feet.

Elaborating on the personalized rhetoric, in a *seliḥah* for the Day of Atonement, *'Ani hu' ha-šo'el*, the poet lectures the Father and urges Him to admit that His son is in need:

Redeem Your captive son and bless his substance;
When will You acknowledge him and say, 'I know, my son, I know;

I have seen you suffer, destroyed by pain;
I have heard your plaint, I will redeem and rescue.'[69]

[68] Habermann, 'Piyyuṭey R. Barukh', p. 83. [69] Ibid. 132.

Combining complaint with polemic in his *seliḥah*, *Beynot ʾarayot*, R. Barukh presses God for an answer to his insistent question:

How long will they boast before me,
Saying, 'This dead man [Jesus] is Your son!'[70]

There is a hint of provocation in the poet's tone. His question ('How long will they boast') is a rhetorical charge: 'How can You tolerate this perverse claim that the crucified Jesus is Your son?'

R. Barukh is also the author of an eloquent meditation, ostensibly for his personal use. Modelling his style on the meditations of Saʿadyah Gaʾon, the Mainz poet celebrates the virtues of personified Wisdom. The hymn, *Be-roʾš ʾilan mešoreret*, in the form of a metrically balanced *qaṣīdah*, is based on sources in rabbinic literature (*bBB* 26b–27a). In 1894 it was published as an appendix to the Babylonian Talmud.[71]

'On the treetop I sing, I am Wisdom of good fortune.'
Beneath lie the shepherds on a floor of pearl and onyx . . .
Within its [Wisdom's] shade live many with honour and beauty . . .
'Accept me O Lord like an [altar] offering, like a caring gift . . .
I, blessed Wisdom, sing perched on the treetop.'

FRANCO-GERMAN LANGUAGE AND STYLE

Rabbinic Usage

The language of R. Meir b. Isaac and his contemporaries was derived mostly from Scripture and a sizeable amount of rabbinic usages in Hebrew and Aramaic. For example, in his *ʾofan*, *Malʾakhey ṣevaʾot*, the term *bi-sqirah* is taken from the rabbinic account (in *bRH* 18a) of the New Year when all creatures pass before God, who views them with 'a simple glance' (*bi-sqirah ʾaḥat*).

Rhyme

In addition to the standard eastern rhyming patterns, the pseudo-*muwashshaḥ*, pioneered in France by Joseph Ṭov Elem, gained popularity in Rhine valley synagogues. Following is the last strophe in the *ʾofan* for the intermediate Sabbath of Tabernacles, *Malʾakhey ṣevaʾot*, by Meir b. Isaac.[72]

ʿAl kes ʾorah / watiq yošev be-tifʾarah
Le-ʿolamo mabbit bi-sqirah / mi kamoni yiqraʾ
ʿAl ḥayyot ha-qodeš mitgaʾeh
ʿAl ha-merkavah hadur we-naʾeh.

[70] Ibid. 147. [71] Ibid. 156–7. [72] *Maḥazor Le-Sukkot*, pp. 261–2.

Upon a throne of light / the Lord sits in glory;
He looks down upon his world with a glance; 'Who is My equal?'
 He proclaims;
 He is exalted above the holy creatures
 Surrounding the chariot [throne] magnificent and sublime.

Metre

Meir b. Isaac was the first central European poet to experiment with quantitative metre in the Hispanic style. His *seliḥah*, *Tefillah tiqqaḥ*, for the New Year evening service is built in rhymed hemistichs and its metre is a variation of the Judeo-Arabic *ha-marnin*, – –/– –v (*pe'ulim, nif'al*). This was to be his only halting attempt at quantitative metrics.[73] Other efforts at composing in the new metrics by R. Ephraim of Regensburg and Rabbenu Jacob b. Meir Tam (*c.*1100–71) were likewise unimpressive. When Abraham Ibn Ezra arrived in France in 1147 he came to know and admire Rabbenu Tam, a prominent rabbinic scholar and master of the academy at Champagne. The letters the two men exchanged reveal Ibn Ezra's disdainful reaction to Rabbenu Tam's attempt at metric poetry in Hispanic fashion:

Who let the Frenchman into poesy's mansion?
[Who permitted] the stranger to trample upon the holy place?
Were Jacob's verses as sweet as manna,
I am the sun, and I grow hot and they melt. [Exod. 16: 21][74]

Ibn Ezra's countryman Judah Al-Ḥarizi (12th c.) is even less charitable in his assessment of Franco-German hymnography, in his *Taḥkemoni* (No. 18, p. 190):

I have seen learned men among the French. They shine as the stars in heaven. Their hearts are as wide in wisdom as the broad sea. They leave nothing unstudied. However, I have paid attention to the poetry they write, and what I heard is not authentic [*lo' ken yedabberu*]; their themes are base, not worth the listening; their hymns are stiff as iron and loaded with sins like the scapegoat [Lev. 16: 8]. Their rhymes are full of errors. Seeking to innovate in poesy, their work is incomprehensible without a commentary. Some of them do write commentaries on their verse and these too require commentaries. Suffice it to say that their poems are strange and their metrics fragmented.

By the élite Hispanic standards of Ibn Ezra and Al-Ḥarizi, the Franco-Germans were as fault-ridden in the poetic art as was Eleazar Qillir, their model and mentor. In his response to Ibn Ezra's strictures, Rabbenu Tam admits as much. The allusion to Exod. 16: 21 was not lost on Rabbenu Tam, the younger man, who graciously conceded that he had met his master:

73 *Seder Ha-Seliḥot . . . Polin*, pp. 115–19.

74 Dinur, *Yisra'el Ba-Golah*, II. iii. 83.

I am a servant employed by Abraham [Ibn Ezra];
I bend the knee and bow before him!

Impressed by this allusion to Gen. 23: 17–18, but not to be outdone, Ibn Ezra replied with mock reproach:

Is it proper for the gallant shepherd of God's flock
To abase himself in writing before one despised?
Heaven forbid that the Lord's angel
Should bend the knee and bow before a vagrant.[75]

Polemics

A distinctive feature in the language of the Franco-Germans consists of the neologisms designating the ruling Christian power. Simeon b. Isaac and Ṭov Elem refer to them as 'oppressors' (*'oyen*); Simeon, Ṭov Elem and RaŠI call them 'liars' (*ṭofeley šeqer*); and R. Geršom labels them 'the wicked' (*beney 'awlah*). Ṭov Elem charges that they are idol-worshippers (*kore'ey le-molekh*) and his countryman Reuben b. Isaac (*c.*1300) states they they serve foolishness (*'ovedey hevel*). No less sanguine are the characterizations of the founder of Christianity. Judah b. Kalonymous of Mainz (*c.* 1200) calls him 'a detestable offspring' (*neṣer nig'al*) and his contemporary, David b. Mešullam of Speyer, refers to him as the 'child born in the heat of fornication' (*yiḥum ha-zimmah*). The crucifix is labelled by Judah b. Kalonymous as 'the hanging corpse' (*peger taluy*) while to Ṭov Elem and R. Geršom it is seen as 'the contemptible image' (*'eṣev nivzeh*).[76]

Undoubtedly, these visceral epithets reflect the agonies endured by Rhineland Jewry during the First and Second Crusades. They may also reflect a response to a Christian practice that Jews found particularly offensive. Adding insult to injury, Christian monks often forced Franco-German Jews in the twelfth and thirteenth centuries to hear missionizing sermons. Barukh b. Samuel in his *seliḥah*, *'Eleykha 'adonay nafši 'essa'*, hints at this practice.[77]

The children are ensnared by baptismal waters,
While the mother is sent to a burning place;
Without protection, her lips whisper; she pricks up her ears to the
scandalous tone.

The mother who was not 'ensnared' was consigned to the stake ('burning place') while her children continued to be exposed to the preaching of the monks hoping to convert them with 'baptismal waters'. A similar complaint is heard by the poet Zedekiah delli Mansi of Rome (Zedekiah b. Benjamin the

[75] Ibid.
[76] Zunz, *Die synagogale Poesie*, pp. 461, 467–8.
[77] Habermann, 'Piyyuṭey R. Barukh', p. 101; Chazan, *Daggers of Faith*, pp. 21–3.

Physician) (d. after 1280), who in a pseudo-*muwashshaḥ teḥinnah* laments the missionizing efforts of the Franciscan order:[78]

All manner of heretics appeared; ravaging foxes;
Barefoot, girded with sackcloth, they made claims;
With their staves they pushed their sweets upon the congregation;
They jeered at me; they build roads [for my ruin]. [Job 30: 12]

The widespread missionizing efforts of the thirteenth-century monks are also seen in the hymn *Ya'ir levavi* by the Provençal poet Isaac of Mont Ventoux (*Ha-Seniri*). He protests against their proselytizing practices, which appear ludicrous to him:

He places his faith and hope in a statue;
From wood that will not rot, he makes an image;
That which he cut from the forest,
He proclaims, 'God is your name!'[79]

The degree of success achieved by the monks' campaign among the Jews in central Europe has not as yet been determined.[80] It is known, however, that European Christians became converts to Judaism during the twelfth and thirteenth centuries. They included R. Abraham the Proselyte (mentioned in *Tosafot* on *bQid* 71a); the poet R. Yehosifyah the Proselyte; and R. Ovadiah the Proselyte of Normandy, author of the 'Scroll of Ovadiah' (*Megillat 'Ovadiah*).

In the year 1264 a young convert to Judaism named Abraham, from Augsburg, was emboldened to enter a disputation with the monks in a nearby city. In the course of the heated debate, young Abraham took a crucifix from the monks and broke it in half. This led to a mob attack upon the Jewish community, following which Abraham was brought back to Augsburg in chains and was subsequently burned at the stake. In observance of his martyrdom, a *seliḥah*, *Mah rav ṭuvekha*, was composed by R. Mordecai b. Hillel, author of the 'Mordecai Commentary' on the Talmud, and another, *'Akhalunu hamamunu*, by R. Moses b. Jacob. In the latter work the poet pays tribute to the young martyr:

'Who created courageous souls?
It is God who does no wrong.'
This is what the humble Abraham said to them . . .
Impetuous, he would have none of their soothing words,
And he said, 'I will not join you like the rabble;
I am inscribed in the Books and Records,
And I see the lights of Israel aglow.'[81]

[78] Schirmann, *Mivḥar Ha-Širah*, pp. 100–2.
[79] Habermann, *Toledot Ha-Piyyuṭ*, ii. 129.
[80] Chazan, *Daggers of Faith*, pp. 159–81.
[81] Habermann, *Sefer*, p. 189.

Philosophical Themes

Unlike the late eastern and Hispanic poets, central Europeans were not inclined to inject contemporary philosophy and science into their hymnography. While Sa'adyah Ga'on and Ibn Gabirol and their contemporaries could learn much from Arabic culture, which was at its summit during their lifetimes, there was little in central European civilization in the High Middle Ages that interested Franco-German Jews. Some few attempts to embrace religious philosophy and mysticism are preserved in hymns on God's unity (*širey ha-yiḥud*) and hymns on God's glory (*širey ha-kavod*). These emerge in the thirteenth century from the circle of German pietists (*ḥasidey 'aškenaz*). Following is part of an anonymous central European *šir ha-yiḥud*, reminiscent of the meditations on religious philosophy by Sa'adyah Ga'on, who appears to be its primary source:[82]

> You confuse the wise . . . Your might weakens the bravest heart . . .
> Their thoughts are not Yours . . . our Lord is exalted beyond limit;
> Hidden beyond hiding, borne aloft beyond bearing, concealed utterly . . .
> Quality and quantity do not pertain to Him; nothing is His equal . . .

In stressing God's transcendence, the Franco-German poet invokes some of the ten categories ('quality . . . quantity') in the writings of Aristotle, which were probably available to him through the writings of Sa'adyah Ga'on. Speculations in mysticism centred around the figures of R. Judah the Ḥasid of Worms (d. 1217), whose writings are preserved in the 'Book of the Devout' (*Sefer ḥasidim*), and his disciple, R. Eleazar b. Judah, of Worms, author of the halakhic code, the *Roqeaḥ*, and of kabbalistic tracts. It is likely that the hymn *'Anna', be-khoaḥ*, ascribed to the second-century rabbi Neḥunyah b. Ha-Qanah, originated in the circle of mystics identified with the Ḥasidim in medieval Germany (*ḥasidey 'aškenaz*). The seven-cola unrhymed hymn is in a six-unit word metre. Its initial letters make up the forty-two-letter Name of God. Below are the opening cola:[83]

> [O Lord,] we ask that with the might of Your powerful right hand, You set free the captive;
> O awesome God, accept the prayers of Your people, lift us up, make us pure.

[82] Sa'adyah Ga'on, *Siddur*, pp. 47–58; Habermann, *Toledot Ha-Piyyut*, ii. 204–5.
[83] Trachtenberg, *Jewish Magic*, pp. 94–5; Scholem, *Major Trends*, pp. 82–3.

Folk Legends

Cantor-rabbis in central Europe would often insert folk stories into the synagogue liturgy. Being themselves the rabbinic authorities in the region they had no hesitation about this practice, unlike their classical and late eastern predecessors, whom the rabbis chided for adding legends and mysteries to the standard liturgy. Among the popular folk legends in the Franco-German ritual is the story of Judith, recited during Ḥanukkah. The earliest treatment of this story in the ritual is by the eleventh-century Joseph b. Solomon of Carcassonne, in Provence. Cited as an authority by RaŠI (in his commentary on Ezek. 21: 18), R. Joseph is the author of the *yoṣer 'Odekha ki 'anafta*,[84] for the first Sabbath of Ḥanukkah.

The hymn begins with praise of God, who took revenge against Antiochus after he issued decrees against the Jews. Among the tyrant's rulings was the obligation of Jewish brides to spend their wedding night with the provincial governor. The hymn continues with an account of the nuptials of Mattathias' daughter and her bold plan in rallying her brothers, under the leadership of Judah the Maccabee, to resist the harsh decree. Following is R. Joseph's dramatic description of the daughter's action on her wedding night:

As they gathered by the canopy to drink and rejoice,
The bride appeared without any clothes;
She poured a cup for the assembled revellers
Who hid their faces, now protected from gazing;
Fierce was the brother's anger against her:
'The noble guests are here invited to celebrate,
How could you stand before them like a naked whore!'
The fair lady gave them answer:
'How dare you lecture me with your hypocrisy?
When you allow the unclean Gentile to have his pleasure with my body!'

This bold action causes her brothers to muster forces and launch a rebellion against the ruling power. When word of this reaches Holofernes (commander of the enemy armies), he gathers his forces and lays siege to the city of Jerusalem. The hymn concludes with an account of Judith's courage in slaying Holofernes and liberating her people. In this *yoṣer*, R. Joseph combined three originally independent legends preserved in the book of Judith in the Apocrypha and in three rabbinic sources, the *Megillat Ta'anit* (ch. 6), the *Ma'aseh Yehudit* (otherwise known as *Ḥibbur Yafeh Me-Ha-Yešu'ah*), and *Midraš Le-Ḥanukkah*.[85]

In order to understand the hymnist's method of combining the legends it

[84] Ber, *Seder*, pp. 629–33.

[85] *'Oṣar Midrašim*, i. 204–9.

is first necessary to separate them. Originally the tale of Judith and Holofernes in the Apocrypha was independent of the other two. The story grew in stages until it reached the form in R. Joseph's *yoṣer*. In the earliest rabbinic stage the Judith legend retained most of the personal and place-names of the account in the Apocrypha. In the second stage of the legend there is no mention of place-names and only four characters from the Apocrypha are referred to by name. However, the identities of the four have been altered: Holofernes is 'King of Greece', instead of commander of Nebuchadnezzar's armies, as in the earlier account, and Judith is not 'the daughter of Be'eri', as in the first-stage account, nor is she 'the daughter of Merari', as in the Apocrypha. Only Uzziah ben Micah and Carmi are remembered as 'officers in the Israelite army', whereas in the Apocrypha they are the town magistrates and their names are given as Uzziah ben Micah of the tribe of Simeon and Carmi ben Malkiel. Moreover, the setting of the story is Jerusalem and not Bethulia, as in the earlier account, and the struggle is now between the Jews and the Greeks (not the Babylonians) during the Maccabean period.

There are two tracks in the third stage of the Judith legend. In the first, as exemplified in the *Ma'aseh Yehudit*, the names of the characters have been completely forgotten. There is no mention of Holofernes, or of Greeks, or even of Judith. We learn only that 'the king of the Gentiles came to Jerusalem with forty thousand soldiers, and the Israelites were discomfited before them', and that a 'young woman of the daughters of the prophets . . . took her life in her hands' and saved her people by cutting off the king's head, after getting him drunk. This helped to rally the warriors of Israel and defeat their enemy.

In the second track of this third stage, the Judith legend is firmly connected with the Maccabean uprising and with the evil decrees of 'the king of the Greeks'. One such decree ordered that whoever took a wife was to bring her first to the provincial governor so that he might have intercourse with her before she could return to her husband. This decree and the legend surrounding it is first mentioned in *Megillat Ta'anit* (ch. 6). In this account, the daughter of Mattathias (son of Yoḥanan, the High Priest), on the eve of her marriage, is saved from being disgraced by the provincial governor through the courageous efforts of Mattathias and his sons, who prevail over the Greeks.

This legend in *Megillat Ta'anit* is embellished in the later *midrašim*. There the daughter of the High Priest, now named Hannah, appears naked at her wedding feast. When her brothers are outraged by her behaviour, she taunts them for their hypocrisy, and for their passive compliance with a ruler's decree that allows the provincial governor to take sexual liberties with Jewish brides. Thoroughly shamed, the brothers resolve to resist their oppressors and rally to do battle against the enemy. Subsequently, the story—with some variations—of the High Priest's daughter and the resistance of her brothers is connected with the Maccabean rebellion against Antiochus IV, Epiphanes. Still later, these two are combined with the Judith legend when, in retaliation against the Maccabean resistance, a siege is laid to the city of Jerusalem by Holofernes, acting, presumably, on the orders of Antiochus. The merging of all three stories is not achieved in the extant *midrašim*, but in the *yoṣer ʾOdekha ki ʾanafta* by R. Joseph b. Solomon, cited above.

Characteristically, the French hymnist, like Qillir in the classical period, chose to enlarge upon the legends from rabbinic sources for the edification and entertainment of his congregation. This three-stage development of the Judith legend is supported by a *yoṣer*, *ʾOdekha ki ʿanitani*, and a *zulat*, *ʾEyn mošiʿa we-goʾel*, by R. Menaḥem b. Makhir of Regensburg[86] and a *seliḥah*, *Mi kamokha ʾaddir*, by the Cretan physician and poet Malkiel b. Meir Aškenazi (13th–14th c.).[87] In his *yoṣer*, R. Menaḥem tells of the decrees issued by the Greek authorities, including the privileges of provincial governors with Jewish brides, and continues with the story of the wedding night of Hannah, the sister of Judah, and the subsequent rebellion of Judah and his followers. In R. Menaḥem's more subdued treatment of Hannah's behaviour before her wedding-night guests, the bride, daughter of the High Priest, is concerned that she will be condemned by law to burning (Lev. 21: 9) if she is violated by a Gentile:

> The bride, her hair dishevelled, entered the assembly;
> In lieu of wine, she poured a cup of tears for the evil to come;
> Her coloured coat she tore to shreds;
> Her brother Judah spoke, 'Hannah, why do you cry?
> And why despair like a drunkard and complain?'
> She replied, 'My lord, I am by nature not depressed!
> But if the villian violates me on my wedding night,
> I will have profaned my father and be condemned to burning!'

Notably missing in the *yoṣer* is the Judith legend. However, in his *zulat* R. Menaḥem relates the story of Judith and her heroic act in slaying the commander of the Greek armies, although he does not mention the *ius primae noctis* issued by the authorities, or the story of the daughter of the High Priest and the provincial governor, and the resistance of Judah and his followers. Of equal significance in the *zulat* is the reference to Judith as 'the daughter of Merari', which is similar to the pedigree of Judith given in the Apocrypha and in the earliest midrashic version. This would suggest that at the time of R. Menaḥem these several legends were not as yet combined, although the story of Judith was already connected with the observance of Ḥanukkah.

The *seliḥah* of Malkiel b. Meir is the latest treatment of the Judith legend. As in the *yoṣer* of R. Joseph b. Solomon, the Judith story is merged with that

[86] Ber, *Seder*, pp. 636–44.

[87] Weinberger, *Širat Yisraʾel*, pp. 65–9.

of Judah and his sister and their resistance to the government decree affecting Jewish brides. It is also connected with the story of the Maccabean uprising against Antiochus. However, Judith is not mentioned by name, but only as 'the honourable Judaean lady' (*ha-yehudit ha-kevudah*). Her name has been forgotten![88]

Reflecting the lighter side of Franco-German Jewry is the ballad-like *havdalah*, *'Iš ḥasid hayah*, by the thirteenth-century Franco-German R. Jesse b. Mordecai. The hymn is based on the folk legend concerning Elijah the prophet, expected to come at the close of the Sabbath to announce the arrival of the Messiah. In this account, the prophet sells himself as a slave in order to help a poor man in distress:[89]

> There lived a saintly man without food or provisions,
> Unemployed and confined to his home for lack of clothes;
> Surrounded by five children and a worthy wife
> Who said, 'No longer can you sit idle;
> Are we not without food to eat, naked and destitute;
> You have acquired Torah learning by your efforts, but what shall we eat?
> Give a care, beloved, and go to market,
> The gracious and merciful One on high will, perhaps, have compassion on us . . .'
> 'You have given wise counsel, but I cannot agree
> To be embarrassed and venture out without a stitch of clothes . . .'
> She hastened to borrow from neighbours clothes suitable for wear;
> Now dressed, he put his trust in a loving God
> While his children prayed, 'Let him not return a poor man, disgraced!'
> He walked in the market with his hopes high, and Elijah appeared to greet him;
> He who would announce the redemption assured him, 'Today you will be rich;
> Command me, by your honour, I am now your slave;
> Announce it: Here is an uncommon slave to be bought . . .'
> When a merchant happily made the purchase for 800,000 gold coins,
> He asked [Elijah], 'What are your skills, do you know the building trade?
> On the day that you complete the work on my mansions and palaces, I will set you free.'

88 Weinberger, 'A Note on . . . Judith', pp. 44–8.
89 Habermann, *Toledot Ha-Piyyuṭ*, ii. 206–7.

Needless to say, Elijah was able to finish his labours and regain his freedom. Undoubtedly, the story of the enslaved prophet struck a chord among Rhineland's Jews, who were as yet not freed from the burdens of exile.

Despite the hardships, there were times of rejoicing called for by the religious calendar. On Purim, Franco-German Jews celebrated the fall of Haman and the triumph of Mordecai with liturgical hymns, like the *ma'ariv* in the form of a parody by the thirteenth-century R. Menaḥem b. Jacob. The poem begins with a play on the words from Exod. 12: 42: '[That was for the Lord] a night of vigil' (*leyl šimmurim*), which the poet converts to 'a night of drunkards' (*leyl šikkorim*). (The practice of imbibing intoxicants in celebrating Purim is supported by the rabbinic injunction (in *bMeg* 7b), 'It is the duty of a man to mellow himself [with wine] on Purim until he cannot tell the difference between "cursed be Haman" and "blessed be Mordecai."') Continuing, the poet pursues his theme in a mock-serious tone:

For the Purim (feast) prepare ducks and chickens . . .
Cursed be the man who eats lentils
On the nights of Purim . . .
Cursed be the man who eats ground peas—
It is so decreed by the king and the governor and all the heads;
Every Israelite family shall rise up in arms against him,
And expel him from the holy congregation![90]

The phrase 'cursed be the man' is a parody of the 'cursed be Haman . . . blessed be Mordecai' from rabbinic literature, also preserved in the pre-classical Purim hymn *Šošanat ya'aqov*.[91]

Another festive *ma'ariv* for the Purim evening service was composed by R. Eliezer Dayyan of Amberg, in Bavaria. Presumably, the hymn was a Purim gift sent to his father. R. Eliezer also begins with the parody 'a night of vigil . . . a night of drunkards' (*leyl šimmurim . . . leyl šikkorim*), and pursues a mock-serious tone similar to that of R. Menaḥem b. Jacob. R. Eliezer's hymn elaborates on the merits of Purim rejoicing and is constructed in rhyming tercets with a repeated refrain of the opening parody, *Leyl šikkorim*:

A night of drunkards: no water is permitted in the home
As on the days of the solstice and equinox [when water was
believed to be poisoned] . . .[92]
A night of drunkards: let us toast together many cups
And eat sponge cake instead of *ḥaroset* [the Passover mixture
symbolic of the mortar used to fashion bricks in Egypt] . . .
A night of drunkards: rejoice with your wife often,
Evening, morning and noon.

[90] *Maḥazor Witry*, pp. 583–4. [91] Ber, *Seder*, p. 448.
[92] Trachtenberg, *Jewish Magic*, p. 257.

The humorous folk character of this hymn is seen in its use of the vernacular, such as *leqikhlikh* (l. 34) for sponge cake, and in its play on words, as in the following:

> Coins [*sela'im*] protect the rabbits;
> Give them to the poor and destitute
> On the day of Purim rejoicing . . .

The word play is based on Ps. 104: 18, 'The rocks [*sela'im*] are a refuge for the rabbits', and is here used to urge disbursements to the needy in line with the instructions in Esther 9: 22. Here is another example of word-play humour from the hymn:

> Take a jar of Haman [*ṣinṣenet ha-man*] in your hands
> And fill it with wine from your jugs
> On the day of Purim rejoicing.

This must have elicited a laugh from the congregation, familiar with the verse in Exod. 16: 33, 'And Moses said to Aaron, "Take a jar [*ṣinṣenet*] and put an omer of manna [*man*] in it."'[93]

THE PRINCIPAL FRANCO-GERMAN GENRES

Qedušta': 'Eloheykhem

Although the Franco-Germans did not make significant changes in the *qedusta'*, they favoured an addition to the genre which began with the unit *'eloheykhem*. The poem, comprising six or seven cola in monorhyme, was inserted in the *qeduššah* of the Sabbath and festival Additional Prayer (*musaf*). The hymn was chanted between the fourth verse, 'I am the Lord your God' (*'ani 'adonay 'eloheykhem*), and the fifth verse, 'The Lord shall reign throughout all generations.'[94] Several *'eloheykhem* poems were composed by Franco-Germans, including Judah b. Samuel the Ḥasid (*c.*1150–1217); Eliezer b. Judah of Worms (1165–1230) and Barukh b. Samuel of Mainz (1150–1221). Following is an *'eloheykhem* hymn in the Franco-German ritual for the Sabbath of the Intermediate Days of Tabernacles. The acrostic yields the name Yehudah (the Ḥasid?).[95]

> Your God:
> May He return to Jerusalem, His tabernacle and dwelling;
> May He build His temple and the chamber where He will rest;

[93] Habermann, *'Iyyunim*, pp. 304–6.

[94] It is possible, but unlikely, that the Italian poet Zevadiah pioneered this genre in his *'Eloheykhen zeruyaw ye'esof.* The reason for doubt is that the acrostic in the hymn is not clear. See David, *Širey Zevadiah*, p. 48.

[95] Ibid.; *Mahazor Le-Sukkot*, p. 286.

May He cause to dwell therein the glory of His presence
  [*šekhinato*];
May He in His wrath tread upon the enemy as in a wine press;
May He erect a pavilion to shade the guardians of His tabernacle;
May He who establishes His vault upon the earth
Rule over all the lands from His heights in the heavens.

Yoṣer

The Franco-German *guf ha-yoṣer* generally followed earlier Italian forms. Like Amittai, who in his *'Asiḥah be-divrey nifle'otekha* added a *qadoš* refrain after each strophe, Franco-German poets departed from eastern models and varied the ratio of strophes to refrains. In Ephraim of Regensburg's *yoṣer*, *'Ašer be-ma'amarot 'immeṣ gevurot*,[96] his ratio of strophes to refrains is four to two.

Departing from the eastern practice in which the theme of the *guf ha-yošer* expanded upon the Sabbath Torah reading, the central Europeans varied the focus of this hymn. Their treatment of the *guf ha-yoṣer* for the festivals stressed the laws and traditions of the occasion, whereas for the Sabbath the theme of the *guf ha-yoṣer* centred on creation of the world in six days and celebration of the day of rest.

'Ofan

The Franco-German speculation in the *'ofan* on the nature of creation (*ma'aseh bere'šit*) and on God's chariot throne (*ma'aseh merkavah*) differed from eastern and Spanish practices. While the latter were constrained in their esoteric utterances in the *'ofan* by fear of rabbinic authorities, who forbade these efforts, the Franco-Germans had no such qualms, since the hymnographers were the rabbis in the region. Already Amittai in his *'ofan*, *'Attah 'elohey ha-ruḥot*, anticipates the new freedom in mystical speculation:[97]

You are the Lord of the souls;
You know the innermost feelings;
You reveal man's thoughts;
You are praised by holy songs.
Holy, holy, holy, is the Lord of hosts.

Metatron, prince of the inner chamber,
Teaches the Torah to the young;
Seized from among the earthlings,
He changed into flame and clouds.

[96] Habermann, 'Piyyuṭey R. Ephraim . . . mi-Regensburg', p. 184.
[97] Amittai, *Širey*, p. 97.

According to the legend (in *bAZ* 3b), Metatron, originally the man Enoch taken up to God (Gen. 5: 24), was employed in the heavens as instructor to the young. In this *'ofan*, Amittai shows familiarity with several angelic figures, like Temalyon, the guide (l. 11), Yafi'el, the prince of darkness (l. 16), Zahariy'el, prince of the constellations (l. 26) and Qippod, prince of Gehenna (l. 27).

Rhine valley poets expanded on Amittai's treatment of the *'ofan*. Simeon b. Isaac in his *Ševivey šalhavot* speculates on the esoteric name of God, 'Adiriron', and Meir b. Isaac closes his *'ofan*, *Mal'akhey ṣeva'ot* with a reference to the divine chariot throne.[98] Along with a thematic freedom, the central Europeans allowed themselves latitude in structuring the *'ofan*. In addition to the standard rhyming-quatrains model, they also favoured tercets with internal rhyme and variable refrains, and pseudo-*muwashshaḥāt* forms in the Hispanic fashion.

'Ahavah

The Franco-German *ahavah* is distinctive for its dialogue form. In *Segullati melukhah 'azartikh*, attributed to Mešullam b. Moses, God (*dodi*, the beloved) and Israel (*segullati*, the treasure) exchange, in alternating strophes, words of endearment:[99]

> [GOD:]
> My treasure . . .
> From the furnace I have saved you, and lead you to follow Me;
> Eternally I have loved you, My treasure.
>
> [ISRAEL:]
> My beloved
> Your name gives strength to my sons, Your remembrance illumines my face;
> Fervently I pray You to bring relief from my enemies . . .
> To You I lift mine eyes, my beloved.

Zulat

Following Italian models, the *zulatot* of the Franco-Germans departed from eastern practices, where the *zulat* was a thematic expansion of the reading from the Prophets for Sabbaths and festivals. Instead, the theme of the central European *zulat* varied. The festival *zulat* focused on themes related to the holy day, whereas the *zulat* for the Sabbath dealt in most instances with

[98] Habermann, *Piyyuṭey Rabbi Šim'on*, p. 59, l. 20. Adiriron is a name under which God appears in the *heykhalot* books read by R. Simeon's colleagues, the Ḥasidim, in medieval Germany. See Scholem, *Major Trends*, p. 114, and *Maḥazor Le-Sukkot*, pp. 261–2, l. 17.

[99] Fleischer, *Širat Ha-Qodeš*, p. 459.

contemporary events. Following is a portion of Simeon b. Isaac's *zulat*, *ʾEl ʾel ḥay ʾarannen*, with its sharp staccato call for retribution on Israel's enemies:[100]

> Look upon me, labouring in agony;
> I am like dill beaten out with a stick;
> Remove the whip from me;
> Be not silent.

A similar tone pervades Ephraim of Regensburg's *zulat*, *ʾEli, ʾeli lammah*, for the fifth Sabbath after Passover:[101]

> My God, my God
> Why are my sighs hidden from You?
> Behold, I am a dove afflicted.

ʾEl ʾAdon and *Ševaḥ*

The Franco-Germans introduced into the *yoṣer* cycle two additions to the Sabbath morning hymn preceding the first benediction before the *šemaʿ*, *ʾEl ʾadon ʿal kol ha-maʿasim*. Titled *ʾEl ʾadon* and *Ševaḥ*, the additions were inserted before the first and last strophes of the *ʾEl ʾadon* benediction respectively. Following is part of a *ševaḥ* by the Franco-German poet Mordecai for a Sabbath on which a circumcision is performed. The hymn is built in tercets with refrains ending with the word *qadoš*, thereby rhyming with the last unit of *ʾEl ʾadon ʿal kol ha-maʿasim*:[102]

> Praises are lavished upon Him
> By the hosts on high exalting,
> And His people covenant with Him
> With the blood of circumcision and the holy flesh . . .
>
> The blood and flesh of the infant
> Atones like an altar offering;
> O Holy One, command and forgive
> The guardians of the sacred sanctuary.

Rešut

Learning from the Hispanics, the Franco-Germans composed 'permission requests' (*rešuyyot*) before the Sabbath and festival morning prayer, *Nišmat kol ḥay*. The *rešut* by Menaḥem b. Makhir of Regensburg, *Nišmat melummedey morašah*, for Simḥat Torah,[103] is probably the first of its kind by a central

[100] Habermann, *Piyyuṭey Rabbi Šimʿon*, pp. 14, 40–1.
[101] Habermann, 'Piyyuṭey R. Ephraim . . . mi-Regensburg', p. 135.
[102] Fleischer, *Širat Ha-Qodeš*, pp. 460–1.
[103] *Maḥazor Le-Sukkot*, pp. 331–2.

European hymnist. R. Menahem constructs the hymn in rhyming tercets introduced by the word *nišmat*, in a manner similar to the *rešuyyot* of Joseph Ibn Abitur, Solomon Ibn Gabirol and Judah Ha-Levi. Below is the first strophe:

[In] the soul of the Torah scholars, men who are free [*'Avot* 6. 2],
You have planted the hope of eternal life and rest;
The law of the Lord is perfect, reviving the soul.

Franco-Germans were fond of composing *rešuyyot* for the evening service *barekhu*. This practice followed the model of the Hispanics, although the latter wrote *rešuyyot* for the morning *barekhu* only. The Franco-German *rešut* was, in most instances, a pseudo-*muwashshaḥ* with the 'belt' colon usually rhyming with the unit *barekhu*, as in the following by Solomon b. Eliezer:[104]

Sing to the Lord
Young and old;
In God's assemblies
Bless [*barekhu*].

'Permission' hymns were also composed in Aramaic. The use of Aramaic in the synagogue liturgy appears in pre-classical eastern congregations where selections from the Scripture reading were translated into the more familiar language of the Talmud. The practice was continued in the early Italian synagogue by competent scholars who would introduce their translations with an Aramaic permission (*rešut*) in which they summarized the scriptural reading. In the Italian ritual these permissions are known as *alfabeytin* or *fabeytin*, since they featured an alphabetic acrostic. Franco-German poets were attracted to the Aramaic permission, and in the mid-eleventh century began writing in this genre. The best-known is the monorhyme hymn, *'Aqdamut millin*, by Meir b. Isaac, chanted before the reading of the Torah on the first day of Pentecost.[105]

The popular *rešut* was also involved in the liturgical celebration of weddings. On the Sabbath following the nuptials, the bridegroom was escorted to the synagogue by his groomsmen (*šošvinin*). During the morning service, he would be called to read a Torah lesson appropriate for the occasion, such as the account of Isaac's betrothal to Rebekah in Gen. 24: 1 ff. The invitation to the bridegroom to begin his Scripture reading was preceded by an elaborate introduction with extravagant mock-heroic conceits, composed mostly in monorhyme. The invitation to chant the Torah lesson was framed in the form of a *rešut*, a permission request addressed first to God, then to the Torah, the sages in the congregation and the laity.

The themes of the permission request usually focused on the sanctity of

104 *Maḥazor Witry*, p. 566.

105 *Maḥazor . . . Ha-Šavu'ot*, pp. 56–61.

family life and the joys of marriage, and sought the blessings of the deity upon the young couple. Later embellishments of this *rešut* were in the form of dedications to the groomsmen and to the parents of bride and groom. Following is a portion of Simeon b. Isaac's *Me-rešut šokhen ʿad we-qadoš*, one of the earliest permission requests by a Rhineland poet. In the last section R. Simeon appeals to the congregation:

> With the permission of the holy remnant gathered here,
> Replete with merit like a pomegranate, trustworthy in their dealings . . .
> Accustomed to show love for the bridegroom on his wedding day . . .
> With their permission, rise up Mr . . . the bridegroom from among the people uncounted [Num. 23: 10],
> And stand by me on the wooden platform as decreed by custom;
> Let your groomsmen accompany you with song and refrain;
> Open your lips to recite the proper blessing of praise before and after [the Torah reading],
> And read the select portion from the true testimony [the Torah] . . .
> And let the people respond with, 'Amen', after you, for great is the reward of the covenant [observed].[106]

R. Simeon's *rešuyyot* for these occasions gained wide popularity. Following his model, poets like Meir b. Isaac began to compose *rešuyyot* for other festive events. R. Meir's hymns in this genre were directed to the honorees invited to complete the Torah reading on Simḥat Torah, and those asked to begin the reading anew with the book of Genesis. The latter were designated the 'bridegroom of the Torah' (*ḥatan torah*) and the 'bridegroom of Genesis' (*ḥatan bere'šit*), respectively. In the *rešut*, the honorees were treated to a poetic celebration of the merits of the Torah and their own special gifts. Some of the *rešuyyot* for Simḥat Torah were divided into the four thematic units of the *rešut* for the bridegroom; others, like *Maqdim we-ro'š la-qore'im*, by Meir b. Isaac, focused on the special character of the *ḥatan bere'šit*:[107]

> My heart overflows, giving direction to my eyes,
> Beholding the beacon bright illuminating like a lantern;
> He grows stronger on his watch like a steady pillar in place;
> Standing firm, providing a true foundation stone . . .
> Arise and stand Mr . . . bridegroom of Genesis.

Although this *rešut* is now a part of the Franco-German ritual, it is likely that R. Meir had in mind a particular notable when composing his hymn. The

[106] Habermann, *Piyyuṭey Rabbi Šimʿon*, p. 187.
[107] *Maḥazor Le-Sukkot*, pp. 451–60.

ḥatan bere'šit, like the *ḥatan torah*, was a distinguished community leader. In the rabbinic period they honoured 'the greatest of them all' (*bMeg* 32a) by reading the conclusion of the Torah. In later practice, the congregation's rabbi was the *ḥatan torah*, while its presiding officer was designated *ḥatan bere'šit*.

Nišmat

'Illu Finu

Another Franco-German embellishment of the *Nišmat kol ḥay* was a hymn inserted before the phrase, 'Were our mouths filled with song' (*'Illu finu male' širah*). One of the first central Europeans to compose in this genre was a twelfth-century French convert to Judaism, Yehosifyah the Proselyte. His hymn, 'Were a song as wide as the sea, it would not suffice for the eternal living [God]' (*We-'illu širah ka-yam, 'eyn day ḥay we-qayyam*), was included in the Franco-German ritual.[108]

Ha-Melekh

A new genre introduced by thirteenth-century Franco-Germans was a work beginning with 'The King' (*ha-melekh*). The hymn was injected into the *Nišmat kol ḥay*, between the verses 'The King is enthroned high and exalted' (*ha-melekh ha-yošev 'al kisse' ram we-nissa'*) and 'Abiding forever, exalted and holy is His name' (*šokhen 'ad marom we-qadoš šemo*). The *ha-melekh* hymns were generally constructed in the form of a pseudo-*muwashshaḥ*, with each strophe beginning with *ha-melekh* and ending with *šemo*. Following are strophes from this genre by the Franco-German poet Solomon:[109]

> The King, a freewill song
> Is hymned to Him in every region:
> Extol Him who rides the clouds;
> The Lord is His name . . .
>
> The King, His hand extended high
> When garbed with might on vengeance's day;
> The God is a warrior;
> The Lord is His name.

'El Ha-Hoda'ot

Another central European innovation was titled 'God of Thanksgiving' (*'el ha-hoda'ot*). It was placed before the last blessing in the 'introductory hymns

[108] Fleischer, *Širat Ha-Qodeš*, p. 461. [109] Ibid.

and psalms' (*pesukey de-zimra'*). Appropriately, the *'el ha-hoda'ot* was chanted before the verse 'God of thanksgiving, Lord of wonders who takes delight in songs and psalms, O God and King, the life of the universe' (*'El ha-hoda'ot, 'adon ha-nifla'ot, ha-boḥer be-širey zimrah, melekh 'el ḥay ha-'olamim*). The hymn opens with the word *'El* and is constructed either in the form of a Spanish-style pseudo-*muwashshaḥ* or with a constant refrain in the early Italian mode. Below is a sample of the genre in the latter form, by a thirteenth-century poet named Eliezer:[110]

God of thanksgiving
From the four corners,
Evening and morn,
  King and God, the life of the universe.

Lord from above,
Revered in praises
Above all exalted,
  King and God, the life of the universe.

Ma'ariv

The *ma'ariv* (evening) hymn not often found in eastern liturgies and neglected by Hispanics and early Italians was popular with the Franco-Germans. The Frenchman Joseph Ṭov Elem was the first European to compose in this genre. The tendency to lengthen the evening service with embellishments was frowned upon in many Mediterranean congregations, both so as not to encroach upon dinner time and from fear of attack while returning home late at night. This fear was probably no longer warranted in France under the early Capets in the eleventh century, when there were no special decrees affecting Jews.[111]

The Franco-German *ma'arivim* generally followed classical models, which divided the hymn into six units of generally equal length, save for the longer third. The genre was often adorned with opening and closing scriptural verses in the classical manner. Only one rhyming quatrain was allocated to each of the units, whereas the third was allowed refrains and responses. Occasionally the *ma'ariv* was built in tercets with a pseudo-*muwashshaḥ* rhyme pattern. The third unit concluded with a quatrain similar to the others and led the hymn into the evening service verse, 'Who is like You O Lord among the mighty?' (*mi kamokha ba-'elim 'adonay?*). The theme of the *ma'ariv* units focused on the meaning of the festival, with the expanded third devoted to the particular laws and traditions of the day. Following is the opening of Ṭov Elem's *ma'ariv* for Tabernacles, *'Atanneh ṣidqot 'el*:[112]

110 Fleischer, *Širat Ha-Qodeš*, p. 463.
111 Schwarzfuchs, 'France', p. 153.
112 *Maḥazor Le-Sukkot*, pp. 48–51.

I will proclaim God's love to my people,
In this sanctuary I will voice my song;
I will celebrate His might and will not be silent;
At night His melody is with me.

Beginning in the eleventh century, Rhine valley poets like Meir b. Isaac would add a seventh unit, known as *bikkur* (early, i.e. evening, service) or *tosefet* (addition). This unit, considerably larger than the preceding ones and varied in form, led into the closing benediction after the *šema'*, 'Blessed are You, O Lord, who spreads the tabernacle of peace over us' (*ha-pores sukkat šalom 'aleynu*). Although the addition of the seventh unit disrupted the symmetry of the *ma'ariv*, it was considered necessary to close the hymn with a flourish of prominent proportions rather than with a mere quatrain.

Magen 'Avot

Franco-German poets endowed the Sabbath evening service with an embellishment of the *magen 'avot bi-dvaro* (God's word has ever been our fathers' shield), a liturgical synopsis of the seven benedictions of the evening *'amidah*. This synopsis probably originated in the rabbinic period, where it is indirectly referred to in *bŠab* 24b.[113] The synopsis was also included in the Babylonian synagogue ritual, as may be seen in the Amram Ga'on prayer-book.[114] The Franco-German *magen 'avot* addition generally opened with a short paraphrase of Scripture, followed by a tercet designed to rhyme with the third line of the synopsis hymn, 'The holy God like whom there is none' (*ha-'el ha-qadoš še-'eyn kamohu*). Below is part of a *magen 'avot* addition for Šabbat Šuvah by an anonymous Franco-German poet:[115]

Would that the sinner would fear my words, confess and forsake
  [his sins],
And be reconciled to the Lord and obtain His mercy;
Return O Israel to the Lord our God for He will abundantly
  pardon;
He instructs the wayward. Who can teach like Him?
Turn from evil and do good; His strength is power's paragon;
To sweet song He raises high His hand;
'Our father's shield God's word has ever been;
He revives the dead by His word;
The holy God like whom there is none.'

[113] See RaŠI's comment in *bŠab* 24b on 'The Reader who descends before the desk'.
[114] *Seder Rav 'Amram Ga'on*, p. 64.
[115] Fleischer, *Širat Ha-Qodeš*, p. 467.

Seliḥah

The central European *seliḥot* are distinctive in their reflection of contemporary Jewish disabilities resulting from government decrees and unruly mobs. The early Italian and Franco-German *seliḥot* are noted for their restrained quatrains, unembellished by closing scriptural verses. This was in marked contrast to the late eastern and Hispanic treatment of the genre. With the visit to the region of Abraham Ibn Ezra in the twelfth century, changes occurred in the local hymnography. One result was that the Franco-German *seliḥah* was endowed with enhancements, including quantitative metre. The following groupings of *seliḥot*, *ḥaṭa'nu*, *'aqedah* and *gezerot*, were named after their main theme and structural style.

Ḥaṭa'nu

The later central European *seliḥot* favoured strophic forms, whether in couplets (*šeniyyah*), tercets (*šelišit*) or quatrains (*šalmonit*, complete). These were often preceded by verses from Scripture repeated as refrains, or by the litany 'We have sinned O our Rock; forgive us, our Maker'. Hymns with the latter refrain were identified by the term *ḥaṭa'nu* (we have sinned). The *ḥaṭa'nu*, originating in the classical period, was used in Rhineland synagogues as a confessional. It was built in strophes connected by anadiplosis and interrupted by the litany 'We have sinned'. A memorable sample is R. Geršom b. Judah's *Gadol 'awoni we-la-ḥaṭo' hosafti*.[116]

My sin is great; I add to my transgressions;
My guilt increases; my evil multiplies;
Great are my failings; I should be flogged;
I deserve to be exiled; I have forgotten my homeland.

'Aqedah

A prominent place in the Franco-German ritual is reserved for the *'aqedah*, a *seliḥah* on the Binding of Isaac (Gen. 22). The *'aqedah* makes its debut in Europe in the work of the eleventh-century poet Meir b. Isaac. The Binding of Isaac theme was rarely treated in separate hymns in the classical and late eastern post-classical periods, and hardly at all by the Hispanics. However, given the experience of the central Europeans during the anti-Jewish decrees of 1096, 1146–7 and 1197 and the martyrdom of Rhine valley congregations, Abraham's willingness to sacrifice his son Isaac, in response to God's command, had a familiar resonance.

This familiarity was enhanced by a rabbinic reading (in *Midraš Ha-Gadol* on Gen. 22: 19) of the *'aqedah* in Gen. 22, suggesting that the reason Isaac is

[116] *Maḥazor Le-Yamim*, ii. 566.

not mentioned accompanying his father from Mount Moriah is that, 'although Isaac did not die, Scripture regards him *as though* he had died and his ashes lay piled on the altar. That is why it is written [in Gen. 22: 19], "So Abraham [alone] returned to his young men."' Elaborating on the rabbinic comment, R. Ephraim b. Jacob of Bonn (born in 1133 and witness to the havoc in the ensuing years) wrote the following in his *'aqedah*, *'Et 'avotay 'ani mazkir*:[117]

He [Abraham] hastened to pin him [Isaac] with his knees;
He made strong his two arms;
With a steady hand he slaughtered him as required;
A complete sacrifice prepared.

When a reviving dew fell upon him and he lived,
He seized him to slaughter him again;
Bear witness, Scripture; it is truth confirmed:
And the Lord called Abraham, even a second time from heaven.
[Gen. 22: 15][118]

Gezerot

A distinctive type of Franco-German *seliḥah* came to be called *gezerot* (decrees), in which the martyrdom of Rhineland Jewry by decree during the Crusades was memorialized, often by eyewitness accounts. The *gezerot* differed from other *seliḥot* in their account of atrocities committed against Jews, in a named locality. Following is an example by R. Joel b. Isaac Ha-Levi of Bonn lamenting the suffering of the Cologne congregation during the decrees of 1147. The hymn *Yivkeyun mar mal'akhey šalom*, comprising thirty-three versets in monorhyme with closing couplet, was chanted in Franco-German congregations during the Ninth of 'Av and is included in the region's *Seder Ha-Qinot*.[119]

Alas, fallen into the hands of strangers; the hand of the Lord struck
The King's treasure [Israel], the gentle and fair
Daughter of Cologne; my head is in pain, I have seen a horrible thing:
They sought to baptize them in the accursed putrid waters,
Urged them to worship the dead, a strange god;
They threatened death to the disobedient [lit. those who cursed the 'strange god'], but Jacob chose the Lord!

117 Habermann, 'Piyyuṭey R. Ephraim . . . mi-Bonn', pp. 264–6.
118 Spiegel, *The Last Trial*, pp. 148–9.
119 *Seder Ha-Qinot*, pp. 160–3.

Petiḥah

The *petiḥah* (introduction), thematically related to the *seliḥah*, was chanted before the first recitation of God's Thirteen Attributes (Exod. 34: 6–7) during the vigil nights of 'Elul and the Days of Awe. Characteristically, the *petiḥah* closed with the verse 'For we rely upon Your exceeding mercy' (*ki ʿal raḥamekha ha-rabbim ʾanu beṭuḥim*) or a paraphrase thereof. The closing focused on God's mercy and led into the introductory formula to the Thirteen Attributes, 'The Lord, the Lord is a merciful and gracious God.' Two *petiḥot by* RaŠI, [*ʾAdonay*] *ʾelohey ha-ṣevaʾot* and *ʾAz ṭerem nimteḥu*, are included in Franco-German *seliḥot* collections.[120]

Qinah

The Franco-German elegies (*qinot*) are divided thematically into two sets: general laments voiced on ordained fast-days like the Ninth of 'Av, and threnodies in observance of particular tragedies that befell Rhineland Jewry. Distinctive in their elegies is a fondness for the writings of Judah Ha-Levi on the destruction of the Jerusalem Temple. His zionides, particularly *Ṣiyyon ha-loʾ tišʾali li-šlom ʾasirayikh*, with its elegantly balanced hemistichs, were widely imitated, although the Franco-Germans appeared to be unable to duplicate Ha-Levi's elaborate metrical pattern: – –/–v– –/–v–/–v– –// – –/–v– –/–v–/–v– –. The most notable of the imitation zionides were composed by R. Meir b. Barukh of Rothenburg (*c.*1215–93) and his contemporary Eleazar b. Moses Ha-Daršan of Wuerzburg.[121] Elegies lamenting specific decrees in Crusader days were written by Kalonymous b. Judah of Mainz (11th c.), who wept over the catastrophe that befell the congregations in Speyer, Worms and Mainz; Ephraim of Bonn (d. after 1196), on the fate of Blois Jewry; Menaḥem b. Jacob of Worms (d. 1203), on the martyrs of Boppard; Barukh b. Samuel of Mainz (12th c.), regretting the losses in Speyer, Boppard and Blois; and Yeḥiel b. Jacob, on the destruction of the Lauda and Bischofsheim congregations in 1235, among others.[122]

Some of the personalized elegies are impressive in their uncommon insights into the horrible events in twelfth-century Rhineland. Among these is Barukh b. Samuel's *Beynot ʾarayot*, lamenting the death of a young man named Isaac, in Würzburg, who chose martyrdom to baptism:

> The Binding of Isaac was clear to see,
> In the streets and byways to all revealed;
> One of the Israelites leapt forth
> And sanctified Your name willingly . . .

[120] *Seder Ha-Seliḥot . . . Liṭaʾ*, pp. 65, 139. [121] *Seder Ha-Qinot*, pp. 124–6, 128–30, 135–7.
[122] Habermann, *Sefer*, pp. v–vii; idem, 'Piyyuṭey R. Barukh', pp. 96–9, 133–40.

A charming youth, adored by all;
Alas, he was tortured on a crushing rack.[123]

Eleazar b. Judah of Worms (d. between 1223 and 1232) was moved to write a tribute to his wife, who was murdered, together with his two daughters, in 1197, by two brigands who broke into his home on the twenty-second day of Kislew. Although R. Eleazar is controlled in his elegy, written in the form of a commentary on Prov. 31: 10, his sense of personal loss comes through.[124]

'A capable wife who can find' like my worthy spouse, the matron Dolṣa? . . .
'The heart of her husband trusts in her,' she fed and clothed him with dignity . . .
'She is like the ships of the merchant' providing for her mate that he may study Torah . . .
'She girds herself with strength' . . . cooks her meals and sets her table for all . . .
'She opens her mouth with wisdom' and knows the permitted and forbidden . . .
'She rejoices in obeying her husband' and never causes him distress;
'Give her a share in the fruit of her hands' in the Garden of Eden.

Birkat Ha-Mazon

In honour of the seven feast-days (*šivʿat yemey ha-mišteh*) following a wedding, poetic embellishments of the grace after meals (*birkat ha-mazon*) were customary. In this the Franco-Germans revived a practice that had been neglected since the period of the classical poets. Seeing that their epithalamia were well received, the hymnists began to adorn the grace at the feast of circumcision. Enhancing the grace after the Sabbath and festival meals followed, and some of the leading poets in the region made their contributions, including Simeon b. Isaac, Ephraim b. Isaac of Regensburg and Barukh b. Samuel of Mainz.

ENGLAND'S PRINCIPAL POETS

Caedmon?

The earliest liturgical poetry in England was composed by Caedmon, who, according to the Venerable Bede, lived in the seventh century and composed

[123] Ibid. 147. [124] Id., *Toledot Ha-Piyyut*, ii. 197–200.

poetic paraphrases of the biblical books Genesis, Exodus and Daniel.[125] A. Mirsky has suggested that Caedmon may have been Jewish.[126] Presumably, these biblical paraphrases served a liturgical purpose similar to the *qerovot* of Yannai and Qillir in the synagogue and the *kontakia* of Romanus the Melode in the Byzantine church. In paraphrasing the Scripture reading, Caedmon often embellished the text with non-biblical conceits, in much the same way as did Yannai and Qillir, who were able to draw inspiration from rabbinic sources. It is likely that Caedmon's embellishments likewise derived from extra-biblical sources, whether early Christian or rabbinic. Following is Caedmon's embellishment on Gen. 2: 21: 'So the Lord caused a deep sleep to fall upon the man and he slept; then He took one of his ribs and closed up its place with flesh':

> And he [Adam] knew no pain
> His gift came without hurt.[127]

How did Caedmon know that this procedure was accomplished without suffering? Possibly he had access to the rabbinic source in *Pirqey de R. Eliezer*, No. 12, 'The Holy One blessed be He had compassion upon the first man [Adam] and in order that he should not feel any pain, He cast upon him the sleep of deep slumber.' Presumably, Caedmon was also familiar with the work of the Church Father Tertullian (*c.*155–*c.*222), who discussed Adam's 'sleep' in his *De Anima*, 43.

Noteworthy is Caedmon's paraphrase of Gen. 7: 16: 'And those that entered [the ark] male and female of all flesh, went in as God had commanded him; and the Lord shut him in.' He elaborates:[128]

> The Guardian of the kingdom of heaven
> Shut after him, *with His own hand* [italics mine],
> The opening to the sea vessel.

The figure of God closing the ark in this way is mentioned in *Pirqey de R. Eliezer*, No. 23, 'When all creatures had entered [the ark], the Holy One, blessed be He, closed and sealed with His hand the gate of the ark.' A similar expression is found in *The Book of Adam and Eve*, ed. Malan, III. ix.[129]

Caedmon's embellishment on the drunkenness of Noah and his being uncovered in his tent (Gen. 9: 20 ff.) is instructive:[130]

> First came Ham,
> And as the son of Noah
> Arrived where his father lay

[125] Bede, *A History of the English Church and People* (Harmondsworth, 1964), pp. 245–8.
[126] Mirsky, 'Midrašot'.
[127] Cf. B. J. Timmer, *The Later Genesis*, edited from MS Junius 11 (Oxford, 1948), ll. 179–80.
[128] Ibid., ll. 1363–4.
[129] See *Pirqey de R. Eliezer*, pp. 87 n. 4, 166 n. 6.
[130] Timmer, *The Later Genesis*, ll. 1576–84.

In distress, he did not extend
The honour due to the man who gave him birth;
Even his nakedness he did not conceal from onlookers,
But he laughed lustily
And told his brothers how
The master is sprawled out in his house.

The rabbinic source for this legend is *Pirqey de R. Eliezer*, No. 23: 'Ham entered and saw his [Noah's] nakedness. He did not take to heart the duty of honouring [one's father]. But he told his two brothers in the market, making sport of the father.' Here, too, a similar account is preserved in the *Book of Adam and Eve*, ed. Malan, III. xiii. Josephus, in his *Antiquities of the Jews* (bk. i, ch. 6) also refers to the behaviour of Ham '(Noah) . . . being drunk, he fell asleep, and lay naked in an unseemly manner. When the youngest son saw this, he came laughing, and showed him to his brethren . . . And when Noah was made sensible of what had been done, he prayed for prosperity for his other sons; but for Ham . . . '

Was Caedmon Jewish, as Mirsky suggests? His name is derived from the Hebrew *qadmon* (ancient); he embellishes Scripture for liturgical use after the fashion of Yannai and Qillir; and he may have been familiar with rabbinic sources. Yet he had access to non-rabbinic texts which may have served him, and it is likely that he was familiar with Romanus' Scripture adorning *kontakia* for the Byzantine Church. Caedmon's religious identity remains open to speculation.

Yom Ṭov b. Isaac

The earliest hymns for the synagogue by a Hebrew poet in England were the penitentials and elegies—some in Aramaic—composed by Yom-Ṭov b. Isaac of Joigny, who settled in York around 1180. His metric *seliḥah Yom, yom yidrošun lakh* is built in strophes and refrains after late eastern models. The hymn was included in the Franco-German ritual for the Day of Atonement evening service. In the following sample the poet pleads for divine aid.[131]

Reject the tale-bearer [Satan];
Annul his recorded charges . . .
Silence the prosecutor
And receive the intercessor instead;
See our disgrace,
Consider it instead of our sin.

An elegy on the martyrs of York, where R. Yom-Ṭov and his congregation perished in 1190, was composed by R. Joseph of Chartres, who lived in

[131] *Maḥazor Le-Yamim*, ii. 28–9.

England. In a revealing couplet, he blames Richard I for the anti-Jewish violence that began with the Third Crusade, led by the English king, in company with the German emperor, Friedrich I, and Philippe II of France, and invokes dire punishment upon the ruler and his subjects:[132]

My anger is directed towards you, king of the isles,
Under your wings is found the blood of the innocent;
May God punish the Kitium [English] herd;
May their lot in life be like the corpses of my people;
Let there be no dew or rain on the island land;
From the day your king was crowned [in 1189], woe has come to your land . . .

Meir of Norwich

The most versatile rabbi-poet in England was R. Meir b. Elijah of Norwich. Born in France, where he studied under the Tosafists, R. Samson b. Abraham of Sens and R. Solomon b. Judah of Dreux, R. Meir settled in England and was among the Jews banished in 1290 by Edward I. The poet lamented the expulsion in his *havdalah*, *'Oyevi bi-m'eyrah tiqqov*, bearing the superscription, 'A *me'orah* for the severity of the exile and the killings in the prison and the loss of property.' Following is an excerpt from the hymn in which Israel is referred to in the singular:[133]

They scattered him in all directions;
He sought [in vain] the vision, hidden;
Yes, the visionaries sealed it from light . . .
The wicked men encompassed him, menacingly seeking to devour him;
They imprisoned him and he looked for light in the evening.

The superscription designating the hymn as a *me'orah* is misleading and was probably added by a later editor. *'Oyevi bi-m'eyrah* is connected to R. Meir's *Me'onah 'eloha šamayim*, to be chanted at the close of the Sabbath, as indicated in its refrain, 'Mighty are You and luminous who separated the darkness from the light.' This refrain is based on the *havdalah* service benediction, 'Praised are You . . . who divides light from darkness.' The connection between *Me'onah 'eloha*, and *'Oyevi bi-m'eyrah* is confirmed by the acrostic which begins in the first hymn with 'Meir Be-Rabbi' and concludes in the second with 'Eliyahu Ḥazaq'. R. Meir, like most of the early Italians and Franco-Germans, did not compose *me'orot* as separate liturgical units.[134]

[132] Habermann, *Toledot Ha-Piyyut*, ii. 244–5.
[133] Habermann, *Piyyuṭim We-Širim*, pp. 13–16.
[134] Fleischer, *Ha-Yoṣerot*, p. 673.

Like many central European poets, R. Meir constructed his *mi kamokha* hymn with a Hispanic-style cosmic preface. In his epic 216-cola *Mi kamokha, mitnasse' ba-marom 'al keruvo*, for Passover, he expatiates on the creation of the world, the story of the Patriarchs, the exodus from Egypt and the dividing of the sea. The hymn closes with 'Who is like You, O Lord, majestic among the gods? And they sang . . . this song on that day.' R. Meir varies from the typical Hispanic rhyming quatrains in this genre by constructing the opening four strophes in tercets, with rhyming couplets and closing scriptural verse. The remaining strophes are in quatrains of rhyming tercets and closing verse. All verses are in monorhyme ending with *hu'*. The acrostic, one of the lengthiest in Hebrew hymnography, yields 'Meir, the alphabet, I, Meir son of Elijah from the municipality of Norwich which is in the island country called England; I will strive in the Torah of my Maker and in the fear of Him, amen, amen selah.' Unlike the general practice of the Hispanics, the eclectic R. Meir resorts to an extensive use of rabbinic allusions. Following are some examples:[135]

> Before the foundations were laid,
> Before the cold from the scattering wind,
> Seven creations He made;
> He is the One who formed all things. [ll. 9–10]

The 'seven creations' are cited in *bPes* 54a: 'Seven things were created before the world was created, and these are they: The Torah, repentance, the Garden of Eden, Gehenna, the Throne of Glory, the Temple and the name of the Messiah.'

> He caused the earth to put forth vegetation *a fortiori* [*be-qal wa-ḥomer*]
> And trees by their own shape [*le-ṣivyonam*] were created;
> The awe-inspiring luminaries He made;
> The great and the small are there. [ll. 19–20]

This strophe can be understood only with reference to rabbinic sources. In the first line the poet alludes to the comment in *bḤul* 60a:

> For when the Holy One, blessed be He, enjoined 'after its kind' [Gen. 1: 11] upon the trees, the plants applied unto themselves an *a fortiori* argument, saying: If the Holy One, blessed be He, desired a motley growth, why did He enjoin, 'after its kind' upon the trees? Moreover, if upon trees, which by nature do not grow up in a motley growth, the Holy One, blessed be He, enjoined 'after its kind', how much more so does it apply to us! Immediately each plant came forth after its kind.

[135] Ibid. 575–91; Habermann, *Piyyuṭim . . . Rabbi Meir*, pp. 17–31.

In the second line, R. Meir refers to the statement in *bḤul* 60a:

All the animals of the creation were created in their full-grown stature, with their consent, and according to the shape of their own choice, for it is written [in Gen. 2: 1]: 'And the heaven and the earth were finished, and all their host'; read not 'their host' [*ṣeva'am*] but 'their shape' [*ṣivyonam*].

R. Meir's *tokheḥah* (self-rebuke), *Miqreh beru'im we-sodam*, was probably intended as a private meditation for the ill and infirm. Unlike the central European poets, whose liturgical writings focused on the corporate needs of the congregation and generally disregarded personal concerns, R. Meir's 'admonition', written in the first person singular—probably to his son—is distinctive in the manner in which it individualizes man's concern with death and the grave:[136]

When his time comes [to die],
He cannot escape . . .
The Angel [of Death] stands before him,
His drawn sword, in his hand . . .
The body descends into the grave;
He is buried in the sand;
Alas, after he is covered,
There is no rest for him . . .
He is sent to be punished there;
A lash for each sin . . .
Be fearful of these;
Tremble and sin not;
My son, shun transgression;
Justice, justice pursue . . .
Keep the word of my Rock and Redeemer
Who supports me in my lot . . .

'He is sent to be punished there' is a reference to the legend of 'Judgment and Punishment in the Grave' (*din we-ḥibbuṭ ha-qever*) from the writings of the Babylonian *ge'onim*. The legend was later incorporated into the liturgical writings for the Byzantine synagogue.[137] Like some of the central Europeans, R. Meir tried his hand at composing *qaṣīdah*-type hymns in metrically balanced hemistichs. In some sixteen of these, which he dedicated to a friend, R. Meir displays his virtuosity. The hymns, divided into sets of four, are built in quatrains with rhyming morphemes in both the opening and closing of the colon. The author's name 'Meir' is given in the acrostic of each set.[138]

[136] Fleischer, *Širat Ha-Qodeš*, p. 470; Habermann, *Piyyuṭim . . . Rabbi Meir*, pp. 5–8.
[137] Weinberger, *Seder Ha-Seliḥot . . . Ha-Romaniotim*, pp. 20–2.
[138] Habermann, *Piyyuṭim . . . Rabbi Meir*, pp. 32–9.

4

Synagogue Poets in Balkan Byzantium

GENERAL BACKGROUND

Greece and Anatolia

ALTHOUGH it is likely that Jewish settlements in Balkan Byzantium existed from the time the Eastern Empire was founded by Constantine in 330 until the advent of Alexius Comnenus (1081–1118) and his heirs, the historical record begins with the visit of Benjamin of Tudela to the region in 1168. During his visit to Constantinople, the capital of the Empire, Benjamin was impressed with its sizeable Jewish community of Rabbanites and Karaites. Making his way through the Via Egnatia, the southern Balkan trade route linking the Adriatic to the Black Sea, and the seaport cities, the Tudelan itinerant noted his impressions of some twenty-seven Graeco-Jewish settlements engaged in farming and cloth-dying, silk manufacture and tanning. Jewish communities not mentioned by Benjamin include Kastoria on the Via Egnata, the home of the learned R. Tobias b. Eliezer, author of the *Midraš Leqaḥ Ṭov* (written and revised in 1097–1108) and Selymbria (Silivri), the city near Constantinople where the twelfth-century rabbi Hillel b. Eliaqim lived. Author of commentaries on the *Sifra* and *Sifre*, R. Hillel is cited as an authority in Jewish law by R. Isaac b. Abba Mari of Marseilles (*c.*1120–*c.*1190) in his *Sefer Ha-ʿIṭṭur* and by the thirteenth-century Italian Tosafist, Isaiah b. Mali of Trani.[1]

In the Roman Empire, the Jews as a religious group were tolerated according to law (*religio licita*). Although their status did not change when the Empire came under the control of Christian monarchs, this became subject to several restrictions. In the east the Byzantine emperor Theodosius II (408–50) in his code of 438 prohibited the building of new synagogues and allowed only essential structural repairs on existing buildings. His code also forbade excesses in Purim celebrations. This intrusion into Jewish religious

[1] See Dinur, *Yisra'el Ba-Golah*, II. ii. 157; Bowman, *The Jews of Byzantium*, pp. 333–7.

practice was followed by others under Justinian I (527–65), who sought to regulate the Jewish worship service by forbidding rabbinic interpretations in the Scripture lesson and by being involved in deciding which biblical translation to use (see Sharf, *Byzantine Jewry*, p. 24). Later emperors in the Heraclian (Heraclius I, 610–41), Isaurian (Leo III, 717–41) and Macedonian (Basil I, 867–86, and Romanus I, 919–44) dynasties sought to convert Jews to Christianity by force. The east Roman emperor in Nicaea, John III, Ducas Vatatzes (1222–54), made a similar effort.

Despite these problems, Jewish life flourished in southern Italy under Byzantine control through most of the Phrygian and Macedonian dynasties (820–1081). The Fourth Crusade in 1204, which led to the capture of Constantinople by western Europeans, also brought destruction to the Jewish settlements in the city and its suburb, Pera. Following the recapture of the city in 1261 and the emergence of the Palaelogi dynasty in the same year, there were no legal changes in the status of the Romaniote (the name by which the early settlers in the region were known) Jews in Balkan Byzantium.

Benjamin of Tudela in his travels through the region observed that the larger communities were led by five elders and the smaller by two, and he gives their names. Although Jews were a separate autonomous community, they absorbed some aspects of the Hellenistic world. The president of the congregation was the *archisynagogos*; the synagogue council was called the *gerousia* (elders), its members were named *archontes* (magistrates), and the keeper of the archives and regulations was the *grammateus* (secretary). Tobias b. Eliezer in his *Leqaḥ Ṭov* and Hillel b. Eliaqim in his *Sifra* and *Sifre* commentaries often had to transliterate Hebrew words into Greek and explain obscure passages in the vernacular. The vernacular intrusion is also reflected in the local Romaniote liturgy which calls for the following readings in Greek:

1. Announcements of the New Moon.
2. The reading of the Book of Jonah on the Day of Atonement.
3. More than thirty liturgical offerings from Constantinople, Janina and Corfu. The hymns included threnodies (*qinot*) for the Ninth of 'Av, and additions to the service on the Days of Awe, Pentecost, Purim and the close of the Sabbath.[2]

The Jews in Balkan Byzantium and Asia Minor, known as the Romaniotes or Gregos, preserved their liturgy in the *Maḥazor Romania*. Romaniote hymnists from the eleventh century are Benjamin b. Samuel, Isaac b. Judah

[2] Additional evidence that the Jews absorbed Hellenistic culture is seen in their multilingual liturgical writings, in which the opening strophe in Hebrew is followed by strophes in Greek, and in words and phrases in Greek inserted into the Hebrew hymn. See Sharf, *Byzantine Jewry*, p. 179; Starr, *The Jews in the Byzantine Empire*, p. 212; D. Benvenisti, 'Multi-Lingual Hymns' [Hebrew], *Sefunot*, xv (1981), pp. 214, 221–6, 229–334; J. Matsa, 'Jewish Poetry in Greek' [Hebrew], *Sefunot*, xv. 237–366; Weinberger, *'Antologia*, pp. 12–13, 99, 218.

and Benjamin b. Zeraḥ. Prominent Romaniotes from the twelfth to fourteenth centuries include Moses b. Ḥiyyah, Joseph Qalai, Abraham b. Isaac b. Moses, Moses Ḥazan of Thebes and Solomon Šarvit Ha-Zahav of Ephesus.

The Role of the Poet

It is likely that the Romaniote poet served as the congregational cantor. Like his predecessors in west Asia and his contemporaries in central Europe, Benjamin b. Samuel asked permission to lead his congregation in prayer. The following is from his *mešullaš*, *Be-ruaḥ nišbarah histofafti*, to his New Year *qerovah*, *'Aggan ha-sahar*:[3]

With a broken spirit I approach the door of Your sanctuary
Seeking mercy for Your holy ones [Israel];
May the utterances I make be as sweet as the fragrance of [altar] offerings,
As I lift my hands towards Your most holy sanctuary.

Like Yannai, R. Benjamin is seen taking a position in disputes regarding Jewish law. Fragments of R. Benjamin's *'azharah*, [*Moṣa'*] *sefatayim li-šmor*, discovered in the Cairo Geniza, provide evidence of the author's independence as a hymnist and of his self-image as a legal authority. Unlike Sa'adyah Ga'on's *'azharah*, or the metric *'azharah* of Solomon Ibn Gabirol,[4] R. Benjamin's treatment of the genre offers, in addition to the conventional catalogue of positive and negative commands, a summary listing after sets of ten commands:[5]

Whatever your lips [utter], you must diligently observe and do [Deut. 23: 24]; and recite before bringing the first fruits [Deut. 26: 5]; and declare, I have given to the Levite [Deut. 26: 13];
[Aaron] shall bless the people [Num. 6: 23], the first fruits of His harvest;
The woman suspected of infidelity [Num. 5: 12 ff.]; the beheaded heifer [Deut. 21: 3 ff.]; and one-tenth of the tithe [Num. 18: 26];
The holy congregation in Jerusalem shall consume the tithes of the new grain and wine and the firstlings of their herds and flocks in the presence of the Lord [Deut. 14: 22, 23];
These add up to one hundred and ten.

R. Benjamin counts 'Whatever your lips utter you must diligently observe and do' as two separate commands. This is contrary to the opinion of

[3] *Maḥazor Le-Yamim*, i. 178; see also Fleischer, ' 'Azharot le-R. Binyamin', pp. 23–4.
[4] Sa'adyah Ga'on, *Siddur*, pp. 157–216; Ibn Gabirol, *Širey Ha-Qodeš*, pp. 392–441.
[5] Fleischer, 'Azharot le-R. Binyamin', pp. 44–6.

the *Halakhot Gedolot* from the period of the *ge'onim*, and the views of Maimonides and Naḥmanides, who count 'observe and do' as one command. Presumably, R. Benjamin relied upon an unidentified halakhic code based on the rabbinic opinion (in *bRH* 6a), ' "That which is gone out of your lips" (Deut. 23: 24), this is an affirmative precept . . . "and do" [ibid.], this is an injunction to the *beyt din* [court of law] to make you do.'[6]

After his summary of a ten-set strophe of positive commands, R. Benjamin summarizes the negative commands after two strophes of ten. In numbering the negative commands, R. Benjamin further asserts his independence by following a halakhic code that differed from the authoritative *Halakhot Gedolot*. Following is an illustration from his negative commands: [7]

> [You shall eat] no bread, or parched grain, or fresh ears [until you have brought the offering to your God] [Lev. 23: 14]; [do not eat] the thigh muscle that is on the socket of the hip [Gen. 32: 33];
> [You shall not ill-treat] the widow and the orphan [Exod. 22: 21]; do not act towards them as a creditor [Exod. 22: 24];
> Exact no interest from them [ibid.]; do not importune [a debtor] persistently for payment [Deut. 15: 2];
> When you set the slave free, do not feel aggrieved. [Deut. 15: 18];

Ill-treatment of the widow and the orphan are counted as two separate prohibitions by R. Benjamin, contrary to the opinions of the *Halakhot Gedolot*, Maimonides and Naḥmanides, who consider them as only one negative command.[8]

Isaac b. Judah also takes a stand on issues of Jewish law. R. Isaac's *yoṣerot* for Sabbaths Šeqalim, Zakhor, Parah, Ha-Ḥodeš and Ha-Gadol, are mostly reviews of rabbinic literature and legal opinions pertaining to those observances. At times he chooses between opposing halakhic views, as in his *yoṣer* for Šabbat Ha-Gadol, *'Eli ṣuri wi-yšu'ati*, where he sides with the opinion of Rabbi Isaac b. Melkiṣedek of Siponto (the 'Greek rabbi', an appellation given to him by R. Abraham b. David of Posquières, in Maimonides, *Mišneh Torah*, *Ṭum'at Met*, 1. 11, 25. 3), who permits vessels made of cattle dung to be prepared for Passover use by rinsing alone. In this he is opposed by the North African authority R. Isaac Al-Fasi and by Maimonides, who require scouring in hot water.[9] Below is the relevant couplet from R. Isaac's *yoṣer*.[10]

> Dung [vessels] require rinsing;
> Glazed vessels that expel [what they absorb]
> Are forbidden for [Passover] use.

[6] Fleischer, ''Azharot le-R. Binyamin', p. 44.
[7] Ibid. 53–4.
[8] Ibid. 54.
[9] See *Ṭur*, *'Oraḥ Ḥayyim*, No. 451.
[10] Weinberger, *Re'šit Ha-Payṭanut*, pp. 160–1.

Benjamin b. Zeraḥ undoubtedly served as the rabbi-poet of his community. Later generations referred to him as 'Our rabbi, Benjamin, the great, master of the Name' (*Rabbana' Binyamin Ha-Gadol, Ba'al Ha-Šem*). The latter appellation may derive from his familiarity with both the names of angels—of which he names some twenty-six in his *'ofannim*—and the names of God. Presumably, R. Benjamin employed the theurgic force of the esoteric divine names in the service of his congregation in much the same way as did Samuel Ibn Nagrela in his victory over Seville in 1039.

Romaniote Mysticism

Mysticism, defined as the attempt to attain illumination by the divine, was a leading attraction for the Romaniotes. When Maimonides was asked if the tracts on the 'Measure of [God's] Body' (*ši'ur qomah*) were written by the sages (in the period of the *ge'onim*), he replied disdainfully that these tracts were the work of 'Greek preachers [*ha-daršanim ha-yewanim*] and nothing more.'[11] Benjamin b. Samuel writes in his *'ofan*, *Mah dodekh mi-dod*, commenting on the dimensions of the Beloved (God) in Cant. 4: 11–16, that although the latter is 'hidden, concealed from every breathing soul', he will praise him 'there' in the heights. Isaac b. Judah is thoroughly familiar with the *heykhalot* (celestial palaces) literature and in his *'ofan*, *Yidodun, yidodun*, he speculates on the mystery of the divine chariot throne. Benjamin b. Zeraḥ, master of the divine names, introduces his congregation to the angels surrounding the *merkavah* in his *'ofan*, *Beluley 'eš u-meymot*.

Moses b. Ḥiyyah, one of the later Romaniotes, continued the practice of expatiating on the mysteries of creation (*ma'aseh bere'šit*) and the chariot throne. In his description of the palaces (*heykhalot*) leading to the throne, he refers to the ascent of the Four who entered the Garden (*pardes*) and the warning of Rabbi Akiva (in *bḤag* 14b), 'When you arrive at the stones of pure marble [that look like water], say not, Water, water [and we cannot proceed].' Below are the relevant strophes from his *seliḥah*, *'Adonay 'azkir šemo be-hegyonay*: [12]

> The Lord has aligned His palace;
> Its appearance resembles that of bdellium;
> And encompassing His stronghold
> Round and round goes the wind.

In the same hymn—as in his *rahiṭ*, *We-'attah malki mi-qedem*[13]—R. Moses bases his cosmogonic speculation on the *Sefer Yeṣirah* where God is said to have a created the world by means of the thirty-two secret paths of

[11] Maimonides, *Tešuvot*, No. 118, p. 201.
[12] Weinberger, *Re'šit Ha-Payṭanut*, pp. 36–8.
[13] Ibid. 41.

wisdom, consisting of the ten *sefirot* added to the twenty-two letters of the Hebrew alphabet:

God sealed [the world] with the secret of the letters *ʾalef*, *mem*, *šin*;
He set limits that their foundations not be moved;
He created form from formlessness
And He drew from the spirit.

The poet's sources are *Sefer Yeṣirah* 3. 2 and 2. 6, and his intention is to explain to his congregation its cosmogony; that God employed the three letters *ʾalef*, *mem* and *šin* which he sealed with six rings, and that from them emerged, air (*ʾawir*), water (*mayim*) and fire (*ʾeš*) as the pillars (*yesodot*) for the creation of the world. With the air, or wind (*ruaḥ*), He created all the letters of the alphabet, and with the unbridled waters He made formlessness (*tohu*). God then set limits to the waters in the form of east, west, north and south, and above and below, hence the six rings. With the fire, He carved the Throne of Glory (*kisseʾ ha-kavod*) and the ministering angels.[14] Completing the cosmogonic portrait in his *seliḥah*, *ʾAdonay ʾazkir šemo be-hegyonay*, R. Moses adds an insight not found in the *Sefer Yeṣirah*:

God sanctified by all manner of sanctifications,
Carved out of His throne the souls . . .[15]

The throne made from primordial fire becomes the medium through which the living soul emerges. The poet's conceit was undoubtedly prompted by the rabbinic observation (in *bŠab* 152b), 'The souls of the righteous are hidden under the Throne of Glory.' The cantor-poet ends the last strophe by reassuring his congregation that the immortal soul will re-enter the body at the resurrection of the dead:

He will bring the good news to the dry bones [saying]:
I will cause breath to enter you.

R. Moses, like Benjamin b. Zeraḥ, shared the secrets of divine names with his congregation. In the above *seliḥah*, he writes:

The Lord, God is exalted and concealed;
He is crowned with forty-two [letters]
Which are understood only with reference to the letters
yw[=o]*d heʾ*;
The Maker of mountains and Creator of the wind.

The forty-two letters of the divine name were already known in the talmudic period, although the rabbis warned (in *bQid* 71a) against its misuse: 'The

[14] See Scholem, *Reʾšit Ha-Qabbalah*, pp. 30–1.
[15] Weinberger, *Reʾšit Ha-Payṭanut*, pp. 36–8.

forty-two-lettered name is entrusted only to him who is pious, meek, middle-aged, free from bad temper, sober and not insistent on his rights. And he who knows it, is heedful thereof and observes it in purity.' The forty-two letters were divided into seven sets as follows: *'BGYTṢ QR'SṬN NGDYKS BṬRṢTG HQDTN' YGLPZQ SQWṢYT*. They were known to R. Ha'yyay Ga'on, who wrote, 'Although the consonants of this name are well known, its proper vocalization is not rendered by tradition.'[16]

In the third colon of the strophe, R. Moses suggests that the forty-two-lettered name is understood only with reference to the initial phonemes of the two halves of the Tetragrammaton *YHWH*; that is *yw* (=o)*d*, with the numerical value of 20 ($y = 10$, $w = 6$, $d = 4$) and *wyw*, with the value of 22 ($w = 6$, $y = 10$, $w = 6$; $20 + 22 = 42$). The numerical values of the divine names are treated by Abraham Ibn Ezra (in his *Yesod Mora'*, II. 11), whose writings were probably known to R. Moses. The forty-two-lettered divine name, like the twenty-two-lettered one, was said to have theurgic powers when invoked.

R. Moses is also familiar with the names of angels patrolling the heavenly palaces (*heykhalot*). In the following strophe from his *rahiṭ*, *Yošev me'onah*, he cites the angel Anapi'el, guardian of the seventh palace:[17]

> He dwells concealed traversing the vault of heaven;
> He appoints officers for each district;
> And the prince Anapi'el whose worth increases
> Sits at the gate of the King.

In *Heykhalot Rabbati* 22. 3–4 the angel is referred to as 'Anapi'el *YW"Y* [=God]', who signified to the mystics an aspect of God's glory.[18] In the hymn the *YW"Y is* left out from Anapi'el's name. Presumably, the poet's congregation did not share the insights of the mystics and were not prepared for their bolder figure.

Distinctive among Romaniote hymns is the *seliḥah* for the Ten Days of Repentance, *Halelu 'et 'adonay 'emunay*, by the twelfth-century poet Avrekh b. Isaac. R. Avrekh's *seliḥah* is in rhyming quatrains with closing scriptural verses. Each strophe begins with the unit *halelu* (give praise). The opening colon indicates its purpose as a penitential:[19]

> Praise the Lord, you who are faithful, seek Him where He may be found in the acceptable time [*be'ittah reṣuyah*].

The 'acceptable time' (Ps. 69: 14) is designated as the period between the New Year and the Day of Atonement (*beyn kese' le-'asor*). From the *heykhalot* literature we learn that penitence is achieved when the soul, fortified with the requisite esoteric knowledge, ascends to the 'Throne of Glory'. This reinter-

16 See *'Oṣar Ha-Ge'onim*, iv, Ḥagigah, pp. 20–1.
17 Weinberger, *Re'šit Ha-Payṭanut*, pp. 52–4.
18 See Scholem, *Major Trends*, p. 56.
19 Weinberger, *Širat Ha-Qodeš*, pp. 49–50.

pretation of repentance is reflected in the rabbinic comment (in *bYoma* 86a), 'Great is repentance for it leads to the Throne of Glory.' Yehuday Ga'on (8th c.), in elaborating on this comment, notes that the penitent ascends heavenward through the seven firmaments. In a *heykhalot* tract, Rabbi Akiva describes his passage through the seven palaces making moral progress at each stage until he is able to stand before God and praise Him as 'the Sublime in the chambers of grandeur.' In the strophes that follow, the poet provides directions to the soul on making the 'ascent' to its heavenly home, armed with the knowledge of the ten *sefirot*, which he identifies as both *middot* and *sefirot*, after the manner of the author of *Sefer Ha-Bahir*.[20]

Enquire after the eternal (God), recite His attributes [*middot*] in the towers of Zion rebuilt . . .
Your soul lives because they [the *sefirot/middot*] are the source of life . . .
Praise the Lord who founded and emanated His world from nothing and renewed it [*himṣi' we-he'eṣil me-'ayin 'olamo we-ḥiddešo*] . . .
From the day when it entered His 'conception' [*he'elahu be-maḥašavah*] until the moment when it weakens and its days are ended . . .
Praise Him who created concealed beings [*hawayot nistamot*] who relate His fearful might . . .
When He overturned the mountains from their roots and divided the rivers with the attribute of this 'wisdom' [*be-middat ḥokhmah zo*] . . .
Praise [Him] . . . who engraved small signs in His thirty-two paths [*ba-ḥarot rešimot daqqot be-lev netivotaw*]
With 'understanding' [*binah*], numbered the third in His *sefirot* [*ha-nisperet šelišit bi-sfirotaw*], He carved them [*ḥaqaqam*] . . .
Praise the first of His glory divided into several colours of light in His domain . . .
All gain merit with 'lovingkindness' [*ḥesed*] . . .
Praise with song the name of God . . .
And the faithful with 'power' [*bi-gvurah*]; seek Him with fear . . .
Praise the fearful and awesome [God] . . .
That He may be gracious while He waits [for your repentance] and from His 'beauty' [*tif'eret*] give you in abundance a flow of life channelled [*šofe'a ḥayyim ka-ṣinnor*].
Praise the Lord . . .

[20] See Scholem, *Major Trends*, pp. 78–9; idem, *Re'šit Ha-Qabbalah*, p. 263; *Sefer Ha-Bahir*, No. 127, p. 61.

. . . that the goodness of His 'victory' [*niṣḥo*] embrace you like sand multiplied . . .
Praise . . . the Lord . . .
That the rays of His 'majesty' [*hodo*] be abundant and constant for you . . .
Praise the merciful and compassionate [God] . . .
The foundation [*yesod*] of the world . . .
Praise the holy One sanctifies by the attribute that is known to all [*be-middah ha-yedu'ah la-kol*] . . .
Called the diadem of the 'kingdom' [*'aṭeret malkhut*] . . .
Praise be to the mighty and powerful God, ineffable, named, *hawayah*
Which is [known] and will be and was;
Therefore whosoever desires . . . shall thank Him [*yeho(w)dehu*], as the man who made the ascent has spoken [*ke-na'am 'iš 'aliyah*] . . .
Give praise always to [God] abiding forever in adoration, understood through the thirty-two [*mi-sekhwi sekhuyah*]
Appointed from the natural [*menuyah mi-muṭba'*], built from the psychic [*benuyah mi-murgaš*] and covered with the intellectual [*u-mi-muskal 'aṭuyah*]
And say: 'Whoever comprehends this, will succeed [in making the "ascent"].'

It is apparent that R. Avrekh borrows terms and conceits from *Sefer Ha-Bahir* and the Gerona mystics. In addition to his reference to the *sefirot* as *middot* and *sefirot*, a practice of the *Bahir* author, he divides the *sefirot* of *maḥašavah*, *ḥokhmah*, *binah*, *ḥesed*, *gevurah*, *tiferet*, *neṣaḥ*, *hod*, *yesod*, and *malkhut* into three stages, 'the natural', 'the psychic' and 'the intellectual', as proposed by R. Azriel. However, the poet agrees with the *Bahir* in designating 'conception' (*maḥašavah*) as the first of the *sefirot*, and differs from R. Azriel, for whom 'crown' (*keter*) heads the list. In the remaining *sefirot* the poet's list coincides with that of R. Azriel and the *Bahir*.

The poet's terminology is indebted to *Sefer Yeṣirah* and the writings of the Gerona mystics and Jewish Neoplatonists. The view that the *sefirot* are the 'source of life' is similar to that of R. Azriel, for whom 'the existence of created beings is brought about by the *sefirot*.' God who 'engraved small signs in His thirty-two paths' is a reference to the combination of the twenty-two letters in the Hebrew alphabet with the ten *sefirot*, mentioned in *Sefer Yeṣirah*, chapter 1. The 'flow of life channelled' (*ka-ṣinnor*) is based on the perception that the *sefirot* radiate both direct and reflected light through a channel (*ṣinnor*), a view held by the Gerona mystics and later kabbalists.

In the cryptic strophe 'Praise be to . . . God, ineffable', etc. the poet hints that the ineffable Tetragrammaton is known to the mystic, in line with the view of R. Ezra of Gerona, 'From that time [of Moses] to the present there was not one generation in Israel which did not have the tradition of "wisdom"—that is, knowledge of the [ineffable] name [of God].' Moreover, he is suggesting that 'whosoever desires' to make the ascent shall use the divine name in thanksgiving (*yeho(w)dehu*) as the 'man who made the ascent has spoken.' The Hebrew *yeho(w)dehu*, it will be seen, comprises the four Tetragrammaton letters, *YHWH*. In the last colon the poet, careful in what he reveals, closes with the hint that whoever is privy to the secrets of the *sefirot* and the divine name ('the man who made the ascent') will have success (*tušiyah*) in his own effort to ascend.[21]

Romaniote Folk Practices

A widespread folk tradition preserved in the synagogue liturgy and frowned upon by rabbinic authorities[22] was the cantor-poet's habit of appealing to angels and other intermediaries to intercede before God on Israel's behalf. In support of this practice, the poets relied upon the rabbinic observation (in *Exod. Rabbah* 21. 4), 'When they [Israel] have all finished [praying], the angel appointed over prayers collects all the prayers that have been offered in all the synagogues, weaves them into garlands and places them upon the head of God.' Among the other intermediaries to whom the poets appealed were the Torah, the Divine Throne of Glory (*kisse' ha-kavod*), the Patriarchs and the personified Thirteen Attributes. The hypostatizing of the Attributes was suggested by the rabbis in *bSan* 94a, where the Attribute of Justice is portrayed as communicating with deity, and/or in *bSan* 97b, delaying the coming of the Messiah.

An appeal to the 'Attributes bearing the Throne of Glory' to intercede before God is prominent in the *heykhalot* literature (*Heykhalot Rabbati* 11. 2). In the synagogue liturgy, one of the earliest examples of an appeal to intermediaries is preserved in the hymn from the period of the *ge'onim*, *Makhnisey raḥamim*, attributed to R. Amram Ga'on: [23]

> Angels of mercy,
> Usher in [our petition for] mercy
> Before the Lord of mercy;

[21] Azriel of Gerona, 'Še'elot', Nos. 33–4; idem, 'Explanation', p. 91; Scholem, *Re'šit Ha-Qabbalah*, pp. 273–5; idem, 'Kabbalah'. Ezra of Gerona's statement is preserved in *Haqdamah Le-Peruš Šir Ha-Širim*, in Naḥmanides, *Kitvey Ha-Ramban*, ii. 477–8; Weinberger, 'Seliḥah'.

[22] See Maimonides in his commentary on *mSan* 10. 5.

[23] *Seder Ha-Seliḥot . . . Polin*, p. 16.

Angels of prayers,
Make heard our prayers
Before Him who listens to prayers.

The earliest European hymns exemplifying this practice are seen in Amittai's *'Ezkerah 'elohim we-'ehemayah* and Simeon b. Isaac's *Ševet ha-kisse' 'ašer le-ma'alah menusse'*. The former appeals to the Attribute of Mercy hypostatized, and the latter to the 'Throne of Glory'. The Thirteen Attributes, which the rabbis (in *bRH* 17b) identified in Exod. 34: 6, were invested with the power to intercede on Israel's behalf, as indicated in the *seliḥah Šeloš 'esreh middot ha-'amurot ba-ḥaninah*, by the twelfth- to thirteenth-century hymnist Solomon b. Menaḥem, presumably from Byzantium.[24]

In the Balkan synagogue, the practice of seeking the intercession of intermediaries is seen in Moses Ḥazan's *rahiṭim We-hegyon mešartekha* and *Pi 'eftaḥ le-hallelkha*, albeit in a more reserved manner. The poet does not directly refer to angels or personified figures, but to 'advocates' (*meliṣey*) and 'advocates of the right' (*meliṣey yošer*), on Israel's behalf: [25]

WE-HEGYON

O exalted One, receive favourably the prayers of the advocates of the right;
O fearful and awesome One, banish the adversary and prosecutor . . .

PI 'EFTAḤ

Heed the declaration of my beloved advocates:
'All our words are just.'

Although Moses Ḥazan does not name the 'advocates', it may be assumed that he had in mind the speech of Elihu, in Job 33: 23, describing the intercessory role of an angel in a judgment process. The rabbis expand on the verse from Job, adding (in *bSab* 32a), 'Even if nine hundred and ninety-nine parts of that angel are in his [man's] disfavour and one part is in his favour, he is saved, for it is said [Job 33. 23] 'an angel, an advocate, one part in a thousand.'

THE PRINCIPAL POETS: EARLY ROMANIOTES

Benjamin b. Samuel

Whereas the data on the Jews in Byzantine Italy is plentiful thanks to the journal of Aḥima'aṣ b. Paltiel, information about their Romaniote brethren in the Balkans during the Macedonian and Comnenian dynasties is scant. It is

[24] Ibid. 95–8, 174–5, 208.

[25] Weinberger, *Širat . . . Rabbanim*, pp. 87, 110.

likely that one of the earliest hymnists in south-eastern Europe was Benjamin b. Samuel (11th c.), author of *qedušta'ot*, *yoṣerot* and *'azharot*. This conjecture is supported by the twelfth-century Provençal rabbi Joseph b. Plat. Cited in *Sefer Ha-Pardes* (from the school of RaŠI),[26] he mentions the poet Benjamin b. Samuel, who is said to have been R. Joseph's grandfather from Balkan Byzantium. R. Joseph also observed[27] that congregational choral responses, a common practice in central European synagogues, were notably absent in the Romaniote synagogue, where 'the cantor recites the benediction [introducing the *Hallel*, Pss. 113–18], and all others remain silent.' Distinctive in Benjamin b. Samuel's liturgical writing is his treatment of the *guf ha-yoṣer* for Tabernacles, *'Akhof we-'ikkaf wa-essa' de'iy la-gavoha*. Unlike central European hymnists, he constructs his *qadoš* refrain, following the third strophe, with anadiplosis:

> . . . *'eyno ra'uy le-virkat 'eḥad*
> *'Eḥad barukh šemo . . . qadoš.*

> [A palm-branch obtained through robbery] is not fit for benediction of the One
> The One, blessed be His name . . . holy.[28]

Although the poet does not sign his full name in the hymn's refrain, he spells his first name *Binyamin*, without the letter *yod* before the closing *nun*, in line with his practice in some of his other liturgical writings.[29]

In his Tabernacles hymn, R. Benjamin reviews the laws pertaining to the festival, a practice he follows in his *rešut* for Šabbat Ha-Gadol, *'Az ke-gulgal ši'bud horim*, in which he informs his congregation about the rules pertaining to Passover observance. The poet's instructions for the festival are in line with rabbinic teaching (in *bPes* 6a): 'Questions are asked and lectures are given on the laws of Passover for thirty days before the Passover. R. Simeon b. Gamaliel said: Two weeks.' Following is a revealing couplet from R. Benjamin's *rešut*:

> What is the reason that the table is removed from its place?
> In order that the young people should ask, 'Why is this night different?'[30]

In instructing his congregation to lift the Seder table in order to prompt the curiosity of the children, R. Benjamin is following the practice from talmudic times. This is noted in *bPes* 115b: 'R. Simi b. Aši said: We remove the table . . .

[26] *Sefer Ha-Pardes*, p. 208.

[27] Ibid.

[28] *Maḥazor Romania* (Venice, 1522–3), p. 405b.

[29] See Schirmann, *Širim Ḥadašim*, p. 421; cf. Fleischer, who argues for a Franco-German provenance for R. Benjamin in his ' 'Azharot le-R. Binyamin', pp. 5–6, 10–44; see also Fleischer, *Ha-Yoṣerot*, p. 616 n. 27.

[30] *Maḥazor Romania*, Bibliothèque Nationale, Paris, MS No. 606, fo. 71.

before him who recites the *Haggadah*.' This practice continued in Balkan homes, as seen in the directions given by the editor of the Romaniote Prayer-Book, the *Maḥazor Romania*: 'The table is to be lifted' (*we-ʿoqrin ha-šulḥan*).[31] From the comments of RaŠI and from *tosafot* on the statement of R. Simi in *bPes* 115b, we learn that the practice of removing the Seder table was discontinued. The reason was that it became too burdensome to remove the large tables used in French homes, as distinct from the smaller tables in use in the eastern Mediterranean region.

The change of practice in the French home is reflected in the *silluq*, *'Eyn ʿarokh 'eylekha le-haggid*, for the Sabbath before Passover (Šabbat Ha-Gadol) by the early French hymnist R. Joseph Ṭov Elem, in which he reviews for his congregation the laws pertaining to the Seder:

Why do you remove the *plate* [italics mine] before its time?
In order that the child may see and ask, 'Why is this different?'[32]

Like R. Benjamin in his *rešut*, Ṭov Elem in his *silluq* instructs his congregation on the laws of Passover through a series of rhetorical questions. Presumably, their differing opinions on whether to lift the table, or make do with the lighter plate because the table is too heavy, is reflective of the diverse practices in the regions in which they lived.[33]

Characteristic of R. Benjamin is his tendency to load his hymns with neologisms, allusions to rabbinic sources and polemics modelled after his classical predecessors. Following is his anti-Christian diatribe in hymn No. 5 of his *qedušta'*, *'Arukkah me-'ereṣ middah*:[34]

You shall not have loathsome symbols
Crafted in the image of man;
Pursue the name [of God] renewed [in praise] by the 'Er'ellim,
And do not profane it with idols.

Although indebted to the practice of the classical hymnists, R. Benjamin is eclectic in his hymnography. For example, in his *qerovah*, *'Aggan ha-sahar*, he signs his name in the strophe preceding the *meḥayyeh* benediction, and connects the strophe by anadiplosis to the set of preceding scriptural verses.[35] However, in his *qedušta'* for Pentecost, *'Arukkah me-'ereṣ middah*, he signs his name 'Binyamin' in the strophe preceding the *meḥayyeh* benediction but he does not connect the strophe by anadiplosis to the preceding set of scriptural verses.[36]

31 Ibid. 66, and *Maḥazor Romania* (Constantinople, 1510), p. 98.
32 Ber, *Seder*, p. 720; Weinberger, 'Hebrew Poetry'.
33 Cf. Fleischer, ' 'Azharot le-R. Binyamin', p. 31 n. 109; see Weinberger, 'Ha-payṭan'.
34 Weinberger, *'Antologia*, p. 42.
35 This is also the practice of R. Simeon b. Isaac of Mainz, but not of Amittai, the Apulian.
36 See *Maḥazor Le-Yamim*, i. 89, 178; Amittai, *Širey*, p. 12; Weinberger, *'Antologia*, p. 40.

R. Benjamin further asserts his independence in the treatment of the strophe preceding the *magen* benediction in *'Aggan ha-sahar*. Following classical models, he connects this strophe by anadiplosis to the set of preceding scriptural verses. Unlike his classical forebears, however, he signs his name in this strophe and begins his signature with the unit after the anadiplosis:[37]

> 'In the path of Your judgments, O Lord, we wait for You; Your name and Your renown are the soul's desire [*ta'awat nefeš*].' [Isa. 26: 8]
> The soul of Your chosen one [*nefeš beḥirekha*], please [*na'*] do not distress;
> Fulfil our hopes from above and protect us [*yiḥulenu me-rum tašlim le-hagen*].

The underlined letters *bnymn* coming after the anadiplosis unit spell the poet's name Binyamin, minus the *yod* before the closing *nun*. In his *qedušta'* for Pentecost, *'Arukkah me-'ereṣ middah*, R. Benjamin connects the last strophe before the *magen* with the scriptural verse preceding it by anadiplosis, but he does not sign his name in that strophe as he does in the above *qerovah*. Given that the treatment of the last strophe before the *magen* and *meḥayyeh* benedictions had not been standardized, poets felt free to improvise in this respect. This may also explain the unusual occurrence of two consecutive *qiqlar* strophes in R. Benjamin's Pentecost *qedušta'*, hymn No. 6. As indicated, the classical-era *qedušta'*, beginning with Qillir, featured the *qiqlar* strophe as a choral response ending with the unit *qadoš*. The response appeared in hymn No. 6, after sets of three strophes. Below are translations of R. Benjamin's uncommon consecutive choral responses, from his Pentecost *qedušta'*:[38]

> As You have encompassed us around the mountain [Sinai],
> Like a skylight visible to all,
> So may You hearken on high to the 'rounded bowl' [Israel, Cant. 7: 3], O exalted and holy [*marom we-qadoš*].
>
> As You have announced the ten commands
> To the nation exalted by tithing,
> So will You proclaim the arrival of the herald,
> Bringing news of comfort and redemption, holy One [*qadoš*].

[37] Signing the poet's name in the strophe preceding the *magen* was also the practice of Amittai and of Simeon b. Isaac. See *Maḥazor Le-Yamim*, i. 89, 176; Amittai, *Širey*, p. 10; Fleischer, ''Azharot le-R. Binyamin', pp. 24–5.

[38] See Weinberger, *'Antologia*, p. 43; Habermann, *Piyyuṭey Rabbi Šim'on*, p. 90; Fleischer, ''Azharot le-R. Binyamin', pp. 26–7.

R. Benjamin's liturgical writings were preserved mostly in Balkan prayer-books, and some were also adopted by Franco-German congregations.

Isaac b. Judah

The hymns of R. Benjamin's younger contemporary Isaac b. Judah, author of *yoṣerot*, *zulatot* and *'ofannim*, survive only in the rituals of southern Europe, in Italian, Romaniote and Corfiote congregations. That R. Isaac lived in the latter half of the eleventh century we learn from his *zulat*, *'Aqumah we-lev 'akhinah*, where he laments the loss of Israel's national home in the latter third of the first century:[39]

Hear the suppressed, imprisoned
A little over a thousand years;
Tearful bread You have fed them.

Isaac b. Judah's work also reflects the pervasive influence of Solomon Ha-Bavli's neo-classicism.. This is seen in his consistent word metre, and in his end rhyme which comprised two morphemes, in the manner of Qillir which Ha-Bavli revived. As indicated, late classical poets like Phinehas Ha-Kohen found the two-morpheme end rhyme too cumbersome, and made do with one only.[40]

Departing from classical models, R. Isaac, like his colleagues in central Europe, uses scriptural verses, albeit sparingly, in embellishing his hymns. The only surviving work in which he employs verses from Scripture in closing the strophe is his *zulat*, *'Aqumah we-lev 'akhinah*. However, in line with classical and eastern practices, R. Isaac favours anadiplosis,[41] even as he loads his hymns with neologisms and allusions to rabbinic sources.

Benjamin b. Zeraḥ

Benjamin b. Zeraḥ, prolific author of *yoṣerot* and *seliḥot*, informs us that he lived a little over 1,000 years after the destruction of the Temple in the first century CE. We learn this from his *zulat*, *'Anna' hašqifah*, and his *seliḥot*, *'Afefu we-hiqqifu ʿalay* and *'Adabberah we-yirwaḥ li*. Following are the revealing couplets in the latter hymn, in which he laments Israel's lot in exile:[42]

Am I made out of iron? Is my heart copper-coated
That I should be able to bear and suffer these many pains?
These many years [the Temple] lies wasted and ravaged;
A thousand years and more I am widowed and barren.

39 Weinberger, *Re'šit Ha-Payṭanut*, pp. 131, 8, English section.
40 See Fleischer, 'Širatenu', p. 211.
41 See Weinberger, *Re'šit Ha-Payṭanut*, p. 150.
42 See Zunz, *Literaturgeschichte*, p. 120; Brody and Wiener, *Mivḥar*, p. 212.

Both L. Zunz and Ḥ. Schirmann suggest that the poet flourished in Byzantium, and with good reason. Like Isaac b. Judah, Benjamin b. Zeraḥ was eclectic and innovative in his writings for the synagogue. His *yoṣer*, *'Itti mi-levanon kallah*, for the Sabbath before Passover, is built, like R. Isaac's *'Otot yemey ge'ullah*, with the uncommon five-cola *qadoš* refrain coming at the end of the first strophe and at the close of the hymn. Moreover, R. Benjamin in his *yoṣer*, *'Ihel be-'oz gevurotaw*, for Šabbat Bere'šit, connects the third strophe to the *qiqlar* refrain by anadiplosis. This is a habit of Benjamin b. Samuel in his *yoṣer*, *'Akhof we-'ikkaf*, and Isaac b. Judah in his *'Aḥalleh peney bore'*. This distinctive feature of the poets in Balkan Byzantium is absent from the hymnography of the early Italians or Franco-Germans. Below are the relevant strophes from R. Benjamin b. Zeraḥ's hymn:[43]

Qaddešuhu romem šifrotaw;
Takhlit binyan mif'alotaw;
Nafaš we-šavat tehillotaw.

Tehillotaw 'abbi'a be-miqdašo,
Le-ha'ariṣo u-le-haqqedišo;
U-le-romem 'et šem qodšo, qadoš.

Sanctify Him, exalted in the heavens,
Perfect in His constructive work;
He rested and was refreshed in His praises.

His praises I utter in His sanctuary,
To adore and sanctify Him,
And to exalt His sacred name, holy.

Benjamin b. Zeraḥ was eclectic in his choice of themes. In his *yoṣer 'Ahallel be-ṣilṣeley šama'*, he engages in the uncommon practice of commenting at length on the letters of the Hebrew alphabet. The special character of the alphabet is noted by the rabbis (in *bBer* 55a), 'Bezalel knew how to combine the letters by which the heavens and earth were created.' In the mystical literature of the *Sefer Yeṣirah* and the *heykhalot* writings, the twenty-two Hebrew letters are personified as spiritual essences emanating from God and invested with esoteric meaning. R. Benjamin's hymn is based in large part on the *Alphabet of Rabbi Akiva* (*c.*700)—a favourite text of the *heykhalot* mystics—from which he drew much of his theosophical speculation. Below is part of the *yoṣer*'s introduction and some relevant samples: [44]

The letters of His Torah I will explain to the general public;
Upon which He wondrously expanded and transmitted to Moses
at Sinai:

[43] Fleischer, *Ha-Yoṣerot*, p. 634.

[44] See Ber, *Seder*, 753–5; Scholem, *Major Trends*, p. 66.

[Letter] *Waw*:
Six seals on pillars of fire facing the Lord of all the angels;
They are the ineffable Names [*šemot ha-meforašim*], preferred above others;
The *'er'ellim* [a class of angels] use them in their secret meanings . . .

[Letter] *Yod*:
With a lasting memorial [*yad wa-šem*] and a crown of glory
He will bind His treasure [Israel] with text and tradition [saying]:
'The [Ineffable] Name eternal and unrevoked, I will give to him.'

With mastery of the secret names comes power strong enough to summon angelic forces and open the doors of the palaces (*heykhalot*).[45] Even the Divine Presence (*šekhinah*) can be coerced by the might of the esoteric names, as indicated in R. Benjamin's comment on the letter *mem*:

What is the reason that the two [letters, medial *mem* and final *mem*] are separate, but sound similar [when read from either direction]?
Because they praise the throne of glory, they prostrate themselves in their rendition:
'Your kingdom is a kingdom for the ages and Your dominion for all generations.' [Ps. 145: 13]

The obscure second colon, with a paraphrase of the *Alphabet of Rabbi Akiva*,[46] is explained by the thirteenth-century Bohemian commentator on the liturgy, R. Abraham b. Azriel: [47]

The two letters [medial and final *mem*] stand by the hidden Throne of Glory [*kisse' ha-kavod*] and fashion on their heads crowns of the Torah. When the time approaches to recite the *qedušsah* [Trisagion] and the Holy One does not descend from His heights to the Chariot [*merkavah*], the two letters [medial and final *mem*] approach each other and ask, 'When will the Holy One descend from His heights upon the Chariot that we may behold the image of His face and sing [his praises] before Him?' . . . Then as the Holy One descends upon the Chariot . . . all the letters that are in the Chariot receive the *šekhinah* with mighty song . . . What do they sing? Medial *mem* chants, 'Your kingdom is a kingdom for the ages,' and final *mem* sings, 'And Your dominion for all generations.'

Following the paraphrase of the *Alphabet of Rabbi Akiva*, R. Abraham notes the comment of R. Eleazar b. Judah of Worms that the angels standing

[45] Ibid. 56.
[46] See 'Alpha Beta de Rabbi Akiva', 418–19.
[47] See Abraham b. Azriel, *Sefer*, i. 130–1.

before the Throne were created in the form of letters, and when medial and final *mem*, representing 'kingdom' (*malkhut*) and 'dominion' (*memšalah*) appeared, all the heavenly hosts began to tremble before them (i.e. before the power that they personified). Therefore, they were made to prostrate themselves and recite the verse said by King David, 'Your kingdom . . . Your dominion.'

R. Benjamin's observation that the alphabet's esoteric lore was transmitted to Moses at Sinai and his reference to 'text and tradition' (*ba-re'ayah u-masoret*)—in his comment on the letter *yod*—are repeated in his *seliḥah* for the Day of Atonement morning service, *'Anna' 'adonay ha-'el ha-gadol*, which is built in rhyming couplets (*šeniyyah*). Of particular interest is the Divine Name of twenty-two letters, *Anaqtam Pastam Paspasim Dionsim*, written in the acrostic of the hymn. This name, believed to have theurgic powers, is mentioned in the *Sefer Raziel*, which preserved traditions in Jewish mysticism dating from the period of the *ge'onim*. Below is a selection from the *seliḥah*: [48]

I beseech the Lord God, great, mighty and awesome,
Fittingly named, and the Name helps the one who repeats it;
The humble one [Moses, after Num. 12: 3] was summoned in the cleft of the rock
[And ordered] to seize the tradition [*masoret*] in his hand before Galiṣur [the angel] attacks;
When he carried off the mighty stronghold [Torah] from the warriors' city to which he had ascended,
The Divine Name in his prayer he remembered to utter;
He passed on its secret to [Joshua] the attendant at his tent;
He [Moses] revealed its power [which Joshua used] when he fell prostrate in prayer [Josh. 7: 6];
He [Joshua] delivered it to the elders and the elders to the prophets of the treasured [Israel] . . .
Whosoever is familiar with it [the Name] and knows how to pronounce it with clarity,
Should be careful to invoke it in [a state] of purity and holiness . . .
Because its force is great and its power mighty.

The poet emphasizes that the esoteric tradition concerning the twenty-two-letter Divine Name was received by Moses at Sinai, and delivered to Joshua and the elders, prophets and Men of the Great Assembly (l. 6), in a manner similar to the exoteric Torah. The names of the parties to the transmission are similar to those listed in *'Avot* 1. 1. There the rabbis attempt to

[48] *Maḥazor Le-Yamim*, ii. 235–7; see also *Sefer Razi'el* (Amsterdam, 1701), pp. 42b, 44b and 45a.

establish the authority of the Oral Torah (*Torah še-baʿal peh*), which is believed to have been revealed to Moses at Sinai, along with the Written Torah (*Torah še-bi-ktav*). However, both Written and Oral Torah are exoteric literature available to the public, unlike the esoteric traditions—alleged by R. Benjamin to have been revealed at Sinai—which are available only to the favoured few in a state of 'purity and holiness.'

THE PRINCIPAL GENRES OF THE EARLY ROMANIOTES

Qedušta'

Benjamin b. Samuel's *qedušta'*, *'Arukkah me-'reṣ middah*, is constructed on nine topics after the classical model of Yannai, although he differs in some respects from the earlier practice. His *magen* is built in rhyming quatrains with a complete and uninterrupted alphabetic acrostic, unlike the practice of Yannai and Qillir, who insert the *magen* benediction and/or scriptural verses between the letters *lamed* and *mem*. However, like Qillir, R. Benjamin begins the strophe leading into the *magen* benediction with the unit ending the last of the *magen*'s scriptural verses. Below are samples from Qillir's *qedušta'* for Šabbat Ḥatanim, *'Ahavat neʿurim*, and R. Benjamin's *'Arukkah me-'ereṣ middah*:[49]

[QILLIR]
He is like a tree planted by streams of water, which yield their fruit in its season, and his leaf does not wither. In all that he does he prospers. [*yaṣliaḥ*, Ps. 1: 3]

'May the sprig of our planting ever prosper [*yaṣliaḥ*]
And not be led to stray from You;
In rejoicing establish Your house [Temple] as before,
And with the power of Your shield protect us.'

Blessed are You, shield of Abraham.

Note that R Benjamin also begins the strophe leading in to the *magen* benediction 'Blessed are you, shield of Abraham' with the unit *yam* which ends the last of the *magen*'s scriptural verses:

[R. BENJAMIN]
Its measure is longer than the earth and broader than the sea. [*minni yam*, Job 11: 9]

'The great sea [*yam gadol*] filled up its boundaries,
And the sun added to its lustrous crown

[49] See Fleischer, *Širat Ha-Qodeš*, p. 156; Weinberger, *'Antologia*, p. 39.

When He bequeathed 'the stronghold which they trusted [the Torah, Prov. 21: 22]
To the treasured [Israel], longing for protection in His shade.'

Blessed are You, shield of Abraham.

R. Benjamin's second hymn, the *meḥayyeh*, has a reverse alphabetic acrostic in rhyming quatrains, followed by a set of scriptural verses and a quatrain strophe leading into the *meḥayyeh* benediction. The third hymn, the *mešullaš*, R. Benjamin (like Qillir) builds in sets of quatrains and spells out his name in the acrostic. Following the model of the earlier master, R. Benjamin ends the set of *meḥayyeh* quatrains with the unit that opens the following scriptural verse. In this he reverses the practice in the *magen*, where he begins the quatrain with the unit that ends the scriptural verse. In this manner of interlocking hymn and verse, the poet effects a closure of the *magen*, *meḥayyeh* and *mešullaš* topics, thereby ending the first section of the *qedušta'*.

R. Benjamin's second section begins with the fourth hymn, preceded by *'el na'* (Please O Lord), and ends with *qadoš*.[50] Like the classical models, this hymn is a relatively short work in monorhyme prose, lacking strophes or acrostics. Since the fifth hymn was not standardized and received varied treatment by classical poets, R. Benjamin felt free to construct it in an abridged *dibrin* form, popularized by Qillir in his *qedušta'ot* for Pentecost.[51] The final third section of the *qedušta'* comprised non-standardized hymns as well, and poets were at liberty to innovate. However, R. Benjamin follows the model of Qillir in the sixth hymn of this section, and constructs it in rhyming tercets and alphabetic acrostic, with intermittent *qiqlar* strophes closing with *qadoš*.[52] In the seventh hymn, the *rahiṭ*, R. Benjamin also follows the Qilliric practice in the latter's *qedušta'ot* for Pentecost, *'Ereṣ maṭah we-ra'ašah* and *'Agmey qarim 'ad lo' hurequ*, and likewise devotes the hymn to the legend in which God seeks a suitable mate for the Torah. Both poets introduce this *rahiṭ* with the verse from Prov. 8: 22: 'The Lord created me [Wisdom, = Torah] at the beginning of His work, the first of His acts of long ago.' R. Benjamin's second *rahiṭ*, the eighth hymn in his *qedušta'*, is, like Qillir's Pentecost *qedušta'*, *'Ereṣ maṭah we-ra'ašah*, introduced by the verse from Exod. 19: 14, 'So Moses went down from the mountain to the people', and is constructed in a *dibrin* form, similar to his mentor's hymn No. 8 in the above *qedušta'*. R. Benjamin's *silluq*, the ninth hymn, is, like Qillir's, introduced with the litany, 'And thus may the sanctification ascend unto You, for You are the Holy One of Israel and the Redeemer', and, like the latter's, is written in non-strophic monorhyme prose, leading to the recitation of the *qeduššah*.[53]

50 Fleischer, ' 'Azharot le-R. Binyamin', p. 72 n. 4.
51 Weinberger, *'Antologia*, pp. 41–2; Fleischer, *Širat Ha-Qodeš*, pp. 180–2.
52 Weinberger, *'Antologia*, pp. 42–3; Fleischer, ' 'Azharot le-R. Binyamin', pp. 74–5.
53 Weinberger, *'Antologia*, pp. 43–51; *Maḥazor Le-Ḥag*, pp. 107–22.

Yoṣer

Benjamin b. Samuel's *yoṣer* for the Sabbath during the intermediary days of Passover, *'Az be-ha'avir sorarim*, has been preserved only in the *guf ha-yoṣer, silluq*, *'ofan* and *zulat*. His *guf ha-yoṣer* is constructed in rhyming quatrains with closing scriptural verses from Canticles. The absence of intermittent *qiqlar* refrains, after the manner of Qillir, is instructive. It is likely that in this practice R. Benjamin was influenced by Solomon Ha-Bavli's *yoṣer* for Passover, *'Or yeša' me'uššarim*, likewise built in rhyming quatrains with closing verses from Canticles, and without *qiqlar* refrains. Like Ha-Bavli's Passover hymn, R. Benjamin's *guf ha-yoṣer* spans the complete alphabetic acrostic, twofold, even as he employs the identical scriptural verses from Cant. 1: 1–3: 10. However, unlike his Italian colleague, R. Benjamin adds a set of strophes after completing the acrostic. In the latter he spells his name, *Binyamin Bi-Rabbi Šemu'el Ḥazaq.*[54]

Like Ha-Bavli's *'Or yeša'*, R. Benjamin follows his *guf ha-yoṣer* with the *silluq*, *'Ani yešenah be-galut bavel*, in monorhyme strophes opening with verses from Canticles and without alphabetical acrostic. R. Benjamin's *'ofan*, like Ha-Bavli's, is built in strophes which open with verses from Canticles, and, in line with Italian and Franco-German practices, he is not shy in his speculations on the nature of the divine chariot throne. As indicated above, this practice was generally avoided by the classical and late eastern poets out of regard for rabbinic authorities who forbade mention of the chariot throne in public.

Isaac b. Judah's *guf ha-yoṣer* is constructed on a modified neo-classical model, with an opening set of three rhyming tercets interrupted by a choral refrain, which reappears at the end of the hymn. R. Isaac employs this practice in his *yoṣerot*, *'Aḥalleh peney bore'*, *'Eli ṣuri wi-yšu'ati*, and *'Arannen la-boqer ḥasdekha*. These works encompass a complete alphabetic acrostic with first-name signature in the choral refrain. The exception to this pattern is the hymn *'Eqra' yomam we-lo' 'edmeh*, with its three choral refrains—one after the first set of three tercets, the second after the alphabetic acrostic, and the last at the hymn's end—and the signature of the author's first name and that of his father.[55] At other times, R. Isaac builds the *guf ha-yoṣer* on the Solomon Ha-Bavli model with sets of rhyming quatrains. However, unlike Ha-Bavli, who dispenses with the choral refrain since Italian congregations did not employ professional choirs, R. Isaac adds a closing, name-signature choral quatrain ending with *qadoš*, after his quatrains spanning the alphabet. R. Isaac's *yoṣerot* on this model are *'Essa' de'iy le-meraḥoq* and *'Afiq ron be-tokh ḥeleq*. Like Benjamin b. Samuel, R. Isaac is eclectic in his choice of *yoṣer*

[54] Bernstein, *Piyyuṭim*, pp. 44–57; Fleischer, *Piyyuṭey . . . Ha-Bavli*, pp. 191–203; Habermann, *Piyyutey Rabbi Šim'on*, pp. 27 ff; Fleischer, ''Azharot le-R. Binyamin', p. 22.

[55] Weinberger, *Re'šit Ha-Payṭanut*, pp. 140, 150, 160, 168.

configurations, as may be seen in his *'Otot yemey ge'ullah*, built in rhyming quatrains with a five-cola choral strophe, coming after the first quatrain and repeated at the close of the hymn. The five-cola *qadoš* strophe in a similar configuration is also used in the *yoṣer* by the eleventh-century Byzantine hymnist R. Benjamin b. Zeraḥ, in his *'Itti mi-levanon kallah*, for the Sabbath before Passover.[56] The *qiqlar* choral refrains in the liturgical writings of both Benjamin b. Samuel and Isaac b. Judah suggest that Joseph b. Plat's observation that the Romaniote congregation 'remain[ed] silent' occurred only when the cantor recited the benediction introducing the *Hallel*.

Of particular significance is R. Isaac's manner of connecting, by anadiplosis, the first set of tercets in his *guf ha-yoṣer*, *'Aḥalleh peney bore'* for Šabbat Ha-Ḥodeš, with the following *qadoš* refrain. This would appear to be a distinctive Romaniote practice followed by R. Benjamin b. Samuel, but not by the early Italians or Franco-Germans. Below are the relevant strophes from R. Isaac's hymn: [57]

Ge'ulay bo ḥofeš maṣa'u,
Me-'avdut le-ḥerut 'az nimṣe'u;
Kol ṣiv'ot 'adonay yoṣe'u.

Yoṣe'u ṣeva'ay ḥamušim;
Qibbuṣ 'eḥad me-ḥamiššim;
Bi-šlošah ḥalfu maššim, qadoš.

My redeemed were liberated therein [in the month of Nisan];
They found themselves freed from slavery;
All the hosts of the Lord went forth.

They went forth, my hosts, with their weapons,
One out of a group of fifty found their freedom;
On the third day the lenders [Egyptians] changed [and pursued the Israelites, Exod. 11: 2-3, 14: 5], O Holy One.

Benjamin b. Zeraḥ's *yoṣer*, *'Itti mi-levanon kallah*, for the Sabbath before Passover is built, like R. Isaac's *'Otot yemey ge'ullah*, with the uncommon five-cola *qadoš* refrain coming at the end of the first strophe and at the close of the hymn. Most unusual is R. Benjamin's *guf ha-yoṣer*, *'Eloheynu 'elohim 'emet*, for the Šabbat Bere'šit (according to the Italian rite). The hymn is composed in rhyming tercets, but without a *qadoš* refrain, a practice not found in the writings of the early Italians or Franco-Germans. The rarity of this poem

[56] Ibid. 128, 134, 172. The text of R. Isaac's *yoṣer* on p. 172 should be corrected. The choral refrain comprises 5 cola only, not 8 as given. As L. Zunz has indicated, the 5-cola *qadoš* refrain in the *yoṣer*, *'Ayelet 'ahavim matnat sinay*, for Pentecost, is incorrectly attributed to R. Simeon b. Isaac; see Zunz, *Literaturgeschichte*, p. 115, and Fleischer, *Ha-Yoṣerot*, p. 654 n. 45; see also Ber, *Seder*, pp. 706 ff.

[57] Weinberger, *Re'šit Ha-Payṭanut*, p. 150.

was observed as early as the twelfth century, by the Franco-German R. Eliezer b. Nathan: 'The poet R. Benjamin did not include a *qadoš* [refrain] in his *yošer* [*'Eloheynu 'elohim 'emet*], not in the second strophe or at the end.'[58]

In his *yoṣer*, *'Ihel be-'oz gevurotaw*, for Šabbat Bere'šit, Benjamin b. Zeraḥ connects the third strophe to the *qiqlar* refrain by anadiplosis. As observed above, this is a distinctive mannerism of Balkan Byzantine poets like Benjamin b. Samuel in his *yoṣer*, *'Akhof we-'ikkaf* and Isaac b. Judah in his *'Aḥalleh peney bore'*.

Silluq and *'Ofan*

The *silluq* which follows the *guf ha-yoṣer* is preserved in two hymns by Benjamin b. Samuel, *Ani yešenah be-galut bavel*, for Passover, and *U-mošeh qibbel torah*, for Pentecost. In the latter, R. Benjamin connects the *silluq* to the *guf ha-yoṣer* by completing the latter's alphabetic acrostic in the first four cola of the *silluq*. The *silluq* itself is constructed in three separate monorhyme strophes. The six-cola opening strophe begins with units that complete the verse, 'Moses drew near to the thick darkness where God was' (Exod. 20: 21). The twelve-cola second strophe spells out the poet's name *BNYMYN*, and the third, six-cola strophe leads into *Ha-me'ir la-'areṣ we-la-ddarim 'aleyha be-raḥamim* (In mercy You bring light to the earth and to those who dwell thereon), the opening verse in the first benediction before the recitation of the *šema'*. In the eleventh century, synagogue poets began the practice of bridging the *guf ha-yoṣer* with this benediction through the *silluq*. Following is the last strophe in R. Benjamin's *silluq*.[59]

And they took upon themselves and their children to preserve it
  [the Torah] for generations;
Whereupon they were adorned and wreathed with crowns and
  diadems,
And the seas were empowered, even the settled lands and deserts;
And they were liberal in their praise and thanks and esteem
Of the King who conducted the nation with words purified;
He who is glorified in the assembled circle of angels on high:
'In mercy You bring light' [etc.]

R. Benjamin's eclecticism is seen in his *silluq*, *'Ani yešenah be-galut bavel*, for Passover. The hymn is built in one monorhyme strophe, but there is no leading up to *Ha-me'ir la-'areṣ*, as there is in his Pentecost *silluq*. The practice of connecting with the benediction 'In mercy You bring light', etc., through the *silluq* is also observed in the *silluq*, *Ṣe'enah u-r'enah*, by Solomon

[58] See Zunz, *Literaturgeschichte*, p. 120; Schirmann, *Širim Ḥadašim*, p. 421; Abraham b. Azriel, *Sefer*, iv. 29.

[59] *Maḥazor Romania*, Bibliothèque Nationale, Paris, MS No. 606, fo. 103b; Fleischer, *Ha-Yoṣerot*, p. 229 n. 90.

Ha-Bavli, who, presumably, was R. Benjamin's mentor. The following is from the closing cola of Ha-Bavli's *Ṣeʾenah u-rʾenah*.[60]

> *Qayyem le-dor dorim,*
> *Ha-meʾir la-ʾareṣ we-la-ddarim.*
>
> Preserve [us] for all generations,
> You who bring light to the earth and its dwellers.

In R. Benjamin's *silluq* for Passover, *ʾAni yešenah*, the closing cola lead not into the benediction, 'In mercy You bring light', but directly into the *qeduššah* (Trisagion, based on Isa. 6: 3) of the *ʾofan*.[61]

> I make you [Israel] promise, protected by the shade of the world's architect;
> Holy seed, inheriting the land,
> To extol and sanctify Him as do heaven's angels . . .
> Who when calling [Him] holy beg permission from each other.

Presumably, R. Benjamin lived at a time when the practice of connecting the *guf ha-yoṣer* and *silluq* to the benediction 'In mercy You bring light' had not been standardized. Hence, poets were free to vary the closing strophes of the *silluq*.[62]

R. Benjamin's two *ʾofannim*, *Mah dodekh mi-dod*, for Passover, and *Ba-ʿaloto ha-harah*, for Pentecost, are also different in form. The first is a one-strophe monorhyme hymn after classical models, while the second is a longer, three-strophe poem, reminiscent of the *ʾofannim* of Solomon Suleiman and Saʿadyah Gaʾon in the late eastern period. Following is a selection from the latter. Its theme is Moses' ascent to heaven to receive the Torah, and his encounter with the angels who were reluctant to part with it.[63]

> When he ascended the mountain to receive the Torah pearls,
> Tranquil [angels] gathered against him;
> His friend Mitatron [*sic*] brought him into the inner chambers, guiding him through the twenty-four gates . . .
> He taught him the Torah identified
> With his name . . .[64]

[60] Fleischer, *Piyyuṭey . . . Ha-Bavli*, pp. 210, 96–7.

[61] The text is based on Paris, MS No. 606, fo. 103b; Oxford, MS Opp. Add. 4to 171, No. 2501, fo. 9a; and on New York, MS Enelow, No. 615. The latter was published in Bernstein, *Piyyuṭim*, p. 94.

[62] See Fleischer, *Ha-Yoṣerot*, pp. 622–3.

[63] Paris, MS No. 606, fos. 103a–b; see Fleischer, *Ha-Yoṣerot*, pp. 256–7.

[64] See *bŠab* 88b; 'Midraš ka-tapuaḥ ba-ʿaṣey ha-ya-ʿar' and 'Midraš maʿyan ḥokhmah', in *ʾOṣar Midrašim*, i. 262–4, ii. 306–7.

Like his central European colleagues, Benjamin b. Samuel finds the *ʾofan* a suitable medium for speculating on the nature of the deity. In his *ʾofan*, *Mah dodekh mi-dod*, he comments on those verses from Cant. 4: 11–16 which describe the dimensions of the Beloved who in rabbinic and kabbalistic literature is equated with God. In a revealing couplet, the poet observes:[65]

My Beloved is hidden, concealed
From every breathing soul;

There I shall sing of His wonders
And thrice extol Him with blessing [*ʾašallešem be-varukh*] like the
ʾofannim on high.

R. Benjamin's disclosure that he has reached ('There') the Beloved's 'concealed' abode is in line with statements in the *heykhalot* (celestial palaces) literature, where the mystic, armed with the requisite esoteric knowledge, ascends to the 'chariot throne'. In this regard, the comment attributed to Rabbi Akiva in a *heykhalot* text is instructive:

When I ascended to the first palace, I was devout; in the second palace I was pure; in the third, sincere; in the fourth I was wholly with God [*tamim*]; in the fifth, I displayed holiness before God; in the sixth I recited the *qeduššah* before Him who spoke and created, in order that the ministering angels might not harm me; in the seventh I held myself erect with all my might, trembling in all limbs, and spoke the following: O living and eternal God . . . I will magnify the blessings of Your glory [*birkat kevodekha*]. Praised are You, sublime in the chambers of grandeur.

Like the ministering angels, R. Benjamin, master of the esoteric code, reaches the 'hidden' place of the 'chariot throne', recites the Trisagion and magnifies the Lord's blessings.[66]

R. Benjamin's revelation of his 'ascent' is matched by Solomon Ibn Gabirol's in his *seliḥah*, *Šeney ḥayyay u-maʾawayyay*, and by the twelfth-century Byzantine hymnist Moses b. Ḥiyyah in his *rahiṭ*, *Yošev meʿonah*:

[GABIROL]
The Lord of the universe who is concealed,
Stands [revealed] before me;
I will sing Your praises and entreat You wherever I may be.[67]

[MOSES B. ḤIYYAH]
God who abides with unobserved might . . .
Is concealed from view . . .
I have seen Him in the holy place, and though He is unknowable,
He sits before me.[68]

[65] Bernstein, *Piyyuṭim*, p. 53.
[66] See Scholem, *Major Trends*, pp. 78–9 n. 136.
[67] Ibn Gabirol, *Širey Ha-Qodeš*, p. 577.
[68] Weinberger, *Reʾšit Ha-Payṭanut*, p. 53.

Common to these conceits is the figure of contrast between the poet, who is privy to the vision of the Godhead, and others from whose view it is hidden. A similar figure is projected in the above *heykhalot* text: 'God who is concealed [*ne'elam*] from all creatures and hidden from the ministering angels, reveals Himself to Rabbi Akiva in the "chariot throne" [*ma'aseh merkavah*].'[69]

Isaac b. Judah in his *'ofan*, *Yiddodun, yiddodun kol ḥayyaley qarṭon*, elaborates on the theme of the divine chariot throne in the manner of the early Italians and Franco-Germans. R. Isaac's hymn is built in rhyming quatrains with the Trisagion from Isa. 6: 3 as repeated refrain. The poet's signature is spelled in the acrostic of the strophes. The verse from Isaiah was also used by Amittai as the refrain for his two *'ofannim*, *'Er'ellim u-mal'akhim* and *'Ešnabey šeḥaqim*. The latter hymn, like R. Isaac's *'ofan*, was constructed in rhyming quatrains with the author's name in the strophes' acrostic.[70] However, unlike Amittai, R. Isaac drew extensively on *heykhalot* literature in his speculation on the chariot throne. Below are some excerpts from *Yiddodun, yiddodun*, and their parallels in *Heykhalot Rabbati*:

> The supernal hosts tremble before Him
> Encompassing Him, they are agitated like the palace angels;
> The bearers of His throne, the *ḥayyot* and *'ofannim* [classes of angels] praise Him in six voices:
> Holy, holy, holy is the Lord of hosts.

The reference to the six voices is found in *Heykhalot Rabbati* 4. 1: 'With six voices they minister to Him . . . the bearers of His throne of glory, the *keruvim* and the *'ofannim* and the holy *ḥayyot*, as it is written [in Isa. 6: 3]: Holy', etc.[71] In describing the ceremony of adulation preceding the recitation of the Trisagion, the poet observes that the celestial orchestra presents a musical prelude to the offering of the angelic choir:

> The *ḥašmalim* [Ezek. 1: 4] similar in feature [*qelaster panim*]
> Fly and soar and do not repeat themselves;
> The choir presents after the musicians,
> With a mighty sound and much trembling, they respond:
> Holy [etc.]

The source for the features of the angelic *ḥašmalim* who fly and soar is again *Heykhalot Rabbati*, 8. 3 and 26. 5: 'The features [*qelaster panaw*] of one are similar to those of the other . . . they soar like an eagle and fly like an eagle.' Also in this work (7. 2) is the observation that the playing of the musicians precedes that of the choir: 'Each day with rejoicing the music excites and the

[69] See Scholem, *Major Trends*, p. 364 n. 80.
[70] Weinberger, *Re'šit Ha-Payṭanut*, pp. 176–9; Amittai, *Širey*, pp. 106–15.
[71] See *'Oṣar Midrašim*, i. 111–22.

multitudes sing.' The conceit of angels not repeating themselves is undoubtedly based on *Gen. Rabbah* 78. 1: 'The celestial company does not praise [God] and repeat [their praises], but . . . every day the Holy One, blessed be He, creates a company of new angels and they utter songs before Him and then depart.' The manner in which the angelic choir performs is also dealt with in R. Isaac's hymn. Expanding on Isa. 6: 3–4, 'And one [seraph] called to another and said, Holy, holy holy is the Lord of hosts,' the poet suggests that the choral offering was given in antiphonal responses:

> They exalted His majesty with their lips, responsively;
> A glowing fire encompassed the camp;
> The seraphim stood and each named the other;
> One recited and the other responded,
> Holy [etc.]

The responsive offerings of the angelic choir are reported in *Perek Mi-Pirkey Heykhalot*:[72] 'The choir of angels in divided into three sections . . . one section chants *qadoš* [holy] and falls upon its face, another responds *qadoš*, and a third closes with *qadoš, 'adonay ṣeva'ot, melo' khol ha-'areṣ kevodo* [holy is the Lord of hosts, the whole earth is full of His glory].' Commenting on the rotating Throne of Glory (*kisse' ha-kavod*) in Ezek. 1: 17, R. Isaac notes that the angel who stood at its right side now stands at its left (*'omed yamin meḥazzer semo'l*). Here, too, he draws upon *Heykhalot Rabbati* 8. 3: 'The angels who stood at the right [side of the throne] now stand at the left; those who stood at the left are now at the right.' It is clear that R. Isaac was thoroughly familiar with the *heykhalot* texts and borrowed freely from their conceits and their language.

Benjamin b. Zeraḥ, like his colleagues in Balkan Byzantium, uses the *'ofan* as a medium for speculating on the divine chariot throne and the names of God and the angels. Following is a selection from his *'ofan, Beluley 'eš u-meymot*. The hymn is contructed in quatrains with internal rhyme, modelled after Amittai's *'ofan, 'Er'ellim u-mal'akhim*:[73]

> A blend of fire and water,
> Heroes of the city on the heights;
> Like walls, they stand erect [before Him];
> Trembling and fearful, they applaud the mighty
> Lord who fashioned the earth . . .
> Michael growls and Gabriel wails;
> Uriel cries out and Raphael rages;
> Hadarniel celebrates
> The majesty of God [*Yah*], Akhtariel.

[72] Ibid. 122–3.

[73] See Zunz, *Literaturgeschichte*, p. 122; Ber, *Seder*, p. 709; Amittai, *Širey*, pp. 111–12.

Akhtariel is a name for the deity, as indicated in *bBer* 7a:

R. Ishmael ben Elisha says: I once entered into the innermost part [of the Sanctuary] to offer incense and saw Akhtariel Yah, the Lord of hosts, seated upon a high and exalted throne. He said to me: Ishmael, my son, bless Me!

This name and others, like Ḥasdiel and Shemaiel—listed in Benjamin b. Zeraḥ's *'ofannim*—figure prominently in the *heykhalot* literature, a subject with which R. Benjamin was undoubtedly familiar. In the *heykhalot* texts, Akhtariel is dramatically portrayed as sitting on the divine chariot throne (*merkavah*).[74]

Zulat

Three *zulatot* by Benjamin b. Samuel have been preserved in Romaniote prayer-books: *'Aṣaltikh qenuyati*, *Bittaqti zero'a* and *'Emunat 'ittey ha-qeṣ*, from his *yoṣerot*, *'Az ke-gulgal*, *'Ani ḥokhmah* and *'Akhof we-'ikkaf*, for Passover, Pentecost and Tabernacles respectively. His *zulat* for Passover, with alphabetic acrostic and name signature, is built in rhyming tercets with closing scriptural verse and is in line with similar practices by Solomon Ha-Bavli in his *'Ahevukha nefeš le-hadekh* and Simeon b. Isaac's *'Ezor-na' 'oz li-mlokh*. Also, following Ha-Bavli, R. Benjamin's acrostic spans the complete alphabet and gives the signature of the author, albeit only in part, *Binyamin bi-rabbi* (Benjamin, son of Rabbi . . .).[75]

However, in R. Benjamin's *zulat* for Pentecost, he varies from conventional practice by omitting the alphabetic acrostic and moving directly into the name signature, *BNYMYN BRRBY ŠMW'L*. In the latter *zulat*, built in rhyming tercets, the poet comments on the Ten Commandments, with which he closes each strophe save the sixth. The hymn is constructed in sixteen strophes in order to accommodate the poet's name signature. R. Benjamin's *zulat* for Tabernacles varies from his others in its structure of eight strophes in rhyming quatrains with closing scriptural verse, reminiscent of Sa'adyah Ga'on and Joseph Ibn Abitur. Another uncommon feature in this hymn is that R. Benjamin presents an alphabetic acrostic without a name signature.[76]

Isaac b. Judah, like R. Benjamin, is eclectic in the construction of his *zulatot*. His *'Aqumah we-lev 'akhinah*, *'Ellu šaloš miṣwot*, *'Imrot 'adonay 'imrot ṭehorot*, *'Az mero'š huddaḥti* and *'Elkha li wa-'ašuvah* are built on conventional central European models of the *zulat*. All but the first are constructed in rhyming quatrains with complete alphabetic acrostic and closing strophe with the author's name signature. *'Aqumah we-lev 'akhinah* is built in rhyming tercets with closing signature strophe, a pattern prevalent in

[74] See Zunz, *Die synagogale Poesie*, pp. 501, 504; Scholem, *Major Trends*, p. 356 n. 3.

[75] See Bernstein, *Piyyuṭim*, pp. 53–7; Fleischer, *Piyyuṭey . . . Ha-Bavli*, pp. 213–20.

[76] Fleischer, *Piyyuṭey . . . Ha-Bavli*, pp. 213–20; *Maḥazor Le-Yamim*, i. 56–7; *Maḥazor Romania*, Paris, MS No. 606, fo. 103b; *Maḥazor Romania* (Venice, 1522–3), p. 406a; Zulay, *Ha-'Askolah*, pp. 176–8; Fleischer, *Ha-Yoṣerot*, pp. 290–2.

eleventh-century central Europe.[77] Of particular interest is the innovative rhyming pattern in R. Isaac's *zulat* for Šabbat Ha-Ḥodeš, *'Az me-ro'š huddaḥti*. The hymn, in quatrains, forms the uncommon rhyme *aa / bb / cc / dd / ee / ff / gg / hh / ii /*, etc. This pattern is the only one of its kind in eleventh- and twelfth-century central and eastern Europe. Following is the first strophe: [78]

'Az me-ro'š huddaḥti / lo' šalawti we-lo' naḥti;
Halakhti ba-golah u-va-ševi / mi-ymey 'avraham 'avi;
U-mi-yom nolad yiṣḥaq / hayyiti nidḥeh we-nidḥaq;
Kol 'aḥ ʿaqov yaʿaqov / me-'az seṭamo ʿesaw le-yaʿaqov.

When at first I was cast out, / I had no repose and no rest;
I went into exile and was a captive, / yet in the days of Abraham, my father;
And from the time that Isaac was born, / I was rejected and repressed;
Every brother takes advantage, / from the moment that Jacob was hated by Esau.

Benjamin b. Zeraḥ also varies the construction of his four *zulatot*, which survive only in manuscript collections. Three, *'Omeret 'ani maʿasay la-melekh*,[79] for Šabbat Ha-Gadol, *'Anna' hašqifah u-r'eh*[80] and *'Elohim 'al dami lakh*,[81] are built in rhyming quatrains with alphabetic acrostic and name signature. However, *'Ašrey ha-kallah 'ašer be-ḥesed kelulah*,[82] also for Šabbat Ha-Gadol, is constructed in rhyming octets holding an alphabetic acrostic and name signature, with each strophe encompassing two letters. Following is a selection from his emotionally charged *'Elohim 'al dami lakh*:

Lord, be not silent,
Do not remain unconcerned and keep still,
For Your elegant palace is laid waste and ploughed over;
The nations claim it; therefore it is fitting to avenge
The spilled blood of Your servants, as yet unavenged.

Seliḥah

No *seliḥot* by Benjamin b. Samuel appear to have been preserved. Isaac b. Judah's one surviving hymn in this genre, *'Agagi 'az ke-ʿamad*, for the Fast of

77 Weinberger, *Re'šit Ha-Payṭanut*, pp. 131, 137, 146, 155, 165; Fleischer, *Ha-Yoṣerot*, p. 691.
78 Weinberger, *Re'šit Ha-Payṭanut*, p. 155; Fleischer, *Ha-Yoṣerot*, p. 690.
79 London, British Library, Add. MS 17867, No. 651, fos. 112a–113b.
80 Oxford, Bodleian MS Michael 161, fos. 132–3.
81 London, British Library, Add. MS 27086, No. 650, fos. 225b–226a.
82 Munich, National Library, MS No. 21, fos. 17b–18a.

Esther, is in ten-quatrain strophes with closing cola from the Book of Esther. This is one of the few occasions when R. Isaac employs scriptural verses for strophe endings.[83] Benjamin b. Zeraḥ makes up for this scarcity by composing more than thirty hymns in this genre. At this time the *seliḥah* in its several forms became a highly visible genre in Romaniote hymnography. The dominant themes in the Romaniote *seliḥot* are derived from Ps. 130: 4, 'there is forgiveness in You' (*ki ʿimmekha ha-seliḥah*). Principally, the hymn seeks divine aid in line with the expectation that 'the Lord [will] answer us when we call' (Ps. 20: 10). As in the Hispanic and central European tradition, the Balkan *seliḥah* focused on the rabbinic assurance (in *bRH* 17b) that God showed Moses the order of prayers and said to him, 'Whenever Israel sin, let them carry out this service before Me, and I will forgive them.' The 'service' refers to the reading of the Thirteen Attributes in Exod. 34: 6–7, which formed the basic unit in the order of *seliḥot* prayers (*seder ha-seliḥot*). Like their European colleagues, the Romaniotes embellished the basic unit of the *seliḥot* service by composing introductions to the Thirteen Attributes. Among the earliest adornments of the attributes was 'O God You have taught us to recite the Thirteen Attributes [*ʾel, horeyta lanu lomar šeloš ʿesreh*]; remember this day in our favour,' preserved in the prayer-book of R. Amram Ga'on. To this introduction was added the litany, 'Almighty King, who sits on the throne of mercy' (*ʾEl melekh yošev ʿal kisseʾ raḥamim*). Later, both introduction and litany were preceded by *petiḥot* as permission requests.

Among the *petiḥot* for the vigil-nights *seliḥot* service in the month of 'Elul is Benjamin b. Zeraḥ's *ʾEykh niftaḥ lefaneykha dar metuḥim*. The monorhyme hymn holds an alphabetic acrostic and author's signature. Below is part of R. Benjamin's *petiḥah* with its indictment of the Christian ruling power:[84]

They who enslave Your people, the worshippers of the dead one
  [Jesus],
Continue to prosper morning and night;
Rebelling against You with abusive speech,
'You [Israel] are in shambles, in whom have you placed your
  confidence?'

Pizmon

This form of the *seliḥah* is constructed in strophes with a refrain. The refrain may consist of a complete strophe or a single colon. Following is Benjamin b. Zeraḥ's *Ḥoreyta derekh tešuvah* in rhyming quatrains with repeated opening

[83] *Maḥazor Romania* (Venice, 1522–3), p. 77.

[84] Similar in form are the Days of Repentance *petiḥot* to the vigil-nights service, *ʾAz ṭerem nimteḥu nivley šekhavim*, and [*ʾAdonay*] *ʾelohey ha-ṣevaʾot noraʾ ba-ʿelyonim*, by R. Benjamin's contemporary R. Solomon b. Isaac (RaŠI) of Troyes. See *Seder Ha-Seliḥot . . . Polin*, pp. 21, 66, 120.

strophe. Note the opening colon paraphrasing the introduction to the Thirteen Attributes:[85]

> You have taught [*horeyta*] the way of repentance to the faithless daughter,
> Between the New Year and Day of Atonement to return to You . . .
> You had Repentance precede the world's creation . . .
> Sincere repentance is accepted before Your [throne] of glory . . .
> Restore us for Your sake that we may duly repent.

The refrain in rhyming tercets is presumably modelled after the Apulian Shefatya b. Amittai's *Yisra'el nošaʿ ba-'adonay*.[86]

Šeniyyah, Šelišiyyah, Šalmonit

The above *seliḥot* are built in strophes of two, three or four cola, respectively. Unlike the Italians and Franco-Germans, who favoured the *šeniyyah* and *šelišiyyah*, Balkan hymnists neglected the first two and preferred the *šalmonit*. Following is Benjamin b. Zeraḥ's [*'Eloheynu we-'lohey 'avoteynu*], *betulat bat yehudah*, in this genre. In the hymn, Israel is personified as a maiden held captive:[87]

> O virgin daughter of Judah, her mourning and lamenting increases;
> Sadly she lifts her hands from the pit of captivity . . .
> With eyes raised for help, she looks around;
> The decrees of the sybarite cause her anguish like a woman bringing forth her first child;
> Dejected, she claps her hands and moans in her prayer,
> 'Where then is my hope?'

The 'sybarite' (*ʿadinah*) is from Isa. 47: 8 and refers to the Christian ruling power.[88]

ʿAqedah

This *seliḥah* recalls the Binding of Isaac and his readiness to be sacrificed at God's command. Notable *ʿaqedot* by Benjamin b. Zeraḥ are *'Emunim beney ma'aminim* and *'Ahavat ʿezez we-toqef ḥibbah*, for the Day of Atonement. As in his other hymns, R. Benjamin is eclectic in constructing the *ʿaqedah*. His *'Emunim* is built in rhyming couplets, while *'Ahavat ʿezez* is in monorhyme. In the following from his *'Emunim*, the poet boldly embellishes the biblical account of the *ʿaqedah* in Gen. 22: [89]

85 Ibid. 9–10; 132–4, ll. 1–2, 4, 27, 31.
86 Ibid. 38.
87 *Seder Ha-Seliḥot . . . Liṭa'*, pp. 57–8.
88 Zunz, *Die synagogale Poesie*, p. 455.
89 *Maḥazor Le-Yamim*, ii. 228–9.

They [Israel] recollect the binding [of Isaac] at Moriah as a whole burnt offering [in the Temple] . . .
The father [Abraham] rejoiced at the sacrifice, as if attending a feast for his son;
The son [Isaac] exulted at being the victim, as if standing under his wedding canopy.

A similar conceit is found in the anonymous *Sefer Ha-Yašar*, on *Wa-Yera'*, 'Isaac spoke to his father, "All that the Lord has spoken to you, father, I will do gladly and willingly" . . . And Abraham and Isaac rejoiced at God's command. Although tears were in their eyes, their hearts were happy.'

In R. Benjamin's *'Ahavat 'ezez*, he reaffirms the view that the Binding of Isaac is comparable in merit to the Temple sacrifice and suggests that Isaac's ashes, from the burnt offering made by his father, remain piled on the altar:[90]

[POET:]
He [Abraham] tied his [son's] hands and feet with a double knot,
Lest he kick and thereby render invalid the required holocaust offering . . .

[GOD:]
He [Isaac] lives though his ashes are gathered up before Me;
I regard him as if he were sacrificed, a burnt offering to Me.

The seeming contradiction between Isaac 'living' and 'his ashes are gathered up before Me' is prompted by the biblical account (in Gen. 22: 19), 'So Abraham returned to his young men.' Both father and son went up to Moriah to sacrifice (Gen. 22: 6) and only the father returned! One rabbinic answer (in *Midraš Ha-Gadol*, on Gen. 22: 19), borrowed by the poet, was, 'Although Isaac did not die, Scripture regards him as though he had died and his ashes lay piled on the altar. That is why it is said, "So Abraham returned to his young men." '[91]

'Azharah

These hymns were designed as a warning (*'azharah*) to the congregation to observe the 613 commandments and were often chanted on Pentecost, the anniversary of the giving of the Torah. Although *'azharot* were already in vogue in the period of the pre-classical poets, the best-known hymns in this genre were composed by Sa'adyah Ga'on and Solomon Ibn Gabirol. The Cairo Geniza has preserved a fragment of an *'azharah* for Pentecost [*Moṣa'*] *sefatayim li-šmor*, by Benjamin b. Samuel. In his treatment of this genre, R. Benjamin not only provided a catalogue of the commandments but, unlike

[90] *Maḥazor Le-Yamim*, ii. 522–3.

[91] Spiegel, *The Last Trial*, pp. 3–4.

Sa'adyah or Gabirol, added a summary of the negative and positive commands.[92]

THE PRINCIPAL POETS: LATER ROMANIOTES

Moses b. Ḥiyyah

With the hymns of Moses b. Ḥiyyah (12th c.), Byzantine Hebrew hymnography began its long and affectionate affair with Hispanic-style prosody. The perceptive critic Judah Al-Ḥarizi (d. before 1235) was prepared to concede in his *Taḥkemoni* that, although the Byzantine Hebrew poets were generally inept, there were some exceptions, like Moses b. Ḥiyyah, because 'in his youth he travelled to Spain and studied there.' A study of the seventeen hymns by R. Moses that have been preserved in the Italian, Romaniote and Karaite rituals reveals a decided Hispanic influence. Unlike Benjamin b. Samuel, Isaac b. Judah and Benjamin b. Zeraḥ, who employ scriptural verses sparingly, R. Moses loads biblical passages onto his hymns, after the manner of the Hispanics. The scriptural reference may appear at the beginning, middle or end of the hymn, or as a repeated refrain. Below is a sample from his *tokheḥa* (self-rebuke), *We-'attah malki mi-qedem*, the first and last lines in whose strophes begin with *we-'attah* (And You), the first unit in the scriptural verse.[93]

And You my ruler in heaven from of old,
  To You I lift my eyes;
  In my thoughts I praise You this day;
And You my Lord are on high forever. [Ps. 42: 9]

And You have arranged the heavens fair;
  Those too feeble to stand firm
  Until they hardened fast;
And You did tread on their backs. [Deut. 33: 49]

In his use of biblical texts, R. Moses often recontextualizes a verse, after the model of Solomon Ibn Gabirol. There follows an example from R. Moses' *Mi kamokha mesim netivah be-mayim 'azzim,* for Šabbat Ḥatanim. He pays tribute to the bridegroom by invoking the verse from Ezek. 31: 3, but in a different context:[94]

His [the bridegroom's] stately form is like a palm;
His cheeks are like beds of spices and his bouquet is unspoiled;
All who behold him exclaim,
Behold, I see a cedar in Lebanon.

92 See *bMak* 23b and Fleischer, ''Azharot le-R. Binyamin', pp. 44–58.

93 Weinberger, *Re'šit Ha-Payṭanut*, pp. 40–2; see Al-Ḥarizi, *Taḥkemoni*, No. 18, pp. 177 ff.

94 Weinberger, *Re'šit Ha-Payṭanut*, pp. 3–5; Fleischer, 'Širatenu', p. 215 n. 115.

The last colon in its source in Ezek. 31: 3 reads: 'Assyria [*'aššur*, with a *pataḥ* under the *'alef*] was a cedar in Lebanon.' In its recontextualized form, *'aššur* is written with a *qameṣ*, meaning 'I see'. Word-play with scriptural verses to suit the poet's rhetorical needs is a commonplace in R. Moses' hymns. Another example comes from his *tokheḥah*, *'Et peney mevin ṣefunay*, recited during the month of 'Elul in Italian and Romaniote congregations:[95]

When your calamities increase,
And flames [of *geyhinnom*, hell] come upon you,
Where is your brother, vanity [*hevel*]?

The cantor-poet, in seeking to turn his congregation away from the pursuit of wordly pleasures, reminds them of the punishment that awaits after death. In the last colon of the tercet, R. Moses intends a new meaning for the verse (from Gen. 4: 9), 'Where is Abel [*hevel*] your brother?' The play on the words *hevel* (Abel) and *hevel* (vanity) was not lost on the congregation.

In recontextualizing the scriptural text, R. Moses employed a rhetorical device in which he divided the verse into halves for rhyming purposes, thereby highlighting the poetic conceit. Below are sample strophes from his *seliḥah*, *Šaḥar miflaṭ li 'aḥišah*, with segmented verses from Isaiah and Genesis.[96]

In the morning the enemy pursued me and mocked with his speech [*be-mivṭa' sefatayim*]:
'How you are fallen from heaven [*mi-šamayim*], O Day Star, son of Dawn!' [Isa. 14: 12] . . .

In the morning your people are fearful and struggle earnestly with their passions [*wa-yyillaḥem 'im yiṣro be-ḥumo*];
'And a man wrestled with him [*wa-yye'aveq 'iš 'immo*] until daybreak.' [Gen. 32: 14]

Although R. Moses' literary remains do not include hymns in quatitative metre counting both long and short vowels, his *muḥarrak* (a Hispanic-style introduction to the *nišmat*), *'Odeh ṣuri hifli' ḥasdo*, for Tabernacles, is in the form of a metric *muwashshaḥ*, counting only long syllables. Other hymns are constructed in the manner of the pseudo-*muwashshaḥ*. His use of language is primarily biblical and relatively free from allusions to rabbinic sources; in this, too, he reflects the Hispanic influence. Yet there are limits to how far R. Moses was prepared to follow Iberian models. Unlike the latter, who closed their pseudo-*muwashshaḥāt* with variable units, R. Moses was content with the same unit, repeated. Moreover, his non-metric *tokheḥah*, *'Etayu 'amelalim*, built in rhyming couplets, varies from the practice of the Hispanics,

[95] Weinberger, *Re'šit Ha-Payṭanut*, p. 27; Fleischer, 'Širatenu', pp. 201, 215 n. 115.
[96] Weinberger, *Re'šit Ha-Payṭanut*, pp. 33–4.

who constructed their rhymed couplet *tokheḥot* with quantitative metre, as, for example, Ibn Gabirol's *Šokhney batey ḥomer*.[97]

In his role as poet, Moses b. Ḥiyyah sought to improve the aesthetic quality of his compositions with assonance, alliteration and internal rhyme. Following are examples from his phonetically intensive *qinah*, *'Aval tiroš*, and *rahiṭ*, *Mivtaḥi we-goḥi*:[98]

[QINAH]
'Aval tiroš u-mey roš wi-ygonim;
Be-khaf qela' niqla'ti, nivla'ti ba-mayim ha-zedonim;
Gafni 'umlalah, 'ovlah novlah, ruṭṭašti 'aḥor u-fanim;
Ki te'enah lo' tifraḥ we-'eyn yevul ba-gefanim.

The wine dried up and poisoned water and grief [remain];
From the hollow of a sling I am tossed about, swallowed by the
raging waters;
The vine languishes, I am torn apart, fore and aft;
The fig tree does not blossom and no fruit is on the vines.

[RAHIṬ]
Ḥanon yaḥanon we-yignon ba-levanon we-yinnon le-qarev
li-khmehim
'Elohim
Dibber be-qodšo.

Truly, He will be gracious and protect Judah [Lebanon, Jer. 22: 23]
and bring Yinnon [the Messiah] near to those who yearn;
The Lord
Spoke in His holiness.

Joseph Qalai

Joseph b. Jacob Qalai, a contemporary of Moses b. Ḥiyyah, is the author of some twenty-four *piyyuṭim* in the *yoṣer* and *seliḥah* genres, most of which were adopted by Romaniote, Italian, North African and Karaite congregations. Several of his hymns were preserved in the Cairo Geniza. To his acrostic name signature he adds *ḥazan* (cantor) and *payyaṭ* (poet), and, occasionally, *karfan*. The latter is possibly a derivation from the Greek *chorufaios* (cantor). Although Qalai's family may have originated in Spain or North Africa, or possibly in Chufut-Kale in the Crimea, it is likely that either R. Joseph or his father moved to the Balkans and settled there. An early sixteenth-century rabbi of Spanish origin, Samuel Qalai, son of R. Moses

[97] Ibid., Nos. 2, 7, 10, 11, 14, 17; Ibn Gabirol, *Širey Ha-Qodeš*, pp. 213–15; Fleischer, 'Širatenu', p. 217.

[98] Weinberger, *Re'šit Ha-Payṭanut*, pp. 7–8, 56–7.

Qalai, served as a *dayyan* (religious-court judge) in Arta (Epirus), and is recorded as having rendered a decision in Jewish law in a dispute involving merchants from nearby Lepanto, in the year 1521.[99]

The Hispanic influence observed in the work of Moses b. Ḥiyyah is more pronounced in the hymns of Qalai, whose considerable familiarity with Andalusian prosody is seen in his *muwashshaḥāt* and pseudo-*muwashshaḥāt*. Also based on Iberian models is his *mustajāb*, *'Aromimkha 'elohay ha-melekh*; an epithalamium, *Liqra't peney ḥatan*, in quantitative metre; a metric *tokheḥah*, *Ha-le'el yirbu 'omer* (counting long syllables only), with variable rhyme; and an unsparing use of scriptural verses as refrains. In the following *tokheḥah*, built in quatrains, he imitates the rhyming pattern of Solomon Ibn Gabirol's *Šokheney batey ḥomer*, *aa / bb / cc / dd / ee / ff//*, and borrows the latter's opening half-colon for his own strophe:[100]

They who continue to speak for God,
He binds their hands with judgment;
How much more those who live in houses of clay
[*šokhney batey ḥomer*],
Whose foundation is in the dust!

Qalai's *qinah*, *'Eykhah 'avi 'iššo bi hiv'ir*, is built in rhyming quatrains with closing scriptural verse; each colon opens with the unit *'eykhah*. This configuration is presumably modelled after Judah Ha-Levi's *qinah*, *'Eykhah yeḥidah ba-banot*. Following are the opening strophes from Qalai and Ha-Levi respectively:[101]

Alas, my Father set a fire within me;
Alas, His anger and fury were aroused against me;
Alas, He exiled me among Muslims and Christians;
Alas, lonely sits the city.

Alas, they make sport of me, those who are younger than I and I am their delight;
Alas, the Senior [God] on the day of His anger rained upon me fury's storm;
Alas, the Lord in His anger has humiliated daughter Zion; how the gold has grown dim;
Alas, lonely sits the city that was once full of people.

Qalai's hymns are models in clarity of phrasing and precision in language, even as he employs stylistic mannerisms that set him apart. Among the latter

[99] Zunz, *Literaturgeschichte*, p. 339; Fleischer, *Ha-Yoṣerot*, p. 508 n. 37; Habermann, *'Ateret*, p. 227; Benjamin Ze'ev, *Responsa*, Nos. 36, 74, 222, 290.

[100] Weinberger, *Re'šit Ha-Payṭanut*, Nos. 29 (pp. 93–5), 30 (pp. 96–7), 31 (pp. 98–9), 35 (pp. 110–13); Fleischer, 'Širatenu', p. 218; Ibn Gabirol, *Širey Ha-Qodeš*, p. 213.

[101] Weinberger, *Re'šit Ha-Payṭanut*, p. 81; Ha-Levi, *Širey Ha-Qodeš*, p. 551.

is his use of enjambment, a straddling of a conceit over two (or more) cola. It is possible that he found this practice in the hymns of Solomon Ha-Bavli, who, as indicated, was a notable influence on European cantor-poets. Following is a sample from his *tokheḥah* for the Fast of Esther, *'Eleykha 'adonay*. The enjambment is in the first two cola: *mošiv yeḥidim / Baytah.*[102]

'Eleykha 'adonay mošiv yeḥidim
Baytah, qiwwu 'aleyhem yom šodedim;
Qamu, be-rifyon yedeyhem, maḥamadim,
Wa-yavo' 'amaleq wa-yyillaḥem 'im yisra'el bi-rfidim.

For You, O Lord who gives the desolate
A home, they had hope on the day that the brigands
Fell upon them, the precious, in their weakness;
And Amaleq came and made war on Israel at Refidim.

Qalai displays his virtuosity in a wonderful *ḥaṭa'nu*, *'Essa' 'išon,* built in rhyming quatrains of strophes and cola, both of which are connected by anadiplosis. This remarkable hymn is part of the Romaniote ritual for the midnight service during the Days of Awe and has been preserved, in part, in the Cairo Geniza.[103] There follow the opening cola:[104]

'Essa' 'išon / 'išon be-rigšon / be-rigšon we-raḥašon / le-marom me-ri'šon
Me-ri'šon noṣeri / noṣeri we-'ozeri / we-'ozeri mi-ṣari / 'adonay 'ori
'Ori ya'irah / ya'irah we-yaṣhirah / we-yaṣhirah mi-ṣarah / mi-mi 'ira'?
'Ira' yomo / yomo we-za'ammo / we-za'ammo be-qumo / la-din 'ammo.

I pray at midnight, / at midnight excited, / excited in pleas, / to the heights from the first [day, Gen. 1: 1];
From the first, He preserved me, / preserved me and saved me, / saved me from my enemy, / God my lamp;
My lamp illumines; / illumines and brightens, / brightens my sorrow, / whom shall I fear?
I fear His day [of judgment], / His day and His fury, / His fury when He arises / to judge His people.

[102] Fleischer, *Piyyuṭey . . . Ha-Bavli*, pp. 110–11; Weinberger, *Re'šit Ha-Payṭanut*, p. 85.

[103] A *ḥaṭa'nu* for the Franco-German ritual Days of Awe midnight service, *'Arid be-siḥi / be-siḥi le-goḥi*, by Isaac b. Yaqar (from central Europe?) is identical in its structure to the *ḥaṭa'nu* of Qalai, who may have been familiar with it. See *Seder Ha-Seliḥot . . . Liṭa'*, p. 228.

[104] Weinberger, *Seder . . . Ha-Romaniotim*, p. 129.

Qalai pioneered the expanded dialogue in the Balkan synagogue, and was the first among the region's poets to employ a variant form of the pseudo-*muwashshaḥ*, in which the 'belt' is doubled. This practice, which he probably learned from Solomon Ibn Gabirol's *tokheḥah*, *Šikhḥi yegonekh*, for the Day of Atonement, is seen in Qalai's Ninth of 'Av *qinah*, *He'asfi golah*. E. Fleischer reconstructed the hymn from fragments preserved in the Cairo Geniza. Following is the reconstructed first 'belt' and strophe with the uncommon rhyme *aaaa*, *bbb*, *cc*:[105]

Assemble, O exiled [*golah*], with tears and wailing [*bi-vkhi wi-ylalah*]
In place of joy and merriment [*we-gilah*], tremble this moment and at midnight [*wa-ḥaṣot laylah*]
Lift your voices [*biš'onekh*]
With a bitter cry in your prayers [*hegyonekh*];
Do not, though your pain increases [*bi-rvot 'onekh*],
Give respite to your eyes [*ʿeynekh*]
Year by year [*šanah*];
Cut off your hair and throw it away; raise on the bare heights a lamentation [*qinah*].

Although influenced in large part by the Hispanics, Joseph Qalai also borrows from earlier Romaniote poets. This tension may be seen in his *zulat* for Šabbat Zakhor, *'Et 'adonay darašti*. While it is built on Spanish-style rhyming quatrains with closing scriptural verse, the hymn reviews the laws pertaining to the reading of the Scroll of Esther on the Sabbath before Purim. In the latter practice Qalai is following the example of Benjamin b. Samuel and Isaac b. Judah[106] in informing his congregation of their obligations for Purim. In the *zulat* Qalai, like R. Benjamin and R. Isaac before him, has to choose between differing Esther Scroll-reading regulations. In his choices he relies upon earlier rabbinic rulings. The following, from his *zulat*, is based on *bMeg* 4a:[107]

Men and women alike, [saved] by miracle and wonder, are obligated
To hear the [reading of the] Scroll and to erase the memory of Amalek . . .

[105] The Geniza fragment is at Cambridge University; Taylor–Schechter (TS) collection, Misc. 22.124; TS N.S. 102.142, 139.103; see Ibn Gabirol, *Širey Ha-Qodeš*, pp. 289–91; Fleischer, 'Širatenu,' pp. 191–2; Weinberger, *Re'šit Ha-Payṭanut*, p. 127.

[106] See R. Benjamin's *'Az ke-gulgal* and R. Isaac's *'Eli ṣuri*.

[107] Weinberger, *Re'šit Ha-Payṭanut*, p. 65.

Abraham b. Isaac b. Moses

In the fourteen surviving *seliḥot* by Abraham b. Isaac b. Moses the Hispanic influence continues. Like his contemporaries Moses b. Ḥiyyah and Joseph Qalai, R. Abraham closes his hymns with scriptural verses, and opens his strophes with a repeated use of the verses' first unit. This mannerism, which may be seen in Moses b. Ḥiyyah's *taḥanun*, *Qadoš mistatter be-miškan rumo*, is often employed by R. Abraham, as in the following *rahiṭ*: [108]

Give thanks [*hodu*]
to Him who stretches out the heavens like a curtain and is wrapped in light as with a garment;
His majesty covers the heavens and He alone does wonders;
He created all with the letter *heh* and suspends the world like an amulet [see *bMen* 29b and *jḤag* 2. 1]
Give thanks [*hodu*]
to the Lord for He is good and His mercy endures forever.

It is likely that this is one in a series of *rahiṭim* added to a Day of Atonement *qedušta'*. Presumably, the series was prefaced by the verse from Ps. 106: 1, *Hodu la-'adonay ki tov ki le-'olam ḥasdo* (Give thanks to the Lord, for He is good, etc.). The other surviving *rahiṭim* in the set are R. Abraham's *Ki* (For) *'eqqaḥ mo'ed; Ṭov* (Good) *'adonay le-qowaw*; *Le-'olam* (Forever) *'ašir 'oz ha-mafli'*, and *Ḥasdo* (His mercy) *'eloha yir'af'*. The poet's *rahiṭim* for words No. 2 and No. 5, in the verse from Psalms, have apparently been lost.[109]

R. Abraham is also the author of hymns with patterns of contrast using the figures 'I' and 'Thou' (*'ani we-'attah*). In the *seliḥah*, *'Ani 'aniti 'aniti*, for the Ten Days of Repentance, built in rhyming quatrains, he compares his wretched life with the sovereign might of God, and asks, in the last colon of each strophe, 'How long' (*'ad 'anah*): [110]

I call from the walls of my heart with eyes tear-filled;
I am sated with unnatural sorrow; I am drunk with vipers' venom;
But You, mighty and exalted, take heed of the poor, in exile buried;
How long must I cry and You not listen?

In another notable 'I–Thou' *seliḥah, 'Attah 'eli 'el 'elim*, there is no hint of complaint or pleading, only a profound awareness of God's majesty, contrasted with man's unworthiness. The hymn, in rhyming tercets with closing verse, is charged with alliteration, assonance and internal rhyme designed to enhance its choral quality:[111]

[108] The *rahiṭ* (bar or beam) was originally part of a *qedušta'* and was built on the several units of a biblical verse. Because of its length it was chanted as an independent hymn. Weinberger, *Re'šit Ha-Payṭanut*, pp. 48–9; idem, *Širat . . . Rabbanim*, pp. 39–40.

[109] Ibid., Nos. 18–22.

[110] Ibid., pp. 35–6.

[111] Ibid. 37–8.

You my God are Lord of the angels, Mighty One of the armed
hosts; the *'er'ellim* [class of angels] dance before You;
You are revered in the councils, powerful in their circles; they
break into song in greeting You;
I am a clod of earth and ashes, ashamed to tell Your praise:
Lord, who is like You, awesome in holiness, doing wonders!

R. Abraham's most ambitious project, modelled after Ibn Gabirol's *silluq*, *'A'amir 'a'ddir* is his brilliant phonetic-intensive *'Oyevet šoqetet*, a twenty-seven-strophe hymn with internal and closing monorhyme, *et*. The first nine cola, spanning the letters *alef–ṭet*, are devoted to a staccato indictment of Israel's enemies characterized as a sinister female and 'lover of pleasures' (*'adinah*, Isa. 47: 8), and the remaining cola present Israel's plea for relief. Following are the cola for letters *alef*, *gimel* and *ḥet*:[112]

'Oyevet, šoqetet, šo'evet, šo'efet . . .
Go'eret, go'elet, bohah, meḥarefet . . .
Ḥomedet, ḥomeset, 'ošeqet, we-ṭorefet . . .

She is hostile, unconcerned, absorbed, oppressive . . .
Reproachful, loathsome, frightening, abusive . . .
Covetous, violent, exploitative, beastly . . .

R. Abraham is careful to limit each colon to four units. This use of word metre patterned after Solomon Ha-Bavli's influential *yoṣer*, *'Or yeša' me'uššarim*, is also evident in R. Abraham's *ḥaṭa'nu*, *'Azelu be-khillayon wa-ḥereṣ*, with its three units in each colon. Like his Balkan contemporaries, R. Abraham was open to influences from central Europe as well as Spain. Following is the first strophe from his *ḥaṭa'nu*, built in rhyming tercets with closing scriptural verses ending with the repeated unit *'areṣ*:[113]

'Azelu be-khillayon wa-ḥereṣ;
'Emunim maqdišekha be-'ereṣ;
'Eyn 'omed be-fereṣ;
'Avad ḥasid min-ha-'areṣ.

They have vanished, fully demolished by decree,
Even the faithful sanctifying You with fear;
There is no one to stand in the breach;
The pious are gone from the land.

As well as bitterly denouncing the ruling power, R. Abraham laments over the martyrs who died for the sanctification of God's name (*'al qidduš ha-šem*) and grieves over the heavy tax burden that his people are forced to pay. This

112 Zunz, *Die synagogale Poesie*, pp. 456–7; Weinberger, *Širat . . . Rabbanim*, p. 26.
113 Fleischer, *Piyyuṭey . . . Ha-Bavli*, pp. 191–203; Weinberger, *Širat . . . Rabbanim*, pp. 27–9.

is seen in selections from his *seliḥah*, *Ḥasdo 'eloha yir'af*, and his *ḥaṭa'nu*, *'Akhin qerev we-sar'appayim*:[114]

[SELIḤAH]
May He enlarge His love for the poor nation, separated from
others and their counsels;
Throughout the day they are martyred affirming God's unity;
The faithful are no more, though many
Proclaim themselves loyal.

[ḤAṬA'NU]
They cry to You, 'Violence';
They wail from the heavy taxes [*mi-koved ha-mas*];
They are shrivelled up and depressed,
Even the lights of heaven.

Moses Ḥazan of Thebes

Moses Ḥazan b. Rabbi Abraham of Thebes, presumably the son of R. Abraham b. Isaac b. Moses, composed over twenty hymns in the *seliḥah* genre. In his acrostics, he reveals that his home is in Thebes and that he is employed as congregational cantor (*ḥazan*). To his name he adds the title *memuneh*, indicating that he held the office of syndic, a prominent position in the governance of Greek Jewry in the Balkan settlements. Cecil Roth,[115] writing about the congregation of Greek Jews on the island of Corfu, notes that 'it had its own council of administration, presided over by two syndics, or *memunim*, and two *parnasim*. The former were elected each year by the council . . . [and] were responsible for the maintenance of internal discipline.' It is likely that Moses Ḥazan lived before 1187, when Jerusalem was still in the hands of the Crusaders. This is suggested in his *seliḥah*, *Minḥat marḥešet*:[116]

The Temple mount, O Lord, how will the sons of Zibeon and Aiah
Descecrate it? they have despoiled its field, now a nesting-place for
kite and vulture;
Restore the remnant of Jacob's house and may
The field [Jerusalem] released in the Jubilee [year] be holy to the
Lord.

Zibeon and Aiah (Gen. 36: 24), descendants of Esau, are a metaphor for Christians. Note the poet's use of enjambment in the first two cola and

[114] Weinberger, *Širat . . . Rabbanim*, pp. 41–2, 18–19.
[115] Roth, *Venice*, p. 315.
[116] Weinberger, *Širat . . . Rabbanim*, pp. 112–14.

again in cola three and four. This stylistic feature of Hispanic poetry was also observed in the writings of Joseph Qalai.

Many of Moses Ḥazan's hymns were built around word- and verse-play. Some were probably intended as *rahiṭim* for a Day of Atonement *qedušta'*. As indicated, the *rahiṭ* was introduced by a scriptural verse, followed by a series of hymns embellishing each unit in the verse. Observed earlier in the work of R. Abraham b. Isaac, it is also seen in Moses Ḥazan's hymns, *Yihyu 'imrey fi*, *Le-raṣon meyaḥalim*, *Pi 'eftaḥ*, *We-hegyon meśartekha*, *Libbi 'a'orer*, *Lefaneykha 'odeh*, *'Adonay mesan'i*, *Ṣuri maḥasi* and *We-go'ali ḥay*. The opening units in these hymns (with the exception of one, 'words', *'imrey*) consist of the verse from Ps. 19: 15, 'Let the words of my mouth and the meditation of my heart be acceptable to You, O Lord, my rock and my redeemer' (*Yihyu le-raṣon 'imrey fi we-hegyon libbi le-faneykha, 'adonay ṣuri we-go'ali*). Presumably, these *rahiṭim* formed part of a *qedušta'* for the Day of Atonement, as indicated in the hymn beginning with, *Libbi 'a'orer*:[117]

> O my heart, sanctify a fast, call a solemn assembly;
> Seek mercy in fasting and prayer;
> Do not despise my plea, O awesome on high
> I call to You when my heart is faint.

The use of repeated units as a rhetorical device is seen in Moses Ḥazan's *seliḥah*, *'Attah 'addir*. The hymn is in eighteen strophes of rhyming quatrains with each colon beginning with the unit 'You' (*'Attah*). In the classical period, Yannai made effective use of the repeated unit *'el* in his *qerovah* on Gen. 35: 9: 'God appeared to [*'el*] Jacob.' The following is from Moses Ḥazan's hymn:[118]

> You hewed the seven pillars before all else;
> You contemplated making the four [elements] without speech
> [*beli qol*];
> You fastened the Dragon and suspended the world like a grape;
> You, O God are above all.

The 'seven pillars' refer to Prov. 9: 1, 'Wisdom has built her house, she has hewn her seven pillars.' The pillars, according to the rabbis (in *bSan* 38a) are the seven days of creation. The reference to the view of the Greek philosophers that four elements, water, earth, air and fire, are the building-blocks of the universe is found in Philo, *De Decalogo* 8. Moses Ḥazan may have found the reference in Sa'adyah Ga'on's *Siddur* (p. 248): '[He] who created the world with four elements.' The 'Dragon' is a constellation of stars in the form of this mythical figure mentioned in the *Sefer Yeṣirah* 6. 7.

117 Weinberger, *Širat . . . Rabbanim*, p. 95, and see Nos. 41, 47, 50, 39, 43, 46, 42, 51, 38.
118 Ibid., pp. 80–2; Rabinovitz, *Maḥazor*, i. 217–19.

Moses Ḥazan is one of the Balkan poets who focused on the theme of judgment and punishment in the grave, in his *tokhehah*, *'Enoš binah mišpat ha-ḥereṣ*. Like Moses b. Ḥiyyah's *'Et peney mevin ṣefunay* on this subject, Moses Ḥazan's hymn is built in rhyming tercets with closing scriptural verse. Characteristically, the poet does not shrink from embellishing upon the theme's bare outline in rabbinic sources, reconstructing the drama of the sinner's death and punishment in the grave and recontextualizing biblical verses for rhetorical effect: [119]

He [the Angel of Death] strikes him and his limbs separate;
His bones are ground into thin dust,
And from there it divides and becomes four branches.

His carcass is spoiled and its stench rises;
His belly is split; his excretion spills forth
With his parts and his head . . .

On his back they [the worms] race like horses,
Eager to eat his flesh,
And the dead they shall also divide.

In its context, the third colon, from Gen. 2: 10, refers to the river that flows out of Eden to water the garden and from there divides into four branches. The sixth colon is from Exod. 29: 17 and refers to the consecration of the sons of Aaron and the sacrificial ram whose entrails and legs were to be placed with its other parts and its head. In the ninth colon the poet enlists the ruling from Exod. 21: 35 regarding the goring ox and its victim. Both are to be sold, and the price of the live and dead animal is to be divided.

Moses Ḥazan's *ḥaṭa'nu* hymn, *'Ef'eh ka-yyoledah*, is prefaced by its identifying litany from classical times, repeated after each strophe: 'We have sinned, O our Rock; forgive us our Creator.' As in the central European treatments of this genre, Moses Ḥazan devotes the hymn to retelling the story of the Ten Martyrs. Relying on rabbinic sources, which do not agree on the names of the ten, or on the order in which they were put to death, R. Moses, like other poets writing on this theme, has to choose between varying versions of the story.

In the closing strophes of the *ḥaṭa'nu*, Moses Ḥazan notes a comparison between the tragic deaths of the ten in talmudic times and the plight of the Jews living under Christian rule in his own day:[120]

The perverted have ruined and degraded me;
I am crushed and vanish like smoke;
To the four corners I am chased;
I am not at ease, nor am I quiet, I have no rest.

[119] Weinberger, *Širat . . . Rabbanim*, pp. 60–4.

[120] Ibid. 119.

The 'perverted' (*to'ey ruaḥ*) as a metonym for Christians is used in the *yoṣer 'Elohay bekha 'eḥaveq*, by the Franco-German hymnist R. Ephraim b. Isaac of Regensburg, to condemn the anti-Jewish violence of the Crusaders:[121]

The perverted have ruined me;
Your beloved they have frightened and bereaved,
And the remainder they have devoured.

Attack my adversaries who are spilling my blood like water . . .

Balkan poets like Moses b. Ḥiyyah and Joseph Qalai were fond of composing *tokhaḥot*, featuring the dialogue between body and soul with each blaming the other. Moses Ḥazan was also attracted to this theme and, like Qalai in his *Ke-fo'oli le-ḥeyqi*, he constructed his *tokheḥah*, *'Enoš 'el ṣur ma'ariṣkha*, in rhyming tercets, after earlier Spanish models. The arguments of body and soul are, as before, based on rabbinic sources in *Lev. Rabbah* 4. 5 and *bSan* 91 with characteristic elaborations of the poet. Expanding on the treatment of the theme by Moses b. Ḥiyyah and Qalai, Moses Ḥazan added the parable of the watchmen of the vineyard, one lame and the other blind, who stole their master's figs by subterfuge. The parable (from the above rabbinic sources) is included in God's argument condemning both body and soul:[122]

Heavy is the burden of your sin;
Like the lame and blind [upon whose shoulders he climbed] you
have all betrayed me.

Solomon Šarvit Ha-Zahav

In his commentary to Abraham Ibn Ezra's *Sefer Ha-Šem* (Vatican MS 105), the fourteenth-century philosopher-poet Solomon b. Elijah Šarvit Ha-Zahav ('Golden Sceptre', from the Greek *chrysokokos*) informs us that in his wanderings he moved to Ephesus—presumably from Salonika, where his father lived—and wrote his commentary in 1387. Šarvit Ha-Zahav also wrote two volumes on astronomy (Bibliothèque Nationale, Paris, MS 1042.3, dated 1374, and Vatican MS 393), and translated from Greek into Hebrew Ptolemy's 'Treatise on the Astrolabe' (Paris MS 1047.5). In addition to his monograph, *Ḥešeq Šelomo*, on Hebrew grammar, and his playful poetic debate among the letters of the Hebrew alphabet, *Merivah nihyatah beynot ḥaverim*, the Ephesian philosopher-poet composed for the synagogue. In some of the ten *piyyuṭim* that have been preserved he introduces themes from

121 See Habermann, 'Piyyuṭey R. Ephraim . . . mi-Regensburg', p. 131.
122 Weinberger, *Širat . . . Rabbanim*, p. 76.

contemporary science and philosophy into the liturgy, after the fashion of late eastern and Hispanic poets. Below is a selection from his *baqqašah*, *Yeš yešut ʾemet*, where he paraphrases the first of Maimonides' Thirteen Principles of Jewish faith:[123]

[First Principle:] It is certain that there is an existent [*yešut*], an eternal reality, a being concealed from reach . . . the cause [*sibbah*] of all things; all are in need of it [*ʾeleha*, i.e. the 'cause'], but she is not in need of them . . . The sum of Your word is truth [as it written in Exod. 20: 2; Deut. 5: 6]: 'I am the Lord your God who brought you out of the land of Egypt and the house of bondage.'

Abraham Ibn Ezra's popularity and influence already noted in our discussion of the Franco-Germans is again seen in Šarvit Ha-Zahav's commentary on the Spaniard's *Sefer Ha-Šem*. In his *taḥanun*, *Šadday hizkartani*, the Ephesian poet echoes Ibn Ezra's view[124] that God has delegated to the stars the governance of the sublunar world:[125]

[I remember] when You showed me the stars in Your heaven;
They informed me of Your gracious deeds.

Like earlier Balkan and central European poets, Šarvit Ha-Zahav denounces the Christian ruling power in his *baqqašah*, *Yeš yešut*:

Our voices will call upon God and He will answer us from His holy mountain. [We will not be deluded] by the designs of the [Christians] who pursue vanity. They fall into the tangle of their imagination and are consumed . . . Far be it from us to forsake God . . .[126]

The poet's vow, 'Far be it from us to forsake our God' suggests that Christian missionaries were active in their efforts to proselytize among the Jews of Ephesus in Šarvit Ha-Zahav's time.

Other Balkan poets whose hymns are preserved in the Romaniote ritual include Mordecai of Nicaea (13th c.) and his contemporaries David of Byzantium, Joseph and Avtalion Meyuḥas,[127] Elnatan Ha-Kohen of Arta and Moses Qilqi of Chios. Romaniote poets from the fourteenth century are Moses Kapuṣato Ha-Yevani ('the Greek') and his kinsman Elijah Kapuṣato, Ḥananyah b. Šelaḥyah and his son Šelaḥyah, Isaac b. Qalo (from the Greek *kalos*), Samuel b. Nathan Ha-Parnes, Samuel Qir b. Šabbetai and Šabbetai b. Caleb.[128]

123 Ibid. 225–32.

124 See Ibn Ezra on Exod. 23: 33, and his '*Sefer Ha-Šem*', 2. 4–5.

125 Weinberger, *Širat . . . Rabbanim*, p. 223.

126 Ibid. 226. The text is preserved in the Bodleian Library, Oxford, MS No. 1168, fo. 128b. The subject of the poet's diatribe was presumably erased by censors.

127 Meyuḥas is a translation of the Greek *eugenes*.

128 For a full listing see Weinberger, *Širat . . . Rabbanim*, English section, pp. 20–30.

THE PRINCIPAL GENRES OF THE LATER ROMANIOTES

Rahiṭ

Although there are no complete *qedušta'ot* in the late Romaniote period, Moses b. Ḥiyyah's *rahiṭim*, *We-'attah malki*, *Kal 'emuney 'ammim*, *Me-'eyn kamokha*, *Qadoš mistater*, *Yošev me'onah* and *Mivtaḥi we-goḥi*, were originally part of a Day of Atonement *qedušta'* built on the several units in Ps. 22: 4, 'You are holy, enthroned on the praises of Israel.' R. Moses' *qedušta'ot* fragments recall an earlier period when hymns of this genre were chanted with all their component parts intact. Presumably, because of the inordinate length of the full *qedušta'* and the limited tolerance threshold of the congregation, the genre was separated into manageable portions, of which the *rahiṭ* became a leading survivor. Below is the *rahiṭ*, *Qadoš mistatter*, embellishing the unit 'holy' in the above verse from Psalms.[129]

The holy One is concealed in His heavenly home;
He contains Himself in zero space [*be-'efes maqom*],
And no one knows its location;
Holy and fearful is His name.

To the Balkan *rahiṭim* by Abraham b. Isaac and Moses Ḥazan should be added the *rahiṭim* by Ḥananyah b. Šelaḥyah. His *Yisra'el ḥallu peney 'el* is built in rhyming quatrains which open and close with the unit, *Yisra'el*. Presumably, the *rahiṭ* was part of a series embellishing Ps. 22: 4, 'You are holy, enthroned on the praises of Israel.' The latter verse, with which the hymn closes, undoubtedly served as the superscription to a *rahiṭim* series in the *qedušta'*. Of interest in the hymn is the poet's use of Aramaic, a not uncommon habit of the Romaniotes:[130]

Israel's hands are raised [in prayer] to the holy One, creator of lights:
May Your right hand save and give drink to the weak;
Your congregation awaits Your help, and to You, who refreshes the hopeful,
They cry, 'My God, we—Israel—know You.'

The 'weak' (*šelahay*, colon 2) is an Aramaic term found in *Targum 'Onkelos*, on Deut. 25: 18—needed to rhyme with 'lights', *negohay*. In another *rahiṭ*, *Ṣeva'ot ḥeyli migdoli*, R. Ḥananyah plays on two units, *ṣeva'ot* and *qodšo*. In

[129] Weinberger, *Re'šit Ha-Payṭanut*, pp. 40–57; Fleischer, 'Širatenu', pp. 194–5; see also *bḤag* 13b.

[130] Weinberger, *Širat . . . Rabbanim*, p. 206.

this instance, it is likely that the *rahiṭim* series was introduced by the verse, 'But the Lord of hosts [*ṣeva'ot*] is exalted through justice and the Holy God shows Himself holy by righteousness' (Isa. 5: 16) and 'My mouth will speak the praise of the Lord, and all flesh will bless His holy name' (*šem qodšo*, Ps. 145: 21).

Other likely *rahiṭim* separated from *qedušta'ot* include *Melekh 'elekha 'etḥannan*, by R. Ḥananyah's contemporary Caleb b. Eliaqim. The hymn is constructed in quatrains, beginning and ending with *melekh*. Presuambly, the *rahiṭ* was designed to embellish Jer. 10: 7, 'Who would not fear You, O King [*melekh*] of the nations? for that is Your due; among all the wise ones of the nations and in all their kingdoms there is no one like You.'[131]

O King, the stated cause of His people, He will not dismiss;
Adorn Him as with a necklace and you may be ransomed;
And have an advocate for the right, and be inscribed in the book
Of chronicles before the King.

The 'advocate for the right' is a reference to an angelic intermediary. The 'book of chronicles' refers to the rabbinic view (in *jRH* 1. 57a) that before God seated in judgment are three books, one for the perfectly righteous, one for the wicked and one for whom judgment has not been decreed. The popular *rahiṭim* also served as a means of calling for judgment on Israel's enemies. The following was written by Caleb b. Moses, a contemporary of R. Ḥananyah. R. Caleb's hymn *Ḥayyim 'etnah lifneykhem* begins and ends with *ḥayyim* (life/living), and is probably taken from the verse 'Those of you who held fast to the Lord your God are all alive today' (Deut. 4: 4).[132]

O living One who remembers the covenant, keep in mind what is left of the lion [Judah] and the proud beast [Israel];
Stifle the Christians and devour the Muslims; [think of] those who are crushed by the armed force;
O gracious and forgiving One, forgive the sins [of Israel], and if he has rolled in blood impure, he repents and returns to wash
His flesh in the living waters.

Another contemporary, Samuel Qir b. Šabbetai, is more sanguine in his *rahiṭim* as he pleads for punishment of the Christian ruling power, whom he condemns as 'the servants of Molokh' (*'ovedey molekh*) and 'the worshippers of idols' (*'ovedey teref*). He is enraged at the efforts of Christian missionaries seeking to subvert Israel's faith in its God. He is incensed at the attempt by Christians to assume the mantle of Israel and proclaim themselves God's people, even as he charges that their invocations of God (as three persons) are not supported by 'truth or mercy'. Moreover, he is not impressed with the

131 Ibid. 266–7.

132 Ibid. 278.

worldly success of Christian rulers, invoking the verse from Ps. 33: 16, 'A king is not saved by his great army.' Samuel Qir's *rahiṭim* embellished the verse 'But I, through the abundance of Your steadfast love, will enter Your house' (Ps. 5: 7). In three of these hymns, each strophe in the quatrain begins with one of the units in the verse. These include *Be-rov* ('Through the abundance') *'arešet sefatay*; *Ḥasdekha* ('Your steadfast love') *'addir ba-marom*; and *'Avo* ('I . . . will enter') *'edroš 'el 'el*. The following are from his *Be-rov* and *Ḥasdekha*.

[BE-ROV]

[God] good and gracious, gather Your folk from among the servants of Molokh,
For the glory of a king is a multitude of people . . .

Defiled men have come together to force me to abandon You and not cleave to You;
Because of their many transgressions cast them out, for they have rebelled against You . . .

Salvation is from You [O God], while a king is not spared from plunder or captivity;
Though he lead a mighty army, neither is the warrior delivered by his great strength.

[ḤASDEKHA]

Return Your nation's captives and redeem them from the idol-worshippers;
Your steadfast love endures forever; do not forsake the work of Your hands . . .[133]

Other fourteenth-century authors of *rahiṭim* include Samuel b. Natan and Šabbetai b. Caleb. Samuel b. Natan, in the superscription to his *rahiṭ*, *Ḥayyim 'avaqqešah*, is named, Rabbana', a common Romaniote rabbinic designation. In the acrostic to his *rahiṭ*, *Ḥayyim ša'alti bi-š'elati*, he adds the title *Ha-Parnes.* [134]

Šabbetai b. Caleb's *rahiṭim* focused on the verse 'The living, the living [*ḥay*, *ḥay*] he [*hu'*] thanks You [*yodekha*] as do I [*kamoni*] this day [*ha-yom*];

[133] Weinberger, *Širat . . . Rabbanim*, No. 145, ll. 11–12, 15–16, 39–40; No. 146, ll. 15–16. In line with the judgmental tone of Samuel Qir's *rahiṭim* is his *seliḥah*, *Šokhen 'ad marom*; ibid., No. 149, ll. 9–10, 15–16: 'My oppressors . . . though they invoke the God of Israel, / It is without truth or mercy . . . / The traitors wear the mantle of Your chosen one; / They that have forsaken You have removed his cloak; / Bring him [Israel] back [to his land] that he may sleep in his garment and bless You.'

[134] Ibid. pp. 285–6. In the governance of Venetian Jewry, the Parnas was one of 7 heads of the congregation forming the *Wa'ad Qaton*, a deliberative body representing Jewish interests. See Roth, *Venice*, p. 128. Presumably, Balkan Jewry followed a similar practice.

fathers make known [*yodiʿa*] to children [*banim*] your faithfulness [*ʾel ʾamittekha*],' from Isa. 38: 19. The poet embellished this verse by composing a hymn for each unit, which opens the strophe and may open (or close) the scriptural verse at the end of the quatrain. In his *Ḥay ʾel ʾelohim*, the *rahiṭ*-unit is at the beginning of the strophe and begins the closing verse:[135]

The living [*ḥay*, God], who sits concealed in His upper chambers,
With mercy He restrains His measure of judgment;
He will not despise my prayer, my cry will reach His ears,
The living [*ḥay*] God before whom I stand.

In Šabbetai b. Caleb's *ʾAmittekha šeḥaqim yaʿidu*, the *rahiṭ*-unit closes the scriptural verse at the end of the quatrain-strophe:[136]

Your faithfulness [*ʾamitekha*] the heavens witness; they relate the work of Your hands;
The tribes of Jeshurun [Jacob, Isa. 44: 2] sing the praises of Your might and glory;
With seven [words: *qadoš*, *ʾadonay ṣevaʾot*, *melʾo khol ha-ʾareṣ kevodo*, Isa. 6: 3] each day commending You, they who stand in Your presence;
For Your steadfast love and Your faithfulness (*ʾamitekha*).

Other hymns by R. Šabbetai in this *rahiṭim* series are *Ḥay šofeti malki u-qdoši*, *Huʾ ʾeḥad u-myuḥad*, *Yodekha ʾaddir niflaʾ*, *Kamoni šefal berekh*, *Banim ʾammiṣ ʾonim*, *Yodiʿa šemo ha-nisgav* and *ʾEl ʾeloha ʾeʿetar*. It is likely that Samuel Qir's hymn, *Laylah ʾelekhaʾ šiwwaʿti*, in which each strophe opens and closes with *laylah*, was part of a *rahiṭ* based on the verse 'But their delight is in the teaching of the Lord, and he studies that teaching day and night [*laylah*]' (Ps. 1: 2).[137]

Yoṣer

Guf Ha-Yoṣer Dialogue

Balkan Romaniote poets were attracted to the dialogue *yoṣer* as a rhetorical medium designed to heighten the experience of worship. In adapting the dialogue form from earlier Qilliric and Hispanic models, the Romaniotes usually prefaced the speeches of the parties with introductions. At times, the poet would add a chorus-type strophe commenting on the unfolding drama. Moses b. Ḥiyyah's elegant *yoṣer*, *Malki noṭeh ka-ʾohel meʿonay*, for Šabbat

[135] Weinberger, *Širat . . . Rabbanim*, pp. 303–4. [136] Ibid. 316.

[137] Ibid. 293, 300–16. As late as the 16th c. Balkan poets composed *qeduštaʾot rahiṭim*. The same verse from Isa. 38: 19 served the *rahiṭ* of Elijah b. Benjamin Ha-Levi, in his *ʾAv le-vanim yodiʿa ʾel ʾamittekha*; see Weinberger, *Sirat . . . Rabbanim*, No. 234.

Ḥatanim is crafted in Hispanic-style dialogue between God and Israel, represented as husband and wife. R. Moses' hymn is built in sets of rhyming tercets interrupted by refrains ending with the unit *qadoš*. The sets alternate between the speeches of Israel and God in continuing sequence. The choral stanza, like the chorus in the Greek tragedy, comments on the proceedings and encourages the pair. As in the Hispanic treatment of the *yoṣer*, R. Moses signs his name in the acrostic beginning with the opening tercets, and dispenses with the alphabetic acrostic commonly employed by classical and early central European poets. The Balkan poet enlists the theme of the separated lovers from Canticles in his portrayal of Israel's estrangement from her God and her hope for reconciliation. The cantor-poet seeks to reassure his congregation that God has not forsaken his beloved, Israel. Following are selections from the dialogue:[138]

> [ISRAEL:]
> My Sovereign who tented in my Temple,
> Shine Your face upon the faithful sons;
> They are a stock the Lord has blessed . . .
>
> [CHORAL REFRAIN:]
> Would that the bridegroom stand aloft,
> Together with the loving perfected doe,
> Rejoicing like a groom with His bride, holy . . .
>
> [GOD:]
> Hide yourself for a little while, My sweet one,
> And we will take our fill of love, My gazelle;
> You are altogether beautiful, My beloved.

Joseph Qalai's *guf ha-yoṣer*, *Mah matequ ta'amey šabbat*, is in the form of a dialogue between the Sabbath and the New Month. The poem is built in rhyming tercets interrupted after sets of three strophes by choral refrains ending with the unit *qadoš*. The structure is similar to Moses b. Ḥiyyah's *Malki noṭeh*. However, unlike the latter, Qalai prefaces the speeches of the two parties with 'The Sabbath said to the [New] Month' and 'The [New] Month replied, saying to the Sabbath.' He may have learned this practice from Qillir's dialogue between Mordecai and Esther in his Purim *qerovah*, *'Amittekha we-ḥasdekha 'al tirḥaq*, with its preface formula, 'And Mordecai spoke in reply to Esther,' and 'Esther spoke in reply to Mordecai.'[139] Unlike the serious tone in Qillir's hymn, Qalai's *yoṣer* is a playful exchange between the Sabbath and New Month, with each claiming preference over the other:[140]

[138] Weinberger, *Re'šit Ha-Payṭanut*, pp. 1–3.
[139] Fleischer, *Ha-Yoṣerot*, pp. 506–7.
[140] Weinberger, *Re'šit Ha-Payṭanut*, pp. 67–9.

[SABBATH:]
My cup was exalted
When the Lord said, 'Rest is My delight.'
And God blessed the seventh day . . .
It brings joy to the living and the dead with its pleasure;
For six days the 'Judgment in the Grave' brings distress,
But on the seventh day, the Sabbath, [judgment] is not made.

[NEW MONTH:]
O Sabbath, surely you know the honour due to me;
In me the moon renews itself and I enable it;
Behold the heavens are my witness;
Why persist in spinning words before me?
Do you not know that I preceded you by three days? [Gen. 1: 16, 19]
Those older than your father [are on our side]. [Job 15: 10]

The New Month has the last word, and it is not mock-confrontational as before, but fully conciliatory and reflective of Israel's hopes for national restoration:

In the time to come, God will create for the nation ill unto death,
Ensnared this day by the enemy's fowler,
New heavens and a new earth. [Isa. 65: 17]

He will gather His flock into His ornamented home,
Where they will proclaim His glory and sovereignty,
From new moon to new moon and from Sabbath to Sabbath.

They will sing and rejoice and flourish unconcealed;
When their exiles return, they [Sabbath and New Month] will make ready together:
Two are better than one.

The final colon, from Eccles. 4: 9, with its focus on the value of a supporting friend, is recontextualized by the poet. In the hymn the biblical verse underscores the reconciliation of Sabbath and New Month in the age of national restoration and the ingathering of Israel's exiles.

In the Balkan synagogue, the practice of building the *guf ha-yoṣer* in dialogue form, with speeches prefaced by reference to the parties, was pioneered by Qalai, who wrote two hymns in this manner. The dialogue form gained popularity and was much imitated by poets in the region, including Šabbetai b. Mordecai, Jonathan b. Abraham Ha-Kohen, Solomon Šarvit Ha-Zahav and Elijah Ha-Kohen Šelebi from Ottoman Anatolia. Qalai's other *guf ha-yoṣer* in dialogue, *'Agagi 'aleykha be-fošṭo ke-yeleq*, features a debate between

Ahasuerus and Haman. It was chanted on Šabbat Zakhor. Like his *Mah matequ*, the hymn is built in rhyming tercets with a similar ratio of strophes to *qadoš* refrains. Although the tone of this hymn is serious, compared to his light-hearted *Mah matequ*, Qalai manages to find humour in Haman's choice of arguments against the Jews, based on Esther 3: 8, 'Their laws are different from those of every other people, and they do not keep the king's laws.'

Much of the following, from *'Agagi 'aleykha*, is based on *bMeg* 13a:[141]

[HAMAN:]
They pervert the laws and accumulate festivals for rejoicing:
Today the Sabbath, tomorrow a day of rest;
They do not know how to do right.

They would dash [the king's] cup to the ground and despise it,
And if he touch it they would not drink therefrom;
It is pronounced unclean.

But if a fly fell therein and polluted it,
They would cast it [the fly] to the ground, unafraid of it [as a pollutant],
And drink, draining it down to the dregs.

In addition to the dialogue hymns by Moses b. Ḥiyyah and Joseph Qalai, there is the *guf ha-yoṣer* for the Sabbath before Purim (Šabbat Zakhor), *'Eymun u-šluḥo 'el 'ereṣ megurayikh*, by the thirteenth-century poet Jonathan b. Abraham Ha-Kohen. Constructed in the form of a dialogue between Ahasuerus and Haman, the hymn is based on Esther 3: 8–12 and the speeches are prefaced by introductions. Like earlier Balkan writers in this genre, R. Jonathan opens with an introductory three-strophe set of rhyming tercets, followed by a choral refrain ending with *qadoš*. In the remainder of the hymn the poet assigns alternating three-strophe sets with *qadoš* refrains to each speaker. The speeches of Ahasuerus and Haman are based on rabbinic comments on the verses from Esther, which are embellished and expanded.

Unlike Qalai's *yoṣer*-dialogue on this theme, *'Agagi 'aleykha be-fošṭo ke-yeleq*, with its playful interludes, R. Jonathan's tone is consistently serious. Following is the latter's treatment of Haman reassuring the king that he will go unpunished for annihilating the Jews in his kingdom:[142]

His [God's] power over enemies is now yours;
Their [Israel's] Lord has forsaken them these many days;
He is like an old man, well advanced in years;

[141] Weinberger, *Re'šit Ha-Payṭanut*, p. 61.
[142] Ibid. 59–62; idem, *Širat . . . Rabbanim*, pp. 149–52.

This bold conceit is based on the rabbinic comment (in *bMeg* 13b), 'There never was a traducer so skilful as Haman.' Haman's argument, which the poet adapts, is taken from *Esther Rabbah* 7. 13:

The God who drowned Pharoah in the sea and performed for Israel the wonders and mighty deeds of which you have heard is now old and cannot do anything, since Nebuchadnezzar has ere this gone up and destroyed His house and burned His temple and taken Israel captive and scattered them among the nations.

The popularity of the *yoṣer*-dialogue with Romaniote poets continued. Šabbetai b. Mordecai (14th c.) composed his *yoṣer*, *'Adon me-qedem tamim po'olo*, for Šabbat Ḥatanim, borrowing from Moses b. Ḥiyyah's *yoṣer*, *Malki noṭeh ka-'ohel me'onay*, for a similar occasion, and from the hymns in this genre by Joseph Qalai. Like the former, R. Šabbetai constructs his hymn in a dialogue between the bridal pair, and he imitates the latter in his prefaces introducing the speakers. As in previous Balkan treatments of the genre, R. Šabbetai assigns to each party an alternating set of four strophes in rhyming tercets, including a closing choral refrain ending with *qadoš*. The tone of the hymn is festive and the language is strongly flavoured with images from Canticles. There is a *double entendre* in the poet's conceit. The nuptial pair are both the bride and groom of the special Sabbath and the hypostatized lovers, God and Israel. The imagery of the poet, based on rabbinic comments to Canticles, sympathizes with Israel, God's bride, abandoned to a life in exile but ever hopeful of her lover's return and their happy reunion:[143]

[ISRAEL THE BRIDE:]
He is my saintly husband and I will adorn Him;
O that I knew where I might find Him;
Let Him kiss me with the kisses of His mouth . . .

The day the slave will be freed,
The time when my sun will rise,
Tell me, You whom I love so well.

[GOD THE BRIDEGROOM:]
Your graceful inclination toward Me I have observed;
Of all the lovely maids, I eagerly await only you;
Ah, you are beautiful, My beloved . . .

The memory of you and your utterance are with Me always,
When you gathered My myrrh and My spice;
I would lead you and bring you into the house of My Mother.

In the concluding strophes, God, Israel's bridegroom, hinting at the approaching 'time' of their reunion, urges His bride:

[143] Weinberger, *Re'šit Ha-Payṭanut*, pp. 180–3.

My beloved, flee now and forsake the nations,
And be espoused to Me with steadfast love and mercy
Upon the mountains of spices.

Some Balkan poets chose to omit the dialogue from their *yoṣerot* and were content with rhyming tercets and *qadoš* refrain. In this manner, they revived the earlier practice of Isaac b. Judah. An example of this trend is seen in the *yoṣer*, *'Anovev we-siḥi 'ešpekhah*, for the Sabbath of the New Moon in Ḥanukkah (Šabbat Ro'š Ḥodeš Ḥanukkah) by the thirteenth-century poet Avmelekh b. Yešua. In addition to building his *yoṣer* on the model of earlier forms, he also tends to favour the use of ellipses, after the fashion of classical poets. The following is from his choral refrain:[144]

I will speak of the Torah restoring [*mešivat*, the soul],
Given to the preserved like an apple [*ke-vavat*, of the eye, i.e. Israel],
A psalm, a song for the Sabbath day, holy.

Fittingly, the poet combines the themes of all three occasions, in the closing strophes praying for the fall of Byzantium:

O Redeemer, hasten the deliverance
And we will delight in You
When You destroy Greece's evil kingdom [*malkhut yawan ha-riš'ah*].

Maṣdar

The influence of late eastern post-classical poets on Qalai is evident in the *maṣdar*, *Wa-yehi ha-kol be-ma'amar*, to his *yoṣer* for the Sabbath of a New Moon, *Mah matequ ta'amey šabbat*. The *maṣdar*, a short introduction to the *yoṣer*, is a nine-cola hymn in monorhyme ending with the unit *qadoš*. Following is the closing tercet to Qalai's *maṣdar*:[145]

May He hasten the perfection of His Temple and His people in His homeland,
That we may ascend and worship in the elegance of His holy place
From new moon to new moon and from Sabbath to Sabbath, holy.

'Ofan

The later Romaniotes, unlike their forebears, Benjamin b. Samuel, Isaac b. Judah and Benjamin b. Zeraḥ, were not inclined to compose *'ofannim*. The

[144] Weinberger, *Re'šit Ha-Payṭanut*, pp. 122–5.
[145] Ibid. 66; Fleischer, 'Širatenu', p. 188.

few hymns in this genre that have survived from the twelfth and thirteenth centuries show the influence of Hispanic prosody. A telling example is the metric pseudo-*muwashshaḥ 'ofan*, *Dar ḥevyon be-'apiryon*, for Šabbat Ḥatanim by the thirteenth-century poet David from Byzantium. Notable in this hymn is the absence of references to *heykhalot* literature or angelic names, as was common in the *'ofannim* of the earlier Romaniotes. The tone of R. David's hymn is festive in its calling upon God to renew in Israel the joy of Temple days. The only reference to angels is the hope that their myriads will provide protection for God's people and join in celebrating Israel's restoration.[146]

He who dwells in the hidden canopy will renew song and merriment;
From His heights, God of awesome deeds, commands the release of his people;
He will redeem and console them and announce the city's [Jerusalem's] renown;
And the sound of mirth and gladness, the voice of the bride and the bridegroom.
Set the tranquil angels [*we-šin'annim we-ša'anannim*] eternally over Your people;
Command from Your Temple that they provide relief and gaiety
For the faithful assembled, delivered and exulting in You . . .

The similarity between R. David's *'ofan* and Solomon Ibn Gabirol's *Šin'annim ša'anannim ke-niṣoṣim yilhavu*[147] (Tranquil angels blaze like fire-sparks) is noteworthy. Both are built in the form of a metric (not counting the short syllables) pseudo-*muwashshaḥ* and employ similar figures of speech, and it is likely that the Byzantine hymnist was familiar with the work of the renowned Andalusian.

'Ahavah

Balkan *me'orah* hymns embellishing the antepenultimate benediction before the *šema'*, *Yošer ha-me'orot* (Creator of the heavenly lights), have not been preserved. The *'ahavah* hymn designed to adorn the last benediction before the *šema'*, *Ha-boḥer be-'ammo yisra'el be-'ahavah* (. . . who in love has chosen His people Israel), has survived in a hymn, preserved in the Cairo Geniza, *'Eynay mi-levavi*, by Joseph Qalai. His metric *'ahavah*, built in the form of a *muwashshaḥ*, is modelled after Hispanic forms in this genre. Its theme is a dialogue between God and Israel in which the pair profess their

[146] Weinberger, *Širat . . . Rabbanim*, pp. 141–2; Zunz, *Literaturgeschichte*, p. 546.
[147] Ibn Gabirol, *Širey Ha-Qodeš*, pp. 89–92.

love for each other combined with the expectation that they will be reunited in their national home:[148]

[ISRAEL:]
For my wandering beloved [i.e. God], my eyes draw
Blood from my heart, now a widened stream . . .

I wait in silence for the Lord and am put to shame
Being a migrant in a land not mine
Until He looks out and sees the enemy exalting himself over me . . .

[GOD:]
I will cause My face to shine upon My people and with wonders
I will redeem them and My judgment will go forth as the light . . .
I am jealous for Zion, plundered this day;
Rejoice, you will walk erect on her behalf;
Do not fear [My beloved], say to her [Zion];
My love for you is like the roaring sea;
On the day your beloved arrives, all will be secure.

Zulat

The eclectic Joseph Qalai builds his *zulat*, *'Et 'adonay darašti*, in quatrains with closing biblical verse. The hymn varies from central European models in that the poet in the acrostic provides only his name signature and not the alphabet. This practice is reminiscent of Benjamin b. Samuel's *zulat* for Pentecost, *Bittaqti zero'a*.[149]

Jonathan b. Abraham's *zulat*, *'Aširah na' li-ydidi*, for Šabbat Ha-Gadol is constructed as a dialogue, a common rhetorical device of Romaniote poets. The parties to the debate are Moses and Pharoah, and their exchange is based on Exod. 7: 15 and its rabbinic commentaries:[150]

While bathing, the crocodile fool [i.e. Pharoah] spoke [to Moses],
Who in my [Israel's] behalf had protested,
'Remove yourself from me. Who sent you?
I know not God and will not send Israel free!'

The humble one (Moses) responded, 'The Rock [God] of the pure [Israel] ordered it.'

Moses then complains to God about Pharoah's intransigence even as he is upset with the Lord for His failure to act:

[148] Weinberger, *Re'šit Ha-Payṭanut*, pp. 123–4; Fleischer, 'Širatenu', p. 198.
[149] Weinberger, *Re'šit Ha-Payṭanut*, pp. 64–5, 131–2, 137, 146–7, 155–7; Zunz, *Literaturgeschichte*, p. 122.
[150] Weinberger, *Širat . . . Rabbanim*, pp. 147–8.

I appealed [to him] speaking in Your name,
He has mistreated this people and You have done nothing to
deliver Your people.

The poet then shifts the scene to the present and reminds his congregation that God did act to redeem Israel from slavery in Egypt, and, it is hoped, will again save His people from their enemies.

Later treatments of the Balkan *zulat* do not vary from the standard rhyming quatrains with closing scriptural verse, alphabetic acrostic and name signature. Solomon Šarvit Ha-Zahav's *zulat*, *'Efes zulatekha*, for Passover, follows this model. In the following selection he recounts God's mighty acts in Egypt and prays that they be repeated in the present.[151]

Return Your treasured people,
Redeem them once again;
Assemble Your congregations;
Bring them in and plant them on the mountain of Your own
possession.

Send us Your sweet anointed [king]
To regale the daughters in Ariel's [Jerusalem's] abode,
Even the prized prophets and the seven [after *bSukk* 52b] glorified
shepherds,
And may He gather up in his arms the stray sheep.

Mi Kamokha

Like their Hispanic colleagues, the Balkan poets were fond of composing in the *mi kamokha* genre. The earliest surviving *mi kamokha* by a Romaniote is Moses b. Ḥiyyah's *Mi kamokha mesim netivah*, for Šabbat Ḥatanim. The hymn is styled like its Andalusian model in quatrains with a pseudo-*muwashshaḥ* construction and identical units from scriptural verses at the close of each strophe. The theme of the hymn is a celebration of the marriage union, with fitting tributes to the bridal pair, after Iberian models. The following strophes from R. Moses' *mi kamokha*, in which the bridegroom invites his beloved to hasten into the perfumed garden, reflects the influence of themes in Canticles and Judeo-Arabic *ghazal*-type love poetry:[152]

Come, fly on the wings of the soaring bird;
Dwell in the garden perfumed
With spices of myrrh and fragrance;
Your garments have the scent of Lebanon

[151] Ibid. 240–1.
[152] Weinberger, *Re'šit Ha-Payṭanut*, pp. 3–5; Fleischer, *Ha-Yoṣerot*, p. 575.

Fair-eyed maid, bejewelled;
Your speech is the dew-drop wished for in the islands;
A well of living waters;
A flowing stream from Lebanon

Another hymn in this genre, *Mi kamokha la-ʿad ʾazamrah we-ʾasiḥah*, for Šabbat Ḥatanim, was composed by the thirteenth-century poet and administrator Leon b. Michael *Ha-Parnes*.[153] R. Leon's *mi kamokha* is built on the Hispanic model in theme and structure. The tone of the hymn is festive and the espousal of bride and groom is recontextualized to embrace the love between God and Israel, even as the language of affection is borrowed from Canticles. In a variation from the standard Hispanic *mi kamokha*, R. Leon uses the third and fourth cola in the opening strophe as repeated refrains after the second and following strophes. The acrostic gives the poet's name and that of his father.[154]

Seed of sacred teachers,
Of Torah pure to the ages;
When the players' timbrels are raised,
The Bridegroom [God] will surely come forth from His chamber and the bride [Israel] [from her canopy, (after Joel 2: 16)]
[To the] sound of mirth and gladness; the voice of the bride and the Bridegroom.

In the ellipsis in the last colon before the refrain, the congregation was expected to fill in the balance of the verse from Joel 2: 16.

Later treatments of the genre include *Mi kamokha ʾeloha qedem meʿonah*, by the fourteenth-century poet Elijah b. Moses Kapuṣato.[155] R. Elijah's *mi kamokha*, chanted on Pentecost, was a review of the Ten Commandments and the reasons for their observance. The hymn is built in standard Hispanic fashion with identical units at the end of the strophes, complete name signature and a cosmic preface introducing the main theme. The following selection uses a rhetorical mix of precept and the reason for its observance:[156]

The reason that murder of one like you in form and image is forbidden
Is that in the image of God was the form fashioned . . .

[153] R. Leon may be identified with 'Mar Leon', one of 3 communal leaders in Andravida in the Morea. The others, named in an account of 1257 preserved in the Cairo Geniza, were, 'R. Elia *Ha-Parnes* (leader) and R. David *Ha-Melammed* (teacher).' Bowman, *The Jews of Byzantium*, pp. 224–7.

[154] Weinberger, *Širat . . . Rabbanim*, pp. 166–7.

[155] His kinsman, Moses the Greek (*Ha-Yewani*) Kapuṣato, was a vigorous opponent of the Karaites in Byzantium. See Elijah Bašyatchi, *ʾAdderet ʾEliyyahu*, 7. 3b.

[156] Weinberger, *Širat . . . Rabbanim*, pp. 189–91.

The reason that you should not commit adultery with your
neighbour's wife
Is that you may be distinguished and holy, you and your seed . . .

The reason that you should not steal the wealth of your friend
Is that you are unjust in taking this course . . .

The reason that you should not covet your neighbour's possessions
Is that you will thereby be seduced and led astray.

An uncommon form of the *mi kamokha* is Solomon Šarvit Ha-Zahav's dialogue hymn for the Sabbath of Ḥanukkah, *Mi kamokha šabbat we-ḥanukkah niggešu*. Varying from earlier practice, the poet omits the repeated unit at the close of the strophes and dispenses with the cosmic preface. Instead, he presents a playful debate between the two festivals, with each promoting its special merits. The light-hearted tone of the work is reminiscent of Joseph Qalai's festive dialogue-*yoṣer* for Šabbat Ro'š Ḥodeš, *Mah matequ ṭa'amey šabbat*. Like Qalai, R. Solomon prefaces the speeches of the parties to the dialogue; but unlike his mentor, he introduces himself into the debate, urging the pair to settle their dispute.[157]

The Sabbath and Ḥanukkah approached and debated before me:
One saying, 'I am the Lord's', and the other claiming it in my
hearing;
What is to be done to them this day in the presence of the
discerning?
The rich and the poor have this in common: the Lord is the maker
of them all.

Said the Sabbath to Ḥanukkah:

'Mine is the right of the first-born,
But who are you and your upstart family!
The Lord, great and fearful, rested on me
From all the work that He had done in creation . . . '

Replied Ḥanukkah to the Sabbath:

'My light's lustre is kindled first while yours is later,
And the memory of me is in the *ha-'areṣ* benediction while the
reference to you is in the *raḥem* blessing [that follows it];
All that pertains to you and yours shall set out last by companies'
[Num. 2: 31].

[157] Ibid. 238–40.

Said the Sabbath to Ḥanukkah:

'Note that I am consistent like the wife of one's youth, pure,
Appearing on the seventh day like a princess decked in her chamber robes led inside,
While you are like a concubine fearfully appearing at night
At your proper time from year to year.'

Replied Ḥanukkah to the Sabbath:

'By your lights one sees [in the dark], they serve for public use,
Whereas I am the spouse forbidden to men and women;
Moreover, your songs are many whereas my one [the *Hallel*] will be sung by the children
When the Temple will house the Holy of Holies.'

At the close of the hymn, the poet counsels the pair to be reconciled:

I responded:

'Turn away from your quarrels
For today you are joined in affection.'

The fine points in the arguments of the two protagonists were not lost on Šarvit Ha-Zahav's learned congregation. They knew the ruling in the rabbinic codes that on a Sabbath in Ḥanukkah, the lights of the latter are kindled first; to do otherwise would be a violation of the law prohibiting the lighting of fire on the Sabbath. They understood the reference to the *ha-'areṣ* benediction in the grace after meals (*birkat ha-mazon*) and its Ḥanukkah component, the *'Al ha-nissim* (We thank You for the miracles [of Ḥanukkah]), which was recited before the *Reṣeh we-haḥaliṣenu* . . . (Strengthen us O Lord our God with Your commandments and with the commandment concerning the . . . holy Sabbath). They were informed of the rabbinic objection to making use of the Ḥanukkah lights, and were familiar with the Sabbath songs for the dinner table, even as they knew that the *Hallel* chanted on Ḥanukkah would be sung on the day of the Messiah's arrival.[158]

Undoubtedly, R. Solomon's congregation appreciated his subtle play on words and *double entendre* in the argument made by the Sabbath against Ḥanukkah:

'I am like a man praised and esteemed,
Whereas you are like the brazen female out to plunder;
And did not the most splendid sages teach:
One is forbidden to have relations with her at all.'

The Hebrew in the last colon, *'eyn mištamšim be-'iššah kelal*, can also be translated, 'One is forbidden to make use of its [the Ḥanukkah candle's]

[158] See *Ṭur*, *'Oraḥ Ḥayyim*, Nos. 188, 673; Kahane, *Rabbi Salomo*, pp. 25–6.

flame', in line with the rabbinic ruling. However, given the two ways of reading the text, the poet playfully turns Ḥanukkah into a harlot—in the Sabbath's argument—with whom one is forbidden to have relations. The Hebrew *mištamšim* is thus intended to mean *tašmiš ha-miṭṭah*, sexual intercourse.

Ge'ullah

Following the *mi kamokha* hymn in the *yoṣer* cycle is the *ge'ullah* designed to adorn the benediction, 'God, redeemer of Israel.' The designation of this hymn as a *ge'ullah* probably originated with Hispanic poets, and several specimens of this genre by Ibn Gabirol and Abraham Ibn Ezra have been preserved. It appears that Balkan poets were not as attracted to this genre as to the *mi kamokha*. The earliest surviving *ge'ullah* from the region is *'Averu ha-'ivrim*, for the seventh day of Passover, by the fourteenth-century poet Moses b. David.[159]

R. Moses' hymn is a metric *muwashshaḥ* similar to Abraham Ibn Ezra's *Ṣur ha-meqora' be-ṣur yisra'el.* The metre in both hymns is – – –/–v–/–v– –. R. Moses recounts the exodus from Egypt and highlights the drama of Israel being pursued by the Egyptians to the sea's edge:[160]

> To the faithful [Moses] He said, 'Is the Lord's power limited?
> My children I will preserve in life and bring death to every
> enemy!
> For he oppressed my servants and discomfited them;
> Divide now the sea
> And I will make my flock pass through and drown the foe.'

Rešut

The request for permission (*rešut*) to chant the liturgy is heard in Isa. 6: 3, 'and one (angel) called to the other.' In the early liturgy, the 'call' was interpreted as a request for permission ('Each grants leave to the other to join in hallowing their Creator,' morning service), given the humility of the angels in God's presence. The earliest permission formula was probably *Mi-sod ḥakhamim u-nvonim* (With the inspired words of the wise . . . I will open my lips in prayer and . . . implore the Presence of the King), chanted before the *qerovot* for Sabbaths and festivals. Beginning with the Hispanic poets, the *rešut* developed into an independent genre to which the Golden Age Andalusians were attracted.

[159] Presumably the poet is the Rabbanite teacher Moses b. David from Nicomedia in Anatolia, mentioned by the Karaite Aaron b. Elijah (in his *Gan 'Eden*, *Šeḥitah* 84a), relating an event which took place in 1339.

[160] Weinberger, *Širat . . . Rabbanim*, pp. 250–1; A. Ibn Ezra, *Širey Ha-Qodeš*, i. 79.

Qaṣīdah-style *Rešuyyot*

By the fourteenth century Romaniote poets were attracted to Hispanic *qaṣīdah*-style *rešuyyot*. Following is an elegant example by Elijah Kapuṣato. His *rešut* for the *qaddiš*, *'Asapper nifle'ot yoṣer šeḥaqim*, is in *qaṣīdah* form with *ha-merubbeh* metre. The hymn, chanted during the morning service of Passover, closes with a reference to the *qaddiš*:[161]

> My Sovereign, have regard for the cry of Your people and be merciful,
> And restore their fortunes like the water-courses—
> That they may magnify and sanctify [*yigdal we-yitqaddeš*] Your praise
> Like the mouths of babes and infants at the Sea of Reeds.

The congregation was expected to complete the ellipsis in the second colon, based on Ps. 126: 4, '. . . like water-courses in the Negev.'

Another *qaṣīdah*-style *rešut* from this period is a permission request before chanting the *barekhu*. The *rešut*, *Meromam 'at 'aley kol šir we-zimrah*, is the only surviving hymn by Mosqoyo.[162] The poet signs his name *MSQWYW* in the acrostic to his one-strophe, six-cola *reṣut*. His *qaṣīdah*-form poem with balanced hemistichs is in *ha-merubbeh* metre. Mosqoyo's hymn closes with *barekhu 'et 'adonay ha-mevorakh* (Praise the Lord, Source of blessing). A similar closing is used by Ibn Gabirol in his *barekhu rešut*, *Šaḥaq we-khol hamon zevul*, and in Abraham Ibn Ezra's hymn in this genre, *'El pe'alaw gaveru*. Following is part of Mosqoyo's hymn:[163]

> Exalted are You above all poetry and song
> And poor is the power of your clay creature;
> Your praise O Lord, with all his ability
> He offers You for Your people assembled . . .
> You, the nation [of God], lift up your hands to the holy place,
> And praise the Lord, Source of blessing.

Simḥat Torah *Rešuyyot*

Romaniote *rešuyyot* for Simḥat Torah had a distinctive character. On this festival the spiritual leader of the synagogue was honoured with reading the closing section from Deuteronomy, and the administrative head would read the first part of Genesis. The former was designated 'the bridegroom of the

[161] Weinberger, *Širat . . . Rabbanim*, p. 192.

[162] The poet's name, Mosqoyo, suggests a connection to Moscow, which was established as a metropolitan seat in 1326. Presumably the city had a Jewish presence similar to that of Kievan Russia. Records of Jewish settlements in Kiev date from 1018.

[163] Weinberger, *Širat . . . Rabbanim*, p. 144; Ibn Gabirol, *Širey Ha-Qodeš*, p. 458; A. Ibn Ezra, *Širey Ha-Qodeš*, i. 290.

Torah', *ḥatan ha-torah*, and the latter, *ḥatan bere'šit*, 'bridegroom of Genesis'. In central and eastern European congregations, both honorees were treated to festive permission requests (*rešuyyot*) in which praise was lavished upon the Torah in the *ḥatan ha-torah* hymns, and upon God, the Creator, in the *ḥatan bere'šit* poems. The extravagant length and lavish hyperbole of the *rešuyyot* composed by the Franco-Germans were not duplicated by Balkan hymnists, although the general festivity of Simḥat Torah elicited some uncommon practices. A notable example is the fourteenth-century Yose b. Abraham's *rešut* for the *ḥatan bere'šit*, *Nodeh u-nšabbaḥ le-'attiq yomin*, in Hebrew, Aramaic and Greek rhyming couplets.[164] A distinctive folk quality is discernible in R. Yose's work, and its Aramaic and Greek vernacular usage reflects its popular appeal on the festive holiday. The following strophe from R. Yose is in Aramaic and Greek:[165]

> *'Aqalles le-malka' ton pandon ḥey 'olamim;*
> *Modan u-mvarkhin kol nagwat 'amemin.*
>
> I will praise the King, all-powerful, abiding forever;
> Praised and thanked by all the island people.

In the closing strophes the poet prays for divine blessings upon the honoree:

> He, the great God, feared thoughout the world
> May He bless this bridegroom and grant him long life.
>
> O King of kings, grant that this bridegroom sire worthy sons learned in the Torah
> And may the Temple be rebuilt in our day and we alive and prospering.

Petiḥah

A *petiḥah* (opening) is often another name for the *rešut*. Like the latter, this hymn is a permission request to chant the *nišmat*, *qaddiš*, *barekhu* parts of the *yoṣer* complex, and daily and life-cycle events. It can also have a *seliḥah* function, as with Judah Ha-Levi's *petiḥah* hymns praying for rain or for relief from persecution. Most of the Balkan *petiḥot* served as *rešuyyot*. Two such hymns in the form of pseudo-*muwashshaḥāt* were composed by David from Byzantium, *Ri'šon le-ṣiyyon 'eloheykhem yevasserkhem*, for Šabbat Ha-Ḥodeš and *Dofeq pitḥey yešenah*, for the morning service of Šemini 'Aṣeret. The

164 The refrain which opens R. Yose's hymn is similar to the opening in the *rešut* for the *ḥatan ha-torah* by his contemporary, the Cretan philosopher, poet and translator Šemaryah b. Elijah Ha-Ikriti. Presumably both hymns are based on an older Aramaic text.

165 Weinberger, *Širat . . . Rabbanim*, pp. 199–200.

former was presumably a permission hymn before the *ge'ullah*, as indicated in the following strophe:[166]

Raise Your nation's banner and prepare his
Way; hearken to his prayer,
And bring the news to Your son [Israel]: 'Thus
Spoke the Lord your redeemer [*go'alekhem*] . . . '

The poet's skilful use of enjambment in the last two cola is reminiscent of similar figures employed by Joseph Qalai. R. David's second *petiḥah* was probably intended as a permission request before the recitation of the *qaddiš*, given that the poet paraphrases one of its responses:[167]

[Their prayers] gliding over lips and teeth,
The sons sanctify Him;
The righteous that preserve the faith
Respond, 'Amen, may His great name [be blessed] ['*amen, yehe' šeme*']';
And on the merits of the patriarchs' love,
May our prayers be accepted [*titqabbel ṣelotana*'].

Unlike his other pseudo-*muwashshaḥ petiḥot*, R. David's *'Adati le-'el meyaḥelet*, for Šabbat Šeqalim, is in quatrains with rhyming tercets and closing colon ending with the unit *ha-šeqel* (the coin). Here, as in the other two, the poet favours the short colon of two to four units. In the hymn, the poet asks when Israel's banners will be restored to their national home:[168]

The beloved [await] the time of the banners [replaced];
Hidden is [that time] and they are fearful.

A *petiḥah* for Šabbat Ḥatanim, *'El la-ḥatani zeh*, by the fourteenth-century poet Tobias, has been preserved in a manuscript edition of the Romaniote prayer-book, the *Maḥazor Romania*.[169] Tobias's epithalamium-*petiḥah* is built as a pseudo-*muwashshaḥ* with *ha-mitpaššet* III (see p. xxiii). It is likely that the hymn was a permission request before the grace after meals (*birkat ha-mazon*), given its focus on providing food for the new family, as in the following:[170]

O Lord hasten to give strength for this bridegroom;
That he may succeed in all his endeavours.

[166] Weinberger, *Širat . . . Rabbanim*, p. 137. [167] Ibid. 141. [168] Ibid. 143.

[169] London, Jews' College, MS Montefiore No. 220, fo. 268b. The hymn is headed by a superscription describing the Romaniote practice on Šabbat Ḥatanim. The congregation would assemble in the home of the bridegroom and there recite the preliminary 100 benedictions. Then they would accompany him to the synagogue, where the remainder of the service was held.

[170] Weinberger, *Širat . . . Rabbanim*, pp. 247–8.

Food for his nourishment
Provide for him . . .
See that he is fed
Evermore and bring contentment
To him and his spouse . . .

The *petiḥah* also provided an opportunity for Romaniote poets to experiment with exotic rhyming patterns. Evidence of this is seen in the metric pseudo-*muwashshaḥ* hymn for Passover, *'Imrey hegyonay*, by Moses Ha-Yewani (the Greek) Kapuṣato, a contemporary of Tobias. R. Moses' uncommon rhyming pattern, *aa*, *ba*, *ba*, *ba*, *bccca*, *aa* / *de*, *de*, *de* / *dfffa*, *aa* / etc., is one of a kind in the later Romaniote period. In Ottoman times, Elijah Ṣelebi is also drawn to elaborate rhyming mannerisms. R. Moses' hymn was presumably a permission request before the chanting of the *'ofan*, as indicated in his closing strophe:[171]

Israel assembled, make your offerings to the Lord revered among the holy [*na'araṣ bi-qdošim*];
God, mighty in strength, His name is praised and esteemed;
[The angels] *qaddiš*, *'ir* and *'el* all sanctify His holiness;
Therefore, ye pure of heart, compose a song and chant, and relate the mercy of God.

Of special interest is the poet's reference in the *petiḥah* to Rome and Byzantium:

Owner of the heavens, living and eternal God dwelling on high,
Gather Your faithful, scattered among the nations,
And on our behalf, O my Rock, show wonders in the *ṣorayim* nation as in the past.

The term *ṣorayim* is the dual form of *ṣor*. The rabbis, commenting on Ezek. 26: 2, 'Because Tyre [*ṣor*] gloated over Jerusalem', perceived the term as a metaphor for Edom, or Rome. The use of the dual form designating both Rome and Byzantium appears in the Hebrew *Vision of Daniel*, from the ninth to tenth centuries,[172] and in an anonymous hymn preserved in the *Maḥazor Romania* (p. 68b). See also *bPes* 42b for Tyre as a metaphor for Rome. The phrasing in the latter hymn, similar to that of R. Moses, follows:

[171] Moses Kapuṣato was known as a vocal opponent of the Karaite, Aaron b. Joseph 'the Elder', on the issue of when the new month was to be declared. Against the Karaite view, that argued for the monthly testimony on the appearance of the new moon, R. Moses, in line with the view advanced in the 11th c. by the Rabbanite Tobias b. Eliezer of Thessalonica and Kastoria, declared that such testimony was frequently impractical, as e.g. when the sky is cloudy. See Elijah Bašyatchi, *'Adderet 'Eliyyahu*, 7. 3b; Tobias b. Eliezer, *Leqaḥ Ṭov*, on Exod., pp. 54 (27b) and 55 (28a); Weinberger, *Širat . . . Rabbanim*, pp. 188–9.

[172] See Ginzberg, *Ginzey Schechter*, i. 320.

You have performed wonders in Egypt
Do now wondrously in *ṣorayim*.

By the thirteenth century, a distinctive pattern is observed in the Balkan permission *petiḥah* for the 'Elul and Days of Repentance midnight vigil service. The pattern, which gained wide popularity in the region, featured an opening scriptural verse followed by a one-strophe set of rhyming tercets, with a closing colon repeating a segment of the opening verse. Ending the strophe was a colon paraphrasing Dan. 9: 18, 'Because of Your abundant mercies', the verse that precedes the recitation of God's Thirteen Attributes (*middot*) in the midnight service. It is not known who pioneered this practice, which by the thirteenth century had become a common feature in the Romaniote ritual. A prominent opening verse for this pattern of *petiḥah* was 'How can young people keep their way pure? By guarding it according to You word' (Ps. 119: 9). At least four *petiḥot* were built on this verse, beginning with a five-cola hymn featuring rhetorical questions designed by the poet Šabbetai:[173]

How can a young person keep his way pure?
Absorbed in desire, in sullied waters defiled, with what will he be made pure?
Smitten by sin befouling, if not cleansed by Your mercy, how can he keep pure?
When his heart is constant in devising evil, his mouth opened without restraint, can the young be pure?
From the day he emerged from the womb, he is perverse whether standing or sitting, the young on his way;
Compassionate [God] receive the repentant, be gracious to the poor returning, trusting in Your abundant mercy.

Solomon Šarvit Ha-Zahav's *petiḥah*, prefaced by this verse from Psalms, is a nine-cola hymn, because the poet sought to sign his name in the acrostic, *SRBYṬ HZHB*. Given his wider purpose, R. Solomon's hymn is divided into two strophes. The first, in six cola, is an extended commentary on 'How can a young person keep his way pure?', and the second is a plea for divine mercy.

Šarvit Ha-Zahav's contemporary, Gur Arye Judah b. David Ha-Levi, also favoured vigil-nights *petiḥot* in this pattern. However, his choice of scriptural headers was 'Bless the Lord, O my soul, and all that is within me bless His holy name' (Ps. 103: 1). Moreover, instead of rhyming tercets, R. Gur Arye, in his *Godlo zikhri tamid we-ʿirkhi*, prefers quatrains. However, like his contemporary from Ephesus, his closing colon in the strophe holds a segment of the scriptural header. Following the now-established pattern for the vigil-

[173] Weinberger, *Seder . . . Ha-Romaniotim*, p. 30.

nights *petiḥot*, the colon in the last strophe is an ellipsis from Dan. 9: 18 and leads to the introduction of the Thirteen Divine Attributes.[174]

Be-ʿizzuz ʿoṣmekha
Nahel ʿammekha
Wa-ʾavarkha wa-ʾagaddelah šemekha
Ki ʿal raḥamekha—

With Your mighty power
Lead Your people
And I will bless and exalt Your name,
For Your mercy [abundant].

Later Ottoman hymnists—Aaron b. Abaye of Constantinople, an older contemporary of Elijah Mizraḥi (1450–1526), and R. Aaron's contemporary Isaiah b. Joseph of Missini (from Mesene in the Morea)—wrote *petiḥot* for the *seliḥot* services using as a header Ps. 119: 9.

While the above *petiḥah* pattern was distinctive in the Romaniote synagogue, other types of vigil-nights *petiḥot* reflect the influence of Hispanic models. Among them is Šarvit Ha-Zahav's metric (*ha-šalem* III; see p. xxii), *Šafel we-gowe ʿa ʾani*, for the Ten Days of Repentance. The hymn is built in strophes of sestets with rhyming quintets, and a scriptural verse as closing colon ending with the unit *melekh* (king). In the opening strophe the cantor-poet, aware of his responsibility as emissary of the congregation, prays for divine aid:[175]

Afflicted and weak am I, poor and destitute,
Despised and shunned by others with no end to their contempt;
Yet the leaders of Zion have appointed me,
[Knowing] that it is good to praise You and sing to the Most High.

In the first colon, the cantor-poet's disclosure that he is weak (*goweʿa*) can be attributed to the practice of fasting on the Ten Days of Repentance. Evidence of fasting during this 'acceptable time' (*ʿet raṣon*) between the New Year and the Day of Atonement is found in the liturgical writings of central and eastern European poets.[176] Pressing his point, Šarvit Ha-Zahav intimates that, in addition to his weakened body, he suffers from the contempt of enemies who delight in pointing to Israel's Temple mount in ruins:

Behold, Your first-born [Israel], his enemies reproach him,
'Where is the house of your God, and where its builders?'

Šarvit Ha-Zahav's two other *petiḥot* for the Ten Days of Repentance, *Šimkha ʾelohay niqraʾ ʿaleynu* and *Šadday zekharnukha be-miškavenu*, were

[174] Weinberger, *Širat . . . Rabbanim*, pp. 253–4. [175] Ibid. 234–5.
[176] *Seder Ha-Seliḥot . . . Polin*, p. 10; Weinberger, *Seder . . . Ha-Romaniotim*, p. 18.

composed in the form of a pseudo-*muwashshaḥ* with *ha-šalem* metre. The former is notable for an extended conceit on divine omniscience. Note the use of enjambment in both couplets: [177]

We are unable to conceal in our hands
The sin; though Your throne is in the heavens,
Your ear is extended, and Your eyes
Behold humankind, probing them.

In *Šadday zekharnukha*, the cantor-poet repeats a familiar conceit in penitential hymnody by confessing his congregation's lack of merit:[178]

We come before You without much merit
Our heads are not raised, we wave no [banners];
We surely rely on Your holy word:
May it please the good Lord to forgive those who find refuge
In Your name . . .

Gur Arye Ha-Levi, Šarvit Ha-Zahav's contemporary, also composed vigil-nights *petiḥot* after Hispanic models, in addition to his distinctively Balkan hymn, *Godlo zikhri tamid we-ʿirkhi*. Two of R. Gur Arye's *piyyuṭim*, *Be-ḥin libbi we-hegyon* and *Yom ʾefteḥah delet*, are in the form of a pseudo-*muwashshaḥ*, and a third, *Yah ḥon ʿammekha*, is in strophes of rhyming quatrains ending with *raḥamekha*, from the verse in Dan. 9: 18.

Muḥarrak

The Balkan poets followed their Hispanic colleagues in favouring the *muḥarrak* (from the Arabic 'moved'), an introduction to the Sabbath and festival morning prayer 'The breath of all that lives praises You' (*Nišmat kol ḥay tevarekh*). The reason why this introductory prayer is called by this name is, as yet, unknown. A characteristic of the hymn is that the last unit in each strophe rhymes with the last unit in the header opening. Moses b. Ḥiyyah's *muḥarrak*, *ʾOdeh ṣuri hifliʾ ḥasdo*, for Tabernacles, a *muwashshaḥ* in quantitative metre with internal rhyme, was doubtless modelled after Moses Ibn Ezra's *Ruaḥ sesoni we-ḥen manʿammaw* for Passover and Judah Ha-Levi's *Mi yitneni ʿeved ʾeloha ʿoseni*.[179] However, unlike the Hispanics, R. Moses reviews for his congregation the laws pertaining to the festival, the construction of the booths and the rules relating to the four species (Lev. 23: 40–2). Below is the closing strophe leading into the *nišmat*.[180]

177 Weinberger, *Širat . . . Rabbanim*, p. 236.
178 Ibid. 237–8.
179 Schirmann, *Ha-Širah Ha-ʿIvrit*, i. 411–12, 519–20.
180 Weinberger, *Reʾšit Ha-Payṭanut*, p. 7.

He has chosen us from among the nations
And has led us by His commands;
He pitied us at the outset;
By day the sun did not bruise us . . .
The merciful One gave us His instruction
And gladdened body and soul
He will surely bless His only one [Israel];
The breath of every living being abides with Him.

Seliḥah

The *seliḥah* (penitential hymn) in its several forms continued to have wide appeal in the late Romaniote period. As in earlier times, hymns in this genre were most prominent during vigil nights in the month of 'Elul and the Ten Days of Repentance, when Romaniote poets would compose embellishments of the Thirteen Divine Attributes, the basic unit of the *seliḥot* service. Following are the types of *seliḥot* for the vigil nights and for fast-days in the religious calendar.

Pizmon

In this *seliḥah* with a refrain the repeated element may be a complete strophe or a single colon. The fourteenth-century poet Isaac b. Qalo (from the Greek *kalos*) chose the latter form in his *Yešuʿatekha galleh*. The *pizmon* opens with a rhyming quatrain whose closing colon, a verse from Exod. 15: 1, is repeated after each of the following quintet strophes. The hymn's theme combines a plea for forgiveness with a prayer for relief from Israel's enemies. A noteworthy theme is the poet's fear that the Greek language (and culture?) is having a deleterious effect on his congregation:[181]

For the time of vengeance raise Your arm on high
To break the yoke of Seir [Christians] and the son of the maid
[Hagar, Muslims] . . .
The language of the Greeks [*u-lšon yewanit*] destroy utterly with the
might of Your spirit,
And pave the way for the shattered [remnant].

The Hispanic influence on Romaniote writing in this genre is seen in the *pizmon* of Šabbetai Ha-Oreg b. Mordecai, Isaac Qalo's contemporary. R. Šabbetai's *Šeḥartikha deraštikha* is a metric pseudo-*muwashshaḥ*. The verse from Ps. 25: 11 provides the closing colon in the 'guide', and this colon is repeated after each strophe. Here, as in Benjamin b. Zeraḥ's *pizmon*, *Horeyta derekh tešuvah*, there is a reference to the now standard introduction to

[181] Ibid. 242.

the Thirteen Attributes section in the *seliḥot* service, as in the following example:[182]

> You have taught [*horeyta*] and revealed the secret of the
> repentant's value;
> Man suffers when he turns away from the virtuous deed,
> And is deceived by seductive voices leading him astray;
> I desire Him when I repent, and He responds, 'Here I am!'
> 'For Your sake O Lord, forgive my sin.' [Ps. 25: 11]

The 'secret of the repentant's value' refers to the rabbinic comment (in *bYoma'* 86a), 'Great is repentance . . . for it leads to the Throne of Glory,' which came to be regarded by Yehudai Ga'on (8th c.), as the mystical ascent of the soul through the stages of moral perfection.[183]

Mustajāb

The *mustajāb* (Arabic, 'response') is a *seliḥah* headed by a scriptural verse with whose closing unit each strophe is rhymed. Often the closing unit in the verse is identical with the close in the strophes. This simplified form of the pseudo-*muwashshaḥ* was introduced by Hispanic hymnists; it was frequently employed in their *qedušta'ot* for the Day of Atonement, and later served their *seliḥot* as well. Balkan poets were not widely attracted to this genre and few samples are extant. Following is a part of Joseph Qalai's *mustajāb*, headed by the verse, 'I will extol You, my God and King' (Ps. 145: 1). It is likely that the hymn was chanted either on the New Year or the Day of Atonement: [184]

> O Lord observe the prayers of Your children
> As they pass before You this day like a flock of sheep,
> If I have found favour in Your eyes
> And the matter seems right before the King.

The phrase 'they pass before You this day [*ki-vney maron*] like a flock of sheep', taken from *mRH* 1. 2, was incorporated into the *silluq*, *U-ntaneh toqef* from the period of the anonymous poets and chanted on the Days of Awe.

The hymn by the fourteenth-century Caleb b. Moses, *Ḥayyim 'etnah lifneykhem*, for the Day of Atonement, incorrectly designated a *ḥaṭa'nu* by the editor of the *Maḥazor Romania*, is a *mustajāb* with an implied scriptural header 'Which of you desires life?' (Ps. 34: 13). Its quatrain strophes begin and end with the unit 'life' (*ḥayyim*). The hymn appeals for divine forgiveness

[182] Weinberger, *Re'šit Ha-Payṭanut*, p. 319.

[183] See Scholem, *Major Trends*, p. 78.

[184] Weinberger, *Re'šit Ha-Payṭanut*, pp. 110–12.

and reconciliation, and offers a prayer that Israel be spared from the snares of the prevailing culture.[185]

> O [source of] life, make us clean from sin, that we may be, as in
> the past, friends and companions [*re'im 'amitim*];
> Why would You have us stray from Your path like the Greeks
> [*lammah tat'enu mi-derakhekha ke-goyim keretim*]?
> Choose to be merciful and set us among the mortals [*mimtim*]
> Whose portion in this world is life.

The choice of the term *keretim*, literally 'Cretans', is in order to protect the rhyme with *'amitim* and *mimtim*. The poet's indictment of the Greeks who have strayed from God's path is undoubtedly a reference to the Byzantine Church.

Šeniyyah, Šelišiyyah, Šalmonit

These *seliḥot* are constructed in strophes of two, three or four cola respectively. Romaniote poets preferred the *šalmonit* to the *šeniyyah* and *šelišiyyah*, unlike the Italians and Franco-Germans, who favoured the latter two. Benjamin b. Zeraḥ's *šalmonit*, [*'Eloheynu we-'lohey 'avoteynu*], *betulat bat yehudah*, is an early example of this form. Later Romaniote poets also chose this medium, including Joseph Qalai and his contemporary the learned Hillel b. Eliaqim of Silivri. Qalai's *seliḥah*, *'Ani 'ahuvah hayyiti*, is built in repetitive figures of contrast, 'I was' (*'ani hayyiti*) and 'But now' (*we-'attah*). The effect recalls Yannai's pattern poems with which Qalai was undoubtedly familiar. The latter poet compares the plight of Israel in exile with her former prominence as God's beloved. A similar pattern contrast is employed by Qalai's contemporary Moses b. Joseph of Rome in his *seliḥah*, *'Ezkerah wa-'etmogeg we-nafši 'amulah*. Following is part of Qalai's emotionally charged lament:[186]

> I was beloved from earliest times,
> Carefree and peaceful in my Temple and palace;
> But now I am forsaken, despised, forlorn because of my guilt;
> I went away full, but the Lord has brought me back empty . . .
>
> I was fertile and favoured by the Awesome in deeds;
> Of all the virgins I won His favour and devotion;
> But now I am set [as a mark] for His arrow, I am plucked like an
> ear of corn by every hand;
> I was a wall and my breasts were like towers.

185 *Maḥazor Romania* (Venice, 1522–3), p. 378; Zunz, *Literaturgeschichte*, p. 379; Weinberger, *Širat . . . Rabbanim*, p. 279.

186 Cf. Zunz, *Literaturgeschichte*, pp. 340, 346; Weinberger, *Re'šit Ha-Payṭanut*, p. 121.

Less sanguine is Hillel b. Eliaqim's *seliḥah*, *'Attah 'eloha ha-ri'šonim*, for the Fast of Esther. In it he displays his considerable narrative talent based on biblical, rabbinic and folk sources:[187]

You are God of the Fathers
Performing wonders at every moment;
When the foe determined to demolish the faithful
Men, women, children and aged.

He [the foe] prevailed over them with a ruse;
When they feasted on the king's [unclean] offerings and disgraced themselves,
The pre-eminent [God] decreed destruction upon them,
And Satan rejoiced and went to bring the scroll!

The Torah went forth clothed in mourning and lament,
And all heaven's hosts cried at her bitter wail,
And [Elijah] the Tishbite ran panic-stricken
To inform the faithful [Moses] and those who sleep in the Makhpelah [Cave, i.e. the Patriarchs] . . .

Upon his return, he revealed the news to [Mordecai] the Benjaminite
That he might stand by him in prayer;
He [Mordecai] arranged a fast and summoned the communities
To deprive themselves for three days and nights . . .

He assembled the lads in the school house and sat with them
And both he and they wept;
At the sound of their voices the foe [Haman] entered upon them
And found them gathered with Mordecai among them.

Instantly he ordered that they be counted,
And that chains and bonds be placed about their necks,
Saying, 'In the morning I will have them put to death
And then I shall hang Mordecai their teacher.'

Now their mothers stormed and bleated like cows
And brought bread and water to them;
But [the lads] rebelled, saying, 'Food shall not enter our mouths,
For those about to be slaughtered have no need of nourishment.'

[187] See S. Schechter, 'Notes on Hebrew MSS. in the University Library at Cambridge', *JQR* o.s. 4 (1892), pp. 94–6; Weinberger, *Širat . . . Rabbanim*, pp. 10–11.

With moans and shrieks the mothers hovered over them
Hugging and kissing each one;
All were sobbing bitterly, piteously
And angels were tearful at the sound of their cry;

Their voices were heard in the second hour of the night
As the humble [Moses] and the Patriarchs were standing in prayer;
The exalted [God] said to his hosts on high,
'A voice like that of young goats ascends the heights!'

[They responded], 'Hear before You the Patriarchs and angels among them,
O merciful and compassionate, they are not lambs or goats, they are Your children;
Your people's infants are bound in chains
And on the morrow all will die.'

Mindful of the covenant, He was instantly filled with compassion
And ordered that the scroll decreeing destruction be torn up . . .

In this account of Israel's crisis, the poet deftly combines legends in *Esther Rabbah* 7. 13, 8. 6 and 9. 4 and embellishes them with folk accounts. An example of the latter is the response of the lads refusing the food offered them by their mothers, saying, 'Those about to be slaughtered have no need of nourishment.' In the rabbinic account (in *Esther Rabbah* 9. 4) they are recorded as saying that they swore by the life of Mordecai that they 'will neither eat nor drink, but will die while still fasting.' The dramatic impact of the angels' pithy response to God is carefully crafted: 'They are not lambs or goats, they are Your children.' Contrast this sparse yet forceful reply with the wordy answer given in the above rabbinic source: 'Sovereign of the Universe, they are neither kids nor lambs, but the little ones of Your people who have been keeping a fast now for three days and for three nights, and tomorrow the enemy means to slaughter them like kids and lambs.'

Other composers of *šalmonit seliḥot* were Moses Ḥazan of Thebes and the thirteenth-century poet Šabbetai b. Joseph.[188] There follows a selection from R. Šabbetai's phonetic-intensive *'Attah seter li go'ali,* for the Ten Days of Repentance, featuring alliteration, assonance and internal rhyme. These mannerisms he may have learned from Joseph Qalai and Moses Ḥazan, and from Solomon Ibn Gabirol in his *silluq*, *'A'amir*, *'a'addir*, *'afuddat 'aguddat 'oratekha.*[189]

[188] Šabbetai b. Joseph is listed in a 14th-c. catalogue of *seliḥah* composers. See Zunz, *Literaturgeschichte*, p. 625.

[189] Ibn Gabirol, *Širey Ha-Qodeš*, p. 243; Weinberger, *Širat . . . Rabbanim*, pp. 126–7.

Qomem šifli we-nifli, 'eli we-qoni;
Romem qarni we-'armoni we-naḥem da'avoni;
Šorari, ṣorari yevoš we-yaḥpor moni;
'Im barekh tevorkheni.

Rehabilitate me in my weakness and degradation, my God and creator;
Re-establish my dignity and my palace and comfort my sorrow;
My master, my enemy, may he wither and be put to shame, even my oppressor,
If but the Lord would bless me.

The popularity of the phonetic-intensive *ṣalmonit* continued into the fourteenth century, as seen in Samuel b. Ḥiyyah's seven-strophe *seliḥah, 'Ayyeh ḥasadeykha ha-ri'šonim*, for the Ten Days of Repentance. Like Šabbetai b. Joseph's *'Attah seter*, R. Samuel's hymn is enhanced by its assonance, alliteration and internal rhyme. Note the author's reference to the calculations regarding the time of Israel's redemption:[190]

By now You have made me weak and have punished me severely;
I have waited patiently and the delay has been unbearable;
A thousand years and more I am a captive;
The [love]sick [dove] has had her wings clipped; [she is] like a woman in hard labour.

The phrase 'a thousand years and more' from Dan. 12: 12, 'Happy are those who persevere and attain the thousand three hundred and thirty-five days', was a source of intense messianic speculation in the Middle Ages.[191] In the poet's imagery, Israel is the helpless, lovesick dove patiently awaiting the return of her lover, even though the promised time of his arrival has long since passed. The poet's reference to contemporary events is significant. In the following strophe Israel continues her plea:

I have placed You before me at my right hand, I shall not be moved;
Do remove the stone dashing at my foot about to slip;
Punish the one who instigates resentment among us that he fail
And announce the time when the yoke of exile will be broken.

The 'one who instigates resentment among us' may be a reference to Christian missionaries, who argued that Israel's anointed king had already come in the person of Jesus of Nazareth.

Two *šalmonit seliḥot* for the Day of Atonement, *'Anšey levov hitwaddeu*

[190] Weinberger, *Širat . . . Rabbanim*, pp. 248–9.
[191] See Silver, *A History of Messianic Speculation*, pp. 81–101.

piš'eykhem and *'Ani qera'tikha ki ta'aneni*, by R. Samuel's contemporary Caleb b. Eliaqim, are relatively free of phonetic-intensive mannerisms. Devoid of stylistic excesses, R. Caleb's hymns reflect a profound personal awareness of impending judgment and fear of its verdict, as in the following from *'Ani qera'tikha*:[192]

Terror throbs within me and I sink into the dust;
My heart melts like wax and there is no relief;
My flesh trembles from fear [of You], night and day; the sun has set on all joy.
My life is spent in sorrow and my years with sighing.

Turning now to his congregation, the cantor-poet in his *'Anšey levav* warns against the seductive power of the wicked (Satan).[193]

Rise up and confront the presence of the evil [Satan, *peney raša'*] and subdue him;
Lurking at the door [Gen. 4: 7], he kidnaps the innocent and brings them to ruin.

Caleb b. Eliaqim's contemporary, Caleb b. Solomon, in his *šalmonit*, *'Eykhah ro'š ha-pisgah* for the Seventeenth of Tammuz fast-day, revives a practice of Hillel b. Eliaqim in his *'Attah 'eloha ha-riš'onim*. Like the latter, Caleb b. Solomon focuses on the historical events that prompted the fast, and laments the five misfortunes that befell Israel on that day: the Tables of the Decalogue were broken; the daily burnt offering ceased; the city of Jerusalem was breached; Apostomos burned the Scroll of the Law and set up an idol in the Sanctuary. All are reported in *mTa'an* 4. 6. The poet adds another misfortune to the list by mourning the murders of Gedaliah b. Aḥikam, governor of Judaea, and a group of pilgrims by Ishmael b. Netanyah (Jer. 41: 1 ff.):[194]

They [pilgrims on the way to Jerusalem] were delivered into the hands of ben Netanyah, eighty men with their beards shaved and their clothes torn,
Men wise, discerning and reputable.

Although the death of the governor of Judaea is mourned on a separate fast, the Fast of Gedaliah, the poet connects his martyrdom and that of the pilgrims with the calamities that befell Israel on the Seventeenth of Tammuz, when a breach was made in the city wall of Jerusalem and an idol was placed in the Temple. The reason for the poet's action may be understood in light of the rabbinic teaching (in *Sifre* No. 31): 'The death of the righteous was as difficult for God to bear as was the destruction of the Temple.'

[192] Weinberger, *Širat . . . Rabbanim*, pp. 265–6.
[193] Ibid. 263–4.
[194] Ibid. 271.

Ḥaṭa'nu

The distinguishing feature of the *ḥaṭa'nu seliḥah* is its generally recurring header, 'We have sinned, O our Rock; forgive us, our Creator.' Its theme is focused on the hardships endured by Israel and the death of its martyrs. Two of Moses b. Ḥiyyah's hymns in the *ḥaṭa'nu* genre have been preserved. Both are built in rhyming quatrains, as in earlier models with anadiplosis. The strophes close with the conventional refrain of the *ḥaṭa'nu*, 'We have sinned, O our Rock; forgive us, our Creator.' The first, *'Ezkerah 'elohim we-'ehemayah*, in forty-four strophes, tells of the tragic deaths of the Ten Martyrs, a dominant theme in the *ḥaṭa'nu*. As in earlier treatments, R. Moses draws upon rabbinic sources, and chooses from among the differing versions with regard to the order in which the ten were put to death.[195] R. Moses' *ḥaṭa'nu*, *'Eškolot baṭelu we-'umlalnu*, laments the loss of Israel's national home and prays for its restoration. The poet complains about the efforts of Christian missionaries attempting to convert the Jews:[196]

> The evil men drew their swords to lead us astray,
> And divert us from God's way;
> They would have swallowed us alive,
> Had not the Lord been with us.

In addition to Moses b. Ḥiyyah's *ḥaṭa'nu* hymns, Joseph Qalai composed two, the virtuosic *'Essa' 'išon* and *'Essa' besari be-šinnay,* in rhyming quatrain and closing scriptural verse. Abraham b. Isaac's *ḥaṭa'nu*, *'Azelu be-khillayon wa-ḥereṣ*, in rhyming tercets, condemns the ruling power in a manner reminiscent of Moses b. Ḥiyyah's *'Eškolot baṭelu*. Moses Ḥazan's *ḥaṭa'nu*, *'Ef'eh ka-yyoledah*, also focuses the death of the Ten Martyrs and calls for judgment on Israel's enemies. His hymn, *'Abbirim nisḥafu be-'evrah*, preserved in the Vatican *Maḥazor Candia*, has the superscription *ḥaṭa'nu*, although it lacks the litany that accompanies hymns in this genre. *'Abbirim nisḥafu be-'evrah*, like Moses b. Ḥiyyah's *'Eškolot baṭelu we-'umlalnu* and Abraham b. Isaac's *'Akhin qerev we-sar'appayim*, is built in rhyming tercets and closing scriptural verse. A characteristic of hymns in this genre is the lament over Israel's helplessness in exile, as in the following from Moses Ḥazan's *'Abbirim nisḥafu*.[197]

> Downcast and barely surviving they suffer,
> Your loved ones, at the hands of creditors [*nošim*].

[195] Whether the Martyrs died at one time as a result of a specific decree, and the order in which they were killed, are questions that await an answer. In addition to the rabbinic literature on the subject, there are some 15 hymns devoted to the theme, of which the earliest, *Zekhor tevusat ṣo'n tivḥah*, was composed by Sa'adyah Ga'on. See idem, *Siddur*, pp. 327 ff.; Weinberger, *Re'šit Ha-Payṭanut*, p. 19; *Seder Ha-Qinot*, p. 12.

[196] Weinberger, *Re'šit Ha-Payṭanut*, p. 21.

[197] Weinberger, *Širat ... Rabbanim*, p. 67.

The reference to 'creditors' is probably a euphemism for government tax-collectors, who apparently exacted exorbitant payments from Byzantine Jews. A similar complaint is seen in the above-mentioned *ḥaṭa'nu* by Abraham b. Isaac, 'They cry to You, "Violence," / They wail from the heavy taxes.'[198]

Several *ḥaṭa'nu* hymns in the Romaniote ritual tell the story of the Ten Martyrs. Thirteenth-century treatments include *'Isfi nafši me-'ereṣ kin'atekh*, by Joseph b. Šelaḥyah Meyuḥas (from the Greek *eugenes*). Unlike earlier accounts, however, which included the names of ten martyred sages, R. Joseph's *ḥaṭa'nu* ends with the death of Rabbi Akiva, the third of the victims, although he too mentions that there were ten in the group:[199]

> Of the ten sages, one from the family of priests spoke [the divine name]
> In order to ascend the secret heights and explain to them [the sages] God's will.

The reason for the reluctance to give the names of the other seven may be due to the difference of opinion among rabbinic sources with regard to the identity of the ten. The central theme presented by R. Joseph is similar to the earlier accounts. The ruling power assembles the ten sages and charges that they be put to death for the unpunished sin committed by the sons of Jacob when they kidnapped their brother Joseph. Rabbi Ishmael b. Elisha, after ascending to heaven and ascertaining that such is God's judgment, returns to prepare his colleagues for martyrdom. After describing their tragic end, the poet prays that their deaths serve as an atonement for the sins of Israel, past and present:

> Consider [O Lord] the blood of the saints [*qedošim*]
> Spilled by the hands of idolaters [*qedešim*]
> As burnt offering of fatlings presented
> On God's altar.

In the Balkan synagogue, as in other Jewish centres, the legend of the Ten Martyrs served to vindicate divine justice, albeit delayed. It also had the effect of protecting the traditional theodicy. The improbable assertion that a pagan emperor should quote from Deut. 24: 7, 'If someone is caught kidnapping another Israelite, enslaving or selling the Israelite, then that kidnapper shall die', was made to justify God's judgment on a Jewry subject to the erratic

198 Ibid. 18–19. Whether Jews in Byzantium were subject to a special tax during the period from Justinian to the Fourth Crusade is a topic of debate. However, in light of the complaints by the synagogue poets in the region it is likely that 'the financial consequences of their [the Jews'] legal disabilities from the Code of Theodosius onwards . . . make it inherently probable that they were also subject to some sort of discriminatory, fiscal burdens' (Sharf, *Byzantine Jewry*, p. 189).

199 Weinberger, *Širat . . . Rabbanim*, pp. 153–4.

whim of imperial power. In this *ḥaṭa'nu* hymn, sinful Israel alone was to blame for her predicament. The paronomasia of *qedošim . . . / qedešim* is one of several stylistic features employed by the poet.

A *ḥaṭa'nu* by another contemporary of the Meyuḥas family, Avṭalion b. Samuel, is modelled after Joseph Qalai's hymn in this genre, *'Essa' 'išon, 'išon be-rigšon*. Like Qalai, Avṭalion employs a consistent pattern of anadiplosis and internal rhyme with stylistic enhancements of alliteration and assonance in his twenty-strophe hymn of rhyming quatrains. Below are the opening strophes:[200]

'Oyah li šeḥaṭa'ti / šeḥaṭa'ti we-šepaša'ti / we-šepaša'ti we-šenikhšalti / nilkadti ba-ḥaṭṭa'ti

Ba-ḥaṭṭa'ti u-vi-zdoni / u-vi-zdoni 'azavani / 'azavani noṣereni / u-v-'ašmotay ṭilṭelani.

Woe is me for I have sinned, / sinned and transgressed, / transgressed and come to grief; / I am ensnared by my sin.

Because of my sin and my malice; / for my malice He forsook me; / He forsook me, my Creator / and for my trespass He exiled me.

The death of the Ten Martyrs remained a dominant theme in the *ḥaṭa'nu* hymns of Joseph and Avṭalion Meyuḥas' successors in the fourteenth century, Elia b. Yoqtan and Ḥananyah b. Šelaḥyah. In the former's *ḥaṭa'nu*, *'Asiḥah be-mar siḥi*, lamenting the martyrdom of the ten, R. Elia, in giving their names and the order in which they died, chooses one of several differing rabbinic sources. There is a hint of protest in the tone of this hymn that is not found in earlier Balkan treatments:[201]

Lord, highly exalted,
Your judgments You conceal as the deep waters;
How can You approve that Your beloved be delivered to their enemies?
Is this a small thing in Your sight?

In the closing strophes, the poet urges God to avenge the deaths of the martyrs:

Let not the blood of Your beloved be taken lightly by You;
Hasten and avenge the outpoured [blood] of Your servants;
Be zealous for Your name and Your honour;
Why should the wicked renounce God [and say in their hearts, 'You will not call us to account!' (Ps. 10: 13)]?

200 Weinberger, *Širat . . . Rabbanim*, pp. 155–6.

201 Ibid. 195.

Another *ḥaṭa'nu* by R. Elia, *'Oyevi gavar u-memšalo fasah*, reveals his personal struggle against a pervasive evil inclination:[202]

The evil one insinuates himself like a princely friend,
While he amasses a bundle of sins for me;
Now repenting with regret, I confess my flaw;
I am sorry for my faults.

The conceit in the first colon is based on the rabbinic comment (in *Gen. Rabbah* 22. 6) on Gen. 4: 6, 'Sin is lurking at the door': 'At first it is like a [passing] visitor, then like a guest [who stays longer], and finally like the master of the house.' It is likely that this hymn was chanted during the midnight vigil service, as the following reveals:

O Rock, Your nearness is more desirable than sleep;
Your hint of passion [more precious] than my slumber at midnight.

Ḥananyah b. Šelaḥyah's *ḥaṭa'nu* hymn on the Ten Martyrs, *Ḥeṭ'i ke-nifkad*, is identical in both theme and construction with that of his contemporary R. Elia b. Yoqtan, save for one item: R. Ḥananyah tends to emphasize the sinless nature of the martyrs. An indication of this tendency is seen in the statement of the Angel of the Face (*sar ha-panim*) to R. Ishmael, justifying the divine decree:[203]

'The Lord chose you [ten] from among all the prophets and seers;
Before the One who discerns secrets [*ḥakham ha-razim*] You are
  the equal
Of the brothers of Joseph . . . '

It is also seen in the poet's characterization of R. Simeon b. Gamaliel:

The first to be taken [for execution] was the prince [Simeon] who
  fed and provided,
[He,] the mighty shepherd.

This assessment of R. Simeon is based on the rabbinic account (in *'Avot de-R. Natan*, No. 38) of Rabbis Ishmael and Simeon who wondered aloud why they were to be slain. Said Rabbi Ishmael to Rabban Simeon, 'Perhaps when you sat down to dinner, poor folk came and stood at your door and you did not let them come in and eat?' 'By Heaven!' Rabban Simeon protested, 'I did not act in that way. On the contrary, I had doormen sitting at the entrance; when the poor came, the doormen would bring them in to me and the poor used to eat and drink with me and recite a blessing in the name of Heaven.' The poet's emphasis on the sinless nature of the ten was in line with the biblical view of the atonement sacrifice. Only the ten who were without blemish

[202] Ibid. 197. [203] Ibid. 202–4.

could, by their sacrificial deaths, serve as a vicarious atonement for the sin committed by the sons of Jacob/Israel. This assumption is echoed in the poet's plea, as follows:

O my help, receive the spilled blood [of the ten]
As if it were the blood of the holy altar sacrifice and burnt offering.

In the closing strophe, God is said to respond to the poet's plea on behalf of Israel:

I will lead you exonerated and will forgive your sins;
No longer will you remember the disgrace of your widowhood;
I will settle your kids secure
Beside the shepherds' tents.

R. Ḥananyah's *ḥaṭa'nu* hymns for the Seventeeth of Tammuz, *'Afiq mayim naḥalayyim* and *'Ehgeh ke-yonim hegyon*, recount Israel's loss of national independence, on the basis of biblical and rabbinic sources. In the following from *'Afiq mayim naḥalayyim*, the poet is undoubtedly referring to the Crusader wars in his lifetime, and observes that Jerusalem remains a city coveted by the nations:[204]

[The] Scion [of Esau] is determined to make desolate
The comely [land]; I suffer from terrors
I throb at the sight of the nations
Waging war over Jerusalem.

Other fourteenth-century authors of *ḥaṭa'nu* hymns include Samuel Qir b. Šabbetai and Šabbetai b. Caleb. Šabbetai Qir's *ḥaṭa'nu*, *Šokhen 'ad marom*, for the Day of Atonement, built in quatrain strophes with repeated closing unit, laments Israel's life in exile and bemoans the pretensions of Christians who consider themselves the new Israel. As in the *ḥaṭa'nu* by R. Ḥananyah, God consoles Israel and reassures her of His love.[205]

[POET:]
The traitors [Christians] have taken on the mantle of Your chosen one [Israel];
Those who forsake You have removed his [Israel's] cloak . . .

[GOD:]
I remember the devotion of your youth, I shall lead my congregation
Who is like a bride adorned with her jewels . . .
My servant Ṣemaḥ [Zech. 3: 8] will arrive and the traitors [Christians] he will devour
Before the coming of the terrible day of the Lord—who can endure it?

[204] Weinberger, *Širat . . . Rabbanim*, pp. 212–14, 216–18.
[205] Ibid. 297.

Šabbetai b. Caleb's *ḥaṭa'nu*, *Šikhnekha 'iwwiti li-nhor*, like Samuel Qir's, is constructed in rhyming quatrains with repeated closing unit. In lamenting Israel's exile and loss of its national home, the poet begins with a rhetorical question:[206]

> I do wish for Your dwelling to glow [*li-nhor*];
> Why cannot Your flock throng to it [*tinhor*]?
> [Alas] the foe has inherited the dowry;
> The polluted spits on the pure.

R. Šabbetai's homonym construction in the opening cola is matched by another:

> In You I place my hope [*kisli*];
> Remove my stupid folly [*kisli*];
> O Lord create in me
> A pure heart.

The term *tahor* (pure) is a repeated unit in the hymn. Its focus is to draw a contrast between the pollution of the exile and the purity to come with national restoration and God's presence in His 'dwelling'.

Tokheḥah

This is a didactic poem and its theme is self-admonition. Like the *mustajāb*, the *tokheḥah* is headed by a scriptural verse which establishes the main theme of the hymn. However, unlike the former, the *tokheḥah* strophes do not rhyme with the scriptural header. In developing his theme, the poet employed rhetorical figures for effect. Such was the practice of Abraham Ibn Ezra in his *tokheḥah*, *Ben 'adamah yizkor be-moladto*, in which the admonition is made under the guise of a 'discourse on the ages of man' leading to senility and death. Moses b. Ḥiyyah constructed his *tokheḥah*, *'Etayu 'amelalim*, in the form of a dialogue between body and soul, as did Joseph Qalai in his *Ke-fo'oli le-ḥeyqi* and Moses Ḥazan of Thebes in his *'Enoš 'el ṣur ma'ariṣkha*. They followed the model of the Hispanic poets Joseph Ibn Abitur, Isaac ben Mar Saul and Solomon Ibn Gabirol, who used a similar rhetorical theme in their treatment of this genre. A distinctive theme in the Romaniote *tokheḥah* is 'judgment and punishment in the grave', as seen in the hymns in this genre by Moses b. Ḥiyyah, Moses Ḥazan, Mordecai b. Isaac, Šabbetai b. Joseph and Elnatan Ha-Kohen.

To appreciate fully the Romaniote *tokheḥah* we should examine the theme of 'judgment and punishment in the grave' (*din we-ḥibbuṭ ha-qever*). The theme embodied in rabbinic literature from the time of the *ge'onim* was treated extensively by Romaniote poets, who embellished the earlier legends

[206] Ibid. 301.

on judgment in the grave. While the early sources, *Masekhet Ḥibbuṭ Ha-Qever* (Tractate on Punishment in the Grave) and *Keyṣad Din Ha-Qever* (How is Judgment Carried Out in the Grave?), present a bare sketch of the travails that await the sinner in the grave, the poets, characteristically, are less controlled and readily provide the missing details. A composite account emerges from several hymns:[207]

The sick man, lying on his death-bed, gapes in fear as the Angel of Death, sword in hand, approaches. He dies from fright when he sees the Angel, hears his commanding voice urging him to leave this world, and feels the blows from his sword coming down upon him. The Angel then places the man upon his wings and carries him to heaven, where he is privileged to behold the face of the Divine Presence (*šekhinah*) before being dispatched to the grave.

Buried in the grave, the man sees the Angel of Death perched on its edge reading from the Book of Records, wherein all human deeds are recorded. [Prior to his death, it is believed man sets his seal in the Book in witness to his deeds.][208] When the Angel completes his reading and discovers that the man's sins are more numerous than his virtues, the judgment and punishment begin. His soul is tossed from place to place, and his body beaten by the Angel for three days, until his belly bursts.

The beating continues on every part of the man's body until it turns to dust. Then the worms take over and feast on what is left. After the worms have gorged themselves and can eat no more, the remains are thrust into the fires of *geyhinnom* [hell], where they are consumed.

A prominent elaboration of this theme is Moses b. Ḥiyyah's *tokheḥah*, *'Et peney mevin ṣefunay*, where he describes the carcass of the sinner being devoured by worms. Note how he recontextualizes scriptural verses in the Hispanic fashion.[209]

The worms ascend onto his back;
They cast lots for him;
  They shall have an equal portion to eat.

He is fed to them as a feast;
His body is completely vanished;
  None of the meat shall remain.

The source of the third colon in the first tercet, Deut. 18: 8, deals with the law of town Levites, whose former role was changed by the centralization of worship 'in the place that the Lord will choose'. They '*shall have equal portions to eat* even though they have income from the sale of family possessions.' The last colon in the second tercet, from Deut. 16: 4, tells of the Passover sacrifice that is to be slaughtered and eaten on the eve of the fourteenth day of the month of 'Aviv: 'none of the meat of what you slaughter on

207 Weinberger, *Seder . . . Ha-Romaniotim*, pp. 20–2.

208 See *Sifre on Deuteronomy*, No. 307.

209 Weinberger, *Re'šit Ha-Payṭanut*, p. 30.

the first day [of Passover] *shall remain until morning*.' It is likely that R. Moses' congregation, thoroughly shaken by the graphic image of the sinners' fate, found some relief in the poet's play on familiar scriptural usages.

Moses b. Ḥiyyah's *tokheḥah* dialogue, *'Etayu 'amelalim*, also relates to this theme. The hymn is largely based on a rabbinic legend (in *Lev. Rabbah* 4. 5):

Even so will the Holy One, blessed be He, in the time to come, say to the soul: 'Why have you sinned before Me?' and the soul will answer: 'It is not I that sinned, but the body it is that sinned' . . . God will also say to the body: 'Why have you sinned before Me?' and the body will reply: 'O Master of the Universe, not I have sinned, but the soul it is that has sinned' . . . What will the Holy One, blessed be He, do to them? He will bring the soul and inject it into the body, and judge both as one.

Building on this rabbinic theme, the poet connects the exchange between the parties to judgment and punishment in the grave, and embellishes the responses of body and soul. In this setting, God confronts the sinner, now lying in his grave, and receives an answer from his body in which he blames the soul for deceiving him:[210]

[BODY:]
'I have been a wanderer
From the time the heat consumed me [by day] and the frost at night;

The pack of sins comes from the breathing soul,
Which You placed within me; she gave it to me

I walked about in gloom, my dross has been melted away [through my agony];
I have done nothing to warrant putting me into the pit;

O merciful One, do not hold the soul guiltless; make her an example
After she has been defiled; she is an abhorrence;

She has forgotten her deeds and blames me for the criminal acts;
Hear my voice and go, get [her] for me.'

The soul will now reply to these charges and place blame on the body. Here, too, the poet expands on the outline of the rabbinic legend in order to achieve the desired rhetorical effect:

[SOUL:]
'His [own] words to the Lord condemn him;
You must not yield or listen to him;

[210] Ibid. 23–4.

The burden of sin collect from him and make him pay;
Your own hand shall be the first to execute him;

He reached out to eat the fruit of his sins and devoured them,
[After hearing:] "I commanded you: you shall not eat of it."

He cast his lot with the nations and their idols;
He drew them near to him and kissed them;

Why, O Lord would You slay me? Did I conceive him,
Or give birth to him that You should say to me: Carry him?'

Not content with protesting her innocence to God, the soul now directs her angry complaint directly to the body:

[SOUL:]
'Your bad habits
Led you to be unmindful of the Rock that bore you; you forgot the God who gave you birth . . . '

God, however, is not fooled by these tactics, and judges body and soul combined. Man, now in his grave, would have the last word as he turns to the Angel of Death with the plea, 'Take my body and all that I possess, only let me have my soul!' The soul, however, will have none of it and leaves him, never to return. In this hymn, the cantor-poet allows his imagination to give an added dimension to the familiar rabbinic legend, even as it permits his congregation to experience its dramatic impact.

Like Moses b. Ḥiyyah's *tokheḥah*, *'Etayu 'amelalim*, Qalai's *tokheḥah*, *Ke-fo'oli le-ḥeyqi*, for the Day of Atonement, features the dialogue between body and soul standing in judgment before God, with each blaming the other. Although Qalai's hymn is built in rhyming tercets, unlike R. Moses' couplets, their rabbinic sources (in *Lev. Rabbah* 4. 5) are similar. Qalai's choice in building this *tokheḥah* in tercets is undoubtedly modelled on earlier tercet *tokhaḥot* on this theme composed by the Hispanics Joseph Ibn Abitur (*'Ammiṣ šokhen 'ereṣ*), Isaac b. Mar Saul (*Ha-kol yifḥadu we-yirhu*) and Solomon Ibn Gabirol (*Šeṭar 'alay we-'edim*). However, Qalai's *tokheḥah* differs from the hymns of Mar Saul and Ibn Gabirol. Unlike the latter's tercets, which spell out the author's name at the very beginning of the hymn, Qalai's tercets, like those of Ibn Abitur and earlier eastern models, begin with an alphabetic acrostic, and only after its completion is the author's name given. Moreover, unlike all three Hispanic *tokhaḥot,* which spell the author's name and his provenance, Qalai gives only his name. In his treatment of the *tokheḥah* Qalai is eclectic, choosing from both late eastern and Hispanic models.[211]

[211] Weinberger, *Re'šit Ha-Payṭanut*, pp. 102–7; Schirmann, *Širim Ḥadašim*, pp. 154–5; idem, 'Yiṣḥaq ben Mar Šaul'; Ibn Gabirol, *Širey Ha-Qodeš*, pp. 31–4.

Later Balkan poets attracted to the theme of judgment in the grave for the *tokheḥah* include the thirteenth-century poet Elnatan Ha-Kohen of Arta.[212] Below is a selection from R. Elnatan's *tokheḥah*, *'Im yo'mar li qoni*, built in rhyming tercets with closing scriptural verse.[213]

All my days and nights
I am occupied in my work,
Yet all this does me no good!

Glorious [God] my mind will degenerate
When I descend into the gloom [grave]
In a narrow place where there is no way to turn.

Baqqašah

This *seliḥah* hymn can be in rhymed prose or in metric strophes. Examples of the former are the *baqqašot* of Sa'adyah Ga'on and the epic *Keter Malkhut* by Solomon Ibn Gabirol. Metric *baqqašot* were composed by the Hispanic poets Isaac Ibn Mar Saul, Baḥya Ibn Paqudah and Judah Ha-Levi. The *baqqašah* in rhymed prose is generally headed by the unit *'adonay* (Lord) or *'anna'* (please). In most instances the *baqqašah* forms part of the 'Elul vigil-night and fast-day services known from the time of the *ge'onim* by the name *ma'amad* (standing). Two hymns in this genre in rhymed prose were composed by Solomon Šarvit Ha-Zahav for use during the Ten Days of Repentance. Both are modelled after Sa'adyah Ga'on's *baqqašah*, beginning with the verse, 'O Lord, open my lips and my mouth will declare Your praise' (Ps. 51: 17), which likewise serves as their header. The smaller of Šarvit Ha-Zahav's two *baqqašot*, *Tehillatekha 'eyn lah teḥillah*, focuses on the contrast between God, who is beyond limit and definition, and mortal man searching, in vain, for the ineffable. In one of the Romaniote liturgies in which this hymn is preserved (MS Oxford No. 1168, fo. 65b) it is described as a 'supplement' (*hosafah*) to the 'morning prayer' by R. Sa'adyah. The 'morning prayer' in Sa'adyah's *Siddur* begins with his first *baqqašah*. The following is from Šarvit Ha-Zahav's *Tehillatekha*:[214]

Your praise has no beginning and Your glory is without end; there is limit to our knowledge beyond which one cannot grasp; how then can he with limits encompass the One who is limitless? Therefore silence befits You most . . .

The last colon is based on Ps. 65: 2 and the commentary of RaŠI: 'Silence is Your praise since there is no limit to Your glory and adding thereto decreases

[212] R. Elnatan's Arta, with its sizeable Jewish community, was the commercial and administrative centre of Epiros and a river port on the crossroads of the east–west and north–south trade routes.

[213] Weinberger, *Širat . . . Rabbanim*, pp. 163–4.

[214] Sa'adyah Ga'on, *Siddur*, pp. 47, 64; Weinberger, *Širat . . . Rabbanim*, pp. 232–3.

it.' The poet may also have had in mind the comment of Maimonides on this verse (in *Moreh Ha-Nevukhim* I. 59) and his angry diatribe against the hymnists who, he writes

are extravagant in praise, fluent and prolix in the prayers they compose and in the hymns they make, in the desire to approach the Creator. They describe God in attributes which would be an offence if applied to a human being . . . Treating the Creator as a familiar object, they describe Him and speak of Him using any expression they think proper . . . and believe that they can thereby influence Him and produce an effect on Him.

Šarvit Ha-Zahav's other *baqqašah*, *Yeš yešut 'emet*, is a much larger work, similar in scale to the two hymns in this genre by Sa'adyah and Gabirol's *Keter Malkhut*. Like the latter, the Ephesian poet's hymn is divided into an opening philosophical excursus and a closing confession. It is headed by the verse from Ps. 65: 21, similar to the header in Sa'adyah's second *baqqašah*, and continues with an elaboration on the Thirteen Principles of Jewish faith presented by Maimonides (in the introduction to his comments on chapter 10 (*Ḥeleq*) of *mSan*). The opening section of Šarvit Ha-Zahav's *baqqašah*, quoted above on page 237, with its dense set of terms from contemporary Neoplatonic and Aristotelian philosophy, implies that his Ephesian congregation was learned enough to follow the argument.[215] The verse in the last colon is also the proof text for the existence of a Creator given in Maimonides' First Principle, in his introduction to the chapter *Ḥeleq*.

[Second Principle:] You are God alone without partners or associates, without opposition [*hefekh*] or change [*temurah*] . . . You are one not like the unit one to be counted, or like one in a relationship to others in gender or species, or like one composed of fractions, or like one that can be divided . . . Your oneness is simple and absolute and there is none like it . . . [as it is written in Deut. 4: 35], 'Hear O Israel, the Lord our God, the Lord is one.'

In the argument for God's unity, the poet draws upon conceits in Gabirol's *Keter Malkhut*, No. 2, and employs the proof text used by Maimonides.

[Third Principle:] There is no one like You, Lord . . . corporeal measurements or its accidents [*middot ha-guf u-miqraw*] cannot apply to You, since whatever a body perceives is impaired. Even when we stood at Mount Sinai, we did not observe any image, but only heard the voice emerge from the darkness and the mountain seared with fire that reached the heavens . . .

The poet's argument for God's incorporeality, based on Israel's experience at Sinai in which it heard a voice but saw no form, is similar to that advanced by Maimonides (in chapter *ḥeleq*).

[215] Weinberger, *Širat . . . Rabbanim*, pp. 225–7. The text of the closing confession, as yet unpublished, is at Oxford, MS No. 1168, fos. 131b–141b.

[Fourth Principle:] You have preceded all and none came before You, or is prior like You . . . Your name [*YHWH*] points to Your eternality . . . [as it written:] Long ago You laid the foundation of the earth and the heavens are the work of Your hands. They will perish, but You endure [Ps. 102: 26–7].

In citing the proof text for God's eternality from Psalms, the poet differs from Maimonides, who finds support for this principle in Deut. 33: 27, 'The eternal God is a dwelling-place.'

[Fifth Principle:] Our voices will be raised to God . . . not like the designs of the [Christians] who fall into the tangle of their imagination and are consumed . . . The earth is full of Your glory . . . We direct ourselves to You and we refer to no one but You . . .

In the principle that God alone must be worshipped, R. Solomon warns against Christian trinitarianism. In both the printed edition of *Maḥazor Romania* (p. 293a) and the manuscript version (MS Oxford 1168, fo. 128b) of Šarvit Ha-Zahav's hymn, the text reads 'not like the designs of . . . who pursue vanity' (*lo' ke-maḥševet . . . 'ašer šaw' rodefim*). Undoubtedly the *nomen rectum* in the genitive was *noṣerim* (Christians), which was removed by censors. Maimonides, not living in Christian lands, warns against idolatry in the form of astral worship and the adoration of angels.

[Sixth Principle:] You have enlightened with Your holy spirit and have influenced through an emanation of Your glory . . . the pure in spirit, holy and clean, and they have prophesied in Your name . . . each according to his ability, coming to him through the ornament of perfection and the rays of intellect adorned . . .

In the principle that Israel's prophets are true, Šarvit Ha-Zahav follows the view of Maimonides that both superior intellect and perfection of character are essential for the prophet.

[Seventh Principle:] The greatest of the prophets and their master was the humble one, high and exalted, Moses son of Amram . . . entrusted with all [Your] house enduring; face to face You spoke with him—clearly and not in riddles and he beheld the form of the Lord [Num. 12: 7–8].

Again, following Maimonides, the poet cites the verses from Numbers to show that Moses, unlike other prophets, was addressed directly by God, unaided by intermediaries. Moreover, his prophetic message came during his waking hours, and not in a dream, and God spoke to him directly face to face. In his comment on 'face to face', Maimonides emphasizes that this conceit is not to be taken literally, unlike the practice of the authors of 'the Dimensions of (God's) Body' (*ši'ur qomah*), whose brazen anthropomorphisms he condemns as the writings of 'Greek preachers' (*ha-daršanim ha-yewanim*).[216]

[Eighth and Ninth Principles:] The Torah from heaven You gave us through Moses, tablets written by Your finger and the Torah copied by Your direction, explained by

216 Maimonides, *Tešuvot*, No. 118 (i. 201).

him in Your presence; a Torah fully complete with nothing superfluous in it, and not in need of extraneous comment, or change and emendation . . . All that is secret or hidden is not removed from it, all is there to be explained in the Book of the Torah elucidated.

The poet combines the principles that the entire Torah was divinely given to Moses and that it is immutable. Maimonides adds the warning that it is forbidden to deny that any verse in the Torah is divinely inspired, and that the established rabbinic interpretations of Scripture, the Oral Torah, are likewise divinely sanctioned.

[Tenth Principle:] You are the Lord God . . . nothing is too difficult for You . . . Your eyes are opened to all the ways of mortals . . . the Lord looks down from heaven; He sees all humankind. From where He sits enthroned, He watches all the inhabitants of the earth . . .

Maimonides adds a polemical note in his comment on God's omnipotence, omniscience and providence and chides those (mentioned in Ezek. 8: 12) who say, 'The Lord has forsaken the land.'

[Eleventh Principle:] You repay all according to their work; they shall eat the fruit of their chosen way and be sated with their own devices. He does good to those who are good . . . and those who turn aside to their own crooked ways, the Lord will consign them to the sinners . . .

For the principle that God rewards and punishes, Maimonides adds as proof text the exchange between God and Moses (in Exod. 32: 31–3), '[Moses:] But now if You will only forgive their sin—but if not, blot me out of the book that You have written. [God:] Whoever has sinned against Me I will blot out of My book.'

[Twelfth Principle:] At that time I will raise up a true branch of David's line and he shall do what is just and right in the land. In those days Judah shall be delivered and Israel shall dwell secure . . .

On the principle that the Messiah will come, Maimonides also adds a polemical note, warning against attempts to calculate the time of redemption. Quoting Hab. 2: 3, 'if it seems to tarry wait for it', he cites the rabbinic dictum (in *bSan* 97b): 'Blasted be the bones of those who calculate the end.'

[Thirteenth Principle:] The Lord deals death and gives life, casts down into *šeol* and raises up. Your dead shall live, their corpses . . . and the earth will give birth to those long dead.

Maimonides' comment on the principle of the resurrection of the dead is unusually brief, consisting of only the words 'as we have explained' (*u-kvar be'arnuha*).[217]

[217] Maimonides was criticized for this brief comment, and it was suspected that he held this principle lightly. It is not mentioned at all in his *Moreh Ha-Nevukhim*. It is presumed that for this

While adopting the basic outline of Maimonides' Thirteen Principles for the first part of his *baqqaśah*, Šarvit Ha-Zahav is selective in the choice of citations from his mentor, as we have seen. The second confessional section in Šarvit Ha-Zahav's *baqqaśah* is a lengthy discourse in rhymed prose on human experience from birth to the grave. The Hebrew text, as yet unpublished, provides a revealing insight into the creative mind of a Romaniote poet from Byzantine Ephesus. Most of Šarvit Ha-Zahav's confessional, which is unlike any other in Balkan synagogue hymnography, is here translated.[218]

O Lord what are human beings that You regard them, or mortals that You think of them? They are like a breath; their days are like a passing shadow [Ps. 144: 3–4]. On first emerging from the womb of his birth, the Lord appears and breathes in his nostrils the breath of life and the man becomes a living being. Likewise his children and their descendants are dispatched from Your presence. They dwell in fear of their Father and their end approaches as the days accumulate to seventy years, or perhaps eighty; even then their span is only toil and trouble.

Perforce is he created, compelled to be born; he lives with shame and disgrace and dies with worms and maggots. How You have nurtured him, like milk carefully stirred and cheese prepared to harden; You have clothed him with skin and flesh and covered him with with bones and sinews. Life and love You bestowed upon him and by Your command has he been preserved.

Who gave him his teeth? Who prepared breasts for his mother? It was You who took him from the womb, made him secure on his mother's breast. Still unable to walk, he crawled on his belly and ate dirt. Beset by all manner of hurts and bruises, he was in pain, though unable to speak. Were it not for Your guidance accompanying him [he would not have survived]. He narrowly escaped death in his restive persistence until he became a lad.

The days of a lad. His hair grows longer and who can rein in an ass with restraints? Like a roaring lion and growling bear, he does not hear the voice of the Lawgiver. Though punished from anger, he persists in perversion. Folly and cunning are knotted up in the lad's heart. The fool schemes, 'In a little while I shall build me a mansion and buy expensive clothes with all common luxuries—coffers and coffers of them.'

And there stands Satan at his right hand to tempt him . . . a bronze helmet upon his head . . . [he knows] that the inclination of the human heart is evil from its youth. The deceitful [Satan] inhabits his chamber waiting for the chance to pervert him and lead him astray. Today he [Satan] begs to give him but a little room and tomorrow he expels him from the house. With cunning he entices him to live the life of a sybarite and to allow himself the forbidden.

The dogs are greedy; they are never satisfied. The hard-hearted falls into evil while his enemy stands laughing and his friend is sad and dejected . . . Yet by the mercy of God he can free himself from the net; God will not abandon him to be delivered into his [Satan's] hands neither will he condemn him in judgment. All our steps are ordered by the Lord; how then can we understand our own ways? Perhaps when we

reason he composed the tract 'On the Resurrection of Dead' in 1121—23 years after completing his introduction to chapter *ḥeleq*—giving a defence of the resurrection of the dead.

218 Oxford, MS No. 1168, fos. 131b–135b.

come to the age of wisdom, between youth and old age [when] the flesh has come to rest and the raging fire is diminished. Passion's grave is dried up and man is at a turning-point. His plans vacillate: at one time he is wayward, at another, he regrets. In time of trouble, he calls upon You and prays with passion that his pain is great. Then, finding relief, he stubbornly returns to follow the dictates of his heart.

Know that the sinner will be afflicted. [Sin] will bind him with cords and bring him near the grave and execute him. [Again] he will pray and make promises. You will listen to him, do as he asks and help him, lying on his sick-bed, and heal him. Now recovered he attends to his business and an enchanter seeks him out to break his word, or he himself will annul his vow and make it void, retroactively.

If You graced him with children, the sin of his soul, the fruit of his body, they will cause him pain and anger all his days. Every year a fearful voice rings in his ear. Much agony and little joy. [He fears] that an accident will befall them. Even if he wax rich and his wealth increases, his days are spent in anguish and his nights, all his life, without rest, lest these [possessions] slip away from him. What do people gain from all the toil at which they labour under the sun?. Their lives embittered by hard work with lime and bricks; [their riches] they leave to others, as do the bees. What will your heart carry away and what boast will enter your thought? Man, together with his prominent peers, will be made to account for his donation to the poor and destitute, a paltry sum causing much disgrace.

He thinks to himself, 'Because of my virtue I am enriched and for my honesty I have prospered.' Or he may say, 'By the strength of my hand I have done it, and by my wisdom, for I have understanding; I have made a pact with death and have a contract with the grave. My power and the might of my own hand have gotten me this wealth.' Is not his vaunted power flawed and his glory shame and embarrassment?

[O Lord], man born of woman, You have refined him by Your will and tested him in the furnace of adversity. When he is hungry and enraged, he turns heavenward complaining, 'What is my offence? What is my sin that You have hotly pursued me? Why have You been distant from me while supporting the councils of the wicked? Even if I felt in my hand the weight of a thousand pieces of silver like the man [speaking to Joab, 2 Sam. 18: 12], and days of affliction had not come to meet me, I would remain, unlike others, observant of the commands and charitable at all times.' This man does not know that Your thoughts are not his thoughts, nor are his ways Yours; for You, O Lord, do as You please. And if You have given him a share in his Torah which affords him respite from his labours, he is not saved from [the desire] to transgress it. Due to his eminence, his inclination [to sin] is greater than that of another, for he stands in the vineyard's path searching in the heights and he that increases knowledge increases sorrow.

[Speculating on the forbidden:] what is above and what beneath and what before and what after [see *mḤag* 2.1], or in his opinion, refusing [the evil] and choosing [the good—as did R. Meir from Aḥer, the apostate; see *bḤag* 15b]. Even in this, he lusts after his heart and is seduced by his thoughts, and he takes lightly a serious matter. Sometimes a good man perishes in spite of his goodness. Yet sweet is the sleep of the servant [of God] whether he eats little or much, for wisdom excels folly as light excels darkness. If God's Torah is in his heart, his foot will not falter.

[O Lord], when You have been slow to anger and have lengthened his days and guided him consistently, he will forget that he is mortal. From year to year he will come to believe that the withered can have pleasure and that he was born only yesterday . . . Yet who can live and never see death? Who can escape the power of the grave? But he does not consider it, nor does he think about it. No man knows when his time is come. They are like fish caught in the malicious net, or like birds fallen into a trap. A human [being], when times of trouble come upon him, suddenly [realizes] that he has spent his days with vanity and his years in confusion.

By then he is into old age, reaching those years when desire has left him. Brokenhearted, he finds that the mule that was under him is gone [see 2 Sam. 18: 9]. His eyes begin to weep even when there is no smoke and his teeth fall out though he disdains vinegar. He is hard of hearing, though his ears are not diseased, and without fainting, his countenance changes. His head is bowed like a reed [before a storm] and he weeps for his soul [saying], 'The haughty mortal shall be humbled and the pride of men brought low' [see Isa. 2: 17].

He places the staff upon his face [as if he were dead; [see 2 Kgs. 4: 29]. He makes no response, as if he were not the one who [earlier] burst forth and shocked the world, leaping upon the mountains, bounding over the hills, light on his feet like a gazelle. He saw the fortified city and was determined to take it by storm. He would break down the brass doors and cut through the bars of iron. And now he cuts a tomb in the rock since he is at his wit's end; his sight is dim and his spittle runs down his beard.

At that moment he begins thinking to himself, 'O that I were as in the months of old I would lead them in procession to the House of God. [O that] I were in my prime, my mouth would sing the praises of the Lord. He was then accessible but I was unwilling, now I am willing but He is not present.'

At this point the poet notes, in parenthesis, the reason for God's absence.

(All his days on earth God left him to himself, in order to test him and to know all that was in his heart.) He now tried to prove his innocence as he took his mantle and rolled it up and curbed his temper. He fancied himself immune saying, 'I am safe because I am on God's side and no longer have an interest in women.' But he forgets his ways as a lad and does not bear the disgrace of his youth—as on the day of judgment he will forget every practice and principle. Now his memories of love are fled, even his hates. His envy vanishes and is no more. There is now no room for them among the labours under the sun. Their courage melts away in their calamity. But before they are laid to rest she [the soul] comes upon them on the roof [of the world] to give an account of his deeds, malicious or inadvertent. And she is cleansed from her impurities and returns to her home in the heights where she dwells. Her alliance with the body; the compact with the grave annulled.

Into the cave [where the body is buried] rocks are placed and dirt is set in the burrows. The [mourning] voices have ceased and the visitors are no more. They [the mourners] have lifted him on their shoulders and carried him. They have placed him [in the cave] underneath, and he stood mute and did not move. They shouted at him and he did not reply. He no longer feared their shouts, their crowds did not intimidate him. No one could do him any good. He will not awake nor stir from his sleep until the time of the resurrection, when, like the grass, the dead will blossom and many asleep in the dust shall rise. This is the record of man's life and the fate of mortals . . .

In the following paragraphs Šarvit Ha-Zahav observes that in addition to the problems that he faces as a human, subject to old age, disease and death, the Jew in exile is beset with a wider range of difficulties in being a member of a barely tolerated minority. The *baqqašah* ends with a plea for divine mercy, an expanded confessional and a catalogue of sins committed. The framework of the confession is loosely based on the Ten Commandments, and on an earlier model in alphabetical order from the period of the *ge'onim*:[219]

I [confess] that we have trespassed without being [intentionally] rebellious; we have decreed [*gazarnu*] by Your name in vain; we have profaned the rules of the Sabbath; we have scorned our parents; we have killed; we have prostituted ourselves and have committed adultery; we have kidnapped and stolen; we have given false witness against friends; we have coveted the wealth of associates; we have perverted the innocent and ruled them with corruption; we had the ability to protest [against evil] but did not; we have procrastinated, hoping to be forgiven; We are factious in Your congregation and disobey the instruction of our teachers; we have degraded Your commands and have despised their interpreters; we hate admonition and are insulting to others; we are quarrelsome with many and we keep items lost by a brother. We take part in robbing the unfortunate and we pervert justice with bribery; we have taken food from the helpless and we have used their [garments given as] pledge [see Deut. 24: 12]; we listened to disgrace heaped on friends and felt exalted; we suspected the innocent and went tale-bearing; we slandered and were overcome by anger; we were enticed by crafty schemes and had a hand in the work of the wicked. From *'alef* to *taw* we have transgressed.

'Aqedah

Unlike the Franco-German poets, whose many hymns on the Binding of Isaac (*'aqedat yiṣḥaq*) echoed the atrocities committed against Rhineland Jewry during the First and Second Crusades, Balkan *'aqedot* are few, since Romaniote Jews were relatively unmolested during that turbulent period. In addition to the two hymns in this genre, *'Emunim beney ma'aminim*, and *'Ahavat 'ezez we-toqef ḥibbah*, by Benjamin b. Zeraḥ, there is the *'aqedah*, *'Az dibbarta ba-ḥazon 'iš ṣaddiq*, by Moses Ḥazan of Thebes. His hymn is built in quatrains with rhyming tercets and closing scriptural verse, after Hispanic models. Moses Ḥazan's *'aqedah* is more subdued that Benjamin b. Zeraḥ's and relies mainly on the biblical narrative, albeit with some embellishments. His focus is on Abraham who successfully passed the last of his ten trials, and on the innocent compliance of Isaac:[220]

Thus You have spoken in a vision to the pure and righteous man
[Abraham]:
'I have tried and tested you these ten times [see *'Avot* 5. 4]

[219] Oxford, MS No. 1168, fos. 137a–b.
[220] Weinberger, *Širat . . . Rabbanim*, pp. 70–1.

Even through your son, a sacrifice of well-being,
An offering by fire of pleasing odour to the Lord . . . '
He, the bundle of myrrh [Abraham], ran quickly . . .
The sacrifice he prepared without knowing the intentions of the [Lord] trying him;
The delightful gazelle [Isaac] seeing what transpires asks,
'All is in readiness for the holocaust offering, but where is the lamb?'
He did not know that it would cost him his life.
'Child of my delight, you have been chosen by [the Lord], the light in my darkness;
My soul longs to do the will of my King.'

Taḥanun/ Teḥinnah

This *seliḥah* focused on the relationship between God and Israel. In the *Seder R. ʿAmram Gaʾon*, the *taḥanun* generally ends with the verse, 'Turn from Your fierce wrath; change Your mind and do not bring disaster on Your people' (see Exod. 32: 12). In the liturgy for fast-days, the *taḥanun is* generally recited at the end of the service. In Joseph Qalai's two hymns in this genre, *ʾOholi šuddad* and *Yom dallah we-neʾenaḥah*,[221] Israel in exile presents its complaint in the opening strophes, with God responding with words of comfort and reassurance at the close of the hymn. The first hymn is in rhyming quatrains and the second is a pseudo-*muwashshaḥ*. Later thirteenth-century treatments of the genre include Šabbetai b. Joseph's *Šullaḥah mi-meʿonah*, for the Tenth of Ṭevet fast. His hymn is built in the form of a pseudo-*muwashshaḥ* with internal rhyme in both the 'guide' and the strophes. In the poet's imagery—recalling Abraham Ibn Ezra—Israel is represented as a forsaken dove driven from home into an inhospitable exile by her Master:[222]

The dove was sent away from her home into a foreign land;
On a cold and rainy day, her Master drove her angrily into exile;
Terrified and helpless, she is pursued by archers with shields,
She makes every effort to escape, but the enemy has enfeebled her
And the dove found no place to set her foot . . .
She raises a lament on the heights; her heart is broken and dejected;
She lives among lions and no one sees or cares;
Wild beasts surround her and a raven flies above;
Would that He hasten and come to her, lie down and sleep at her side . . .

221 Zunz, *Literaturgeschichte*, p. 340; Weinberger, *Reʾšit Ha-Payṭanut*, pp. 96, 100.
222 Weinberger, *Širat . . . Rabbanim*, pp. 125–6.

The lions' (*leva'im*) and 'wild beasts' (*pera'im*) are references to Christians and Muslims, respectively.[223]

R. Šabbetai's contemporary Jonathan b. Abraham Ha-Kohen is the author of two pseudo-*muwashshaḥ taḥanunim*, *Yemot 'olam be-'ol sivlam*, for the Seventeenth of Tammuz fast, and *Yahir 'aṣ wa-yyin'aṣ*, for Purim. The former hymn is built in Hispanic metre and the closing colon in the 'guide', 'On the day that the enemy, Nebuchadnezzar, came and exiled me to Babylon', is repeated after each strophe. In his *taḥanun* the poet pleads for relief from the Christians, whom he calls 'the worshippers of Baal' (*'ovedey ba'al*). Lamenting Israel's martyrs, he compares them to the heifer that was slain in expiation of a murder when the slayer was unknown (Deut. 21: 4):[224]

I will strike hand to hand and weep
I am to be beheaded like the heifer.

The reference to the unknown slayer may be linked to the rabbinic comment (in *bYoma'* 9b): 'Why was the first Sanctuary destroyed [by Nebuchadnezzar]? Because . . . bloodshed [prevailed].' The poet echoes the traditional theodicy which holds that Israel suffers, like the heifer, because of the blood shed in an earlier time, even as it continues to be punished for its sin with the Golden Calf committed by its ancestors, as in the following:

I am violently shaken unto despair;
My foot keeps slipping
Because I have been wayward and have hastened
To make the Golden Calf [Exod. 32: 4].

In his *Yahir 'aṣ*, R. Jonathan focuses on divine providence and omniscience in retelling the Purim story. Embellishing the biblical account, the poet reveals that when the Jews of Persia were distraught on hearing the news of Haman's designs against them, Mordecai offered them words of comfort:[225]

'He [God] knows all our plans,' said Mordecai to the hopeful,
'The Rock will not abandon His people who beseech Him in their assemblies.'

The poet's conceit is related to the rabbinic comment in *bMeg* 13b, 'The Holy One, blessed be He, does not smite Israel unless He has created a healing for them beforehand.'

Another contemporary, Moses Qilqi of Chios,[226] composed a metric *taḥanun*, *'Uri 'ayyumati*, also in the form of a pseudo-*muwashshaḥ*. As in

[223] A. Ibn Ezra, *Širey Ha-Qodeš*, i. 197.
[224] Weinberger, *Širat . . . Rabbanim*, p. 145.
[225] Ibid. 146.
[226] Chios, an island colony off the coast of Anatolia, was noted for its Jewish scholars. See Moskoni, 'Haqdamah', pp. 6–8.

Šabbetai b. Joseph's *Šullaḥah mi-meʿonah*, the central purpose of the poem is achieved within a rhetorical framework highlighting the tension between protagonists:[227]

Awake, you who are as terrible [as an army with banners] at the
  beginning of the watch;
Rouse yourself and put on garments of might and glory;
Come to the threshold of God's house and enter the sanctuary;
Bow down and kneel before the Seat of Mercy.

When will you awaken to thrice behold the beauty
Of the Lord and His Temple?
I would hope to see your procession again;
  I will be glad and rejoice in you with spiced myrrh;
  Awake [etc.]

Set your heart on ascending the highway,
It is a level road well paved;
Hasten, erect a ladder with its top reaching to the heights;
  Thereon you will speak of God's wonders;
  Awake [etc.]

Take counsel with me, receive my instruction;
Do not be tempted by the enemy that is in my flesh;
Hasten to Gilead and take balm
  To heal your [leprous] swelling and eruption;
  Awake [etc.]

The subject addressed by the poet is both the congregation of Israel and the soul, personified. 'Terrible as an army with banners' from Cant. 6: 10 is perceived by the rabbis (in *Cant. Rabbah* 6. 10) as a metonym for Israel. However, the subject who is being urged to ascend the ladder whose top reaches unto the heavens and 'speak of God's wonders' is presumably the soul. The poet's Neoplatonist imagery is undoubtedly borrowed from Solomon Ibn Gabirol. Abraham Ibn Ezra in his commentary on Gen. 28: 12 reports that Gabirol saw in Jacob's ladder an 'allegory of the Universal Soul' (*remez la-nešamah ha-ʿelyonah*), and the 'angels of God' ascending and descending on it, 'the thoughts of wisdom' (*maḥševot ha-ḥokhmah*). Qilqi is suggesting that the congregation of Israel and the soul share a similar predicament in that both are exiles—Israel from its native land and the soul from its domicile in the heavens—and both are urged to be reconciled with their true source.

The poet as interlocutor in the first two strophes speaks for God address-

[227] Weinberger, *Širat . . . Rabbanim*, p. 165.

ing Israel. In the last two strophes he speaks for himself to his soul. In the last strophe, the phrase 'Do not be tempted by the enemy that is in my flesh' is a continuation of his self-admonition.

Fourteenth-century *taḥanunim* are represented by Ḥananyah b. Šelaḥyah's *Ḥanot 'etkhem yeḥezeh*, for the Day of Atonement; Zekhariah Ha-Kohen's *'Anna' 'adon 'olam* and *Zevaḥ u-minḥah ne'daru*, for the New Year; and Menaḥem b. Judah's *Mequṭṭeret mor u-lvonah*, for the Ten Days of Repentance. All are in the form of a pseudo-*muwashshaḥ*, with the conventional repeated colon, or unit, from the 'guide' closing the strophes. Each has a distinctive quality worth noting. In R. Ḥananyah's hymn the poet speaks in God's name and urges the congregation to repentance. Of particular interest is the practice of Romaniote congregations on the Day of Atonement to which the hymn alludes:[228]

> If you will be pure, arise at midnight with supplication and song;
> Wake up and be reconciled in your assemblies with the Creator of the world
> And the ends of the earth; with festal apparel
> He commanded [to clothe you] and to forgive you.

The practice of arising at midnight on the Day of Atonement, or remaining awake throughout the night, was not uncommon in European congregations.[229]

Zekhariah Ha-Kohen was a poet and philosopher.[230] His *'Anna' 'adon 'olam*, was chanted during the *zikhronot* (remembrance) portion of the service, prior to the sounding of the *šofar*. Its central theme is an appeal to deity to remember the Binding of Isaac, prompted by the sound of the horn recalling the ram caught in the thicket on Mount Moriah (Gen. 22: 13):[231]

> Weeping and ashamed we call upon You
> Knowing that You are near on the day of our supplication;
> The day is very short and the Master is urgent.

The conceit in the last colon is taken from 'Avot 2. 15, where the 'day' refers to a lifetime. R. Zekhariah's *Zevaḥ u-minḥah ne'daru*, was part of the *šoferot* service. Its refrain colon repeated at the end of each strophe is 'God is gone up amidst shouting; the Lord amidst the sound of the horn' (Ps. 47: 6), on which the rabbis commented (in *Lev. Rabbah* 29. 3), 'When [the children of] Israel take their horns and blow them in the presence of the Holy One, blessed be He, He rises from the Throne of Judgment and sits upon the

[228] Weinberger, *Širat . . . Rabbanim*, p. 211.

[229] *Maḥazor Le-Yamim*, ii. 29, introd.; Agnon, *Yamim Nora'im*, pp. 309–10.

[230] Zekhariah Ha-Kohen is the author of a defence of Maimonides against charges brought by Naḥmanides. There are indications that R. Zekhariah was the grandfather of the poet and Bible commentator Menaḥem Tamar. See Zunz, *Literaturgeschichte*, pp. 378–9.

[231] Weinberger, *Širat . . . Rabbanim*, pp. 220–1.

Throne of Mercy.' Building on this comment, the poet makes a rhetorical argument in his plea for atonement:[232]

> Many are the sins we committed against You,
> Greater still, however, is Your merciful love.

Menaḥem b. Judah's *Mequṭṭeret mor u-lvonah*, for the Ten Days of Repentance, employs the now familiar imagery of Israel as the forlorn 'dove' abandoned by her Master. It is distinctive, however, in its dialogue form, in which God and the poet exchange views. In the opening four strophes the poet laments the dove's predicament, and in the closing God responds with reassurance. An added stylistic touch is the unit 'alas' (*ʾEykh*), reminiscent of Lam. 1: 1, 2: 1 and 4: 1, which begins the second colon in the opening four strophes. In his argument, the poet favours a rhetoric of contrast between the dove's happy past, when she was pampered by her Beloved, and the present, when she is neglected and abused. In the closing strophe, God reaffirms His everlasting love for her:[233]

> [POET:]
> She that was scented with myrrh and frankincense
> And was bathed in fragrant oils,
> Alas, she is exiled and is taunted by her oppressors . . .
> She sits [lonely] like a widow and there is no comfort for her;
> And the dove found no place to set its foot.
>
> [GOD:]
> I will take you for My wife with faithfulness,
> Whereas you have been forsaken,
> And on the hill of frankincense
> We will delight ourselves with love

Like the Hispanics, Menaḥem b. Judah—and Šabbetai b. Joseph, in his *Šullaḥah mi-meʿonah*—recontextualize the 'dove' that could find 'no place to set its foot' (Gen. 8: 9). It is likely that both poets borrowed the imagery of the forlorn dove from the widely popular *seliḥah*, *ʾElohey qedem meʿonah*, by Abraham Ibn Ezra, who likewise employed this verse in closing his strophes.[234]

Widduy

The hymn which usually begins with 'Master of the Universe' (*ribbono šel ʿolam*) is a confession of sins. The late eastern poet Nissi Al-Nahrawani composed his *widduyyim* in rhymed prose, as did many of his later imitators. Balkan confessionals, however, tended to use strophic forms, and the early

[232] Ibid. 222–3. [233] Ibid. 283–4.
[234] A. Ibn Ezra, *Širey Ha-Qodeš*, ii. 76–7.

hymns in this genre by Abraham b. Isaac and his contemporary Mordecai b. Yinnon are built in rhyming tercets with closing scriptural verse. R. Abraham's *widduy*, *'El yom ha-mehumah*, combined the themes of confession and admonition as in the following:[235]

To the day of judgment
My thoughts are now drawn
And I am troubled in my moaning.

I have sinned greatly and I think
On Your judgment; remembering in my bed,
Fear and dread overcome me . . .

He is scarred by his transgression and isolated;
His soul will not be saved from the fire;
Flames surround him and he does not understand.

The confessional portion of the hymn in the first two strophes is in the first person singular, as expected, whereas the last strophe in the third person is an admonition. R. Mordecai's *widduy*, *'Etwaddeh lekha qoni*, is, unlike R. Abraham's hymn, primarily in the confessional first person singular, save for the closing strophes, where the cantor-poet pleads for forgiveness for his congregation. Note from the following that the poet borrows the language of the confessional from the period of the *ge'onim*:[236]

I confess to You, my Creator, I tell You my sins . . .
I have counselled evil [*ya'aṣti ra'ah*] . . .
I have strayed [*ta'iti*] . . .
I have acted wickedly [*raša'ti*], I have comitted iniquity [*ni'aṣti*] . . .

'Elohim qedošim 'el 'ayom we-norah, by the fourteenth-century Menaḥem b. U[ri], is designated a *widduy* by the editors of the Romaniote prayer-book, although its theme is unlike that of other hymns in this genre. Built in quatrains with rhyming tercets, the poem closes with verses from Exod. 34: 6–1 listing the Thirteen Divine Attributes. In this distinctive hymn, R. Menaḥem skilfully combines the themes in the tercets with the closing biblical verse. His language is a fluent blend of rabbinic and biblical usages:[237]

When the holy Lord God, fearful and awesome
Presented to Moses the protocols of prayer,
He wore the fringed [prayer shawl] and phylacteries, a resplendent image;
The Lord passed before him and proclaimed—
He identified the attributes which make the desolate heart rejoice;

[235] Weinberger, *Širat . . . Rabbanim*, pp. 20–1. [236] Ibid. 59–60. [237] Ibid. 280–1.

He showed him, ever available and competent, how to sing the
prayer,
And in time of distress to cry out and entreat repeatedly:
The Lord, the Lord, a merciful God and gracious . . .

He puts aside every first iniquity as though it never was;
[When] a life [is] in the scale of balance, He determines if there is
merit to be found
And aids with His finger to tilt the full balance of sins,
Forgiving iniquity, transgression and sin.

The latter conceit is based on the rabbinic comment (in *bRH* 17a), 'He puts aside every first iniquity; and therein lies the attribute [of grace].' RaŠI interprets this to mean that if without the first iniquity the good deeds are in excess, then the first iniquity is not put back in the scale.

Qinah

The liturgical elegy chanted on the Ninth of 'Av and other fast-days was a prominent feature in the Romaniote ritual. A distinctive feature of the Romaniote (and Italian) prayer-book is the practice of embedding the Ninth of 'Av elegy into the *qerovah* that embellished Benediction 14 of the *'amidah*, 'Builder of Jerusalem'. The elegies of Moses b. Ḥiyyah, *'Aval tiroš* and *'Ešpekhah 'alay nafši*, followed classical models in their rhyming quatrains, alphabetic acrostic and name signature. The scriptural verse with which R. Moses closed his strophe was a practice he learned from the Hispanics. The theme of *'Aval tiroš* is focused on relief from exile and national restoration. In the following strophe the poet calls for judgment on Byzantium and Islam:[238]

You shepherded the first-born [Israel] in the valley of death, even
his descendants in the islands of Kitium;
With trumpet blasts they declared war upon You, even the rulers
of Tarshish and the islands;
Run through my enemies with Your sword, even the Cushite
sons;
In fury You trod the earth, in anger You trampled nations.

The 'islands of Kitium' are a reference to Greece in synagogue hymnography, and the 'Cushite sons' are the Muslims.[239] R. Moses' other surviving *qinah*, *'Ešpekhah 'alay nafši*, laments that the worshippers of idols now occupy his national home:[240]

238 Weinberger, *Re'šit Ha-Payṭanut*, pp. 7–8.
239 See Zunz, *Die synagogale Poesie*, pp. 454, 465.
240 Weinberger, *Re'šit Ha-Payṭanut*, p. 10.

My beloved has been torn away and exiled, even all my princes and captains;
Foolish men rioted and the wicked were exalted;
Now the worshippers of cedar and holm oak [statues] remain at the flagstaff,
Like chaff that swirls from the threshing floor.

In his reference to '[statues] of cedar and holm oak' the poet has in mind Christian iconolatry, a common reference of synagogue poets.[241]

Joseph Qalai's elegies include *'Arakh ḥevli*, in rhyming quatrains, featuring a rich mix of assonance, alliteration and internal rhyme, recalling the sonority in Ibn Gabirol's *silluq*, *'A'amir, 'a'ddir 'afuddat 'aguddat 'oratekha*. Following is a selection from Qalai's phonetic-intensive *qinah,* showing how the constant repetition of rhyming morphemes increases the emotional intensity of the lament:[242]

Yašavti meqonen, mit'onen, mitronen we-'eyn ḥonen mištonen ʿim kilyotay;
Kaluy we-'aluy u-valuy we-ḥaluy we-šaluy we-galuy miškenotay;
Le-khol zar we-'akhzar mefuzzar we-neʿezar soṭeni wa-'ani be-tugotay
Nišbar libbi be-qirbi, raḥafu kol ʿaṣmotay.

I sit lamenting, protesting, shouting and there is no mercy, my feelings are numbed;
Imprisoned and cursed, withered and sickly, uprooted and exiled from my home;
Scattered among strangers and barbarians, my enemy is given aid and I am grief-stricken;
My heart is crushed within me, all my bones shake.

In his *qinah*, *'Iyyevani 'avi u-ntivi*, Qalai reveals his impatience with the seeming interminable length of the exile and seeks to calculate the time for the Messiah's arrival. In this practice he is following the example of earlier notables like RaŠI, Judah Ha-Levi and Abraham b. Ḥiyyah. Even Maimonides, known for his disapproval of eschatological speculation, was persuaded that the birth-pangs of the Messianic period had begun in his time. Following is Qalai's lament:[243]

Through his [Israel's] tears, he awaits redemption, his sins have distanced him [from God] and played him [a fool]; like a pebble [in a shoe] they have distressed him;

241 See Zunz, *Die synagogale Poesie*, pp. 466–8.
242 Ibn Gabirol, *Širat Ha-Qodeš*, p. 243; Weinberger, *Re'šit Ha-Payṭanut*, p. 78.
243 See Silver, *A History of Messianic Speculation*, p. 74; Weinberger, *Re'šit Ha-Payṭanut*, p. 75.

Day and night he endures new troubles worse than the old and no
  one pays him heed;
He sits and calculates his [exile's] end; resolute is his quest, 'How
  long must I wait to see him [the Messiah]?
Perhaps [*'ulay*], it was an oversight [that he was not sent]?'

Joseph Qalai in his *qinot*, *'Umlelah gafni* and *'Iyyevani 'avi*, added a stylistic embellishment to his rhyming quatrains with a repeated unit, *'Eyn* (no, in the former), and *'Ulay* (perhaps, in the latter), at the beginning of the closing scriptural verse. A more elaborate stylistic effort is seen in Qalai's elegy for the Ninth of 'Av, *'Eykhah 'avi*, in quatrains with each colon beginning with *'eykhah* (alas), after Lam. 1: 1.[244]

Alas, my Father set me afire with His torch;
Alas, He vented his fierce anger upon me;
Alas, I am exiled among Qedar [Muslims] and Seir [Christians];
Alas, how lonely sits the city [of Jerusalem].

Later forms of the Balkan elegy show a more pronounced Hispanic influence, as in the metric pseudo-*muwashshaḥ qinot* of the thirteenth-century poets Mordecai of Nicaea, David from Byzantium, and Šemayah Ha-Kohen b. Solomon.[245] R. Mordecai's elegy, *Mivṣar 'ir homiyyah*, mourns the fall of Jerusalem to Babylon and Rome in times past, even as he laments the continuous struggle by Christians and Muslims in his own day for control of the city:[246]

Shame has covered my face since the day the lion [Christians]
  came upon the land;
My dwelling he turned to ruin, even Šepho [from the house of
  Edom, (Gen. 36: 23)] and the son of the maid [Muslims]
With thunderous war shouts; on that day he mobilized his
  cavalry;
By the anger of God this happened; for these things I weep . . .

David from Byzantium composed two elegies for the Ninth of 'Av, *'Oy [li] ki faqad 'awwon beyt yisra'el* and *'Eykh 'ovlah we-'umlalah*. The poet's themes and figures are largely from Jeremiah and Lamentations. In the latter hymn he achieves a mournful sonority through the use of alliteration and assonance:[247]

244 Weinberger, *Re'šit Ha-Payṭanut*, pp. 81–2.

245 R. Mordecai, serving as cantor-poet in Nicaea, is of historic interest. His office suggests that, despite the conversion attempts by John Vatatzes in the Empire of Nicaea in 1254, the Jewish community appears to have flourished. See Bowman, *The Jews of Byzantium*, p. 89.

246 Weinberger, *Širat . . . Rabbanim*, p. 136.

247 Ibid. 138–40.

'Eykh 'ovlah we-'umlalalah ha-ʿir ha-yefeyfiyyah;
We-nadammah we-našammah we-husamah li-še'iyyah
Be-mar teqonen we-tit'onen be-ta'aniyyah wa-'aniyyah;
Bakho tivkeh ba-laylah we-dimʿatah ʿal leḥyah.

Alas, she is in mourning and misery, the magnificent city;
She is despoiled and desolate and set for destruction;
Bitterly she laments and complains with moaning and dirge;
She weeps much into the night with tears on her cheeks.

Šemayah Ha-Kohen's elegy *Šuddad neweh roʿi*, like R. Mordecai's, laments both past and present events. In a moving plaint the poet laments Israel's helplessness:[248]

Has Israel no heir? Has he no son?
Esau dwells in the hills of the Lord and he defiles them;
Qedar, Hadad, Adbel [Ishmael's tribes] are encamped about his tent;
[Lord], restrain the polluter, him and his hosts . . .
I say to God, my rock, 'Why have You forgotten me?'

In addition to composing *qinot* in a strophic pseudo-*muwashshaḥ*, Balkan poets were also attracted to the use of paronomastic (a figure of speech depending on a similarity of sound and disparity of meaning) rhyme in metric couplets. This stylistic enhancement—known in Arabic as *tajnīs* and in Hebrew as *šir ṣimudim*—they learned from the Hispano-Hebrews,[249] and put into practice in three *qinot* for the Ninth of 'Av. They are *Bekhu šovevim meʿullafim* by Šemayah Ha-Kohen b. Solomon (13th c.), *Šamem netiv galgal* by Šemaryah Ha-Kohen b. Aaron (14th c.) and *'Im 'eyn menaḥem lah* by his contemporary, Abraham b. Menaḥem. Šemayah b. Solomon adds a further embellishment by introducing each strophe with the unit *Bekhu* (weep). Below is a selection from his elegy. The punning figure comes at the end of the colon.[250]

Bekhu šovevim meʿullafim be-ṣiṣiyyot meʿuṭṭafim
U-va-raʿav u-va-ṣṣamah be-khol ḥušot meʿuṭṭafim;

Bekhu melekh 'ašer banaw lefanaw nišḥatu ka-sseh;
Demeyhem šuppekhu 'arṣah we-'eyn 'omer 'enoš kasseh.

Weep, wayward sons in fright, with [bare] fringes you are clothed,
And from hunger and thirst you faint in the streets;

[248] Weinberger, *Širat . . . Rabbanim*, p. 134.
[249] See Pagis, *Ḥidduš*, pp. 129–30.
[250] Weinberger, *Širat . . . Rabbanim*, pp. 132–3.

Weep, O king [Zedekiah], whose sons were slaughtered like lambs
before his eyes;
Their blood was spilled upon the ground and no one wishes to
cover it [Lev. 17: 13].

The shorter couplets in the hymns of Šemaryah b. Aaron and Abraham b. Menaḥem enhance the urgency of the lament. Below are selections, beginning with the former. Again, the punning figure closes the colon.[251]

Šamem netiv galgal we-gam bokhim;
ʿUgav halo᾽ hayah le-kol bokhim . . .

Ha-ʿir ᾽ašer zakku nezireyha
᾽Az ʿolalu ṣarim nezireyha . . .

Hisgir betulotay le-ʿarley gat;
Sillah le-᾽abbiray ke-dorekhey gat.

Desolate are the carriage roads, even they weep;
The flute has become a voice for tears;

The city whose princes were purer [than snow]
Has been gleaned thoroughly of its teachers by the foe . . .

He delivered my maidens to the uncircumcised of Gath;
He disposed of my warriors, trodden as in a wine press.

In Abraham b. Menaḥem's paronomastic lament, the poet draws heavily upon rabbinic legends in his narrative:

Hevi᾽ ᾽appistomos kemo saraf
Torat ᾽elohim be-᾽ur saraf

Reʿo ke-vo᾽ ṭiṭus be-qol paraš
Zonah ʿaley torah halo᾽ paras . . .

Ṣaʿqat zekharyahu ʿašer damam;
Damim be-damim nageʿu damam . . .

Apostomos, serpent-like,
Brought God's Torah into the fire to be burned [cf. *mTan* 4.6].

His colleague Titus violently seized
A prostitute and spread her out upon the Torah [cf. *bGiṭ* 56b] . . .

The cry of Zekhariah was silenced
Bloodshed following bloodshed joined his blood . . .

[251] Ibid. 245–6, 243–4.

The final strophe is based on the account in *bGiṭ* 57b, 'Nevuzaradan, the captain of the guard . . . in Jerusalem, he killed ninety-four myriads on one stone, until their blood went and joined that of Zekhariah [the son of Yehoiada, the high priest], to fulfil the words [in Hos. 4: 2], "Blood touches blood." '

Even as some Balkan poets were composing elegies in paronomastic couplets, others, like Caleb b. Šabbetai (14th c.) and his contemporary David Peppi, favoured earlier strophic forms for their Ninth of 'Av *qinot*. The former is the author of *Kalu dimʿot ʿeynayim*, built in rhyming quatrains, without repeated unit embellishment. His metric hymn counts long syllables only. Distinctive in his lament is an irony of situation, as in the following:[252]

Peninah was the mother of sons
Who are the slaves of her handmaiden;
They wander far from their home
Which strangers have embraced.

In rabbinic literature, Peninah is a metaphor for Sarah (see *Tanḥuma'*, *Ḥayyey Sarah*, 3), whose handmaiden, Hagar, was mother of Ishmael. As in earlier treatments of the Ninth of 'Av elegy, the poet's diatribe against the ruling power is unusually harsh, even as it is revealing:

With a perfect hatred they despise me;
The villians' chains enthral me;
Often have they attacked me from my youth;
They cherish enmity against me.

David Peppi's strophic elegy *Diršu negidim le-vat yaʿanah*, in quatrains with internal tercets, is, like R. Caleb's, without repeated unit embellishments, and, similarly, his metric hymn counts long syllables only. The poet calls upon the universe to join in mourning the fall of Jerusalem:[253]

Princes have removed the ornaments
Of gold on the day of my calamity;
Universe, come down from your majesty
And return to earth.

A conventional conceit in the Hispanic eulogy was the call to nature to join in the general lament for the deceased. Such urging is seen in the dirge composed by Moses Ibn Ezra on the death of his brother Joseph:[254]

Have you fallen from heaven,
O Day Star son of Dawn,
And the hosts on high do not tremble at the sound of your fall?

[252] Weinberger, *Širat . . . Rabbanim*, p. 268. [253] Ibid. 269.
[254] M. Ibn Ezra, *Širey Ha-Ḥol*, No. 113.19 (p. 115); Pagis, *Širat*, p. 207.

Ṣidduq Ha-Din

Related to the *qinah* is the *ṣidduq ha-din* (justification of the divine decree) hymn originating in the classical period. The *ṣidduq ha-din* was chanted during the burial service, when selections from Scripture are recited acknowledging God's righteous judgment. In their burial service hymns, the cantor-poets sought to exhort the survivors to repent and to comfort the mourners. Following is a portion of Joseph Qalai's pseudo-*muwashshaḥ*, *ṣidduq ha-din* hymn, *Ba-yom din 'eykh yig'al*:[255]

> How will he redeem himself on judgment day,
> Covered with disgrace and shame? . . .
>
> See him borne to the grave;
> His soul is in mourning;
> She remains to account for his foolishness;
> In a little while; [she is left] like a shelter in a cucumber field . . .
>
> His soul has fled
> And he returns to the earth;
> But in his treason against Him,
> She will not be blameless.

Unlike the dirges for prominent men that were included in the Romaniote liturgy, Joseph Qalai's lament is designed to serve a wider constituency. His hymn is addressed to whom it may concern, as seen in the following strophe:

> [Lord], look kindly
> And without malice on Mister so and so [*'al revi peloni*];
> Cover his sin with love
> [As You have done] in the law of Moses our possession.

Epithalamia

Hymns celebrating the nuptial union probably originated as embellishments of the grace after meals (*birkat ha-mazon*) for the Seven Days of Repast (*šiv'at yemey ha-mišteh*) in honour of bride and groom. On Šabbat Ḥatanim, when the latter was called to the reading of the Torah, the cantor-poets would enhance the benedictions of the *šema'* with hymns celebrating the nuptials. Such is the *'ofan*, *Dar ḥevyon be-'appiryon*, for Šabbat Ḥatanim by David of Byzantium. Other Balkan epithalamia bear the superscription *zemer le-ḥatan* or *šir la-ḥatanim*. Among these is Michael Namer b. Judah's (late

[255] Weinberger, *Re'šit Ha-Payṭanut*, pp. 98–9.

13th c.) *Mah na'amu dodim*.[256] R. Michael's hymn is a pseudo-*muwashshaḥ* with an uncommon metre, a variation of *ha-šalem*, thus, reading from right to left: – – –/–v– –/–v– –/–v– –//–v– –/–v– –/–v– –/–v– –. The hymn's language is a blend of scriptural, rabbinic and philosophical usages. The festive images celebrating the excellence of the bridal pair are drawn from both Canticles and the Hispanic amatory prelude (*nasīb*). Following is a selection:[257]

How delightful is love's season, now the bridegroom
Spreads the edge of his cloak;
Bride, deck yourself with ornaments of gold;
Rejoice and be glad . . .
Go [bridegroom], win your purchase [*miqqaḥakha*, see *bQid* 2a],
Charming as a graceful doe . . .
Her lustre reflected in light's prism
Reveals more than the moon's;
Her beauty puts to shame the stars

In heaven; she lightens the darkness . . .
Bridegroom, rejoice in your portion . . .
Satisfy your thirst from your cistern
And flowing water [from your well] . . .
May the Lord grant His favour
And bestow love and wondrous desire
Between them and may no
Illness afflict them . . .
[Lord] merciful, gracious in abundance and good . . .
[You are] the cause of all causes [*'illah le-khol ha-'illah*].

[256] Michael Namer's son, Judah b. Namer, copied A. Ibn Ezra's commentary on the Pentateuch in 1387 in the city of Manissa (Magnesia) in Anatolia. See Bowman, *The Jews of Byzantium*, p. 291.

[257] Weinberger, *Širat . . . Rabbanim*, pp. 159–60.

5

Cantor-Poets on Greece's Periphery: Macedonia, Bulgaria, Corfu, Kaffa (Crimea) and Crete

GENERAL BACKGROUND: MACEDONIA AND BULGARIA

JEWISH SETTLEMENTS in Macedonia date from 140 BC and were prominent in Kastoria and Salonika. Kastoria on the Via Egnatia, a strategic hub in the Balkans linking Dyrrachium with Constantinople, attracted Jewish merchants and artisans. Although Jewish life was already flourishing in the region in the eleventh and twelfth centuries, under the leadership of Rabbi Tobias b. Eliezer of Kastoria and Salonika, a dramatic increase in the Jewish population began in the twelfth and thirteenth centuries. This was the period of the Second Bulgarian Empire under the rule of the ambitious Assenide dynasts who encouraged Jewish immigration into their country in order to gain a commercial and industrial advantage over their Dalmatian and Aegean rivals. A further increase in Bulgaria's Jewish population occurred in the latter half of the fourteenth century with the arrival of refugees from Hungary and Bavaria, following their expulsion from those countries in 1360 and 1376.[1]

Soon afterwards, friction arose between the native Jewish settlers, who followed the Romaniote synagogue ritual, and the immigrants from the north. Presumably the conflicts resulted from disputes regarding the decree of Rabbenu Geršom of Mainz banning polygamy. The special session called in Vidin in 1376, reaffirming R. Geršom's decree and ruling on matters relating to dowry and inheritance, was designed to set standards for the diverse Jewish population in the region.[2] It is likely that during this transitional

[1] See Baron, *Social and Religious History*, xvii. 102.

[2] See Bowman, *The Jews of Byzantium*, pp. 289–90, for the text of the Vidin rulings.

period the native Kastorean Jews decided to compile their own prayer-book reflecting their synagogue practices and thereby preserving the special character of their congregational life. The Kastorean ritual was never published, and survives in one manuscript copy at the Bodleian Library, Oxford (No. 1168).

Macedonian Messianism

A distinctive feature in the Macedonian liturgy of the eleventh and twelfth centuries is the rise of messianic hopes. Mordecai b. Šabbetai seeks to ascertain the 'end-time', and Menaḥem b. Elia is persuaded that Israel's redeemer–king riding on a donkey is fast approaching. Following is Israel's part of R. Menaḥem's dialogue *ḥaṭa'nu*, *'Amarti la-'adonay*. The speaker is God:

> The calculation of the end-time is clear,
> Only a few years remain;
> Now Edom will be consumed in flames
> And the last remnant with return . . .
>
> Exile's end has passed;
> The yoke of wickedness is broken
> And Judah has prevailed,
> This is the word from God.
>
> Behold the prince Michael,
> And with him the prince Gabriel
> And between them, the redeemer Messiah;
> Be glad Jacob, O Israel, rejoice.

The exuberant optimism of R. Menaḥem reflects the high messianic hopes during the period of the Crusades in the eleventh and twelfth centuries. The suffering that Jewish communities endured at the hands of the Crusader mobs in 1096 was interpreted as the 'birth-pangs' of the Messiah, and led Jewish notables to calculate that the 'end-time' was near. When 1096 passed without relief, Tobias b. Eliezer wrote (in his *Midraš Leqaḥ Ṭov*, p. 20 on Exod. 3: 20), 'I . . . have searched our divine books and considered the length of our exile . . . and how all the "end-times" have passed [*we-hinneh kalu kol ha-qiṣim*] and redemption is now dependent upon repentance alone.' The perception that the time for Israel's deliverance had already passed could lead to despair and the mocking jibes of her enemies, as reported by R. Tobias's contemporary Benjamin b. Zeraḥ in his *seliḥah*, *'Adabberah we-yirwaḥ li*, for the Tenth of Ṭevet:[3]

[3] Brody and Wiener, *Mivḥar*, p. 212.

You have calculated the time of redemption and it has passed,
And the hope for deliverance is over and gone.

Menaḥem b. Elia's hopeful tone is in contrast to the earlier pessimism. His language appears to be borrowed from Solomon Ibn Gabirol's writings. Gabirol sought to allay the fears that the 'end-time' had passed, and stressed the need to be watchful and patient. This is seen in his *ge'ullah*, *Šekhulah, 'akhulah lameh tivki*, and his *yoṣer*, *Šezufah nezufah be-šibbolet šeṭufah*.[4] In the former hymn, constructed as a dialogue between God and Israel, the latter complains:

The end [*qiṣṣi*] is long drawn
And my gloom is extended . . .
My God, my God, how long must I wait?
How long will it continue, this exile wall?

To which God replies:

Here is your king, in a while he will come to you . . .
Soon you will be Mine and I yours.

A similarly hopeful message is featured in Gabirol's *yoṣer*, also in the form of a dialogue between God and Israel. To the latter's plea for relief from the oppressive years of exile, God replies:

Hear this, you who are humbled and pilloried;
Hope and wait for Me; very soon
I will send My angel to prepare My way . . .

THE PRINCIPAL MACEDONIAN AND BULGARIAN POETS

Tobias b. Eliezer and Eliezer b. Judah

The earliest liturgical writing in Macedonia comes from the above-mentioned Tobias b. Eliezer, a rabbi-poet in the Franco-German tradition. Leader of the Rabbanites in his time and author of the *Midraš Leqaḥ Ṭov* (written and revised, 1097–1108) on the Pentateuch, his role in Balkan Byzantium would be comparable to that of R. Simeon b. Isaac and R. Geršom b. Judah among Rhineland Jews. R. Tobias's *seliḥah*, *'Ehyeh 'ašer 'ehyeh*, preserves an anti-Karaite polemic characteristic of his vigorous defence of the rabbinic Oral Torah. In the following selection from his *seliḥah*, the poet has God addressing Moses:

4 Ibn Gabirol, *Širey Ha-Qodeš*, pp. 362–3, 364–6.

Scion of the noble [Jacob], you shall in this way fence in [*li-gdor*]
your edifice [the Torah];
This is My name forever, and this is My title for all generations . . .

In the opening strophe, R. Tobias reaffirms the opinion (in *'Avot* 1. 1) that the rabbinic rulings, the 'fence' around the Torah, are ordained by divine decree. His emphasis on this issue is directed against the Karaites who denied the authority of rabbinic interpretations of Scripture. This anti-Karaite polemic is in line with his comment (in his *Midraš Leqaḥ Ṭov*, *Wa-'etḥannan*, p. 13) on Deut. 3: 28, '[The Lord said to Moses], "But charge Joshua", with the Oral Torah.'

As with his colleagues in Byzantium, Benjamin b. Zeraḥ and Moses b. Ḥiyyah, R. Tobias is familiar with divine and angelic names which he invokes in his liturgical writings. The following is from the above *seliḥah*:

'This is my God' [Exod. 15: 2], my possession and portion *'Itti'el*
The mighty Lord, the Rock who saves and redeems,
Ṭeṣ"s, the Ineffable Name, awesome and sublime, *'Akkatri'el*;
And You are holy enthroned on the praises of Israel . . .
I trust in Your name, *'Addiriron*, I desire Your forgiveness;
You are unique, without equal, ruling the world and its fullness . . .

The names *'Itti'el*, *Ṭeṣ"s*, *'Addiriron* and *'Akkatri'el* are manifestations of diverse forms of divine energy. The latter name, derived from the Hebrew *keter* (crown), implies the sovereignty of God, as indicated in the report (in *bBer* 7a) by Rabbi Ishmael b. Elisha, 'I once entered into the innermost part [of the Sanctuary] to offer incense and saw *'Akkatri'el Yah*, the Lord of Hosts seated upon a high and exalted throne.' In a similar context, the rabbis observe (in *bḤag* 13b) that the angel Sandalfon stands behind the 'chariot throne' and 'wreaths crowns for His Maker,' that is, he offers up to God the prayers of the righteous. Likewise, in *Exod. Rabbah* 21. 4, 'The angel appointed over prayers takes the prayers . . . and makes of them crowns.' The name *Ṭeṣ"s*, as found in *Heykhalot Rabbati* 2. 2, is followed by *YHWH 'elohey yisra'el*, the full formula of the mystical name, to which the poet refers by adding to *Ṭeṣ"s* 'the Ineffable Name' (*šem ha-meforaš*). It is likely that R. Tobias, the cantor-poet, is appealing to these manifestations of deity to bear the prayers of his congregation to the divine chariot throne and form them into wreaths for God's crown, thereby affirming His sovereignty.[5]

Tobias b. Eliezer merited mention by Abraham Ibn Ezra, who disapproved of his method of interpreting Scripture. In the latter's introduction to his commentary on the Pentateuch he singles out 'the scholars of Greece, who ignore rational and grammatical considerations, and rely on the homiletical

[5] Scholem, *Major Trends*, p. 363 n. 57; idem, *Re'šit Ha-Qabbalah*, p. 158; Weinberger, *'Antologia*, pp. 35–6.

method, as in [*Midraš*] *Leqaḥ Ṭov* . . .' However, the Kastorean rabbi-poet won approval from the Bible commentator and philosopher Judah b. Moses Moskoni (b. 1328), from Ocrida in Bulgaria, who praised him as 'a great scholar'. In addition to his influential *Midraš Leqaḥ Ṭov*, R. Tobias was one of the earliest commentators on the *qerovot* in the synagogue liturgy.[6] A younger contemporary of R. Tobias is the twelfth- to thirteenth-century poet Eliezer b. Judah, presumably a nephew of the former. R. Eliezer is eclectic in styling his hymnography, favouring both a Hispanic *qaṣīdah*-type structure with quantitative metre and a compulsory word metre in the fashion of the Italian master Solomon Ha-Bavli. In his *ḥaṭa'nu*, *'Ašuvah 'adekha misgabbi*, he laments the restrictive decrees of the ruling power:

> We live in fear of the laws from evil rulers and their mortal wounds;
> Their anger overflows their lips.[7]

Mordecai *Ha-'Arokh*

Mordecai b. Šabbetai *Ha-'Arokh* (Greek *makros*), the scribe, is a contemporary of Eliezer b. Judah. L. Zunz, in his magisterial study of the liturgy's literary history, gave the provenance of Mordecai b. Šabbetai as 'Italy or Greece'.[8] However, recent studies have shown that R. Mordecai hailed from Kastoria, a fact that he reveals in the acrostic to his *seliḥot*, *Me'anah hinnaḥem* and *Male'u matenay ḥalḥalah*. R. Mordecai was one of the Balkan hymnists whose *piyyuṭim* were included in the Franco-German ritual and were commented upon by Abraham b. Azriel (13th c.), one of the 'elders of Bohemia', in his study of the liturgy, *'Arugat Ha-Bosem*. R. Mordecai's works were also included in the Italian and Karaite prayer-books, and, like Benjamin b. Samuel and Benjamin b. Zeraḥ, his popularity extended into central and western Europe. In the superscriptions to his hymns he is referred to as *rabbana'* (our teacher), and in his acrostics he informs us that he is a scribe, presumably of phylacteries, *mezuzot* and Torah scrolls. He is the author of a *petiḥah* (introduction) for Šabbat Bere'šit and of some sixteen *seliḥot*-type hymns.

A distinctive feature in R. Mordecai's hymnography is his pervasive yearning for national restoration. Below is an example from his *ḥaṭa'nu*, *Male'u matenay ḥalḥalah*, headed by the refrain, 'We have sinned, O our Rock! Forgive us, O our Creator.' Although there is no mention of the Ten Martyrs, as is commonly the practice in the *ḥaṭa'nu*, the poet focuses on Israel's travail in exile and yearns for its end at long last:[9]

[6] Starr, *The Jews in the Byzantine Empire*, pp. 215–16; Ginzberg, *Ginzey Schechter*, i. 246.
[7] Weinberger, *Širat . . . Rabbanim*, pp. 129–32; Dinur, *Yisra'el Ba-Golah*, II. iii. 388.
[8] Zunz, *Literaturgeschichte*, p. 336.
[9] Weinberger, *Širey . . . Kastoria*, pp. 35–7.

I am likened to one who lies at the bottom of the sea, since the
end-time travail is long-lasting;
The prophecy is hidden and sealed up and my anointed is cut
off and without resources;
When the greatly beloved [Daniel] saw it in a dream and all did
tremble and enquire of him:
What is the meaning of this dream?

The intense desire to know when to expect the end of Israel's exile is echoed in R. Mordecai's moving *seliḥah*, *Me'anah hinnaḥem nafši 'al-ḥorban miqdaši* (My soul will not be comforted after the destruction of my Temple):

I have asked the prophets and seers who prophesied on my behalf:
'How long until the end of these awful things and my promised
redemption?' [Dan. 12: 6]
They responded, 'Why do you ask seeing that it is unknowable?'
And no one tells me;
I pine away, I pine away. Woe is me![10]

It is likely that in his personalized search for the end-time R. Mordecai was influenced by Abraham Ibn Ezra's *ge'ullah*, *'Im 'oyevay yo'meru ra' li*. R. Mordecai, like his Hispanic predecessor, closes his strophes with the unit *li* (me). Like Ibn Ezra, who appeals to Ezekiel for an answer to his question, 'How long until the end of these awful things?' (Dan. 12: 6), R. Mordecai asks the 'prophets and seers'. The similarity continues in the response given to the two poets. Ibn Ezra, after receiving no answer from Ezekiel, turns to Daniel, who surely must know since he is 'privy to every parable and riddle'. The cryptic response given to the Spanish poet—recontextualized from Judg. 13: 18—is identical to the one heard by R. Mordecai, 'Why do you ask? It is unknowable.'[11]

Like earlier poets, R. Mordecai defends the traditional theodicy and reaffirms his belief in divine providence. He rebukes the view—undoubtedly held by some—that Israel's suffering is unrelated to her sinful behaviour:

Since He has crushed my life to the ground and in His anger made
me sit in the darkness,
My inclination provokes me, rebellious still, and says,
It is not the Lord who brought this on, and he blesses himself,
Thinking, I am safe.

The opinion, based on Deut. 29: 19, that God is not in control of the world ('It is not the Lord who brought this on') is expanded in rabbinic theology by the comment attributed to R. Akiva (in *Gen. Rabbah* 26. 6),

[10] Weinberger, *Širey . . . Kastoria*, pp. 57–9.

[11] A. Ibn Ezra, *Širey Ha-Qodeš*, ii. 25–6.

'Why do the wicked renounce God and say in their hearts, "You will not call us to account", meaning that there is no judgment or judge? [In truth] there is judgment and there is a judge.'

Šabbetai Ḥaviv

Šabbetai Ḥaviv b. Avišai is presumably the son of R. Avišai from Zagora in Bulgaria. Judah Moskoni reports that R. Avišai wrote a commentary on the writings of Abraham Ibn Ezra—a favourite subject of Balkan scholars—in 1170.[12] R. Šabbetai appears to be well versed in the writings of Maimonides and the Jewish Neoplatonists. He is probably the earliest Macedonian hymnist to introduce themes from medieval philosophy into the synagogue liturgy. The following is from his introduction to the *qaddiš*, *Sesoni rav*, for the Pentecost service:[13]

Would that my Beloved dwelt in my Temple
As in earlier days, He that is absolute existence [*meḥuyyav ha-meṣi'ut*].

In his *Mi kamokha šamayim konanta*, he explains God's creative activity in terms borrowed from Jewish Aristotelians:[14]

You have created all that exists [*ha-nimṣa'im*], divided all into two modes [*minim*];
Among these are the non-material [*gešem*], nor prepared with matter;
They are the angels who praise and respond:
Blessed in the glory of the Lord.

You formed the second mode of several materials,
Among which are the simple [*pašut*] comprising the four elements [*yesodim*],
As well as composite [*murkavim*] in which there is generation and corruption [*howim we-nifsadim*];
How great are Your works, O Lord.

Like other cantor-poets, Šabbetai Ḥaviv felt obliged to inform his congregation regarding the laws of forthcoming festivals. This practice is observed in his *šalmonit seliḥah*, *'Agagi šaqad be-khol me'odo le-haḥariveni*, for the Fast of Esther, in which he focuses on the rules pertaining to the reading of the Scroll of Esther. Of particular interest is his ruling with regard to the ink used in writing the Scroll:[15]

[12] Moskoni, 'Haqdamah', pp. 6–9.
[13] Weinberger, *Širat . . . Rabbanim*, pp. 172–3.
[14] Ibid. 186. On God as 'absolute existence', see Maimonides, *Moreh Ha-Nevukhim*, 1. 52 and 2, introd., No. 20.
[15] Weinberger, *Širat . . . Rabbanim*, p. 177.

Written with *kalkanthos* [Greek, copperas] treated with gall-nut
On parchment that is not coarse, the Scroll is permitted.

The poet bases this opinion on the statement of the third-century *'amora'* Rabbah b. Ḥana (in *bMeg* 18b–19a). In commenting on this ruling, the Tosafot commentary on the Talmud asks, 'How are we [in western Europe] able to write Scrolls of the Pentateuch, *tefillin* and the Scroll of Esther, since the parchment is not treated with gall-nut?' To this Rabbenu Jacob Tam replies, 'The lime that we use in treating the parchment is as effective as gall-nut.' Maimonides in his *Mišneh Torah*, Laws of *Tefillin* (1. 6), anticipates the problem of the Franco-Germans, in whose region gall-nut-producing oak trees did not grow, and rules that gall-nut *or the like* can be used in treating the parchment.

However, R. Šabbetai does not hesitate to recommend the use of gall-nut in treating the parchment, since it is a common growth that develops on the Mediterranean oak (*Quercus lusitanica*). Moreover, the Balkan poet refers to it by its Greek name, *kalkanthos*, instead of *kankantom*, as in *mMeg* 2. 1. The latter usage is probably an Aramaic treatment of the Greek. Of equal interest in this hymn is the poet's use of Aramaic terms, which he lifts verbatim from the rabbinic text (in *bMeg* 16b and 19a):

And the sons of the Aggagite [Haman] who were hung on one pole [Aramaic *'izdaqifu ba-ḥada' zeqifatah*],
[Their names] are to be said in one breath [when reading from the Scroll] . . .

It is forbidden to read the Scroll from a volume containing the rest of Scripture;
If the Scroll is a little shorter than the rest, or a little longer [Aramaic *miḥasra' purta' 'o miyyatra' purta'*], it is permitted.

The influence of Andalusian style and form is clear in R. Šabbetai's hymnography. He experiments with quantitative metre and constructs his hymns in *qaṣīdah* style, or in the form of a pseudo-*muwashshaḥ*. Some of Šabbetai Ḥaviv's hymns have been preserved in the Cairo Geniza.[16]

Menaḥem b. Elia

The thirteenth-century poet Menaḥem b. Elia of Kastoria is the author of several *seliḥot*, including a virtuosic *baqqašah*, *Malki mi-qedem*, in fourteen strophes comprising five cola in monorhyme with five units in each hemicolon. Added to this carefully constructed word metre is the poet's impressive effort to spell his name and that of his father in the fourteen strophes by

[16] Weinberger, *Širat . . . Rabbanim*, pp. 168–9.

repeating each of its units fifty times, thus: MNḤM BN KR ʾELIA ZL (*Menaḥem ben kevod rav ʾElia zikhrono li-vrakhah*, Menaḥem son of the honourable Rabbi Elia of blessed memory). His achievement recalls that of the Provençal poet and philosopher Yedayah Ha-Penini Bedersi (*c.*1270–1340) and his *baqqašat ha-memim*, comprising 1,000 units beginning with the letter *mem*. Hispanic prosody was a major influence in R. Menaḥem's liturgical hymns, some of which he constructed in quantitative metre and in the form of a *muwashshaḥ* or pseudo-*muwashshaḥ*.

Of particular interest in Menaḥem b. Elia's hymnography is his conviction that the time of Israel's redemption from exile is approaching. Following are the closing strophes of his *ḥaṭa'nu*, *ʾAmarti la-ʾadonay ʾeli*, featuring a dialogue between God and Israel in which God announces that Israel's national restoration is imminent:

Riding on a donkey, see him coming;
Fresh troops and armed men are with him;
Ruddy and distinguished among ten thousand;
How you have stirred up the love!

I have heard your complaints;
I know of your wanderings;
You have been punished by the guilt of your sins
To atone for your souls . . .

Why do you speak evil [against Me],
Am I not with you in your troubles?
The Garden of Delight is preserved for you,
Gems and precious stones . . .

Other Macedonian poets include Elia b. Abraham *He-ʿAluv* (the hapless) from Kastoria, a contemporary of Menaḥem b. Elia. Like the latter, R. Elia merits the title *rabbana* in the superscriptions to his hymns. He is the author of an *ʾofan* and *zulat* in the *yoṣer* cycle and a *ḥaṭa'nu*. Macedonian hymnists from the fourteenth century include the Kastoreans Abraham b. Jacob, author of an epic *mi kamokha* in Hispanic style, and R. David b. Eliezer, author of *seliḥot* and the probable editor of the *Maḥazor Kastoria*. Like Šabbetai Ḥaviv, R. David is familiar with the writings of the Jewish Neoplatonists and Aristotelians, and in his hymns he shares their thinking with his congregation. He, like Menaḥem b. Elia, constructed some of his hymns in quantitative metre and in the form of a pseudo-*muwashshaḥ*. In several of his hymns R. David gives his first name as *ʾAvihu*, *ʾAḥiyah* or *ʾAvḥiyah*. He also adds to his name, *ḥay we-nošaʿ* (living and saved). S. D. Luzzatto has suggested that the name change may have been an anti-demonic strategy resulting from the poet's illness. According to this folk practice the invalid adopts an alias—in this case a variation of *ḥay* (living)—in order to deceive the harmful spirits.[17]

THE PRINCIPAL MACEDONIAN GENRES

Qedušta' and *Rahiṭ*

Although no *qedušta'ot* from Macedonia have been preserved, it is likely that sections from larger works have survived. The most likely prospects are the four hymns by Mordecai b. Šabbetai, *Laylah mi-meʿon qodšekha*, [*Ha-yom*] *malki mi-qedem*, [*ʿErev*] *me-'ittekha tehillati* and [*Ḥesed*] *me-'az konanata*, built in quatrains that open and close with identical units. As indicated above, such features were common in the *qedušta' rahiṭim* headed by a scriptural verse whose units were embellished in separate hymns. The excessive length of the *qedušta'* prevented its use in the Macedonian synagogue, although its *rahiṭ* component—now renamed *seliḥah*—retained its popularity. Like his colleagues in the Balkans, R. Mordecai was influenced by Hispanic practices. Observe the use of enjambment in his [*Ḥesed*] *me-'az konanta*.[18]

In mercy preserve [Israel] and the covenant of the fathers and do
with us
As You have agreed compacting with them, even this day answer
our prayer;
Turn to us with Your goodness and rebuke the Tempter because
He has not remembered to do mercy.

Menaḥem b. Elia's hymns, *'Adonay melekh meyuḥad be-'emet* and *'Attah 'ošyotay konanta*, were probably *rahiṭim*, now separated from a *qedušta'* and renamed *seliḥah*. In both hymns the strophes begin and end with *'Adonay* and *'Attah* respectively, and it is likely that the units formed the scriptural header to the *rahiṭ*. In the latter hymn the opening unit in each colon in the rhyming tercets and the closing unit in the quatrain strophes is *'attah*. Its structure recalls Solomon Ibn Gabirol's *rahiṭim*, *'Attah 'ippadta šafrir ʿal qaw memadekha* and *'Attah 'amon qanita*, *'attah eṣlah ḥanita*, and may have been R. Menaḥem's models. Below is a selection from the Kastorean poet's *'Attah 'ošyotay konanta*:[19]

'Attah 'ošyotay konanta;
'Attah be-qirbam hitlonanta;
'Attah ga'yoni hitbonanta;
Mi-beṭen 'immi 'eli 'attah.

[17] Zunz, *Literaturgeschichte*, pp. 383–4. Zunz observed that the name *'Avihu* has the numerical value of 'David'. See Trachtenberg, *Jewish Magic*, p. 168.
[18] Weinberger, *Širey . . . Kastoria*, pp. 39–40.
[19] Ibid. 96; Ibn Gabirol, *Širey Ha-Qodeš*, pp. 165–71.

'Attah dar bi-nharah;
'Attah harari le-'ezrah;
'Attah we-ne'zar bi-gvurah,
'Ezrati u-mfalleṭi 'attah . . .

You have built the bulwarks [of the Temple]
You have lodged therein;
You have taken into account my pride;
Since my mother bore me, You have been my God.

You dwell with brilliance;
You are my mountain of aid;
You are girded with strength;
My help and deliverer are You . . .

Menaḥem b. Elia's hymn *'Adonay me-'eyn temurah we-ḥevrah*, in which each strophe begins with the unit *'adonay*, may also have been intended as a *rahiṭ* for the *qedušta'*, although it, like the above two, is designated as a *seliḥah* in the Romaniote prayer-book.[20]

David b. Eliezer's hymn *Ḥayyim deraštikha mi-ṣarah*, in quatrains with rhyming tercets and closing biblical verse, begins and ends with the unit *ḥayyim*. It is headed by the verse from Ps. 34: 13, 'Which of you desires life' (*Mi ha-'iš he-ḥafeṣ ḥayyim*). Although in the manuscript of the *Maḥazor Kastoria* (fo. 184) it is set among the *seliḥot* for the 'Elul vigil nights, it is likely that the hymn originally served as a *qedušta' rahiṭ* headed by the above verse from Psalms. The poet draws attention to the predicament of the soul seeking to be reunited with its divine source:[21]

[With] life, courage, and the might of growing authority
You have endowed the soul, even with an abundance of light;
Let my soul, from the fear of You, be tied up
And bound in the bond of life.

The divine 'light' granted to the soul is a conceit that the poet presumably adapted from Solomon Ibn Gabirol's *Meqor Ḥayyim* (3. 45) and his *Keter Malkhut* (No. 7). From a concern for the soul, the poet shifts to admonishing his congregation—in terms borrowed from contemporary philosophy—to use their intellect in the service of the deity:

You, the living, truly God's people and His creation,
Make known His reality [*yešuto*] and with your intellect establish
His presence [*u-v-sikhleykhem šakkenuhu*];
That we may be aided by His truth and be able to explain His unity;
Truly He is the living God.

[20] Weinberger, *Širey . . . Kastoria*, p. 79.

[21] Ibid. 130.

The concern for the soul and cultivation of the intellect are also themes prominent in the writings of Ibn Gabirol. The Andalusian sage believed that the soul, which belongs to the spiritual world, can return to its divine source only if it is aided by knowledge and pious practice, and that 'the knowing part being the best part in man, that which man must seek is knowledge.'[22]

Yoṣer

Zulat

Elia b. Abraham's *zulat*, *'Az be-vo' 'oyevay u-monay*, for the last day of Passover is constructed in rhyming tercets with closing scriptural verses from the Song at the Sea (Exod. 14: 30–15: 21). The hymn is modelled after Solomon Ha-Bavli's *zulat*, *'Ahevukha nefeš le-hadekh*, and Samuel Memeli's, *'Uyyam ne'eman we-nikh'av*:

> The troops of angels descended;
> Even the stars waged war from the heavens;
> At the blast of Your nostrils, the waters piled up . . .
>
> The angels on high rose up
> To humble the enemies of Your people;
> The nations heard, [they trembled] . . .

Mi Kamokha

Šabbetai Ḥaviv b. Avišai is the author of three *mi kamokha* hymns. *Mi kamokha šomer 'ammekha yisra'el*, for Šabbat Ha-Ḥodeš, and *Mi kamokha šamayim konanta bi-tvunah*, for Šemini 'Aṣeret, follow conventional Hispanic models, with repeated units closing the strophes. However, his *Mi kamokha šokhen bi-šmey qedem*, for Šabbat Parah, varies from the others by omitting the identical repeated unit after the strophes. In this practice, the Macedonian poet follows the models of Sa'adyah Ga'on and Joseph Ibn Abitur, whose *mi kamokha* hymns were without the repeated unit embellishment. The following selection is from R. Šabbetai's Šabbat Parah hymn, where the poet ponders the mystery of the water treated with the ashes of the red heifer. The ashes and water had the puzzling effect of purifying the unclean while defiling those who handled it (Num. 19: 1–22).[23]

> Regarding the command of the red heifer,
> I [Solomon] said, 'I thought I could fathom it,
> But it eludes me mightily,
> The right teaching of the Lord;

[22] Ibn Gabirol, *Meqor Ḥayyim*, I. 1, 4; idem, 'Keter Malkhut', No. 30.

[23] See Zulay, *Ha-'Askolah*, p. 299 for a listing of Sa'adyah's *mi kamokha* hymns; Fleischer, *Ha-Yoṣerot*, pp. 580–2; Weinberger, *Širat . . . Rabbanim*, pp. 180–7.

How is it that contact with it defiles,
But its sprinkling purifies?
No sacrifice or sin offering is like it;
It defies wisdom, understanding and awe!'

R. Šabbetai's *Mi kamokha šamayim konanta bi-tvunah* is heavily endowed with references to contemporary religious philosophy and suggests that the congregation was sufficiently informed to appreciate his discourse. In introducing themes of this nature into the synagogue liturgy, the Macedonian poet is following precedents set by Sa'adyah Ga'on in Babylon and Ibn Gabirol in Spain. Although the major focus of this hymn is Šemini 'Aṣeret and the water-drawing ceremony associated with it, the poet opens with an *'avodah*-type historical introduction. This habit he undoubtedly learned from the Hispanics, who initiated the practice of giving a cosmic preface to their *mi kamokha* hymns.[24]

Who is like You, appointing the heavens with wisdom,
And establishing the earth firmly upon nothing;
The earth is given over to humans,
But the heavens are the heavens of the Lord.

Abraham b. Jacob's *Mi kamokha 'el nora' tehillot* is a forty-seven-strophe hymn for the Sabbath before Passover (Šabbat Ha-Gadol). Like Mordecai b. Šabbetai, Menaḥem b. Elia and Elia b. Abraham, R. Abraham takes pride in mentioning his native city in the acrostic signature, 'Abraham b. Jacob from Kastoria.' His massive *mi kamokha*, in quatrains with rhyming tercets and closing scriptural verse, opens with a cosmic preface in the Hispanic style. He follows with an account of Israel's enslavement and the exodus, combining biblical and rabbinic sources with the rhyming requirements of the hymn. In accommodating such requirements, R. Abraham even resorts to Greek usage:[25]

The sea looked and fled
Seeking refuge from fear of the Lord;
Its waters rose to the heavens [*le-ouranos*]
At the presence of the Lord.

Rešut and *Petiḥah*

One of the earliest Macedonian hymns in the *rešut* genre is Eliezer b. Judah's *qaṣīdah*-style *rešut* before the *qaddiš* for Šemini 'Aṣeret. The Hispanic manner pervades the hymn, which features a quantitative *ha-merubbeh* metre. The

[24] Ibid. 186–7; Fleischer, *Širat Ha-Qodeš*, p. 90.
[25] Weinberger, *Širey . . . Kastoria*, p. 118.

indication that the hymn was designed as a permission request before the *qaddiš* is seen in the closing stich. Following is a selection from the hymn:[26]

With a broken heart I approach You in prayer;
The offerings of my lips are in place of a Temple sacrifice . . .
O Lord, the heavens cannot contain Your glory,
How can I with little understanding? . . .
Yet I, the merest of mortals, presume to stand
Glorifying You, with much fear and trepidation;
Show me Your favour as if I were seasoned and sage
And I will sanctify You [*we-ʾaqdiškha*] in the assembly of the wise.

A *rešut* before the *qaddiš* in the Pentecost service was composed by Šabbetai Ḥaviv b. Avišai. The hymn, *Sesoni rav be-ʿomedi ʿim seganay*, is also in the Hispanic *qaṣīdah* style, with balanced hemistichs in *ha-merubbeh* metre. The *rešut* closes with the opening phrase of the *qaddiš*, 'Magnified and sanctified be the name of God throughout the world,' a common practice of Hispanic poets, as seen in Abraham Ibn Ezra's *qaddiš rešuyyot*, *ʾOdeh le-ʾeli* and *ʾAgaddelkha ʾelohey kol nešamah*. Focusing on Israel receiving the Torah at Mount Sinai, R. Šabbetai combines themes in biblical and rabbinic literature with contemporary religious philosophy. In the following selection from the hymn, the speaker is Israel:[27]

Great was my joy when I stood with my officers
By the mountain longing for God's seat, even Sinai . . .
Your love greeted me
With, 'I am' and 'You shall not have before Me.'
With all my heart I am aware of these two;
They are basic, my ears have heard . . .
My soul left me when God spoke,
Then He revived me with gracious dew descending . . .

According to rabbinic legend (in *Gen. Rabbah* 99. 1), Mount Sinai was chosen as the seat of divine revelation because it was never used for idol worship. The first two of the Ten Commandments, which are basic to all the others (see *bHor* 8a) God Himself spoke. However, the People of Israel had not the strength to endure the impact of the revelation, and their souls left their bodies, whereupon, God summoned a reviving dew and restored them to life.[28]

Another *rešut* by Šabbetai Ḥaviv was designed for the Sabbath preceding the month of Nisan (Šabbat Ha-Ḥodeš). The hymn, beginning with the

[26] Weinberger, *Širat . . . Rabbanim*, p. 129.
[27] Ibid. 172–3; A. Ibn Ezra, *Sirey Ha-Qodeš*, i. 31, 43–4.
[28] *Exod. Rabbah* 29. 4 and *Pirqey de-Rabbi ʾEliezer* (Warsaw, 1852), No. 41.

words *Še'eh 'eli 'eley šaw'i*, is in *qaṣīdah* style with *ha-merubbeh* metre, and may have served as a permission request before the *šema'* benediction, *'eyn 'elohim zulatekha* (there is no God beside You). Following is the relevant colon from the hymn:[29]

O singular in the world where there is none beside You [*'eyn biltekha*];
You are God who revives the weak.

Mordecai b. Šabbetai's *petiḥah*, *'Ahallel la-noṭeh*, was chanted before the first benediction of the *šema'* in the Sabbath morning service, *La-'el 'ašer šavat mi-kol ha-ma'asim* (To God who rested from all His labours). R. Mordecai's hymn focuses on the creation story in Gen. 1. This *petiḥah*, built in rhyming tercets, is uncommon in that the closing colon is not a scriptural verse but versets from the first *šema'* benediction for the weekday morning service, 'Our praiseworthy God with vast understanding' (*'El barukh gedol de'ah*), as follows:[30]

I will sing of Him who on the first [day] stretched out the heavens like a curtain;
Awesome, He set the earth on its foundation and spread it out;
Our praiseworthy God with vast understanding.

From the luminosity of His glory He is wrapped in light as with a garment;
He saw that it was very good to form the earth;
He fashioned the rays of the sun.

On the second day He said: Let there be a dome to separate the waters below;
He Himself collected and gathered up on the third [day] the waters of the sea;
The good [light] He created reflects His splendour . . .

Šabbetai Ḥaviv is the author of several *petiḥot* that served to introduce the obligatory benedictions and prayers. His *Mah na'amu dodim* and *Be-mivṭa' ha-kol yaṣar*, both preserved in the Cairo Geniza, are in the form of a pseudo-*muwashshaḥ*. The former was probably an epithalamium chanted on the Sabbath before the *nišmat* prayer. R. Šabbetai's theme focuses on the bond between man's body and his God-given soul:[31]

How delightful is the meeting of lovers
They clasp each other and cannot be separated . . .

[29] Weinberger, *Širat . . . Rabbanim*, p. 172.
[30] Weinberger, *Širey . . . Kastoria*, pp. 47–8.
[31] Weinberger, *Širat . . . Rabbanim*, pp. 168–9.

Following the opening 'belt' celebrating the union of bride and groom, the poet prepares the congregation for the *Nišmat kol ḥay tevarekh 'et šimkha* (Every breathing soul praises You) prayer. The following strophe extends the metaphor of the bridal pair and focuses on the body, which, having encountered the divine soul, is captivated by her charms:

> With bands of love by Your soul
> I am restrained, having met You, I am bound
> From the day the sun shone upon me . . .
> My heart's resolve is shattered.

The hymn closes with the body's promise to mend its ways:

> I will abhor venality and flee from it;
> No matter how attractive the price I will disdain it.

R. Šabbetai's *Be-mivṭa' ha-kol yaṣar* for Šabbat Bere'šit is an introduction to the benediction before the *šemaʿ*, 'Praised are You, O Lord, Creator of lights.' Its theme is the first chapter in Genesis and its focus is the creation of the two great lights and their dispute (based on *bḤul* 60b):[32]

> With wisdom and discernment He thinned out the two luminaries;
> When one wished to be magnified above the other;
> He spoke to the complainer: 'Go and make yourself smaller.'
> Therefore He separated the lights . . .

The hymn closes with the hope of national restoration and 'the continuous light' predicted by the prophet Zechariah (14: 7).

Šabbetai Ḥaviv's two other surviving *petiḥot*, *Širu ne'emanay* and *Simḥu 'av we-yoladto*, are built in strophes ending with a repeated unit, similar to hymns in this genre by his contemporary, David from Byzantium. *Širu ne'emanay*, chanted at the Passover morning service, opens with a rhyming tercet, followed by rhyming couplets and closing scriptural verse. Presumably the hymn served as an introduction to the *barekhu*, as seen in the following:[33]

> O house of Jacob, bless [*barekhu*]
> The Lord, make ready to sing,
> For it is God's Passover

Simḥu 'av we-yoladto, for the circumcision service (*berit milah*), is a metric *petiḥah* in rhyming tercets with closing scriptural verse ending with *šalom*. The hymn celebrates the entrance into the covenant of Abraham with a personalized conceit in the form of a dialogue between God and the poet:[34]

[32] Weinberger, *Širat . . . Rabbanim*, pp. 169–70. [33] Ibid. 171. [34] Ibid. 170–1.

[GOD:]
Rejoice, father and son with family and friends
My covenant with him [Abraham] was a covenant of life and well-being

[POET:]
When You hear his [the infant's] cry, send help to his providers
And bring full [healing] to his organ, Lord of peace.

The poet concludes with blessings for the infant:

May he be constant in his virtue and take his stand on the high ground . . .
May he be blessed in his world and healed in his seal.

Menaḥem b. Elia's *petiḥah*, *Mah-yaqru reʿim be-qum ʾašmoret*, for the 'Elul vigil nights *seliḥot* service is a metric pseudo-*muwashshaḥ*. Its theme, based on Hos. 14: 3, is a plea to the deity to receive the prayers of his congregation in lieu of Temple altar offerings.[35]

How dear are the friends who arise at the watch of the night;
They pour out heart and soul before the Seat of Mercy;
In place of sacrificial bullock and ram they pray;
Consider their supplications, O Rock, as incense;
How dear is the golden tongue and the mantle! [Josh. 7: 24]

Elia b. Abraham's *petiḥah* for Šemini 'Aṣeret, *ʾImru la-ʾel todah*, introduces the second benediction before the *šemaʿ*. It is built in rhyming tercets with closing scriptural verse. Its final strophe ends with 'To praiseworthy God they sing sweetly' (*le-ʾel barukh neʿimot yitenu*), the said *šemaʿ* benediction. The hymn gives an account of the dedication of Solomon's Temple in the month of Tišre on Šemini 'Aṣeret. The poet characteristically combines scriptural and rabbinic sources with narrative embellishments:[36]

On this day stood [*ʿammedu*]
Israel with the king in assembly [*noʿadu*],
They lost heart and trembled [*wa-yeṣeʾ libbam wa-yeḥeradu*].

The closing colon, which is not based on scriptural or rabbinic sources, is an added embellishment prompted by the poet's rhyming needs: *ʿammedu . . . no-ʿadu . . . wa-yeḥeradu*. In the following strophes, the poet again combines the three sources:

35 Weinberger, *Širey . . . Kastoria*, p. 81.
36 Ibid. 103–4. The hymn is incorrectly designated an *ʾofan* in the above text.

He [Solomon] took counsel with himself and determined
[To ask others] what to say:
And one called upon the other to speak.

When he saw that the gates [of the Holy of Holies] were shut,
He rose from where he had knelt twice,
With his hands outstretched towards heaven.

When the servants of the Lord saw
That they were unable to take the Ark into the innermost chamber [*lifnim we-lifnay*],
And it was then that Solomon had finished offering his prayer to God.

He thought of his father's error and the sin
He committed, and he beseeched the Rock with affection
Asking, 'Show me a sign of Your favour.' . . .

The gates shook and opened up,
And the Ark was entered and they rejoiced,
And a light brilliant and clear shone upon them.

The major source of the poet's narrative is 1 Kgs. 8. This he supplements with the rabbinic account (in *bŠab* 30a):

When Solomon built the Temple, he desired to take the Ark into the Holy of Holies, whereupon the gates clave to each other. Solomon uttered twenty-four prayers, yet he was not answered . . . But as soon as he prayed, 'O Lord God, turn not away the face of Your anointed: remember the good deeds of David, Your servant' [2 Chr. 6: 42], he was immediately answered. In that hour the faces of all David's enemies turned [black] like the bottom of a pot, and all Israel knew that the Holy One, blessed be He, had forgiven him that sin [with Bathsheba].

Again, the poet's embellishments are prompted by the hymn's rhyming needs. The image of Solomon rising from the place where he had knelt, twice, is unsupported by the sources; it is included in the hymn because *paʿamayim* (twice) rhymes with *delatayim* (gates) and *šamayim* (heaven). 'And a light brilliant and clear shone upon them' is, likewise, not supported by Scripture or rabbinic literature, but its closing unit in the tercet, *zaraḥu* (shone) rhymes with *pataḥu* (opened) and *samaḥu* (rejoiced).

Seliḥah

The earliest Macedonian *seliḥah* is Tobias b. Eliezer's *ʾEhyeh ʾašer ʾehyeh paṣtah la-ʾavi-gedor*. The hymn ends with the colon 'Almighty King who sits on the throne of mercy' (*ʾel melekh yošev ʿal kisseʾ raḥamim*), the introductory litany prior to the recitation of the Thirteen Divine Attributes in the *seliḥot* service. All the other closing cola in this fourteen-strophe hymn are scriptural verses after the Hispanic model. Tobias's references in the hymn to divine and angelic names and to sources in Jewish mysticism is a characteristic feature in the hymnography of early Byzantine poets like Benjamin b. Samuel, Isaac b. Judah and Benjamin b. Zeraḥ.[37]

Mordecai b. Šabbetai's *seliḥah*, *'Ahuvah 'ašer 'orasah*, employs the now familiar conceit from Hispanic prosody in which Israel is the forlorn, abandoned bride who is mocked by her unfeeling neighbours:[38]

The beloved betrothed, He set apart like a princess,
With embroidery of gold and silver endowed;
She was supreme and sovereign in her abundant glory;
[Alas,] Judah has gone into exile with suffering and hard
servitude . . .

Forsaken, living as if in widowhood, she has no respite;
Her husband hid His face and left her in anguish;
He took a bag of money with Him for the discounts on the new
moon,
Then He wrote her a certificate of divorce, put it in her hand and
sent her away.

She turned to her lovers and called for their help;
They betrayed her, harassed her, seized her without mercy;
She sought Him, whom her soul loved, to save her;
The betrothed cried for help, but there was no one to rescue her!

Unlike other treatments of this conceit, there is no response of reassurance from the Beloved at the close of the hymn, only the hope that the pair will ultimately be reconciled.

The fervent nationalism of Mordecai b. Šabbetai is seen in his *seliḥah*, *Mi-qoṣer ruaḥ u-me-'avodah qašah*. Israel is there portrayed as 'Judah's daughter' cast out by her royal father, in whose affections she is replaced by other maidens. Following is her bold complaint echoed by the poet:[39]

Your help is extended to another who wears her ornaments;
Her reign is long and prosperous and her cup overflows;
From Judah's daughter in captivity and exile, You avert Your gaze
And You embrace the bosom of a stranger.

In line with Israel's complaint in *Mi-qoṣer ruaḥ* is her need to know when she can expect an end to her exile. Her desire to be reconciled with her God is

[37] Weinberger, *'Antologia*, pp. 35–6.
[38] Weinberger, *Širey . . . Kastoria*, pp. 54–6.
[39] Ibid. 51–3.

movingly expressed in R. Mordecai's *seliḥah*, *Me'anah hinnaḥem nafši 'al ḥorban miqdaši* (My soul will not be comforted after the destruction of my Temple).

Šabbetai Ḥaviv's *'Agagi šaqad be-khol me'odo le-haḥariveni*, for the Fast of Esther, is uncommon in its theme. Unlike Hillel b. Eliakim's narrative hymn, *'Attah 'eloha ha-ri'šonim*, for the Fast of Esther, in which he combines biblical and rabbinic Purim legends, R. Šabbetai in his twenty-one-strophe *seliḥah* focuses on the laws pertaining to the reading of the Scroll of Esther. Of particular interest are the poet's rulings reflecting practices in his region.[40]

Šeniyyah

Menaḥem b. Elia is one of the few Balkan poets who composed *seliḥot* in couplets, known as *šeniyyot*. His *'Ayyaḥekha be-morah*, in rhyming couplets, is preserved in the Romaniote ritual for the 'Elul vigil nights; its second colon comprises verses from Ps. 145. Distinctive features of the hymn are its phonetic-intensive character and its thematic focus. Following is a sample illustrating the assonance, alliteration and internal rhyme:[41]

Nevu'ah nora'ah / teluyah bi-qriyah / na'ah mufla'ah / mi-pi doreš we-šo'el . . .

Qašševet 'ozno le-mitḥanneno / 'im ra'yono mekhino / u-kh-'eyno be-'eyno / nekhšav u-va' ka-met;
Qarov 'adonay le-khol qore'ayw, le-khol 'ašer yiqra'uhu ve-'emet . . .

The attainment of awe-inspiring prophecy is dependent upon the proper articulation [of the letters of the alphabet] by one seeking [to attain this goal] . . .

[The Lord] will hear those who pray to Him if they prepare their thoughts and think of themselves as non-existent, as if they had died;
The Lord is near to all who call upon Him, to all who call upon Him in truth.

There is a resemblance in these cola to the teaching of the Hispanic mystic Abraham Abulafia (1240–*c.*1291), for whom meditation on the letters of the Hebrew alphabet aided the soul in freeing itself from preoccupation with its natural self and enabled it, in Abulafia's words, 'to untie the knots which bind it.' The layers of meditation on the alphabet include articulation (*mivṭa'*), writing (*mikhtav*) and thought (*maḥšav*). By renouncing his attachment to

[40] Weinberger, *Širat . . . Rabbanim*, p. 177.
[41] Weinberger, *Širey . . . Kastoria*, p. 92.

the phenomenal world the individual, ascending the steps of the mystic ladder, is ultimately able, with the aid of meditation on the letters of the Divine Name, to attain prophetic inspiration. In describing the preparations for meditation, ecstasy and prophecy, Abulafia (in his *Ḥayyey Ha-ʿOlam Ha-Baʾ*, Jerusalem, National and University Library, MS No. 8⁰ 540, fos. 44–5), comments on the verse (in Amos 4: 12), 'Prepare to meet your God, O Israel':

Prepare yourself to focus your heart on God alone . . . begin to combine a few or many letters, to permute and to combine them with rapidity until your heart becomes warm . . . Then turn all your true thoughts to imagine the Name and His exalted angels in your heart as if they were human beings sitting or standing about you . . . And know, the stronger the intellectual flow within you, the weaker will become your outer and inner parts. Your whole body will be seized by an extremely violent trembling, so that you will think that surely you are about to die, because your soul, overjoyed with its knowledge, will leave your body. At this moment, be ready consciously to choose death, and then you will know that you have come far enough to receive the flow [of divine power].

When Abulafia left the city of Acre after his futile search for the mythical river Sambatyon, he returned to Europe via Greece, where he was married. It is known that in the 1270s he visited Thebes and Patros, where he taught Maimonides' *Guide of the Perplexed* in Greek. Presumably, his influence extended north into Macedonia.[42]

Ḥaṭaʾnu

An early Macedonian *ḥaṭaʾnu*, *ʾAšuvah ʿadekha misgabbi*, comes from the pen of Eliezer b. Judah. Its twenty-four strophes are connected by anadiplosis and its cola are consistently limited to three units, after the manner of the much-imitated Solomon Ha-Bavli. As indicated above, Ha-Bavli's neo-classicism featured a revival of the Qilliric two-root-consonant rhyming pattern which the Macedonian R. Eliezer also sought to emulate. However, combined with a loyalty to Ha-Bavli's model, the eclectic Eliezer b. Judah chose to end his rhyming quatrains with scriptural verses in the Hispanic manner. In the following excerpt from the *ḥaṭaʾnu*, note the balanced word count, the anadiplosis, and the two-root rhyme in the second strophe:[43]

Ṭovim hemmah la-mevin
Dinekha, rokhev ʿavim;
Pešaʿim taʿavir we-talbin;
Šegiʾot mi yavin.

[42] See Scholem, *Major Trends*, pp. 135–7; Idel, *The Mystical Experience*, pp. 2–3, 142–3.
[43] Weinberger, *Širat . . . Rabbanim*, pp. 130–1.

Yavin devarkha u-mgalleh,
Yešʿakha lo tegalleh,
We-ʾom ʿammekha mekhalleh,
Kalleh be-ḥemah kalleh—

Your ordinances, O Rider of the Clouds
Benefit those who understand;
You pardon iniquity and make white [the scarlet-like sin];
Who can detect their errors?

He who understands Your word and reveals it [lawfully]
To him Your salvation is disclosed;
And the nation that seeks to destroy Your people,
Consume them in wrath, consume them—

The term *megalleh*, translated 'reveals it [lawfully]', is taken from a rabbinic statement in *ʾAvot* 1. 15, 'He who misinterprets the Torah (*ha-megalleh panim ba-torah šeloʾ ka-halakhah*) . . . has no share in the world to come.' It is likely that R. Eliezer, in praising those who interpret the Torah in line with lawful rabbinic teaching is, at the same time condemning the Karaites who do not acknowledge the Oral Torah.

Mordecai b. Šabbetai's *ḥaṭaʾnu*, *Maleʾu matenay ḥalḥalah*, is headed by the refrain characteristic of the genre, 'We have sinned, O our Rock; forgive us, our Creator.' The hymn is built in rhyming tercets with closing scriptural verse ending with a repeated unit. The neo-classical revival of Eliezer b. Judah, with its display of consistent word metre and two-root-letter rhyme is not seen in the *ḥaṭaʾnu* of R. Mordecai (or in any of his other hymns). It is likely that, as in other regions, the Macedonian poets found the Qilliric rhyming pattern too demanding.

Although there is no mention of the Ten Martyrs in *Maleʾu matenay ḥalḥalah* (or in Eliezer b. Judah's *ḥaṭaʾnu*), as in other treatments of the genre, R. Mordecai focuses on Israel's travail in exile and its hope for relief.[44]

Menaḥem b. Elia's *ḥaṭaʾnu*, *ʾAmarti la-ʾadonay ʾeli*, is built, like Eliezer b. Judah's, in rhyming quatrains with closing scriptural verses. Here, as in the previous two treatments, there is no reference to the Ten Martyrs. In its place is a dialogue between God and Israel in which the latter recalls their earlier intimacy:[45]

[ISRAEL:]
I have declared that the Lord is my God;
I must speak, so that I may find relief;
He heard me from His palace [*me-heykhalo*]
And He is settled next to me.

[44] Weinberger, *Širey . . . Kastoria*, pp. 35–7.

[45] Ibid. 87–8.

In holiness I have seen Him in His brilliance;
The hem of His robe filled the palace
And thick darkness was under His feet,
Because the Lord had descended upon it.

In the following strophes Israel contrasts her idyllic past with her current life in exile, and asks why the all-powerful Lord does not act on her behalf:

You who are mighty and strong,
Why have You delivered Your people to plunder?
Even the abomination that desolates is in Your palace;
He has come into Your house and remained.

In the closing strophes Israel's God responds, urging her to be patient and await her imminent restoration.

Elia b. Abraham's *ḥaṭa'nu*, *'Essa' 'eynay we-libbi be-ra'yon*, reviews the narrative in Num. 13, and the majority report of the scouts that formidable obstacles stood in the way of taking the Land of Canaan. The rabbis (in *bSot* 35a), in commenting on the verse in Num. 14: 1, 'Then [after hearing the report of the scouts] all the congregation raised a loud cry, and the people wept that night,' observe, 'That day was the Ninth of 'Av [the date the two Temples were destroyed]; and the Holy One, blessed be He, said, "They are now weeping for nothing, but I will fix [this day] for them as an occasion of weeping for generations." ' For the synagogue poet, the theme of Israel's faithlessness on hearing the report of the scouts was a fitting subject for a *ḥaṭa'nu*.

R. Elia's hymn is built in quatrains with rhyming tercets and closing biblical verses ending with the unit *'areṣ* (land). The *ḥaṭa'nu* opens with an acknowledgement of God's sovereignty, and an admission that He had instructed the ruling powers in Canaan to relinquish their authority over the land:[46]

Indeed we have sinned, Lord God;
I am fully aware of Your instruction
That God had commanded my master
To give up the land.

Paraphrasing the biblical narrative, the poet castigates the pessimistic scouts:

Did not Your sons affirm, 'There is none like the Lord,
O Jeshurun, riding in the heavens,' and since God is with us,
Why do you hinder the sons of Israel
From entering the land?

In closing, the poet turns his attention to contemporary issues and observes Israel's pitiful conditions in exile, even as he prays for national restoration:

[46] Ibid. 106–8.

Remember our prayers and establish with much love
The nation set apart, now forced to rely [for protection] on a broken staff to be removed;
She cleaves to You to find delight among her brothers, and for [the tribes of] Joseph,
To rule over the land.

In the closing strophes the poet reaffirms God's dominion over the land of Israel, and urges his contemporaries not to repeat the error of the rebellious scouts and abandon hope of ever recovering the land promised to them:

The sovereign over the land is He alone,
The provider for all who live on earth

After this, know my thoughts and give witness;
Consider it with your intellect, and without malice in your hearts;

Only do not rebel against God
And do not fear the people of the land.

David b. Eliezer is the author of three *ḥaṭa'nu* hymns. *'Elohay qedem me'onah, peney le-qol teḥinnah* and *'Anšey ḥesed ba'aley tevunah* are in quatrain strophes connected by anadiplosis after classical models. R. David adheres to the conventional theme of the genre, lamenting the plight of Israel in exile, which he blames on 'the sins of the fathers and our own' (*ba-'awwon 'avoteynu we-riš'enu / hirkavta 'enoš le-ro'šenu*).[47] Resolving to repent, he pleads for divine forgiveness and in an uncommon request asks that his intellect be improved:[48]

May the Lord support mercifully,
The man filled with the knowledge of God;
May He endow him with intellect
Being gracious to His anointed.

The emphasis on the intellect is further seen in R. David's *ḥaṭa'nu*, *'Anšey ḥesed ba'aley tevunah*, relating to the Ten Martyrs, who are praised as 'men of understanding' and 'knowledgeable in the sciences' (*meviney madda'*); they are put to death by 'people of an obscure speech that you cannot understand.' In his treatment of the martyrs, the poet chooses from among the differing rabbinic sources with regard to the names of the slain and the order in which they were executed. A notable feature of the hymn is the attention given to the princess who is infatuated with Rabbi Ishmael, one of the ten, and who pleads with her father, the Emperor, to spare him. Fully eight strophes are devoted to this story, whereas Rabbi Akiva merits only one strophe and the seven martyrs who perished after him are lumped together in

[47] Ps. 65: 12 and comment of RaŠI.

[48] Weinberger, *Širey . . . Kastoria*, p. 147.

one strophe. In telling the tale of the princess's infatuation, the poet embellishes the account with conceits borrowed from Hispano-Hebrew love-poetry. Following is the plea she makes to her father:[49]

May the handsome one find favour in your eyes;
Issue an order to save him from calamity;
His radiance I desire above all other intimates;
Behold, how good and how sweet.

Delightful and lovely [is] his beauty to behold,
I desire his form and the look on his face;
His glorious splendour I lust after and will have it;
It is my meditation all day long.

R. David's *ḥaṭa'nu*, *'Etayu 'am 'el qeru'im*, is a fourteen-strophe hymn, relatively short compared to his other works in this genre. He opens with a meditation on the soul praying that it be endowed with wisdom and understanding. In line with contemporary Neoplatonism, this endowment will enable it to make the cosmic journey heavenward. He closes with an appeal for Israel's redemption, adding the hope that her travail in exile will be forgotten:[50]

May we be redeemed for eternity and may Israel forget
The earlier years and receive the good [news]
And repent, its eyes opened;
And take from the tree of life as well.

In his paraphrase of the Garden of Eden story in Gen. 3, the poet is hopeful that Israel will partake not only of the tree of knowledge ('its eyes opened') but also of the tree of life. In his focus on the intellect, R. David echoes the view of Solomon Ibn Gabirol that the soul requires both knowledge and pious deeds in order to purify itself and return to its divine source.[51]

Tokheḥah

Menaḥem b. Elia's *tokheḥah*, *Me'on 'ehyeh 'ašer 'ehyeh*, for the 'Elul vigil-nights service follows earlier Romaniote models for this genre in its reference to 'judgment and punishment in the grave'. His hymn is a metric *muwashshaḥ*, and its guide strophe closes with Job 25: 4, 'How then can a mortal be righteous before God? How can one born of a woman be pure?'—a verse commonly employed by Balkan poets in their *seliḥot*. R. Menaḥem's elaborate internal rhyme is distinctive: *aab*, *ccb*, *ddb*, *eeb*, *ffb*, *ggb*, verse / *hhi*, etc. / *bb* / etc. Below is the first strophe after the guide:[52]

49 Weinberger, *Širat . . . Rabbanim*, p. 488.
50 Weinberger, *Širey . . . Kastoria*, p. 156.
51 Sirat, *History of Jewish Philosophy*, p. 72.
52 Weinberger, *Širey . . . Kastoria*, pp. 84–5.

Be-vo' ʿitto / be-yom moto / we-'az yašuv le-'admato;
Ne-wat beyto / we-ḥelqato; / we-'im yarbeh kevod beyto
Ke-ven zolel / u-mistolel, / tehi ruḥo we-nišmato
Re'ot ṣuro / be-ʿet šivro / we-'af ki 'aḥarey moto;
We-'eykh yarum / 'ašer yarum / be-toleʿah we-yiv'ašah,
We-'aḥrito / ʿamidato / peney melekh melo' bušah . . .

Comes his time / on the day of his death / he returns to his earth,
His mistress / and his portion; / and if he increases the wealth of his house
Like a glutton / and exploiter, / then will his spirited soul
See [God] his Rock / when disaster comes / and later when he dies;
Why then be proud / he, the maggot infested and odious
When he is destined / to stand / before the King fully disgraced! . . .

Baqqašah

Menaḥem b. Elia's most ambitious work is his epic *baqqašah* for the 'Elul vigil nights named in the superscription, *Širey Ha-Yad Ha-Ḥazaqah* and *Malki'el.* The hymn begins with selections from Pss. 100, 118 and 119 and from Judg. 5 and 3, and continues with a personal plea to the deity in rhymed prose. The cantor-poet, though unworthy, is hopeful that his prayers will be accepted:[53]

Who am I and who is my father's family? My family is the youngest in Israel and I am the youngest in my tribe, with little education . . . How is it possible that this lowly servant . . . could stand and speak before the Lord, King of kings, high and exalted? . . . I am best advised to be silent . . . I, a wretched beggar and vagrant. Do I have the ability to petition and seek the welfare [of my congregation]?

In the following section the poet shares his doubts with the congregation regarding his credentials as their emissary:

As I turned the matter over in my mind I found myself on the horns of a dilemma: should I speak or remain silent? Yet a mass of ideas welled up inside me, more precious than gold . . . The spirit of the Lord now began to pulsate within me, endowing me with understanding and wisdom unforgettable . . . [The spirit] aroused me as if I had awakened from sleep and it spoke, 'Take your position [at the reading lectern]. Why do you hesitate to approach the King? Be strong and bold. Fear not . . . Call upon the Lord your God with integrity of heart, with pure thoughts and clean hands . . .

When these words came to me, I reconsidered and said, 'Come what may, one is to be commended for good sense; I will sing to my Beloved . . . with the little talent that has been given me. Perhaps He will make His face to shine upon me and be gracious to me . . . and from His great abundance He will bring splendour to my intellect [*yevareq sikhli*].'

[53] Oxford, *Maḥazor Kastoria*, Opp. Add. MS 4to, 80 (No. 1168), fos. 108–10.

The first section of the *baqqašah* ends with another selection of verses from Scripture and leads to the *tour de force* hymn *Malki mi-qedem*, in fourteen strophes comprising five cola in monorhyme with five units in each hemicolon. Repeating each unit fifty times, the poet spells his name and that of his father, imitating the practice of Solomon Ibn Gabirol in his *silluq*, *'A'amir, 'a'dir, 'afuddat 'aguddat 'oratekha*, and the *Baqqašat ha-Memim* of the Provençal poet Yedayah Ha-Penini. In the later Ottoman period, Elia Ha-Levi b. Benjamin of Constantinople would attempt to equal R. Menaḥem's achievement with his own impressive *baqqašah*, *Bet Ha-Lewi*. Below is the first strophe from R. Menaḥem's hymn:[54]

Malki mi-qedem mehullal mi-kol ma'asekha,
Mi-šamayim mi-mezarim mi-mazzalot mi-maḥanot mešortekha;
Me-'araṣot: mi-mizraḥ mi-teyman mi-ṣafon mi-yammekha;
Meraḥami moši'i meqimi me-'afar marglotekha;
Meromemi mi-ša'arey mawet mi-mišlaḥat mal'akhekha;
Malleṭeni mi-ṣaray me-'oyevay mo'asey miṣwotekha;
Mešeni mi-mayim mi-kaf me'awweley maqdišekha;
Mi-ma'arakhtam maṭṭim maher mis'adam mi-mattenotekha;
Mesan'ay meḥaṣ motneyhem meḥem mi-sifrekha;
Mitqomemay, mehorsay malle' miš'alotam me-'alatekha.

My King eternal, praised in all Your deeds
From the heavens, the stars, the constellations and Your servant hosts;
From the lands to the east, the south, the north and the west;
He shows me mercy and helps me; He lifts your feet from the dust;
He raises me up from the gates of death with its contingent of angels [of death];
He saves me from my foes, the enemies who despise Your commands;
He draws me up from the abyss, from the hands of sinners who deal wickedly with those who sanctify Your name;
Hasten now Your gracious aid to those who are urged to defect from your company;
Crush the loins of my enemies, erase them from Your book;
Those who rise up against me with destructive designs, requite their requests with Your curses.

Closing the *baqqašah* is a personal confession in rhymed prose revealing the poet's struggle within himself, with which his congregation could presumably identify:[55]

[54] Weinberger, *Širey . . . Kastoria*, pp. 67–70.

[55] Oxford, *Maḥazor Kastoria*, fos. 114 ff.

I am deeply distressed and greatly perplexed; I know not the way that will bring respite and relief to my soul . . . given the two choices that have been with me since my birth . . . They are like a woman and her rival. If I please one I anger the other . . . One leads me with sure integrity on just paths; the other to trackless wastes, darkness and chaos . . . I am stretched out between two poles . . .

The poet asks for divine aid to help him make the wise choice so that his congregation will not be disgraced. Now persuaded of divine guidance, he seeks to know how he can best represent his people. In his appeal for forgiveness, the poet confesses his sins in an alphabetic paraphrase of the earlier confessional litany from the time of the *ge'onim*:[56]

I have sinned before You; I have walked the way of falsehood; I have said, 'None will see me'; I have trampled upon Your commands; I have dealt falsely with Your ordinances; I have despised Your laws; I have stolen from brothers and strangers . . . I have belittled the elders . . . I have coveted wealth and have done violence to my soul; I have been a sycophant; I no longer take pleasure in Your Torah; I have been a hypocrite . . . I have been jealous and have borne a grudge against members of my people; I have been greedy and have not given charity as required . . . I have judged unfairly, forgetting Your judgments . . .

Adding to the alphabetic acrostic litany in the *Seder Rav Amram Ga'on*, which lists twenty-two sins for each of the letters, R. Menaḥem counts two sins for each letter, bringing the total to forty-four. Unlike the *baqqašot* of Sa'adyah Ga'on and Solomon Ibn Gabirol, Balkan poets like Menaḥem b. Elia and Solomon Šarvit Ha-Zahav included the confessional litany in hymns of this genre.

Following the confession, the poet blames his 'impulse' (*yeṣer*) for his failings and employs Adam's language (in Gen. 3: 12) in his attempt at self-justification:[57]

My King and my God . . . I have been a sinner from my youth because of the impulse in my heart [*yeṣer libbi*] stirring within me . . . accursed, evil and cunning, 'The woman [i.e. the impulse] whom You gave to be with me, she gave me the fruit from the tree and I ate.' And now, O Lord God, if You will punish me for the sin of this woman [*'im tifqod 'alay 'awon ha-'iššah ha-zo't*] . . . and bring me to judgment and repay me according to my deeds . . . there will be nothing left of me to stand before You.

In his plea for divine mercy, the poet refers to the disability of living in exile and in bondage. A similar argument was used by Šarvit Ha-Zahav, comparing Israel's current exile with its earlier bondage in Egypt:[58]

I have tried to walk before You upright in Your path these many years, but what can I do since I am sold as a slave? I, Your servant, the son of an Israelite, am in bondage to an Egyptian residing here. He is rebellious and cruel and thinks of me as a stranger. He despises and tortures me and puts me to work at hard labour. He allows me no

[56] Oxford, *Maḥazor Kastoria*, fos. 118b–119. [57] Ibid., fo. 119b. [58] Ibid., fo. 120b.

respite, neither does he permit me to return to the land of my fathers to do Your will and Your service . . . Evening and morning he plots against me . . . and lurks in order to dissuade me from serving You . . .

The last section of the *baqqašah* is prefaced by a superscription, 'The following is a prayer for Jerusalem to be recited if there is time before sunrise.' In developing his theme the poet contrasts the history of the city, once full of people and great among the nations, with its present desolation and despair, and prays for its restoration.

'Aqedah

Mordecai b. Šabbetai's *'aqedah*, [*Boker*] *mefalleti 'eli*, is in rhyming tercets with closing scriptural verse. Each strophe begins and ends with the unit *boker* (morning). This hymn, which was included in the Franco-German vigil-nights *seliḥot*, was favoured with a commentary by Abraham b. Azriel in his *'Arugat Ha-Bosem*. The poet focuses on the eagerness of Abraham to do God's bidding to slay his son Isaac:[59]

In the morning [Abraham] acknowledged Your sovereignty, obeyed
  Your command and showed his love;
With all his heart he rejoiced to do Your will;
Love upsets the natural order and driven by his happiness,
  Abraham arose early in the morning.

The rabbis (in *Gen. Rabbah* 55. 8) comment on the phrase 'And Abraham arose early in the morning and saddled his ass': 'Love upsets the natural order . . . surely he had plenty of servants [to saddle his ass].' In a later strophe R. Mordecai underlines Abraham's determination to obey God's command by noting that 'he took the knife and *did not care that a man* [*would die*]' (*we-lo' ḥašav 'adam*). On this, Abraham b. Azriel in *Sefer 'Arugat Ha-Bosem* comments, 'The spilling of Isaac's blood mattered less to him than his love of God.' Given the martyrdom of Rhineland Jews during the Crusades it is understandable why R. Mordecai's *'aqedah* would be adopted for use in the Franco-German synagogue ritual.

Taḥanun

Mordecai b. Šabbetai's pseudo-*muwashshaḥ taḥanun*, *Mi-beyt ṣevi 'armonah*, imagines Israel as the homeless 'dove', lost and friendless:[60]

From her elegant palace, her pleasant dwelling-place,
The dove has been driven; now she sits lonely far from her home;
Instead of delighting in the shade of her royal chamber,

[59] Abraham b. Azriel, *'Arugat Ha-Bosem*, iii. 571; Weinberger, *Širey . . . Kastoria*, pp. 33–4.
[60] Ibid. 61–3.

She is like a vagrant hut removed from house and home;
She strays from her land; in the forest she wearies;
And the dove found no place to set its foot.

The last colon, recontextualized from Gen. 8: 9, became a commonplace scriptural close for European poets—beginning with the Hispanics—who were attracted to the imagery of Israel as the exiled 'dove'. Unlike his *seliḥah*, *'Ahuvah 'ašer 'orasah'*, which ends without divine reassurance, R. Mordecai ends the *taḥanun* with the conventional words of comfort from God:

O dove, entrapped, imprisoned and confined
Upon cliffs and and rock-strewn wastes, you are sick unto death;
I will summon the force to search you out [and take you] from there,
And I will raise you up with timbrels and song and will betroth you as my wife;
Upon your head will be a crown and I will bind your turban.
[He shall bring out] the top stone amid shouts of 'Grace, grace to it.'

Mordecai b. Šabbetai's other *taḥanun*, *Meromim 'essa' 'eynay*, is a pseudo-*muwashshaḥ* with internal rhyme and and an uncommon (for this genre) synthetic parallelism in which the second colon (or several consecutive cola) supplements or completes the first, as in the following:[61]

I lift my eyes and entreat the Lord:
Remember the patriarch's covenant and hear the cry of the multitude . . .
See my wretchedness and weeping, and forgive my trespass and guilt;
Have no regard for my stubbornness, You, my King and Father;
Bring me up from my captivity, bind my wound and hurt . . .
The Mighty who humbles the haughty and raises the poor from the dust;
Erect the Temple on earth and the altar and vestibule,
And forgive our sins this day and bring us up from the gates of hell [exile] . . .

David b. Eliezer is the author of two *taḥanunim* for the vigil nights, *'Et mey yešu'ah* and *Diršì newat beyti*. Both are in the form of a pseudo-*muwashshaḥ* and the latter is built in Hispanic *ha-šalem* metre. In *Diršì newat beyti*, the poet singles out the role of the angels through whom the prayers of Israel are transmitted:[62]

[61] Weinberger, *Širey . . . Kastoria*, pp. 37–8. [62] Ibid. 143.

May He inscribe in mercy for a memorial in His book,
And be adorned with the sweet [songs] woven into His crown
By the angels standing round the chariot of the King.

In this conceit the poet adapts the rabbinic statement (in *Exod. Rabbah* 21. 4), 'The angel appointed over prayers collects all the prayers that have been offered in all the synagogues, weaves them into garlands and places them upon the head of God.' R. David is consistent in his appeal to angelic intermediaries, which he reaffirms in his *rahiṭ*, *Ḥayyim deraštikha mi-ṣarah*, where the angel's role is to banish the sins of Israel from God's presence:[63]

Would that I may hear, 'Away, do not touch my sins,'
The angel warning them [the accusers] in my hearing,
And in God's presence in the land of the living.

In the practice of appealing to intermediaries in Israel's behalf, R. David follows an earlier habit of Balkan and Franco-German poets, to the dismay of rabbinic authorities like Maimonides, who frowned upon such hymns. In line with the latter's concern R. Menaḥem b. Elia, in his *baqqašah* in rhymed prose, *Malki we-'lohay*, emphatically rejects this practice:[64]

Why should I appeal to the holy ones standing concealed before You to intercede for me? Are You not the Lord, God of all flesh, and is there anything hidden from You? You are acquainted with all my ways. You discern my thoughts from afar. Even before a word is on my tongue, O Lord, You know it completely.

GENERAL BACKGROUND: CORFU, KAFFA (CRIMEA) AND CRETE

Corfu, the second largest of the Greek islands in the Ionian group, was sparsely settled in the late twelfth century. Benjamin of Tudela, travelling through the Balkans from 1160 to 1173, found only one Jew on the island, Rabbi Joseph. When Corfu was conquered in 1214 by Michael I (Angelos), ruler of Epirus, the Jewish population increased. Presumably this was the result of a favourable policy towards the Jewish minority. The new arrivals, attracted by news of the policy change, came from the Greek mainland, which at that time suffered from political and military unrest. In 1267, when Corfu came under the control of the Kingdom of Naples, its Angevin monarchs found a sizeable Jewish settlement on the island.

Although the government published periodic orders to defend them from hostile mobs, Corfiote Jewry were disadvantaged by having to provide lodgings for soldiers acting as public executioners. In 1386 Corfu was conquered by Venice, which in 1406 restricted the Jews from acquiring land and forced

[63] Ibid. 130. [64] Ibid. 7, bottom.

them to wear a distinguishing badge. Added to this was the imposition of huge taxes which the Jews were forced to pay the Venetians in support of their wars against the Ottoman Turks. Like the Jews in mainland Greece, the Corfiotes used the Romaniote synagogue ritual, with slight variations in the order of service and the choice of hymns. It is likely that the hymns preserved solely in the manuscript editions of the Corfiote prayer-book—a *Maḥazor Corfu* was never published—were composed by natives of the island.

THE PRINCIPAL CORFIOTE POETS

Samuel Memeli and Abraham Marino

The earliest Corfiote writing for the liturgy comes from the twelfth- to thirteenth-century poets Samuel Ha-Kohen b. Memeli and Abraham Kohen b. Marino. Their hymns are preserved primarily in the *Maḥazor Corfu*. The former is the author of a *yoṣer*, *'Ayummah tamid mevorakha*, for Simḥat Torah complete with a *silluq*, *'ofan* and *zulat*. The latter composed two hymns for the Sabbath before Purim (Šabbat Zakhor) embellishing the *nišmat kol ḥay* prayer. The first belongs to the *'illu finu* genre, in which the poet inserts a hymn before the verse, 'Were our mouths filled with song as the sea [is with water]' in the *nišmat* prayer. The second of R. Abraham's Šabbat Zakhor hymns is of the *kol 'aṣmotay* genre based on Hispanic models, notably Judah Ha-Levi's *Kal 'aṣmotay . . . yiṣri wi-yṣuray mi-makh hayu* and Abraham Ibn Ezra's, *Kal 'aṣmotay . . . 'efes biltekha be-'et ṣarah.*

The Later Corfiotes

Corfiote poets in the fifteenth century continued to compose for the *nišmat*. A *rešut* for the *nišmat*, *Me-'eyn sof ḥuṣṣavah*, by Menaḥem b. Šabbetai Ha-Kohen is distinctive in its imagery. The hymn, built in four quatrains with rhyming tercets and closing monorhyme scriptural verses, reflects the poet's interest in the Gerona school of Jewish mysticism. Abraham b. Gabriel Zafrano, returning to earlier genres, is the author of hymns in the *yoṣer* cycle, a *taḥanun* and an epithalamium. With Moses Kohen of Corfu, a new era begins in the hymnography of the Stato del Mar—the name given to the Greek islands and the surrounding coastlands. R. Moses is the author of two *seliḥot* for the Ten Days of Repentance and an elegant *terzina* for Šabbat Zakhor. This first attempt at a *terzina* in syllabic metre by a Balkan poet represents a watershed in the hymnography of the region.

The *Maḥazor Corfu* preserves one hymn by the sixteenth-century poet Abraham b. Elijah de Mordo. The de Mordos, a prominent Jewish family in Corfu, aided the Venetian forces in defending the island against the Ottoman invaders in 1537 and 1716, and distinguished themselves by their bravery. R.

Abraham's *'Anna' ṣuri barekh*, a *rešut* for the *nišmat* on the Sabbath of the Intermediate Days of Tabernacles, bears the name 'Abraham bar Elijah' in the acrostic. In the *rešut*, the poet also adds his family name, 'de Mordo.'[65]

A contemporary of Abraham de Mordo, Elijah b. Mazal Ṭov, is the author of a *ge'ullah* and two *petiḥot* preserved in the *Maḥazor Corfu*. R. Elijah served as both physician and rabbi in Corfu. His hymns are headed by a dedication in the superscription, 'to the memory of our teacher and rabbi the renowned physician, Eliezer de Mordo, may he rest in Eden.' The honoree, a member of the Corfiote de Mordo family, was presumably the poet's patron, as well as his teacher.[66]

THE PRINCIPAL CORFIOTE GENRES

Yoṣer

Samuel Memeli's *guf ha-yoṣer*, *'Ayummah tamid mevorakha*, for Simḥat Torah is in rhyming quatrains with closing scriptural verse, in the Hispanic manner. However, the hymn is without a *qadoš* refrain and holds a consistent word metre of three units to a colon, following the widely imitated neo-classical revival by Solomon Ha-Bavli. Imitating the latter and his model, Eleazar Qillir, the Corfiote R. Samuel favours phonetic-intensive mannerisms in the form of allusions, neologisms and elliptic syntax. Memeli also attempts to revive the Qilliric two-root-consonant rhyme, as in the following, based on Num. 25: 11 ff.:[67]

Ḥaš massat me'ereykha,
Ḥillaqto khevod me'orekha;
Ḥeleq be-'iššey 'ureykha,
U-l-lewi ʿamar: tummekha we-'ureykha

[Because Phinehas] hastened to avert the curse arising from temptation,
[God] awarded him the honour of the [High Priest who wears the] Urim [breastplate];
[In addition] he received a portion of the altar offerings,
And of Levi he said: Let your Tummim and Urim [be with your faithful one, Deut. 33:8].

The closing verses in the strophes are from Deut. 33: 1–25 and the theme of the hymn is focused on the final blessings of Moses for the Israelite tribes, based on rabbinic comments in *Sifre*. Below is the opening strophe:[68]

[65] Roth, *Venice*, p. 323; Bernstein, *Piyyuṭim*, No. 43, pp. 83–4; New York, *Maḥazor Corfu*, MS No. 4588, fo. 56.

[66] See Zunz, *Literaturgeschichte*, p. 531.

[67] Weinberger, *Širat . . . Rabbanim*, p. 1.

[68] Ibid. 1–2; Fleischer, *Piyyuṭey . . . Ha-Bavli*, pp. 191–203.

The formidable [*'ayummah*, Israel, Cant. 6: 4], ever praising
The name of God in prayer;
Treasures of goodness are stored [for her]
And this is the blessing [with which Moses . . . bade the Israelites farewell before he died].

Silluq

Samuel Memeli's *silluq*, *'Eyn ka-'el šaliṭ gozer gezerah*, built in monorhyme couplet strophes introduced by scriptural verses from Deut. 33: 26–9—a continuation of the verse sequence from the *guf ha-yoṣer*—is identical in form to Solomon Ha-Bavli's *silluq*, *Ṣe'enah u-r'enah, maskil šir yedidim*. As indicated above, Ha-Bavli's *silluq* also continues the verse sequence begun in the *guf ha-yoṣer*, and it is likely that the Corfiote poet consciously sought to pattern his hymn after the earlier model from nearby Italy. Following is a selection from Memeli's *silluq*:[69]

'There is no one like the Lord,'
He issues rules and decrees;
Who, like the Lord, punishes those who violate them?

'O Upright One' [*yešurun*];
He assembled a nation apart and special;
Beloved and wise, fair as the sun and bright.

'Ofan

Samuel Memeli's *'ofan*, *Kevodo šikken be-tokh 'am mešallešim*, built in monorhyme couplet strophes introduced by individual units from Deut. 33: 29, comprises twenty strophes. Here the Corfiote poet departs from the model of Ha-Bavli's five-strophe *'ofan*, *Ro'šo ketem paz*, in rhyming octets. The reason for the variation is that Ha-Bavli had five verses left in Cant. 5 from his *guf ha-yoṣer* and *silluq* and therefore built a strophe around each verse, whereas R. Samuel had only the last verse, Deut. 33: 29, in reserve and therefore chose to build his couplet strophes around each unit in that verse:[70]

'Happy are you' [Moses], a faithfully stable tutor to the holy,
Abundantly helpful and wise in the laws of purity.

'Israel', a unique nation sanctified among the holy,
Seeking [the Beloved of] rounded gold set with jewels [Cant. 5: 14].

[69] Weinberger, *Širat . . . Rabbanim*, pp. 5–6; Fleischer, *Piyyuṭey . . . Ha-Bavli*, pp. 204–10.
[70] Weinberger, *Širat . . . Rabbanim*, pp. 6–7; Fleischer, *Piyyuṭey . . . Ha-Bavli*, pp. 210–13.

Zulat

Samuel Memeli's *zulat*, *'Uyyam ne'eman we-nikh'av*, is formed in word metre with three units to a colon. Its rhyming tercets with ending verses from Deut. 34 is again closely modelled after Ha-Bavli's *zulat*, *'Ahevukha nefeš le-hadekh*. The Corfiote poet even adds a one-strophe coda to his *zulat*, similar to Ha-Bavli's three-strophe *piyyuṭ siyyum* (concluding hymn), *'Al harey besamim sov*. Following is a selection from Memeli's *zulat*:[71]

Terrified and pained was the faithful [Moses]
At the decree of the Master and Father,
And Moses went up from the plains of Moab.

The border of Menasseh was concealed
Mocking him was Ephraim's gallop,
Even all of Naftali.

Like Ha-Bavli, Memeli connects by anadiplosis the closing strophe of the *zulat* which ends with the verse, 'And for all the mighty deeds' (Deut. 34: 12), with his *piyyuṭ siyyum* (concluding hymn) as follows:

The mighty deeds send forth; make wondrous Your awesome redemption,
Draw near with Your love those awaiting Your glory
That all may know the power of Your strength;
There is no one like You among Your creatures;
Garbed in majesty, fearful in might,
Strengthen Your prophets looking for Your help.[72]

Abraham Zafrano's *zulat*, *Be-noteno torah qedoši*, for the Sabbath before Pentecost, is constructed in rhyming tercets with closing scriptural verse. His hymn is modelled after Abraham Ibn Ezra's *zulat* in tercets, *'Az be-'ereṣ miṣrayim bekhori kinnitikha*. Zafrano's theme is an account of Israel's preparations to receive the Torah, based on Exod. 19 and its rabbinic interpretation:[73]

When He gave the Torah holy
To a threefold nation
On the third month . . .

[71] Weinberger, *Širat . . . Rabbanim*, pp. 8–9; Fleischer, *Piyyuṭey . . . Ha-Bavli*, pp. 213–20.

[72] Fleischer in his *Piyyuṭey . . . Ha-Bavli*, pp. 378–9, lists 14 European hymnists who composed their *yoṣerot* for Passover on the model of Ha-Bavli's *'Or yeša' me'uššarim*. To these should be added Samuel Ha-Kohen b. Memeli's *yošer*, *'Ayummah tamid mevorakhah*, for Simḥat Torah.

[73] Weinberger, *Širat . . . Rabbanim*, pp. 454–5; A. Ibn Ezra, *Širey Ha-Qodeš*, ii. 403–4.

He overturned the mountain upon them like an [inverted] cask,
Even upon the nation He chose;
They took their stand at the foot of the mountain.

The 'threefold nation' is Israel, after Eccles. 4: 12 and the rabbinic comment (in *mQid* 1. 10), ' "And a threefold cord is not quickly broken"; but he who is not versed in Scripture and in Mišnah and in good conduct is of no benefit to the public weal.' The opening colon in the second strophe is taken from *bŠab* 88a, ' "And they stood under the mount" [Exod. 19: 17] . . . this teaches that the Holy one, blessed be He, overturned the mountain upon them . . . and said to them, "If you accept the Torah, it is well; if no, there shall be your burial." '

Another *zulat* by Zafrano, *'El bara' 'olamim be-yah*, for Šabbat Ḥatanim is also composed in rhyming tercets with closing scriptural verses. The hymn features a dialogue between God the bridegroom and Israel, His bride. The poet's sources are Canticles and the dialogue *yoṣer*, *'Adon mi-qedem tamim po'olo*, by an earlier Balkan poet, Šabbetai b. Mordecai. It appears that Zafrano lifted several strophes verbatim from R. Šabbetai's hymn and passed them off as his own.[74]

Mi Kamokha

Abraham Zafrano is the author of two *mi kamokha* hymns, *'Addir nora' we-'ayom*, for the Sabbath of the intermediate days of Tabernacles, and *'Emunim simḥu we-gilu*, for Simḥat Torah. Both hymns are built in quatrains with rhyming tercets, closing scriptural verses and repeated unit endings. In his *'Addir nora'* he follows the Hispanic conventions of the genre with an opening cosmic preface and continues with speculation on the 'end of the days' and the epic struggle against 'Gog of the land of Magog':[75]

[God], mighty, dreadful and fearsome,
Hasten to bring near the appointed day,
When at the given time
Gog will come upon the land of Israel . . .

At that time in the days to come
Seventy nations will join him
To wage war in the land of Ramim,
While Israel my people dwell secure . . .

Gog and all his troops will fall,
Their carcasses devoured by birds of prey and wild animals,
Because they have profaned My name
Among the children of Israel.

[74] Weinberger, *Širat . . . Rabbanim*, pp. 463–5, and nn. to ll. 8–25. On this widespread practice, see Abramson, *Be-Lašon Qodemim*, pp. 31–53.
[75] Weinberger, *Širat . . . Rabbanim*, pp. 457–8.

The 'land of Ramim', which sounds like Rome, may be a metaphor for Byzantium, the eastern Roman Empire, and the 'war' refers to its capture by the Ottomans in 1453 during Zafrano's lifetime. The poet, like others, including Isaac Abrabanel and Moses b. Joseph di Trani, saw messianic implications in the struggle between Christian Byzantium and the Ottoman Turks. Added to this was the prevailing view (enunciated by R. David Kimḥi in his commentary to Ezek. 38: 8) that Gog is to be identified with the Persians of antiquity, who, according to the observation of Abrabanel, may be 'the [Ottoman] Turks of today.'[76]

Zafrano's *'Emunim simḥu we-gilu* is a large, seventy-cola *mi kamokha* with the standard cosmic preface punctuated by terms from the writings of Jewish Aristotelians and Neoplatonists. The uncommon feature in the hymn is the strophes' third colon, which begins with the opening verse from the weekly Torah reading in the annual cycle. In order to accommodate all the readings, the poet combines several in one strophe. Closing the hymn is the dialogue between God and Moses just before the latter's death.[77]

O ye faithful, rejoice and be glad with God's Torah
And have faith in the renewal of His world, O lily among thorns;
In the beginning when God created the heavens and the earth—

He made two inclinations—the Lord, mighty in strength—
To be with man for reward and punishment in the afterlife;
These are the descendants of Noah
[Who were commanded:] Be fruitful and multiply and abound on the earth.

The first principle [*ro'š ha-ʿiqqarim*] is to believe in the existence [*meṣi'ut*] of God;
The decrees of the Lord are sure—
Now the Lord said to Abram, 'Go from your country that is debauched
To the land . . . '

When the humble [Moses] saw that God's decree was firm,
He asked the Torah to seek God's mercy;
Perchance on her account Yekutiel [Moses] would be allowed to live
And see the land.

The dialogue, based in part on rabbinic sources (in *Deut. Rabbah* 11. 9), begins with God's response to Moses' request:

[76] See Abrabanel, *Yešuʿot Mešiḥo*, p. 35a; Silver, *Messianic Speculation*, pp. 112–13.
[77] Weinberger, *Širat . . . Rabbanim*, pp. 459–63.

[GOD:]
'O more beloved than Adam, I have sentenced to death all men;
Who can live and never see death? Who can escape the power that leads to Sheol?
How abundant is the goodness that I have laid up for you, O meekest of men!
I will make you ride on the heights of the earth.' . . .

[MOSES:]
'Do not hand me over to Samael
Like all who inhabit the world and live on earth.'

[GOD:]
'Why should you be preferred above others, Yekutiel,
That you are unwilling to deliver your soul to Samael
Into whose hands are given the lives of all creatures—by the will of God—
In the four corners of the earth?'

[MOSES:]
'I am not like the others;
For forty days I survived without food or drink [Exod. 34: 28],
They cannot survive even six days [Exod. 16: 5]
Without eating the crops of the land.'

Moses succeeds in persuading God not to force him to present himself to Samael, the Angel of Death:

[GOD:]
'Do not fear,
Because your soul is innocent and pure
And your body is perfect, clean and clear like a precious stone,
[Like] gold in the land,

Therefore, I will not deliver you to Samael;
Rather will I, Myself in person, invite her [your soul],
And peaceful angels will accompany you and I will prepare your grave;
This is witnessed by the ends of the earth.'

The dialogue ends with Moses' reaction to the good news:

At that moment the meek [Moses] rejoiced even as he purified himself like God's *serafim*;
He placed his two hands upon his breast as the angels of the Lord laid out his bier;

He [God] then summoned his soul, 'My daughter go forth and
indulge yourself in the Lord's Eden,
I am the Lord your God who raises you up from the earth.'

Ge'ullah

Elijah b. Mazal Ṭov's *ge'ullah* for the Ninth of 'Av, *'Aḥalay yikkonu ha-yom*, is a pseudo-*muwashshaḥ* in strophes comprising a couplet, a tercet and a refrain with an uncommon rhyming pattern: *aa*, *bbb*, *b* // *cc*, *ddd* / *b* / *ee*, *fff* / *b* / etc. The poet hints that his hymn is designed for the Ninth of 'Av service in the following tercet:

[Israel's] contempt for His power flared up
On the night when they complained;
Then He showed His anger.[78]

The tercet is based on Num. 14: 1 and the rabbinic comment (in *bSan* 104b), ' "And . . . the people wept that night." It was the Ninth of 'Av and the Almighty said to Israel, "You have wept without cause: therefore will I appoint a weeping to you for future generations." ' The indication that the hymn is a *ge'ullah* is seen at the end of each colon, which closes with the unit *go'el* (redeemer).

Rešut

A *rešut* for the *nišmat*, *Me-'eyn sof ḥuṣṣavah*, by Menaḥem b. Šabbetai Ha-Kohen, is built in four quatrains with rhyming tercets and closing monorhyme scriptural verses. The poet makes distinctive use of conceits from the Gerona school of Jewish mysticism:[79]

From the *'Eyn-sof* [No end] it is hewn [*ḥuṣṣavah*]
My soul, and it comes into being;
The Eternal has blessed it
He is concealed, exalted and fearful.

In the opening strophe the poet connects the theme of the *nišmat kol ḥay* (Every living soul) prayer with an observation on the origin of the soul. In so doing, R. Menaḥem employs terms from the *Sefer Yeṣirah* and from the writings of Rabbi Azriel of Gerona. The term *ḥuṣṣavah* (hewn) is from the *Sefer Yeṣirah* 1. 10–12, where God is portrayed as the stonemason hewing His creation from the building blocks of the twenty-two letters of the Hebrew alphabet. Among the items created are the souls, which in the opinion of the poet are hewn from the *'Eyn-sof*. This term originated with R. Azriel of

[78] New York, *Maḥazor Corfu*, MS No. 4588, fo. 4a.
[79] Weinberger, *Širat . . . Rabbanim*, p. 448.

Gerona, who was the first to employ it as an abstract concept and as the source from which the ten *sefirot* radiate. In his hymn, R. Menaḥem retains the imagery of the *Sefer Yeṣirah* in which God is actively involved in the creative process, and combines it with the newer speculation of the Gerona mystic. In the remaining three strophes, R. Menaḥem treats the central theme of Pentecost, the giving of the Torah at Sinai.[80]

Abraham de Mordo's *ʾAnnaʾ ṣuri barekh* is a *rešut* to the *nišmat* in the Sabbath morning service of the Intermediate Days of Tabernacles. In his prayer for national restoration, the poet recalls the legend (in *bḤag* 12a) of the primeval light which God preserved for the righteous. This light is to emanate from Jerusalem's rebuilt Temple and radiate throughout the world. Corfiote Jewry's special attachment to Jerusalem is seen in the *mi kamokha* hymn for Šabbat Šeqalim by the Ottoman poet Judah Qilti. His hymn *Mi kamokha ʾel ʾelohey ha-ṣevaʾot* was preserved in the *Maḥazor Romania*, in use in mainland Greece, and in the *Maḥazor Corfu*. In one of the strophes R. Judah notes that we are no longer obligated to pay the half-shekel for the maintenance of the Temple, which is now in ruins. However, the editor of the *Maḥazor Corfu* substitutes another strophe: 'In some localities, there are Jews who treasure this command [of the half-shekel] despite their being in exile. On this Sabbath they remember to pledge joyfully a gift to be brought to Jerusalem, in lieu of the redeeming shekel [Exod. 30: 12 ff.].'[81]

ʾIllu Finu and *Kal ʿAṣmotay*

Abraham Kohen b. Marino wrote two hymns for the Sabbath before Purim (Šabbat Zakhor), embellishing the *nišmat kol ḥay* prayer. The first belongs to the *ʾillu finu* genre, in which the poet inserts a hymn before the verse 'Were our mouths filled with song as the sea [is with water]' in the *nišmat* prayer. Presumably, R. Abraham was familiar with the hymn in this genre by the French synagogue poet Yehosifya the Proselyte (*c.*1200), built in the form of a metric *muwashshaḥ* with an opening paraphrase from the *nišmat*, *We-ʾillu širah ka-yam / ʾeyn dey ḥay we-qayyam* (Were [our mouths filled] with song as the sea, it would not suffice [to thank] the living and eternal [God]). R. Yehosifya's hymn continues with rhyming tercets and couplet guides. Abraham Marino's pseudo-*muwashshaḥ* hymn is also headed by a paraphrase from *nišmat*, *We-ʾillu finu ka-yam / ka-neharot we-dokhyam* (Were our mouths [filled with song] like the sea, / like the roaring rivers). The latter's paraphrase is followed by rhyming tercets and a closing 'guide' rhyming with the header, as follows:[82]

[80] See Scholem, *Ha-Qabbalah*, p. 149; Azriel of Gerona, 'Explanation of the Ten *Sefirot*', No. 2, p. 90.

[81] See Bernstein, *Piyyutim*, No. 43, pp. 83–4; Weinberger, *Širat . . . Rabbanim*, pp. 414–16.

[82] Weinberger, *Reʾšit Ha-Payṭanut*, pp. 187–8; Yehosifya's hymn is preserved in the *Mahazor Witry*, Poetic Supplement, No. 95, pp. 55–6.

The Valiant [Lord] with vast power
Worked wonders for the nation He possessed,
And to relate His deeds
  The rivers raised a roar [*yis'u neharot dokhyam*] . . .

Anguish turned to joy
Sighing to relief,
And Mordecai at ease
  Established the days of Purim [*yemey purim qiyyam*].

The second of R. Abraham's Šabbat Zakhor hymns is of the *kal 'aṣmotay* genre based on Hispanic models, notably Judah Ha-Levi's *Kal 'aṣmotay . . . yiṣri wi-yṣuray mi-makh hayu* and Abraham Ibn Ezra's *Kal 'aṣmotay . . . 'efes biltekha be-'et ṣarah*. R. Abraham's *kal 'aṣmotay*, like theirs, opens with the verse from Ps. 35: 10, 'All my bones shall say, "O Lord, who is like You?" ' He then builds the hymn in the form of a pseudo-*muwashshaḥ* with a rhyming quatrain guide and a colon refrain, 'O Lord who is like You?' repeated at the end of the tercet strophes and the colon 'guide'.[83]

Father, O Father, I call unto You,
Strong shield and cover;
Yours is the power and might;
Sovereignty becomes You
O Lord, who is like You?

  In the third year of the King [Ahasuerus]
  He invited every noble and vagabond
  To eat at the king's table;
Even Vashti the queen [made a feast]-
O Lord, who is like You?

  My sin was great
  I was called to the gathering
  And added thereby to the offence
And what resulted from it;
O Lord, who is like You?

Here the poet follows the opinion of the rabbis (in *bMeg* 12a), as expressed in other Purim hymns, and attributes the rise of Haman to the sin committed by the Jews of Susa in eating forbidden food at the king's table. In this interpretation of history, the cantor-poets echo the traditional theodicy, which holds that every crisis that comes upon Israel is attributable to her lack of response to the Lord's commands.

[83] Weinberger, *Re'šit Ha-Payṭanut*, pp. 185–6; Ha-Levi, *Širey Ha-Qodeš*, pp. 331–2; A. Ibn Ezra, *Širey Ha-Qodeš*, i. 144–6.

Petiḥah

Elijah b. Mazal Ṭov's *petiḥah* to the *qaddiš*, *Mah rabbu nifle'otekha*, was chanted on the morning service of the seventh day of Passover. The pithy six-strophe hymn in the form of a pseudo-*muwashshaḥ* reveals its intention as an introduction to the *qaddiš* in its closing strophe:

> O awesome One, may Your name soon be sanctified [*yitqaddaš šimkha*]
> When You gather the stray sheep into Jerusalem's Temple.[84]

Among the poet's references is a paraphrase of the 'Reply' to the 'Four Questions' in the Passover *Haggadah*, as seen in following couplet from the hymn:

> We were slandered by evil men, even the traitorous sons of Noph [Egypt];
> We would have remained slaves had not the Lord been gracious.

Elijah b. Mazal Ṭov's *Mi-šamayim 'el hišmi'anu* is a *petiḥah* to the *barekhu* on Pentecost. In the quatrain hymn the poet presents Israel as the obedient bride eager to learn her obligations, as enumerated in her Master's commands:[85]

> The two tablets He commanded to be inscribed,
> And thereby betroth the beautiful folk;
> He wrote the Ten Commands,
> They became the crown of the bride [Israel].
>
> [ISRAEL:]
> 'The instruction from His lips is good for me,
> I desire to learn it . . . '

Seliḥah

Moses Kohen's *seliḥah*, *Mah le-qoni mekharani*, is in four rhyming quatrains which open with repeated *mah*. The hymn is distinctive in its phonetic-intensive character, featuring alliteration, assonance and internal rhyme, reminiscent of earlier works by Joseph Qalai and Moses Ḥazan. Below is the opening strophe in which the poet answers his own rhetorical question:[86]

> *Mah le-qoni mekharani, hippilani we-nafalti?*
> *Ba-'awwon ra'ati, ḥaṭṭa'ti, ḥovati rabbati še-ribbavti;*
> *Wa-'ehi šaduf, naduf, haduf, u-v-nidduf niddaḥti,*
> *Ki 'efer ka-leḥem 'akhalti we-šiqquway bi-vkhi masakhti.*

[84] Bernstein, *Piyyuṭim*, No. 33, p. 66.
[85] New York, *Maḥazor Corfu*, MS No. 4588, fos. 4a and 17b, and MS No. 4580, fo. 1a.
[86] Weinberger, *Širat . . . Rabbanim*, p. 453.

Why, O my Maker, have You sold me, felled me and I am
prostrate?
Because of my offensive perversity, my sin, my huge guilt that I
have amassed;
Thus I have become empty, dispersed, thrust out, driven and
banished;
For I eat ashes like bread, and mingle tears with my drink.

Moses Kohen's hymn *Marom hu' ʿal kol meromim*, in quatrains with rhyming tercets and closing biblical verse, is preserved in the *Maḥazor Corfu* where the superscription reads *piyyuṭ* (poem). However, the reference to the Thirteen Divine Attributes in the hymn suggests that it was intended as a *seliḥah*:[87]

Destroy the servants of idols,
Who is like You, among the gods?
Be reconciled with those who enquire of Your Torah
On account of the Thirteen Attributes.

Moses Kohen's *Terzina*

Moses Kohen's *terzina* for Šabbat Zakhor is the first attempt to compose in syllabic metre by a Balkan poet. Syllabic metre, in which short syllables were counted as equivalents to long syllables, was an alternative to the Hispanic quantitative metre, long the dominant metric form. Pioneering this effort was the Italian poet Moses b. Isaac da Rieti (1398–*c.*1460), called 'Il Dante Ebreo' on account of his book, *Miqdaš Meʿaṭ*, composed in *terza rima* in imitation of Dante Alighieri's *Divina Commedia*. The superscription to Moses Kohen's *terzina*, preserved in the *Maḥazor Corfu*, acknowledges his indebtedness to Moses Rieti. Following are the opening cola with ten syllables to each and with a verse form of iambic tercets rhyming *aba bcb cdc*, etc.—the second colon of the first tercet providing the rhyme for the second tercet, the second colon of the second tercet providing the rhyme for the third, thereby allowing for an uninterrupted narrative flow to the entire hymn:[88]

Wa-yehi vi-ymey melekh 'aḥašweroš
'Ašer naṭah 'ozen li-dvar haman
Le-hašqotenu laʿan u-mey roš.

Hu' ha-mekhin keley mawet wa-yeman
Šemad hereg we-'ovdan we-reṣaḥ;
We-tilkedo rišto 'ašer ṭaman.

[87] Ibid. 452–3.
[88] Ibid. 449–52, 82–90.

'Am zu nafuṣ ke-khammon, ke-qeṣaḥ',
Nam lo: Dato šoneh, 'attah 'aqum,
Hanikhah li 'akhalehu neṣaḥ . . .

This happened in the days of Ahasuerus
Who willingly listened to the voice of Haman,
And make us drink wormwood and gall;

He it was who prepared the fatal vessels and appointed
Pogroms, killing, destruction and murder;
Yet he fell into the trap which he had hidden.

'This nation is scattered like cumin, like fennel,'
He told him, 'Their laws are different; now I shall attempt
By your leave to destroy them forever' . . .

Moses Kohen's *terzina* is an epic work, comprising 414 tercets in syllabic metre. Bearing the title *Sefer Yašir Mošeh*, it was published in Mantua in 1612, in Salonika in 1613 and in several later editions, and was read in Corfiote congregations on the Sabbath before Purim. In his narrative the poet draws upon biblical, rabbinic and folk sources, as in the following description of King Ahasuerus' banquet:

I call upon you to behold these men:
They exchange lecheries at the table,
While Jeshurun keeps to the words of Torah.

There arose their stench and foul smell;
They were overcome with a passion for debauchery
As their bellies were filled with delicacies.

There sat the head as if comforting mourners;
They bragged about the beauty of [their] women,
Their tongues were like sharpened arrows . . .

The first strophe, based on *bMeg* 12b, compares the table talk of the nations with that of Israel (Jeshurun). The second and third strophes—from the same rabbinic source—relate the events at the king's banquet table that lead to the invitation to Queen Vashti to join the men. The poet's narrative, as preserved in the *Maḥazor Corfu*, ends with the latter strophe. A fuller account is given in *bMeg* 12b:

At the feast of that wicked one [words of frivolity were exchanged]: Some said, The Medean women are the most beautiful, and others said, The Persian women are the most beautiful. Said Ahasuerus to them, The vessel that I use is neither Medean nor Persian, but Chaldean. Would you like to see her? They said, Yes, but it must be naked.

GENERAL BACKGROUND: KAFFA

Records of Jewish settlements in the Crimean date from the first century CE. Among the centres of Jewish life in the peninsula during the medieval period were Qirqer in the north, known in Jewish sources as Chufut-Kale, 'The Jews' Fortress', home of Rabbanites and Karaites, and the port of Kaffa (modern Feodosiya). In the first half of the thirteenth century Kaffa, then under Tatar rule, became a major trading centre—in which Jewish merchants took a leading part—linking the Asian caravan trade with central Europe and the Mediterranean world. These commercial links led to wider contacts with European Jewry, as may be seen in the Bible commentary, *Sefat 'Emet*, by the Crimean rabbi Abraham Kirimi (b. 1358). In this work, Kirimi was influenced by Abraham Ibn Ezra and by Šemaryah b. Elijah of Crete, to whose writings he frequently refers.

The liturgy of the Kaffan congregations is preserved in the *Maḥazor Kaffa*, which was edited by Moses b. Jacob of Kiev, known as Moses Ha-Golah (1449–*c.*1520). Like the *maḥazorim* of the Corfiotes and Kastoreans, the *Maḥazor Kaffa* was never published. It is preserved in two manuscript editions in the Jewish Theological Seminary Library, New York: Davidson, No. 0717 and Adler Collection, *Maḥazor Kaffa* (unnumbered). The *Siddur Kaffa*, comprising daily and Sabbath prayers, was published in 1735 at the Hebrew printing press in Chufut-Kale and in Mezirov in 1793. The Kaffans, like the Corfiotes and the Kastoreans, followed the Romaniote ritual, with some variation, and, like the former, they preserved in their prayer-book the liturgical writings of classical, late eastern and European poets, as well as the compositions of their native sons.

THE PRINCIPAL KAFFAN POETS

The earliest Kaffan poet known by name was R. Eliaqim, father-in-law to R. Abraham Kirimi (b. 1358), author of *Sefat 'Emet*. R. Eliaqim composed a *rešut* to the *qaddiš* for Šabbat Bere'šit and a *rešut* for the *barekhu* on Šabbat Naḥamu. Fifteenth- to sixteenth-century poets in Crimea include Moses Mevorakh, Isaac Handali and Moses Ha-Golah. Moses Mevorakh, a member of the family that included the poet Solomon Mevorakh, is the author of a *seliḥah* for the Day of Atonement and two *petiḥot*, for the Sabbath of Consolation and for the Sabbath and New Moon. Isaac Handali composed three songs (*zemirot*) for the Sabbath dinner-table, and Moses Ha-Golah's literary corpus includes only one *seliḥah*, which is preserved in both the *Maḥazor Kaffa* manuscripts, which he edited, and the Chufut-Kale printed edition of the *Siddur Kaffa*.

THE PRINCIPAL KAFFAN GENRES

Memorial Prayer

There are no surviving *qedušta'ot* or *yoṣerot* by Kaffan poets, and it is likely that the editors of Crimean prayer-books were content to use hymns in these genres by better-known eastern and European hymnists. Yet a mixture of Kaffan deference to the more prominent Jewish centres combined with pride in the local settlement can be seen, for example, in the *Sefat 'Emet* of Abraham Kirimi, who acknowledges his indebtedness to Abraham Ibn Ezra, Maimonides and Šemaryah Ha-Ikriti, even as he on occasion disagrees with the commentary of RaŠI. A more revealing example of this ambivalence appears in the distinctive memorial prayer in the *Maḥazor Kaffa* for the 'Elul vigil nights. The prayer begins, 'May the memory of the pious be a blessing' (*zekher ṣadiqim li-vrakhah*), and lists such eminences as Maimonides, Abraham Ibn Ezra, Solomon Ibn Adret, Joseph Karo, Elia Mizraḥi and Moses Cordovero. Interspersed with these notables are the names of local worthies like Abraham Kirimi (who is listed after Abraham Ibn Ezra), Moses Ha-Golah, Moses and Joseph Mevorakh and other Crimean dignitaries. Most of the surviving hymns by Kaffan poets are *rešuyyot*, *petiḥot* and *seliḥot*.

Rešut

Among the anonymous hymns preserved in the Kaffan liturgy is a *rešut* to 'Blessed be He who spoke and the world came into being' (*Barukh še-'amar we-hayah ha-'olam*) for the Days of Awe morning service. The hymn is built in rhyming couplets spanning the complete Hebrew alphabet, with each hemicolon beginning with *barukh*. The *rešut*, of which a portion follows, is similar in form and theme to Joseph Ibn Abitur's hymn in this genre, *Barukh 'ašer 'el qadmon niqra' yošev 'al šiv'ah reqi'im we-sovlam.*[89]

Blessed is He who discloses the hidden and the revealed inscribed before Him . . .
Blessed is He whose dwelling angels encompass . . .
Blessed is He whose palace home is brimming with sapphire.

Another noteworthy anonymous *rešut* is *'Al 'amitekha we-ḥasdekha* to the Sabbath and Festival morning prayer, 'All shall offer You thanksgiving, all shall praise You' (*Ha-kol yodukha we-ha-kol yešabḥukha*). The poet gives gratitude for the gift of the body, in line with rabbinic teaching (in *bSan* 38a and *bBer* 60b) and with the prayer 'Blessed are You . . . who have fashioned man in wisdom' (*Barukh . . . 'ašer yaṣar 'et ha-'adam be-ḥokhmah*). The hymn is in

[89] Bernstein, 'Ha-Maḥazor', pp. 494–8, 527; Fleischer, *Širat Ha-Qodeš*, pp. 396–7.

rhyming couplets, with each strophe beginning with *ʿal* (for). Below is a selection:[90]

For Your manifold steadfast love and faithfulness
From the womb [we are grateful] . . .

For the physical body, the clod of earth skin and flesh,
We thank You, Lord of the spirits of all flesh.

For connecting limb, sinew and bone,
'Who is like You?' all my bones shall say.

For preparing sustenance for the infant from dry breasts,
Your strength is affirmed by the mouths of babes and infants.

The alphabetic acrostic in the hymn ends with the letter *lamed*, allowing the poet to lead directly into 'All shall offer You thanksgiving.' Following is the closing strophe:

For the singing tongue in adoration and praise of Your creation,
For all Your works shall give thanks to You.

The Hispanic influence is evident in R. Eliaqim's *rešut* to the *qaddiš* for Šabbat Bere'šit, *'Adon ha-kol u-vara' kol be-ḥokhmah.* The metric seven-cola hymn in *qaṣīdah*-style monorhyme closes with a paraphrase of the lead verset in the *qaddiš*:[91]

Because He is exalted and magnified eternally,
Therefore is His great name sanctified throughout the world.

R. Eliaqim's *rešut* for the *barekhu* on the Sabbath of Consolation (after the reading from Isa. 51: 12) is a terse summary of the Ten Commandments in recognition of the Torah reading from Deut. 5. Below is a selection:[92]

Indeed, God's Torah is perfect
Written and sealed by the divine hand . . .
The foundations of the world were established with its words,
Even the upper chambers so designed . . .
Consider first, 'I am the Lord,'
And 'you shall not have a foreign god in the world' . . .
Restrain your hand from doing violence to any man,
'You shall not murder' another in anger;
Shut up the mouth of your tempter at all times,
And 'you shall not commit adultery' . . .

90 Bernstein, 'Ha-Maḥazor', pp. 499–500.
91 Weinberger, *Širat . . . Rabbanim*, p. 157; Bernstein, 'Ha-Maḥazor', p. 465.
92 Weinberger, *Širat . . . Rabbanim*, pp. 157–9.

Seliḥah

Moses Mevorakh is the author of *'Elohim be-rov ḥasdekha*, a *seliḥah* for the additional service (*musaf*) on the Day of Atonement. Each of its fifteen strophes begins, 'O Lord, in the abundance of Your steadfast love.' The closing colon in the strophes is a biblical verse, after the Hispanic model. Following is a selection:[93]

> O Lord, in the abundance of Your steadfast love have mercy on
> the children of Your beloved [Abraham];
> They lift their eyes to the throne of Your glory;
> Answer us faithfully, incline Your ear and extend to us Your hand;
> Be not silent, O Lord my God and I will give thanks to You forever.

Moses Ha-Golah's *seliḥah*, *'Elohim ḥay we-'el nora'*, is a metric hymn in rhyming tercet strophes. Among the conventional themes in the *seliḥah* is the following revealing strophe:[94]

> Repay my enemies as they deserve;
> Give them anguish of heart
> And pay no heed to their plottings.

In this invective the poet may have had in mind the incident in his life in 1506, when the town of Lida in Lithuania, where he lived, was attacked by Tatars who carried him off to the Crimea, where he was ransomed by the Salkhat Jewish community.

Petiḥah

Moses Mevorakh's *petiḥah*, *'Adon 'olam, 'adon kol ha-gedolot*, for Šabbat Naḥamu is a metric *qaṣīdah*-style hymn in monorhyme. Following is a selection:[95]

> The chorus of angels and *ḥašmalim* [Ezek. 1: 4, 27] hesitates, their
> hearts are faint . . .
> And if talent, wisdom and enlightenment are wanting in their
> company emanated from Your spirit,
> How can one impeded and slow of speech sing Your praises?
> However, the troubles that have come upon Jacob's children,
> descendants of a special treasure
> Impel me to speak of the hardships, the spilled blood, the violence,
> and the robberies
> Perpetrated by the sons of Esau [Christians] and Hagar
> [Muslims] . . .

[93] Bernstein, 'Ha-Maḥazor', pp. 479–82.

[94] Ibid. 488–9.

[95] Ibid. 482–4.

How much longer, O Lord God, will they be kept down in the
depths like a stone?
They have already received double for each sin in the long exile of
much degradation and poverty.

'They have already received double for each sin' is from Isa. 40: 2. The reference to the prophetic lesson for Šabbat Naḥamu from Isa. 40 in the above hymn, and the reading from Isa. 51: 12–52: 12 in the Šabbat Naḥamu hymn of R. Eliaqim, above, suggests that the Kaffans observed the generally accepted practice of designating seven such Sabbaths with appropriate readings from the Prophets for each.[96]

Moses Mevorakh's *petiḥah*, *'Avarekh šem kevod ha-'el*, for the Šabbat Ro'š Ḥodeš is also built in metric *qaṣīdah*-style monorhyme, after Hispanic models. The poet recalls the practice in Temple days of blowing trumpets on the feasts of rejoicing and at the beginning of the months (Num. 10: 10). He prays that his song offering be accepted in lieu of the trumpet blasts.[97] Mevorakh's *petiḥah* before the reading of the Scroll of Esther, *Mah gadelu ma'asey ha-'el wa-ḥasadaw*, is built in an uncommon form of six strophes in which the odd-numbered have internal rhyme: *ab*, *ab*, *ab*, *ab* / *ccccd* / *ef*, *ef*, *ef* / *ggggd* / *hi*, *hi*, *hi*, *hi* / *jjjjd*. The repeated *d* colon with rhymeme *ti* at the end of the odd-numbered strophes would suggest that the hymn opened with a *ti* rhyming guide, in the manner of a pseudo-*muwashshaḥ*, and that this was omitted by copyists. Below is a sample from two of the odd-numbered strophes:[98]

'Oyevi gavah we-'alah
Ya'aṣ ba-ḥaṣi laylah
Ḥašav le-khallot kallah
Surah we-'umlalah
Wa-'ani be-galuti . . .

'Elyon 'ašer me-'olam
Šama' he'ezin qolam,
Niglah u-miyyad ge'alam;
Yaḥiš zeman ne'elam,
Yašiv 'et ševuti

My foe, ascendant, prevailed,
He plotted at midnight
Hoping to kill the bride [Israel];
Put away and wretched,
I am in exile . . .

96 See *Enṣiqlopedia Talmudit*, x. 20–1, 713–14.
97 Bernstein, 'Ha-Maḥazor', p. 484.
98 Ibid. 484–5.

Exalted [God] who from time immemorial
Listened and took notice of their cries;
He appeared and forthwith redeemed them;
May He hasten the [end] time concealed
  And return my exiles . . .

Zemirot

Isaac Ḥandali's three *zemirot* are in celebration of the Sabbath and were sung at the dinner-table. The Sabbath day of rest was perceived as a foretaste of Israel's national restoration, as seen in his quatrain *zemer*, *Mi-yom ri'šon 'ad yom šišši*:[99]

Although the dove has found no place to set its foot,
When the good Sabbath day comes she will find respite.

R. Isaac's table song, *Yom zeh le-yisra'el 'orah we-simḥah*, preserved in the Kaffan prayer-book, attracted the attention of the Karaites—neighbours of the Rabbanites in Crimea—who included it in their liturgical collections. The hymn, in the form of a pseudo-*muwashshaḥ*, projects an uncommon rhyme scheme: *aa*, *bc*, *bcc*, *aa* / *de*, *dee* / *aa* / *fg*, *fgg* / *aa* / etc. The effect of the Sabbath on a homeless people is suggested in the following:[100]

Delighting the hearts of a depressed people;
For creatures in pain, an enlarged soul; for one in distress,
He removes the sigh on the restful Sabbath.

The conceit in the second colon is based on the rabbinic statement (in *bBeṣ* 16a), 'On the eve of the Sabbath, the Holy One, blessed be He, gives to man an enlarged soul and at the close of the Sabbath, he withdraws it from him.'

R. Isaac's *zemer*, *Yaṣar ha-'el be-vinah*, built in quatrain monorhyme strophes, is an admonition to be guided by wisdom. From the hymn we learn of the Kaffan practice of arising at midnight and studying the Torah until dawn:[101]

The Lord endowed man with wisdom and understanding
When He made him from the earth's void;
He set in his heart the skill to perceive a profound mystery . . .

Midnight is the time to awaken from slumber
And be occupied with God's perfect Torah;
Make this a habit ever firmly established.
And take care not to neglect the time for arising.

[99] Bernstein, 'Ha-Maḥazor', p. 486. [100] Ibid. 487. [101] Ibid. 487–8.

GENERAL BACKGROUND: CRETE

Jewish settlements in Crete date from the middle of the second century BC, when the island was under Roman rule. Although the evidence is scant, Jews continued to live there through the Byzantine and Muslim periods from 395 to 961. In 961 the Byzantines reconquered the island, but were forced to sell it to Venice in 1204 following the Fourth Crusade and the fall of Constantinople to the Latin Crusaders. During the Venetian period (1204–1669) a formidable Jewish community emerged in the harbour cities of Candia, Canea, and Retimo, where they were a dominant force in the Cretan export trade. For their commercial privileges they had to pay special taxes to the state. Despite their usefulness to the Venetian ruling power, they were required to live in segregated quarters and wear distinctive badges. They were often accused of betraying hostility to the Church by desecrating the Host or siding with the Muslim Turks. In a time of troubles they risked attack: during the Greek population riot in 1364, the tiny Jewish settlement in Castelnuovo was massacred.

Much is known about the social and religious life of Cretan Jewry during the Venetian period, thanks to a collection of *Candiote Ordinances* (*Taqqanot Candia*) designed to correct perceived abuses of Jewish law. The abuses, such as misuse of the ritual bathhouse, laxity in Sabbath observance and poor attendance at synagogue services, were observed by the German rabbi, Barukh b. Isaac, who visited the island in 1328. The individual largely responsible for preserving the literary legacy of Cretan Jewry was its native historian and bibliophile Elijah b. Elqanah Capsali (1483–1555), who collected and edited the *Candiote Ordinances* in addition to composing a valuable history of the Ottoman Empire (*Seder Eliyyahu Zuta*) with special emphasis on its Jewish settlers. Capsali's library, which was acquired by the Vatican, also included the archives of the fifteenth-century Cretan scholars Michael b. Šabbetai Kohen Balbo and Moses Kohen Aškenazi, and the one surviving manuscript copy of the island's Jewish prayer-book, the *Maḥazor Candia* (Vatican library, Assemani, No. 320). An examination of this prayer-book reveals that, like the Kastoreans and Corfiotes, Cretan congregations generally followed the Romaniote ritual, but with some variants—presumably intended to affirm their independence and distinctiveness.[102]

Cretans in the Italian Renaissance

A distinctive feature in the life of Cretan Jewry is the involvement of its poets and philosophers in the revival of classical learning in Italy. The Italian renaissance of the fourteenth to sixteenth centuries, which embraced Rome, Milan, Genoa, Venice, Naples and Sicily, attracted Šemaryah Ha-Ikriti, Elijah del

[102] Roth, *Venice*, pp. 294–304; Weinberger, *Širat . . . Keretim*, English introd., pp. 1–3.

Medigo and Elijah Capsali, among others. Šemaryah Ha-Ikriti was invited to the court of Robert of Anjou, King of Naples, for whom he translated the masterpieces of Greek literature. Elijah del Medigo (Elijah Cretensis) was part of a distinguished circle of savants at the home of Lorenzo de' Medici at Florence. Del Medigo taught philosophy at the University of Padua and gave Hebrew lessons to Pico della Mirandola, at whose request he translated works by Averroes from Hebrew into Latin. Elijah Capsali, author of a history of the Ottoman Empire with particular reference to its Jewish subjects, studied Talmud and medicine at the University of Padua. He later succeeded his father as leader of Cretan Jewry.

The renewed interest in Aristotelian philosophy is seen in the work of Elijah Philosof, whose book on logic (*Sefer Higgayon*) is based on the principles of the Greek philosopher. Combined with an admiration for classical thinkers was an apprehension that their views might be harmful to Jewish religious teaching. Aware of this problem, Elijah Philosof, in his *baqqašah*, *'Attah 'eḥad*, informs his congregation—who, it may be assumed, was also caught up in the classical revival—that the Ten Categories of Aristotle cannot be used to define the God of Israel. The tension between philosophy and religion is reflected in the heated exchange which began in 1466 between the Cretan notables Michael Kohen Balbo and Moses Kohen Aškenazi. They disagreed on the question of metempsychosis (transmigration of souls), with Balbo arguing for and Aškenazi against. The larger issue behind their debate was the relation of faith to reason. Are they compatible and can they coexist? This problem was to be addressed by Elijah del Medigo in his *Beḥinat Ha-Dat* (Examination of Religion), written in Candia in 1490, and arguing in favour of the double truth of philosophy and religion: science is concerned with truth that can be demonstrated, whereas the Torah is political in that it seeks to guide humans towards seeking the truth.[103]

THE PRINCIPAL CRETAN POETS

Anatoli Qazani

The earliest synagogue poet in Crete, Anatoli b. David Qazani (12th c.), a member of a prominent Jewish family on the island, is the author of hymns in Hebrew and Aramaic. A Hispanic influence is evident in his *petiḥah* to a *yoṣer* for Passover, *Le-rannen ḥasdekha ta'arog*, and his *tokheḥah* for the New Year, *'Imri yeḥidati*. Both are built in metric *qaṣīdah* style and echo themes adapted from Jewish Neoplatonist philosophy. His *taḥanun*, *'Et se'aray sa'ir gilleaḥ*, for the vigil nights is a metric pseudo-*muwashshaḥ*. However, Qazani's Aramaic *rešut* for the translator of the reading from the Prophets,

[103] Weinberger, *Širat . . . Keretim*, English introd., pp. 2–3; Sirat, History of Jewish Philosophy, p. 405.

'Abba' ševaḥta' bi-v'ituta', is similar to the Pentecost Aramaic *rešuyyot* for the translator, by the Franco-Germans Meir b. Isaac and Jacob Tam, authors of *'Aqdamut millin* and *Yeṣiv pitgam* respectively.

Moses del Medigo

One of the Cretan hymnists under Venetian rule was Moses b. Šabbetai Ha-Ikriti del Medigo (13th–14th c.), a member of the illustrious family of physicians, philosophers and scientists who came from Germany to settle in Crete. R. Moses is the author of a *rešut*, *'Agaddelah šimkha selah*, to his *guf ha-yoṣer*, *'Akhtirah le-ḥonen da'at u-musar*. The latter is built in rhyming quatrains without a *qadoš* refrain, after the model of Solomon Ha-Bavli's much-imitated *'Or yeša' me'uššarim*. To this Šabbat Ha-Gadol *yoṣer* R. Moses adds a *silluq*, *Mi šelo' 'amar 'ellu šelošah devarim*, which he constructs, like his *guf ha-yoṣer*, in rhyming quatrains without scriptural verse endings.

Malkiel Aškenazi

A contemporary of Moses del Medigo, Malkiel ben Meir Aškenazi, the physician (presumably the surgeon Melchiel Theotonicus, known from Latin sources) is the author of a *mi kamokha* for the Sabbath of Ḥanukkah, *Mi kamokha 'addir 'ayom we-nora'*. The hymn opens with the standard cosmic preface after the manner of the Hispanic poets and continues with a modified account of Ḥanukkah legends combined with the story of a 'Judaean lady', a reference to Judith from the Apocrypha.

Jacob b. Eliezer

Jacob son of Rabbi Eliezer is the author of a metric pseudo-*muwashshaḥ petiḥah*, *'Ašer šipper reqi'ey rum*, for the intermediate days of Passover, and a metric *qaṣīdah*-style *tokheḥah*, *'Ani 'et nafši 'odeh tehillah*, for the Ten Days of Repentance. According to the *Candiote Ordinances* 48.5, 50.8, R. Jacob served as cantor-poet and ritual slaughterer (*šoḥet*) in Retimo in 1362, and in Candia in 1369. It would appear that the poet's father was a well-known rabbi in the region, given the acrostic signature in his *petiḥah*, 'I, Jacob son of the Rabbi, be strong (*ḥazaq*).' In the acrostic of his *tokheḥah*, the poet also refers to his father as 'Rabbi Eliezer.'

Šemaryah Ha-Ikriti

The best known of the Cretan hymnists was Šemaryah b. Elijah b. Jacob Ha-Ikriti (1275–1355), author of tracts on logic, grammar and philosophy and translator of classical Greek literature, from the original Greek, for Robert of Anjou, King of Naples. Although several poetic works by Ha-Ikriti survive, including panegyrics in honour of R. David Ha-Nagid, grandson of Maimonides, only one liturgical work, a *rešut* for the Bridegroom of the Torah (*ḥatan ha-torah*), has been preserved. The hymn, *Nodeh u-nšabbaḥ le-ʿattiq yomin*, written in Hebrew and Aramaic with a smattering of Greek terms, is built in rhyming couplets with an Aramaic refrain.

Elijah Philosof

Elijah b. Eliezer Philosof (14th c.), author of *Sefer Higgayon ʿal Derekh Še'elot U-Tšuvot* (Studies in Logic in the Form of Responsa), based on Aristotelian logic (Bibliothèque Nationale, Paris, MS No. 707 and MS Parma, No. 997), composed five *baqqašot*, of which three are in rhymed prose after earlier models by Saʿadyah Ga'on, Solomon Ibn Gabirol and Judah Ha-Levi, and two are in the style of a metric *qaṣīdah*.

Šemaryah b. Elqanah, Elqanah b. Šemaryah and Mattityah b. Joseph

Cretan contemporaries of Elijah Philosof included Šemaryah b. Rabbana' Elqanah and Elqanah b. Šemaryah *Ha-Parnes*, presumably his son. The former is the author of two *seliḥot*, *'Elohim 'essa' nafši*, a hymn in quatrain strophes with identical opening and closing units, and *Šavrah libbi [be]'anḥati*, for the Fast of Gedaliah; a *tokheḥah*, *Šimʿu le-millay ʿam 'emunay*, in rhyming tercets with scriptural endings; and a *ḥaṭa'nu*, *Šiqdu ʿam nidka'*, for the Tenth of Ṭevet fast. R. Elqanah's sole surviving hymn, *'Eyley meromin*, a *seliḥah* for the Ten Days of Repentance, is modelled after Eleazar Qillir's *'Ammiṣey šeḥaqim mi-maʿal* for the Day of Atonement. Mattityah b. Joseph signs his name in his *ḥaṭa'nu*, *Minʿi yeḥidah*, 'Mattityah b[i]r[a]b[bi] Joseph *Ha-Parnes*.' The latter title designated a member of the congregation's seven-member deliberative council (*waʿad qaṭon*) comprising *parnasim* and *memunim* (syndics). Under Venetian rule, the council spoke to the state on matters of concern to the Jewish community. R. Mattityah is also the author of a *teḥinnah*, [*Laylah*] *mahalal malkekh*, in rhyming tercets and with biblical closure.[104]

Moses Ha-Yewani and Abraham Ha-Kohen

Cretan hymnists in the fifteenth century include the learned duo Moses Ha-Yewani (the Greek) b. Elia and Abraham Ha-Kohen. The former translated into Hebrew the treatise on astronomy, *Sefer Mezuqqaq* (Paris, Bibliothèque Nationale, MS No. 1061.3) by Omar Ibn Muhammad, and had copied for

[104] Roth, *Venice*, p. 128.

him a book on geometry and trigonometry that was completed in 1463 (Paris, MS No. 1061.2). Abraham Ha-Kohen copied Abraham Ibn Ezra's *Yesod Mora'* in 1490 (Vatican, MS No. 49) and is presumably the Abraham Kohen listed as the copyist of the above volume of geometry and trigonometry for Moses b. Elia (Paris, MS No. 1061.2). Moses Ha-Yewani is the author of a *seliḥah*, *'El ḥaṣereykha*, for the Fast of Esther in which he reviews the laws pertaining to the Scroll of Esther and the feast of Purim. R. Moses' hymn is similar in form and theme to Šabbetai Ḥaviv's *seliḥah*, *'Agagi šaqad*, for the Fast of Esther. Like his Balkan colleague, R. Moses rules that it is permitted to write the Scroll with copperas (to which the poet refers by its Greek name *kalkanthos* and not by the Hebrew derivative *kankantom*, in *mMeg* 2. 1) on parchment that is not rough or coarse and has been treated with gall-nut.[105] Another *seliḥah* by R. Moses, *Me'on qodšekha 'ammekha 'ussaf*, for the Day of Atonement, is in standard quatrain strophes with closing biblical verses ending with the unit *laylah* (evening).

Abraham Ha-Kohen is the author of an *'ofan*, *'Odeh šem 'el*, in monorhyme, in which he combines themes in medieval philosophy with Jewish mysticism. R. Abraham's two hymns, *'Edbaq bekha raḥum* and *'Ozziy we-zimrat yah*, are metric cameo works consisting of one four-cola strophe. The occasion for which they were written is not clear. The repeated reference to the soul suggests that they may been *rešuyyot* to the *nišmat*. His *'Enoš 'anuš we-'adam me-'adamah*, in rhymed prose, is probably a self-rebuke (*tokheḥah*), after late eastern models.

THE PRINCIPAL CRETAN GENRES

Yoṣer

The *Maḥazor Candia* preserves not only the hymnography of its native sons under Byzantine and Venetian rule but also that of classical, late eastern and European poets. Representing the classical period is the anonymous author of a *guf ha-yoṣer* for Simḥat Torah, *'Iš 'anaw mi-kol ha-areṣ*, built in rhymed tercets without a *qadoš* refrain. This omission implies that the hymn antedates Eleazar Qillir, who is said to have introduced the choral refrain into the *guf ha-yoṣer*. Another *guf ha-yoṣer* for Simḥat Torah, *'Ešme'ah berakhah*, was written by a poet who gives his name as Judah in the acrostic. This hymn in rhyming quatrains also lacks a *qadoš* refrain. In this case, the missing choral refrain may be due to the influence of the Italian, Solomon Ha-Bavli, and his *'Or yeša' me'uššarim* in quatrains minus a *qadoš* refrain. Of particular interest in the *Maḥazor Candia* is the *guf ha-yoṣer* for Šemini 'Aṣeret, *'Iš 'ašer befanim yuqran*, by the ninth-century poet Ḥedveta b. Abraham, whose known hymns survive only in the Cairo Geniza. In this *guf ha-yoṣer*, built in rhyming

[105] Weinberger, *Širat . . . Rabbanim*, pp. 498–502.

tercets with *qadoš* refrain, each strophe ends in a scriptural verse, a practice not seen in R. Ḥedveta's other hymns.[106]

Moses del Medigo's *guf ha-yoṣer*, *'Akhtirah le-ḥonen da'at u-musar*, is built in rhyming quatrains without a *qadoš* refrain, in the style of Solomon Ha-Bavli's *'Or yeša' me'uššarim*. The superscription to the hymn directs that it be sung to the melody of Ha-Bavli's work. However, the eclectic del Medigo, unlike his Italian precursor, does not close his strophes with scriptural verses. The burden of the hymn is a review of the laws of Passover, in line with rabbinic instruction (in *bPes* 6a), 'Questions are asked and lectures are given on the laws of Passover for thirty days before Passover. R. Simeon b. Gamaliel said: Two weeks.' The poet's citations from rabbinic sources are often given in the Aramaic in the very form that they appear in the Babylonian and Jerusalem Talmuds. In citing the Passover laws that his congregation is required to observe, the poet provides a glimpse of the festival practices of Cretan Jewry under Venetian rule:[107]

> One is required to recline while eating the unleavened bread and drinking the four cups of wine;
> Likewise, a prominent woman [is required to recline].

Reclining at the Passover dinner is a sign of freedom, a practice preserved from antiquity (cf. *mPes* 10. 1). Qualifying this practice, the rabbis note (in *bPes* 108a), 'A woman in her husband's [house] need not recline [because she stands under his authority], but if she is a woman of importance she must recline.' Later rabbinic authorities, like the German talmudist R. Mordecai b. Hillel Ha-Kohen (*c.*1240–98) and the Hispanic sage R. Yeroḥam b. Mešullam (*c.*1290–1350), considered all women important and required that they recline. Their view was seconded by the Polish codifier R. Moses b. Israel Isserles (*c.*1525–72). R. Moses del Medigo, apparently, did not share this opinion, and chose to follow the view of Maimonides, in line with the rabbinic view in *bPes* 108a cited above.[108]

Silluq

Moses del Medigo's *silluq*, *Mi šelo' 'amar 'ellu šelošah devarim*, is built, like his *guf ha-yoṣer*, in rhyming quatrains without scriptural verse endings—an uncommon form for the *silluq*, which is generally constructed in monorhyme strophes or in rhyming tercets. The probable reason for the poet's choice of form is that, since his *silluq* continues the review of Passover laws begun in his *guf ha-yoṣer*, he found it convenient to compose the two hymns in a similar manner. Here, as in the preceding hymn, the poet often presents the Passover

106 Weinberger, *Širat . . . Keretim*, pp. 4, 8, 196; idem, 'Yoṣer le-Šimini'.

107 Weinberger, *Širat . . . Keretim*, pp. 42–8.

108 See *Ṭur*, *'Oraḥ Ḥayyim*, No. 472, and comment of Joseph Karo (*Beyt Yosef*); *Šulḥan 'Arukh*, *RaMa*, No. 472. 4; Maimonides, *Mišneh Torah*, Laws of Leavened and Unleavened Bread, 7. 8.

laws in the Aramaic as they are given in the rabbinic sources. Following the conventional practice, del Medigo's *silluq* closes with the verset 'In mercy You bring light to the earth' (*Ha-me'ir la-'areṣ we-la-darim 'aleyha*), preceding the second benediction before the *šema'*. Among the Passover laws reviewed by the poet is the following:[109]

Then he the dips greens in vinegar and offers the benediction,
  '. . . who creates the fruit of the earth';
He lifts the table and recites, 'Why does this night differ?' and all
  of the *Haggadah* . . .

The practice of lifting the table during the Passover *seder* is in line with rabbinic teaching (in *bPes* 115b) as cited above, 'Why do we remove the table? The School of R. Yannai said: So that the children may perceive [the unusual proceeding] and enquire [its reasons].' This practice is also recommended in the *rešut* for the Sabbath before Passover, *'Az ke-gulgal ši'bud ḥorim*, by the eleventh-century Balkan poet Benjamin b. Samuel.[110]

'Ofan

Abraham Ha-Kohen's *'ofan*, *'Odeh šem 'el*, in monorhyme, presents issues in contemporary medieval philosphy and Jewish mysticism. The poet shares with Maimonides (in his *Moreh Ha-Nevukhim* 2. 4) the view that the 'angels,' identified with the Intelligences (*ha-sekhalim*), are the movers of the spheres and that the latter's movement is animated by a desire to be attached to the Intelligences, their movers. In the following selection, the poet refers to the music of the spheres in their heavenly movements, based on Job 38: 7 and the comment of Abraham Ibn Ezra:[111]

Therefore do the spheres sing mightily
In their comprehension [as Gods's creatures] and desire [*mi-ṣiyyuram u-tšuqatam*]
To be joined [*li-daveq*] to them [the 'angels'] speedily.

Mi Kamokha

Malkiel b. Meir Aškenazi is the author of a *mi kamokha* for Šabbat Ḥanukkah, *Mi kamokha 'addir 'ayom we-nora'*. The hymn opens with the standard cosmic preface after the manner of the Hispanic poets and continues with a list of the decrees issued by the Greek ruling power restricting Jewish religious practice. Among these was the requirement that Jewish brides spend their wedding night with the provincial governor. On the eve of her

109 Weinberger, *Širat . . . Keretim*, pp. 59–61.
110 Weinberger, 'Ha-payṭan'.
111 Weinberger, *Širat . . . Rabbanim*, p. 503.

marriage, the sister of Judah the Maccabee seized upon a bold plan to provoke her brothers to revolt:[112]

> The daughter of the Maccabee, Judah,
> While under the canopy removed her clothes
> And walked naked among the invited guests,
> And Judah, enraged, saw her.
>
> Judah, deceived, spoke,
> In rebuke, hot-tempered;
> She responded, 'Tonight I will lie, an adulteress,
> With a man unrepentant in his treason [against God].'

The sister's courageous initiative has the desired effect, leading to the assassination of the provincial governor by Judah, who gains entrance to the palace by flattery. When word of his action reaches King Antiochus, he lays siege to the city of Jerusalem. At this point in the narrative the poet introduces the Jewish heroine, who in the dark of night steals into the king's camp and slays him:

> That evening the sleep
> Of the honourable Judaean lady was disturbed;
> She arose and went alone
> To the king to awaken him.
>
> He asked her: Who are you?
> She replied: I am descended from the prophets of my people;
> Tomorrow, my national home will be delivered into your hands,
> And you will utterly defeat my forces.
>
> Her words appealed to the king,
> And he asked her: Would you sleep with me, O pure and fair?
> She replied: I am not clean
> And unable to lie with the king in his garment.

The lady then seeks permission to leave the king's tent, and assures him that she will return prepared to spend the night with him. The king, satisfied with her response, gives orders to allow her free passage through his camp. Later that evening, she returns and, finding the king asleep, decapitates him:

> She severed his head
> And went out into the city;
> The gates that had been shut in fear
> Were opened for her . . .

[112] Weinberger, *Širat . . . Keretim*, pp. 65–6.

They [the Judaeans] entered and purified the Temple
Which had been polluted by the barbarians;
And they did not find pure oil available
Save for one cruse with its seal intact.

As in the earlier treatment of the Judith legend by the eleventh-century French poet Joseph b. Solomon of Carcassonne in his *yoṣer*, *'Odekha ki 'anafta*, her story is combined with that of the sister of Judah the Maccabee on her wedding night and the account of the Judaean uprising and the re-dedication of the Jerusalem Temple. However, unlike the accounts in the earlier sources from the Apocrypha, the rabbinic literature, and the hymns of R. Joseph Carcassonne and his contemporary, R. Menaḥem b. Makhir (in his *yoṣer*, *'Odekha ki 'anitani*, and *zulat*, *'Eyn mošia' we-go'el*), where Judith is known by her name, in this later treatment by R. Malkiel, her name is forgotten and she is referred to as 'the honourable Judaean lady' (*ha-yehudit ha-kevudah*).

The unifying figure connecting the several legends in both rabbinic and liturgic sources is the term 'deception / deceived' (*mirmah-merammah*). Not only are the provincial governor and king deceived, but so is Judah by the unconventional action of his sister in parading naked before her wedding guests. In Hebrew, the term *mirmah* may also be use to indicate hypocrisy, or a form of deception. Such usage is found in the hymn by R. Joseph Carcassonne where Judah's sister charges her brother, 'How dare you lecture me with your hypocrisy?' (*li 'eykh teyasseruni bi-rmiyyah*).

Both the rabbis and the hymnists make much of the irony of the story. This is seen in the rabbinic *Midraš Le-Ḥanukkah* and in R. Menaḥem's hymn,[113] where Judah and his brothers, members of a priestly family, repelled by their sister's brazen behaviour, order that she be burnt. Burning is the punishment meted out to the daughter of a priest who profanes herself by playing the harlot. They rescind the order when she reminds them of their hypocrisy in permitting her to be defiled by the governor. The irony of situation in the story of Judah and his sister is closely related to the legend of the biblical Judah and his daughter-in-law Tamar, also a descendant of a priestly family. When it is learned that Tamar 'is pregnant as a result of whoredom', Judah orders, 'Bring her out and let her be burned' (Gen. 38: 24). Here, too, the order is revoked when Judah learns that he is the father. The rabbis, sensing the irony of situation in the Judah–Tamar story, comment (in *Gen. Rabbah* 85. 9) on the verse (in Gen. 38: 20), 'When Judah sent the kid [of the goats] . . . to recover the pledge from the woman [Tamar],' as follows, 'The Torah laughs at men. The Holy One, blessed be He, said to Judah: You deceived your father with a kid of goats [Gen. 37: 31–4]; by your life! Tamar will deceive you with a kid of goats.'

[113] See *'Oṣar Midrašim*, i. 192; Ber, *Seder*, p. 637.

Rešut

Anatoli Qazani's Aramaic *rešut*, *'Abba' ševaḥta' bi-v'ituta'*, for the translator of the reading from the Prophets on the seventh day of Passover, is built, like Meir b. Isaac's *'Aqdamut millin* and Jacob Tam's *Yeṣiv pitgam*, in monorhyme strophes. However, unlike the Franco-German treatment, R. Anatoli's hymn is embellished with internal rhyming tercets. Its theme draws attention to the Prophets as witnesses to God's glory and guardians of divine secrets, which some translators, like Jonathan b. Uziel, had sought to reveal:[114]

> Like a flame my heart burns with desire to know
> The secrets concealed in the vision [of Daniel] . . .
> Jonathan the son of Uziel, a man wise and valiant who explained the mysteries of the Torah,
> Wished to reveal the secret [time of redemption] . . .
> [When God], fearsome and holy, wondrous in might, and omniscient, concealed it . . .

Moses del Medigo's *rešut*, *'Agaddelah šimkha selah*, to his *guf ha-yoṣer* (above) is constructed in rhyming quatrains, but without scriptural verse endings. The poet personalizes his permission request and prays that the learned in his congregation overlook his failings:[115]

> I request permission from the Lord, terrifying and awesome
> Before uttering each word and syllable,
> And from His worthy assembly,
> Old and young, I beg leave.
>
> Indeed, my knowledge is limited,
> And if I err, I pray that the Torah sages will absolve me;
> O Lord, my God, I seek Your aid
> In cleansing me from error and choosing the issue of my lips.

Šemaryah Ha-Ikriti's *rešut* for the Bridegroom of the Torah (*ḥatan ha-torah*), *Nodeh u-nšabbaḥ le-'atiq yomin*, written in Hebrew, Aramaic and Greek, is built in rhyming couplets with Aramaic refrain:[116]

> *Nodeh u-nšabbaḥ le-'atiq yomin*
> *Saggi' le-šezavah yitbarakh le-'olmin.*
>
> We thank and praise the Ancient of Days
> He is mighty to save and eternally blessed.

A similar refrain is employed by the fourteenth-century Balkan poet Yose b. Abraham, whose *rešut* for the Bridegroom of Genesis (*ḥatan bere'šit*) is also

[114] Weinberger, *Širat . . . Keretim*, pp. 33–4. [115] Ibid. 38–9. [116] Ibid. 76–80.

built in rhyming couplets in Hebrew and Aramaic with a scattering of Greek terms. The following couplet from the body of the hymn is also employed, with slight variation, by both poets:

'Aqalles le-malka' ṭon paddon ḥay 'olamim,
Le-malkhuteh modan kol nagwwat 'ammemin.[117]

R. Šemaryah's closing couplet in Aramaic, with its blessing for the honoree and the prayer for national restoration, is also strikingly similar to the close in R. Yose's hymn:

[R. ŠEMARYAH]
Yifqun minnakh benin 'osqin be-'orayyta' u-miṣwwata' meqayyemin
We-yitbeneh beyt maqdeša' we-khullana' ḥayyin we-qayyamin.

May the sons that are born to you be studious in the Torah and faithful to the commandments,
And may the Temple be rebuilt, and all of us alive and well.

[R. YOSE]
Melekh malkhayya', yazkineh le-ḥatna' dena' bi-vnin dekhirin me'allefin be-'orayyta' u-l-naṭreh qayyemin
We-yitbeneh be-yomana' beyt maqdeša' we-khullanah ḥayyin we-qayyamin.

King of kings grant this bridegroom sons studious in the Torah and observant of its commands,
And may the Temple . . .

It is likely that both poets used sections from an older Aramaic hymn for their refrains and strophes. In presenting their tributes to the Bridegrooms of the Torah and of Genesis in a mixture of Hebrew, Aramaic and Greek couplets, the poets were presumably following an accepted practice in Romaniote congregations. Following is a selection from Ha-Ikriti's hymn:

Ševaḥ yeqar u-gedullah le-ḥay 'olamim,
Šalliṭ be-'orenos, pandoqrator le-khol ha-domim.

Render praise, distinction and greatness to the Eternal,
Ruler of the heavens, sovereign in all the earth.

The command 'Render praise, distinction and greatness' is taken from the Sabbath morning prayer, 'Unto God who rested from all His work' (*Le-'el 'ašer šavat mi-kol ha-ma'asim*). The Greek term *ouranos* in R. Šemaryah's hymn was not uncommon in the Romaniote liturgy, having been used by

[117] See above, p. 255 for the translation. The text in R. Šemaryah is *paddon*; in R. Yose it is *panddon*.

Abraham b. Jacob from Kastoria in his *mi kamokha* for the Sabbath before Passover. The Greek *pandoqrator* also appears in an anonymous hymn for Pentecost sung in Corfiote congregations:[118]

'Afendi pandoqra'ṭora'
Simfatisemas simerah
Ṭin ge'ullah sṭilemas 'ogligora'
We-Yisra'el 'aleluyah.

Lord, sovereign over all
Forgive us this day;
Thou, hasten to send us redemption,
And Israel, praise the Lord.

Although the thirteen-strophe hymn is mostly in Greek, Hebrew usages (*ge'ullah*, *we-yisra'el 'aleluyah*) are also included. The combination of Hebrew, Aramaic and Greek in the liturgy was a periodic practice of the Romaniotes.

The repeated references to the soul in Abraham Ha-Kohen's hymns, *'Edbaq bekha raḥum* and *'Ozziy we-zimrat yah*, would seem to indicate that they were *rešuyyot* to the *nišmat*. In the former, the poet gives voice to his soul's longing to be connected with its divine source:[119]

I would cleave [*'edbaq*] to You, O merciful One, be my refuge;
Being attached to You is my soul's longing
[*ha-devequt nikhsefah nafši*];
In You is all my desire [*tešuqati*] and joy;
Rejoice my heart, be happy for my reward.

Even as the spheres are animated by a desire to be attached to the Intelligences, the soul, likewise, yearns to cleave to her divine source. The reference for this conceit is Deut. 11: 22, 'If you will diligently observe this entire commandment . . . loving the Lord your God . . . and holding fast to Him [*u-l-dovqah bo*].' The rabbis (in *bKet* 111b), commenting on Deut. 4: 4, 'But you that did cleave unto the Lord, your God are alive every one of you this day,' ask, 'How is it possible to cleave to the Divine Presence concerning which it is written [Deut. 4: 24], "For the Lord your God is a devouring fire"?' However, in the writings of the Neoplatonist philosopher Isaac Israeli (850–*c*.932) cleaving (*devequt*) is defined as the reward of paradise from the Creator,

which is the union with the upper soul, and the illumination by the light of the intellect and by the beauty and splendour of wisdom. When attaining this rank, he

[118] See J. Matsa, 'Jewish Poetry in Greek' [Hebrew], *Sefunot*, xv (1981), pp. 237–366 at 278–80.

[119] Weinberger, *Širat . . . Rabbanim*, p. 504.

becomes spiritual, and will be joined in union to the light which is created, without mediator, by the power of God [*be-hidabqo be-ʾor ha-nivraʾ me-ʿoz ʾel noraʾ beli beynoni*].[120]

Abraham Ha-Kohen's *ʿOzziy we-zimrat yah* is possibly a *rešut* to the *nišmat* on the seventh day of Passover. This is indicated by its paraphrase of the Song at the Sea in Exod. 15: 7. The poet condemns God's enemies, whom his soul despises, and calls for their destruction.[121]

> God is my strength and song; He is the Lord helping me from the heavens:
> Demolish those who have gone astray and despise the truth; in the greatness of Your majesty, You overthrow Your adversaries;
> My soul hates Your enemies and loathes Your opponents;
> Hate them O Lord with eternal enmity, even as You pour out Your wrath upon them.

'Those who have gone astray' (*toʿey lev*) is a reference to the Christian ruling power. This designation is also found in the *yoṣer*, *ʾEloha bekha ʾeḥaveq*, of the Franco-German rabbi-poet Ephraim of Regensburg, who complains, 'Those who have gone astray have destroyed Your wife [Israel]' (*toʿey ruaḥ killu raʿyatkha*).[122]

Petiḥah

Anatoli Qazani's *petiḥah* to a *yoṣer* for Passover, *Le-rannen ḥasdekha taʿarog*, is based on Hispanic models. His hymn, which functions as a 'permission request' (*rešut*), is built in metrically balanced *qaṣīdah*-style hemicola with themes adapted from Jewish Neoplatonist philosophy:[123]

> My soul longs to sing of Your love, O Lord,
> And Your feared name to bless . . .
> The soul which You have hewn [*ḥaṣavta*] from her source in the Intellect [*sekhel*],
> And in the body placed her, preserved and prepared . . .

The idea of the soul emanating from the Intellect is a familiar Neoplatonic conceit enunciated by Solomon Ibn Gabirol (in his *Keter Malkhut*, No. 29), 'You did fashion its [the soul's] form from the flames of the Intelligence and like a burning fire have You wafted it.' Combined with the Neoplatonism is language borrowed from the *Sefer Yeṣirah* 1. 11, where God is represented as the architect and builder who quarries (*ḥaṣav*) His creation into the twenty-

120 Israeli, *The Book of Definitions*, trans. S. M. Stern, in Altmann and Stern, *Isaac Israeli*, pp. 25–6.

121 Weinberger, *Širat . . . Rabbanim*, p. 505.

122 See Habermann, 'Piyyuṭey R. Ephraim . . . mi-Regensburg', pp. 130–2.

123 Weinberger, *Širat . . . Keretim*, p. 26.

two letters of the Hebrew alphabet, the building-blocks of the universe. Following the account of God's role in fashioning the soul, the Cretan poet praises His providential acts in Israel's history from the time of Abraham to the exodus from Egypt. The hymn closes with a plea for relief from the current exile and restoration in Israel's national home.

Jacob b. Eliezer's *petiḥah*, *'Ašer šipper reqi'ey rum*, for the intermediate days of Passover, is designed, like Qazani's, as a *rešut*. However, unlike the latter's *qaṣīdah* style, R. Jacob favours a metric pseudo-*muwashshaḥ* comprising fourteen strophes and an opening 'belt'. This uncommonly long *petiḥah* opens with a cosmic preface of the type commonly found in a *mi kamokha* hymn, following which the poet reviews Israel's sacred history, concluding with the exodus from Egypt and the division of the Sea.[124]

Seliḥah

Šemaryah b. Elqanah's *'Elohim 'essa' nafši*, in quatrain strophes with identical opening and closing units, is marked in the Romaniote ritual as a *seliḥah* for the Ten Days of Repentance. His other hymn in this genre is *Šavrah libbi [be]'anḥati*, for the Fast of Gedaliah, in which he laments the latter's assassination, based on the account in 2 Kgs. 25: 22 ff. and Jer. 40–1.[125] Of special interest is the *seliḥah*, *'Eyley meromin*, for the Ten Days of Repentance by R. Elqanah *Ha-Parnes*. Modelled after Eleazar Qillir's, *'Ammiṣey šeḥaqim mi-ma'al*, for the Day of Atonement, the Cretan's hymn is in quintet strophes with rhyming quatrains and closing scriptural verse ending with the unit *lakh* (to You). The first three cola in each strophe are introduced by alternating refrains:[126]

ANGELS ON HIGH declare, 'There is none holy like You;'
MEN ON EARTH, with fear and trembling, Your unity affirm,
EVEN I [the cantor-poet], the substance of my inner life and thoughts
[In lieu of] burnt offerings of fatlings,
I present to You.

ANGELS ON HIGH compose a song and sing sweetly the treasured words;
MEN ON EARTH direct their prayers and prepare to repent;
EVEN I confess my sins and the inclination that deceived me;
A donation
I offer up to You . . .

124 Weinberger, *Širat . . . Keretim*, p. 70.
125 Ibid. 116–18; idem, *Širat . . . Rabbanim*, pp. 492–8.
126 Weinberger, *Širat . . . Keretim*, pp. 119–22; *Maḥazor Le-Yamim*, ii. 385–7.

R. Elqanah is obviously familiar with the rabbinic view (in *Exod. Rabbah* 21. 4) that angels bear the prayers of Israel to God's chariot throne and weave them into a crown for His use: 'ANGELS ON HIGH crown You with wreaths, Dweller in the Bush' (Deut. 33: 16). He pleads with the angels to intercede on Israel's behalf:

ANGELS ON HIGH appeal to God to hasten my redemption . . .
ANGELS ON HIGH mediate for us, declare us upright before the
King.

Moses Ha-Yewani's *seliḥah* for the Fast of Esther, in which he reviews the laws pertaining to the Scroll of Esther and festival of Purim, is similar in form and theme to Šabbetai Ḥaviv's *seliḥah*, *'Agagi šaqad*, for a like occasion. R. Moses' *seliḥah*, *Me'on qodšekha 'ammekha 'ussaf*, for the Day of Atonement is in quatrain strophes with closing biblical verses ending with the unit *laylah* (evening). In his plea for forgiveness the poet borrows from rabbinic sources:[127]

[Lord] erase the evil judgment and give him [Israel] relief
He has forsaken wickedness; his prayers pour out before You;
His fat and blood he offers; his gift is passed on ahead of him,
And he [Jacob] spent the night [in prayer]— [Gen. 32: 22]

'His fat and blood he offers' is taken from the prayer of R. Šešet (in *bBer* 17a) during a fast, 'May it be Your will to account my fat and blood which have been diminished as if I had offered them before You on the altar . . . '

Ḥaṭa'nu

Šemaryah b. Elqanah's *ḥaṭa'nu*, *Šiqdu 'am nidka'*, for the Tenth of Ṭevet fast is a sixteen-strophe hymn in rhyming tercets with closing scriptural verse closing with the repeated unit *ṣeva'ot* (armies). Although there is no mention of the Ten Martyrs—as is commonly found in hymns of this genre—the tone of R. Šemaryah's *ḥaṭa'nu* reflects Israel's agony in exile and her hope for redemption.[128]

[God], exalted on high, will see the maltreated,
And He will confuse the enemy oppressing them;
He will display wonders to Israel, His very own tribe,
The Lord of hosts [is His name].

Mattityah b. Joseph's *ḥaṭa'nu*, *Min'i yeḥidah ro'a fo'olekh*, is a pseudo-*muwashshaḥ*, with each of its twenty strophes ending with the unit *melekh* (king). Following a confession of sins, the poet recalls the martyrdom of the Ten Sages and lists by name [R. Simeon] b. Gamaliel, R. Ishmael and R.

[127] Weinberger, *Širat . . . Rabbanim*, pp. 502–3.

[128] Ibid. 497–8.

Akiva. In the closing strophes, R. Mattityah asks that the cruel death of the unblemished sages be an atonement for the sins of Israel.[129]

[God], consider the spilled blood of the holy ones
Like the blood of offerings in Your holy [Temple];
Remember the virtue of those who look to You
O Lord, grant victory! May the King [answer us when we call].

Tokheḥah

Anatoli Qazani's metric *qaṣīdah*-style *tokheḥah*, *'Imri yeḥidati*, is the poet's admonition to his soul. Here, as in his *petiḥah*, above, he reveals his Neoplatinist leanings:[130]

Tell me, my soul, will you forever
Be lodged in this mortal house and remain asleep?
Sweet is your slumber; you forget that it ends,
And you will be startled and terrified . . .
Put an end to your animal passions until
They become the mere image of a dream . . .
You who are quarried from the holy [*maḥaṣavakh ha-mequddaš*], awake;
Forsake this mortal dwelling become flesh . . .
Rejoice, my soul, and return to the home
Of your Father and of His bread partake.

Qazani combines a complex of images in this hymn. The sleeping soul is unaware of the reality of the wakeful world where man has to account for his actions. The soul asleep is able to indulge herself in 'animal passions' and is forgetful of her spiritual source. When the poet advises the soul, 'Return to the home of your Father' (God), he is suggesting that she pursue the values of the spirit, such as knowledge and virtue, and forsake the demands of the 'mortal dwelling become flesh.'

Jacob b. Eliezer's *tokheḥah* is a self-admonition comparable in form and theme to Anatoli Qazani's *'Imri yeḥidati*, and based in large part on Ibn Gabirol's *Keter Malkhut*, Nos. 25–31. The Hispanic influence is seen in R. Jacob's use of the metric *qaṣīdah* style for his *tokheḥah*, and his practice of repeating the first hemicolon at the close of the hymn. The latter stylistic device was employed by Moses Ibn Ezra and his contemporaries. Below are the opening and closing cola from R. Jacob's hymn:[131]

With all my soul I will praise and be thankful,
And if she has been perverse and inwardly corrupted,

[129] Weinberger, *Širat . . . Keretim*, pp. 110–12.
[130] Ibid. 30.
[131] Ibid. 73–6; M. Ibn Ezra, *Širey Ha-Ḥol*, i. 1, ii. 3.

[Remember] that I am a vagrant far [from home], lodged in a
wasteland;
Alas, the virgin [soul] has been violated . . .
Graciously heal O Lord, and kindly hasten to one seeking [Your
presence];
With all my soul I will praise and be thankful.

Abraham Kohen's *tokheḥah*, *'Enoš 'anuš we-'adam me-'adamah*, is also in metric *qaṣīdah* style in a tone of self-rebuke. The soul is urged to free itself from its earthly morass by meditating on the wisdom of God's activity, in imitation of the angels who praise Him with their intellect (*be-sikhleyhem*). The reward that awaits the liberated soul is eternal union with the light of the intellect, a theme that the poet alluded to in his *rešut*, *'Edbaq bekha raḥum*. Following is the closing stich from his *tokheḥah*:[132]

This is the secret concerning the union of man with his Intellect
[*sod devequt 'iš we-sikhlo*]:
It makes possible the ascent to the heaven and its heights.

Šemaryah b. Elqanah's *tokheḥah*, *Šime'u le-millay 'am 'emunay*, in rhyming tercets with scriptural closure, enlists the theme of 'judgment and punishment in the grave':[133]

Both poor and rich will stand
In judgment before the Dweller in the Heights,
Even kings and princes will be summoned . . .
Both soul and body will be delivered
To the destructive angels there [in the grave] to be punished,
Because they did not take instruction.

Baqqašah

Elijah Philosof's two *baqqašot* for the Day of Atonement, *'Elohey ha-'elohim wa-'adoney ha-'adonim* and *Yehi raṣon . . . še-tesimeni min ha-'anašim*, show the influence of Sa'adyah Ga'on, Ibn Gabirol and Judah Ha-Levi. The above hymns of the Cretan poet conclude with Ps. 19: 15, as do the two *baqqašot* of Sa'adyah, the *Keter Malkhut* of Gabirol and the *baqqašah 'Avarekh 'et 'adonay* by Ha-Levi. Both *baqqašot* by R. Elijah were designed for private devotional use—as were the *baqqašot* of Sa'adyah—and their tone is characteristically confessional and personal. Following is a selection from *'Elohey ha-'elohim*:[134]

132 Ben-Menaḥem, *Mi-Ginzey Yisra'el*, pp. 169–70.
133 Weinberger, *Širat . . . Rabbanim*, pp. 495–6.
134 Weinberger, *Širat . . . Keretim*, pp. 88–9; Sa'adyah Ga'on, *Siddur*, pp. 47 ff.; Ibn Gabirol, *Širey Ha-Qodeš*, pp. 37 ff.; Ha-Levi, *Širey Ha-Qodeš*, pp. 132 ff.

Much loving kindness have You granted me, even in my mother's womb and later when I issued forth into the airy world. With much goodness have You endowed me throughout the time that You brought me here, notwithstanding that I am stripped bare of good deeds. My few decent traits are pitiful now that I come to present myself before You . . . In my flesh is the sign of Your covenant . . . and in my heart is trust in Your mercy and grace . . .

R. Elijah's second *baqqašah*, *Yehi rașon* . . . , is uncommon in that it paraphrases the Hispanic Neoplatonist, Baḥya Ibn Paqudah's (11th c.) *Duties of the Heart* (*Ḥovot Ha-Levavot*), the 'Gate of Abstinence', chapter 7.[135] R. Elijah's third *baqqašah* in rhymed prose, *'Attah 'eḥad be-sod romemutekha*, is an expanded commentary on Ibn Gabirol's *Keter Malkhut*, No. 2, in which the Cretan poet argues that God's unity is absolute and that the Ten Categories of Aristotle, listed below, cannot be used to define the nature of God. Here also the poet adapts in large part Ibn Paqudah's 'Duties of the Heart', chapter 7. Below is a selection:[136]

The [five] senses cannot reach Him, nor can any creature be likened to Him; He is not a substance [*'eșem*] to be reached by accidents and descriptions . . . He has no quality [*'eykhut*] that can take on appearance, nor quantity [*kammut*] that can be reached by measure, division or character; He is unrelated [*hișṭarfut*] to anything and cannot be scaled by degree; He is not confined to place [*'anah*] and cannot be encompassed by another; He is not bound by time [*matay*] that consigns Him to change; He is not limited by position [*mașșav*]; He is not described by His actions [*qinyan*]; He is not subject to change from one condition to another [*še-yyitpa'el*]; nor is He affected by the action of another [*še-yyif'al*] . . . His uniqueness is a mystery . . . hidden from the eyes of all humans and from the birds of the heavens concealed . . .

Elijah Philosof's two metric *baqqašot* in monorhyme, *Yešir nivzeh* and *'Aqaddemkha be-niv nefeš qedošah*, for the Ten Days of Repentance, are appeals to the soul to remember its divine source and remain pure, as it carries out its mission on earth. The poet borrows extensively from the writings of the Jewish Neoplatonists Solomon Ibn Gabirol and Abraham Ibn Ezra. The above hymns by R. Elijah are similar in form and theme to Jacob b. Eliezer's *baqqašah*, *'Ani 'et nafši 'odeh tehillah*. Like R. Jacob, R. Elijah repeats the opening hemicolon at the close, following Hispanic practice. It is likely that both Cretan poets modelled their hymns in this genre on Abraham Ibn Ezra's metric *baqqašah* in monorhyme, *Lekha 'eli tešuqati*.[137]

Taḥanun and *Teḥinnah*

Anatoli Qazani's *taḥanun*, *'Et se'aray sa'ir gilleaḥ*, for the 'Elul vigil nights is a metric pseudo-*muwashshaḥ* in quatrains with internal rhyme in the

135 Weinberger, *Širat . . . Keretim*, pp. 97–8; Ibn Paqudah, *Sefer Ḥovot*, pp. 551–4.
136 Weinberger, *Širat . . . Keretim*, p. 101.
137 Ibid. 81, 84; A. Ibn Ezra, *Širey Ha-Qodeš*, ii. 33–9.

strophes, but not in the guide. Its theme is a plea for relief from the oppressive policies of Christian and Muslim rulers toward their Jewish subjects:[138]

Byzantium has taken a razor to me;
They pierce my entrails with a cutting arrow;
Who has let the wild ass [Muslims] go free?
Who has loosed the bonds of the swift ass? . . .
O Pure One, how long will You see and be silent?
The son of Šamah [Esau] controls my land,
And the son of the slave [Hagar] has exiled me;
At the noise of the horseman I take flight . . .

Mattityah b. Joseph's *teḥinnah*, [*Laylah*] *mahalal malkekh*, for the Day of Atonement evening service, is a pseudo-*muwashshaḥ* with each of its of its sixteen strophes beginning and ending with the unit *laylah* (evening). Its phonetic-intensive alliteration and assonance recall the mannerisms of Joseph Qalai and Moses Ḥazan. Below is a selection from R. Mattityah's hymn:[139]

Laylah, *tamin we-yašar*, *masbi'a*, *mašpi'a u-mrawweh kemehim* . . .
Laylah, *yahir*, *bahir*, *kabbir*, *'abbir*, *meromam* . . .
Laylah, *zedim heliṣuni*, *heṣiquni*, *hel'uni*.

In the evening, [God], the pure and just, satisfies and endows, and fills the hopes of the hopeful . . .
In the evening, [God] the proud and lucid, mighty, forceful and exalted [hears prayers] . . .
In the evening, evil men mocked us, tortured us, made us weary.

[138] Weinberger, *Širat . . . Keretim*, pp. 35–6. [139] Ibid. 104–6.

6

Ottoman Hymnography

GENERAL BACKGROUND

Under Muslim Rule

WITH THE OTTOMAN CONQUEST of Anatolia, Greece and the Balkans from the Byzantines beginning with the capture of Bursa (Brusa) in 1326, the condition of Jews improved. They could now engage in business without restriction, purchase land and buy homes. They were, however, required to pay a poll-tax and a land-tax and thereby gained the protection of their person and property. Despite these costs Jewish life flourished and its community grew, thanks to the tolerant policies of the Ottoman sultans. In the fifteenth and sixteenth centuries the native Romaniotes were joined by immigrants from central and western Europe.

The *dhimmī* status of Jews as a protected minority in the Ottoman Empire was extended by the 'capitulation' agreements with Christian monarchs introduced by Suleiman the Magnificent (1520–66) and renewed by his heir, Selim II (1566–74). Under these agreements, Jews living and doing business in Christian Europe enjoyed extra-territorial rights and were protected from attack on their person and property. As a result, Jews were attracted to Ottoman lands and the economic opportunities that they offered. Among the newly arrived immigrants were exiles from the Spanish expulsion who, together with the native Romaniotes, ushered in an epochal revival of Jewish learning in the region. A notable academy was founded by the Romaniote Elijah Mizraḥi, where both sacred and secular studies were pursued. Succeeding Elijah Mizraḥi as headmaster was Elia Ha-Levi, editor of the *Maḥazor Romania*. A student of Moses Capsali and Elijah Mizraḥi, whom he succeeded as spiritual leader of the Romaniotes in Constantinople in 1525, R. Elia Ha-Levi was a leading figure in the renaissance of Jewish learning during the early Ottoman period. His responsa volume, *Tana' de-vey 'Eliyahu*, a part of which was published under the title *Zeqan 'Aharon*

(Constantinople, 1734) reveals that his correspondents included the notables Tam Ibn Yaḥya and Joseph Karo, author of the authoritative code of Jewish law, the *Šulḥan ʿArukh*. Like his contemporary, Solomon b. Mazal Ṭov of Constantinople, R. Elia was active in editing classic works in Hebrew literature and preparing them for publication on the printing press recently installed in the city by the brothers David and Samuel Ibn Naḥmias. Among the volumes which R. Elia had a hand in editing were Jacob b. Asher's law code, *Arbaʿah Ṭurim*, in 1504, the code of R. Isaac Al-Fasi in 1509 and the first printed edition of the *Maḥazor Romania* in 1510.

With the influx of refugees from Spain and Portugal following their expulsions in 1492 and 1496, friction often developed between the Romaniotes and the new arrivals. Differences in liturgical practices and betrothal customs added to the disputes. Romaniote leaders, aware of the prestige and learning of the Iberian immigrants, whose influence was soon being felt in the Ottoman community, feared that their congregations would be absorbed by the enterprising newcomers. In attempting to avert this, in 1510 Elia Ha-Levi of Constantinople and his colleagues decided to edit and publish their *Maḥazor Romania* on the Naḥmias brothers' press. In editing the Romaniote *Maḥazor* R. Elia had to choose hymns from among the several thirteenth- and fourteenth-century manuscript versions that were available to him.[1]

For their part the Iberian exiles established their own *yešivot*, with the most notable headed by Joseph Levi, author of *Beyt Ha-Lewi*, and funded by Doña Gracia Mendes Nasi and her son-in-law, Don Joseph Nasi. In addition to its *yešivot*, the region could boast an academy for the cultivation of poetry founded by Gedalyah Ibn Yaḥya in Salonika. Poets like Saʿadyah Longo, Judah Zarko of Rhodes, David Onkeneyra, Jacob Tarfon and Solomon Ha-Levi composed in a variety of secular genres, modelled after the courtier-poets of Andalusia and the sonnets and *maqāmat* of Immanuel of Rome.[2]

The religious life of the Ottoman Jewish community was much enhanced by the installation of a Hebrew printing press in Constantinople by the Naḥmias brothers, and David Naḥmias's son Samuel. In addition to Asheri's *Ṭurim* and the code of Al-Fasi, the Naḥmias published the Pentateuch with the commentaries of RaŠI and David Kimḥi and the works of Abraham Ibn Ezra and Moses Maimonides. Also published were books of regional interest like the *Maḥazor Romania* and the *Širim U-Zmirot We-Tišbaḥot*, a liturgical collection from 1545 under the editorship of the rabbi and cantor-poet Solomon b. Mazal Ṭov.

[1] For a list of the MS texts of the *Maḥazor Romania*, see Weinberger, *Širat . . . Rabbanim*, pp. 847–8. The later edns. of the Romaniote ritual, published in Venice, 1522–3, and in Constantinople, 1574, are generally based on Elia Ha-Levi's 1510 edn.

[2] See Habermann, *Toledot*, i. 232–5; idem, 'Qinot ʿal ḥakhmey Saloniqi'; Yarden, 'Niqbašot mi-širey R. Saʿadyah Longo'.

THE PRINCIPAL POETS

Šalom Enabi and Elia of Istip

Among the leading rabbi-poets in the early Ottoman period were Šalom b. Joseph Enabi of Constantinople and Elia b. Samuel from Istip, in Macedonia. Like his Cretan colleagues, Enabi was attracted to the revival of classical studies in the Balkans. He is known to have copied in 1460 Šem Ṭov ben Isaac Ibn Šaprut's Hebrew translation of Averroes' *Middle Commentary* (preserved in Paris, Bibliothèque Nationale, MS No. 965), and is the author of commentaries on Aristotle's *Physics*, Maimonides' *Hilkhot Yesodey Ha-Torah* (Laws Concerning the Principles of the Torah), and the mathematics of Abū'l-Hassan Ibn Lebhan. An exchange of letters between him and R. Michael Balbo of Crete is preserved in the latter's journal (Vatican Library, MS No. 105), which also contains two panegyrics by Balbo in honour of Enabi. Distinctive in Enabi's hymnography in the *Maḥazor Romania* are the numerous references to medieval science, philosophy and mysticism.

Elia b. Samuel of Istip in Macedonia, a gifted poet and author of a Pentateuch commentary which he completed in 1470, composed a dozen hymns, none of which was included in the *Maḥazor Romania*. The hymns survive in a private collection which may been a part of the poet's journal.[3] It is possible that the Constantinople editor of the *Maḥazor Romania*, R. Elia b. Benjamin, considered Istip a backwater and was not impressed with its cantor-poet. Undoubtedly, Elia b. Samuel's hymns were chanted by his Macedonian congregation which, it may be assumed, was competent enough to comprehend his references to the *Sefer Yeṣirah* and to medieval astronomy. From R. Elia's collection we learn that he corresponded with Moses Capsali, rabbinic leader of the Romaniotes in Constantinople, and with Elijah b. Parnes of Vidin in Bulgaria.

Mordecai Comtino and Elijah Ṣelebi

Mordecai b. Eliezer Comtino (1420–*c.*1487), of Constantinople and Negroponte, was the author of commentaries on Aristotle's *Metaphysics*, on several books by Abraham Ibn Ezra, on Maimonides' *Introduction of Logic*, and studies in Hebrew grammar, mathematics and astronomy. Comtino, like his mentor Ḥanokh Saporta, was a willing teacher of Karaites, who respected him enough to include his liturgical works in their prayer-book, albeit with some alterations. The two surviving hymns by Comtino are a metric epithalamium, *Mi-meʿono ʾor zoreaḥ*, and a metric *zemer* (song) for the festivals. The latter includes a subtle anti-Christian polemic.

[3] Oxford, MS Opp. 218 No. 251, fos. 213a–217b.

Comtino's contemporary Elijah Ha-Kohen b. Israel Ṣelebi of Anatolia composed a *yoṣer* with a Romaniote-style dialogue and experimented with uncommon rhyme forms in his *rešut*, *'Im levavi ba-'aṣato*. His massive *'azharot* for both positive and negative commands, the earliest Ottoman forms of this genre, reveal an anti-Karaite bias. Ṣelebi's two epithalamia, *'Ahuvati kemo sahar* and *Mešakhtini kelulat ḥen*, combine sacred and secular conceits. The latter is distinctive in its refrain based on Turkish melodies. The poet's name, Ṣelebi, is an honorific in Turkish and designates a 'gentleman'.

Menaḥem Tamar and Elia Ha-Levi

Menaḥem b. Moses Tamar lived in the second half of the fifteenth century. Like several of his Balkan colleagues, he wrote explanatory notes on Abraham Ibn Ezra's Bible commentaries and a tract on Hebrew grammar titled *Šir Ha-Širim* (Canticles), which he dedicated to his son Samuel. His liturgical works include *'azharot*, a metric *petiḥah* in the form of a *muwashshaḥ*, and a zionide elegy in the style of Judah Ha-Levi.

Elia Ha-Levi, a younger contemporary of Menaḥem Tamar, wrote a manual on ethics, *Sefer Liwyat Ḥen*, and several volumes of poetry, in addition to his responsa, mentioned above. Among his liturgical works is *Beyt Lewi*, a metric *tour de force* of 100 cola comprising 1,000 units beginning with the letter *bet*. Like his contemporaries, R. Elia favoured themes in medieval philosophy for liturgical use. His hymns reveal hints of anti-Christian and anti-Karaite polemics, despite his agreement to teach Karaites if they did not violate the festivals of the Rabbanite calendar and refrained from abusing Rabbanite teachers.[4] Solomon b. Mazal Ṭov's more than fifty liturgical works include components in the *yoṣer* cycle and *rešuyyot*, various *seliḥot*, a prayer for the seafarer and a tribute to Suleiman the Magnificent.

Other notable poets in the early Ottoman period were Ḥelbo of Ephesus, who had a Pentateuch copied for him in 1419 by Israel Šarvit Ha-Zahav, son of the Ephesian notable Solomon Šarvit Ha-Zahav; Aaron b. Abaye of Constantinople, an older contemporary of Elijah Mizraḥi; Yedidyah Solomon b. Joseph Roch of Rhodes, a correspondent of Michael Balbo of Crete; Joseph b. Solomon, author of the moving *seliḥah*, *Yom zeh levavo 'ammekha qore'a* (On this day your people rend their hearts); and Joseph b. Moses Qilti from the Morea, grandson of Rabbana David Pardoleone, author of *Minḥat Yehudah*, a treatise on Hebrew grammar. His father, Moses, corresponded with Michael Balbo of Crete. Joseph Qilti's *seliḥah*, *Nafši 'ešpekhah lakh*, was included by both Rabbanites and Karaites in their liturgies. Isaiah b. Joseph Missini, physician and poet from Mesene in the Morea, was esteemed by Elijah Mizraḥi, who referred to him as 'my friend, the honourable rabbi Isaiah Missini.' Missini was a vehement opponent of the Karaites: he

[4] See Mizraḥi, *Responsa*, No. 57.

compared them to the Sadducees (who denied the authority of the Oral Torah) and forbade a priest (*kohen*) to marry a Karaite woman. Mazal Ṭov b. David (d. before 1545) was the father of Solomon Mazal Ṭov.[5]

Later Ottoman poets include Isaac b. Joseph Missini, presumably Isaiah Missini's younger brother; Judah Ha-Kohen, whose elegy *Yiddom le-nogen ḥalil* was adopted for liturgical use by Karaites as well as Rabbanites; and Judah Ha-Levi b. Aaron Qilti, member of a prominent Romaniote family. His hymns contain several references to contemporary philosophy. Šelaḥyah b. Ḥananyah was possibly the son of Ḥananyah b. Šelaḥyah; and Solomon Mevorakh, a rabbi-poet from Salonika, is the author of *piyyuṭim* in several genres, including three panegyrics in honour of the Ottoman sultan, Selim II (1566–74).

Solomon b. Mazal Ṭov and the Ottoman Golden Age

Born in the last quarter of the fifteenth century to a Romaniote family with branches in Crete and Corfu, Solomon b. Mazal Ṭov, son of the poet Mazal Ṭov b. David, rose to prominence in Constantinople. Solomon b. Mazal Ṭov is listed among the notables, including Joseph Karo, Elia Ha-Levi and Aaron da Trani, recommending Abraham b. Solomon of Treves' *Sefer Birkat 'Avraham*, a work completed in 1534 in the home of Moses Hamon, physician to Suleiman II. R. Solomon began his career as editor in 1513 with the publication of David Kimḥi's *Sefer Ha-Šorašim* at the Constantinople press; the last book that he edited was the *Sefer Mikhlal Yofi* by Solomon Ibn Melekh in 1549. He worked closely with the local press during the more than three decades during which he edited or wrote encomia for some fifteen volumes published in Constantinople.[6]

A prolific writer of sacred and secular hymns, Solomon b. Mazal Ṭov epitomizes the renaissance of Hebrew literature in an Ottoman Golden Age that included the gifted Karaite poet Caleb Afendopolo and the Academy of Poets in Salonika founded by Gedalyah Ibn Yaḥya. R. Solomon is the author of some fifty-five liturgical works including *Šokhen le-ʾulam zeh*, for the dedication of a new synagogue, as indicated in the hymn's superscription. It is likely that this was the congregation which he served in Constantinople, where, in his day, there were some forty-four synagogues in the city attended by exiles from southern France, Italy and the Iberian peninsula, in addition to the native Romaniotes. Following is a selection from the dedicatory hymn built as a metric pseudo-*muwashshaḥ*. Its revealing superscription directs that the hymn be sung to a Greek melody (*ʿod lo zemer le-niggun yewani*), presumably for the benefit of his Greek-speaking Romaniote congregation.[7]

[5] Weinberger, *Širat . . . Rabbanim*, English section, pp. 30–4; Mizraḥi, *Responsa*, No. 58.

[6] See Markon, 'R. Šelomo'.

[7] *Širim U-Zmirot*, No. 269; Roth, *The House of Nasi*, p. 92.

You who dwell in this hall
Bring joy to this people;
Prophet and priest
Install in Your Temple . . .

Humbly they beg You,
Singers after musicians;
A sanctuary in miniature they build
In lieu of of Your Temple.

R. Solomon's hymns, composed in several genres, enjoyed a wide popularity and were included in the synagogue rituals of Spain, Yemen, Cochin and the Karaites.[8]

Solomon b. Mazal Ṭov's Messianism

Suleiman's order to rebuild the walls of Jerusalem and to repair its water conduits and pools, in addition to his grant of a concession for Tiberias to Don Joseph Nasi, evoked messianic hopes in the writings of Solomon b. Mazal Ṭov. Following is a sample from his metric pseudo-*muwashshaḥ baqqašah* for Simḥat Torah, *'Aḥar nogenim 'ašir širah*, with its exhilarating tone of imminent redemption. In the following strophe the poet speaks in God's name to the congregation:[9]

Why would you tarry in the wilderness waste?
The vine has flowered, the pomegranates are in bloom;
They blossom already from the dew of Hermon;
Come my beloved; awaken O harp.

In his hymns for the seven Sabbaths of Consolation, the poet exults in the hope of national restoration in language reminiscent of Isaiah of Babylon. In his *rešut*, *Ṣiyyon be-qol garon*, R. Solomon announces that 'the time has come to prune the vines,' a verse from Cant. 2: 12 which the rabbis, in *Cant. Rabbah*, interpret, 'The time has come for the land of Israel to be divided among the Israelites.' Reinforcing this good news is the poet's *rešut*, *Šuvi lakh yonah ṣiyyonah*, for Šabbat Naḥamu with the prophetic reading from Isa. 54: 11 ff. Speaking in God's name, R. Solomon assures his congregation that they will witness the fall of Rome even as their ancestors saw the Egyptians drowning in the sea:[10]

[8] See Markon, 'R. Šelomo', pp. 332–3, for R. Solomon's encomium in honour of the volume 'Midraš on the Five Scrolls' (*Midraš Ḥameš Megillot*), which he edited in 1520. There (l. 13) he protests against those 'making a public outcry and [who] with their dumb tongues and impeded speech shout noisily.' It is not clear whether his remarks are directed against the Karaites.

[9] *Širim U-Zmirot*, No. 233.

[10] Ibid., No. 266.

Goodly are your tents and beautiful,
Even your footsteps in sandals;
As at the sea mighty wonders
You beheld so will you see [fulfilled] the prophecy on Rome [*teḥezi massa' roma'*].

In closing, the poet brings hope to the Jews exiled in lands ruled by Christians, called Seir (Esau), after Gen. 32: 4:

To him who calls out from Seir, 'How much longer is the night [of exile]?'
The Rock who causes hinds to calve responds,
'The Day Star has fallen from the heavens!'
Praise Him all that have breath.

The 'Day Star' who 'laid the nations low', after Isa. 14: 12, is a reference to the Western Church in Rome. In this conceit, R. Solomon echoes the view of Isaac Abrabanel (1447–1508), in his *Yešu'ot Mešiḥo*,[11] that the Ottomans, who prevailed against the Eastern Church in Constantinople in 1453, will overcome the Church in the West.

In his *petiḥah*, *Samti megammati 'eli le-negdekha*, R. Solomon calls upon the Jews living in the West to leave the land that is ruled by the progeny of Seir, who set the Temple ablaze, and return to the Land of Israel:[12]

Why would you be ruled by Seir
Who put to the torch the Holy Temple?
Wake up and find a nest in the city
Built by your swallows. [Ps. 84: 4]

Truly, the appointed time has come
For the sheep [Israel] to spread out to Dan;
Return from the grave [exile]
To your Shepherd.

The call to settle in the Land of Israel is a persistent theme in R. Solomon's liturgical writings, as in his *ge'ullah*, *Me-ḥagwey ha-sela'im ṣe'i*:[13]

My dove, come out from the cleft of the rocks
And return to your nest . . .

The invitation, in God's name, is repeated in his *Šuvi yefat 'ayin*, *Šim'i bat u-r'i*, *'Uri yonati, yafati*, and *Širah 'ašir 'al šošannim*.[14]

[11] See Abrabanel, *Yešu'ot Mešiḥo*, p. 79b.
[12] *Širim U-Zmirot*, No. 26.
[13] Ibid., No. 251.
[14] Ibid., Nos. 255, 115, 234, 237.

[*ŠUVI YEFAT ʿAYIN*]
How you cheapen yourself, a fugitive among your tormentors;
Wake up, arise, and return to your cities;
My dove, your time is near and you will take your fill
Of love until morning, adorned in your necklace.

[*ŠIMʿI BAT U-RʾI*]
Why do you tarry, O lily [Israel] among the thorns,
In the courts of Dishon [Gen. 36: 26], the foe?
Come now to the garden of the King's palace,
In the company of the Lord's tribes,

It is now a thousand years
And even half of a thousand
Since a foot has set therein . . .

[*ʿURI YONATI, YAFATI*]
Take now your fledgelings
From the stranger's nest, even your delicate ones . . .

Come to God's house, O graceful gazelle,
Pay homage to the Lord who searches the heart . . .

[*ŠIRAH ʾAŠIR ʿAL ŠOŠANNIM*]
Come now to the King;
Raise your mighty voice,
O my dove, I have set you free.

In his optimistic call for Jews to return to the Land of Israel, R. Solomon was undoubtedly encouraged by the efforts of Joseph Nasi, Duke of Naxos, to rebuild Tiberias, as well as by the growing Jewish settlement in Safed, where Joseph Karo and Moses di Trani were ordained rabbis in 1538. However, nagging doubts remained, and the poet shows his impatience in his *Šir ʿahạddeš beyn ʾemunim*:[15]

Show us, O Lord of hosts,
The end of the wonders decreed;
Gather in the scattered sheep
There in God's courts.

Sometimes, the poet wonders, as in his *Širat dodi, širat karmo*, if Israel's redemption time is imminent:[16]

Lo the winter has passed and is gone,
Why does Seir yet prevail?

[15] Ibid., No. 270.
[16] Ibid., No. 109.

In his *Ṣeviyyah ʿaley siryon*, however, the poet says that Israel is already prepared and ready to return to her home:[17]

The gazelle [Israel] on Mount Siryon awaits her troops,
She will cascade down upon Zion's hills.

THE PRINCIPAL GENRES

ʾAzharah

Only a few *ʾazharot* by Balkan poets have survived. Other than Benjamin b. Samuel's *ʾazharah* fragment, [*Moṣaʾ*] *sefatayim li-šmor*, preserved in the Cairo Geniza, there are no hymns in this genre in the later Romaniote period. Ottoman poets did produce two *ʾazharot*, *ʾAvarekh le-ʾel noraʾ* by Elijah Ṣelebi and Menaḥem Tamar's *Mešokh naʾ ḥasadekha*. Both hymns are closely modelled on Solomon Ibn Gabirol's *Šemor libbi maʿaneh*.[18] Emulating the Saragossan sage, Ṣelebi and Tamar compose their Pentecost hymns in a variation of the *ha-ʾarokh* metre, with monorhyme quatrains enclosing rhyming tercets. Both preface the list of commands with an introductory prayer giving the author's signature.

Notable in Ṣelebi's *ʾazharah* is his tribute to Maimonides, whose rulings he generally follows:[19]

Trained in the lap of wisdom,
And known as the son of Maimon;
He makes clear the concealed basics [of the law]
And reveals their secrets;

May his soul in God's shade
Be bound up in the holy mountain,
That it be a covering for his head
And protect him in its recesses.

In listing the positive and negative commands, the Ottoman hymnist must choose between differing rabbinic opinions. In such cases, Ṣelebi mostly sides with Maimonides. For example, he agrees with the latter's ruling—opposed by R. Abraham b. David of Posquières (RABaD)—that brothers who have not divided up their father's estate are exempt from the surcharge (*qolban*) paid as compensation to the Temple for any loss incurred in the exchange of money. Ṣelebi also sides with the Fustat sage, against RABaD and Naḥmanides, that one is commanded to deduct interest from loans to

[17] *Širim U-Zmirot*, No. 275.

[18] Weinberger, *Širat . . . Rabbanim*, pp. 389–406, 423–45; Ibn Gabirol, *Širey Ha-Qodeš*, pp. 392–441.

[19] Weinberger, *Širat . . . Rabbanim*, p. 402.

foreigners, and he agrees with the former, against RABaD, with regard to forcing the foreigner to pay his debt. However, asserting his independence, Ṣelebi opposes Maimonides and forbids making images not only of men—as ruled by the latter—but of animals as well.[20]

Like Ṣelebi, Menaḥem Tamar generally follows the rulings of Maimonides, even in disputed cases. For example, he agrees with him—against Naḥmanides—that one who turns to ghosts, or enquires of familiar spirits, should be punished by excision (*karet*). However, he disagrees with him in the matter of the afflictions to be endured on the Day of Atonement. In line with the views of *Tosafot Yešanim* and R. Ašer b. Yeḥiel (ROŠ), Tamar rules that only eating and drinking are forbidden by biblical law, while Maimonides maintains that all five prohibitions are sanctioned by biblical law.[21]

Yoṣer

The conventions of the Balkan *yoṣer*-dialogue popularized by Joseph Qalai and Solomon Šarvit Ha-Zahav were continued in the Ottoman period by Elijah Ṣelebi in his *ʾOraḥ ḥayyim la-ṣaddiq meyšarim*, for Šabbat Šeqalim. As in earlier treatments of the genre, the parties are God and Israel, and their speeches are presented in alternating sets of four-tercet strophes including choral refrains ending with *qadoš*. As in earlier models, beginning with Qalai, the sets are prefaced by a formula introducing the speakers: 'And the Lord spoke to Moses, saying,' and 'They responded, all that God has spoken we will do and obey.'

The theme of Ṣelebi's *yoṣer* is the payment of the half-shekel to the Temple treasury, as directed in Exod. 30: 12–16 and interpreted by the rabbis. The importance of rabbinic teaching in elucidating the scriptural text is stressed in the opening set:[22]

> The path of life for the pious upright
> The Lord wondrously made, before weighing the mountains in scales;
> It rises in the darkness as a light for the righteous.
> Only these did He allow to give instruction . . .

It is likely that Ṣelebi's emphasis on the exclusive authority granted to rabbinic teaching in the Oral Torah was directed against Karaite polemicists, whose views on the rabbis interpreting Scripture are best summarized by Salmon ben Yeruḥam's (10th c.) diatribe against Saʿadyah Ga'on:

> It is written, *The Torah of the Lord is perfect* [Ps. 19: 8];
> What profit be there for us, then, in the written *Mišnah*?[23]

[20] Ibid. 381–6, 389–92, 398–402.
[21] Ibid. 432–6.
[22] Ibid. 381–6.
[23] Nemoy, *Karaite Anthology*, p. 78.

The fact that Ṣelebi found it necessary to stress rabbinic teaching suggests that the Karaite–Rabbanite controversy continued well into the fifteenth century in Anatolia. In the remaining strophes of the *yoṣer*, the poet reviews the laws pertaining to the half-shekel in *mŠeq*. Of particular interest is Ṣelebi's use of two alternating *qadoš* refrains as chorus commentaries. The first chorus refrain echoes the biblical-rabbinic ruling that the payment of the half-shekel is decreed for all Israelites:

[CHORUS:]
For all [the Israelites] who crossed the sea [of reeds] in distress,
The half-shekel is decreed
And the shekel is twenty *gerah*.

The second chorus echoes the joy of Moses, following Israel's agreement to contribute the half-shekel:[24]

[ISRAEL:]
We, the faithful progeny, all accept the rule,
Levites, Israelites and Priests,
We together, the honest sons of one man . . .

[CHORUS:]
When the humble one [Moses] heard this,
Fullness of joy showed in his face;
And upon hearing it, he agreed.

'Ofan

Šalom Enabi's *'ofan*, *Le-'el ha-barukh ne'imot notenim*, for Šabbat Šeqalim, is a metric five-strophe *muwashshaḥ*. Its theme reflects Enabi's interest in medieval astronomy and in contemporary religious philosophy, as seen in the following opening strophes:[25]

The Almighty, concealed, creates wonders;
There is the Chariot [*merkavah*], there the secret hidden;
In the heavens He wondrously [conceived] the world's highways;,
 The mystery of the Chariot is counted in the four [letters],
 The last and the first.

In the sphere of the stars are several divisions,
With each one following the other:
North and south in different degrees;
 By the [variations] of climate are they designated;
 Some rest while others journey.

[24] Weinberger, *Širat . . . Rabbanim*, pp. 382–3. [25] Ibid. 331–3.

The 'last and first' of the 'four [letters]' of the Divine Name, *yod* and *he'*, are said by Jewish mystics to be the building-blocks of the heavens. This is suggested in Ps. 33: 6, 'By the word of the Lord the heavens were made.' In a rabbinic text (in *bBer* 55a), Bezalel, the architect of the wilderness tabernacle, is reputed to have known how to combine the letters by which the heavens and earth were created. After the introduction, Enabi turns to the subject of the half-shekel donation to the Temple treasury, the theme of Šabbat Šeqalim. Here too he focuses on the mystical traditions regarding the half-shekel payment:

> Bitter is the measure for measure from the Lord on high;
> In order to forgive and remember [in mercy] the assembly's plot,
> The likeness of the half-shekel [He] revealed in concealed fire
> For the sons that have come of age,
> From twenty [and above], they make an offering.

'Measure for measure' refers to the rabbinic comment (in *jŠeq* 2. 3), 'Because Israel has sinned by making the Golden Calf at midday, they are required to give the half-shekel.' The 'likeness of the half-shekel revealed in concealed fire' is based on the rabbinic note (in *jŠeq* 1. 4) that in response to Moses' uncertainty as to the coin's appearance, God showed Moses a half-shekel freshly minted in the flames of the chariot throne.

Me'orah

Solomon Mevorakh's two *me'orah* hymns, *Šaḥar 'a'irah* and *'Ašorerah le-fo'arah*, in the form of a pseudo-*muwashshaḥ*, feature strophes linked by anadiplosis, a stylistic tactic from the classical and early Romaniote periods. However, unlike the earlier practice of linkage with one unit, Mevorakh links the strophes with a complete colon in *Šaḥar 'a'irah* and with two cola in *'Ašorerah le-fo'arah*. Below is part of *Šaḥar 'a'irah*:[26]

> *Le-'oṭeh 'orah / be-no'am qolot / yamim gam-leylot / ma'uzzi 'eqra*
> *Ma'uzzi 'eqra / ṣuri misgabbi / nafši we-libbi / hoṣeh mi-ṣarah!*

> [I sing] to [God] clothed in light / sweet songs / day and night, / I call Him my strength;
> I call Him my strength / my rock and fortress; / my heart and soul [plead]: / bring us out of distress!

Mi Kamokha

Šalom Enabi's five *mi kamokha* hymns are built on Hispanic models with identical repeated units after each quatrain strophe and an elaborate cosmic

[26] See Jerusalem, National and University Library, *'Osef Piyyuṭim Mi-Turkiyah*, MS No. 421, 8o, fos. 21b, 29a; Weinberger, 'Širim ḥadašim', I, p. 14.

preface liberally laced with references to contemporary religious philosophy and Jewish mysticism. In Enabi's *Mi kamokha šamayim konanta bi-tvunah*, for the New Year, he connects the ten *šofar* blasts with the ten *sefirot* in the *Sefer Yeṣirah*, 1. 2:[27]

The mystery of the ten orderly [*šofar*] voices
Is suggestive of the ten *sefirot*,
Malkhuyyot, *zikhronot*, and *šoferot* . . .

Enabi sees a relationship between the *sefirot*, the agency through which, according to Jewish mystics, all created things came into being, and the blasts of the *šofar* on Ro'š Ha-Šanah, the day on which the world was created, in the opinion of the rabbis (in *bRH* 27a). The connection between the ten blasts and creation is also suggested by the rabbis (in *bRH* 32a), 'To what do these ten kingship [*malkhuyyot*] verses [recited during the *šofar* service on the New Year] correspond? . . . To the ten utterances [*ma'amarot*] by means of which the world was created.' The function of the *sefirot* as creative agents is articulated by the early thirteenth-century mystic R. Azriel of Gerona in his 'Explanation of the Ten *Sefirot*', No. 3:[28] 'The existence of created beings is brought about by means of the *sefirot*.'

In a revealing strophe in his *Mi kamokha šokhen be-tokh 'eser*, for Šabbat Šeqalim, Enabi speculates on the relationship of the One to the Ten:[29]

Who is like You dwelling within Ten?
And the Ten surround You like the peel on a sprig.

Here, as well, Enabi probably drew on the writings of the Gerona mystics, who dealt with the problem of the One *vis-à-vis* the Ten, as seen in Rabbi Azriel's 'Explanation of the Ten *Sefirot*', No. 6:

About this the enquirer persists: How can we possibly say that He is One and the multiplicity of Ten unites within Him? . . . *Answer*: . . . the One is the foundation of the many and that in the many no power is innovated—only in Him. He is more than them and each of them is superior to its antecedent, and the potency of one is in the other.

In the same hymn, Enabi alludes to what Rabbi Azriel, in the above treatise (No. 9), calls 'the nature of the *sefirah*' as 'the synthesis of everything and its opposite':

Who is like You? The crown placed before you is like a roof and canopy;
The crown and the glory are like bride and groom . . .
Who is like You, the hewer of letters into general matter and form?
Their secret resides in the mystery of 'crown' and 'glory' . . .

[27] Weinberger, *Širat . . . Rabbanim*, pp. 336–8.

[28] See Dan, *The Early Kabbalah*, pp. 89–96.

[29] Weinberger, *Širat . . . Rabbanim*, p. 344.

Enabi combines the terminology of Aristotelian philosophy, 'matter and form' (*ḥomer we-ṣurah*) with *Sefer Yeṣirah* speculation on the Hebrew letters *'alef*, *mem*, *šin*, symbolizing fire (*'eš*) and water (*mayim*), the opposites in the universe, similar to male and female. To this the poet adds the two *sefirot*, *malkhut* (crown) and *'aṭeret* (glory), representing bridegroom and bride. In the dynamic interaction of opposites and their synthesis, creation emerges.[30]

Enabi also introduces themes from contemporary astronomy into the liturgy. In his *Mi kamokha šamayim konen bi-gvurah* he echoes the view of Maimonides (in the *Moreh Ha-Nevukhim*, 2. 10) with regard to the 'four spheres which contain stars,' and that 'the spheres must have a soul; for only animate objects can move freely.' Moreover, the poet adds, the spheres move out of desire for their Creator—a conceit he shares with Solomon Ibn Gabirol (in his *Keter Malkhut*, No. 24)—and the four spheres are to be identified with the four 'living creatures' (*ḥayyot*) of the divine chariot throne. Each had four faces and moved in any of the four directions without veering (Ezek. 1: 6–17). The following is from Enabi's hymn:[31]

Who is like You, establishing the [stars] in the heavens with force?
Made from matter and form [*ḥomer we-ṣurah*],
They move in circles uneven . . .
They are endowed with souls and intelligence guides their
movement . . .
Each has four faces . . .
[And] their desire is to be united with their Beloved.

The conceit that the four spheres are the four 'living creatures' of the chariot throne is affirmed in Enabi's *Mi kamokha šamayim naṭita bi-gvurah*, for the New Year:[32]

Who is like You arranging the four spheres by design?
They themselves are the chariot throne [*merkavah*].

Introducing the laws pertaining to the festival of Tabernacles in his *Mi kamokha šiv'ah 'amudey hod hoṭba'ta*, Enabi follows the model of the Macedonian Šabbetai Ḥaviv, who reviews the laws of the heifer ashes in his Šabbat Parah hymn in this genre. Enabi, like past cantor-poets, not only instructs his congregation in matters of Jewish law but chooses between differing opinions on required practice. Below is an example:[33]

An *etrog* [citron] that is [either] white, Ethiopian, speckled or half-
ripe
Is invalid for use.

[30] See Scholem, *Re'šit Ha-Qabbalah*, p. 51; idem, 'Kabbalah', *EJ* x. 574.
[31] Weinberger, *Širat . . . Rabbanim*, pp. 352–3.
[32] Ibid. 333–5.
[33] Ibid. 340–1.

Regarding the use of the half-ripe *etrog*, Rabbi Akiba declares it invalid, while the Sages permit it (in *bSukk* 36a). Maimonides[34] and Joseph Karo[35] agree with the Sages. However, R. Šalom, following the ruling of the thirteenth-century Italian scholar R. Isaiah ben Mali di Trani (in his *Tosefot Rid*), forbids it.

The tendency to introduce themes from religious philosophy in the *mi kamokha* is also seen in the writings of Isaac b. Joseph Missini. His *Mi kamokha ba-'elim 'adonay* for the Sabbath is in quatrain strophes closing with scriptural verses and an identical repeated unit, after Hispanic models. Before the main theme, an exhortation to serve the Lord, there is the following cosmic preface:[36]

Who is like You among the gods, O Lord,
Whose necessary existence [*meḥuyyav ha-meṣiy'ut*] is understood
from [the nature] of God [*ha-muvan me-'adonay*]?

God as a 'necessary existent' is a designation that Missini may have borrowed from Maimonides' *Moreh Ha-Nevukhim*, 1. 52: 'Now, as God has necessary existence, while all other beings have only possible existence, there consequently cannot be any correlation [between God and His creatures].' This may also have been the poet's source for the argument that God's necessary existence derives from His nature, as suggested in the *Moreh* 2, Introduction, Proposition 20: 'A thing [like God] which has in itself the necessity of existence cannot have for its existence any cause whatever.' In the same hymn the poet refers to the soul by three names, a conceit he may have found in the writings of Sa'adyah Ga'on,[37] who designates the three as aspects of the cerebratonic (reasoning), somatotonic (appetition), and visceratonic (anger) character (*koaḥ ha-hekhreḥ, koaḥ ha-ta'awah, koaḥ ha-ka'as*). The following is from Missini's hymn:

You have created man dust, from the waste earth,
With *nefeš*, *ruaḥ* and *nešamah*, wise;
She [the soul] provides for her people;
This is the fair way of the Lord.

The soul as provider for the body brings to mind Ibn Gabirol's comment (in *Keter Malkhut*, No. 29), where the soul is commissioned by God as the body's protector.

Judah Qilti's *Mi kamokha 'el 'elohey ha-ṣeva'ot*, for Šabbat Šeqalim, follows the standard Hispanic structure of the genre, complete with cosmic preface and a repeated unit closing each strophe. A characteristic of the Romaniote

[34] Maimonides, *Mišneh Torah*, Laws of Sukkah, 8. 8.
[35] *Šulḥan 'Arukh, 'Oraḥ Ḥayyim*, 648. 22.
[36] Weinberger, *Širat ... Rabbanim*, pp. 409–11.
[37] Sa'adyah Ga'on, *Sefer*, 6. 121.

mi kamokha is the review of practices governing the half-shekel offering in Temple times. R. Judah's twenty-eight-strophe hymn was preserved in both the *Maḥazor Romania* and the *Maḥazor Corfu*. The Corfiote editor changed one of the strophes to read that, despite their exile, the Jews of Corfu 'pledge joyfully' the 'redeeming shekel' which is 'to be brought to Jerusalem.'

R. Judah's *Mi kamokha 'el 'elohey ha-ruḥot* for Šabbat Parah is also a lengthy twenty-four-strophe hymn with cosmic preface and repeated closing unit. The main theme of the hymn concerns the sacrifice of the red heifer and the use of its ashes mixed with water for purification. Like previous hymns in this genre, the poet closes with a plea for national restoration and, in the rebuilt Temple, resumption of sacrificial offerings for purification and atonement:[38]

> Fearful and mighty [God], from old You have chosen the holy nation
> Purified by the heifer's ashes and altar offerings;
> Make us clean from our defilement now when holiness has vanished
> We hope for redress, and there is none.

Later Ottoman *mi kamokha* hymns are represented by Solomon b. Mazal Ṭov's *Mi kamokha 'alfey šin'an*, for Šemini 'Aṣeret. His hymn is in the standard form for this genre, with strophes in quatrains closing with a repeated unit from Scripture. However, instead of a cosmic preface, the poet in his opening strophe reveals the occasion for which the hymn was written:[39]

> With mighty chariotry, twice ten thousand,
> Their cheers mixed with song, they bow low before You;
> Your heavens dripping with water declare the glory of God,
> For there the Lord ordained His blessing.

The clue that reveals the occasion for which the hymn was intended is 'heavens dripping with water.' This refers to the prayers for rain offered in the synagogue on Šemini 'Aṣeret.[40]

Ge'ullah

Solomon b. Mazal Ṭov is the author of three *ge'ullah* hymns built in quantitative metre. Although Romaniote hymns in this genre are rare, an earlier example by Moses b. David is also in metric form. R. Solomon's *ge'ullah*, *Yonah meqannenet 'el ha-yešimon*, is a pseudo-*muwashshaḥ*, but with an uncommon metre: – –v/– –/– –/–v– – (*pa'alulim*, *nif'al*, *nif'al*, *pe'ulim*).

[38] Weinberger, *Širat . . . Rabbanim*, pp. 418–20.
[39] *Širim U-Zmirot*, No. 294.
[40] See *mTa'an* 1. 1, 2 and *Maḥazor Le-Sukkot*, pp. 402 ff.

The superscription directs that the hymn be sung to the melody (*laḥan*) of Judah Ha-Levi's *Noda' be-khol hamon*, a Pentecost hymn. In R. Solomon's *ge'ullah*, the matron Israel is compared to a dove abandoned in the wilderness and longing to return home. The tone of the poem is hopeful that the matron's wish will soon be fulfilled:[41]

Lo the song of the nightingale [Israel]
Is now heard, even the voice of the turtle-dove;
He prefers the lovely Land [of Israel]
Over Tyre and Cyprus;
Aaron's progeny will kindle
The lamps in the flower knob [of the *menorah* in the Temple];
His land inherited
Will be given to the redeemed [Israel].

It is likely that R. Solomon's optimism reflected the benign policy of Suleiman II toward his Jewish subjects and his attempt to rebuild the walls of Jerusalem, the Damascus gate and the Tower of David.

R. Solomon's other two hymns in this genre, *Me-ḥagwey ha-sela'im ṣe'i yonati* and *Ṣeviyyah 'aley siryon*, are also metric pseudo-*muwashshaḥāt* and their tone is equally expectant and festive. In *Me-ḥagwey ha-sela'im*, Israel is personified both as the dove and as the young maid awaiting her lover's arrival:[42]

The maiden will now rejoice
When the Branch [the redeemer in Zech. 3: 8] comes to dance;
Like a palm tree he shall flourish
  In your garden, my beloved.

In *Ṣeviyyah 'aley siryon*, Israel is the 'gazelle', from Hispanic lore, whom the poet urges to take up arms for the climactic battle that will restore her national home:[43]

The gazelle dressed in armour
Is mustering her troops . . .
  She is drawn by the voice of her lover
  And by her home and its music;
  Behold her lustre and glory increased
Even the band of her prophets.

Two *ge'ullah* hymns by Solomon Mevorakh have been preserved. *Melo' 'eš hod we-hadar* is a pseudo-*muwashshaḥ* for Simḥat Torah with short staccato cola of only two to three units. Following the opening 'belt' couplet, the

[41] *Širim U-Zmirot*, No. 274: 20–3; Ha-Levi, *Širey Ha-Qodeš*, p. 445.
[42] *Širim U-Zmirot*, No. 86.
[43] Ibid., No. 298.

hymn continues with monorhyme in the strophe endings and variable internal rhyme:[44]

Konen ʿir ha-ṣedeq / we-šofeṭay ha-šivah
We-hoṣeh me-ḥedeq / ʾasirat ha-tiqwah.

Build the righteous city / and restore my judges;
Remove from the thorns / the prisoner of hope.

In his *geʾullah*, *ʾEmor le-ʾloheynu noraʾ we-ʾaddir*, Mevorakh also experiments with an uncommon rhyme form: *ab* / *cd* / refrain / *ce* / *ed* / refrain . . .

Rešut

Elia b. Samuel's *rešut*, *ʾImru horim li-vney širim*, for the Sabbath *maʿariv* (evening) service before the *qaddiš* suggests that the fifteenth-century Macedonian cantor-rabbis were not discouraged from embellishing the evening service, as was the practice in other congregations, noted above. Following is part of R. Elia's festive hymn celebrating the arrival of the Sabbath bride:[45]

Ye sages, call forth
The musicians,
The singers in front,
  The musicians last.

Greet the bride
Who is praised
On this eve,
  The night of espousals . . .

We will meet the queen
Highly regarded;
She comes with blessings
  To the children.

Although the hymn does not close with the opening of the *qaddiš*, the poet reveals its purpose in the closing colon:

A good life and pleasant [is enjoyed by] the obedient who respond,
  'Amen' [to the *qaddiš*].

A more traditional *rešut* to the *qaddiš* is Elia b. Samuel's *ʾAni vaʾti be-taḥan*, a four-cola *qaṣīdah*-type hymn in *ha-merubbeh* metre which ends with the opening units of the *qaddiš*:[46]

[44] Jerusalem, MS *ʾOsef Piyyuṭim Mi-Turkiyah*, fo. 31a.
[45] Weinberger, *Širat . . . Rabbanim*, p. 328.
[46] Ibid. 320.

I come with pleas and fears,
With abasement, lowered head and stance . . .
No tongue or language does justice
Sanctifying the Name, renowned in the world [*le-haqdiš ʾet šemey rabbah* . . .]

Judah Qilti's *ʾAšer niqdaš be-sod sarfey qedošim* is another *qaṣīdah*-style *rešut* before the *qaddiš*, as can be seen in its closing cola:[47]

From of old the Rock [God] made known to them His ordinances,
Which called for the erection of a holy sanctuary;
He was exalted [*we-yitgaddal*] in the assembly of venerable sages,
And sanctified [*we-yitqaddaš*] in Nisan, the first of the months.

Notable among the *rešuyyot* to the *qaddiš* is Solomon b. Mazal Ṭov's metric monorhyme hymn *ʾAyummati ke-ʾayyelet ʾahavim*. Uncommon for this genre is the introduction of a dialogue between Israel and the poet. In the opening cola Israel is presented as the beloved *femme fatale*, familiar from Andalusian love poetry:[48]

My fearsome lovely deer,
Her eyes are arrows piercing the inward parts;
Her lips are a thread of crimson and lily
Dripping myrrh, and her face is a flame.

Like the flirtatious cup-bearer at the Andalusian banquet, the beloved can be hard-hearted:

Her hands are like golden sceptres,
They tear open the casings of the heart.

Shifting from the descriptive to the meditative mode, the poet shows the carefree damsel turned into a pitiable mother, shedding tears for her exiled children and for the desolation of her home in Zion and the Temple in ruin. The once stately and proud bride of the Lord who followed Him into a trackless wasteland is now the abandoned wife. Seeing her weeping, the poet seeks to comfort her:

I saw her crying bitterly, her tears
Flowing down her cheeks like raindrops;
I asked her, 'Why do you weep?'
She replied, 'My children are grief-stricken . . .
I am like an owl in the wilderness, like the hawk
And the hedgehog dwelling in cities laid waste;

[47] Weinberger, *Širat . . . Rabbanim*, p. 422.

[48] *Širim U-Zmirot*, No. 273.

All rivers have crested from my tears
Which fill every valley and channel, each den and pit;
Yet they are unable to extinguish the flame of their love
Which increases like the locust and the caterpillar.'

Note the dialectic in the hyperbole of the rhetoric: unrequited love increases passion's flame, evoking a shower of tears whose brave efforts only add to the lovesickness. Presumably, R. Solomon adapted this figure from Hispanic love poetry. A notable example is Moses Ibn Ezra's lament on the parting of friends, 'The chariots that hasten friends in their travels' (*Rikhvey nedodim ba-yedidim 'aṣu*). Saddened by his friend's departure, the poet is in tears, even as his heart is aflame with passion for his company. In considering his predicament, he finds that, in addition to missing his friend, he has to contend with his emotions (tears and passion) which he perceives are competing to destroy him. *'Ayummati ke-'ayyelet 'ahavim* is one of R. Solomon's most insightful liturgical works. In it he effectively telescopes Israel's predicament: she cannot free herself from the God who has abandoned her![49]

Among the *rešuyyot* to the *barekhu*, which follow the *rešut* to the *qaddiš*, is Mazal Ṭov b. David's *Meqorekh meqor ḥayyim*. The hymn features an appeal to the soul to be aware of its mission in man's body, and is based on conceits adapted from the writings of Jewish Neoplatonists:[50]

[O soul], you originate from the source of life [*mi-meqor ḥayyim*]
And are hewn from sapphire; you are girded with the might of
your Rock;
[Remember] the time when you stood in your palace;
Mend your ways and cover yourself with courage
So that you may lead him [man] to true repentance;
Why would you be a vagabond and outcast [*golah we-surah*]?

In the final colon the poet borrows verbatim from Ibn Gabirol's *Keter Malkhut*, No. 30: 'If she [the soul] has been defiled, she shall wander for a time in wrath and anger. And all the days of her uncleanness, shall she dwell vagabond and outcast [*golah we-surah*].' A similar rhetorical question to the soul is found in Abraham Ibn Ezra's *petiḥah*, *'Aṣulah mi-meqor ḥayyim me-'irah*, in which the poet observes, 'Forsake the pleasures of the moment; why would you be a vagabond and outcast when you die?'[51] In the concluding cola, the poet advises the soul of the action she must take in order to free herself and return to her divine source. The influence of Gabirol and Ibn Ezra is also indicated here, as is seen in the following from R. Mazal Ṭov:

49 M. Ibn Ezra, *Širey Ha-Ḥol*, i. 195: 7.
50 Markon, 'Le-David', p. 39.
51 A. Ibn Ezra, *Širey Ha-Qodeš*, i. 55.

Improve your looks and put on adornment
From the pillar of reverence [*yesod mora'*], and the counsel of learning and pious deeds [*we-sod miṣwah we-torah*];
Fortified with these you will be enabled to ascend to the inner holiness
And from its glory and splendour you will be adorned.

The phrase *yesod mora' we-sod miṣwah we-torah* is borrowed from Abraham Ibn Ezra's comprehensive study, *Sefer Yesod Mora' We-Sod Torah*, where he advises the soul to 'acquire wisdom . . . study God's Torah and observe His commands.' Ibn Gabirol is even more explicit in affirming that, notwithstanding the soul's divine origin, it can return to its heavenly source only by cleansing itself from the pollutants of the world through knowledge and pious deeds.[52]

Elia of Istip's *rešut* for the *barekhu*, *'Aromimkha 'eloha ṣur yešu'ati*, is a metric, one-strophe, *qaṣīdah*-type hymn, closing with the phrase, 'Praise the Lord who is blessed.' As noted above, an earlier hymnist named Mosqoyo built his *barekhu rešut* in similar fashion, based on models by Ibn Gabirol and Abraham Ibn Ezra.[53] A more elaborate *rešut* for the *barekhu* was composed by Elijah Ṣelebi. The latter's hymn, in the form of a pseudo-*muwashshaḥ*, has an uncommon rhyme scheme: *ab*, *ab*, *ab*, *cccc*, *b* / *de*, *de*, *de*, *ffff* / *b* / etc. Ṣelebi's *rešut* was chanted on Tabernacles and opens with an account of the poet's personal struggle against his evil inclination:[54]

If I direct my heart by his [Satan's] counsel,
He will prevent me from being faithful [to You] . . .
Would that the Rock, with His bands of love,
Direct me on the way;
  Hold me fast, my Refuge; when I sleep, He is within me
  And when awakened I will sing of the Lord's support.

Later forms of the *rešut* to the *barekhu* are represented by Elia b. Benjamin Ha-Levi's hymn, *'El lekha 'oz wa-'aṭeret*, chanted on Simḥat Torah. Built as a metric pseudo-*muwashshaḥ*, this *rešut* is designed as a poetic commentary on the Scripture reading for the festival from Deut. 33: 1 ff. Before addressing the main theme, the poet paraphrases a rabbinic legend in *Mekhilta'* (tractate *Ba-Ḥodeš*) No. 5 and *Sifre*, No. 348:[55]

When God appeared to me [Israel],
Then in Seir, even in Paran
He passed among them [the nations] His Torah and complained,

[52] See A. Ibn Ezra, *Yesod Mora'*, in Levin, *Yalqut*, 7. 12, p. 332; Ibn Gabirol, 'Keter Malkhut', Nos. 29, 30; idem, *Meqor Ḥayyim*, 1. 3, 5; Sirat, *History*, pp. 72–3.
[53] Weinberger, *Širat . . . Rabbanim*, p. 320. [54] Ibid. 380–1. [55] Ibid. 475–6.

'They refused, [preferring] to transgress.'
His holy ones [Israel] awaited Him;
Your [God's] commands are their pride.

Solomon b. Mazal Ṭov's *rešuyyot* to the *barekhu*, *Šelomey 'el yedidey yah* and *Serafim 'omedim 'afu be-sinay*, return to the earlier metric, *qaṣīdah*-style form.[56] As noted above, permission requests were composed preceding the benedictions of the *šema'*. Judah Qilti's *'Ašallem le-'lohay ḥay nedarim*, was probably a *rešut* before the *ge'ullah* hymn in the *yoṣer* cycle. Following are its closing cola:[57]

The Rock brought them [Israel] to His holy mountain and His land,
And He fully rescued them in all circumstances;
As You redeemed [*ke-ga'alta*] Your people from Egypt,
So may You hasten and gather in the scattered [remnant].

Earlier *rešuyyot* for the *ḥatan bere'šit* by Yose b. Abraham and Šemaryah Ha-Ikriti were in the form of folk hymns in a blend of Hebrew, Aramaic and Greek. In sharp contrast is Elia b. Benjamin Ha-Levi's carefully crafted metric *rešut* in the form of a *qaṣīdah* for the *ḥatan bere'šit* on Simḥat Torah. No less festive than the above is the tone of R. Elia's hymn, which opens with a celebration of the miracle of creation and the honour given to the *ḥatan bere'šit*, who will read the opening chapter of Genesis:[58]

Husband of my betrothal, with this diadem crown
Be adorned when you read, 'This is the Torah' [Deut. 4: 44] . . .
Relate the wonders of creation with time
Renewed by the ten words.

The 'wonders of creation with time renewed' (*ḥuddaš*) is a reference to the benediction before the *šema'*: 'Day after day, He renews creation.' The 'ten words' are based on *'Avot* 5. 1: 'The world was created by ten utterances.' In the remaining strophes the poet comments on contemporary astronomy and employs figures borrowed from Solomon Ibn Gabirol and Maimonides. Reflective of Ibn Gabirol's *Keter Malkhut*, Nos. 19 and 20, is R. Elia's characterization of the seven planets in the twelve constellations:

Derision [*lege'*] in the firmament is in Saturn's sphere;
When 'the waters were gathered up' [and land and life appeared,
  Gen 1: 9] He called to Jupiter,
And 'the earth put forth vegetation' [Gen. 1: 11] . . .

In the closing cola R. Elia pays tribute to the *ḥatan bere'šit* as the administrative head of the community:

[56] *Širim U-Zmirot*, Nos. 260, 261.
[57] Weinberger, *Širat . . . Rabbanim*, pp. 422–3.
[58] Ibid. 474.

Fortunate is the magnanimous one chosen from among God's
people
Who merits being called up from the ranks;
The yoke of office is on his shoulders; would that he be blessed
with peace
By the Most High, and may our brother continue to merit strength
and glory.

Solomon b. Mazal Ṭov's metric, *qaṣīdah*-style *rešut* for the *ḥatan ha-torah* on Simḥat Torah hints at the practice in Romaniote congregations observed on the festival. The rabbinic leader was generally designated the *ḥatan ha-torah*, and his task was to read the closing chapter from the Pentateuch at morning prayers. During both evening and morning services the honoree's groomsmen (*šoševinim*) would escort him from his home to the synagogue. Following are the opening cola in R. Solomon's hymn:[59]

When I invoke God's awesome name in song,
Arise O Bridegroom and read the enlightening Torah while the
groomsmen
Follow behind you with lilies;
They greet you with joyful melodies, singers and choir.
'May God, holy and exalted, lengthen your days.
May He who increases Israel's stock give you children
Studious in God's Torah,' and the singers answered,
Amen . . .

A distinctive example of this genre is Solomon b. Mazal Ṭov's Šabbat Naḥamu metric *rešut*, *Ṣiyyon be-qol garon*, in which he weaves the verset from Isa. 40: 1 into his hymn:[60]

Shout O Zion, call on your fortress;
Return, prisoners of song, I would see you rejoice . . .
The time has come to prune the vines, to stand up
To the tyrant, even to thistle and thorn in your dwelling
place;
Rise up and prepare yourselves to greet the Lord exalted
On the day when your God will say, 'Comfort, be comforted.'

He repeats this practice in another of his Sabbaths of Consolation hymns, for when the reading from the Prophets is Isa. 49: 14–26. The hymn, *Šekhurah mi-demey šalem*, is a metric *rešut* in *qaṣīdah*-style monorhyme. Again, he deftly incorporates the opening verset from the scriptural reading:[61]

[59] Cf. Ya'ari, *Toledot*, p. 142; Weinberger, 'Rešut', p. 16.
[60] *Širim U-Zmirot*, No. 264. [61] Ibid., No. 265.

She [Zion] is drunk from the blood of Jerusalem's faithful and not
From the juice of pomegranates or white wine . . .
Will the ninety-year-old daughter who gave birth and was abandoned,
Be restored to the seat of the seventy?
Then they will proclaim [to Zion], 'Rejoice and sing,' and no longer
Will Zion say, 'The Lord has forsaken me.'

The rhetorical figure in the third and fourth cola refers to Sarah, who gave birth to Isaac at the age of 90 (Gen. 17: 17); the 'seat of the seventy' is an allusion to the Sanhedrin (*mSan* 1. 6).

Petiḥah

Ottoman *petiḥot* were designed as introductions to a hymn or ritual to follow. Such is Elia of Istip's hymn for before the reading of the Scroll of Esther on Purim, *'Aromimkha 'adon kol ha-'alulim*. Its superscription reads, 'A *petiḥah* which he composed for the reading of the *megillah* in the tradition of the *kabbalah*.' The hymn is built in metric *qaṣīdah* form and reflects the poet's (and presumably his congregation's) interest in religious philosophy and Jewish mysticism:[62]

I will exalt You, Lord of all causes [*'alulim*],
Are not all things emanated [*'aṣulim*] with a word [from You]?
To whom shall the parables compare You?
What image is fitting for the Cause of causes [*'alul le-'illah*]?
Did not the awesome esteem of Your majesty [*hod*]
Emanate first and is so inscribed?
Likewise wisdom [*ḥokhmah*] by turning from evil has emanated [first] . . .

The view that the *sefirot* named *hod* and *ḥokhmah* emanated before the creation of the world is found in the writings of Rabbi Azriel of Gerona in his 'Explanation of the Ten *Sefirot*' (p. 91). As mentioned on p. 380 above, the *sefirot* are in his opinion 'the force behind existent being'. In combining the Aristotelian notion of a First Cause with Neoplatonist theories of emanation, R. Elia follows a common practice in medieval religious philosophy. To this the poet adds his speculation on the 'thirty-two paths of wisdom', comprising the ten *sefirot* and the twenty-two letters in the Hebrew alphabet, according to *Sefer Yeṣirah* 1. 1. In line with the teachings of the Gerona mystics, the 'paths' are part of the divine essence through which the absolute

[62] Weinberger, *Širat . . . Rabbanim*, pp. 326–7.

reveals itself in the presence of the 'pure soul'. The following is from R. Elia's hymn:

> The thirty-two paths are contained within God [*kelulim be-ʾelohim*]
> And the pure soul is domiciled there in heaven.

The latter conceit is taken from the rabbinic opinion, in *bSab* 152b: 'The souls of the pious are hidden under the "Throne of Glory".' R. Elia concludes the hymn by warning the soul to remain faithful to her mission and not incur God's wrath:

> If they [the souls] transgress, He will
> Punish them with men [like Haman] bent on destruction.

Petiḥot for other events include Elia of Istip's metric pseudo-*muwashshaḥ*, *ʾEl naʾ šemaʿ qoli*. Although the hymn is without a superscription indicating its purpose, it was probably intended as an introduction to the *zikhronot* section of the New Year liturgy, as the following strophe suggests:[63]

> Coming into Your house, Lord,
> The nation begging
> A redeemer from You, O Rock
> Remembering the Patriarchs.

Šalom Enabi's pseudo-*muwashshaḥāt petiḥot* for Šabbat Bere'šit, *ʾAšorer hillulim le-dar be-ʾulam*, and for Šabbat Parah, *Šaḥarit ʾaqaddemah ʾel ʾel yešuʿati*, are, like his other hymns, replete with references to medieval astronomy and astrology, religious philosophy and Jewish mysticism. In the former hymn, Enabi paraphrases the rabbinic observation, in *bḤag* 12a, that God reduced—because of man's sinfulness—the primeval light with which Adam saw from one end of the world to the other, and stored its excess brilliance for rewarding the righteous in the world to come:[64]

> On the seventh [day] I praise the mighty and brilliant [God]
> For the secret of the seventh [palace], when He said, 'Let there be light';
> And the light of the pious increased in brilliance,
> [Taken] from the [sinful] counsel at the beginning [and given to the pious], the foundation of the world.

Enabi's *Šaḥarit ʾaqaddemah*, for Šabbat Parah, is an uncommon form of the pseudo-*muwashshaḥ*. The hymn opens with a rhyming 'guide' couplet, which serves as a refrain after each strophe of three rhyming tercets. However, in the last strophe the poet adds to the 'guide' three additional cola,

[63] Weinberger, *Širat . . . Rabbanim*, p. 321.
[64] Ibid. 329.

presumably for the purpose of adding *ḤZQ* (= *ḥazaq*)[65] after his name signature, *ŠLWM*. The rhyming scheme of the hymn is: *aa* / *bbb* / *a*, guide / *ccc* / *a*, guide / *ddd* / *aaa*, guide. Enabi's hymns are distinctive in their tendency to open with a cosmic preface in the *petiḥah* as well as in the *mi kamokha*. His preface is generally punctuated by terms from religious philosophy. Following is the opening strophe from his *Šaḥarit 'aqaddemah*:[66]

> To You I bow, the Pre-existent [*qadmon*],
> [The world's] Founder [*mamṣi'*], the basis of Wisdom.

Characteristic of Enabi's hymnody are his references to the 'secret'. In the above *petiḥah*, he speaks of the 'secret of the sacrifice [of the red heifer]' (*sod qorban*) which purifies and defiles at the same time. In his other works he mentions 'the secret of the chariot [throne]' (*sod merkavah*); the 'secret of the phases of the moon in its quadrature elongation' (of 90° or 270°, *sod ha-levanah be-qaw ha-merubba'*); the 'secret of the ten [*šofar*] blasts' (*sod 'eser qolot*); the 'secret of the mating of [*sefirot*] *tif'eret* and *malkhut*' (*sod zug tif'eret wa-'aṭarah*); and the 'secret of the ordinances and God's command' (*sod ha-miṣwah we-ṣiwwuy ha-'el*).[67]

Judah Qilti likewise favours religious philosophy in his *petiḥah*, *'Adon 'olam 'ašer ne'lam be-'elim*, for Šabbat Šeqalim. The hymn, in metric *qaṣīdah* style, touches on the nature of God:[68]

> He [God] cannot be characterized by analogy [*dimyon*] or imagination [*ra'yon*] . . .
> He is the foundation of the [one source] element [*yesod ha-yesod*] . . .
> He is the cause of every cause and condition [*we-hu 'illah le-khol 'illah we-sibbah*] and other than He all things are caused;
> He is without form [*demut*] beyond estimation [*'erekh*] or investigation [*ḥeqer*] as regards accidents [*miqrim*] or general principles [*kelalim*].

'He is the foundation of the [one source] element' is traceable to Ibn Gabirol's *Keter Malkhut*, No. 10. Presumably, 'general principles' refers to the Ten Categories of Aristotle, which cannot be applied to God. After devoting seven cola of his eight-cola hymn to a philosophical discourse on the nature of God, the poet in the last colon refers, in passing, to the half-shekel offering:

> Restore us O living God that we may be restored as of old to be forgiven with the *šeqalim*.

[65] Adding *ḥazaq*, meaning 'be strong (and of good courage)', after Josh. 1: 9, was a common practice of the hymnists. See Zunz, *Die synagogale Poesie*, pp. 369–70.

[66] Weinberger, *Širat . . . Rabbanim*, p. 330.

[67] Ibid. 331, 338, 345–6.

[68] Ibid. 413.

Judah Qilti's *petiḥah*, *'Ašer yaṣar šeḥaqim*, for Šabbat Parah, is free of references to religious philosophy and focuses solely on the celebrated event. The *qaṣīdah*-type hymn with Hispanic metres features internal as well as end rhyme, and was probably introduced before the recitation of the *qaddiš*, as indicated in its ending:[69]

> Since we lack the water [ashes] from the heifer of old,
> The [offering] of our lips we make in its place,
> Even as He is exalted [*we-yitgaddal*] within the congregation pure,
> And sanctified is His holy name for ever [*we-yitqaddaš šemeh rabbah be-ʿolma'*].

Menaḥem Tamar's metric pseudo-*muwashshaḥ* Purim *petiḥah*, *Šoraru la-'el yedidim*, features a distinctive rhyming pattern: *ab*, a*b* / *cd*, *cd*, *cd*, *eeee* / *fb*, *fb* / etc. It is likely that the hymn was chanted before the reading of the Scroll of Esther:[70]

> In 'Adar when the Scroll is to be read, the indicated days
> Are called Purim by the Hebrews who feasted and rejoiced;
> Even gifts are sent to friends, and food;
> Consider the poor and weak, bring relief to the unfortunate;
> Refresh the depressed, extend them an open hand
> On the day of light and joy to the Jews.

Ottoman *petiḥot* for the vigil nights of 'Elul continued the distinctive pattern of the later Romaniotes. Like their predecessors, the Ottoman *petiḥah* for this occasion began with an opening scriptural verse followed by a one-strophe set of rhyming tercets, with a closing colon repeating a segment of the opening verse. Representing this *petiḥah* form in the Ottoman period were Aaron b. Abaye in his two hymns with headers from Job 25: 4 and Ps. 119: 9; Yedidyah Roch with a Ps. 33: 22 header; and Isaiah Missini's hymn headed by Ps. 119: 9. All of the above *petiḥot*, like their late Romaniote counterparts, ended with a paraphrase of Dan. 9: 18: 'Because of Your abundant mercies', the verse that preceded the recitation of the God's Thirteen Attributes in the vigil-nights service.[71]

Day of Atonement *petiḥot* are represented by Elia Ha-Levi's *'Ašer nodaʿ be-yisra'el we-šalem meʿono*. Built in metric *qaṣīdah* style, the hymn is distinctive in its use of homonym metaphors, after Hispanic models. The following is a play on the unit *ri'šon* (first):[72]

> *Yeṣaw ri'šon, neqom ri'šon be-ri'šon*
> *We-ri'šon ʿam be-ṣiyyon hu' yenaḥlem*

[69] Weinberger, *Širat . . . Rabbanim*, p. 418.
[70] Ibid. 446–7.
[71] Ibid. 364–5, 367, 372.
[72] Ibid. 476–7.

Command, O First [God, Isa. 41: 4] that the First [Israel, 2 Sam. 19: 21] take vengeance on the First [Esau, Gen. 25: 25]
And the First [herald of good tidings, Isa. 41: 27] will lead the nation into Zion.

Mazal Ṭov b. David's *petiḥah*, *Maʿon u-me-ʿolam nisgav*, does not indicate the occasion for which it was intended. The metric hymn in five quatrains asks God to keep His promise of restoring Israel to its national home:[73]

Remember the appointed time
Inscribed by the man [*ʾiš*] who gave
Testimony, even the heavens saw it;
Keep our promise!

The 'man' (*ʾiš*) is a reference to Daniel 'the greatly beloved' (*ʾiš ḥamudot*) after Dan. 10: 11.

Seliḥah

Pizmon

As in their treatment of other genres, Ottoman hymnists were much attracted to Hispanic-style quantitative metre, and their *pizmonim* were constructed in one of the eleven standard metric configurations. In this they outdid their mentors, whose metric *pizmonim* generally counted long syllables only. Representing the Ottoman *pizmon is* Joseph b. Solomon's ten-strophe *Yom zeh levavo ʿammekha qoreʿa*. This is an impressive pseudo-*muwashshaḥ* in *ha-šalem*, metre III (see p. xxii), with the closing cola in the 'guide' repeated at the end of the strophes. The hymn's theme is a plea for Israel's national restoration by virtue of the merit (*zekhut*) gained by her biblical heroes. However, instead of identifying the individuals by name, the poet alludes to their identity by means of metaphor and metonym. In this way he engages the congregation by challenging it to make the correct identification:[74]

Disdained and exiled, afflicted and storm-tossed
Send balm for her hurt that she may live . . .
By the merit of one who bound his son on mount Moriah for an acceptable holocaust offering [Gen. 22: 1 ff.] . . .
By the merit of one who said [to his brothers], 'And now your eyes see' [Gen. 45: 12] binding the broken [-hearted] and anguished . . .
By the merit of one drawn from the water [Exod. 2: 1] for whom You descended upon the mountain to speak to him . . .

[73] Markon, 'Le-David', p. 40, l. 2.
[74] Weinberger, *Širat . . . Rabbanim*, pp. 368–9.

[By the] merit of one who sprinkles [the blood of the red heifer, [Num. 19: 3] the son of one who sprinkles [Eleazar son of Aaron]; on their behalf, whose eyes beheld Your glory . . .
By the merit of one who was zealous [Num. 25: 11] when You were angry, exchange the ashes [of mourning] for a diadem to Your beloved . . .
By the merit of one who laid the foundations of God's Temple [David, 1 Chr. 28: 2 and *Cant. Rabbah* 1. 1] hasten the good tidings that a redeemer has come to Zion . . . !
By the merit of Yedidyah [Solomon], father of wisdom, may they amuse thenselves there [in Zion] without hindrance.

Another form of the *pizmon* is Isaiah Missini's *'Anna' 'et 'ašawwe'ah*, for the Ten Days of Repentance. The hymn is built in eight quatrain strophes of hemicola whose closing halves, from Dan. 9: 19, are repeated in each strophe:[75]

Rider of the clouds, / O Lord, hear
Sins and debts, / O Lord, forgive
To the repentant, / O Lord, listen,
And bestow goodness upon them; / act and do not delay!

Elia Ha-Levi's *pizmonim*, *'Adon 'ašer rokhev be-ga'wah šaḥaq*, for the New Year, and *'Elohay 'oz heyeh ma'oz*, for the Day of Atonement, are pseudo-*muwashshaḥāt*, with the closing colon in the 'guide' repeated at the end of each strophe. Presumably *'Adon 'ašer rokhev*, built in *ha-šalem* metre, was part of the *zikhronot* unit in the *šofar* service, as indicated in the following from the 'guide', embellished with homonym rhyme play on the unit *šaḥaq*.[76]

O Lord, riding proud in the sky [*šaḥaq*],
You consider the nations like a drop [in the bucket] and dust [on scales] [*ke-mar u-kh-šaḥaq*];
Have compassion on the people oppressed and ground up in exile [*nidkah be-galut šaḥaq*],
And erase their sins recoded in Your tablet in heaven [*be-sifrakh šaḥaq*];
Exalted Father, remember the eminent father [*'av ram* = Abraham] and the binding of Isaac.

'Elohay 'oz is distinctive by virtue of its internal rhyme in both 'guide' and strophes: *aaab*, *cccb*, *dddb*, *eeeb* [refrain] / *fffb* . . . / *gggb*, refrain / etc. Below is the first of its strophes:[77]

[75] Weinberger, *Širat . . . Rabbanim*, pp. 375–6.
[76] Ibid. 484.
[77] Ibid. 485–6.

To every measure there is an end,
Yet there is no limit to Your mercy;
Redeem Your people, relying upon You
And now brought low by Your design.

Mustajāb

Among the few surviving samples of this *seliḥah* in Balkan hymnography is Joseph Qalai's hymn headed by Ps. 145: 1 and Solomon Mevorakh's *Še'eh na' le-qol renanay, wa-'avarekh šimkha 'adonay* (Hear my prayer and I will bless Your name, Lord). The second colon in the opening couplet is a verse fragment from Ps. 145: 1. Its closing unit, *'adonay*, appears at the end of the strophes. Here is a selection:[78]

I belong to You, save me;
I am Your servant, give me wisdom;
Extend Your hand to help me
For the sake of Your name, Lord.

Šalmonit Seliḥah

The Ottoman *šalmonit seliḥah* was generally designed for the 'Elul vigil nights and the Ten Days of Repentance. Such was the intent of *'Aḥat ša'alti me'et 'adonay*, by Ḥelbo of Ephesus. His plea for divine forgiveness employs a rhetoric of antithesis:[79]

Lord, my God, if I have acted wickedly in my foolishness
I pray that You will act in Your wisdom and forgive me.

An Ottoman revival of phonetic-intensive mannerisms in the *šalmonit* is seen in the hymn *'Essa' 'enay*, for the Day of Atonement, by Šelaḥyah b. Ḥananyah. Here is its opening strophe:[80]

'Essa' 'enay 'el 'adonay be-taḥanunay mi-yegonay le-romemeni;
Bo baṭaḥti nismaḥti niš'anti le-sa'adeni;
Galut zullut dallut be-qallut pit'om qera'uni;
'El 'adonay ba-ṣaratah li qara'ti wa-yya'aneni.

I lift my eyes to God in my plea to relieve my distress;
He is my trust upon whom I rely; He is my support and help;
Suddenly, abominable, despised exile and poverty is decreed for me;
To the Lord I call in my agony and He answers.

[78] Jerusalem, MS *'Osef Piyyuṭim Mi-Turkiah*, fo. 33a.
[79] Weinberger, *Širat . . . Rabbanim*, p. 363. [80] Ibid. 465.

Baqqašah

Elia Ha-Levi's *baqqašah*, *'Enoš bi-tšuvah le-rappe' mešuvah*, for the Ten Days of Repentance is similar in theme and structure to earlier forms of the genre by Sa'adyah Ga'on and Ibn Gabirol, and by the Balkan poet Solomon Šarvit Ha-Zahav of Ephesus. Although his *baqqašah*, like theirs, is in rhymed prose, R. Elia pioneers the use of Hispanic metrics in this genre. Like his predecessors, the Ottoman rabbi-poet divides his *baqqašah* into an opening philosophical preface and a closing confessional and appeal for mercy. He achieved a *tour de force* in constructing his hymn with 1,000 units beginning with the letter *bet*. Added to this Herculean achievement is the poet's successful attempt to build the *baqqašah* in twenty strophes connected by anadiplosis.

R. Elia, aware of the uncommon character of his hymn, designates it *Beyt Lewi* (The House of the Levite) in the opening two couplets, which spell his name and give the title of his work. Below are the opening units after the introductory couplets:[81]

Be-re'šit bara' beriy'ot belimah, banenu be-raḥamaw be-hištaddelo be-qiyyum biryotaw bi-m'od . . .

Be-rokhvo be-koḥo ba-šamayim be-ga'awato ba-šeḥaqim, be-voḥoro bi-škhon ba-'arafel;

Be-ḥaddeš be-khol boker be-ma'aseh be-re'šit, be-haggi'o be-galgalaw be-koaḥ be-ma'amar bi-lvad bi-rṣono.

In the beginning He created a structure upon nothing; He built it with His mercy and His great effort to preserve His creatures . . .

By His might He rides in the heavens, His majesty is in the sky where He chooses to live in thick darkness;

He renews each morning the work of creation as He arrives [borne] on His angels; by the power of His word alone He willed [the world].

The requirement that each unit should open with the letter *beyt* meant that R. Elia's confessional could not be based on earlier models, which sought to encompass a catalogue of sins within the framework of the twenty-two-letter alphabet. Because of this limitation, the poet's confessional is not as structured as the others, and is relatively free to reflect frailties that may have come from his own experience:

> I have built my house, a structure on the heights, an altar to foreign gods . . .

[81] Weinberger, *Širat . . . Rabbanim*, pp. 467–70.

I am ashamed to have been drawn after vain pleasures . . . cheered my body with wine . . . and been gluttonous after meat . . .

I have placed my trust in silver and gold, in things that by nature fade away.

Another classic *baqqašah* by R. Elia is his metric hymn *'Avorekhah 'et 'adonay*, comprising twenty-six cola in monorhyme with complete alphabetic acrostic and poet's signature in each of its units:[82]

'Avarekha 'et 'adonay, 'et 'adonay 'ahodeh, 'el 'emunay 'el 'emunay;
Beḥantihu be-sar'appay be-qirbi, be-galuti be-dallut ba' be-'eynay;
Gevurotaw gedolot gam gemulaw geluyim golelim ge'ut ge'onay . . .

I will bless the Lord, the Lord I shall praise, the faithful God to His loyal [servants]
I have searched for Him in my inner thoughts; being in exile, impoverished, He appeared to me;
His might is great and His graciousness is revealed; He topples the pride of the arrogant.

It is likely that in the styling of both *baqqašot* R. Elia was influenced by the Provençal poet and philosopher Yedayah b. Abraham Bedersi Ha-Penini (*c*.1270–1340). The latter is credited with composing the *Baqqašat Ha-Memim*, a liturgical hymn in which every word begins with the letter *mem* and the prayer *'Elef 'Alfin*, a punning allusion to the fact that each of its 1,000 words begins with the letter *'alef*. It is also likely that Elia Ha-Levi was aware of Menaḥem b. Elia of Macedonia and his *Malki'el* hymn.

Taḥanun

Aaron b. Abaye's *taḥanun*, *'Eloha yom gešet*, for the Fast of Gedaliah, employs the image of *keneset yisra'el* (the community of Israel)—a feminine designation—as the abandoned wife. In this conceit R. Aaron follows earlier Hispanic and Balkan models depicting Israel's travail in exile through metaphors like 'the forlorn dove' or 'the lonely widow'. However, in the Ottoman poet's treatment, 'the wife' admits her infidelity. The following is from the 'guide' to R. Aaron's hymn:[83]

This day the vagabond woman [*nedudah*] approaches with much trepidation;
She wears her guilt like a garment covered with shame:
'O my Lord, do not punish [me] for a sin
[So foolishly committed].'

[82] Ibid. 482. [83] Ibid. 366.

Isaiah Missini's *taḥanun*, *Yom 'eḥševah da'at meṣi'utekha*, for the Ten Days of Repentance is distinctive in both form and theme. Unlike his Balkan colleagues, he builds his *taḥanun* in *ha-šalem* III metre (see p. xxii). Moreover, he charts a new course for this genre by focusing on themes in medieval Jewish philosophy. The following selection shows the influence of Gabirol and Maimonides:[84]

This day I contemplate knowing Your existence [*meṣi'utekha*]
By discovering the mystery of Your divine nature [*sod 'elahutekha*];
My soul's passion is to find You
Since I already know You from Your deeds . . .
You are not like one unit [to be counted] and beside You there is no living God and Rock like You . . .
You are eternal without beginning, prior to all the hosts of heaven;
Might and majesty apply to You alone.

Qinah

The pervasive Hispanic influence in imagery and form on Ottoman hymnography included the elegy. The attractive power of Judah Ha-Levi's epic zionide lament, 'Zion, will you not ask if peace be with your captives [*Ṣiyyon ha-lo' tiš'ali li-šlom 'asirayikh*]?', widely imitated in central Europe, continued its appeal into the Ottoman period. Ha-Levi's elegant dirge in monorhyme with its stately *ha-mitpašet* metre was imitated by Menaḥem Tamar in his *Ṣiyyon ha-lo' ted'iy libbot 'avelayikh*. Tamar also begins with a rhyming couplet in *ha-mitpaššet* I metre, and continues in the remaining cola with *ha-mitpaššet* II. His opening couplet, like Ha-Levi's, is framed in a rhetorical question with similar units, *Ṣiyyon ha-lo'* . . . , even as he employs an identical terminal rhymeme, *ayikh*:[85]

Zion, do you not know the hearts of your mourners
Sighing heavily over the plunder of your tents? . . .
Darkened were heaven's luminaries when they set fire to the sanctuary
Holy; then your stars withdrew their shining . . .
Who will give me a reservoir of tears that I may weep over
The excellence of the slain, Zion's sons, your corpses?

Elia Ha-Levi's zionide, *Libbi le-mo 'av ha-lo' yid'av*, is also built with *ha-mitpaššeṭ* II metre in monorhyme, although its terminal rhymeme, *eynu*, differs from Ha-Levi's, as does its opening colon:[86]

84 Weinberger, *Širat . . . Rabbanim*, p. 374.
85 Ibid. 445.
86 Ibid. 479.

My heart goes out to the father [Abraham], much in grief and pained;
Moaning at his anguish, we shed our tears for him . . .
Alas, [stunned] silence has turned to weeping; alas, he [Israel] has become
A byword and a fantasy. Who will come to comfort us?

Elegies lamenting the deaths of individuals were included in the Romaniote prayer-book. One such hymn, *Yiddom le-nogen ḥalil* by Judah Ha-Kohen, bears the superscription, 'An elegy by Rabbi Judah Ha-Kohen to be recited on the death of a prominent man' (*'adam ḥašuv*). R. Judah's hymn, like the zionides, features *ha-mitpaššeṭ* I metre with rhyming tercets in addition to its terminal monorhyme. The internal rhyme lends a doleful sonority to the lament, as in the following:[87]

Yiddom le-nogen ḥalil;
Yussar le-melekh kelil;
Ki saf be-arṣi pelil;
Hah bat zeman 'umlelah.

Havu le-marim 'asis;
Qarevu le-'ovedim be-sis;
U-thi le-'eynam resis,
Tazzil kemo naḥalah

Silence the music of pipes
Remove the king's crown;
A judge has passed from our land;
Woe to the wretched hour.

Bring sweet juice to the embittered;
Prepare a bed for the forlorn;
Have drops ready for their eyes
That they may flow like a brook.

Epithalamia

Elia b. Samuel of Istip's epithalamium, *'El he-ḥatan 'im ha-kallah*, is a four-strophe metric hymn appealing to the deity for blessings on bride and groom. The hymn, titled *zemer* in the superscription, was sung to the melody of the epithalamium, 'I anoint you with the oil of joy' (*Šemen sason mešaḥtikha*), by another poet named Elia. Here is a translation of *'El he-ḥatan 'im ha-kallah*:[88]

87 Ibid. 412. The correct reading is *le-nogen*, not *le-gonen*.
88 Ibid. 320–1; on the hymn *Šemen sason mešaḥtikha*, see *Širim U-Zmirot*, No. 133.

To the bridegroom and bride,
Almighty, increase joy and delight;
Grant them, Lord of the universe [Aram: *'olmayya'*],
Life and sons like Rabbi Ḥiyyah;
May the groom rejoice with his mate
And know the happiness of kinship;
If they are this day joined in
Righteousness, they will be kissed with peace.

The wish to sire sons like Rabbi Ḥiyyah is legendary. A rabbinic tradition, in *bBM* 85b, states that if R. Ḥiyyah and his five sons prayed at the same time they would bring the Messiah before his scheduled arrival. The poet's use of the Aramaic *'olmayya'* is for the purpose of rhyming with Ḥiyyah.

Elijah Ṣelebi's epithalamium, *Mešakhtini kelulat ḥen be-ḥavley 'ahavah*, combines themes from sacred and secular Hebrew poetry and employs the speech and figures common to the Andalusian 'love-drama'. The lovesick bridegroom languishes in bitter-sweet agony awaiting entrance to the bridal chamber and finds no relief from the enforced separation. He is obsessed with the ravishing beauty of his bride, whose praises he is compelled to sing, and his love-madness brings down upon him the reproach of his 'admonishers' (*merivim*). The hymn is in the form of a metric *muwashshaḥ* which, in addition to the required 'guide', is also given a refrain designated by the Turkish term *bilkülliye*.[89]

I am drawn to you, perfect in grace, by bonds of love
As I behold your comely cheeks with sweet voice.

I am enthralled by fierce desire unbounded;
My heart is a vagabond unencumbered by folly
When her passion's door is closed before me;
I call out to her, 'Lovely-eyed,
Lift your gaze upon the impoverished lover;
Do not stray like a wandering Cain
And add to the anguish.' . . .

My heart is in turmoil like the sea; it roars as the lion;
The long separation [*perud*] fuels my wrath
And I am unable to find relief or healing for my hurt;
Alas for the power of love, it evokes disdain and scorn! . . .

Yet, how remain silent and find repose; how not to be moved
Seeing that my soul is caught up in a knot of love

[89] Weinberger, *Širat . . . Rabbanim*, pp. 406–8; Pagis, *Širat Ha-Ḥol*, pp. 268–9. T. Beeri suggests that Turkish hymns were a staple in the synagogue liturgy in Ṣelebi's time. See Beeri, 'Šelomo Mazal Ṭov'.

Which inflames my inner life like a blazing fire . . .
And cascades of water are unable
To quench desire?

Zemirot

The preliminary service for weekdays, Sabbaths and festivals consists of Pss. 145–50. These, forming the core of the *pesuqey de-zimrah* (verses of song), sometimes called *hallel* (praise), were part of the daily service in talmudic times.[90] Later, the core chapters were introduced by the hymn 'Blessed be He who spoke and the world came into being' (*Barukh še-ʾamar we-hayah ha-ʿolam*), with an added coda, 'Praised be Your name forever, our King' (*Yištabbaḥ šimkha laʿad malkenu*). Other selections from Scripture were added to the *pesuqey de-zimrah*, as were embellishments called *zemirot.*

Zemirot were popular in the Ottoman period and several have survived. Isaiah Missini's hymn in this genre, *Yom ʾaqawweh la-ʿalot ʾel har ʾadonay*, was sung on festival days. It is a metric hymn built in quatrains with rhyming tercets and closing scriptural verse ending with *ʾadonay*:[91]

I hope for the day when I will ascend
The mountain of the Lord in Ariel's house;
I will pass Penuel
And there will I bless the Lord.

'Ariel's house' designates the Temple, based on Isa. 29: 1. In the reference to Penuel, the poet has in mind the verse from Gen. 32: 31, 'The sun rose upon him [Jacob] as he passed Penuel' and the rabbinic comment, in *Gen. Rabbah* 78. 5, 'The sun rose in order to heal him.'

Mordecai Comtino's *zemer*, *Mah mevaqqeš mimmekha ʾel*, is identical to Isaiah Missini's *Yom ʾaqawweh la-ʿalot* in form and metre, including the similar repeated unit, *ʾadonay*, sealing the strophes. It is likely that the former's hymn also served the festival *pesuqey de-zimra*. Comtino's *zemer*, like his epithalamium, was included in the Karaite ritual. Below is a selection:[92]

What does the Lord require of you
Who dwell in Naḥaliel [the wilderness, i.e. in exile]?
Draw near and ascend the heights [*bamot*]; the house of God
Is there in the courts of the Lord's dwelling . . .

All and a portion thereof comes from His heaven . . .
He is gracious to those whose deeds are done in the name of
heaven;
He is God and we are not!

90 See *bŠab* 118b.
91 Weinberger, *Širat . . . Rabbanim*, pp. 376–7.
92 Ibid. 378–9.

Comtino's allusion in the opening strophe is to the verse in Num. 21: 19, '[Israel set out from] Naḥaliel to Bamoth.' Naḥaliel in the wilderness is the poet's way of referring to Israel in exile. With a play on the scriptural verse, Comtino is suggesting that Israel overcome the bitterness of exile by ascending the heights in the house of God. In the first colon of the closing strophe, he has reference to *bBer* 33b, 'Everything is in the hand of heaven except the fear of heaven.' The second colon is a reference to *'Avot* 2. 17 and the third, based on Ps. 115: 1, is probably directed against the Christian belief in Jesus as the God–man.

Blessing for the Ruler of the Land

Prayers for the life of the king are mentioned in Ezra 6: 10. Later formulations of these prayers appear in central European and Hispanic rituals, of which 'Who gives victory to kings and authority to rulers?' (*Ha-noten tešu'ah la-melakhim u-memšalah la-nesikhim*), is the best known. Solomon b. Mazal Ṭov's prayer, *Šadday we-ne'lam, 'el ḥay we-raḥman*, for the well-being of the sultan Suleiman the Magnificent extends well beyond earlier practice, and has more in common with the secular *laudes* composed by the Hispanics in tribute to their patrons. However, in contrast to the hyperbole of the Spanish panegyric and its stock phrasing ('his wisdom is as praiseworthy as the sun', 'his ability is the glory of his generation', 'his generosity is as wide as the sea'), R. Solomon is more restrained, allowing the record of the sultan to speak for itself. The metric hymn is constructed in *qaṣīdah*-style monorhyme, with variable internal rhyme. Here is a selection:[93]

Almighty and concealed, eternal God and merciful,
Preserve forever, the great king, sultan Suleiman;

Like a lion, may he seize, dismantle and prey upon
Cities filled with people from Arbel and Šalman, the great king . . .

May he make Muslims and Christians into stepping-stones
For his people, the great king, and distress and bury them . . .

Before his armies may they fall mortally wounded,
The great king who brought low sovereign and cardinal.

R. Solomon invites Jewish exiles to come to the sultan's city and live happily under the rule of Suleiman, the 'great king'.

Come in joy, O princes and princesses
To Constantinople, city of the great king, capital of the Ottomans . . .

[93] *Širim U-Zmirot*, No. 240.

In the concluding strophes, the poet thanks God for the generous 'great king':

> Give thanks to the Lord exalted who makes kings,
> The eternal God and Father supreme of the great king, mighty and faithful;
>
> He will comfort the exiles protected in His shade;
> He will again have mercy, the great King [God] upon the nation poor and widowed.

The allusion to (Bet) Arbel and Šalman—cited in Hos. 10: 14—in Trans-Jordan may refer to Suleiman's victory over Ghazāli, the rebellious governor of Syria and Palestine, shortly after the sultan's accession to power in 1520. The mention of Suleiman's encounter with Muslims would seem to recall the sultan's victory over Ahmed Pasha in Egypt in 1523–4 and his conquest of Tabriz and Baghdad from the Persians in 1534. The Christians in the hymn are probably the forces of Louis (Ludwig), King of Hungary, defeated by Suleiman in the battle of Mohacs in 1526. When the poet praises the sultan, who brought low sovereign and cardinal, he may have in mind Suleiman's intervention before Pope Paul IV (ruler of the Papal States and formerly Cardinal Giovanni Pietro Caraffa) on behalf of the Marranos threatened by the Inquisition in Italy in 1556. The poet's invitation to come and settle in Constantinople reflects the Ottoman policy of *sürgün*, which forced Jews to emigrate from Hungary to Turkey.[94]

Solomon Mevorakh's three hymns, *'El 'al kol 'elim*, *Sarim u-mlakhim gedolim*, and *Be-gilah be-'ahavah*, asking for divine blessings on the sultan Selim II, are modelled on Solomon b. Mazal Ṭov's earlier tribute to Suleiman, Selim's father. The superscription to *'El 'al kol 'elim*, directs that the hymn be chanted to the melody of Mazal Ṭov's *Šadday ve-ne'lam*. Like the earlier work, Mevorakh's encomia combine praise for the monarch with an account of his exploits and generosity. Below is a selection from *'El 'al kol 'elim*.[95]

> God to all who have power, He raises the lowly, He endows with strength
> The great king, the sultan, Selim . . .
>
> The king in his glory shares his bounty and repels the rebels
> That worship idols; the great king . . .

Mevorakh closes with the hope that Selim will rebuild the Temple, even as his father fortified the walls of Jerusalem and built the Tower of David and the Damascus Gate:

[94] See Capsali, *Seder*, ii. 12, 14–15, 147 ff.; Roth, *The House of Nasi*, pp. 151–2; Hacker, 'Šiṭat', pp. 63–5; Weinberger, 'Širat Šelomo b. Mazal Ṭov'.

[95] Jerusalem, MS *'Osef Piyyuṭim Mi-Turkiyah*, fo. 30a.

Grant O God exalted that which was predicted for Zion; may he
[Selim] build the Temple
And the altar, the great king . . .

Prayer Before Setting Forth on a Journey

The rabbis, in *bBer* 29a, advise that the traveller should say the prayer for a journey (*tefillat ha-derekh*). The prayer given in *bBer* and in all medieval liturgies asks that God lead the voyager peacefully to his destination and deliver him from enemy and ambush. Solomon b. Mazal Ṭov's prayer, *Šemaʿuni we-ʾaširah*, described in the superscription, 'For the seafarer', is a supplement to the traditional *tefillat ha-derekh* and deals with hazards of maritime travel. Living in the city of the 'Golden Horn' flanked by the Black and Aegean seas, it is likely that the rabbi-poet and his congregation had occasion to recite this prayer. Although Mazal Ṭov employs the traditional themes of the *tefillat ha-derekh*, his narrative account of a frail craft venturing into perilous waters is distinctive.[96]

Hear me and I will lament [the time] when I observed
The raging sea; my verse will speak of its rising waves and breakers;

At the sound of His voice there is rage in the waters, as when one
brings forth her first child on the birthstool;
He makes the heart and kidneys whirl with rising waves and
breakers.

The craft flees from His voice; it reels from His force.
He heaves it with the might of His breath by the rising waves and
breakers . . .

I sing of the One who divided the sea, and led the sheep [Israel]
by the hand of the messenger [Moses];
I thank Him as he sang then by the rising waves and breakers . . .

Introduction to Maimonides' Thirteen Principles

Solomon b. Mazal Ṭov's *Širah la-ʾel maṣuy meʾod naʿalah* is a poetic paraphrase of Maimonides' Thirteen Articles of Faith, which were recited in most European synagogue rituals at the close of the morning service. The thirteen-cola hymn, in the form of a metric *qaṣīdah*, has much in common with *Yigdal ʾelohim ḥay* by the fourteenth-century Daniel b. Judah of Rome. The Ephesian poet Solomon Šarvit Ha-Zahav's *baqqašah Yeš yešut*, expatiated on the Thirteen Articles. Following is the opening colon in Mazal Ṭov's paraphrase,

[96] *Širim U-Zmirot*, No. 247.

based on Maimonides' text in his Introduction to the tenth chapter of *bSan.*[97]

> Sing to the Lord, the existent [*maṣuy*], highly exalted
> Above all blessing and lofty praise.

Mazal Ṭov converts into a prayer Maimonides' twelfth article, which calls for faith in the coming of the Messiah:

> Command to hasten the coming of our Messiah
> That he may gather the scattered exiles.

[97] Ibid., No. 263; A. Marx, 'A List of the Poems on the Articles of the Creed', *JQR* 9 (1935), pp. 305–36.

7

Karaite Synagogue Poets

GENERAL BACKGROUND

KARAITE SETTLEMENTS appeared in Balkan Byzantium during the mid-tenth century. It is likely that the earliest of these were in Asia Minor and were linked to the flourishing commercial life in tenth-century Anatolia. Presumably Karaites and Rabbanites profited from the maritime trade between the Byzantine port of Attaleia and Alexandria. A Geniza letter dated December 1028, addressed to the Fustat Jewish community in Egypt, asks for funds to redeem Jewish captives brought to Alexandria by Arab pirates. The group comprised three Karaite and four Rabbanite merchants from Byzantium. It is likely that the Karaites (like the Rabbanites) gravitated to the commercially promising coastal settlements in Asia Minor like Attaleia, Ephesus and Nicaea. An added participant in the Attaleia–Alexandria trade route was the island of Cyprus, which in the eleventh century was the scene of a Karaite dispute with the dissident Jewish Mishawite sect. In the following century, Benjamin of Tudela noted in his journal that Rabbanites and Karaites lived on the island.

In the north, Karaites presumably participated in the profitable Black Sea commerce, and there is documentary evidence of Karaite settlements in the Pontic cities of Trebizond and Gangra from the twelfth century. The commercially advantaged city of Nicomedia, the natural gateway to the Bosporus, attracted Jewish entrepreneurs as early as Roman times. It was the home of 'Karaism's keenest mind', Aaron b. Elijah, who died there in an epidemic in the month of Tišri, 1369. Other likely Karaite settlements in the middle Byzantine period were Adrianople, a thriving commercial centre, and Salonika, the home of the Rabbanite notable Tobias b. Eliezer, whose *Midraš Leqaḥ Ṭov* bristles with anti-Karaite polemics.[1]

Presumably the largest Karaite community in the mid-Byzantine period

[1] Starr, *The Jews of the Byzantine Empire*, p. 241; Ankori, *Karaites in Byzantium*, pp. 46, 119, 122–8, 132, 147–8.

was in Constantinople, the cosmopolitan and commercial centre of the eastern Mediterranean. It was the birthplace of the eleventh-century leader of Karaism, Tobias b. Moses, and in the second half of the twelfth century Benjamin of Tudela reported that Constantinople Jews were mainly engaged in the manufacture of silk garments and lived in a separate quarter of the city which comprised 'two thousand Rabbanite Jews and five hundred Karaites . . . and between them there is a partition.'[2] Although a wall separated the two Jewries they often shared the same fate. In 1077, when the rebel John Bryennios set fire to the wooden houses of the Jews in Constantinople, it is likely that Rabbanites and Karaites suffered alike. Two and a half decades later the mob of the Fourth Crusade in 1203–4 also wreaked havoc on Jewish homes indiscriminately.

Despite their disagreement on the interpretation of Scripture, resulting in differences in Sabbath observances, calendar calculations and dietary practices among others, the Karaites were receptive to Rabbanite embellishments of the liturgy. Although the early Karaites did not look favourably on Rabbanite liturgical poetry and insisted that formal prayer should consist exclusively of readings from the Psalms and quotations from other biblical books, some individuals, if they were 'wise and understanding', were permitted to insert into the liturgy their personal prayers. This led to Karaite experimentation with forms patterned after Rabbanite models, and by the thirteenth century the Karaite prayer-book compiled by Aaron b. Joseph included several Rabbanite-style *piyyuṭim* written mostly by Karaites, and some by Rabbanites as well.[3] The Karaite practice of imitating Rabbanite liturgical models continued in the following centuries, despite the opposition of Karaite worthies from Daniel al-Kumisi (9th–10th c.) to Abraham Firkowicz (19th c.),[4] and the adaptation of their genres, poetics and literary sources became commonplace. In addition to imitating Rabbanite hymnography, the nineteenth-century Karaite prayer-books often adopted Rabbanite hymns, albeit with some alterations.

Karaite hymnography in Europe was largely confined to the south-eastern part of the continent, the area of its major settlements. Beginning in eleventh-century Byzantium under the Comneni and continuing through the Palaiologoi and early Ottomans, a significant Karaite corpus of synagogue literature has emerged. The Karaite sources available for study, while not as numerous as those of the Rabbanites, are sufficient to demonstrate the distinctive character of their hymnography. Among the Karaite liturgical collections are four seventeenth-century manuscripts preserved in Berlin's Staatsbibliothek Preussischer Kulturbesitz, MS Orient. No. 198; in the British Museum, London, MS Or. No. 2536; in Paris at the Bibliothèque Nationale,

[2] Benjamin of Tudela, *Itinerary*, pp. 16 ff.
[3] Ginzberg, *Ginzey Schechter*, ii. 436 ff; Nemoy, *Karaite Anthology*, pp. 273–4.
[4] See Habermann, *Toledot*, i. 87.

MS No. 666; in Oxford at the Bodleian Library, MS No. 2369. Added to these are two nineteenth-century Karaite prayer-books, published in Goslow in 1836 and in Vilna in 1890, and the collection *Tehillat Yisra'el*, printed in Berdichev in 1909.

THE PRINCIPAL POETS

Tobias b. Moses

Tobias b. Moses of Constantinople (11th c.) was instrumental in establishing Karaism in Byzantium. Educated at the Jerusalem academy, where he became a member of the mourners for Zion (*'aveley ṣiyyon*), he visited Egypt, where he gave guidance to the local Karaite community. Tobias, author of the philosophical treatise *Mešivat Nefeš* and a multi-volume commentary on Scripture, *Sefer 'Oṣar Neḥmad*, was also active in translating from Arabic into Hebrew the writings of his teacher, Joseph al-Baṣīr. The Egyptian courtier Abū Sa'd al-Tustarī (d. 1048) wrote of Tobias b. Moses that his authority was recognized by all 'the communities of Edom [i.e. Byzantium] both near and far.' Two hymns by Tobias have survived, a *ševah*, *'Eloheynu mi-kol 'ummah 'ahavtanu*, and a *zemer*, *Ṭov lekha na'eh le-hallel*.[5]

Aaron b. Joseph

Aaron b. Joseph Ha-Rofe (the physician), 'the Elder' (*c.*1250–1320), lived in Crimea and in Constantinople. He is the author of a commentary on the Pentateuch, *Sefer Ha-Mivḥar*, a widely popular work among Karaites. Joseph Solomon Lutzki (d. 1844), Karaite leader in the Crimea, wrote a super-commentary, *Ṭirat Kesef*, on the *Sefer Ha-Mivḥar*. Aaron the Elder's commentary favours the plain meaning of the scriptural text, after the model of Abraham Ibn Ezra, although he strays periodically into homiletic interpretations which he borrows from RaŠI. The Rabbanite influence is also seen in Aaron's work on Hebrew grammar, *Kelil Yofi*, which shows his indebtedness to Judah Ibn Janaḥ, and in the Karaite prayer-book which he edited, featuring Rabbanite-style prayers and the hymns of Gabirol, Judah Ha-Levi and Moses and Abraham Ibn Ezra. Some forty hymns in several genres by Aaron the Elder have been preserved.[6]

Aaron b. Elijah

Aaron b. Elijah 'the Younger' (d. 1369) of Nicomedia is the author of a monumental trilogy comprising *'Eṣ Ḥayyim*, on the philosophy of religion,

[5] Ankori, 'The Correspondence of Tobias b. Moses'.
[6] Idem, *Karaites in Byzantium*, p. 489; Weinberger, *Širat . . . Rabbanim*, pp. 512–61.

Gan ʿEden, on Karaite law, and *Keter Torah*, a Pentateuch commentary. His writings reveal a thorough familiarity with Karaite and Rabbanite thinking, and his *ʾEṣ Ḥayyim* was intended as a Karaite counterpart to Maimonides' *Moreh Ha-Nevukhim.* Aaron the Younger took part in what has been 'perhaps the most flourishing period of all Jewish medieval philosophy', led by Gersonides and Moses Narboni, among others. Three hymns by Aaron the Younger have survived, a *tokheḥah*, *ʾOraḥ ḥayyim le-maʿalah*, a *seliḥah*, *ʾAdon ha-raḥamim* and a *zemer*, *ʾEder yeqar ḥemdah.*[7]

Elijah Bašyatchi

Elijah b. Moses Bašyatchi (*c.*1420–90) was a member of a prominent Karaite family from Adrianople. He moved to Constantinople in 1455. His family pioneered Karaite practices that were more in line with Rabbanite teachings, such as kindling Sabbath lights and beginning the weekly Torah readings from the month of Tišri, instead of Nisan. Elijah Bašyatchi is best known for his authoritative code of Karaite law, *ʾAdderet ʾEliyyahu.* His other works include an anti-Rabbanite polemic, *ʾIggeret Ha-Yerušah*, and two polemical tracts, *ʾIggeret Ha-Ṣom* and *ʾIggeret Gid Ha-Našeh*, directed against Karaites in Egypt, Syria and Ereṣ Yisra'el who did not agree with his liberal legal rulings. Six hymns for the synagogue by Bašyatchi have survived, including an *ʾazharah*-style hymn listing the positive and negative commandments.[8]

Caleb Afendopolo

Caleb b. Elijah Afendopolo (d. 1525) lived mostly in Kramariya, near Constantinople, and died in Belgrade. A polymath, he was taught philosophy, science and rabbinics by the Rabbanite Mordecai Comtino, and taught himself Italian, Greek and Arabic. His wide-ranging learning led him to write on a wide variety of subjects. He composed a supplement to Bašyatchi's *ʾAdderet ʾEliyyahu*; an Arabic-style *maqāmah*, *ʾAvner b. Ner*, on ethics; studies in astronomy, *Gan ʿEynay* and *ʾIggeret Maspeket*; a commentary on the Pentateuch and readings from the Prophets, *Patšegen Ketav Ha-Dat*; and *Gan Ha-Melekh*, a volume of poetry and prose including elegies on the expulsion of Jews from Lithuania and Kiev in 1495. Over forty liturgical works by Afendopolo are included in the Karaite liturgy.[9]

Other Karaites from Byzantium who wrote for the synagogue include Aaron b. Judah and Menaḥem b. Michael, twelfth-century poets from Constantinople. Ottoman Karaite hymnists are Abraham b. Judah (15th c.) from Constantinople and his contemporary Mordecai b. Jacob Politi of Adrianople. Later Ottoman poets are Judah Gibbor (15th–16th c.) of

[7] Ibid. 561–6; Sirat, *History of Jewish Philosophy*, p. 342.
[8] Weinberger, *Širat . . . Rabbanim*, pp. 594–612.
[9] Ibid. 613–68.

Constantinople, and his contemporaries Šabbetai b. Elijah of Parvoto (in Turkey) and Judah b. Elijah Tišbi, Constantinople. The sixteenth century is represented by Moses Paša b. Elijah of Kalé in Crimea In addition to the above, whose age and provenance are known, the following are identified only through their acrostic signatures: Abraham the Physician Boba, Barukh b. Ezra, Jacob ha-Ḥazan, Joseph Kohen, Daniel the Physician, Šemayah Kohen, Abram Levi, Aaron the Karaite, Elijah the Karaite b. Moses, Moses, Abraham, Eliezer, Solomon, Joseph, Judah, Israel, Ephraim, Yošaiah, Mešullam, Mordecai and Menaḥem.

LANGUAGE AND STYLE

Karaite Poetics

In their poetics the Balkan Karaites favoured the strophic *muwashshaḥ* and its variants, and the *qaṣīdah*-style hymn in monorhyme, and embellished both in quantitative metres. Unlike their Rabbanite colleagues, the earliest Karaite hymnists in Byzantium, like Tobias b. Moses, Aaron b. Judah and Menaḥem b. Michael, were not influenced by the Italian neoclassicism of Solomon Ha-Bavli. Like their Hispanic contemporaries, the Karaite poets were composing in the newer Arabic style as early as the eleventh century. As the same time, they did not neglect the older Rabbanite forms, including anadiplosis, a rhetorical device employed by the classical and early Italian hymnists.

Karaite poets employed almost all of the twelve basic metres adopted by Hebrew Rabbanites from classical Arabic versification, and introduced variations of their own. Early examples of Arabic influence are the *zemirot*, *Ṭov lekha na'eh le-hallel*, by Tobias b. Moses and *'Ašorer šir le-'el nora'* by Aaron b. Judah. The former is a metric *qaṣīdah*-style poem in monorhyme and the latter is a metric hymn in rhyming couplets. Menaḥem b. Michael's pseudo-*muwashshaḥ*, *Miškenotay ḥaṣerotay hiṣṣitu qoraḥ*, is probably the earliest Karaite example of this form.[10] The likely reason that the Balkan Karaites were attracted to Arabic models earlier than their Rabbanite brethren in the region was the influence of Tobias b. Moses, who travelled widely in Arabic-speaking countries and was familiar with their poetry, as were his Karaite contemporaries in the eastern Mediterranean. The Karaites also experimented with variations of terminal rhyme, disregarding stress or morphology, and freely resorted to linguistic innovations in the manner of the classical Rabbanites and their European successors. Moreover, they were not averse to the use of the dense set of epithets, neologisms, elliptic syntax and allusions to rabbinic literature popularized by their Rabbanite colleagues.

Some of the more gifted Karaite poets like Aaron b. Joseph the Elder experimented with sound parallelism of both roots and endings of words and

[10] Weinberger, *Širat . . . Rabbanim*, pp. 506–9.

discontinuous rhyme, thereby creating a rich sonority reminiscent of earlier Rabbanite models. Following is an example from R. Aaron's phonetic-intensive *seliḥah*, *'E'erokh mahalali*, for the Ten Days of Mercy:[11]

'E'erokh mahalali le-'eli go'ali meḥolali be-ma'aneh ra'ayonay;
Siḥi meqom zivḥi we-niḥoḥi le-mevin ṭuḥi 'atanneh be-ma'anay;
Ha-'oṭeh 'or u-ma'or we-ye'or 'addir we-na'or 'adonay
'Elohey yisra'el.

I offer my praise to my Lord, redeemer and creator, with the speech of my thoughts;
My prayer in place of sacrifice and sweet savour I present in response to One who knows my mind;
Dressed in light, a beacon, the mighty and glorious Lord, illumines, [He is the] God of Israel.

The most notable influence on Karaite poetics came from the Golden Age Hispano-Hebrew poets. This is seen in such works as the *meliṣat ha-miṣwot* of Elijah Bašyatchi *'Anašim maskilim* and *Be-šem 'el ha-mekhasseh* for Pentecost. The genre is a counterpart to the Rabbanite *'azharot* for that festival. R. Elijah's hymn is identical in both strophic structure and metre (*ha-'arokh*: ---/--v/---/--v), as well as in the terminal rhymeme, to Solomon Ibn Gabirol's *'azharot* for Pentecost. Both hymns list the positive and negative commands and are chanted in Rabbanite and Karaite synagogues on Pentecost, the anniversary of the giving of the Torah. Below are samples from Gabirol's *Šemor libbi ma'aneh* and from Bašyatchi's *'Anašim maskilim*, beginning with Gabirol and followed by Bašyatchi:[12]

Šemor libbi ma'aneh
Heyeh vi-m'od na'aneh;
Yera' ha-'el u-mneh
Devaraw ha-yešarim

Guard my speech, O my heart,
And be exceedingly humble;
Fear the Lord and count
His just commands.

'Anašim maskilim
We-yišrey mif'alim,
Heyu ki-vney 'elim
Le-havin meyšarim.

[11] Ibid. 522–3; also see B. Hrushovski, 'Prosody, Hebrew', *EJ* xiii. 1207–8.
[12] Ibn Gabirol, *Širey Ha-Qodeš*, p. 392; Weinberger, *Širat . . . Rabbanim*, p. 601.

Men of wisdom
And just deeds,
Be like the angels
His equity to comprehend.

More striking yet is the resemblance between the two lists of negative commands:[13]

[GABIROL]
Be-ṣel šadday ʾeḥseh
We-ṣidqo loʾ ʾekhseh
Be-miṣwot loʾ taʿaseh,
We-ʾaggid meyšarim.

In God's shade I seek shelter
And His rightness I will not conceal;
With the negative commands,
And I shall relate His equity.

[BAŠYATCHI]
Be-šem ʾel ha-mekhasseh
Šeḥaqim gam maḥseh,
Be-miṣwot loʾ taʿseh
ʾAḥawweh meyšarim.

In the name of God who covers
The heavens [with clouds] and protects,
By the negative commands
I shall declare His equity.

Among the Rabbanite imitators of Judah Ha-Levi's classic zionide, *Ṣiyyon ha-loʾ tišaʾli li-šlom ʾasirayikh*, was the Karaite Menaḥem b. Michael, whose moving elegy *Ṣiyyon teqonen* 'for the Tenth of 'Av' (when Karaites mourn the destruction of the Temple), like Ha-Levi's, employs the *ha-mitpaššeṭ* II metre in *qaṣīdah*-style monorhyme.[14] Caleb Afendopolo, noted for both his sacred and secular poetry, owed much to the poetics of the Hebrew Hispanics. Below is a sample from his *widduy ʾAlelay li* for the Ten Days of Mercy, in which he makes skilful use of the homonym, a practice of Moses Ibn Ezra, Todros Abulafia and other Golden Age poets.[15] In this selection from Afendopolo the terminal rhyme in the quadrilinear strophe has the same sound and the same spelling but differs in meaning:[16]

[13] Ibn Gabirol, *Širey Ha-Qodeš*, p. 414; Weinberger, *Širat . . . Rabbanim*, p. 607.

[14] See Schirmann, *Ha-Širah Ha-ʿIvrit*, i. 485 ff.; Weinberger, *Širat . . . Rabbanim*, p. 508, No. 250.

[15] See Pagis, *Ḥidduš U-Masoret*, p. 130.

[16] Weinberger, *Širat . . . Rabbanim*, p. 628.

'Alelay li we-'aḥ
Be'et tiv'ar ha-'aḥ
U-ven-gil we-'aḥ
Yomar 'aleykhem: he'aḥ!

Woe unto me, alas,
When the [destroying] fire is in the brazier
And the twin brother [Esau]
Responds to you [shouting], Hurray!

Rhetorics and Philosophy

A common feature of Karaite poetics is the rhetorical device of polarity and parallel. The polarity is between the material world of nature and one's body, characterized as 'an obstacle' (*naguf*), as 'filth' (*zevel*) and 'loathsome' (*meto'av*), to be avoided and shunned, and as a prison-house from which one yearns to be freed.[17] At the other end of the continuum is the world of the spirit, characterized as the 'flower-beds' (*'arugey gan*) and 'pleasure palaces' (*heykhley 'oneg*), populated by the righteous whose souls are 'beloved' (*'ahuvay*) and 'honoured' (*kevudah*), as sweet as a honey-bee (*devorah ... ne'imah*) and as beautiful as the full moon (*yafah ka-levanah*).[18] The philosophical premisses behind this polarity are to be found in the writings of the Rabbanite Neoplatonists, Isaac Israeli, Solomon Ibn Gabirol, Baḥyah Ibn Paqudah, Abraham Ibn Ezra and the author of the *Kitāb Ma'ānī al-Nafs* (A Treatise on the Nature of the Soul), all of whom had considerable influence on Karaite thinking as regards the 'science of the soul', that is, the knowledge that man has of his soul.[19]

The Karaite poets who write about the nature of the soul agree in principle with several assumptions found in the writings of the Rabbanite Neoplatonists. The view that the soul 'emanates from the "Throne of Glory" ' is expressed in the term used by Aaron b. Joseph the Elder: *'aṣulah me-'oṣem ha-keruvim.* Similar language is found in Abraham Ibn Ezra's poem *'Aṣulah mi-kevodo 'el bera'ekh / we-'al 'arba' demut ḥayyot nesa'ekh* ([O soul], emanated from the glory of God, your creator, who bears you on the figures of four creatures).[20] Like Solomon Ibn Gabirol, Ibn Ezra equates the Throne of Glory with the Intellect.[21] Caleb Afendopolo writes that the soul 'emanates from You [God]' (*'aṣulah mimmekha*).[22] It is likely that he means from God's 'Glory',

[17] Ibid. 585, No. 312: 5; p. 589, No. 316: 25; p. 621, No. 332: 13; p. 594, No. 319: 10–11.

[18] Ibid. 634, No. 339: 5, 41; p. 688, No. 394: 10; p. 707, No. 412: 3; p. 632, No. 338: 17; p. 706, No. 411: 8.

[19] Sirat, *History of Jewish Philosophy*, p. 71.

[20] Weinberger, *Širat ... Rabbanim*, p. 519, No. 260: 11; A. Ibn Ezra, *Širey Ha-Qodeš*, i. 54: 1.

[21] Ibn Ezra's commentary on Ps. 8: 4 and Ibn Gabirol, *Keter Malkhut*, No. 24.

[22] Weinberger, *Širat ... Rabbanim*, p. 652, No. 349: 9.

which the Rabbanite Neoplatonists equate with the Intellect.[23] Succumbing to the liberties that a poet is tempted to take, Afendopolo is imprecise with regard to the source from which the soul emanates, and resorts to generalities like 'emanated from the holy place' (*ʾaṣulah mi-meqom qadoš*), or 'emanated from the heights' (*ʾaṣulah mi-meromim*).[24]

A variation of this view emerges from Abraham b. Judah: 'Keep distant from the filth of the abhorrent soul so that the maid-servant may not have dominion over her mistress, and give preference to the younger over the older' (*raḥaqi mi-ṭinnuf ha-nefeš ha-keʿurah / še-llo' timšol ha-šifḥah ʾet ha-gevirah*).[25] This comment calls for an explanation, since the poet addresses this warning to the soul itself, as may be seen from the context of the poem, where in the very next colon he gives the reason for his admonition: 'Since you are hewn from a quarry that is eternal therefore you must always seek to ascend by the [light] of the Intellect' (*yaʿan heyotekh gezurah mi-maḥṣav ha-niṣḥiyyim / tamid baqqeši la-ʿalot ba-sikhliyyim*). The poet here assumes that his congregation is familiar with the hierarchical universe of the Neoplatonists, in which the more or less perfect essences are interposed between the perfect God and the imperfect lower world of matter. As formulated by Rabbanite Neoplatonists, the first emanation is the Intellect, followed by the Universal Soul, from which the rational soul is detached and invested with a body. However, the human body, as the most 'composite' of all creation, comprises also an animal and vegetative soul. The animal soul is governed solely by the imagination and by the perception of its senses and not by reason. The vegetative is only capable of desire and of procreation and is inferior to the other two.[26] It is likely that the latter is the poet's referent which he characterizes as 'the abhorrent soul'.

In his poetic hymn on Gen. 28: 10 ff. (*piyyuṭ le-parašat wa-yeṣe'*), *ʾEl ʿelyon nitʿaleh*, Abraham b. Judah suggests that the story of Jacob's ladder (Gen. 28: 12) is an allegory that alludes to the composition of the soul that is invested with a body:[27]

> The meaning of the 'ladder' was revealed to the upright man
> [Jacob] alluding to the cause of the soul
> Which is the Universal Soul dwelling in the heights,
> And she is the reason that the seeker attains wisdom and
> understanding;
> Resting on the ground its head reaches the heavens.

Abraham Ibn Ezra, in his commentary to Gen. 28: 12, reports that Solomon Ibn Gabirol saw in Jacob's ladder an 'allusion to the Universal Soul'

[23] Sirat, *History of Jewish Philosophy*, p. 85.
[24] Weinberger, *Širat . . . Rabbanim*, p. 648, No. 346: 1; p. 614, No. 328: 4.
[25] Ibid. 589, No. 316: 19.
[26] Sirat, *History of Jewish Philosophy*, pp. 62–3, 85, 90.
[27] Weinberger, *Širat . . . Rabbanim*, p. 592, No. 318: 5–8.

(*remez la-nešamah ha-ʿelyonah*) and in 'the angels of God' ascending and descending it 'the thoughts of wisdom' (*maḥševot ha-ḥokhmah*). In line with this is Ibn Ezra's comment that Ibn Gabirol considered the phrase *kol ha-nešamah* in Ps. 150: 6 an 'allusion to the Universal Soul which is in heaven' (*remez la-nešamah ha-ʿelyonah še-hiʾ ba-šamayim*). In Ibn Gabirol's *Fons Vitae* the term *anima universalis*[28] is rendered by Šem Ṭov b. Joseph Ibn Falaquera, the thirteenth-century translator into Hebrew of excerpts from this work, as *ha-nefeš ha-kelalit* (the Universal Soul),[29] the identical term used by the Karaite poet Abraham b. Judah, who was undoubtedly familiar with Falaquera's translation. The poet's statement 'And she is the reason that the seeker attains wisdom' refers to the rational soul and its ascent on the graded stages of wisdom, in line with the interpretation of the ladder by Ibn Gabirol, who in the *Fons Vitae* uses the terms 'ascent' and 'ladder' in the sense of grades of wisdom.[30]

For Elijah Bašyatchi the soul which is 'bound in chains' (*ʾasurah ʿim neḥuštayim*) can free itself by 'knowing its source' (*deʿeh nafši ʿaley šorši*) and can be worthy of gaining the 'wisdom' (*le-haskilah*) needed to 'gain access to the Garden of Eden and its trees of life and to behold the [celestial] world and the "ladder" whose top reaches the heavens' (*le-hanḥilah be-ʿeden gan ʿaṣey ḥayyim; ḥazot ʿolam we-ha-sullam we-roʾšo huʾ le-šamayim*).[31] Here the reference is not to Ibn Gabirol's interpretation of the 'ladder' but to that of the twelfth- to thirteenth-century Provençal writer Samuel Ibn Tibbon, who in his *Maʾamar Yiqqawu Ha-Mayim* interprets Jacob's dream as a prophetic vision similar to the visions of the Celestial Throne by Isaiah and Ezekiel. In Ibn Tibbon's interpretation Jacob's vision, like those of Isaiah and Ezekiel, allegorizes 'the way by which man's intellect attained to its ultimate perfection.'[32] The 'way' taken by Jacob is one of ascent by a ladder made from the trunk of the Tree of Life reaching from the earth to heaven. Bašyatchi's use of the term 'trees of life'—something he is forced to do by the requirements of the metre—is the clue leading to his connection with Ibn Tibbon. In this interpretation Bašyatchi is in the company of his Karaite predecessors Aaron b. Joseph the Elder and Aaron b. Elijah the Younger, who likewise interpret Jacob's ladder in the manner of Ibn Tibbon.[33]

[28] Ibn Gabirol, *Fons Vitae*, iii. 15, p. 111, 19; iii. 51, p. 194, 8; iii. 56, p. 204, 22.

[29] Munk, *Mélanges*, Hebrew section, 11b (3: 14).

[30] Ibid. 166; Altmann, 'The Ladder of Ascension', pp. 13–15.

[31] Weinberger, *Širat . . . Rabbanim*, p. 597, No. 321: 4, 6–7, 9.

[32] Ibn Tibbon, *Maʾamar Yiqqawu Ha-Mayim*, p. 54.

[33] Aaron b. Joseph, *Sefer Ha-Mivḥar*, p. 52b: 'And some say that Jacob's dream resembles the vision seen by Ezekiel and Isaiah who beheld God sitting upon a high and exalted throne . . . there being no difference between them [i.e. the three accounts] except that Jacob began his story [*sippuro*] from below upward.' And see Aaron b. Elijah, *Keter Torah*, p. 65a: 'Some explain . . . each part of the allegory subject-matter . . . and they put together Jacob's dream with the visions of Isaiah and Ezekiel in the sense that the three mean the same thing. However, they call Jacob's understanding one by means of synthesis [*derekh ha-harkavah*], because he apprehended

For Bašyatchi, the knowledge that a person has of his soul not only 'helps him to become free from sin' (*tekhapper ʿal ʾenoš maʿal ḥaṭaʾaw hem be-muskalaw*)[34] but also makes available to him the knowledge of the celestial world, a theme commonly found in Neoplatonic thinking.[35] And the nature of this knowledge includes the sciences as well as the arts, as Bašyatchi makes clear in his *ʾAdderet ʾEliyyahu*,[36] where he recommends not only the study of the Torah but also secular studies such as logic; the 'science of numbers by Nicomachus' (*ḥokhmat ha-mispar šel niqqomaʾqo*); astronomy, and in particular 'the great volume titled *Almagest*' (*ha-sefer ha-gadol ha-niqraʾ almag"isti*); the study of geometry, physics and metaphysics; Al-Ghazālī's *Opinions of the Philosophers*; and the study of music. Here too Bašyatchi follows the lead of his predecessor, Aaron b. Joseph the Elder, who counsels the soul to be the 'gatekeeper at the gates of science, for the impure soul does not gain entrance to God's presence' (*šaʿari be-šaʿarey ha-maddaʿ ki ha-nefeš ha-temeʾah la-ʾel me-ʾeyn mavoʾ*).[37]

However, knowledge alone will not help the soul gain access to its heavenly home. The performance of pious deeds is required. This is explicitly stated by Aaron b. Elijah the Younger, who counsels the soul 'to ascend on the steps of truth and find knowledge and understanding and in the company of the body to do righteousness and justice [and] return to the [celestial] fortress' (*la-ʿalot be-maʿalot ha-ʾemet li-mṣoʾ daʿat we-khišron / we-ʿal yedey ḥevrat ha-guf ʿaseh ṣedaqah u-mišpat, šuvi le-viṣṣaron*).[38] This is in line with Ibn Gabirol's recommendation to the soul that in order to purify itself from the pollutants of the material world and return to its celestial source it must gain knowledge and perform meritorious deeds.[39]

There is drama in the polarity between spirit and matter, body and soul. The soul is unwilling to leave the security of its celestial home and brave the dangers of its journey earthward. Once installed in the body it seeks to liberate itself from the temptations of the material world and return to its native home. The drama of the soul's exile is best seen in the *Sefer Torot Ha-Nefeš* (*Kitāb Maʿānī al-Nafs*),[40] and is reflected in the writings of the Karaite poets. In the *seliḥah* for the Ten Days of Mercy by Mordecai Politi, *Melekh malkhey ha-melakhim*, God has to issue an 'urgent decree' (*dataʾ mehaḥṣefah*) to the soul (*ʿal ner ʾadonay*) in order for it to 'put on the garb of the earth

from below and ascended upward.' The allegory of the ladder is also found in the epithalamium by Joseph Kohen, *Yizlu mey ševaʿ ḥokhmot* (in Weinberger, *Širat . . . Rabbanim*, p. 734, No. 438: 9), where the bridegroom is praised as one 'who has brought to light that which is concealed and has conquered the secret heights of the ladder' (*we-hoṣiʾ leʾor taʿalumim, we-ʿalah be-sod sullam*).

[34] Ibid. 597, No. 321: 15.

[35] Sirat, *History of Jewish Philosophy*, p. 71.

[36] Bašyatchi, *ʾAdderet ʾEliyyahu*, p. 82a.

[37] Weinberger, *Širat . . . Rabbanim*, pp. 519–20, No. 260: 27. Jacob Al-Qirqisānī, a leading Karaite thinker writing in the first half of the 10th c., argues that the study of science and philosophy is not prohibited by Scripture. Nemoy, *Karaite Anthology*, pp. 55–9.

[38] Weinberger, *Širat . . . Rabbanim*, pp. 561–2, No. 292: 6–7.

[39] Ibn Gabirol, *Meqor Ḥayyim*, A. 2.

[40] *Sefer Torot Ha-Nefeš*, pp. 81–2.

dwellers' (*le-halbišo levuš lo me-hamonay*).[41] God is concerned for the comfort of the soul away from home. Therefore, he decrees the blessing over spices at end of the Sabbath in order to bring relief to the soul who mourns the loss of her Sabbath companion.[42] God's purpose in sending the soul earthward is that it be 'fulfilled and returned to its divine source'.[43]

Aaron b. Elijah the Younger is more specific with regard to the purpose of the soul's mission. It is, he writes (in his *tokheḥah*, *'Oraḥ ḥayyim le-ma'alah*), to 'convert the material inclination to do Your will' (*we-hašivi yeṣer ha-ḥomer 'el reṣonekh*), and he concludes: 'For this reason have you been sent into the finite body in order to fulfil yourself and ascend happily in good [time]' (*ki 'al ken šulaḥt be-gomer ha-ḥomer le-hašlimekh 'alot ba-ṭov sesonekh*).[44] It is likely that the term 'material inclination' is a reference to the vegetative soul, whose desirous nature must be curbed by the rational soul in order for the latter successfully to complete its mission on earth. This is somewhat akin to the view stated in the *Sefer Torot Ha-Nefeš*, (pp. 81–2) where 'the mission of the rational soul is to purify the two souls [i.e. vegetable and animal] through knowledge and meritorious deeds' (*'al ha-nefeš ha-sikhlit ha-ḥovah le-haṭhir 'et šetey ha-nefašot ha-'aḥerot be-ḥokhmah u-v-ma'aseh*). Having fulfilled its mission, the soul is rewarded by being allowed to return to its source, where, as described by Aaron b. Elijah the Younger (in *'Oraḥ ḥayyim le-ma'alah*), 'you will be united with your Intellect and attach yourself to God in the company of his faithful ones' (*tityaḥadi be-sikhlekh le-dovqah be-šem ha-meyuḥad be-sod ne'emanay*). The soul's goal is realized through 'attachment' (*devequt*) to God, a term used by Solomon Ibn Gabirol (and other Neoplatonists) to describe the final fulfilment of the soul.[45]

The polarity in Karaite poetics is complemented by the parallel between the predicament of the soul imprisoned in the body and the agony of Israel in exile. Both are forced to live in a strange domicile and both are anxious to return to their native land. Even the conditions that each must meet in order to be rehabilitated are essentially the same. In order to indicate the similarity between the two, the poet resorts to the use of words and phrases that describe the situation of each. For example, in Aaron b. Joseph's *taḥanun* for the Day of Atonement, *'Eloha ram 'ašer huram*,[46] God desires that Israel, His

41 Weinberger, *Širat . . . Rabbanim*, pp. 573–4, No. 301: 9–10.

42 See ibid. 569–70, No. 297: 21–4, Mordecai Politi's *havdalah*, *Male' 'olam kevod yofi*. See Maimonides, *Mišneh Torah*, Laws of the Sabbath, 29: 'Why do we recite the blessing over spices at the end of the Sabbath? Because the soul grieves at the end of the Sabbath [since her companion has left; see the statement of R. Simon b. Laqiš in *bBeṣ* 16a], we therefore attempt to make her happy and calm with a fragrant scent.'

43 See Mordecai Politi's *Melekh malkhey melakhim*, in Weinberger, *Širat . . . Rabbanim*, pp. 573–4, No. 301: 9–11.

44 Ibid. 561–2, No. 292: 22, 37, 39, 42.

45 See Ibn Gabirol, *Meqor Ḥayyim*, 5. 43, where the soul realizes its ambition when it attains 'deliverance from death and attachment to the source of life' (*šiḥrur me-ha-mawet u-dvequt bi-mqor ha-ḥayyim*).

46 Weinberger, *Širat . . . Rabbanim*, pp. 541–2, No. 274: 16, 19–20.

chosen one, 'fulfil itself through His Torah' (*le-haślimam be-torato*). The term *le-haślim* is used also by Mordecai Politi with regard to the soul.[47] In the above *taḥanun* by Aaron b. Joseph, Israel is informed that 'when they repent with all their heart then God will receive them in His mercy and forgive their sins and then return Israel to His sacred dwelling' (*be'et śuvam be-khol libbam yeqabbel ṣur be-ḥemlato, we-yislaḥ la-'awonam la-haśivam 'el neweh qodeś*). The linking word in this instance, *le-haśiv* (to return) is used to describe the successfully completed mission of the soul and its return heavenward, as in Mordecai Politi's *Melekh malkhey ha-melakhim*. The failings of both Israel and the soul are described in similar language. In his *ḥaṭa'nu* for the Day of Atonement, *'Omnam heqalnu*, Aaron b. Joseph laments: 'We have spent our days in the pursuit of vanity and our power has weakened' (*ba-hevel kalu yameynu we-khaśal koḥenu*),[48] even as in his *'Oraḥ ḥayyim le-ma'alah*, Aaron b. Elijah faults the soul with these words: 'You have immersed yourself in delusions of vanity' (*davaqt be-ta'tu'ey hevel*).

Most revealing in this regard is the *zemer*, *'Aqawweh la-'el bo' yavo' go'el*, by Aaron Ḥazan, where the commonly used metonym for the soul as 'the only one' (*yeḥidah*) is used as a reference for Israel and the regularly used image of Israel as 'the dove' (*yonah*) is used to describe the soul. Not only is there an exchange of metonyms, but in the four-strophe hymn focusing on a plea for redemption, the soul and Israel are inextricably combined. The first strophe begins with a prayer for the coming of the 'redeemer from the tribe of Judah' and a plea that God send the 'prince Michael' and fulfil the words of the prophet Malachi. Strophe two describes the waiting of Israel, 'the only one', for the redemption. In strophe three, the poet appeals to the soul 'emanated from on high' (*'aṣulah mi-marom*) to seek God's mercy and return to Him. In the last two lines of the strophe, the poet urges the soul to repent in haste; 'perhaps your Rock will rebuild Jerusalem' (*'ulay yivneh ṣurekh binyan 'ari'el*, after Isa. 29: 1). In the last strophe, the poet prays that God who 'resurrects the dead, rebuild the Temple' (*meḥayyeh ha-metim, beneh 'appiryon*) and ends with the hope that God's 'glorious presence' will return to Zion in the person of His 'anointed one', the branch (of Jesse) (*yaśiv le-ṣiyyon śekhinat kevodo, ṣemaḥ meśiḥo*). Of particular interest here is that, although the poet describes the separation of the soul from its source in language used by the Rabbanite Neoplatonists—'emanated from on high'[49]—he does not resolve the soul's predicament in the manner of the

[47] See Weinberger, *Śirat . . . Rabbanim*, p. 573, No. 301: 11; p. 583, No. 310: 26, Politi's *seliḥah*, *Melekh malkhey melakhim*, and the phrase *le-haślimo u-lhaśivo 'el 'adonay* (to be fulfilled and returned to its divine source) and his epithalamium, *Mah yafu pa'amey regel śulamit . . . hiśba'ti 'etkhen te'oraru ha-śalem* (I adjure you to stir up the fulfilment).

[48] Ibid. 543–4, No. 275: 16.

[49] A. Ibn Ezra, *Śirey Ha-Qodeś*, i. 54, *'Aṣulah mi-kevodo 'el bera'ekh* (Emanated from God your creator), and i. 55, *'Aṣulah mi-meqor ḥayyim me'irah* (Emanated from the source of life illuminating).

Neoplatonists, in terms of reunion with the Intellect, but in the traditional context of Israel's reconciliation with God and its national restoration. The goals of both Israel and the soul are now identical! Here is a translation of Aaron Ḥazan's poem:[50]

I hope in the Lord that the redeemer will surely come
From the tribe of Judah, from the shoot of the mighty Jesse
O fearful [Lord], please send the prince Michael;
My Maker, fulfil, I pray, the prophecy of Malachi.

The 'only one' [*yeḥidah*] awaits the desired time:
O my Rock, take me out of the fortress [exile]
And bring me to mount Moriah, where the binding [of Isaac] took place
And there will the seed of Abraham blossom like the lily.

Pray for mercy and renew your repentance,
You who are emanated from on high, seek your King;
My innocent dove (*yonati tamati*), hurry and hasten [to repent]
Perhaps your Rock will rebuild Jerusalem.

O exalted One, hear now the cry of the poor;
You who resurrect the dead, rebuild the Temple;
Lord, who is eternal will bring back to Zion
His glorious presence [*šekhinah*], even His anointed one [after Zech. 6: 12].

Literary Influences

The Karaites not only borrowed from the Rabbanites in their poetics, but also in their use of literary sources, despite the anti-Rabbanite polemics in the Karaite liturgy. Mostly, Karaite objections focused on the Rabbanite Oral Law, which they saw as a distortion and corruption of the authentic scriptural reference. Thus, in a *ḥazanut* hymn for the seventh day of Tabernacles, *'Akhen ye'eteh yavo'*, Aaron b. Joseph writes: 'In it [i.e. the Torah] a person will find counsel and logical argument, for it alone was given to Israel; Yet now it is made weak by those who would attach to it another Torah' (*bah yimṣa' 'enoš sod u-svara' / ki hi' levaddah li-yšurun nimsarah / we-'attah hi' nefogah mi-meḥabberim 'immah 'aḥeret torah*).[51] Alongside the anti-Rabbanite polemics in the Karaite liturgy is a sense of regret that there is such rancour among 'brothers', as may be seen in three penitentials for the Ten Days

[50] Weinberger, *Širat . . . Rabbanim*, pp. 745–6, No. 449.

[51] Ibid. 549–50, No. 280: 15–17; Salman b. Yeruḥam, *Sefer*, 2: 75: 'It is written: "The Law of the Lord is perfect" [Ps. 19: 8]; what profit be there for us, then, in the written Mišnah?' (*Katuv, 'Torat 'adonay temimah', mah no'il be-mišnah rešumah*). Nemoy, *Karaite Anthology*, p. 78.

of Mercy, one by Aaron b. Joseph and two by Caleb Afendopolo. In a *taḥanun* beginning *ʾAšer yivḥar lekha*, R. Aaron prays: 'Scatter [and cause to vanish] the contention' (*zereh madon*).[52] Using the same term *madon* in a *ḥaṭa'nu*, *ʾIm ʾozen ʾaṭamnu*, Afendopolo confesses: 'We jeered in order to incite contention among brothers' (*paṣinu finu le-šallaḥ beyn ʾaḥim medanim*),[53] and in a *widduy*, *ʾEtwaddeh rov ʿawonay*, he writes: 'I am dismayed by the contention between brothers; [I am dismayed] by the sins that have grown like cedars' (*nivhalti beyn ʾaḥim medanim / me-ʿawonot gaveru ka-ʾallonim*).[54]

Clearly, there is much more in the way of borrowing from the Rabbanite Oral Torah by the Karaite poets than of condemning it. The borrowing is to be found in several areas, ranging from the use of single Rabbanite terms found in the Talmud and Midraš to the employment of whole homilies preserved in Rabbanite sources. There follow some examples, beginning with Aaron b. Joseph the Elder. In his *ševaḥ* for the Sabbath morning service, *ʾAddir we-noraʾ kevod ʾel*, he deals with the theme of the chariot throne upon which God is seated, and concludes that 'the story is related [in this way] to facilitate the reporting of it to the observers' (*we-khol sippur le-šemaʿ ha-roʾim*).[55] The referent here is the statement by the rabbis (in *bBer* 31b): 'The Torah uses an ordinary form of expression' (*divrah torah ki-lšon beney ʾadam*), a lesson also utilized by Maimonides in explaining the anthropomorphisms in Scripture.[56] A slight variation of the above appears in Aaron b. Joseph's *berakhah* for the seventh day of Tabernacles, *ʾEt šem ʾaddir we-noraʾ*: 'A secret was related to the Prophets in such a way as to facilitate its report to the listener' (*sod ha-nevuʾah le-hašmaʿut ʾozen memallela*). In the same work Aaron writes about God: 'He knows all things that are known before they happen except who will become enlightened' (*yodeaʿ be-khol yaduaʿ ṭerem heyoto zulati le-histakkelah*). The likely referent is the statement in *ʾAvot* 3. 15: 'Everything is foreseen but the right [of choice] is granted.'[57]

Karaite poets used *ʾAvot* on other occasions as a source of reference. In his *widduy* for the eve of Yom Kippur, *ʾEykhah ʾessaʾ rʾoš*, Aaron b. Joseph prays for forgiveness and adapts a statement from Hillel in *ʾAvot* 1. 14: 'for the king's mission is urgent and if I am not for myself, who is for me?' (*ki devar ha-melekh naḥuṣ, we-ʾim ʾeyn ʾani li mi li?*).[58] Similarly, we find in the penitential prayer of Joseph Kohen, *Yeḥidah yaḥeli*, for the Ten Days of Mercy, a paraphrase of R. Tarphon's homily from *ʾAvot* 2. 15, as the poet urges the soul to 'rouse yourself from the depths of sloth; the day is short and

[52] Weinberger, *Širat . . . Rabbanim*, p. 524, No. 263: 12.
[53] Ibid. 641–2, No. 342: 17.
[54] Ibid. 642–3, No. 343: 3.
[55] Ibid. 512, No. 253: 8.
[56] Maimonides, *Moreh Ha-Nevukhim*, i. 26.
[57] Weinberger, *Širat . . . Rabbanim*, pp. 545–6, No. 277: 7, 9.
[58] Ibid. 539, No. 272: 24–5.

the work [to be performed] is much' (*we-hitnaʿari mi-tehom ha-ʿaṣlut, ha-yom qaṣar ve-ha-mela'khah rabbah*).[59]

Mordecai Politi is another Karaite poet who adapts Rabbanite homilies. In a *baqqašah* for Pentecost, *Mi yaʿarokh la-'adoneynu*, the poet observes that 'Mount Sinai was chosen as the site for Moses to bring down the Torah because of its humility *vis-à-vis* the other mountains' (*we-gam torah horid mošeh ʿaley sinay šafal neged ramim*).[60] This is based on the rabbinic statement (in *Num. Rabbah* 13. 3): '"But he that is of lowly spirit shall attain to honour" [Prov. 29: 23], applied to Sinai which humbled itself by saying, "I am low," and because of this the Holy One, blessed be He, placed his glory upon it and the Torah was given thereon.' The poet who most often utilizes rabbinic sources is Judah Gibbor. In his poetic commentary on the Scripture reading *Noaḥ*, *We-noaḥ 'iš tamim*, he writes about the 'secret of the city that was built and the matter of the Tower' (*we-sod ʿir ha-binyan / u-migdal kol ʿinyan*),[61] a reference to Gen. 11: 1–9. The source of the 'secret' is the rabbinic homily in *Gen. Rabbah* 38. 5: 'the [evil] deeds of the generation of the Flood are explicitly stated [in. Gen. 6: 11], whereas those of the generation of the Separation are not explicitly stated.' In his comment on the reading *Lekh lekha*, *'Elohim 'az nir'eh*, Gibbor writes that 'the removal of the foreskin and the commandment of circumcision are a secret [reference] to the circumstance [of a lifetime], [even as it refers] to austerity in sexual relations' (*hasarat ha-ʿorlah / u-miṣwat ha-milah / we-sod kol ha-ʿillah / le-maʿeṭ 'eyvarim*).[62] The 'secret' to which Gibbor alludes is revealed in the rabbinic comment (in *Tanḥuma'*, *Lekh lekha* 23) on Ps. 25: 14:

> 'The secret of the Lord is for those who fear Him; to them He makes known his covenant [*berito*].' And what is God's secret? It is circumcision, God did not reveal the mystery of circumcision to anyone save Abraham . . . And what is the secret? The years of a person's life: sixty [*sameḥ*], six [*waw*] and four [*dalet*] [i.e. the numerical value of the letters 'sod'] make seventy.

The clue to the source regarding 'austerity in sexual relations' is the word *'eyvarim* (organs). The referent is probably the rabbinic observation (in *bSanh* 107a): 'There is a small organ (*'eyvar*) in man which satisfies him in his hunger but makes him hunger when satisfied.' In Gibbor's comments on *Wa-yera'*, *We-qol šadday qore'*, he writes about Abraham publicizing his love of God in an excessive manner: 'And he continued to advertise his love, and all men saw in it an attempt to exaggerate his great devotion to the Creator' (*we-ʿod pirsum 'ahavah / we-khol 'iš ir'eh vah / le-haflig rov ḥibbah / le-vore' ha-yeṣurim*).[63] Gibbor's referent is the comment of the rabbis (in *Gen. Rabbah* 55. 8): '"And Abraham rose early in the morning" [Gen. 22: 5]. Surely he

[59] Ibid. 732, No. 436: 2.
[60] Ibid. 581, No. 308: 11–12.
[61] Ibid. 669–70, No. 379: 21.
[62] Ibid. 670–1, No. 380: 7.
[63] Ibid. 671–2, No. 381: 16.

had plenty of slaves? But the reason was that love upsets the natural order.' Gibbor, like his Rabbanite counterparts, felt it necessary to explain Jacob's behaviour towards Laban in placing the streaked rods over against the ewes in order to affect the colouring of those about to be born (Gen. 30: 37). In his poetic comment on *Wa-yeṣe'*, *Gevir ḥalam sullam*, he writes: 'Far be it from the Prince [Jacob] to be unethical since this is forbidden' (*we-ḥalilah mi-sar / ʿavor zeh ha-musar / u-middah zo't ne'esar*). According to Judah Gibbor, the reason for Jacob's action is that he saw it 'as payment for his twenty years of labour' (*ʿavodato li-gbot be-šanim ha-ʿesrim*).[64] A variation of this apologetic for Jacob's behaviour is given by the rabbis in *Gen. Rabbah* 74. 3: 'The Holy One, blessed be He, foresaw what Laban would do to Jacob [i.e. alter the agreement], and so He made the appearance to correspond [i.e. He made the flock bear lambs of the appearance finally agreed upon as belonging to Jacob].' The number of references to rabbinic sources in Gibbor's poetry is explained by the fact that Gibbor, along with Caleb Afendopolo, studied with Rabbanite teachers, and Gibbor's writings, the *Minḥat Yehuda* (a poetic paraphrase of the Pentateuch) and the *Sefer Ha-Moʿadim* (an excursus on the New Year, Tabernacles and Purim), show a preference for Rabbanite over Karaite sources.[65]

Karaite poets borrowed not only from Rabbanite exoteric literature but from the esoteric sources as well. Revealing in this regard is the passage from a *hoda'ah*, *'Attah qadoš yaʿariṣukha hamonay*, for the Sabbath morning service, by Aaron b. Joseph: 'Blessed and praised is He among his angels of fire; concealed from everyone but revealed to his loved ones' (*barukh u-mvo-rakh be-mal'akhey ševivaw / nistar me-ʿeyney khol we-nimṣa' le-'ohavaw*).[66] A similar passage in a *heykhalot* text speaks of 'God who is concealed from the sight of all creatures and hidden from the ministering angels, but who has revealed himself to Rabbi Akiva in the vision of the Chariot' (*ha-'el . . . še-hu' neʿelam me-ʿeyney khol ha-beriyyot we-nistar mi-mal'akhey ha-šaret, we-niglah lo le-rabbi ʿaqiva' be-maʿaseh merkavah*).[67] In both Aaron's work and in the *heykhalot* text there is a common language of contrast 'concealed . . . revealed' and a common conceit wherein only 'the loved ones' are privy to His presence, which is hidden even from the angels.[68]

The several references in Karaite poetry to the influence of the planets on the sublunar world may be traced to readings from the literature of Ibn Gabirol and Abraham Ibn Ezra. Aaron b. Joseph, in his *taḥanun* for the Ten

64 Weinberger, *Širat . . . Rabbanim*, pp. 674–5, No. 384: 8–9. See Gen. 31: 8.

65 See Miller, 'Twilight', p. 88.

66 Weinberger, *Širat . . . Rabbanim*, pp. 514–15, No. 256: 10.

67 See Scholem, *Major Trends*, p. 364 n. 80.

68 See Weinberger, *'Antologia*, p. 10, for the *'ofan* by the 11th-c. Rabbanite poet Benjamin b. Samuel: 'My Beloved [God], hidden and concealed from all that breathes, I shall sing of His wonders in praise like the angels on high' (*Dodi ṭamun we-ḥavuy me-'eyn kol nefuḥey nešamot / 'ani nor'otaw 'ašaršer ke-'ofaney meromim*). See also P. B. Fenton, 'De quelques attitudes qaraïtes envers le qabbale', *REJ* 142 (1983), pp. 5–19.

Days of Mercy, *'Eloha 'al 'awon ma'al*, writes in praise of the spheres which 'do the will of their Rock and [carry out] the decree of their Creator upon earth' (*reṣon ṣuram / we-ḥoq yoṣeram / heyot 'osim le-'admati*).[69] God's command's are entrusted to the spheres, which then proceed to carry them out in the governance of the sublunar world. Compare Abraham Ibn Ezra's commentary on Exod. 33: 21, which was available to Aaron b. Joseph: '[God's] ministers [i.e. the spheres] are unable to change their courses and they are not capable of disobeying the command that God gave them. Even so [are] the stationary stars [in the eighth sphere]. And the inhabitants of the lower world are governed by them according to their status.' Likewise, Abraham b. Judah writes in his poetic comment on *Wa-yeṣe'*, *'El 'elyon nit'aleh*, about 'Jacob's ladder' whose 'top reaches the height of the spheres providing instruction about the luminous [upper] world and the knowledge about their influence on the lower world' (*we-ro'šo ha-nissa' le-ma'alah ba-galgallim / yoreh le-sod 'olam ha-bahir we-li-ydi'at ha-šepa'at ha-šefalim*).[70] The connection that Abraham b. Judah makes between 'Jacob's ladder' and the influence of the spheres is probably the result of his reading of Abraham Ibn Ezra's commentary on Gen. 28: 12. There, Ibn Ezra cites Ibn Gabirol's interpretation of 'Jacob's ladder' as an 'allegory of the Universal Soul' and 'the angels of God' as the 'thoughts of wisdom'. Ibn Ezra disagrees with this interpretation, and suggests that the ladder teaches him that 'nothing is hidden from God and that the events that happen below depend on the supernal beings; there is, as it were, a ladder between them.'

Rabbanite and Karaite Liturgical Exchanges

Rabbanite hymns by Hispanic and Balkan poets were often included in the Karaite ritual. Andalusian Golden Age poets were particularly popular, as were the hymns of Romaniotes like Moses b. Ḥiyyah, Joseph Qalai, Mordecai b. Šabbetai, Hillel b. Eliaqim, Caleb b. Eliaqim, Judah Qilti, Šabbetai b. Caleb and Mordecai Comtino. The latter, a teacher of Karaites, was highly regarded by them, as was his mentor, Ḥanokh Saporta, who, according to a report by Elia Mizraḥi,[71] was prepared to instruct them in 'whatever they desired to learn, whether it be the Talmud or the [later] rabbinic authorities . . . without any hesitation.' Comtino's epithalamium, *Mi-me'ono 'or zoreaḥ*, with conventional themes based on scriptural and rabbinic sources, is included in the Rabbanite Romaniote ritual and in the nineteenth-century editions of the Karaite prayer-books, albeit with some alterations in the latter collections. Here is a selection:[72]

[69] Weinberger, *Širat . . . Rabbanim*, pp. 533–4, No. 269: 24.

[70] Ibid. 592–3, No. 318: 9–10.

[71] Mizraḥi, *Responsa*, No. 57, p. 180.

[72] Weinberger, *Širat . . . Rabbanim*, pp. 377–8; J.-C. Attias, *Le Commentaire biblique: Mordekhai Komtino ou l'herméneutique du dialogue* (Paris, 1991), pp. 176–7.

May the light from His abode shine
Upon you, O bridegroom, and blossoms of joy [appear];
You shall have nothing but joy!
The year of vindication [*šenat šillum*] for Zion's cause,
The end day concealed, in your lifetime,
May it be revealed to you, even the man of peace,
The anointed [*mašiaḥ*], reviving the dead;
You shall have nothing but joy!

In the Karaite ritual, 'a year of vindication' was changed to read 'a year of peace' (*šenat šalom*). In the nineteenth-century editions of the Karaite prayer-book, published in the Crimea under the watchful eye of Abraham Firkowicz, care was taken not to offend the ruling authorities in the region. Following are examples of Karaite sensitivity to the feelings of Russia's Christian rulers. In the *ḥaṭa'nu*, *'Eykh 'ozlat yadi*, the Rabbanite Caleb b. Eliaqim blames Christians and Muslims for 'putting to death' God's 'first-born son [Israel]' (*'eykh horegim beney ṣarekha / 'et binkha bekhorekha*), and laments that Israel 'the great nation whom You loved is ruled by a shameless people whom You rejected' (*'eykh goy gadol 'ašer ḥibbavta / be-yad goy 'az panim 'azavta*). Continuing, the poet charges that God's 'enemies', the 'haughty and conceited' Muslims and Christians, are 'violent men' who have subjected 'the heirs of the Patriarchs' to forced labour and treat them with 'ruthless severity'. Ishmael and Esau (i.e. Muslims and Christians) have made heavy the burden upon the neck of Israel, even as they 'utter their blaspheming assertions about God which He had not commanded.'[73] In the Karaite edition of R. Caleb's hymn, his indictments of the ruling power are completely omitted. While preserving the hymn's pattern structure built on the repetition of the unit 'Alas . . . alas' (*'Eykh . . . 'eykh*) and its rhyming scheme, the Karaite editor, by deft changes in wording, argues that the People of Israel's suffering in exile is caused by their sins, including their inclination 'to invent in their dismay decrees from the Lord which He had not commanded them' (*wa-yaḥpe'u devarim 'al 'adonay mi-ṣaratam / 'ašer lo' ṣiwwah 'otam*).[74]

Although the Crimean Karaites were anxious not to offend Russian Christendom, they were not reticent in condemning the Muslim Turks, Russia's historic enemy. This may seen in the Karaite adaptation of an anonymous Rabbanite elegy, *'Eyaluti be-galuti*,[75] which in the original version calls upon God to 'diminish' (*dal*) the Ishmaelites for their cruelty against Israel and to 'make desolate, like Sodom, the land of Edom [Christians], the destroyers of my mansions' (*hafokh ki-sdom / 'ereṣ 'edom / maḥarivey*

[73] Weinberger, *Seder . . . Ha-Romaniotim*, pp. 94–6, No. 38: 4–5, 26.
[74] Weinberger, 'A Note on Karaite Adaptations'.
[75] The hymn is preserved in Oxford, *Maḥazor Calabria*, MS No. 1081, fo. 227b.

'armonay). Here too the Karaite editor did not retain the latter passage calling for judgment against the Christians; however, he did not hesitate to substitute for 'diminish' (*dal*) the fiercer term 'destroy' (*kalleh*) when invoking punishment against the Muslims.[76]

While there is no direct evidence of Rabbanite borrowings from Karaite hymnography, there is an occasional adoption of a Karaite hymn in the Rabbanite liturgy. Whereas the Karaite editors of the liturgy were motivated by political considerations in determining the content of their prayer-book, the Rabbanite editors were prompted by religious concerns. Although the Karaites included in their liturgy the hymns of Rabbanite poets from Spain and Byzantium, Karaite liturgical works in the Rabbanite prayer-book are rarely found. One such exception is the twelve-strophe epithalamium *Pe'er ḥatanay we-'am 'emunay*, preserved in both Karaite and Rabbanite liturgical collections. In the Karaite editions from Goslow (1836), 4: 39 and from Vilna (1890), 4: 52, the acrostic identifies its author as 'Tišbi Rofe', referring to the Karaite notable Judah b. Elijah Tišbi. In the Rabbanite *Maḥazor Romania*, the hymn makes its first appearance in the 1510 Constantinople version under the editorship of Elijah b. Benjamin Ha-Levi, a student of Moses Capsali. The hymn is also included in the later editions of the Romaniote ritual. However, in these editions the epithalamium yields the acrostic 'Šabbetai Rofe'. Below are the first five strophes; the sleight of hand is achieved by reversing the order of strophes two to four:

Pe'er ḥatanay / we-'am 'emunay / lekhu we-nelekhah / be-'or 'adonay;
Temim derakhim / u-mahalakhim / lekha meḥakkim / 'adat 'adonay;
Ševu yedidim / we-neḥemadim / 'aneh le-'omedim / be-veyt 'adonay;
Be-'oz u-verekh / ṣe'ad be-derekh / lekha 'avarekh / be-šem 'adonay;
Yeḥal we-qawweh / le-'el we-tirweh / be-no'amo we-/'emet 'adonay.

The bridegroom's adorned / and the faithful folk, / come let us walk / in the light of the Lord;
[God], upright / and just, / You are awaited / by the congregation of the Lord;
Return, beloved / and charming, / respond to those who stand / in the house of the Lord;
With praise and humility / make your way / and I will bless you / in the name of the Lord;
Await and hope / for God and take your fill / of His love / in the certainty of the Lord.

The acrostic in the above Karaite text yields the name 'Tišbi Rofe' through the opening units in colas 2–5: *Temim . . . Ševu . . . Be-'oz . . . Yeḥal* (*TŠBY*).

[76] See Weinberger, 'A Note on Karaite Adaptations', pp. 269–71.

Changing the order of the strophes in the Rabbanite version spells 'Šabbetai Rofe': *Ševu . . . Be-ʿoz . . . Temim . . . Yeḥal* (*ŠBTY*). Helping to ascertain the identity of the author is the *Širim U-Zmirot We-Tišbaḥot*, a liturgical collection published in Constantinople in 1545 under the editorship of the Rabbanite, Solomon b. Mazal Ṭov. The hymn *Pe'er ḥatanay*, which is included in this collection (No. 131), yields the signature 'Tišbi Rofe'. Supporting the likelihood that its author was a Karaite is the reference to his work as a physician. Rabbanite poets rarely advertised their profession, whereas Karaite physician-poets often did.

How this hymn came to be included in the Romaniote liturgy is open to speculation. Since it first appears in the 1510 Constantinople edition, it is possible that its editor, Elia Ha-Levi, teacher of Karaites, was attracted to the elegance of the hymn. However, being reluctant to offend his mentor, Moses Capsali, who forbade teaching Karaites, and fearful of antagonizing the Rabbanite worthy Isaiah Missini and his colleagues, who considered Karaites to be the equivalent of Kutians (i.e. idolators), R. Elia presumably rearranged the strophes in order to conceal the identity of the Karaite author.[77]

Karaite Usages

The Karaite prose writings themselves provided source material for their poets, although not nearly as extensive as that offered by Rabbanite literature, given the greater availability of the latter. The use of Karaite terminology and doctrine is in evidence in their poetry. For example, Elijah Bašyatchi in his *ḥaṭa'nu* for the Ten Days of Mercy, *'Et 'imrat 'adonay*, confesses: 'We have mocked and despised the practical ordinances which are "the road and the entrance" [*ʿiṭṭim we-nihulim*] to the [reception] of the rational ordinances.'[78] The term *ʿiṭṭim we-nihulim* is a Karaite usage going back to the twelfth-century Judah Hadassi.[79] And in line with Karaite doctrine Bašyatchi writes in his *Meliṣat Ha-Miṣwot*, *'Anašim maskilim*, that there are many ordinances which are not expressly mentioned in the Torah but which are derived by means of 'analogy' (*heqeš*), and that they are the 'traditions' (*haʿataqot*) handed down to the generations . . . and the scholars of Scripture [i.e. the Karaites: *ḥakhmey ha-miqra'*], after considerable study, have listed the three fundamentals upon which the observance of Scripture rests: the written text, analogy, and 'the burden of inheritance' (*ketav ʿim heqeš we-sevel ha-yeruššah*).[80]

[77] See *bḤul* 6a; Mizraḥi, *Responsa*, Nos. 57, 58; Weinberger, 'Piyyuṭ', p. 23.

[78] Weinberger, *Širat . . . Rabbanim*, p. 594, No. 319: 6.

[79] See Klatzkin, *Thesaurus Philosophicus*, i. 38; Nemoy, *Karaite Anthology*, p. 240.

[80] Weinberger, *Širat . . . Rabbanim*, pp. 601–3, No. 324: 75–8; Nemoy, *Karaite Anthology*, p. 249; see also N. Wieder, 'Three Terms for Tradition', *JQR* 49 (1958–9), pp. 108–21.

Polemics

Occasional references to polemical issues are preserved in Karaite poetic writings. The polemics were directed against the Rabbanites and against other adversaries. The animosity between Rabbanites and Karaites in eleventh-century Constantinople is reflected in the lament of Tobias b. Moses:

> They have made me desolate, they have chastised me;
> Always they quarrel with me!
> Included among them are fierce ones like bears,
> And whereas I am but one, they are many;
> Save me from the tyrants![81]

In his *ševaḥ* for a 'festival that falls on the Sabbath', *'Eloheynu mi-kol 'ummah 'ahavtanu*, Tobias b. Moses prays to God 'to vindicate and sanctify [the counting of] evening, morning and noon as we have taught' (*ṣaddeq we-qaddeš 'erev wa-voqer we-ṣohorayim ke-limmudeynu*). In this prayer Tobias asks for vindication of the lunar calendar, which measures the Days of Creation from evening to evening after Gen. 1: 5. His polemic here is directed against the disciples of Mišawayah of Baalbek, who followed a solar calendration. In his *'Oṣar Neḥmad*[82] Tobias has harsh words for the Mišawites:

> Know ye, our brethren, that at no time has there arisen in Israel a man who would argue that the [different categories] of days—the Days of Creation as well as the Days [legally circumscribed for the Order] of Sacrifices—were all [to be counted] from morning to morning, and that no days were [to be counted] from evening to evening. The only [person who took] exception [and did insist on a general morning to morning count of days] was that second Jeroboam, that man of a stammering tongue, the accursed one [*Mišawayah al-Ba'albekī*].[83]

The Karaite poets, like their Rabbanite counterparts, prayed for relief from domination by Christian and Muslim powers. Some of the prayers reflect the tension between master and subject, and the Karaites' intense longing for redemption from exile and national restoration. In his *baqqašah* for the Ten Days of Mercy, *'Elohey yiš'i, 'ad matay*, Aaron b. Joseph asks: 'And how long will the blasphemer persist in not allowing me to swallow my spittle; he keeps telling me that my fixed time has already passed' (*we-'ad matay meḥaref lo' yarpeni 'ad bilti ruqqi / be-'emor 'elay ki 'avar zeman ḥuqqi*).[84] The reference is to the Christian argument that the Messiah has already come in the person of Jesus of Nazareth. In the same poem R. Aaron, following the model of

[81] Weinberger, *Širat . . . Rabbanim*, pp. 505–6, No. 248: 5–6; Ankori, *Karaites in Byzantium*, pp. 352–3.

[82] The text was published by S. Poznanski in *REJ* 34 (1897), pp. 181–91.

[83] Ankori, *Karaites in Byzantium*, pp. 394–5.

[84] Weinberger, *Širat . . . Rabbanim*, pp. 517–18, No. 259: 21–2, 25–6.

Abraham Ibn Ezra,[85] prays: 'Would that you allow me into the grave of the greatly beloved [Daniel] so that he may make me understand the prophecy regarding the End [time]' (*mi yitneni be-qever 'iš ḥamuddot we-qeṣ ḥezyonay yevineni*). Caleb Afendopolo is more forceful in his condemnation of Israel's masters. In a *ḥaṭa'nu* for the Ten Days of Mercy, *'Eykh 'elohim zenaḥtanu*, he observes: 'How [sad] for Your treasure and Your possession [Israel] who turn to Your laws, that a man who has gone astray has laid claim to them' (*'Eykh segullatkha we-naḥalatkha 'ašer be-ḥuqqekha šo'eh / yimṣa'ehu 'iš we-hinneh to'eh*). The term *'iš* (man) is a metonym for Jesus of Nazareth,[86] and the reference is to the Christian power.

THE PRINCIPAL GENRES

Karaite genres include the *ševaḥ*, described by Aaron b. Elijah as 'adulation of God in sumptuous praises and thanksgiving for His abundant kindness in presenting us with the world and directing it with loving kindness.'[87] Related in theme to the *ševaḥ* is the *zemer*, a popular genre with eleventh- and twelfth-century Karaite poets. The *ševaḥ* hymns and their companion, the *hallel*, at the beginning of the morning service, are comparable to the Rabbanite 'Introductory Hymns and Psalms' (*pesuqey de-zimrah*). Following the *ševaḥ* is the *yiḥud*, a prayer affirming God's unity, similar to the Rabbanite *šema'*. The Karaite *qeduššah* follows; its theme is like the Rabbanite prayer of that name. The Karaite *hoda'ah* is the giving of thanks 'apart from prayer', in the words of Aaron b. Elijah,[88] and would be comparable to the Rabbanite blessings on various occasions (*Seder Ha-Berakhot*). The Karaite penitentials (*seliḥot*) include the *widduy*, confession of sins, and the *taḥanun* and *baqqašah*, prayers of supplication. Closing the essential Karaite service is the Silent Prayer for Personal Needs (*tefillah be-laḥaš*) which is comparable in theme to the benedictions of the Rabbanite *'amidah* following 'Blessed are You, O Lord, holy God' (*Barukh 'attah 'adonay, ha-'el ha-qadoš*).[89]

In addition to the daily service, special prayers for Sabbaths, festivals and fast-days were composed. These include elegies by Menaḥem b. Michael for the seventh and tenth days of 'Av, and genres based on Rabbanite models by Aaron b. Joseph. His hymns include *haqdamot* (introductions) for the 'Day of Trumpet-Blowing' (*yom teru'ah*) for the Sabbath of the intermediate days of Tabernacles, for Šabbat Bere'šit, and for Passover and the Sabbath of the intermediate days of Passover; *tokhaḥot* (self-rebuke) and *ḥaṭa'nu* (we have

85 A. Ibn Ezra, *Širey Ha-Qodeš*, ii. 26: 'Would that I could associate with Daniel . . . and ask him regarding the [time] of the End and ascertain if it has already passed.'

86 See the *qedušta'* of Benjamin b. Samuel, *'Arukkah me-'ereṣ middah*, in Weinberger, *'Antologia*, p. 42: 'You shall not have loathsome symbols crafted in the image of man' (*lo' yihyeh lekha gi'ul semalim / be-tavnit 'iš 'amalim*).

87 Aaron b. Elijah, *Gan 'Eden*, 70d.

88 Ibid. 69b.

89 See Goldberg, *Karaite Liturgy*, pp. 59–61.

sinned) for the Ten Days of Mercy[90] and the Day of Atonement; a *berakhah* (benediction) hymn, a *qeduššah* (sanctification) and *ḥazzanut* (cantillations) for Šemini 'Aṣeret. Mordecai Politi is the author of *mi kamokha* hymns complete with a cosmic preface after the model of Rabbanite Hispanics and a *havdalah* hymn for the close of the Sabbath, also based on Rabbanite models. Abraham b. Judah composed a *piyyuṭ le-yoṣer*, a hymn in praise of God's creative work, and *piyyuṭ le-parašat 'wa-yeṣe'*, a poem on the Torah lesson from Gen. 28: 10 ff. Judah Gibbor wrote metric *qaṣīdah*-style hymns for all the Scripture readings from the Pentateuch, and Elijah Bašyatchi's *meliṣat ha-miṣwot* for Pentecost is a catalogue of the positive and negative commands, modelled after the Rabbanite *'azharot*.[91]

90 The Karaite Ten Days of Mercy are comparable to the Rabbanite Ten Days of Repentance.

91 Weinberger, *Širat . . . Rabbanim*, pp. 508–10, 516–17, 519–22, 525–6, 543–5, 545–55, 567–70, 574–5, 586, 592, 668–81, 601–12.

Glossary

'adonay malkenu (lit. 'our father, our king'). A hymn in the *yoṣer* series, introduced after the paragraph that concludes 'God will be king for ever' (*'adonay yimlokh le-'olam wa-'ed*) as a meditation on the concept of God's kingship.

'ahavah (lit. 'love'). A hymn of the *yoṣer* series, introduced before the benediction 'who chooses His people Israel with love' (*ha-boḥer be-'ammo yisra'el be-ahavah*) as a meditation on the concept of God's love for His people.

'amidah (lit. 'standing [prayer]'). The devotion that forms the central part of each service. It is recited standing and in silence. In all services other than evening services the silent recitation is followed by a public repetition out loud by the cantor. Also known as *tefillah* (lit. 'prayer').

anadiplosis. Word repetition serving to link two units of discourse such as consecutive stanzas or sentences, refrains, and introductory scriptural verses.

'aqedah (lit. 'binding'). A *seliḥah* on the theme of the Binding of Isaac (Gen. 22), invoking Abraham's willingness to sacrifice his son Isaac at God's command as a reason for his descendants' sins to be forgiven.

Aškenaz (adj. Aškenazi). The term Aškenaz, mentioned in Gen. 10: 3, has since the tenth century been identified with Germany. From medieval times, German and French Jews, and their descendants in Poland and elsewhere, who preserved common religious and cultural traditions have been referred to as Aškenazim, in contrast to the Spanish and Portuguese Jews, who have been called Sefardim (Sefarad being the Hebrew for the Iberian peninsula).

'avodah. The Day of Atonement liturgy describing the sacrificial ritual performed by the High Priest on the Day of Atonement in Temple times, based on Lev. 16 and as elaborated in Mišnah Yoma', chs. 3–5.

'azharah (lit. 'warning'). A poetic listing of the 613 positive and negative commands in the Torah, chanted on Pentecost—the anniversary of the giving of the Torah at Mount Sinai—to warn people of their obligations.

baqqašah (lit. 'request'). A petition for forgiveness of sins.

barekhu (lit. 'Bless!'). A hymn chanted by the cantor before the formal call to prayer that starts 'Bless ye God, the blessed!' (*Barekhu 'et 'adonay ha-mevorakh*), in which he requests God's permission to pray on behalf of the congregation.

birkat ha-mazon (lit. 'blessing of the food'). A series of benedictions comprising the grace after meals.

Days of Awe. An alternative name for the Ten Days of Repentance that begin with the New Year and culminate in the Day of Atonement. The name derives from the awesome nature of this period as set forth in the liturgy itself: 'On New Year's Day [God's] decree is inscribed, and on the Day of Atonement it is sealed . . . who shall live and who shall die.'

Eighteen Benedictions. The weekday version of the *ʿamidah*, so called because it contains eighteen benedictions (Heb. *šemoneh ʿesreh*).

Eighth Day of Tabernacles. See **Šemini ʿAṣeret**.

'el 'adon (lit. 'God, Master'). A Franco-German addition to the *yoṣer* series, introduced before the text describing God as the Master of all deeds (*ʾel ʾadon ʿal kol ha-maʿasim*) as a meditation on the concept.

'el ha-hoda'ot (lit. 'God of thanksgiving'). In central European liturgies, a hymn chanted before the last blessing of the introductory hymns and psalms of the morning service (*pesukey de-zimraʾ*) on Sabbaths and festivals, i.e. before the verse that concludes 'God of thanksgiving, Lord of wonders Who takes delight in songs and psalms' (*ʾel ha-hodaʾot, ʾadon ha-niflaʾot . . .*) as a meditation on the concept.

'eloheykhem (lit. 'your God'). A Franco-German addition to the *qedustaʾ*, inserted in the *qeduššah* after the fourth verse 'I am the Lord your God' (*ʾani ʾadonay ʾeloheykhem*).

'Elul vigil nights. In Hispanic congregations, penitential prayers, some of which were called 'vigils' (*ʾašmurot*), were chanted during 'Elul—the month preceding New Year—between midnight and the dawn vigil (*ʾašmoret ha-boqer*).

Fast of Esther. A fast observed on 13 'Adar, the day preceding Purim, to commemorate the three days' fast observed by the Jews of Persia at Queen Esther's behest before she pleaded for their lives before King Ahasuerus. See Esther 4: 16.

gemar (lit. 'conclusion'). A coda to the vigil-night prayers of the Hispanic synagogue.

ge'ullah (lit. 'redemption'). A hymn in the *yoṣer* series, introduced into the liturgy before the benediction 'Praised are You, Lord, Redeemer of Israel' (*. . . gaʾal Yisraʾel*) as a meditation on the concept of redemption.

gezerot (lit. 'evil decrees'). A Franco-German *seliḥah* which memorialized the massacre of Rhineland Jewry during the Crusades.

ghazal (Arabic). Love poetry.

halakhah. Jewish law as expounded by the rabbis in the Talmud and other post-biblical works.

Hallel. A doxology comprising Pss. 113–18, which is chanted in the morning service on Ro'š Ḥodeš, Passover, Pentecost, Tabernacles, and on Ḥanukkah.

ha-melekh (lit. 'the king'). In the Franco-German liturgy for the mornings of Sabbaths and festivals, a hymn that was introduced into the *nišmat* prayer, between the verses 'The King is enthroned high and exalted' (*ha-melekh* *ha-yošev ʿal kisse' ram we-nissa'*) and 'Abiding forever, exalted and holy is His name' (*šokhen ʿad marom we-qadoš šemo*), as a meditation on the concept of God's kingship.

ḥatan bere'šit (lit. 'bridegroom of Genesis'). The person honoured with chanting the benediction before the initial section of Genesis is read from the Torah on Simḥat Torah to mark the recommencement of the annual Torah-reading cycle.

ḥatan torah (lit. 'bridegroom of the Torah'). The person honoured with chanting the benediction before the final section of the Torah is read on Simḥat Torah as the conclusion of the annual Torah-reading cycle.

ḥaṭa'nu (lit. 'we have sinned'). A *seliḥah* with the refrain 'We have sinned O our Rock; forgive us O our Maker'.

havdalah (lit. 'differentiation'). A liturgical embellishment of the benedictions recited at the conclusion of the Sabbath and festival days to praise God for differentiating between the sanctity of holy days and festival days and the ordinary character of weekdays.

hištaḥawayah (lit. 'prostration'). In the Hispanic liturgy, hymns for the 'Elul vigil nights hymns to be chanted while lying prostrate.

Hošaʿna' Rabbah. This is the Hebrew name for the seventh day of Tabernacles. It is marked liturgically by seven processions (*haqafot*) round the synagogue (rather than the single procession of the first six days), in which the celebrants each carry a palm branch (*lulav*) and a citron (*'etrog*) while reciting prayers for Israel's deliverance (*hošaʿna'*, pl. *hošaʿnot*; *hošaʿna' rabbah* means the 'great deliverance').

hošaʿnot. Hymns on the theme of deliverance (*hošaʿnah*) recited during Tabernacles while walking in procession around the synagogue.

'illu finu (lit. 'were our mouths [filled with song]'). The text of the *nišmat* prayer recited in the morning service on Sabbaths and festivals proclaims that we give thanks (*'anaḥnu modim*) to God alone, and that even if our mouths were filled with song, our tongues with jubilation, we would still be inadequate to the task. The *'illu finu* hymns, intended to embellish and meditate on this idea, were introduced into the *nišmat* prayer between the words *'anaḥnu modim* and the words *'illu finu*, and begin with the word *modim*.

kal aṣmotay (lit. 'all my bones'). The *nišmat* prayer in the morning service for Sabbaths and festivals includes the phrase 'all my bones should declare O God who is like unto Thee' (Ps. 35: 10). Hymns in the *kal aṣmotay* genre may be introduced into the *nišmat* prayer before this phrase as meditations on the concept.

maʿarivim (lit. 'evening prayers'). Hymns embellishing the evening service for festivals.

magen (lit. 'shield of [our] fathers'). A hymn of the *qerovah* series. It is based on the *ʿamidah*'s first benediction, praising God as the 'shield of Abraham' (*magen 'avraham*).

magen 'avot. A Franco-German embellishment of the Sabbath evening service hymn, *Magen 'avot bi-dvaro* ('God's word has ever been our fathers' shield').

maḥazor (lit. 'cycle'). Originally the term designating the yearly cycle and the cycle of prayers that mark the notable days of the religious calendar. Later it became the term used for the prayer-book for the festivals.

maṣdar. A one-strophe introduction to the *yoṣer*, giving the name of the hymnist.

meḥayyeh (lit. 'reviver'). A hymn in the *qerovah* series. It embellishes the *'amidah*'s second benediction which ends 'Praised are You, Lord, Who revivest the dead' (*meḥayyeh ha-metim*).

me'orah (lit. 'light'). A hymn in the *yoṣer* series, chanted before the benediction at the end of the penultimate paragraph before the *šema'* that extols God as the creator of lights (*yoṣer ha-me'orot*).

mešalleš (lit. 'threefold'). A hymn of the *qerovah* series, introduced before the *qeduššah* in the public repetition of the *'amidah* as a meditation on the threefold praise of God's holiness in the Trisagion from Isa. 6: 3 that forms part of the *qeduššah*.

meyuššav (lit. 'seated'). In the Hispanic liturgy, hymns for the 'Elul vigil nights to be chanted while seated.

mi kamokha (lit. 'who is like You?'). A hymn in the *yoṣer* series, introduced before the phrase 'Who is like You, Lord, among all that is worshipped?' as a meditation on the concept of God's uniqueness.

mišmarot (lit. 'watches', 'turns of duty'). Hymns recalling the twenty-four watches of priestly and levitical service in the Temple. They were recited on the Sabbath.

muḥarrak (Arabic; lit. 'moved'). A request composed in metrical form for permission to pray on behalf of the congregation that was sometimes recited on Sabbaths and festivals before the morning *nišmat* prayer. The term is perhaps an allusion to the sense of movement generated by the metre.

muqaddimah (Arabic; lit. 'preface'). In order better to prepare the worshipper for the New Year *šofar* ritual, the Hispanic liturgy added a *muqaddimah* of scriptural verses to introduce it.

mustajāb (Arabic; lit. 'that which recurs'). A *seliḥah* introduced by a scriptural verse whose last word then either recurs as the last word of each strophe or rhymes with it.

muwashshaḥ (Arabic: 'belt poem'). A strophic genre comprising sets of contrasting variable and constant rhymemes.

Ninth of 'Av. According to rabbinic tradition the ninth of the month of 'Av is the date of the destruction of both the first and second Temples. It is commemorated by a twenty-five-hour fast.

nišmat (lit. 'the breath [of every living creature]'). A hymn that may be introduced into the *nišmat* prayer recited in the morning service on Sabbaths and festivals. It is inserted after the first segment of the prayer, and each of its strophes begins with the word *nišmat.*

'ofan. A hymn of the *yoṣer* series intended to embellish the idea of *'ofannim* and other celestial creatures praising God. It is introduced before the phrase 'and the *'ofannim* and holy creatures . . . praise [Him] and say: *we-ha-'ofannim we-ḥayyot ha-qodeš . . . mešabbeḥim we-'omerim.*

'oseh ha-šalom (lit. 'the maker of peace'). A *qerovah* hymn embellishing the last paragraph of the *'amidah*, where God is extolled as the maker of peace.

petiḥah (lit. 'opening'). An opening prayer in a series of petitions for forgiveness of sins.

pilgrimage festivals. The festivals of Passover, Pentecost, and Tabernacles, when adult Israelites were required to make a pilgrimage to the Temple in Jerusalem. See Exod. 23: 14–17.

piyyuṭ. A liturgical hymn.

pizmon (lit. 'refrain'). A strophic *seliḥah* with a refrain.

qaddiš (lit. 'sanctification'). The cantor's request for Heavenly permission to recite the *qaddiš* prayer sanctifying God's name.

qaṣīdah (Arabic). Poetic genre; the term is traditionally translated as 'ode'.

qeduššah (lit. 'holiness'). A compilation of extracts from Isa. 6: 3, Ezek. 3: 12, and Ps. 146: 10 extolling God's holiness and chanted during the public repetition of the *'amidah.*

qedušta' (Aramaic; lit. 'holiness'). A multi-part liturgical genre embellishing the *qeduššah* for the mornings of Sabbaths and festivals.

qerovah. A generic name for hymns embellishing the public repetition of the *'amidah* on Sabbaths and festivals.

qidduš yeraḥim (lit. 'sanctification of moons [months]'). Hymns embellishing the Šabbat Ro'š Ḥodeš liturgy.

qinah. An elegy; the form is most developed in the liturgy for the Ninth of 'Av.

rahiṭ (lit. 'bar', 'beam'). A hymn that originated as an embellishment of the *'amidah* for festivals and holy days. Parts of these hymns (the 'bars' or 'beams' on which they were based) later came to be used as independent liturgical units.

rehuṭah (lit. 'flowing'). A Spanish and Provençal genre for the 'Elul vigil nights, featuring variations on scriptural verses. The term indicates that the hymn was supposed to flow.

rešut (lit. 'permission'). A cantor-poet's request for divine permission to pray on behalf of the congregation.

Ro'š Ḥodeš (lit. 'beginning of the month'). Liturgically, the beginning of a new month—which coincides with the new moon, since the Jewish calendar is lunar—is marked with special prayers. The day on which the new month will begin is announced publicly in the synagogue on the preceding Sabbath, again through a special liturgy.

Šabbat Bere'šit. The first Sabbath in the annual Torah-reading cycle, when the reading is from the first section of Genesis (Gen. 1: 1–6: 8), which starts with the word *bere'šit*—'In the beginning'.

Šabbat Ha-Gadol. The Sabbath preceding Passover is thus designated because the reading from the Prophets is Mal. 3, which ends *yom . . . ha-gadol we-ha-nora'* ('the great and terrible day of the Lord').

Šabbat Ha-Ḥodeš. The last Sabbath preceding the month of Nisan. It derives its name from the special additional reading from the Torah on this day, Exod. 12: 1–20, which proclaims that this month (*ha-ḥodeš ha-zeh*) will mark the beginning of a new calendar to commemorate that this was the month in which Israel was freed from Egyptian slavery.

Šabbat Ḥanukkah. The Sabbath (or Sabbaths) occurring in Ḥanukkah. There is an additional Torah reading (Num. 7: 18–29), and a special reading from the Prophets: Zech. 2: 14–4: 7 if there is only one Sabbath during Ḥanukkah, and Zech. 4: 2–9 if there is a second.

Šabbat Ḥatanim (lit. 'Sabbath of bridegrooms'). The Sabbath following a wedding, when the bridegroom is honoured in the synagogue by being called publicly to chant a benediction over the Torah.

Šabbat Naḥamu. The name given to the Sabbath that follows the Ninth of 'Av is from the opening words of Isaiah 40: 'Comfort ye [*naḥamu*], O comfort ye, My people', from which the reading from the Prophets is taken on that Sabbath.

Šabbat Parah. The special additional Torah reading on this Sabbath, the next to last Sabbath preceding the month of Nisan, is Num. 19: 1–22, which describes the laws of how to become ritually clean through the ashes of a red heifer (*parah 'adumah*).

Šabbat Ro'š Ḥodeš (lit. 'Sabbath at the start of the month'). The name given to a Sabbath that coincides with a new moon. It is marked by a special additional reading from the Torah (Num. 28: 9–15) and a special reading from the Prophets (Isa. 66: 1–24).

Šabbat Šeqalim. The last Sabbath before the month of 'Adar. During Temple times it was the practice on that day to announce a call for the payment of a poll tax of half a shekel by every adult Jew. The obligation is recalled through an additional Torah reading, Exod. 30: 11–16, which details the appropriate biblical injunction.

Šabbat Šim'u. The second of the Sabbaths in the three weeks between 17 Tammuz—the date when, according to tradition, Jerusalem's walls were broken by Nebuchadnezzar and Temple worship ceased during the siege by Titus—and 9 'Av, the traditional date when the Temple was destroyed. The reading from the Prophets on this Sabbath begins at Jer. 2: 4, 'Hear [*šim'u*] the word of the Lord'.

Šabbat Šuvah. The Sabbath between the New Year and the Day of Atonement, when the reading from the Prophets begins at Hosea 14: 2—'Return [*šuvah*], O Israel, to the Lord your God'.

Šabbat Zakhor. The Sabbath before Purim, when the special additional reading from the Torah, Deut. 25: 17–19, begins with the phrase 'Remember [*zakhor*] what Amaleq did to you'. According to tradition Amaleq was the ancestor of Haman, the villain of the Purim story who, like Amaleq, tried to wipe out all the Jews.

Sabbaths of Consolation. The seven Sabbaths that follow the fast-day of the Ninth of 'Av, which marks the destruction of the Temple, are marked liturgically by readings selected from Isaiah 40–63 that offer consolation and comfort for the loss, and the promise of future redemption. The first of the seven Sabbaths is known as Šabbat Naḥamu, and the last is the Sabbath before the New Year.

šalmonit (lit. 'complete' or 'squared off'). A *seliḥah* built in quatrains.

seliḥah (pl. *seliḥot*; lit. 'pardon'). A penitential prayer petitioning God for forgiveness of sins; the term derives from Ps. 130: 4, *ki 'immekha ha-seliḥah* ('but forgiveness is with You'). Practices differ as to the period during which *seliḥot* are recited, but they are always recited from before the New Year till the Day of Atonement, and in some traditions for up to a month before the New Year, up to and including Hoš'ana' Rabbah. They are also recited on fast-days.

šelišiyyah (lit. 'trio'). A *seliḥah* built in tercets.

šema' (lit. 'Hear!'). The liturgy affirming God's unity and characterizing the Jew's relationship with God. It begins with the phrase: 'Hear, O Israel: The Lord our God, the Lord is One' (Deut. 6: 4).

Šemini 'Aṣeret (lit. 'eighth day of assembly'). This festival concludes the Feast of Tabernacles. It is mentioned in Lev. 23: 36 and Deut. 16: 18.

šeniyyah (lit. 'second'). A *seliḥah* built in couplets.

ševah. (lit. 'praise'). A Franco-German innovation to the *yoṣer* series, introduced into the *'el 'adon* prayer, before the final strophe which begins 'All the heavenly host praise Him' (*ševaḥ notenim lo kol ṣeva' marom*) as a meditation on the concept of praising God.

Seventeenth of Tammuz. The calendar date of a fast-day in remembrance of the breaking down of Jerusalem's walls by Nebuchadnezzar and the suspension of Temple worship during the siege of Titus. This is the first day of three weeks of mourning that culminate with the Ninth of 'Av.

ṣidduq ha-din (lit. 'justification of the verdict'). A poetic acknowledgement of the justice of the divine decree, chanted during the burial service to embellish the readings from Scripture acknowledging the righteousness of God's judgment.

siddur (lit. 'arrangement'). A prayer-book in which there is an arrangement of daily prayers as well as prayers for Sabbaths, festivals, new moons, and life-cycle events such as circumcision and marriage. Also included are Sabbath hymns, the Song of Songs, which was traditionally read before the service on the eve of the Sabbath, and the Ethics of the Fathers, to be studied on summer Sabbath afternoons. The arrangement of prayers dates from the time of the *ge'onim*, and the first of these was the *Seder Me'ah Berakhot*, edited by Natronay Ga'on. This was followed by the *Seder R. ʿAmram Ga'on*, and later by the *Siddur R. Saʿadyah Ga'on*.

silluq (lit. 'departure'). The closing hymn in the *qerovah* series.

Simḥat Torah (lit. 'Rejoicing of the Torah'). This festival marks the conclusion and recommencement of the annual cycle of Torah reading: the last section of the Torah is read for the *ḥatan torah* and the cycle is immediately recommenced by reading the first part of the Torah for the *ḥatan bere'šit*. In the Land of Israel, this festival coincides with Šemini 'Aṣeret; in the Diaspora it is observed on the following day.

šir ševaḥ. An encomium.

šiv'ata' (Aramaic; lit. 'seven'). Verset embellishments of the seven benedictions of the *ʿamidah* to be chanted during the additional service for Sabbaths and festivals (*musaf*) when, in the old Ereṣ Yisra'el ritual, the *qeduššah* was not recited.

tajnīs (Arabic: paronomasia). A form of pun.

tefillah (lit. 'prayer'). See ***'amidah***.

teḥinnah (lit. 'supplication'). A type of *seliḥah* beginning 'O Lord, turn from Your fierce wrath and renounce the plan to punish Your people'. It was generally chanted on 'Elul vigil nights and on fast-days.

Ten Days of Mercy. This is the Karaite name for the period known as the Days of Awe or Ten Days of Repentance, which start at the New Year and culminate in the Day of Atonement. According to Karaite tradition, the gates of God's mercy are opened on these days.

Ten Days of Repentance. An alternative name for the Days of Awe, recognizing that this period is marked by remorse for sins committed and a resolution to sin no more.

Tenth of Ṭevet. The calendar date of a fast-day commemorating the beginning of Nebuchadnezzar's siege of Jerusalem in 586 BC. The event is described in Jer. 52: 4 and 2 Kgs. 25: 1.

terzina. A hymn in syllabic metre in which short syllables are counted as the equivalent of long syllables. The rhyming scheme of its iambic tercets is *aba bcb cdc* etc.

tokheḥah (lit. 'self-rebuke'). A type of *seliḥah*.

tosefta. This work, like the Mišnah, which it closely resembles, is a collection of statements by the early rabbis (*tanna'im*).

we-ʿal zoʾt (lit. 'and for this'). A *yoṣer* hymn introduced before the phrase *we-ʿal zoʾt šibbeḥu ʾahuvim* ('For this [i.e. the redemption from Egypt] the beloved [i.e. Israel] praised [God]') to embellish the concept and as a meditation on God's uniqueness as expressed in the next passage, the *mi kamokha*.

widduy. A formal confession of sins recited on the Day of Atonement.

yoṣer (pl. *yoṣerot*; lit. 'creator'). A sequence of hymns introduced into the morning liturgy for Sabbaths and festivals between the formal call to prayer (*barekhu*) and the *ʿamidah*. The name derives from the first benediction after *barekhu*, which praises God as *yoṣer ʾor*, the creator of light. The individual hymns of the *yoṣer* series are introduced at specific points in the liturgy to embellish and meditate on particular concepts expressed there, after which they are named.

zemer. A table-hymn chanted during Sabbath meals.

zuhdiyyāt (Arabic). Ascetic poetry.

zulat (lit. 'besides'). A *yoṣer* hymn introduced before the phrase 'There is no God beside You'.

Select Bibliography

Manuscripts

Cambridge, University Library, Taylor-Schechter (TS) collection, Misc. 22.124; TS, new series, 102.142; 139.103

Jerusalem, National and University Library:

Ḥayyey 'Olam Ha-Ba', MS. 80 540, fos. 44–5.

'Osef Piyyuṭim Mi-Turkiyah, MS 421 8vo.

London, British Library:

Add. MS 27086 (No. 650).

Add. MS 17867 (No. 651).

London, Jews' College, Montefiore *Maḥazor Romania,* MS 220.

Munich, National Library, MS 21.

New York, Jewish Theological Seminary:

Maḥazor Corfu, Enelow MS 615.

Maḥazor Corfu, MS 4580.

Maḥazor Corfu, MS 4588.

Oxford, Bodleian:

Maḥazor Calabria, MS 1081.

Maḥazor Kastoria, Oppenheim Add. MS 4to, 80 (No. 1168).

Michael MS 161.

Oppenheim MS 218 (No. 251).

Oppenheim Add. MS 4to 171 (No. 2501).

Paris, Bibliothèque Nationale:

Fonds Hébreu, *Maḥazor Romania,* MS 606.

Fonds Hébreu, MS 707.

Fonds Hébreu, MS 1042.4.

Fonds Hébreu, MS 1047.5.

Fonds Hébreu, MS 1061.3.

Parma, Biblioteca Palatina, MS 997.

Vatican:

Assemani, MS 105.

Assemani, MS 106.

Assemani, MS 393.

Maḥazor Candia, Assemani, MS 320.

Printed Works

AARON B. ELIJAH, *Gan 'Eden*, ed. J. Savuskan (Gozlow, 1866).

AARON B. ELIJAH, *Keter Torah*, ed. J. Savuskan (Gozlow, 1867).

AARON B. JOSEPH, *Sefer Ha-Mivḥar* (Gozlow, 1834).

ABRABANEL, ISAAC, *Yešu'ot Mešiḥo* (Königsberg, 1861).

ABRAHAM B. AZRIEL, *Sefer 'Arugat Ha-Bosem*, ed. E. E. Urbach (4 vols., Jerusalem, 1939–63).

ABRAMSON, S., *Be-Lašon Qodemim: Meḥqar Be-Širat Yisra'el Bi-Sfarad* (Jerusalem, 1965).

AGNON, S. Y., *Yamim Nora'im* (Jerusalem, 1938).

AL-ḤARIZI, JUDAH, *Taḥkemoni*, ed. Y. Toporowsky (Tel Aviv, 1952).

'Alpha Beta de Rabbi Akiva', in *'Oṣar Midrašim*, ed. J. D. Eisenstein (New York, 1915), ii. 408–24.

ALTMANN, A., 'The Ladder of Ascension', in E. E. Urbach, R. J. Z. Werblowsky, and Ch. Wirszubski (eds.), *Studies in Mysticism and Religion Presented to Gershom G. Scholem* (Jerusalem, 1967), pp. 1–32.

—— and STERN, S. M. (eds.), *Isaac Israeli: A Neo-platonic Philosopher of the Early Tenth Century* (Oxford, 1958).

AMITTAI B. ŠEFATIAH, *Širey Amittai*, ed. Y. David (Jerusalem, 1975).

ANKORI, Z., 'The Correspondence of Tobias b. Moses the Karaite of Constantinople', in J. Blau (ed.), *Essays on Jewish Life and Thought: Presented in Honor of Salo Wittmayer Baron* (New York, 1959), pp. 1–38.

—— *Karaites in Byzantium* (New York, 1959).

ASHTIANY, J., *et al.* (eds.), *'Abbasid Belles-Lettres* (Cambridge, 1990).

AZRIEL OF GERONA, 'Explanation of the Ten *Sefirot*', in Dan (ed.), *The Early Kabbalah.*

—— 'Še'elot u-Tšuvot R. Azriel 'al ha-Sefirot', in *Liqqutim Me-Rav Ha'yyay Ga'on*, ed. G. Berros (Warsaw, 1798).

BARON, S., *A Social and Religious History of the Jews* (18 vols., Philadelphia, 1952–60).

BAŠYATCHI, ELIJAH, *'Adderet 'Eliyyahu*, ed. I. Beim (Odessa, 1870).

BEERI, T., *Maṣdarim We-Yoṣerot Be-Piyyuṭey Yosef Al-Baradani* (2 vols., Jerusalem, 1990).

—— 'Šelomo Mazal Ṭov we-niṣaney hašpa'atah šel ha-širah ha-Turkit 'al ha-širah ha-'Ivrit', *Pe'amim*, 59 (1994), pp. 65–76.

BENJAMIN OF TUDELA, *The Itinerary of Rabbi Benjamin of Tudela*, ed. M. N. Adler (Jerusalem and Frankfurt a. M., 1903–4).

BENJAMIN ZE'EV B. MATTATHIAS OF ARTA, *Responsa, Binyamin Ze'ev* (Venice, 1539).

BEN-MENAḤEM, N., *Mi-Ginzey Yisra'el Be-Watikan* (Jerusalem, 1954).

BEN SIRA, 'The Wisdom of Ben Sira', in *The New Oxford Annotated Bible* (Oxford, 1991).

BER, S. (ed.), *Seder 'Avodat Yisra'el* (New York, 1937).

BERNSTEIN, S., 'Ha-Maḥazor Ke-Mihnag Kaffa, Toledotaw We-Hitpatḥuto', in *Festschrift in Honor of Samuel Mirsky* (New York, 1958), pp. 451–538.

—— *Piyyuṭim U-Fayṭanim Ḥadašim Min Ha-Tequfah Ha-Bizantinit* (Jerusalem, 1941).

Beyt Yosef (Joseph Karo's commentary on the *Ṭur*), 4 vols. (Jerusalem, 1962).

BLUMENKRANZ, B., 'Germany, 846–1096', in Roth (ed.), *World History of the Jewish People*, pp. 162–74.

BOWMAN, S., *The Jews of Byzantium, 1204–1453* (Tuscaloosa, Ala., 1985).

BRANN, R., *The Compunctious Poet: Cultural Ambiguity and Hebrew Poetry in Muslim Spain* (Baltimore, 1990).

BRODY, Ḥ., 'Piyyuṭim we-širey tehillah me-Rav Ha'yyay Ga'on', *Studies of the Research Institute for Hebrew Poetry*, 3 (1936), pp. 3–63.

—— 'Širey Mešullam ben Šelomo Dapiera', *Studies of the Research Institute for Hebrew Poetry*, 4 (1938), pp. 3–117.

—— and WIENER, M. (eds.), *Mivḥar Ha-Širah Ha-'Ivrit* (Leipzig, 1922).

Canticles Rabbah (London, 1951).

CAPSALI, ELIJAH, *Seder 'Eliyyahu Zuta* (2 vols., Jerusalem, 1975–7).

CARMI, T., *The Penguin Book of Hebrew Verse* (Harmondsworth, 1981).

CHAZAN, R., *Daggers of Faith: Thirteenth-Century Christian Missionizing and Jewish Response* (Berkeley, Ca., 1989).

DAN, J. (ed.), *The Early Kabbalah* (New York, 1986).

DAVID, Y., *Širey Zevadiah* (Jerusalem, 1971–2).

Deuteronomy Rabbah (London, 1951).

DINUR, B., *Yisra'el Ba-Golah* (vol. i, 4 books; vol. ii, 6 books; Jerusalem, 1972).

ELBOGEN, I., *Ha-Tefillah Be-Yisra'el Be-Hitpatḥutah Ha-Historit*, ed. J. Heinemann (Tel Aviv, 1972).

—— *Der jüdische Gottesdienst in seiner geschichtlichen Entwicklung* (Leipzig, 1913); *Jewish Liturgy: A Comprehensive History*, trans. R. P. Scheindlin (Philadelphia, 1993).

ELIA B. ŠEMAYAH, *Piyyuṭey Elia bar Šemayah*, ed. Y. David (Jerusalem, 1977).

ELITZUR, S., *Piyyuṭey Rabbi El'azar Berabbi Qillar* (Jerusalem, 1988).

—— *Piyyuṭey Rabbi Yehudah Berabbi Binyamin* (Jerusalem, 1988).

—— ' "We-ha-yamim me-ṣuwwin me-'eloha," goral 'iwwer we-'emunah datit be-širah ha-'ivrit bi-Sfarad', in *Israel Levin Jubilee Volume* (Tel Aviv, 1994), pp. 27–43.

Enṣiqlopedia Talmudit (Jerusalem, 1947–).

Exodus Rabbah (London, 1951).

FLEISCHER, E., ' 'Azharot le-R. Binyamin (ben Šemu'el) Payṭan', *Koveṣ 'Al Yad*, 11/21 (1985), pp. 3–75.

—— 'The "Gerona School" of Hebrew Poetry', in I. Twersky (ed.), *Rabbi Moses Naḥmanides (Ramban): Explorations in his Religious and Literary Virtuosity* (Cambridge, Mass., 1983), pp. 35–49.

Fleischer, E., *Ha-Yoṣerot Be-Hithawwutam We-Hitpatḥutam* (Jerusalem, 1984).
—— 'Hebrew Liturgical Poetry in Italy', *Italia Judaica*, 1 (1983), pp. 415–26.
—— *Piyyuṭey Šelomo Ha-Bavli* (Jerusalem, 1973).
—— *Pizmoney Ha-'Anonymus* (Jerusalem, 1974).
—— *Širat Ha-Qodeš Ha-ʿIvrit Bi-Ymey Ha-Beynayim* (Jerusalem, 1975).
—— 'Širatenu ha-qedumah bi-derom mizraḥ 'ayropah', *Jerusalem Studies in Hebrew Literature*, 12 (1990), pp. 179–222.
Genesis Rabbah (London, 1951).
Ginzberg, L., *Ginzey Schechter* (2 vols., New York, 1969).
Goitein, S. D., *A Mediterranean Society* (4 vols., Berkeley, Ca., 1967–83).
Goldberg, P. S., *Karaite Liturgy and its Relation to Synagogue Worship* (Manchester, 1975).
Guttmann, J., *Philosophies of Judaism*, trans. D. W. Silverman (New York, 1964).
Habermann, A. H., *ʿAteret Renanim* (Jerusalem, 1967).
—— 'Berakhot meʿeyn šaloš u-me'eyn 'arba' ', *Studies of the Research Institute for Hebrew Poetry*, 5 (1939), pp. 43–105.
—— *ʿIyyunim Be-Širah U-Va-Piyyuṭ* (Jerusalem, 1972).
—— 'Piyyuṭey Rabbenu Barukh bar Šemu'el mi-Magenṣa', *Studies of the Research Institute for Hebrew Poetry*, 6 (1945), pp. 47–160
—— 'Piyyuṭey Rabbenu Ephraim b. Yiṣḥaq mi-Regensburg', *Studies of the Research Institute for Hebrew Poetry*, 4 (1938), pp. 119–95.
—— 'Piyyuṭey Rabbi Ephraim b. Rabbi Yaʿaqov mi-Bonn', *Studies of the Research Institute for Hebrew Poetry*, 7 (1958), pp. 215–96.
—— *Piyyuṭey Rabbi Šimʿon bar Yiṣḥaq* (Berlin and Jerusalem, 1938).
—— *Piyyuṭim We-Širim Me'et Rabbi Meir Berabbi Eliyahu Mi-Norviṣ* (London, 1966).
—— 'Qinot 'al ḥakhmey Saloniqi mi-Rabbi Šelomo mi-beyt ha-Lewi we-ha-mešorer Saʿadyah Longo', *Sefunot*, 12 (1971–8), pp. 71–80.
—— *Sefer Gezerot 'Aškenaz We-Ṣorfat* (Jerusalem, 1945).
—— *Toledot Ha-Piyyuṭ We-Ha-Širah* (2 vols., Ramat Gan, 1970–2).
Hacker, J., 'Šiṭat ha-"surgün" we-hašpaʿatah 'al ha-ḥevrah he-yehudit be-'imperyah ha-ʿottomanit be-me'ot ha-ṭ"w—ha-y"z', *Zion*, 54 (1990), pp. 27–82.
Ha-Levi, Judah, *Diwan*, ed. H. Brody (4 vols., Berlin, 1894–1930).
—— *Širey Ha-Qodeš Le-Rabbi Yehudah Ha-Lewi*, ed. D. Yarden (Jerusalem, 1978–85).
Heinemann, Joseph, *ʿIyyuney Tefillah* (Jerusalem, 1983).
'Heykhalot Rabbati', in *'Oṣar Midrašim*, ed. J. Eisenstein (New York, 1915), i. 111–22.
Hoffman, L. A., *The Canonization of the Synagogue Service* (Fort Bend, 1979).
Ibn al-Tabbān, Levi, *Širey Lewi Ibn Al-Tabbān*, ed. D. Pagis (Jerusalem, 1967).
Ibn Daud, Abraham, *Sefer Ha-Qabbalah*, ed. G. Cohen (Philadelphia, 1967).

IBN EZRA, ABRAHAM, 'Sefer Ha-Šem', in I. Levin (ed.), *Yalqut Avraham Ibn Ezra* (New York and Tel Aviv, 1985), pp. 419–28.

—— *Širey Ha-Qodeš Šel Avraham Ibn Ezra*, ed. I. Levin (2 vols., Jerusalem, 1975–80).

IBN EZRA, MOSES, *Širey Ha-Ḥol*, ed. Ḥ. Brody and D. Pagis (3 vols., Berlin and Jerusalem, 1935–77).

IBN GABIROL, SOLOMON, *Fons Vitae*, ed. C. Baeumker (Munster, 1892).

—— 'Keter Malkhut', *Ha-Širah Ha-'Ivrit Bi-Sfarad U-Ve-Provans*, ed. H. Schirmann (2 vols., Jerusalem, 1959), i. 257–85.

—— *Meqor Ḥayyim*, ed. A. Zifroni (Jerusalem, 1971).

—— *Širey Ha-Ḥol Le-Rabbi Šelomo Ibn Gabirol*, ed. D. Yarden (Jerusalem, 1975).

—— *Širey Ha-Qodeš Le-Rabbi Šelomo Ibn Gabirol*, ed. D. Yarden (Jerusalem, 1971).

IBN GIY'AT, ISAAC, *Širey R. Yiṣḥaq Ibn Giy'at*, ed. Y. David (Jerusalem, 1987).

IBN NAGRELA, SAMUEL, *Ben Qohelet*, ed. S. Abramson (Tel Aviv, 1964).

—— *Divan Šemu'el Ha-Nagid: Ben Mišle*, ed. D. Yarden (Jerusalem, 1982).

——*Divan Šemu'el Ha-Nagid: Ben Tehillim*, ed. D. Yarden (Jerusalem, 1966).

IBN PAQUDAH, BAḤYA BEN JOSEPH, *Sefer Ḥovot Ha-Levavot*, ed. A. Zifroni (Tel Aviv, 1964).

IBN TIBBON, SAMUEL, *Ma'amar Yiqqawu Ha-Mayim*, ed. M. L. Bisliches (Pressburg, 1827).

IDEL, M., *The Mystical Experience in Abraham Abulafia* (Albany, NY, 1988).

JUDAH B. BARZILAY, *Sefer Ha-'Ittim* (Cracow, 1900–3).

KADUSHIN, M., *Worship and Ethics* (Chicago, 1964).

KAHANE, D., *Rabbi Avraham Ibn Ezra* (Warsaw, 1922).

—— *Rabbi Salomo Scharwit Hasahav* (Warsaw, 1894).

KLATZKIN, J., *Thesaurus Philosophicus* (2 vols., New York, 1968).

Lamentations Rabbah (London, 1951).

LEVIN, I. (ed.), *Yalqut Avraham Ibn Ezra* (New York and Tel Aviv, 1985).

—— ' "Zeman" we-"tevel" be-širat ha-ḥol ha-'ivrit', *'Oṣar Yehudey Sefarad*, 5 (1963), pp. 68–79.

Leviticus Rabbah (London, 1951).

LOEWE, R., 'Ibn Gabirol's Treatment of Sources in the *Keter Malkhut*', in S. Stein and R. Loewe (eds.), *Studies in Jewish Religious and Intellectual History Presented to Alexander Altmann* (Tuscaloosa, 1979), pp. 183–94.

Maḥazor Kol Ha-Šanah Ke-Fi Minhag 'Italiani, ed. S. D. Luzzatto (2 vols., Livorno, 1856).

Maḥazor Le-Ḥag Ha-Švu'ot, ed. W. Heidenheim (Rödelheim, 1857).

Maḥazor Le-Regalim: Pesaḥ, ed. Y. Frankel (Jerusalem, 1993).

Maḥazor Le-Šaloš Regalim: Pesaḥ, ed. B. Alfes (Vilna, 1912).

Maḥazor Le-Sukkot, Šemini 'Aṣeret We-Simḥat Torah, ed. D. Goldschmidt and Y. Frankel (Jerusalem, 1981).

Maḥazor Le-Yamim Ha-Nora'im, ed. D. Goldschmidt (2 vols., Jerusalem, 1970).

Maḥazor Romania (Siddur Tefillot Ha-Šanah Le-Minhag Qehillot Romaniah), ed. Elia Ha-Levi (Constantinople, 1510).

Maḥazor Romania (Venice, 1522–3).

Maḥazor Witry, ed. S. Horowitz (Jerusalem, 1963).

MAIMONIDES, MOSES, *Haqdamot Le-Peruš Ha-Mišnah*, ed. M. D. Rabinovitz (Jerusalem, 1961).

—— *Mišneh Torah* (5 vols., New York, 1947).

—— *Moreh Ha-Nevukhim*, ed. Y. Even-Šemuel (Jerusalem, 1959).

—— *Tešuvot Ha-Rambam*, ed. J. Blau (4 vols., Jerusalem, 1989).

MALACHI, Z., 'Sefer Yonah be-estriota šel RŠB"G le-Yom Kippur', *Sinai*, 68 (1971), pp. 138–43.

MANN, J., *The Jews in Egypt and in Palestine under the Fāṭimid Caliphs* (2 vols., New York, 1970).

MARKON, D., 'Le-David, širey Mazal-Ṭov', in *Nir David* (Frankfurt a. M., 1923), pp. 37–40.

—— 'R. Šelomo b. Mazal Ṭov', in *Alexander Marx Jubilee Volume* (New York, 1950), pp. 325–46.

MARMORSTEIN, A., and HABERMANN, A. M. (eds.), *Qiduš Yeraḥim De-Rabbi Pinḥas* (Jerusalem, 1973).

Megillat 'Aḥima'aṣ, ed. B. Klar (Jerusalem, 1964).

Mekhilta de-Rabbi Išma'el, ed. J. S. Lauterbach (Philadelphia, 1933).

Midraš 'Eykhah Rabbati, ed. S. Buber (Vilna, 1899).

Midraš Ha-Gadol, ed. M. Margulies (Jerusalem, 1947).

Midraš Rabbah, ed. M. Romm (2 vols., Vilna, 1878).

Midraš Tehillim, ed. S. Buber (Vilna, 1891).

MILLER, P., 'At the Twilight of Byzantine Karaism: The Anachronism of Judah Gibbor', Ph.D. thesis (New York University, 1984).

MIRSKY, A., 'Gidrey ha-piyyuṭ šel ha-payṭanim 'alumey ha-šem', *Peraqim*, 1 (1967–8), pp. 109–13.

—— 'Ha-ziqah še-beyn širat Sefarad li-drašot ḤaZaL', *Sinai*, 64 (1969), pp. 248–53.

—— 'Maḥṣavatan šel ṣurot ha-piyyuṭ', *Studies of the Research Institute for Hebrew Poetry*, 7 (1958), pp. 3–129.

—— 'Midrašot ḤaZaL be-širey ha-miqra' ha-'Anglo-Saxim', *Sefer Ḥayyim Širman* (Jerusalem, 1970), pp. 179–94.

—— *Piyyuṭey Yose ben Yose* (Jerusalem, 1977).

The Mishnah, ed. H. Danby (Oxford, 1933).

MIZRAḤI, R. ELIA, *Responsa* (Jerusalem, 1938).

MOSKONI, J., 'Haqdamah le-'Even ha-'Ezer,' in *'Oṣar Ṭov*, ed. A. Berliner (Berlin, 1878).

MUNK, S., *Mélanges de philosophie juive et arabe* (Paris, 1927).

NAḤMANIDES, MOSES, *Kitvey Ha-Ramban, ed.* H. D. Chavel (2 vols., Jerusalem, 1963).
NEMOY, L., *Karaite Anthology* (New Haven, 1952).
The New Oxford Annotated Bible (Oxford, 1991).
NICHOLSON, R. A., *Studies in Islamic Poetry* (Cambridge, 1922).
Old Testament Pseudepigrapha, ed. J. H. Charlesworthy (2 vols., New York, 1983).
'Oṣar Ha-Ge'onim, ed. B. M. Lewin (13 vols., Haifa and Jerusalem, 1928–43).
'Oṣar Midrašim, ed. J. D. Eisenstein (2 vols., New York, 1915).
PAGIS, D., *Ḥidduš U-Masoret Be-Širat Ha-Ḥol* (Jerusalem, 1976).
—— *Širat Ha-Ḥol We-Torat Ha-Šir Le-Mošeh Ibn Ezra U-Vney Doro* (Jerusalem, 1970).
Pesiqta' de. R. Kahane', ed. S. Buber (Lyck, 1868).
Pirqey de Rabbi Eliezer, ed. G. Friedlander (New York, 1965).
Pirqey de Rabbi Eliezer (Warsaw, 1852).
RABINOVITZ, Z. M., *Maḥazor Piyyuṭey Rabbi Yannai* (2 vols., Jerusalem, 1985–7).
REIF, S., *Judaism and Hebrew Prayer* (Cambridge, 1992).
ROTH, C., *The House of Nasi, Doña Gracia* (Philadelphia, 1947).
—— *Venice* (Philadelphia, 1930).
—— (ed.), *World History of the Jewish People,* xi (New Brunswick, 1966).
SA'ADYAH GA'ON, *Sefer Ha-'Egron,* ed. N. Allony (Jerusalem, 1969).
—— *Sefer Ha-'Emunot We-Ha-De'ot* (New York, 1947).
—— *Siddur Rav Sa'adyah Ga'on,* ed. I. Davidson, S. Asaf and B. I. Joel (Jerusalem, 1941).
SALMAN B. YERUḤAM, *Sefer Milḥamot 'Adonay,* ed. I. Davidson (New York, 1934).
SCHEINDLIN, R. P., *The Gazelle: Medieval Hebrew Poems on God, Israel and the Soul* (Philadelphia, 1991).
—— *Wine, Women and Death* (Philadelphia, 1986).
SCHIRMANN, Ḥ., *The Battle Between Behemot and Leviathan According to an Ancient Hebrew Piyyuṭ* (Jerusalem, 1970).
—— 'Ha-mešorarim beney-dorom šel Mošeh Ibn Ezra wi-Yehudah ha-Lewi', *Studies of the Research Institute for Hebrew Poetry,* 4 (1938), pp. 247–96.
—— *Ha-Širah Ha-'Ivrit Bi-Sfarad U-V-Provans* (2 vols., Jerusalem, 1959).
—— 'Hebrew Liturgical Poetry and Christian Hymnology', *JQR* 49 (1953–4), pp. 123–61.
—— *Le-Toledot Ha-Širah We-Ha-Dramah Ha-'Ivrit* (2 vols., Jerusalem, 1979).
—— *Mivḥar Ha-Širah Ha-'Ivrit Be-'Italiyah* (Berlin, 1934).
—— *Širim Ḥadašim Min Ha-Genizah* (Jerusalem, 1965).
—— 'Yiṣḥaq ben Mar Šaul, ha-mešorer mi-Lusena', in *Sefer Asaf* (Jerusalem, 1953), pp. 496–514.
SCHOELER, G., 'Bashshār b. Burd, Abu 'l-'Atāhiyah and Abū Nuwās', in Ashtiany *et al.* (eds.), *'Abbasid Belles-Lettres.*

SCHOLEM, G., *Ha-Qabbalah Bi-Provans* (Jerusalem, 1970).

—— 'Kabbalah', *EJ* x. 489–653.

—— *Major Trends in Jewish Mysticism* (New York, 1946).

—— *Re'šit Ha-Qabbalah We-Sefer Ha-Bahir* (Jerusalem, 1969).

SCHWARZFUCHS, S., 'France Under the Early Capets', in Roth (ed.), *World History of the Jewish People*, pp. 143–61.

Seder Ha-Qinot Le-Tiš'ah Be-'Av, ed. D. Goldschmidt (Jerusalem, 1968).

Seder Ha-Seliḥot Ke-Minhag Liṭa' U-Qhillot Ha-Perušim Be-'Ereṣ Yisra'el, ed. D. Goldschmidt (Jerusalem, 1965).

Seder Ha-Seliḥot Ke-Minhag Polin We-Rov Ha-Qehillot Be-'Ereṣ Yisra'el, ed. D. Goldschmidt (Jerusalem, 1965).

Seder Rav 'Amram Ga'on, ed. D. Goldschmidt (Jerusalem, 1971).

Sefer Ha-Bahir, in Dan (ed.), *The Early Kabbalah.*

Sefer Ha-Pardes, ed. Ḥ. J. Ehrenreich (Budapest, 1924).

Sefer Ha-Yašar, ed. L. Rosenthal (Berlin, 1898).

Sefer Qerovot Hu' Maḥazor Le-Yom Ševi'i U-Šmini Šel Pesaḥ, ed. W. Heidenheim (Hanover, 1739).

Sefer Razi'el (Amsterdam, 1701).

Sefer Torot Ha-Nefeš, Hebrew trans. of *Kitāb Ma'ānī al-Nafs*, ed. Isak Broydé (Paris, 1896).

Sefer Yeṣirah, ed. I. Gruenwald (Tel Aviv, 1971).

SHARF, A., *Byzantine Jewry: From Justinian to the Fourth Crusade* (New York, 1971).

Siddur Ha-Tefillot Ke-Minhag Ha-Qara'im (Gozlow, 1836).

Sifra, ed. I. H. Weiss (Vienna, 1862).

Sifre on Deuteronomy, ed. L. Finkelstein (New York, 1967).

SILVER, A. H., *A History of Messianic Speculation in Israel* (Boston, 1959).

SIRAT, C., *A History of Jewish Philosophy* (Cambridge, 1985).

Širim U-Zmirot We-Tišbaḥot, ed. E. Soncino (Constantinople, 1545).

SPIEGEL, S., *The Last Trial* (New York, 1967).

STARR, J., *The Jews in the Byzantine Empire, 641–1204* (Athens, 1939).

Šulḥan 'Arukh (Joseph Karo's Code of Jewish Law with glosses by Moses Isserles) (4 vols., Jerusalem, 1966).

Tanakh: The Holy Scripture (Philadelphia, 1985).

Tanḥuma', ed. S. Buber (Vilna, 1885).

'Targum 'Onkelos', in A. Sperber (ed.), *The Bible in Aramaic* (4 vols., Leiden, 1959–73).

Targum Pseudo-Jonathan of the Pentateuch—Text and Concordance, ed. E. G. Clarke [*et. al.*] (Hoboken, 1984).

TOBIAS B. ELIEZER, *Leqaḥ Ṭov*, ed. S. Buber (Vilna, 1880).

TRACHTENBERG, J., *Jewish Magic and Superstition* (New York, 1977).

Ṭur (Jacob b. Ašer's Code of Jewish Law) (4 vols., Jerusalem, 1962).

ULLAH, N. (ed.), *Islamic Literature* (New York, 1963).

WALLENSTEIN. M., *Some Unpublished Piyyuṭim from the Cairo Geniza* (Manchester, 1956).

WEINBERGER, L. J., *'Antologia Šel Piyyuṭey Yawan, 'Anatoliah We-Ha-Balqanim* (Cincinnati, 1975).

—— 'Ašer šipper reqi'a rum, petiḥah le-ḥoh"p le-Ya'aqov ben Eliezer', *Sinai*, 79 (1976), pp. 26–9.

—— 'God as Matchmaker', *Journal of the American Academy of Religion*, 40 (1972), pp. 238–44.

—— 'Ha-payṭan ke-poseq halakhah', *Ha-Doar*, 72/21 (1993), pp. 21–2.

—— 'Hebrew Poetry from the Byzantine Empire: A Survey of Recent and Current Research', *Bulletin of Judaeo-Greek Studies*, 3 (1988), pp. 18–20.

—— *Jewish Prince in Moslem Spain: Selected Poems of Samuel Ibn Nagrela* (Tuscaloosa, Ala., 1973).

—— 'The Liturgical Poetry of Samuel Ibn Nagrela', in J. Kabakoff (ed.), *Jewish Book Annual*, 50 (1992–3), pp. 240–8.

—— 'Malki mi-qedem, tefillah le-R. Menaḥem bar Elia mi-Kastoria', in Z. Malachi (ed.), *The A. M. Habermann Memorial Volume* (Lod, 1993), pp. 27–39.

—— 'Midraš 'al peṭirat Mošeh še-ne'evad', *Tarbiz*, 38 (1968), pp. 285–93.

—— 'A Note on Karaite Adaptations of Rabbinic Prayers', *JQR* 74 (1984), pp. 267–79.

—— 'A Note on the Translations of the Judith Legends for Chanuka', *Journal of Reform Judaism*, 32/2 (1985), pp. 44–8.

—— 'On the Provenance of Benjamin b. Samuel Quštani', *JQR* 68–9 (1977–9), pp. 46–60.

—— 'Piyyuṭ qara'i be-maḥazor rabbani', *Ha-Doar*, 69/35 (1990), p. 23.

—— *Re'šit Ha-Payṭanut Be-Balkanim* (Cincinnati, 1988).

—— 'Rešut le-ḥatan ha-Torah be-ḥag Simḥat Torah li-Šlomo b. Mazal Ṭov', *Ha-Doar*, 68/39 (1989), p. 16.

—— *Seder Ha-Seliḥot Ke-Minhag Kehillot Ha-Romaniotim* (New York, 1980).

—— 'Seliḥah le-fi torat ha-sod be-Maḥazor Romania', *Bitzaron*, 7–8 (1980), pp. 10–13.

—— *Širat Ha-Qodeš Le-Rabbanim We-Qara'im Bi-Drom Mizraḥ 'Eyropah* (Cincinnati, 1991).

—— 'Širat Šelomo b. Mazal Ṭov li-khvod ha-sulṭan Suleiman', *Ha-Doar*, 73/21 (1994), pp. 16–17.

—— 'Širat Šemaryah ha-Ikriti li-khvod ha-nagid R. David nekhed ha-Rambam', *Ha-Doar*, 68/34 (1988), pp. 28–9.

—— *Širat Yisra'el Be-'i Keretim* (Cincinnati, 1985).

—— *Širey Ha-Qodeš Li-Yhudey Kastoria* (Cincinnati, 1983).

—— 'Širim ḥadašim me-ha-tequfah ha-Bizantinit', I, *HUCA* 39 (1968), Hebrew section, pp. 1–62.

WEINBERGER, L. J., 'Širim ḥadašim me-ha-tequfah ha-Bizantinit', II, *HUCA* 53 (1972), Hebrew section, pp. 1–39.

—— 'Yoṣer li-Šmini 'Aṣeret li-R. Ḥedweta' bi-Rabbi Avraham', *Sinai*, 107 (1991), pp. 151–7.

WEISSENSTERN, N., *Piyyuṭey R. Yoḥanan Ha-Kohen Bi-Rabbi Yehošu'a* (Jerusalem, 1984).

WERNER, E., 'Hebrew and Oriental Christian Metrical Hymns: A Comparison', *HUCA* 23 (1950–1), pp. 398–401.

—— *The Sacred Bridge* (New York, 1979).

YA'ARI, A., *Toledot Ḥag Simḥat Torah* (Jerusalem, 1964).

YAHALOM, J., *Piyyuṭey Šim'on bar Megas* (Jerusalem, 1984).

—— *Sefat Ha-Šir Šel Ha-Piyyuṭ Ha-Ereṣ-Yisra'eli Ha-Qadum* (Jerusalem, 1985).

YARDEN, D., 'Niqbaṣot mi-širey Rabbi Sa'adyah Longo be-darkey ha-šir we-ha-meliṣah', *Sefunot*, 12 (1971–8), pp. 83–122.

—— *Sefuney Širah* (Jerusalem, 1967).

ZIMMELS, H. J., 'Scholars and Scholarship in Byzantium and Italy', *World History of the Jewish People*, pp. 175–88.

ZULAY, M., *Ha-'Askolah Ha-Payṭanit Šel Rav Sa'adya Ga'on* (Jerusalem, 1964).

—— 'Eine Ḥanukkah-qerovah von Pineḥas ha-Kohen', *Studies of the Research Institute for Hebrew Poetry*, 1 (1933), pp. 149–74.

—— 'Le-toledot ha-piyyuṭ be-'Ereṣ Yisra'el', *Studies of the Research Institute for Hebrew Poetry*, 5 (1939), pp. 107–80.

—— 'Piyyuṭey Rabbi Neḥemiah ben Šelomo ha-Nasi', *Studies of the Research Institute for Hebrew Poetry*, 4 (1938), pp. 197–246.

—— *Piyyuṭey Yannai* (Berlin, 1938).

—— 'Piyyuṭim le-zekher me'ora'ot šonim', *Studies of the Research Institute for Hebrew Poetry*, 3 (1936), pp. 151–83.

—— *Zur Liturgie der babylonischen Juden* (Stuttgart, 1933).

ZUNZ, L., *Literaturgeschichte der synagogalen Poesie* (Berlin, 1865).

—— *Die synagogale Poesie des Mittelalters* (Frankfurt a. M., 1920).

Index of Piyyuṭim (*Hebrew*)

נ

Index of Piyyuṭim (*Transliterated*)

T

U

W

General Index

Piyyuṭim are listed under the poets' names; for a listing by first line, in transliteration and in Hebrew, see separate indexes. For themes of *piyyuṭim* see under 'themes, hymnographic'.

ʾEšpekhah ʿalay nafši 291
ʾEt peney mevin 226, 235, 274
ʾEtayu ʾamelalim 226, 273, 275, 276
ʾEzkerah ʾelohim we-ʾehemayah titʿaṭṭef 268
Kal ʾemuney ʿammim 238
Malki noṭeh 241, 245
Me-ʾeyn kamokha 238
Mi kamokha mesim netivah 225, 249
Mivtaḥi we-goḥi 227
ʾOdeh ṣuri 226, 260
Qadoš mistatter 238
Šaḥar miflat 226
We-ʾattah malki 197, 225, 238
Yošev meʿonah 199, 217
Moses b. Isaac da Rieti:
Miqdaš meʿaṭ 13, 150
Moses b. Israel Isserles 354
Moses b. Jacob (Franco-German poet):
ʾAkhalunu hamamunu 168
Moses b. Jacob of Kiev (Moses Ha-Golah) 343, 344
ʾElohim ḥay 346
Moses b. Joseph of Rome:
ʾEzkerah we-ʾetmogeg 263
Moses b. Joseph di Trani 335, 375
Moses b. Kalonymus 53, 136, 137
ʾEymat norʾotekha 145
Moses Kohen Aškenazi 349, 350
Moses b. Maimon, *see* Maimonides
Moses Mevorakh 343, 344, 346
ʾAdon ʿolam ʾadon kol ha-gedolot 346
ʾAvarekh šem 347
ʾElohim be-rov ḥasdekha 346
Mah gadelu 347
Moses b. Naḥman, *see* Naḥmanides
Moses Narboni 411
Moses Paša b. Elijah of Kalé 412
Moses Qalai 227
Moses Qilqi of Chios 237
ʿUri ʾayyumati 286
Moses b. Šabbetai del Medigo:
ʾAgaddelah šimkha 351, 358
ʾAkhtirah le-ḥonen daʿat 351, 354
Mi šeloʾ ʾamar 351, 354
Mosqoyo:
Meromam ʾat 254
muḥarrak 124–5, 260–1
muqaddimah 128
mustajāb 117, 262–3, 397
muwashshaḥ 10, 15, 44
in Balkan Byzantium 226, 230, 247, 253, 260
in Karaite *piyyuṭim* 412
in Macedonia 307
in Ottoman lands 402
in Spain 91–2, 93, 103, 104, 112, 124
see also pseudo-*muwashshaḥ*
mysticism in *piyyuṭim* 119, 353, 355, 380, 392, 393
of alphabet 118, 201, 208–11, 231, 318–19, 337–8, 361–2, 391
and angelology 176, 177, 199, 202–3, 218–20, 302, 317, 328–9, 355
of Creation 118, 188, 191, 197, 198, 314, 391
divine chariot-throne 57, 153, 163–4, 176, 197, 213, 218–19
divine names 169, 177, 198–9, 202, 209–10, 219–20, 317, 379
of Gerona mystics, influence of 201, 330, 337–8, 380, 391
mystical works, influence of: *Alphabet of Rabbi Akiva* 208–10; *heykhalot* literature 30, 153, 154, 197, 200–1, 202, 208–10, 217–20; *Sefer Ha-Bahir* 201; *Sefer Yeṣirah* 118, 201, 208–10, 337–8, 330, 391

N

Naḥmanides (Moses b. Naḥman) 11, 89, 196, 376, 377
Me-roʾš mi-qadmey ʿolamim 89, 90
Naḥšon Gaon 68
Nathan Ha-Bavli 47
Nathan b. Yeḥiel delli Mansi 146
Naṭronay Gaʾon 57, 67, 68
natural phenomena 12–14
moon: eclipse of 4; new, appearance of 4, 64–6; role of 105–6; sanctification of 4, 65
stars, role of 237
sun: eclipse of 4; role of 269–71, 322–3
Nehemiah b. Solomon b. Heman Ha-Nasi 69, 74, 77
ʾAnʾim gevurot ʾel 78
ʾEloha ba-kol memšalto 78
ʾIm yimmalʾu he-ʿavim 78
Neḥunyah b. Ha-Qanah 169
ʾAnnaʾ be-khoaḥ 169

Q

Solomon Mevorakh 343, 372
'Ašorerah le-fo'arah 379
Be-gilah be-'ahavah 405
'El 'al kol 'elim 405
'Emor le'loheynu 385
Melo' 'eš hod 384
Šaḥar 'a'irah 379
Sarim u-mlakhim 405
Še'eh na' le-qol 397
Solomon b. Moses de Rossi 143
Solomon Šarvit Ha-Zahav 15, 258, 277–84
'Efes zulatekha 249
Merivah nihyatah 236
Mi kamokha šabbat we-ḥanukkah 251–2
Šadday hizkartani 237
Šadday zekharnukha 259, 260
Šafel we-gowe'a 259
Šimkha 'elohay 259
Tehillatekha 'eyn lah teḥillah 277
Yeš yešut 237, 278, 406
Spain 9, 87–134
stichera 81 n.
Sukkot, *see* Tabernacles
synagogue service, distinctive features of 3, 4

T

Tabernacles (Sukkot), compositions for 63, 77, 159, 182, 204, 220, 226, 260, 353, 381, 388
Eighth Day of Tabernacles (Šemini 'Aṣeret) 52, 53, 54, 77, 119, 255, 310, 311, 315, 353, 383, 431
Hoša'na' Rabbah 63–4, 422
Sabbath of Tabernacles 165, 175, 331, 334, 338, 430
Simḥat Torah 12, 178, 180–1, 254–5, 331, 334, 353, 373, 384, 388, 389, 390
taḥanun 231, 237, 285–9, 327–9, 367–8, 399–400
teḥinnah 126, 127, 168, 285–9, 352, 367–8
Ten Days of Mercy 413, 414–15, 418, 424–5, 428, 429, 430, 431
Ten Days of Repentance, compositions for 128
in Balkan Byzantium 199, 229, 231, 258, 259–60, 261, 265, 266, 277, 288, 289
in Crete 351, 352, 362, 366
in Crimea 344
in Ereṣ Yisra'el 27
in Franco-Germany 186
in Italy 144, 149
in Ottoman hymnography 396, 397, 398, 400
in Spain 125
Ten Martyrs 17, 235, 268–71, 320, 322, 363–4
Tenth of Ṭevet, *see* fast-days
teqi'ata' 52
themes, hymnographic:
ages of man 109, 273, 281–4
alphabet, Hebrew, *see under* mysticism in *piyyuṭim*
angelology, *see under* mysticism in *piyyuṭim*
'aqedah, see separate entry
bridegroom, characteristics of 225
Christianity: missionizing of, deplored 167–8, 268; polemic against 36–7, 38, 40, 145–6, 147–8, 159, 165, 167–8, 190, 205, 239–40, 263, 361, 370, 371; ways of, exhortation not to follow 147, 161
contemporary events: anti-Jewish decrees 151, 232–3, 355; anti-Jewish violence by Crusaders 13, 79, 157, 159, 164, 177, 185, 186–7, 190, 236, 268, 272; anti-Jewish riots by Muslims 9, 79; Jerusalem, Christian–Muslim struggle for 127, 293; Tatars, attacks by 346; wars 110–11
cosmology 114, 118, 119, 197–8
Creation, the 106, 118, 120, 176, 389
death 192; of Moses 54–6, 331–2, 333, 335–7; of sages, as atoning for Israel's sins 60–1, 364
dissenters, denouncement of 140–1
end of days, the 334–5
ethical guidance 149
Exodus from Egypt 85, 159, 191, 214, 249, 253, 311, 362
festivals, themes of and commandments pertaining to 33, 114, 176, 177, 182, 204–5, 230, 251–2, 260, 305–6, 310–11, 318, 355, 363, 381
folk-legends, *see separate entry*
food, provision of 256–7
God: centrality of, 106; compassion of 127, 129, 131, 258, 265, 328, 397; complaints against 80, 231; as controlling natural world 64, 147; covenant of, with Israel 160–1, 240, 241, 315; dominion of 112, 175–6;